LATIN AMERICA'S WARS

RELATED TITLES BY ROBERT L. SCHEINA

Latin America: A Naval History: 1810–1987

Latin America's Wars, Vol. 1: The Age of the Caudillo, 1791–1899

Santa Anna: A Curse upon Mexico

LATIN AMERICA'S WARS

The Age of the Professional Soldier, 1900–2001

VOLUME 2

Robert L. Scheina

Brassey's, Inc.
Washington, D.C.

Library of Congress Cataloging-in-Publication Data

Scheina, Robert L.
    Latin America's wars / Robert L. Scheina.—1st ed.
        v. cm
Includes bibliographical references and index.
Contents: v. 1. The age of the *caudillo*, 1791-1899
    ISBN 1-57488-449-2 (cloth : v. 1 : alk. paper—ISBN 1-57488-450-6 (pbk. : v. 1 : alk paper)
    1. Latin America—History, Military—19th century. 2. *Caudillos*—Latin America—History—19th century. I. Title.
    F1413 .S34 2003
    355'.0098—dc21

                                                            2002008029

Brassey's, Inc.
22841 Quicksilver Drive
Dulles, Virginia 20166

First Edition

10 9 8 7 6 5 4 3 2 1

This work is dedicated
to my lifetime partner, Linda;
thank you for all the sacrifices
that made this work possible.

CONTENTS

ILLUSTRATIONS
AND MAPS

ILLUSTRATIONS

MAPS

PREFACE

In a sense, the South American military can hardly be blamed for seeking to exercise political power. After all, they otherwise would have almost nothing to do. Their countries are not in danger either from outside attacks or surprise raids by neighbors.

—*Time* Magazine

WHY STUDY TWENTIETH-CENTURY LATIN AMERICAN MILITARY OPERATIONS?

In 1968 a *Time* magazine reporter wrote the above statement.[1] These patronizing sentiments have been echoed over the decades throughout the United States, including in the halls of the U.S. Congress. The truth is, Latin American militaries fought innumerable wars during the twentieth century against "all enemies foreign and domestic."[2]

Today, many U.S. citizens naively speculate that U.S. military involvement in Latin America could solve the region's problems, whether they be the chaos of narco-terrorism in Colombia, a closing of the Panama Canal, or the downfall of Fidel Castro in Cuba. And yet, we have little comprehension of the causes, magnitudes, or consequences of military operations within Latin America. Until now, no general history of twentieth-century Latin American military operations existed. Many scholars who have studied Latin American militaries in the twentieth century have chosen to focus on their involvement in politics which is but one of their activities.

HOW TO MEASURE THE IMPACT OF MILITARY OPERATIONS?

Many yardsticks are available, but like those of the nineteenth century, which were addressed in a companion volume, they are very inaccurate.

DEATHS AND INJURY

In spite of the fact that death and casualty statistics are as inaccurate for the twentieth century as they were for the nineteenth, these numbers do give a sense of the magnitude of national sacrifice.

We can gain some appreciation of the difficulty in determining the number of casualties sustained by examining one very small engagement: the capture of Güeppí during the Leticia Conflict between Colombia and Peru in 1932. Guillermo Plazas Olarte, writing about the Colombian army, states: "Results of the action [were]: on the Colombian side dead 5, hurt 9.

Peruvians, dead 10, hurt 2, prisoners, 24." Jesús Torres Almeyda, examining the role of the Colombian navy writes: "According to official records, the Colombian casualties amounted to 8 dead 9 hurt and the Peruvian casualties were estimated at 10 dead, 2 hurt, and 24 prisoners." Addressing the Peruvian side, Guillermo S. Faura Gaig concludes: "As a result of the Battle of Güeppí the Colombians had 8 dead and 7 hurt. For our forces 1 officer, 2 2nd class sergeants, 4 corporals, and 32 soldiers were killed, wounded or prisoners, to which were added during the retreat at Pantoja 2 officers and 1 soldier." All of these statements may be accurate, each author choosing a different beginning, ending, and definition to the battle. Or, they may all be wrong, each possessing incomplete or inaccurate information. But these figures are similar and convey the same sense of loss. Throughout this work, I have chosen the figures I believe to be the most accurate.[3]

Latin American combat-related casualties (killed, missing, and wounded) rivaled those of the United States even after the United States emerged as a superpower. The United States sustained 1,100,000 casualties during World War II; Mexico's population decreased by 824,000 persons between 1910 and 1920 as a consequence of its revolution—admittedly, some of this number through emigration. In Vietnam (1964–74) the United States sustained approximately 210,000 casualties of which 54,000 were deaths; it is estimated that 180,000 Colombians *died* in an intraclass war known as *La Violencia* (1948–57).[4]

PERCENTAGE OF POPULATION LOST

During the Chaco War, Paraguay lost 36 percent of those mobilized and Bolivia lost 21 percent of those who served. By comparison the most severe North American losses during the twentieth century were 3.6 percent of those in uniform during World War I.[5]

POLITICS AND POWER

Rafael Trujillo, Anastasio Somoza, Fulgencio Batista, and others like them proved during the twentieth century that within Latin America political power frequently came out of the muzzle of a gun.

SOCIAL CHANGE

More than fifty million Latin Americans had their social rights as citizens significantly altered by three interclass revolutions—the Mexican (1910–20), the Bolivian (1950), and the Cuban (1956–59).

These few examples bear testimony to the importance of Latin American military operations and demonstrate the inaccuracy of the 1968 quotation from *Time* magazine.

HOW TO CONVEY AN APPRECIATION OF GEOGRAPHY?

As in my companion volume, I reference the distance and direction "as the crow flies" (unless otherwise stated) of important sites to a strategic location, most often the capital, in order to convey an appreciation of size. As the twentieth century progressed, technology had an increasing impact on travel time—first at sea, then on land, and finally through the air. However, it can be challenging to know what technology to apply when.

For example, to travel from Lima to Iquitos, Peru's most important Amazonian port, a distance of 612 miles, typically required twenty-one days prior to the introduction of the airplane. After its introduction, the trip could be made in a few hours. But one should not assume that because a technology existed, it was available. During the late 1920s the U.S. Marines moved much of their supplies by ox-drawn cart during their campaigns in Nicaragua, and during the mid-1950s much of Fidel Castro's logistics were carried by burros in the Sierra Maestra. And those geographical obstacles—mountains, rivers, and deserts—that made it hard to calculate travel time during the nineteenth century were still significant factors in the twentieth.

WHAT IMAGES DO WORDS OF VIOLENCE CONVEY?

As in the nineteenth century, conflict terminology was loosely applied to events in Latin America during the twentieth century. Undoubtedly, the most overused word has been *revolution*. Mr. Webster defines revolution as "a fundamental change in political organization . . ."[6] Few revolutions occurred during the twentieth century within Latin America, but when they did—in Mexico (1910–20), in Bolivia (1950), and in Cuba (1956–59)—they caused "fundamental change."

Within this text I have endeavored to convey magnitude by choosing the word which I believe conveys the most accurate image. This frequently differs from that which these events have traditionally been called. Of course my choice is subjective; a magnitude of violence that I would call a war in small Ecuador might not justify my using the term for a similar event in large Mexico.

The views expressed in this book are those of the author and do not reflect the official policy or position of the National Defense University, the Department of Defense, or the U.S. Government.

ACKNOWLEDGMENTS

Azad Ajamian, president of Brassey's Inc., boldly agreed to publish this, the second of two mammoth companion volumes, and I wish to sincerely thank him for his confidence in my abilities. Once again my champion and friend in court has been Rick Russell, Brassey's acquisitions editor. And without my agent, Fritz Heinzen, these two companion volumes may never have been published. Throughout the process he has remained enthusiastic and dedicated to a successful outcome.

I am deeply indebted to the following individuals for their substantive research, face-saving corrections, and thoughtful additions. They have persevered through a decade of research and a second of writing. Without their help, this book would have failed to meet my expectations.

Name	Contributions
Eduardo Alimonda Professor of Economics and Captain (ret.) Argentine Navy	Argentina, Dominican Intervention 1965, and translations throughout
Reginaldo J. da Silva Bacchi Military Analyst and Journalist	Brazil
Robyn Scheina Brown Attorney at Law	Editorial review; troubleshooter
Carlos Hernández González Attorney at Law	Venezuela
David Mahan Medical Doctor and Bibliophile of Chilean Naval History	Chile
Jurg Meister Historian and Author	Entire book

I wish to thank the following individuals for their contributions, which have strengthened specific chapters of this book. Without their help, my work would have been significantly less complete. For those in the military, the rank cited was that held when they made their contribution. Some have since been promoted.

Roxanne Andersen   Troubleshooter
Researcher

Meliton Carvajal Pareja   Peru
Rear Admiral (ret.) Peruvian Navy

Carlos Chavarria   Guatemala
Colonel, Guatemalan Army

Hugo Contreras   Colombia
Colonel (ret.), Colombian Army

Andres Duarte   Paraguay
Colonel, Paraguayan Air Force

Adrian English   Entire book
Scholar and Author

Jon Glassman   "Fidel's Legacy, 1974–91"
Former U.S. Ambassador to Paraguay

Eduardo Guelfo   Argentine urban guerrilla warfare
Captain, Argentine Navy

Nancy Westfall de Gurrola   Mexico
Professor, Universidad Iberoamericana

Julio Hang   Argentina
Brigadier General, Argentine Army

Jerry Hannifin   Caribbean and Central America
Roving correspondent for
Time-Life International

Thomas Hauser   The modern era
Colonel, U.S. Army

Terry Hooker   Research support
President, El Dorado Society

Robert Hughes   Panama
Professor, Industrial College of Armed Forces

Matt Kenny   Caribbean and the cold war
Journalist for United Press International

John Klingemann   Mexico
Scholar

Carlos Lopez   Chile
Professor, Menlo College

Daniel Masterson   Peru
Professor, U.S. Naval Academy

Diego Mantilla Jaramillo   Ecuador
Captain, Ecuadorian Navy

Jay Mallin   Cuba and the cold war
Journalist for major newspapers

Guillermo Montenegro   Argentina
Professor, Escuela de Guerra Naval

Jorge Ortiz Sotelo   Peru
Secretary General, Thalassa Society

Eduardo Pesce   Brazil
Scholar, Universidade do Estado do Rio de Janeiro

Sergio Reyes   El Salvador
Colonel, Salvadoran Army

Patrick Roth   Early twentieth century
Captain (ret.),   U.S. interventions
U.S. Navy

Linda Scheina   Editorial review
Confidante

David Spencer   Cold war
Author

Barbara Tenenbaum Hispanic-American Division, Library of Congress	Mexico
Paul Walsh Bibliophile of Latin American Military	Twentieth century
Robert Wilcox Colonel, U.S. Marine Corps	Dominican Intervention 1965 & Grenada 1983
Catherine Wilson Researcher	Troubleshooter
John D. Waghelstein Professor, U.S. Naval War College	Cold war
César de Windt Lavandier Rear Admiral (ret.), Dominican Navy	Dominican Republic

ABBREVIATIONS

ca.	about
E	east
ed.	editor or edition
fnu	first name unknown
ft	feet
mi	miles
N	north
n.d.	no date of publication cited
n.p.	no publisher cited
OAS	Organization of American States
S	south
unk	unknown
vol.	volumes
W	west

INTRODUCTION

WHAT WERE THE CAUSES FOR WAR
IN TWENTIETH-CENTURY LATIN AMERICA?

> Those who make peaceful revolution impossible will make violent revolution inevitable.
> —President John F. Kennedy, 1962

Three causes for conflict within Latin America were twentieth-century phenomena—interclass war, extrahemispheric conflicts, and communist initiatives. These need to be added to at least six causes that occurred during the nineteenth century and continued into the twentieth—the controversy of separation versus union, boundary disputes, *caudilloism*, intraclass struggles, interventions caused by capitalism, and religious wars.

INTERCLASS WARS

In spite of the fact that the masses provided the cannon fodder for the Wars of Independence and subsequent conflicts, with rare exception, the lower classes won few political, economic, or social concessions for their sacrifices during the nineteenth century. The first of the great interclass struggles was the Mexican Revolution of 1910.

The causes for interclass warfare were political, economic, and social injustices that had roots in the colonial experience. Compared to North America, the Latin America nations had very modest experience with representative government prior to their declarations for independence. Latin America was the property of the King and he ruled it as an absolute monarch. Independence was thrust upon Latin America by the actions of Napoleon Bonaparte. This sudden change precipitated by the wars for independence without prior conditioning meant that throughout the nineteenth century, and for many countries the twentieth century as well, most Latin Americans lived through an era of political turbulence.

Also, a fundamental difference existed in the selection criterion between Latin American colonial administrators and those chosen for North America. The Spanish King made unquestioning loyalty to the Crown the prerequisite for appointment. For pragmatic reasons the English King had to balance the need for loyalty with efficiency. And the Spanish King succeeded in instilling political loyalty, for until 1808, the year he was taken prisoner by Napoleon, not one successful revolution had taken place in his Latin American realm. The

English King could not say the same. And between 1810 and 1815 practically all of Spanish America declared its independence not from Ferdinand VII but from the Junta in metropolitan Spain which declared itself his regent while he was in captivity. Even José de San Martín's military commission issued by the United Provinces of Río de la Plata in 1812 to fight the Spaniards read, "in the name of Ferdinand VII."[1] The colonial legacy of placing loyalty to the King above efficiency to those being served left Latin America with the tradition that the first loyalty of the government servant, whether civilian or military, was to his superior and not the nation.

Interclass conflict is also rooted in past economic practices. Latin American economies could not, and in some cases still cannot, provide the basic social necessities for all their people. Many reasons contribute to this. Wealth was poorly distributed, in large part due to the colonial heritage. The Crown rewarded its conquistadores with large tracts of land. The King required from his new subjects, the Indians, many days of labor each year in exchange for the few services he provided. This collectivism of land and labor, reinforcing the preconquest traditions of the Indians, remained unbroken in many areas until well into the twentieth century and proved to be poor breeding ground for representative government.

Other problems contributed to slow economic development. Many Latin American nations were dependent upon monocrop economies which was susceptible to boom or bust cycles. A high birth rate, particularly in the tropical belt, outstripped resources. Latin America's infrastructure—challenged by formidable geographical barriers—remained underdeveloped. Many well-intentioned but naive attempts to rectify these imbalances only compounded the problems. Thus, far too many citizens lived on the marginal edge of subsistence, and as a result the economic pyramid within Latin America lacked stability.

Third, the social structure inherited from the colonial era contributed to interclass wars. The sixteenth-century conquistador was confronted in many areas by potentially overwhelming numbers of native Americans. To compensate for his inferior numbers, the conquistador attempted to destroy the Indian's social structure and superimpose his own. This created a rigid class structure that suppressed the majority. It also created a dual culture which persists to this day in many Latin American nations, thus making it difficult to create a national identity and the modern nation-state.

These conditions—political immaturity, inadequate economic development, and social discrimination—created a seedbed for interclass warfare. And the twentieth-century communications' revolution—first the radio, then the television, and finally the Internet—made even the poorest person increasingly aware of his political, economic, and social plight.

EXTRAHEMISPHERIC WARS

By the twentieth century some Latin American nations assumed global interests which ultimately led them to extrahemispheric military operations. Brazil went to war with Germany during World War I for many reasons, some pragmatic, but also to show solidarity with its northern sister republic, the United States. Brazilian and Mexican participation in World War II further evidenced that a broadening view of the world could lead to extrahemispheric military operations. Following World War II Latin American nations fought outside the region in support of their allies in the Cold War. Colombia participated in the Korean War and Argentina and Venezuela sent naval units to the Cuban Quarantine of 1962. These contributions were dwarfed when compared to the more than 200,000 Cubans who served in Africa during the 1970s and 1980s for Communism.[2]

COMMUNIST INITIATIVES

Between 1928 and 1935 Joseph Stalin, through his Communist International, attempted to exploit the political, social, and economic injustices within Latin America and to create inter-class war in order to bring Communists to power. Then, Stalin abandoned his attempt to promote class strife throughout the world (including Latin America) in order to focus on the nearby formidable threat of fascism to the Soviet Union.

Following World War II the Communist ranks split between the orthodox who followed Moscow's orders to work within the Latin American political systems (many Communist parties had gained legitimacy during World War II) and the young, radical Communists, who believed armed conflict to be the only recourse to gain power.

The U.S. strategy of casting the Cold War as a bipolar struggle forced many less radical Revolutionaries to choose to side with the Communists in order to receive arms and finances. Within the context of the Cold War, the United States perceived three potential dangers arising from Latin America: the draining of its resources in this peripheral area; the realigning of a nation when it fell to Communism; and the creating of a platform within the hemisphere from which Communists could project power.

To meet these threats, the United States organized the hemispheric defenses. The United States emerged from World War II as the leader of the Western World and the preeminent power in the Western Hemisphere. The building tensions between East and West coincided with increased class unrest within Latin America influenced in part by the communications revolution. As these internal Latin American tensions evolved into open fighting, U.S. decisions concerning which were Communist controlled and which merely had Communist participation, as well as how near or far from its shores the event, significantly influenced the extent of American involvement.

Ideology became the basis upon which the United States chose to support military operations in Latin America. And the United States was far less willing to be patient in Central American than farther south.[3] Brazilian President Juscelino Kubitschek attempted to defuse the potential for communist intervention by proposing to President Dwight Eisenhower the "Pan American Operation," a Marshall Plan for Latin America, but this conflicted with Eisenhower's desire to limit federal spending.[4]

The struggle against Communism raged for some forty years. The Communists attempted three strategies, each of which lasted over a decade and overlapped: the "Foco" (1956–68); the "Urban Guerrilla" (1964–78), and "United Front" (1978–91). The United States tenaciously clung to global containment with Latin America receiving a low priority except for Cuba.[5] Communism failed to spark interclass war within Latin America; nonetheless, the region paid an incredibly high price in talent, treasure, and time!

SEPARATION VERSUS UNION

Colombia and Brazil were the primary victims of wars caused by separation versus union—the spinning apart of the nation. For Colombia, it was the continuation of the unresolved nineteenth-century problem. Brazil had escaped much of the chaos caused by separation versus union throughout the nineteenth century primarily because its leader—a politically constrained emperor—was a continuation of its colonial experience. This changed in 1889 when the Emperor, who had been the glue that bonded this vast nation together, was deposed. Beginning in the late nineteenth century and continuing into the twentieth, Brazil experienced serious separatist movements, not completely uniting until the 1930s.

BOUNDARY DISPUTES

Although some boundary disputes were settled in the nineteenth century, through both wars and negotiations, others continued into the twentieth. They remained a primary cause of conflict within Latin America.

CAUDILLOISM

The weaknesses of the Latin American judicial systems contributed to the continuation of *caudilloism* where the "toughest of the tough" placed themselves above the law. This was in spite of the fact that a few Latin American militaries had begun to professionalize in the closing decades of the nineteenth century. As in the nineteenth century, a few *caudillos* climbed to be "giants"; the mere utterance of their names—Pancho Villa, Emiliano Zapata, Luis Prestes— could turn out thousands of fighters.

INTRACLASS WARS

During the twentieth century wars continued among the "haves" over distributing the spoils of the nation. This was particularly true in the Caribbean and at times involved only a handful of combatants although the entire nation would suffer the consequences. Only twenty-six military and civilian persons joined Fulgencio Batista in his March 10, 1952, Cuban coup!

INTERVENTIONS CAUSED BY CAPITALISM

By the very end of the nineteenth century, the United States had been smitten by imperialism. The closer a Latin American nation lay to the United States, the more likely the possibility of military intervention. The 1903 intervention in the Colombian province of Panama was a watershed event. For one of the first times, the goal of an intervention was to establish political hegemony and not economic security for nationals or political advantage over Great Britain.[6]

Accompanying this U.S. shift in motivation was a change in the level at which the decision to intervene was being made. Now it was the President of the United States and not a naval squadron commander who decided when to put the Marines ashore and the size of the force significantly increased. Also, at this time the United States declared itself the collector of bad debts owed by Latin American nations to whomever. This was outlined in the 1904 Roosevelt Corollary to the Monroe Doctrine.[7] The Good Neighbor policy of the 1930s briefly ended unilateral intervention by the United States. Some seventy-five interventions took place in Latin America during the twentieth century.[8]

RELIGIOUS WARS

As in the nineteenth century, religion continued to be a prime motivator of conflict. The Mexican *Cristero* War (1926–28) pitted the "faithful" against the "agnostics," or at least that is how the *Cristeros* saw the war. Religion was a contributor to the Colombian civil war known as *La Violencia* (1948–57). And a number of Roman Catholic priests chose to fight as Leftist guerrillas during the Cold War (1946–91). Even today, particularly in Central America, the sympathies of many priests and ministers are split. The lower clergy champions the poor and the higher echelon is identified with the rich.

Two nineteenth-century causes for war—race and resources—although contributors to conflict during the twentieth century, were overshadowed by other causes, while two other causes—the ideology of independence and territorial conquest—did not resurface in the twentieth century. However, this does not necessarily mean that these four—race, resources, ideology of independence, and territorial conquest—cannot reemerge as primary causes for conflict in the twenty-first century.

PART 1

CHAPTER 1

THE GIVING AND THE TAKING OF PANAMA, 1903

I am interested in the Panama Canal because I started it. If I had followed traditional, conservative methods I should have submitted a dignified state paper of probably two hundred pages to Congress, and the debate on it would be going on yet; but I took the Canal Zone and let Congress debate and while the debate goes on the canal does too.

—Theodore Roosevelt, 1911

THE SPARK

On November 3, 1903, a mob that included Colombians and some foreigners, financed by U.S. businessmen, declared Panamanian independence from Colombia.

BACKGROUND

Throughout the first half of the nineteenth century, the United States and Great Britain had competed for the economic and political domination of Central America. A key issue was transit rights across the isthmus, first by stagecoach and canoe, then by rail, and later by canal. The United States gained a preferential position within the province of Panama by the Bidlack-Mallarino Treaty (1846) with Colombia (then called Nueva Granada); the United States guaranteed the neutrality of the isthmus and Colombian sovereignty over it in exchange for the same transit rights as Colombian citizens. However, two years later, the United States was forced to make concessions to Great Britain. The two nations concluded the Clayton-Bulwer Treaty (1850) which stipulated that any canal must be jointly built and owned by the two nations. On numerous occasions during the second half of the nineteenth century, the Colombian government permitted and even requested U.S. intervention to restore order.

In 1881 a French corporation headed by Ferdinand de Lesseps, the builder of the Suez Canal, began digging a canal through Panama under license from the Colombian government. Within the United States this was denounced as a violation of the Monroe Doctrine.[1]

1

The United States did not interfere with the French Company but rather chartered an American corporation, the Maritime Canal Company of Nicaragua, to develop the Nicaraguan route. At the same time, the U.S. State Department continued to pressure Great Britain to abrogate or amend the Clayton-Bulwer Treaty of 1850. By the 1890s the French company had gone bankrupt after having accomplished a small portion of the necessary digging.

The Maritime Canal Company of Nicaragua failed to attract the necessary funds to develop the alternate route. A second French effort, the new Panama Canal Company, was franchised and given an extension to 1904 (subsequently extended by executive agreement until 1910) to complete the canal. It resumed work on a modest scale but by 1898 was unable to attract investment and was anxious to dispose of its access rights to the United States. In order to do this, it was necessary to win the consent of the Colombian government.

Following the Spanish-American War, the United States emerged as a world power. In 1902 the United States and Great Britain signed the Hay-Pauncefote Treaty, whereby Great Britain surrendered its rights under the Clayton-Bulwer Treaty to share in the building and control of the canal. This treaty affirmed America's domination within the hemisphere and virtually gave the United States a free hand in any future canal across Central America.

America now had to choose between the Panamanian and Nicaraguan routes. Both had their advantages and disadvantages as well as their champions both within and outside of Congress. At the height of the debate, Philippe Bunau-Varilla, a champion of the Panama route, placed a Nicaraguan postage stamp featuring a smoking volcano in the middle of Lake Nicaragua on the desk of each senator. Fresh in everyone's mind was the eruption of Mount Peleé on the Caribbean Island of Martinique in May 1902 which destroyed the town of St. Pierre, killing 30,000 people. This and other factors caused the U.S. Senate to prefer the Panama route.

The question remained whether the United States would acquire the French companies assets (a hole in the ground and rusted equipment) at a reasonable price, or whether Colombia would grant the rights that the United States considered essential to complete and operate the canal. The first problem was resolved after some price bickering; after all, those holding the stock issued by the French company had no other offers.

Obtaining Colombia's acquiescence was more difficult. A destructive civil war which raged between 1899–1902 (see companion volume) had just ended in Colombia. President José Manuel Marroquín's hold on the reigns of government was precarious, and the canal was potentially a no-win issue for him. If he made the necessary concessions of Colombian sovereignty to satisfy the Americans, he would deprive Colombia of the future benefits of having the canal within his territory. Marroquín vacillated. In 1900 he sent his foreign minister, Martinez Silva, to Washington to negotiate with the United States but failed to give him adequate instructions; shortly, he was recalled. Next José Vicente Concha was sent to Washington, but he intentionally failed to make progress.[2] Then in November 1902, Tomás Herrán, the former secretary of the legation in Washington, was sent. He was faced with a dilemma: agree to a canal without sovereignty or territorial integrity, or retain integrity and sovereignty but without a canal.[3] He and Secretary of State John Hay signed a treaty on January 23, 1903.[4] Three days later, Herrán received a telegram from Bogotá instructing him not to sign. Herrán did not renounce his action and the treaty was sent to the U.S. Senate and approved on March 17. In June Marroquín submitted the proposed treaty to the newly elected Colombian Senate for its approval. On August 12 the Colombian Senate rejected the treaty by a vote of twenty-four to zero, arguing that the financial compensation was too small and that the virtual perpetuity of the concession was too long. After the Colombian Congress rejected the proposed treaty, Roosevelt ordered Secretary Hay, "make it as strong as you can to Beaupré [U.S. Ambassador to Colombia]. . . . These contemptible little creatures in Bogotá ought to understand how much they are jeopardizing their future."[5] Beaupré threatened the Colombia government if it did not reconsider, "our [U.S.] Congress would take steps in the coming winter that every friend of Colombia would painfully regret."[6]

Four options lay open to the United States—renegotiate with Colombia; develop the Nicaraguan route; seize Panama under the pretext that Colombia had not fulfilled its obligations under the 1847 treaty; or support the independence of Panama. This last option was even discussed openly in at least one U.S. newspaper. In August the Indianapolis *Sentinel* wrote, "The simplest plan of coercing Colombia would be inciting a revolution in Panama . . . and supporting the insurrectionary government. . . . It is hypocritical, but it preserves appearances, and in this case it would be almost justifiable."[7]

In May 1903 a small group of conspirators, allied with the Panama Railroad (a subsidiary of the New Panama Canal Co.), began planning the secession of Panama from Colombia should the treaty be rejected. They approached William Nelson Cromwell (the counsel for the New Panama Company) and received assurances of financial and political help. However, when Dr. Manuel Amador Guerrero, the leader of the conspiracy, arrived in New York in September, he was refused access to Cromwell. The Colombian government learned of the plot and Cromwell feared that the company's concessions might be canceled.[8] On September 23 Bunau-Varilla arrived in New York from Paris and lifted Guerrero's spirits. He promised $100,000 to finance the revolution and secured interviews with President Roosevelt and Secretary Hay for Guerrero. Bunau-Varilla gave Guerrero assurances that if the Panamanians would revolt, the United States would intervene. For serving as the conspiracy coordinator between the Americans and the Panamanians, Bunau-Varilla (a French engineer) asked to be named the plenipotentiary minister of the new Panamanian government in Washington.

OPPOSING FORCES

The United States possessed overwhelming strength when compared to Colombia. Typically, six U.S. warships (generally older cruisers and gunboats) were available for contingencies in the Caribbean. Additionally, since September 1902 a Marine battalion (approximately ten officers and 325 men) was continuously maintained afloat in the Caribbean area within a few days' steaming of Panama. In November 1903 no U.S. troops were stationed in Panama. As the Caribbean region became increasingly important to the United States, the Navy was reorganized and in October 1902 a Caribbean Division was detached from the North Atlantic Squadron (which was reorganized into a "fleet").[9]

Colombia was emerging from decades of devastating civil wars. Although many citizens remained under arms, their loyalties were to local *caudillos*; the central government possessed few professional soldiers. Colombia maintained a 300-man garrison in Panama City although its loyalty was suspect. The Colombian navy operated a few dilapidated, second-hand gunboats, which had been worn out in the service of someone else.[10]

OPENING STRATEGY

For Colombia, Panama might as well have been an island since it was only accessible by sea. The U.S. strategy was to prevent (illegally, since war had not been declared) Colombian troops from landing.

A FALSE START

The Colombian authorities were nervous concerning the possibility of unrest in Panama following their rejection of the proposed canal treaty. In late October 1903, Colombian authorities in Bogotá learned that Panamanian Governor José de Obaldía had sent troops to the interior to repel an incursion. Accordingly, Colombia expedited the preparations of a relief force under Gen. Juan Tovar. These reinforcements took the only route possible to Panama City, the provincial capital—they sailed to Colon on the Caribbean coast and then were to ride the American-owned railway to Panama City on the Pacific coast. Trailing overland between Colombia and Panama was impossible due to dense, disease-infested jungle. Colombia was predominantly a Caribbean nation, as reflected by its population distribution, whereas Panama was a Pacific nation.

THE CREATING OF A NEW NATION

While the Colombian government was dispatching these troops, the Roosevelt administration, anticipating a rebellion in Panama, ordered warships to both the Pacific and Caribbean coasts of the isthmus. Due to unforeseen difficulties and encumbering secrecy, the ships were late arriving. Commander John Hubbard, the commanding officer of the cruiser *Nashville*, found the following cable waiting for him at Colon the evening of November 2:

> Maintain free and uninterrupted transit. If interruption threatened by armed force, occupy the line of railroad. Prevent the landing of any armed force with hostile intent, either Government or insurgent either at Colon, Porto Bello, or other point. . . . Government force reported approaching the Isthmus in vessels. Prevent their landing if in your judgment this would precipitate a conflict. Acknowledgment is required.[11]

That same night, the Colombian gunboat *Cartagena* arrived with General Tovar's command of some 400 soldiers. Hubbard had the *Cartagena* boarded in the morning but did not believe he had grounds to oppose the disembarkation of the troops; they landed at 8:30 A.M.

The General Superintendent of the Panama Railway, J. R. Shaler, being privy to the conspiracy, took the precaution of sending most of the rolling stock to the Pacific side of the isthmus. Shaler persuaded General Tovar to board a special train with his staff and travel to Panama City, a distance of 48 miles, with the understanding that the remainder of his command would follow within hours. Shaler then declined to transport the troops without a request by the Governor of Panama.

After decoding his instructions from the Navy Department, Commander Hubbard accurately perceived that he was to prevent these Colombian troops from proceeding to Panama City. The only practical avenue available was the American-owned Trans-Panama railway. While at the railroad station during the evening of November 3, Hubbard learned of a rebellion in Panama City. The nucleus proved to be the Colombian garrison in that city which was bribed with some of the $100,000 advanced by Bunau-Varilla. Late in the afternoon on the third, Shaler received the request and he told Commander Hubbard that the troops would depart at 8 A.M. on the fourth. Hubbard prohibited the transportation of the troops, "in order to preserve the free and uninterrupted transit of the Isthmus."[12] The official justification for refusing to permit Colombian troops to use the railway was that the United States was bound by the 1846 treaty to prevent fighting that would interfere with peaceful transit.[13]

In Panama City General Tovar, General Castro, and Commander Tovar learned of the impending revolution and tried to prevent it. The two generals rushed to the barracks and Commander Tovar returned to his gunboat, the *Bogotá*. The generals were arrested by General Esteban Huertas, second in command of the Panama garrison. The revolution started at 6 P.M. At 8 P.M. a boat from the *Bogotá* carried a message demanding the release of the generals or the gunboat would bombard the city. Two hours later, the *Bogotá* fired its only six shells at Panama City, killing one Chinese and a burro. A harbor fort returned fire. The *Bogotá* hoisted its anchor and sailed off. The Colombian gunboat *21 de Noviembre* laying off the city passively watched. On the morning of the fourth, the *21 de Noviembre* anchored near the fort, and that afternoon she hauled down the Colombian flag and hoisted that of Panama.[14]

On the Caribbean side, Colonel Torres twice attempted to pressure concessions from the U.S. consul on the fourth and the fifth. Both times Commander Hubbard successfully intervened.[15] Finally, at 7:35 P.M. on the fifth, Colonel Torres and 473 Colombian soldiers departed for Cartagena on board the Mail Steamer *Orinoco*.

Events moved fast. On November 4 Panama declared its independence; this was unofficially recognized by the United States on the sixth (and officially a week later). By November 7 the United States had secured the anchorages at either terminus of the railroad, thus being in a position to prevent additional Colombian troops from landing. Two days later the U.S. Navy extended its undeclared blockade along the coast, following rumors that the Colombian government might attempt to land troops outside the normal areas of disembarkation. In December another rumor circulated that Colombia would attempt an overland expedition; however, clear heads prevailed in the United States before wasteful defensive measures had been taken. The polite reception of the cruiser *Olympia* at Cartagena on December 27 gave evidence that Colombia would not resort to military action.[16]

OBSERVATIONS

The revolution succeeded because of the U.S. insistence on maintaining "peaceful transit" across the isthmus. On December 7, 1903, Roosevelt reported to Congress, "Under the circumstances the Government of the United States would have been guilty of folly and weakness, amounting in their sum to a crime against the Nation, had it acted otherwise than it did when the Revolution of November 3 last took place in Panama."[17] No good reason exists to doubt President Roosevelt's words that he chose to guarantee the success of the Panamanian revolution.

The Panama revolution had far-reaching effects within Latin America. These nations were already suspicious of America's imperialistic designs because of U.S. actions in Cuba and Puerto Rico during the Spanish-American War (see companion volume). The shock of the loss of Panama heaped upon the decades of civil wars finally caused Colombian Federalists and Centralists to compromise.

The 1903 intervention was fundamentally different from previous interventions. The American objective here was the independence of Panama under U.S. protection, whereas in the past the United States had intervened to protect threatened economic and political interests and had withdrawn once these threats subsided.

This 1903 intervention demonstrated the ability of the United States to rapidly project military power into the region, making the Caribbean truly "an American lake." The U.S. Marine

Corps could put together a 400-man battalion (or even a 2,000-man brigade) from Marines scattered in barracks from Portsmouth, Virginia, to Pensacola, Florida, and transport it anywhere within the Caribbean within two weeks.[18]

PART 2

CHAPTER 2

THE ACRE WAR, 1903

Colonel, we only made war to take what is ours.

—Placido de Castro accepting the surrender
of Puerto Alonso, on January 24, 1903

THE SPARK

On January 2, 1899, Bolivia opened a customhouse at Puerto Alonso (now Puerto Acre, Brazil) in Bolivia. This angered Brazilian settlers, who wanted the Bolivian authorities to leave. Dr. José de Carvalho led an unsuccessful revolt against the Bolivians on April 30, thus beginning an on-again, off-again conflict for control and possession of the Acre.[1]

BACKGROUND

The province of Acre, about five times the size of Belgium, lies buried in the heart of South America. In 1867 the Treaty of Ayacucho set the general boundary between Bolivia and Brazil but the details were never worked out. Nominally, the Acre was considered to be Bolivian. The Acre attracted little interest because of its inaccessibility and apparent lack of commercial value. Its population was composed of a small number of Indians without a national identity and a few Bolivians and Brazilians.[2]

When the price of rubber, which was harvested from wild trees, skyrocketed at the end of the nineteenth century, nearly 18,000 adventurers and settlers, mostly Brazilians, poured into the Acre to exploit the wild trees. Almost no roads existed, so a few river steamers, canoes, and rafts were the primary means of transportation.[3]

OPPOSING FORCES

Initially, Bolivia relied on a few civil officials and a tiny garrison which was rarely paid. Brazil's interests were championed by its citizens who were exporting rubber from the remote province.

7

OPPOSING STRATEGIES

The strategy for both sides was to seize and hold the river towns.

THE FIRST "REPUBLIC OF ACRE"

Within a few months of the April 1899 uprising, a Spanish adventurer, Luís Gálvez Rodrígues de Arias, who had served as the Bolivian consul at Belem, Brazil, led a second revolt. On July 14, 1899, he declared the independent republic of Acre at Empresa. The Bolivians reacted by dispatching a 500-man force. Before their arrival, Gálvez was imprisoned by Antonio Sonza Braga, who declared himself president of Acre. Shortly thereafter, however, he reinstated Gálvez to power. In March 1900 a Brazilian flotilla reached Puerto Alonso (510 mi N of La Paz and 1,940 mi NW of Rio de Janeiro) and put an end to the republic, returning the port to Bolivian control.[4]

THE SECOND "REPUBLIC OF ACRE"

A force primarily composed of Brazilians organized another revolt in November 1900. Its objective was to wrestle control of Acre from Bolivia and create an independent republic. Known as the "Expedition of the Poets,"[5] this quasi-Brazilian force was built around the river steamer *Solimoes*, outfitted with the aid of the governor of the Brazilian province of Amazonas, Silverio Neri. The *Solimoes* operated on the Purus River and seized the Bolivian launch *Alonso*, which was renamed the *Rui Barbosa*. Rodrigo de Carvalho became the president of the newly declared republic of Acre; his authority rested in one light cannon, a machine gun, and some two hundred men. Around Christmas 1900 this force attacked Puerto Alonso and was beaten back, losing the cannon and machine gun. On December 29 the Bolivian armed launch *Río Afua* brought relief to the embattled Puerto Alonso garrison.[6]

In an attempt to solve its problem, Bolivia leased the Acre region to the Bolivian Trading Company (also known as the "Bolivian Syndicate of New York City") incorporated in Jersey City, New Jersey. This business concern had some very influential shareholders, including the King of Belgium and relatives of William McKinley, then President of the United States. Bolivia awarded to the lessees almost total control over the Acre province in an attempt to protect its sovereignty.[7]

Brazil and Peru (which also claimed the territory) vehemently objected. Brazil recalled its consul from Port Alonso and closed the Amazon tributaries to commerce bound to or from Bolivia. The major world powers, who considered the river system to be international waters, protested, so Brazil reduced the ban to war materials and Bolivian goods cleared for foreign nations.[8]

In the Acre José Plácido de Castro, a gaucho and former professional soldier, now took charge of the quasi-Brazilian force. At five o'clock in the morning on August 6, 1902, he and some thirty-three armed men landed in canoes and captured the river town of Xapuri on the Acre River, whereupon Plácido proclaimed a revolution and an independent republic. On September 18 a 180-man Bolivian battalion, led by Col. Rosendo Rojas, surprised Plácido's force, now numbering some seventy men. The Brazilians, armed only with Winchester rifles, short of munitions, and suffering from tropical diseases and desertion, lost twenty men. They were defeated.[9]

Undaunted, Plácido now recruited another force of about a thousand men. Part of this group laid siege to Puerto Alonso on May 10, 1902. On October 14 the force captured some outer defenses along with the Bolivian armed launch *Río Afua*, which had become stranded during the fighting. The river craft was renamed the *Independencia* and used against its former owners. In spite of this setback, the Bolivians stubbornly held onto Puerto Alonso.[10]

Elsewhere, the Brazilian adventurers laid siege to Empresa, which surrendered on October 15. Other engagements, most of them victories for Plácido's quasi-Brazilian force, took place at Bom Destino, Santa Rosa, and various other river towns. On January 15, 1903, the Brazilian force assaulted and captured some of the Bolivian positions outside Puerto Alonso. The *Independencia*, which lay upstream from the Bolivians, loaded thirty tons of high-quality rubber and forced her way past the Bolivian river batteries to carry the rubber downstream where it could be sold. Plácido's force used the money to buy weapons and munitions. On January 24, the Bolivians at Puerto Alonso surrendered.

The besieging force, now seven hundred strong, occupied the port and advanced to where the Chipamanu (also called the Manuripe) and Tauamanu Rivers meet to form the Orton River. Soon, a Bolivian force under Gen. José Manuel Pando, President of Bolivia, occupied the opposite bank.[11]

At this time the Brazilian government formally stepped in, sending troops into the disputed area then held by the quasi-Brazilian force. Bolivia now reluctantly agreed to sell the province of Acre, a concession formalized in the Treaty of Petropolis and signed on November 17, 1903. Within three years the taxes that Brazil collected in the Acre offset the cost of the indemnities and the loan for the construction of the railroad.[12]

OBSERVATIONS

The Acre War demonstrated the strategic advantage Brazil held over its Spanish-speaking neighbors due to its downstream location on the rivers that flowed across almost the entire continent, beginning in the Andes Mountains and ending in the Atlantic Ocean. Brazil could sail assistance to the disputed area up the river systems, whereas the Bolivians had to carry theirs across the Andes Mountains.

Apparently, the losing Bolivian effort was entirely funded by national rubber barons, Nicolás Suárez, in particular. For a second time (the first being the War of the Pacific; see companion volume) Bolivia lost in war a major part of its sparsely populated lowlands to a stronger, better-governed neighbor.[13]

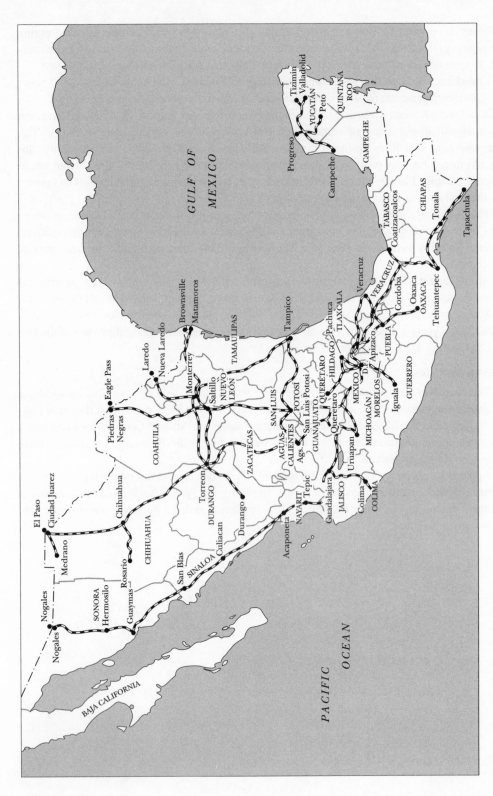

Map 1. The Mexican Revolution 1910–20.

PART 3

CHAPTER 3

THE MEXICAN REVOLUTION, 1910–1920

The true, underlying causes of the revolution had little to do, in the eyes of the masses, with "no re-election" or "real suffrage"; they sprang from the motive of "no poverty and real food, cheaper and more abundant."

—Francisco Bulnes, December 1911

THE SPARK

On October 5, 1910, Francisco Madero[1] denounced the reelection of President José de la Cruz Porfirio Díaz[2] from San Antonio, Texas, and called for an armed rebellion to take place on November 20. This proclamation of the Plan of San Luis Potosi[3] was the signature event in an increasing crescendo of happenings that began the Mexican revolution.[4]

BACKGROUND

In 1910 Porfirio Díaz sought his eighth term as President of Mexico. Internationally, he was at the height of his prestige. Díaz' Mexico was "mother of the foreigner and step-mother of the Mexican." Díaz' source of power was the *Cientificos* (the elites) who wanted order, especially for the bourgeois middle class. Porfirio Díaz maintained order through the federal police (*Rurales*), the military, and the Church much as the Conservatives had done prior to *La Reforma* (see companion volume).[5]

During their more than three decades of dominating influence, the *Cientificos* developed many enemies. The planters were angry with them because of the 1908 banking reforms which made it more costly to borrow money. Businessmen were upset because José Limantour, leader of the *Cientificos* and finance minister, tried to end smuggling. The workers opposed the *Cientificos* because they were against a minimum wage. Feminists were against the *Cientificos* because Limantour had closed the Treasury Department to female employment. Newspapers were opposed to the *Cientificos* because Limantour would not subsidize them. School teachers

11

were against the *Científicos* because Limantour opposed the increase of their salaries and the appropriation of money for rural schools. Protestants opposed the *Científicos* because Limantour never rewarded them with public office. Masons were opposed because *Científicos* did not approve of secret societies. And the list goes on. Until 1910 these factions lacked focus and commitment; it is one thing to be angry and another to rebel.[6]

Since Don Porfirio retained power by playing one rival against another, he had no obvious successor. Underneath the seemingly tranquil Mexican landscape were the accumulating frustrations of the disenfranchised Indians, the oppressed laborers, and the ignored intellectuals. In 1908 Francisco Madero published a book that catapulted him to national prominence. In his book, *The Presidential Succession in 1910*, Madero urged that, should Díaz choose to run again, the people should be given a voice in the selection of the vice president. After all, in 1910 Díaz would be 80 years old.[7]

The 1910 election might have been as uneventful as those preceding it, had it not been for an interview granted by Díaz to James Creelman of *Pearson's Magazine*. Published in March 1908, Don Porfirio stated that he would not accept another term, that Mexico was ready for democracy, and that he would welcome the establishment of an opposition party and hold free elections. These statements, probably intended only for foreign consumption, caused a stir in Mexico. Madero's campaign slogan began "Effective Suffrage and No Reelection." Madero emerged as the old dictator's most dangerous rival. An anti-*Porfirismo* began to develop. Díaz had Madero jailed until after the election on June 26, which Díaz won through fraud. Madero was freed on bond, escaped to the United States, and issued his Plan of San Luis Potosi.[8]

OPPOSING FORCES

Mexico's population in 1910 was almost 12 million. Of these, only 195,000 were laborers, 500,000 artisans, and 11 million peasants. The laborers were concentrated in Mexico City, Monterrey, Puebla, Guadalajara, and Veracruz.[9]

During the three-and-one-half decades of rule by Porfirio Díaz, Mexico gained a reputation for being domestically tranquil and safe for foreign investment, in large part because of the effectiveness of the *Rurales* and the Mexican army. Few outside of Mexico in 1910 would have disputed Thomas Janvier's analysis a decade earlier: "[T]he Mexican army is an honor to the government that has created it, and affords the surest guarantee that in Mexico the days of revolutions are ended, and that the existing constitutional government will endure."[10]

The truth was far different. The Mexican army of 1910 was composed of 29,000 men. It was a mixture of the new and the old. The Chapultepec Military School was graduating well-trained, young officers. Although the graduates from Chapultepec represented half of the officer corps, the most senior officers held their rank because they were old friends of the President. And most of the soldiers were forced conscripts, a system known as the *leva*.[11]

Although some corruption by senior officers was tolerated in order to assure their loyalty, finance minister Limantour did not permit those in the army to steal promiscuously, something they had been accustomed to doing throughout the century-long struggle between the Liberals and Conservatives.[12]

Many Mexicans responded to Francisco Madero's call to arms during the winter of 1910–11, first in northern Mexico and then in the central and southern states. Madero drew support from the growing number of laborers. Their political consciousness had been awakened by the spread of literacy, a product of the Porfiriato's National Preparatory Schools. The artisan class wanted political and legal justice and feared losing its economic gains should the succession problem destroy the nation's economy. Many of the revolution's ideologies and the military advisors came from the teacher training schools. And large numbers of illiterate peasants rose up in support of Madero. Many peasants had gained their first exposure to the world outside their hamlets when building (frequently by force) the extensive railroad system, yet another Porfiriato achievement. The peasants wanted freedom from oppression (a by-product of Porfirio Díaz' modernization) *and land*. In the north, the peasants fought to break up *latifundia*, while in central and southern Mexico they fought for the restoration of their *ejidos* (communal lands). The Revolutionaries came from diverse backgrounds and were motivated by a variety of interests, some of which would prove to be incompatible in the long run. Estimating the number of rebels may be less important than knowing how many guns they had because more frequently that decided the number of troops the rebels could field. [13]

The strength of the rebel forces rested upon the loyalty given to individual leaders by their followers. In most cases, this loyalty had been earned through acts of bravado. Few of these leaders had any formal military education or training. Some were bandits such as Pancho Villa,[14] who had fought against the Mexican army and *Rurales* for more than a decade. Others were social Revolutionaries such as Emiliano Zapata,[15] who had led attacks against wealthy landowners.

Throughout the years of fighting, the opposing sides were armed with the same weapons, the only significant difference being that the Federal troops had more, particularly in the early years. The most common rifles were the Model 1895 German Mausers, the standard issue of the Mexican army, and the Model 1871 Remington carbine, purchased in large numbers from American arms merchants.[16]

OPENING STRATEGY

Porfirio Díaz did not immediately perceive the severity of the threat, and, once he did, he was reluctant to commit his entire army against the rebels for fear that the outside world would lose confidence in his government. Besides, almost half the army was already garrisoned in the northern states, where the uprising was the most serious because of the activities of bandits, Indians, anarchists, and dissidents.

Initially, the Insurgents had no strategy, only a goal, and that was to overthrow Porfirio Díaz. This was the glue that held their fragile fraternity together.

THE ANTI–DÍAZ CAMPAIGN

Due to the lack of central control, numerous uncoordinated acts of rebellion broke out throughout Mexico following the 1910 elections. Among the first, Aquiles Serdán led an uprising in Puebla on November 18; wounded, he was hidden but discovered the next day and executed. Some fifty people died in that uprising. Throughout the north numerous leaders such as Pascual Orozco,[17] Francisco Villa, José Mayorena, and Luís Gutiérrez rose up. And in the south, the Figueroa and Zapata brothers led the Insurgents.[18]

Finally, in the state of Chihuahua in northern Mexico, the Insurgents began evolving from hit-and-run guerrillas into an army. On November 21, Madero crossed the Rio Grande, lost his way, and finally found twenty men waiting for him, only half of whom were armed. Disillusioned and believing that the rebellion had failed, he re-crossed into the United States.[19]

One of the first victories for the rebels occurred when Pascual Orozco defeated a Federal force at Pedernales and then captured Ciudad Guerrero on November 30. On January 2, 1911,

Figure 1. The Mexican Revolution (1910–20). This hardly looks like the beginning of a great revolution. Francisco Madero wearing a business suit reads behind a make-shift table while his supporters rest in the shade of some rocks. Directly behind him in the dark hat and dress is his wife. The individual to her right with the hat on his knee is Madero's brother Raúl. The fighting throughout the Mexican Revolution was dominated by the *vaqueros* (cowboys) of the north and they are very much in evidence in this photograph. *Courtesy Library of Congress, Washington, D.C.*

Orozco ambushed a Federal column. He stripped the dead soldiers of their clothing and sent the clothes back to Porfirio Díaz with the note, "Here are the wrappers; send me some more tamales."[20] After some fierce fighting, Federal troops reoccupied the city on January 6, 1911.[21] But the revolution continued to spread. In Sonora, Salvador Alvarado and Juan G. Cabral occupied Cuquiarachi. In Baja California José M. Leyva captured Mexicali. South of Mexico City, Insurgents captured Guerrero on December 6 but were driven out three days later.[22]

On February 14 Madero again crossed into Mexico from the United States and occupied Zaragoza, Chihuahua, some 10 miles southeast of Ciudad Juárez (1,221 mi NW of Mexico City). He attacked Casas Grandes on March 6 with 800 men. The town was defended by 500 men from the 18th Infantry Battalion who were rescued by the arrival of Federal troops commanded by Samuel García Cuéllar, Chief of the Presidential General Staff (Jefe del Estado Mayor Presidencial). Madero, who was wounded in the arm, was repulsed with significant losses.[23]

In spite of this setback, volunteers poured into Madero's camp, including men led by Pascual Orozco and Pancho Villa. Madero's force swelled to 3,000 men. He now advanced against the border town of Ciudad Juárez, site of an important customs house. Some 800 Federal troops defended the town. Madero became concerned that by attacking Ciudad Juárez he might inadvertently cause the intervention of the United States should stray shells fall into El Paso on the American side of the border. Orozco ignored Madero's order to retreat and instead attacked. The fighting raged from May 8 through May 10. Orozco and Villa led the Insurgents; Col. Manuel Tamborrell, a graduate of the Chapultepec Military School, commanded the Federal garrison. Following three days of hard fighting, the Federal troops, low on ammunition, surrendered. Colonel Tamborrell was among the dead. Madero rescued the overall Federal commander, Gen. Juan Navarro, who had previously executed captured rebels, and escorted him to El Paso, Texas, much to the outrage of Orozco and Villa. Neither Orozco nor Villa were appointed to Madero's new cabinet in spite of their being the key architects of the victory. On May 17 the two sides signed a five-day truce which effectively ended the serious fighting north of Mexico City.[24]

The aging Díaz had failed to send adequate forces against the *Insurgentes* in the north. The capture of Ciudad Juárez gave the rebels access to arms and munitions from the United States. More importantly, this Insurgent victory demonstrated that the Federal army was not invincible.[25]

Díaz' influential financial advisor, Limantour, recognized that given the aging dictator's level of commitment, the struggle could not be won and persuaded Porfirio Díaz to resign. On May 21, 1911, Díaz reluctantly signed the Treaty of Ciudad Juárez, whereby his government stepped down. On June 6 Madero triumphantly entered Mexico City. Surprisingly, it had taken very little time and blood to oust the once seemingly invincible dictator of thirty-five years.[26]

While Madero was winning the political revolution in the north, the Zapata brothers were creating the roots for the social and economic revolutions in the south. The Zapatas led the rebellion in the poor, small state of Morelos, just to the south of Mexico City, where huge sugar plantations with absentee landlords had squeezed the centuries-old communal land (*ejidos*) during the rule of Porfirio Díaz. Leading the poorly armed and poorly trained peasants, the Zapata brothers' fortunes were mixed. Zapata and others in the south refused to recognize the interim government which had temporarily replaced Porfirio Díaz, and the brutal military campaign in the south continued. Finally, Madero was elected president in a peaceful contest and inaugurated on November 6, 1911.[27]

REBELLIONS AGAINST MADERO

President Madero was neither politically strong enough to deliver on his promises of major social reform, nor militarily powerful enough to deal with the growing opposition from both former colleagues as well as old enemies. In short order, Emiliano Zapata, Bernardo Reyes, Pascual Orozco, and Féliz Díaz rebelled against Madero.

The irrepressible Zapata became impatient for land reform and declared the Plan of Ayala on November 28, 1911. This demanded the immediate restoration of the *ejidos*, stolen from the villages and sold to favorites by Porfirio Díaz. Madero was forced to use the *Porfiriato* army to prevent Zapata from redistributing land at the point of a gun. The army was able to control the towns but Zapata held the countryside.[28]

Gen. Bernardo Reyes was the second major figure to rebel. Toward the end of Porfirio Díaz' rule, Reyes had a substantial following and was frequently spoken of as the old dictator's successor. Reyes secretly crossed into San Antonio, Texas, where he purchased arms. The U.S. government discovered his activities and seized his cache. Reyes escaped to Matamoros on December 13, 1911. The hundreds of followers he anticipated never materialized. After a skirmish between Reyes and troops loyal to Madero, Reyes surrendered on December 25. General Reyes was brought to Mexico City and imprisoned at the Santiago Tlaltelolco military prison to await trial. Although sentenced to death, it was commuted by Madero.[29]

Pascual Orozco was next to rebel. He was motivated by a dislike of Madero, the belief that he should have been appointed governor of Chihuahua, and the prodding of the super-rich Terrazas family which dominated Chihuahua. On March 4, 1912, Orozco denounced Madero in the state capital. On the eighth he dispatched two troop-laden rebel trains from the city of Chihuahua to capture Ciudad Juárez on the border. Orozco commanded some 6,000 men.[30]

In Mexico City the Secretary of War, Gen. José González Salas, asked to be placed in charge of the expedition against Orozco. On March 8, a military train carrying one infantry brigade and two cavalry brigades, totaling 2,150 men, departed Mexico City for the north. It proceeded to Torreón, Durango, where the reinforcements joined 5,000 Federal troops. From there some of the infantry advanced on foot and the cavalry on horseback northward against the rebel stronghold Jiménez in southern Chihuahua. The government train followed carrying additional troops, supplies, General Gonzáles Salas, and his staff. Orozco gathered an army of some 6,000 men. On March 24, as the government troops advanced along the rail line, Orozco's men packed a locomotive, "a Crazy Machine" ("*una máquina loca*"), with dynamite and sent it speeding southward. It struck the government's armored train, exploding and causing numerous casualties. Orozco then defeated the government's troops at Rellano Canyon (850 mi NW of Mexico City) and they retreated to Torreón. The Federal troops sustained 600 casualties and those of Orozco 220 casualties. General Gonzáles Salas committed suicide by shooting himself in the head.[31]

Madero was forced to call upon the Porfiriato army headed by Brig. Gen. Victoriano Huerta[32] and the remaining loyal revolutionaries to put down the rebellion. In April, Huerta proceeded north by train bringing with him reinforcements which would increase the Northern Division to 4,800 men. Joining the Federal force were 700 irregular cavalry loyal to Pancho Villa. On May 12 Huerta defeated Orozco at Conejos, Durango. The rebels lost 400 killed, 200 wounded, 107 railroad cars, 2 locomotives, plus weapons and munitions. Then Orozco was defeated at Rellano Station, sustaining 650 casualties. Orozco retreated to Jiménez, destroying the rail line as he went.

Orozco sustained another defeat at La Cruz, Chihuahua, on June 16. On July 3 and 4 Orozco was completely routed at the Canyon of Bachimba in Chihuahua. He retreated to Ciudad Juárez but evacuated it on August 20. The rebellion was finished although scattered elements continued to raid Federal troops for months. Huerta, who expected to be rewarded by promotion to General of a Division, was retired.[33]

General Félix Díaz, nephew of Porfirio Díaz, was next to rebel. Following his uncle's downfall, Félix Díaz retired from the army and took up residence in Veracruz. Díaz believed that he commanded wide support in his uncle's army, which was still intact. On October 16 Díaz, supported by his cousin, Col. Jesús María Díaz Ordáz, who commanded the 21st Infantry Battalion, seized Veracruz (285 mi E of Mexico City). Federal troops reacted rapidly and on October 23 a 2,000-man force recaptured the port. Two days later Félix Díaz was sentenced to death by a local military court. Friends interceded and Díaz was transferred to the Penitentiary of Mexico City where Madero commuted the death sentence.[34]

THE TEN TRAGIC DAYS (FEBRUARY 9-18, 1913)

Mexico began 1913 filled with rumors of new uprisings. On Sunday, February 9, retired Gen. Manuel Mondragón, former Chief of the Artillery Department, led eighty men of the 1st Cavalry Regiment, an artillery battery of the 2nd Regiment, and eighty men from the 5th Infantry Regiment station at Tacubaya into rebellion. They marched to the Santiago Tlaltelolco Prison and freed Gen. Bernardo Reyes; other units joined the rebels.

Simultaneously, the students of the Candidates' Military Academy, founded by General Reyes in Tlalpan, rebelled. They took street cars to Mexico City. These rebels were also joined by other units as they approached the center of the city. Some of the rebels advanced on the National Palace while others went to the Penitentiary of Mexico City and freed Gen. Félix Díaz.[35]

In the meantime, Gen. Lauro Villar, commander of the city's garrison, prepared to defend the National Palace and the Madero government with the loyal 20th and 24th Battalions. Gen. Gregorio Ruiz, first of the rebels to arrive, was captured and shot. An intensive fight broke out between the two forces. Within twenty minutes, 805 bodies littered the plaza in front of the National Palace, most of them civilians caught in the crossfire. Among the dead was General Reyes. The rebels retreated to the Citadel, some twelve blocks from the National Palace. They captured the armory which housed 55,000 rifles, 30,000 carbines, 100 Hotchkiss machine guns, and 26 million 7mm cartridges.[36]

Madero hurried from his residence in the Chapultepec Castle to the National Palace, escorted by the cadets from the military academy; along the way his column was joined by General Huerta. Finding General Villar seriously wounded, Madero placed General Huerta in change. On February 11 Huerta ordered Federal cavalry and infantry to attack the rebels, but the government troops were easily scattered by machine-gun fire. On the thirteenth Huerta attacked with the 2nd and 7th Infantry Battalions but this also failed. Next, the two sides settled into an artillery duel with practically all of the shots falling among civilians. Only one shot hit the Citadel and two hit the National Palace. The innocent dead were stacked like firewood, soaked in gasoline, and burned.[37]

Sickened by the loss of life, frustrated by the lack of progress, and perhaps suspicious of Huerta's intentions, Madero ordered Gen. Felipe Angeles, who was directing operations against Zapata in the state of Morelos, to return to the capital. The general returned with 400 men and four machine guns. Poor cooperation by Huerta led to more unsuccessful attacks against the Citadel.[38]

Beginning on Saturday, February 8, the U.S. Embassy had become the meeting place for those opposed to Madero with the blessings of the U.S. Ambassador, Henry Lane Wilson.[39] Many of those in attendance were American and Mexican businessmen and former leaders of the Porfirio Díaz army. As the fighting raged between February 9 and 18, these conspirators drew up the Pact of the Citadel (*Pacto de la Ciudadela*). On February 16 Ambassador Wilson invited Huerta, the commander of Madero's forces, and the younger Díaz, the chief rebel, to the embassy and urged them to unite against Madero. Huerta arrested the President and Vice President on February 18. Madero's brother Gustavo died while being tortured.

That night the major conspirators and Ambassador Wilson met at the U.S. Embassy and agreed to publish the Pact of the Citadel. On February 22 at 11:30 P.M., President Madero and Vice President José María Pino Suárez were assassinated. In addition, thousands, many of whom were innocent civilians caught in the crossfire, died during the fighting of the "ten tragic days."[40]

Madero had made military and political mistakes. He would not or could not disband the irregular troops who had brought him to power and thus became dependent upon the Porfiriato army to deal with his former supporters who demanded immediate changes. Neither the army nor the irregulars were being regularly paid, thus undermining their loyalty to the central government and reinforcing their loyalty to their officers and leaders, who provided for their needs, frequently by extralegal means. Politically, Madero ignored the interests of potential supporters, such as the Catholic Party, who could have been logical allies.[41]

THE ANTI-HUERTA CAMPAIGN

Much of the "industrialized world" was reassured by Huerta's seizure of power. Most world powers recognized his government; the Church loaned him large sums; and English banks floated huge bonds for Huerta. However, many Mexicans as well as the new liberal President of the United States, Woodrow Wilson, were horrified by Madero's assassination. President Wilson refused Huerta's government recognition in spite of the advice given by Ambassador Henry Lane Wilson, whom the U.S. President recalled for his meddling.

Venustiano Carranza,[42] Governor of Coahuila and a supporter of Madero, refused to recognize Huerta as the new head of state, as did many of the Insurgents who had supported Madero prior to the 1911 election such as Villa and Zapata. On March 26, 1913, Carranza issued the *Plan de Guadalupe* which was a call to arms against Huerta.[43]

At first glance, it seemed that Carranza, governor of a poor, sparsely populated state, stood little chance against Huerta who controlled the resources of the central government. Huerta inherited Porfirio Díaz' army, which, in spite of its shortcomings and previous defeats, had not been destroyed. Also, some of those who had rebelled against Madero in 1912, including Pascual Orozco, joined Huerta against Carranza. They were known as *colorados* because of their red insignia.[44]

Within Coahuila, Carranza could count on only 500 mounted men, mostly irregulars. More importantly, former revolutionary leaders throughout Mexico rallied to Carranza's side. These included Francisco Villa, whose small band of followers would swell into the "Villa Brigade" and later become the feared "Division of the North" (*Division del Norte*). Abraham Gonzáles, Governor of Chichuahua, also refused to recognize Huerta, but he was immediately captured and assassinated. Benjamin Hill, Alvaro Obregón,[45] and Juan Cabral influenced the state of Sonora into joining the rebellion against Huerta. The revolution spread southward and included the uncompromising Zapata.[46]

The only Federal successes were against Carranza, a politican and not a soldier, in Coahuila where he sustained a severe beating at Saltillo (677 mi NNW of Mexico City) between March 21 and 23. Elsewhere, the Insurgents were immediately victorious along the border. In Sonora, Obregón captured the border town of Nogales on March 14, 1913. The Southern Pacific of Mexico railroad line ran through the town and tied into the American system running to Tuscon, Arizona. On April 13 Obregón captured the border town of Naco which was the Mexican northern terminus of a spur of the American El Paso and Southwest Railroad Line. Holding these two towns allowed him to export cattle to the United States and to import arms.[47]

In the state of Chihuahua, Pancho Villa won a series of victories over Federal troops and by the end of May was threatening the large Federal garrison in Chihuahua City, the state capital. Federal forces were only able to hold the northeast and had lost the remainder of the border.[48]

After having won control of northern Sonora, Obregón turned south. He won battles at Santa Rosa (May 9–11, 1913) and Santa María (June 15–26), and besieged the port of Guaymas on June 27. Obregón employed aerial reconnaissance during the battle of Santa María. He extended his operations southward into the state of Sinaloa.[49]

In the south, Zapata continued his hit-and-run tactics. Huerta responded with draconian measures, which increased the hostility of the peasants toward the government. As a consequence, the government controlled the towns and Zapata the countryside. Zapata's nearness to Mexico City required Huerta to commit significant resources against him. Zapata's lack of arms and munitions prevented him from being more of a potent threat.[50]

The struggle might have taken on an increasingly sinister character after May 24 when Carranza, citing a similar order by Benito Juárez of January 25, 1862, announced permission for summary executions of captured soldiers as well as those who recognized or aided the enemy. Most rebel leaders, however, chose to ignore the order. If it had been carried out, the consequences might have significantly damaged their cause by dissuading desertions from the Federal army.[51]

On July 4 Carranza reorganized the Revolutionary army. The most important commands given to Gen. Alvaro Obregón (Northwestern Army Corps—which included the Division of the North commanded by Gen. Francisco Villa), and Gen. Pablo González (Northeastern Army Corps).[52]

Pancho Villa swept southward out of north-central Mexico, his force growing stronger by the day. On October 1, 1913, Villa captured Torreón, a railroad center. He personally executed *Huerista* generals.[53]

Subsequently, Villa abandoned Torreón and turned northward. He attacked Chihuahua City (1,094 mi NNW of Mexico City) on November 5. Garrisoned by 6,300 Federal troops, Villa made little progress. On November 15 Villa abandoned the attack and fell upon a sleeping Ciudad Juárez some 225 miles to the north. Trains loaded with Villa's troops entered the border town uncontested and surprised the garrison. This was an important victory because it

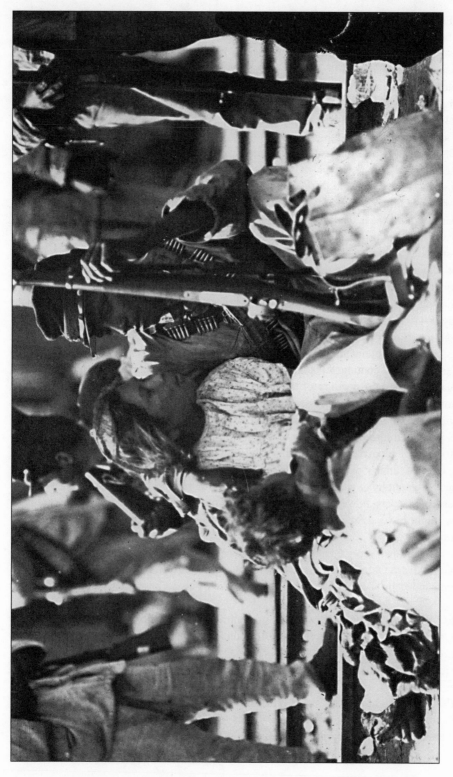

Figure 2. The Mexican Revolution (1910–20). A federal soldier rests with his family. Typically, Mexican families followed their males on campaigns. The family members gathered food and firewood, plus cooked and washed clothes for their husbands, brothers, sons, and sweethearts. The march of a large Mexican force frequently appeared like a migration. *Courtesy of Casasola, Mexico City.*

opened one more avenue for weapons and supplies from the United States. Villa then defeated belated reinforcements sent to Ciudad Juárez on November 25 at the Battle of Tierra Blanca just 20 miles south of the border town. Federal troops abandoned Chihuahua City and ultimately sought sanctuary in the United States.[54]

While the fighting raged, Huerta attempted to transform Mexico into a military arsenal. Non-war-related businesses were forbidden to remain open on Sundays so that reservists could be trained; military cargos choked out all other railroad traffic; technology and machinery necessary to manufacture munitions and weapons flooded into Mexico. Although Huerta constantly decreed increases in the size of the army until it reached 250,000 men on paper on March 16, 1914, these goals could not be realized by any means. The ultimate and most notorious recruitment method was the *leva*, or forced conscription. By late 1913 it was the only source of men. The officer corps expanded and many advanced in grade rapidly, primarily as rewards for non-military activities. By late 1913 the army had grown to its ultimate size, perhaps 80,000 men.[55]

These untrained, poorly led troops frequently surrendered in mass. When they fought, they wasted ammunition at a vociferous rate. Although national production of 7mm rifle bullets had more than doubled between 1910 and 1913, the Federal army frequently expended more ammunition in a single battle than could be produced in Mexico during the entire month. Huerta ordered weapons and munitions from anyone who would sell to him. In the case of the United States, which would not, his agents attempted to smuggle the arms out. Within this procurement system, graft and corruption grew to overwhelming proportions. It was in the financial interests of many of Huerta's supporters to prolong the fighting and not end it.[56]

Movement of Huerta's ill-trained, poorly led, reluctant army was tied to the railroads. This transportation system fell easy prey to the fast-moving, hard-hitting cavalry of the Insurgents. The Insurgents always had the choice of the time and place of the battle.

In an effort to gain U.S. recognition, Huerta held elections in October 1913. In spite of the fact that the *Carrancistas* held the majority of the country, Huerta was declared the winner by his hand-picked national congress. In February 1914 the United States lifted the arms embargo which it had imposed in 1912. This favored the *Constitucionalistas*, as the anti-Huerta forces called themselves, since they controlled the border areas.[57]

THE UNITED STATES SEIZES VERACRUZ

While fighting raged throughout Mexico, the United States seized Veracruz on April 21, 1914, on the pretext that the Huerta government (which it did not recognize) refused to properly apologize and salute the American flag following an incident at Tampico earlier in the month.[58] In part, the United States wanted to block the delivery of seventeen million rounds of ammunition being carried in the German merchantship *Ypiranga*. The *Ypiranga* was warned of the American trap and diverted to Tampico where it successfully delivered its cargo to the *Huertistas*. The *Huertistas* guarding Veracruz were intimidated by the U.S. Marines and chose to flee without a fight; not so for the naval academy cadets and infuriated civilians. Armed with antiquated weapons, they fought a losing battle throughout the day. The Mexicans lost 193 dead and 600 wounded. The Americans lost 19 dead and 70 wounded.[59]

The American action won Huerta sympathy among some Mexicans who now perceived the United States as a bigger threat than the continuation of the Huerta government. The United

Figure 3. The Mexican Revolution (1910–20). Federal forces form a firing line at a street corner to fight U.S. marines and sailors who landed at Veracruz on April 21, 1914. Those wearing white uniforms are possibly cadets from the Mexican Naval Academy, which at that time was located in the port city. *Courtesy U.S. Naval Historical Center, Washington, D.C.*

States accepted the proffered mediation of Argentina, Brazil, and Chile in order to lessen the appearance of meddling. Wilson backed his insistence that Huerta must leave by withholding recognition, blocking trade, and continuing to allow the *Constitutionalistas* to acquire arms across the Rio Grande.[60]

THE 1914 *INSURGENTE* OFFENSIVE

In the spring of 1914 the Insurgents launched a major offensive. Obregón continued to fight southward through the states of Sinaloa and Nayarit. He destroyed the Federal army in the west at the battles of La Venta (July 6), Orendáin (July 7), and El Castillo (July 8), taking 5,000 prisoners, 16 cannons, 18 trains, 40 locomotives, half a million pesos, and large quantities of weapons and ammunition.[61]

Once again, Villa rode southward against Torreón, which had been reoccupied by the government. He captured it between March 27 and April 2. Villa then destroyed the retreating *Huerista* army in a series of battles between April 10 and 13. In May, Carranza ordered Villa to capture Saltillo. Villa defeated the *Hueristas* at Parédon, Coahuila, on May 17, which forced them to evacuate Saltillo.

Next, Carranza ordered Villa to send reinforcements for an attack on the important mining city of Zacatecas. Disobeying, Villa marched with the entire Northern Division and attacked it himself. Garrisoned by 7,000 Federal troops, the battle was bloody, but Villa won on June 23. This defiance of Carranza caused an open break between himself and Villa.[62]

While Villa was winning the north-central region and Obregón the northwest, the less tal-ented Pablo González was taking the northeast. In April 1914 Monterrey and in May Tampico fell to the Northeastern Army Corps.[63]

The combined weight of the loss of the north and to a lesser extent the American capture of Veracruz caused the collapse of the Huerta government. Huerta resigned on July 15, 1914. His defeat also marked the end of the Federal army. On August 13 Federal Gen. Gustavo A. Salas signed the Treaties of Teoloyucan on the fender of an automobile which required the disband-ing of the Federal army. Mexico's traditional power brokers—the army, the landed aristocracy, the business magnates, and the Church—were irretrievably damaged by Huerta's defeat.[64]

CARRANZA, VILLA, AND ZAPATA—WHO WOULD RULE?

While the Huerta government was disintegrating, Obregón and Villa were racing south to see who could seize Mexico City and reap the rewards of holding the capital. Carranza inten-tionally delayed a shipment of coal to Villa, temporarily delaying Villa's train-bound army in Zacatecas (440 mi NW of Mexico City). Obregón won the race, entering Mexico City on Au-gust 15. Villa was outraged, retired to Chihuahua, and bided his time.[65]

In late 1914 Mexico was disintegrating into anarchy. Venustiano Carranza, a pragmatist to some and an opportunist to others; Emiliano Zapata, the champion of agrarian reform; and Pancho Villa, part-time bandit, part-time patriot, now wrestled for control of Mexico. Zapata controlled the south; Villa held the north-central region; and Carranza controlled the coasts north of Mexico City and northeast. The three Revolutionary chiefs each sent representatives to Washington knowing that President Wilson controlled the flow of arms into Mexico and could decide their fates.

While chaos reigned in Mexico and Mexican politicians maneuvered for support in Wash-ington, a group of Revolutionaries managed to call a National Revolutionary Convention at Aguascalientes in October 1914 in an attempt to bring the feuding factions together. The three major Revolutionary forces were represented. Meeting in November, the convention elected Gen. Eulalio Gutiérrez as interim president, tasked to restore order and hold national elections. Carranza refused to recognize Gutiérrez and abandoned Mexico City on November 21, tacti-cally retreating to Veracruz. Forces loyal to Gutiérrez occupied the capital and tried to restore order but had little success controlling either the *Villistas* or the *Zapatistas*. In January 1915 Gutiérrez signed a decree attempting to remove Villa from command of his forces but he had the strength neither to enforce the decree nor to hold the capital. Gutiérrez abandoned the capi-tal for San Luis Potosí where he believed that he had adequate support to maintain his army. Eventually, his force disintegrated.[66]

When Gutiérrez abandoned the capital, Villa and Zapata occupied Mexico City, called a con-ference (naturally dominated by their supporters), deposed Gutiérrez, and named Roque González Garza as provisional president. Mexico thus had three interim presidents— Carranza, self-proclaimed on August 20, 1914, after the signing of the Teoloycan Convention; Eulalio Gutiérrez, chosen by the convention at Aguascalientes on November 6, 1914; and González Garza, elected by the Mexico City Convention on January 15, 1915, under orders from Villa.

While Villa and Zapata controlled two-thirds of Mexico, including the capital, Carranza held Veracruz (recently evacuated by U.S. troops), the oil export center of Tampico, and the north-

Figure 4. The Mexican Revolution (1910–20). A U.S. Marine outpost outside Veracruz in 1914. Woodrow Wilson found himself in a difficult position after seizing Veracruz. He did so to help remove Victoriano Huerta from power, which in fact did happen. But now Mexico had numerous competing factions—The *Carrancistas, Villistas, Zapatistas*, to name only the most prominent—and diplomatically getting out of Veracruz with some guarantees was perhaps more difficult than militarily taking the port. *Courtesy of U.S. Marine Corps, Washington, D.C.*

east frontier with the United States. Controlling the customs house at Veracruz and Nuevo Laredo permitted Carranza to finance his operations and gave him access to American arms.

In order to win followers, Carranza adopted many of Zapata's agrarian reforms. On January 6, 1915, he reinstated the *ejidos*. This nullified the land concessions to the large landholders made by the Porfirio Díaz regime. Also, Carranza supported the fledgling labor movement, thus winning additional supporters.

Carranza also had the loyalty of the best strategist in the field, Alvaro Obregón. While Carranza was attending to political matters, Obregón was organizing an army. On January 5, 1915, the *Carranzanistas* occupied the city of Puebla and within three weeks they entered Mexico City, which had been abandoned by the *Villistas* and *Zapatistas*. Obregón recruited, trained, and organized new recruits. Six battalions known as the "Red Battalions" came from the labor movement known as the "House of World Workers" (*Casa del Obrero Mundial*).[67]

Obregón abandoned Mexico City on March 9 and traveled north by train via Tula, Pachuca, and Ometusco to assure his contact with Carranza in Veracruz. Obregón reasoned that to garrison the capital would require a large body of troops and the city held no military importance. The *Zapatistas* immediately reoccupied the city.[68]

BATTLES OF CELAYA

Obregón's 11,000-man army arrived at Celaya (180 mi NW of Mexico City) on April 4. The army was well armed with abundant ammunition. Obregón took up a defensive, protecting his troops with rolls of barbed wire. Villa's army numbered some 22,000 men; its main arm was the cavalry, known for its fierce charges. The fighting erupted on the fifth, in spite of the fact that Villa's brilliant artillery officer, Felipe Angeles, who was still far to the north at Torreón, warned Villa not to fight at Celaya because the terrain favored a defensive strategy.[69] On April 6 Villa defeated an element of Obregón's army at El Guaje, 12 miles from Celaya; only Obregón's arrival prevented a complete rout which could have spread through the entire army.[70]

Villa rushed forward. At 5 P.M. Villa's rapidly advancing forces came upon Obregón's well-prepared defensive lines protected by barbed wire. Without waiting for artillery and infantry, Villa's cavalry charged the fortified line for three hours. Obregón refused to retreat; he reinforced the garrison at Celaya.[71]

Back in Veracruz, Carranza gathered up scattered units and sent them northward. On the seventh Villa attacked with his entire army without holding any forces in reserve. After severe fighting, the *Villistas* were pushed back and their spirit wained. At noon the *Carrancista* cavalry double-enveloped the enemy. Villa's fatigued troops fought their way through the enemy's cavalry which, however, soon became a rout. The *Carrancistas* lost 557 killed and 365 wounded; the *Villistas* lost 1,800 killed, 3,000 wounded, 500 prisoners, and a large quantity of material. The first Battle of Celaya was a *Carrancista* victory but it was not decisive.[72]

The *Villistas* fell back to Salamanca. Villa reorganized and prepared for another attack. Obregón dug in and received significant reinforcements raising his army to 15,000 men. This included 8,000 cavalry, 13 field pieces, and 86 machine guns. The Second Battle of Celaya began on April 13 at 5 P.M. Within an hour, Villa's cavalry was recklessly charging Obregón's well-dug-in infantry. Again on the fourteenth Villa's cavalry charged unsuccessfully, seeking a breakthrough. On the fifteenth Obregón took the offensive and caught Villa by surprise. After a stubborn defense, the *Villistas* retreated. Once again the *Carrancista* cavalry double-enveloped the enemy. This time Obregón possessed enough strength to crush the encircled *Villistas*. The

Carrancista victory was complete. Obregón lost 138 dead and 276 wounded. Villa lost 4,000 dead, 5,000 wounded, 6,000 prisoners, all of his artillery and most of his supplies.[73]

BATTLE OF AGUASCALIENTES

Villa fled northward, tearing up railroad tracks behind him in order to delay Obregón's pursuit. Villa sought reinforcements and advantageous ground for a decisive engagement. *Carrancista* Generals Francisco Murguía and Manuel Diéguez, who had been fighting in the west, joined Obregón with 10,000 men. Obregón now commanded 30,000 men. On the other side, Villa rebuilt his army to 35,000 men. Engagements took place daily. On June 3 a cannon shell tore off Obregón's right arm, seriously wounding him.[74] Gen. Francisco Murguía succeeded Obregón and on the fifth defeated the *Villistas* at the city of Leon. The *Villistas* made their last major stand at the city of Aguascalientes (364 mi NW of Mexico City). There, on July 10, Villa lost 1,500 dead and wounded, 2,000 prisoners, 5,000 deserters, 8 trains, 33 locomotives, 4 million cartridges, 9 cannons, and 22 machine guns. The Northern Division ceased to exist. The *Carrancistas* lost only some 600 men.[75]

Back in the south, *Carrancista* Gen. Pablo González drove the *Zapatistas* out of Mexico City on August 2, 1915, and through a brutal campaign, pushed them back into the mountains of Morelos. Neither Villa nor Zapata were able to recover from these defeats and no longer could they attract large followings.

Following the successes against Zapata and Villa, the United States recognized the Carranza government on October 19, 1915. Most importantly, this recognition cut off Villa's main source of arms across the border.[76]

TWISTING AMERICA'S TAIL

In order to embarrass Carranza and to win support among the anti-American element, *Villistas* executed eighteen Americans who were on board a train they held up at Santa Isabel, Chihuahua, on January 10, 1916. This was followed by a 400-man raid on Columbus, New Mexico, where eight Americans were killed and seven wounded on March 9. Villa seized arms, for which he had already paid. Also, his men robbed and burned some stores and houses. These acts precipitated the Pershing expedition into Mexico which began in March 1916. Villa immediately became a hero among those who disliked the United States and Carranza was placed in a humiliating position of allowing 12,000 American soldiers to invade northern Mexico in an

---

Figure 5 (opposite). The Mexican Revolution (1910–20). Emiliano Zapata in a photograph of contradictions, probably taken in 1915. Zapata wears his "Sunday best" *charro* (cowboy) outfit—short vest, tight trousers, big spurs, and a wide-brimmed sombrero; more typically, he was photographed in a well-worn, everyday *charro* outfit. Zapata is adorned with the presidential sash. He never claimed to hold this office; perhaps adding the sword and saber was the idea of the photographer to dress up the photograph. Zapata appears at ease; more typically, he was uncomfortable having his picture taken. Zapata is armed with a Winchester model 1873 and a heavy cavalry saber. This model Winchester is frequently seen in photographs of Mexican revolutionaries. Although never issued to any army, this carbine was a favorite of many fighters because it was relatively inexpensive, rugged, and easily handled from horseback. The saber, in addition to its utility, was a symbol of authority. Zapata was the revolutionary leader of the impoverished state of Morelos. The peons throughout southern Mexico made him the embodiment of their cause, the restoration of Indian communal lands. *Courtesy of Casasola, Mexico.*

attempt to track down one man in his own backyard! The unsuccessful expedition was withdrawn in March 1917.[77]

THE ANTI-CARRANZA CAMPAIGN

Carranza convened a Constitutional Convention at Querétaro on February 5, 1917, which promulgated the liberal 1917 Constitution. Mexico experienced three years of uneasy peace under Carranza during which time he implemented few programs to achieve the promised goals. Land was not redistributed to any meaningful degree; troops were used to break striking unions; education was neglected; the foreign debt went unpaid; and corruption was rampant. Numerous cronies were rewarded with commissions in the army. On April 10, 1919, Emiliano Zapata was assassinated. There was a tremendous lack of morality in public affairs. Carranza, ineligible for reelection under the new Constitution, tried to retain power through a puppet, Ignacio Bonillas.

In 1920 Obregón, who along with many others viewed himself as Carranza's legitimate successor, announced his candidacy. Obregón was accused of rebellion and his movements were closely watched. He escaped the city disguised as a railroad worker. Gen. Plutarco Calles, who had resigned as Minister of Industry and Commerce, led an uprising against Carranza in the north. Other military leaders joined him and opposition to the rebellion melted away. Carranza tried to escape with five million pesos but was caught and murdered. By November 1920 Obregón was in power and for the first time in a decade Mexico found a measure of peace.[78]

OBSERVATIONS

Above all else, the Mexican upheaval was a social revolution equal in magnitude to the Bolshevik experience. For the first time the common Mexican was enfranchised with political, social, and economic rights. Between 1910 and 1920 the Mexican population decreased by 824,000 persons; this was caused by deaths during the revolution and emigration.[79] Neither of the initial protagonists was around at the finish. At least to the early Revolutionary leader, Francisco Madero, this uprising was to be significantly less than a class war. However, the revolution soon took on a life of its own and became exactly that. The old guard—Díaz and Huerta—failed to contain the forces of revolution. The Revolutionaries—the fledgling bourgeoisie and the peasants—failed to grab the opportunity. The vacuum was filled by pragmatic, industrious, self-made men from the north as personified by Alvaro Obregón.[80]

The revolution remained a national affair and did not spill outside its boundaries. Although the ideology of the Mexican Revolution was potentially as frightening to the capitalistic world as that of the Russian Communists, the aims of the Mexican Revolutionaries were nationalistic with no design to export their experience.

The Mexican Revolution discredited the professional army and caused the destruction of the military elite. "Amateurs" like Obregon, Villa, and Zapata consistently defeated the reputedly professional soldiers.

Following the revolution, officers were given only short tours of duty in order to break down the loyalty between the officers and their men. Military units were permitted to store only a few days' provisions in order to prevent extended, unauthorized operations. Although these measures adversely affected the efficiency of the army, they did contribute to making the army apolitical.

Mexico developed a foreign policy of nonintervention.

CHAPTER 4

THE CRISTERO REBELLION, 1926–29

Long Live Christ the King!

—Battle cry of the *Cristeros*

THE SPARK

On July 31, 1926, Archbishop José Mora y del Río declared a strike by the Roman Catholic clergy and for the first time since the landing of Hernán Cortés in 1519, the sacraments were not administered on Mexican soil.[1]

BACKGROUND

Many Mexican Revolutionaries believed that the Roman Catholic clergy had been more sympathetic to the losing Conservatives during the Mexican Revolution (1910–20) than they had been to their cause. Therefore, the Revolutionaries enacted anti-Church provisions in the 1917 Constitution to reduce the influence of the Church, which further alienated the two groups. Between 1920 and 1924 President Alvaro Obregón chose to ignore these provisions, but his successor, Plutarco Calles, did not.[2]

Violence against church members and the church's property continued following the revolution. In 1921 a group of Catholics gathered in the city of Morelia (228 mi W of Mexico City) to protest anti-Church acts; they were attacked by socialists and fifty persons died. Shortly afterward on November 14, a bomb exploded beneath the altar of the Virgin of Guadalupe at the Guadalupe church, the most sacred of all the Catholic shrines in Mexico. On May 1, 1922, a street fight erupted in Mexico City between the Catholic Association of Mexican Youth and the "Reds" (followers of the Communist Party). On January 19, 1923, Mexico expelled the Vatican's representative, Monsenor Ernesto Filippi, after he had participated in an outdoor religious ceremony, violating the constitutional provision which prohibited worship outside government-designated churches. In 1924 the government and Roman Catholic Church verbally clashed during a Eucharistic Congress held in Mexico City.[3]

The antagonisms intensified under the Calles presidency (1924–28). In February 1925 the Mexican government gave a schismatic element from the Roman Catholic Church the sixteenth-century Soledad de Santa Cruz church in Mexico City for its use. This infuriated the

Roman Catholics who attacked the schism's "Patriarch," José Joaquín Pérez, when he endeavored to hold religious services on February 23. As a consequence, President Plutarco Calles decreed that La Soledad should be turned into a library and that the church of Corpus Christi should be given to the schism instead. Archbishop Mora y del Río reacted by placing an interdict (invalidating the practice of the sacraments) against the church building.[4]

In April 1925 the Bishop of Huejutla forbid the priests in his diocese from complying with civil laws that conflicted with those of the Church. Reacting against this, state legislatures set the number of and condition under which Roman Catholic priests could administer the sacraments within their boundaries. For example, the legislature of Tabasco declared on October 30, 1925, that only married priests could practice within the state![5]

The confrontation reached fever pitch in February 1926. In that month the Archbishop signed a protest published in the newspaper *El Universal* which stated that the Church would resist the implementation of the 1917 Constitution.[6] The Archbishop also sent a circular letter to all parish priests, chaplains, and clergy stating, "We forbid priests to communicate to the civil authorities the churches administered by them and we likewise forbid them to enter their names in the civil register."[7] As a consequence, Calles took stern measures against the Church. On February 13 he wired federal authorities to enforce Articles 3 (education), 27 (property), and 130 (religion) of the 1917 Constitution.

On the seventeenth, 156 Catholic schools in the Federal District were closed. Also on that day, the government seized the College of the Sisters of Saint Teresa in Mixoac and evicted the sisters and 350 students, including a hundred orphan girls who were receiving a free education. The government closed the Catholic hospital at Guadalajara. On the twentieth the Catholic orphan asylum in Victoria was closed and the orphans put out on the street. The seizures of church property continued throughout February and March. Also, all foreign-born priests were evicted from Mexico.[8]

On March 1, 1926, the Bishop of Huejutla issued a pastoral letter, considered to be inflammatory by the government, for which he was arrested in mid-May. He was sentenced to prison but allowed to remain free (within Mexico City) while his case was being appealed.[9]

On March 18, 1926, Mexico expelled the Apostolic Delegate, Jorge José Caruana, the third papal representative to be evicted. He had entered Mexico without disclosing his identity.[10] On June 14 the Mexican Congress ratified the *Ley Calles* (Law of Calles) which gave the President additional leverage against the Church. Under these laws priests were forbidden to teach at primary schools; priests were prohibited to speak against the government or Constitution; priests could not wear distinctive garb in public; and the government could close any church for failure to abide with these laws. Ten days later Calles put these and the anti-Church statutes in the Constitution into effect. Priests were required to be of Mexican birth and to register with the civil authorities, effective July 31, and only lay teachers were permitted to teach in public schools.

The National League to Defend Religious Liberty (*La Liga Nacional Defensora de la Libertad Religiosa*—LNDLR) called for a national economic boycott and the Episcopate Committee (the Bishops of Mexico) called for the suspension of the administering of the sacraments. The leaders of the League were arrested and both sides worked to rally popular support. The Archbishop called a strike by the clergy.[11]

OPPOSING FORCES

Many Mexicans had fought in the recently concluded revolution (1910–20); therefore, experienced soldiers were available to both sides. By early 1927 perhaps 12,000 Catholics had taken up arms against the government; most of these individuals were rural peasants. Most of the senior officers who had supported the losing, Conservative side in the revolution had been killed, discredited, or driven from Mexico. Therefore, the *Cristeros* were particularly short of experienced officers. The National League to Defend Religious Liberty formed a war committee from exile. It was headed by René Capistrán Garza. Former Revolutionary officers Rodolfo L. Gallegos, Enrique Gorostieta Jr., and Anacleto Gonzáles Flores championed their cause. The primary strength of the *Cristeros* was in the states of Jalisco, Michoacán, and Guanajuato to the northwest of Mexico City.[12]

The *Cristeros* obtained their arms and munitions by stealing or buying from the enemy. Also, the National League to Defend Religious Liberty, operating principally in Mexico City, clandestinely acquired arms on the black market. The League sabotaged governmental infrastructure and spread propaganda in Mexico City. The *Cristeros* also formed women's brigades known as "The Brigades of Saint Joan of Arc" (*Las Brigadas de Santa Juana de Arco*) which carried munitions and messages. These female brigades were very independent, frequently leading to friction between themselves and the National League to Defend Religious Liberty.[13]

The Mexican army of 1926 numbered about 50,000 men. The Revolutionary government was in the early stages of converting it from a collection of private armies, whose loyalties were to *caudillos*, into a professional force.[14]

OPENING STRATEGY

The *Cristeros* did not have a coordinated strategy. Those in Mexico City attempted to provide intelligence and munitions to the rural *Cristeros* in the states of Jalisco, Guanajuato, Colima, and Michoacán. The strategy of the rural *Cristeros* was to drive federal authorities out of the remote areas.

The government's strategy was to fully implement the anti-Church provisions of the 1917 Constitution. It refused to restrain the zeal with which its representatives executed the law.

EARLY ACTIONS

On August 1, 1926, organized labor turned out 50,000 persons in Mexico City who marched in support of Calles' decrees against the Church. In September the Archbishop petitioned the Mexican Congress but this was rejected on the grounds that under the Constitution a cleric could not participate in the political process.[15]

In November the *Cristeros*, led by General Gallegos, attacked a train while stopped at the Banderillas Station, killing the entire military escort. In January 1927 the *Cristeros* captured the villages of León, Guanajuato, and Atotonilco, Jalisco. They executed a number of government officials before being driven out by federal troops. Shortly afterward, government soldiers executed forty-five Catholics who were accused of sedition.[16]

THE *CRISTEROS* ATTACK TRAINS

Unable to withstand the government's superior firepower and better-trained officers, the *Cristeros* began ambushing trains. On March 19, 1927, General Gallegos attacked the Mexico City to Laredo train, killed the escort, and seized one million pesos in federal funds which were on board. On April 19 the *Cristeros*, commanded by Father [first name unknown] Reyes Vega and Victoriano Ramírez ("El Catorce"), dynamited the Mexico City to Guadalajara train near Jalisco. The entire train jumped the tracks; the *Cristeros* shot the crew, guards, and 113 passengers.[17] On the twenty-first the Minister of the Interior (*Gobernación*) Adalberto Tejeda charged Archbishop Mora y del Río with complicity in the train disaster. The Archbishop denied his involvement but declared that Catholics had the right to fight for their faith. He and five other prelates were deported the next day.[18]

The government made no attempt to protect the Church from violence. Priests were murdered, churches looted, and suspected *Cristeros* shot without trials.[19] On May 23 Col. José María Dávila hunted down General Gallegos in the state of San Luis Potosí. Father Gumersindo Sedano and five others were also captured; all were shot. Gen. Enrique Gorostieta now headed the *Cristeros*.[20]

Some military officers abused the power that they had been given to deal with the crisis. Gen. Jesús Ferreira forced the evacuation of 6,000 square miles in northern Jalisco of some 50,000 persons and then used his troops to harvest the crops for his own profit.[21]

EXECUTION OF FATHER PRO

On November 13, 1927, four *Cristeros* tossed two bombs at Alvaro Obregón's Cadillac in Chapultepec Park. The former president escaped uninjured. Four accused conspirators were shot on November 23, including Jesuit Father Miguel Pro Juárez. Although the father had nothing to do with the plot, President Calles wanted to send a message to the *Cristeros* that he would not tolerate opposition. By the end of the year many League members and sympathizers had been sent to jail, some serving at the Islas Tres Marías penal colony off the Pacific Coast.[22]

In spite of severe losses, the *Cristeros* continued their attacks. In April 1928 "El Catorce" burned the railway station at La Piedad, Jalisco. On May 24 *Cristeros* led by Lucas Cuevas attacked and briefly held the port of Manzanillo (600 mi W of Mexico City). The executions by both sides continued.[23]

OBREGÓN IS ASSASSINATED

In June 1928 President-elect Alvaro Obregón advised moderation in dealing with the captured *Cristeros*, particularly the peasants. He proposed sending them to a remote region, such as the Yucatán, from where they could not reunite with their comrades in arms as opposed to shooting them, as was then practiced.[24] On July 17 the religious fanatic José de Léon Toral assassinated Obregón at La Bombilla restaurant in Mexico City, thus eliminating any moderating influence Obregón might have had. The U.S. Ambassador to Mexico, Dwight Morrow, urged both President Calles and his successor, Emilío Portes Gil, to exercise moderation.[25]

Federal troops captured Gonzales Flores, the commander of the *Cristero* National Liberating Army (*Ejercito Nacional Liberador*), and executed him on October 28, 1928. He was succeeded by Enrique Gorostieta, a West Point graduate.[26]

On February 10, 1929, Portes Gil's presidential train was dynamited in the state of Guanajuato by the *Cristero* underground from Mexico City. One person was killed and the engine destroyed; however, the President and his entourage escaped serious injury. Most of the conspirators were caught and imprisoned on Islas Marías.[27] On February 11 Portes Gil required all priests to register their addresses within fifteen days or be declared rebels. On June 4 Generals Maximino Avila Camacho and J. Jaime Quinoñes defeated the last band of organized

Cristeros at Villa Hidalgo, Jalisco. Among those captured and executed was General Gorostieta.[28]

U.S. Ambassador Dwight Morrow helped open negotiations among Calles, Portes Gil, and Father John Burke, a prominent American Catholic. In June 1929 several exiled bishops were permitted to return to Mexico and by the end of the month an accommodation had been reached.[29]

OBSERVATIONS

On Sunday, June 20, 1929, church bells rang out and the clergy openly administered the sacraments in church buildings made available by the government for the first time since July 31, 1926. Although a compromise had been reached, it surely favored the Mexican government. Priests were required to register with the government and no religious education would be taught in the schools. The government declared that it had no intention of destroying the integrity of the Church and religious instruction would be permitted inside government-designated churches.[30]

The Church sustained significant losses in the rebellion. Before the rebellion 4,500 priests resided in Mexico. By 1935 the number had been reduced to some 300 through emigration, expulsion, and assassination. Apparently, ten states had no priests at all.[31]

The Cristero rebellion provided many with the excuse to settle old scores held over from the 1917 revolution. In particular, corrupt officials and rural *caudillos* exploited the rich. Some 90,000 people died or emigrated from Mexico as a consequence of the *Cristeros* rebellion.[32]

Although militarily the *Cristeros* never posed a serious threat to the Mexican government, their activities did have serious international and economic repercussions. The war against the *Cristeros* worsened Mexico's already poor relations with the United States. And the attacks on the trains and the government's need to divert rail service from commercial to military needs strained an economy that was beginning to feel the effects of the Great Depression.[33]

PART 4

AN EXTRAHEMISPHERIC WAR

CHAPTER 5

WORLD WAR I AND BRAZIL, 1917–18

When you cannot do what you should, you must do what you can.

—Rear Admiral Pedro Max Fernando de Frontin, Commander, Brazilian Naval Division in War Operations (Divisão Naval em Operações de Guerra—DNOG)

THE SPARK

On October 18, 1917, a German U-boat torpedoed the Brazilian merchantship *Macau* off the coast of Spain. This followed frequent German violations against Brazilian merchantshipping as agreed to in the Declarations of Paris (1856), and London (1909), concerning the freedom of the sea. As a result, Brazil declared war on October 26.

BACKGROUND

Brazil was the only major Latin American country to declare war on the Central Powers in World War I.[1] Before she had done so, the war had caused her economic disaster. One of her chief exports, natural rubber, which the war machines of the early twentieth century did not need in huge quantities, fell sharply in price. So did her other major export, coffee. The British, after imposing a blockade on the Central Powers, ended the importation of coffee, arguing that shipping tonnage used to carry that commodity was needed for more essential items. Britain placed coffee on the contraband list so that shipments going to the Central Powers were subject to seizure, and she restricted coffee going to European neutrals to prevent any excess from finding its way to Germany.[2]

The British also blacklisted numerous Brazilian firms merely on suspicion of trading with the Germans. While belligerents were buying munitions and grain from the neutral United States, Brazilian agricultural goods sat in port unsold. The value of the country's exports in

1914 was only half of what it had been the preceding year, even though the war had interrupted commerce for only five months. Brazil, like most Latin American countries, derived a large part of her annual income from import taxes. When trade stagnated, government revenues plummeted.[3]

Brazil declared neutrality on August 4, 1914, but from the start her sympathies lay with the Allies. A number of pragmatic considerations influenced the initial neutrality. Germany owed Brazil between six and seven million pounds sterling for coffee seized at Hamburg at the outbreak of the war. If any action were taken against Germany, she might renounce this debt. Also, the loyalty of a large number of German immigrants in southern Brazil was suspect.[4]

Friction between Brazil and Germany was inevitable. The war created a world shortage of merchantships. Ship construction, largely concentrated in the belligerent nations, could not keep up with the increased demand of the war. Brazil possessed the largest merchant marine in Latin America, and one of respectable size by world standards—377 steamers of 290,637 net tons in 1916.[5] As the war took its toll on the merchantships of other countries, Brazilian vessels extended the area of their operations to ports previously dominated by British merchantmen. Soon Brazilian merchantships were regularly found in U-boat-infested European waters. Moreover, hundreds of German merchantmen lay interned in neutral ports throughout the world, 45 of them in Brazilian ports. Commercial interests in Brazil argued for the requisition of these vessels, but for almost three years the government respected their sanctuary.

Brazilian merchantships were sunk despite Brazil's neutral stance. The first loss came on May 2, 1916, when the steamer *Rio Branco* was torpedoed. This action helped solidify the pro-Allied attitude of Brazil, but not enough to draw the country into the war. The *Rio Branco* had been leased to British subjects and no lives were lost in the torpedoing, facts which tempered Brazil's reaction.[6] It did not remain tempered for long. On the night of December 8–9, 1916, the Brazilian steamer *Rio Pardo*, en route from England to Holland, was seized by German destroyers, adding to tensions.

On January 31, 1917, Germany announced a blockade of Allied coasts to be enforced by unrestricted submarine warfare. Now a submarine might attack without warning, whether surfaced or submerged. The Brazilian government protested this action on February 9 and again on the thirteenth, but to no avail; on April 4 the Brazilian merchantship *Paraná* was torpedoed without warning. Brazil severed relations with Germany on April 10.[7] On April 13 Brazil authorized the arming of its merchantships.[8] Although Brazil reaffirmed her neutrality on April 25, the United States' entry into the war earlier in the month had swayed her further to the Allied side. On May 20, a U-boat sank the merchantship *Tijuca* off the coast of Brest, France.

In the second half of 1917, Brazil moved closer to war. On June 1 she revoked her neutrality in the war between the United States and Germany, and President Wenceslau Brás Pereira Gomes authorized the requisition of interned German merchantships in accordance with the principles of the 1907 Hague Convention concerning the rights and duties of a neutral in naval warfare.[9] All forty-five German merchantships were seized over the next day; thirty-three had been so badly neglected or sabotaged that foreign help would be necessary to put them back in service.[10]

Although Brazil was on the path to war, the visit of four American armored cruisers—the *Pittsburgh, South Dakota, Pueblo,* and *Frederick,* with Adm. William P. Caperton, Commander-in-Chief of the U.S. Pacific Fleet on board—probably sped up the timetable. Caperton was there to influence the South American nations into joining the Allies in the war on Germany, a mission for which his force was well suited. His handsome armored cruisers and smart U.S. bluejackets contrasted sharply with the heavily used British warships and the patrol-weary Royal Navy sailors who frequented Brazilian ports. Caperton was experienced in Latin American affairs. After two weeks of wining and dining in Brazil, Caperton sailed south to Uruguay and Argentina where he was more coolly received.[11]

On June 28 Brazil completed the more limited action of June 1 and revoked her neutrality in the war between the Allied and Central Powers. This made her status—as a nonneutral, non-belligerent—somewhat ambiguous but not without its advantages, for Brazilian merchantships could now travel in convoys guarded by Allied and United States warships.

OPPOSING FORCES

Militarily, Brazil had little to offer the Allies but Germany could not directly threaten Brazil. If they were to clash, only their navies possessed adequate mobility to do so.

On paper the Brazilian navy had some decent warships acquired under the 1904 modernization program. The most important were the dreadnoughts *Minas Gerais* and *São Paulo*, the scout cruisers *Bahia* and *Rio Grande do Sul*, and the ten *Pará*-class destroyers all completed between 1908 and 1910 in British yards.[12] However, all these ships shared technical problems. Boilers and condensers were in poor condition and most of the power plants were unreliable. As a result, none of them could make their design speed. Nor were any of them equipped with modern fire control gear which had come into use during the war. Except for the three small *F* class submarines and the submarine tender *Ceará*, all built in Italy shortly before the war, the rest of the Brazilian fleet was run down or hopelessly obsolete.[13] Brazilian naval aviation was organized in August 1916, when a naval aviation school and a seaplane flotilla were established.[14]

More importantly, Brazil had no antisubmarine capability. Her destroyers did not possess hydrophones for detecting submerged submarines nor depth charges for attacking them. On the other side, the German surface fleet had been driven from the high seas by 1917 and few of her 130 submarines had even in theory the range to operate in Brazilian waters.

OPENING STRATEGIES

Brazil's initial plan was to protect her merchantships sailing in coastal waters against German U-boats and surface raiders. As far as international waters were concerned, Brazil had to rely on the Allies and the United States. Militarily, Germany could do little to threaten Brazil.

PREWAR PATROLLING

The Brazilian government ordered its navy to share patrolling responsibilities with those of France, Great Britain, and the United States. In July 1917 the Brazilian navy established three divisions within their assigned patrol zone in the South Atlantic.

The Northern Division, responsible for the area from Amazonas to Sergipe, was commanded by Rear Adm. João Carlos Mourão dos Santos. The Central Division, commanded by Rear Adm. Francisco de Mattos, patrolled an area from Bahia to Rio de Janeiro. The Southern Division, under Rear Adm. Pedro Max Fernando de Frontin, patrolled the area from São Paulo to Rio Grande do Sul.[15]

The Brazilian navy, however, was in a potentially awkward position, since it alone was not at war with the Central Powers and had no right to take action outside territorial waters.

On July 7 the senior German diplomat in South America, Count Luxburg, wrote to the German Ministry of Foreign Affairs that "a submarine squadron with full powers" could "still save the situation" in Brazil, "where the people under thin veneer are Indians." A month later he was still trying to get his submarine squadron.[16] Unfortunately for Germany, Luxburg's dispatches were intercepted, decoded, and published.

The next few months were filled with tension. Brazilian merchantships were sailing under the protection of Allied warships. On October 18 the merchantship *Macau*, one of the German merchantmen requisitioned by Brazil on June 2, was torpedoed off the coast of Spain, and her captain taken prisoner. On October 24 the Brazilian President sent a message to Congress declaring that a state of war had been forced upon Brazil.[17]

THE BRAZILIAN NAVY GOES TO WAR

Brazil's first belligerent act occurred on October 20, 1917, when her destroyers *Mato Grosso* and *Piauí* attempted to seize the disarmed and interned German gunboat *Eber* at Salvador (750 mi N of Rio de Janeiro). The German crew scuttled her.[18] In late 1917 Rear Adm. Francisco de Mattos was sent to Europe to study Allied fleet operations and to support any Brazilian naval operations that might take place in those waters.[19]

On December 21 the British government requested a Brazilian force of light cruisers and destroyers in the war zone, to be placed under operational control of the Royal Navy. The British Admiralty offered to provide logistical support. On the last day of 1917 the Brazilian government agreed to provide two scout cruisers and four destroyers.[20] On January 30, 1918, Rear Adm. Pedro Max Fernando de Frontin was given command of the squadron, composed of the scouts *Rio Grande do Sul* and *Bahia*, and the destroyers *Paraíba*, *Rio Grande do Norte*, *Piauí*, and *Santa Catarina*. This force was designated the Naval Division in War Operations (*Divisão Naval em Operações de Guerra*, or DNOG) on the same day. The admiral insisted that all of the officers be volunteers.[21]

A truly herculean procurement effort followed. Brazil had neither the industrial base nor the coal to support her war fleet. Nothing the DNOG used was indigenous to the country save the crews and they were in part foreign trained. Even the charts of the African coast had to be taken from interned German merchantships. The tender *Belmonte*, armed as an auxiliary cruiser, and the high-seas tug *Laurindo Pitta* were added to the squadron of two scout cruisers and four destroyers.[22]

On July 31 the DNOG sailed from Fernando de Noronha for Sierra Leone, a British colony on the west coast of Africa. The division was forced to stop several times so that coal and water could be transferred from the *Belmonte* to the cruisers and the destroyers. Emergency repairs had to be made at sea, the tug *Laurindo Pitta* ferrying equipment from the tender to the other ships. These necessities were dangerous; whenever the force stopped, its ships became more vulnerable to U-boat attack, a problem the destroyers, having trouble maintaining a protective ASW screens, could not mitigate. In the end the DNOG managed to deal with these problems, meeting Admiral Sheppard's British squadron off Sierra Leone at midnight August 8–9, 1918. The Brazilian ships entered Freetown on August 9, then left for Dakar on August 23.

During the night of August 25–26, the division believed that it had been attacked by an enemy submarine when the *Belmonte* reported a torpedo track. The suspected U-boat was depth charged, fired at, and supposedly sunk by the destroyer *Rio Grande do Norte*—an action that was never confirmed.[23]

On August 26 the DNOG arrived at Dakar, its new base of operations. The force, with 134 officers and 1,361 enlisted men on board, was responsible for patrolling the Dakar–Cape Verde–Gibraltar triangle, an area believed to be frequented by U-boats lying in wait for Allied convoys. The Brazilian squadron was to guarantee the safe passage of convoys and sweep for mines. While in African waters both cruisers, whose new parts had not arrived from the United States prior to sailing, experienced numerous problems with their condensers, a situation the excessively hot weather off the African coast exacerbated.

INFLUENZA OUTBREAK

On September 6, while the fleet was lying in Dakar, Spanish influenza broke out among the crews of the Brazilian squadron. It started on board the *Bahia* and for seven weeks ravaged the ranks, at its peak incapacitating 95 percent of several ships' companies. One hundred three Brazilian sailors were buried in the Dakar and São Vicente cemeteries. Two hundred fifty disabled by the sickness were sent back to Brazil where many later died.

On November 3 the DNOG sailed from Dakar to Gibraltar leaving behind the cruiser *Rio Grande do Sul*, destroyer *Rio Grande do Norte*, and tender *Belmonte*. The squadron arrived at its destination on November 10 to begin operating in the Mediterranean. On entering the strait, it mistook three American subchasers for U-boats but the error was realized before any damage ensued. World War I, the "war to end all wars," came to a close the following day.[24]

OBSERVATIONS

The Brazilian contribution to the defeat of Germany was militarily insignificant. This, however, ignores Brazil's noble and costly efforts to make what contribution she did. It took five months to prepare a small antisubmarine group that would have required but a few weeks from a major naval power, but this should not overshadow the fact that the squadron materialized and served. In addition to this ASW group, the Brazilian navy sent nine aviators who served in the Royal Air Force, at least one of whom lost his life.[25]

The DNOG lost approximately three hundred sailors, most to influenza. To this must be added those who were killed on board several of the seven Brazilian merchantships lost to German warships.[26]

Brazil's primary contribution to the war was political. And she earned the right to be represented at the Versailles Peace Conference. A major question for her was the disposition of the forty-three surviving vessels of the German merchant fleet requisitioned in 1917. The Brazilian representatives maintained that their country should be allowed to keep them. The conference's finance committee, however, was determined to distribute German merchant marine tonnage proportionately, based on the ratio of losses among the Allies. The Brazilian merchant marine, which had suffered comparatively few casualties when compared to the world shipping powers, would gain little from such arrangements. The Brazilians argued that France had acknowledged Brazilian ownership when she leased thirty requisitioned ships from Brazil, and that the United States had done the same when she attempted to buy them.[27] The Brazilians refused to budge. On May 2, France, the last major holdout, fully recognized the claims of the Latin

American country. On June 28, 1919, the Brazilian representative signed the Treaty of Versailles, and it was ratified by Congress on November 11. In addition to the forty-three merchantships, the treaty gave Brazil the German torpedo boats *V-105* and *V-106* as war prizes.[28]

PART 5

ECONOMIC INTERVENTIONS BY THE UNITED STATES

CHAPTER 6

HAITI, 1915–34

You know I have had something to do with the running of a couple little republics. The facts are that I wrote Haiti's Constitution myself, and, if I do say it, I think it a pretty good Constitution.

—Former Assistant Secretary of the Navy and vice presidential candidate Franklin D. Roosevelt, August 18, 1920

THE SPARK

On July 28, 1915, a mob dragged Haitian President Vilbrun Guillaume Sam from his hiding place behind the French ambassador's bed in the Legation and literally tore him to pieces. That afternoon 330 U.S. Marines and sailors landed in Port-au-Prince from the armored cruiser *Washington* and restored order. Two Marines and one Haitian were killed. One of the dead Marines was William Gompers, nephew of Samuel Gompers, the labor leader. President Woodrow Wilson observed, "'we do not have the legal authority to do what we apparently ought to do. . . . I suppose there is nothing for it but to take the bull by the horns and restore order."[1] The U. S. occupation would last for nineteen years.[2]

BACKGROUND

The United States evolved into an imperialistic nation following its Era of Reconstruction (1865–76). It claimed Guam, Puerto Rico, and the Philippines plus a protectorate over Cuba, prizes of the Spanish-American War in 1898 (see companion volume). And America's empire continued to grow. As a result of the Panamanian Revolution in 1903 (see chapter 1), the United States achieved its century-old dream—the construction and unilateral control over a trans-isthmus canal. Great Britain, which had successfully blocked American domination in Central America by the Clayton-Bulwer Treaty (1850), found it militarily expedient to concede the Americas to Uncle Sam by the Hay-Pauncefote Treaty (1901) and concentrate its energies against the more threatening upstart of Germany.[3]

In order to protect the canal, the linchpin to the new North American empire, the United States believed it necessary to control the Caribbean. The United States was well aware that most nineteenth-century interventions within Latin America had their roots in economic problems between the lending institutions of Europe and the United States and the post-independence, politically immature governments of Latin America. In order to eliminate this as a cause for future European interventions within Latin America, President Theodore Roosevelt stated in his December 6, 1904, annual message to the U.S. Congress:

> Chronic wrongdoing, or an impotence which results in a general loosening of the ties of civilized society, may in America, as elsewhere, ultimately require intervention by some civilized nation, and in the Western Hemisphere, the adherence of the United States to the Monroe Doctrine may force the United States, however reluctantly, in flagrant cases of such wrongdoing or impotence, to the exercise of an international police power.[4]

Given the stated purpose of the Roosevelt Corollary to the Monroe Doctrine and the chaos that had reigned for over one hundred years in Haiti, interrupted frequently by brief periods of exhaustion, it should have come as no surprise that the United States sooner rather than later not only would intervene in Haiti but would linger. Between 1900 and 1915 five Haitian presidents were overthrown and exiled; one was blown up in the palace; and one was poisoned.[5]

By 1914 Haiti was once again in turmoil. In January, British, French, German, and U.S. Marines landed from warships to protect their respective consulates. In March the government of Davilmar Theodore was overthrown by Vilbrun Guillaume Sam.[6]

The Haitian foreign debt soared to $21.5 million, requiring 80 percent of the annual budget to be used just to service the debt. This was primarily owed to French and German bondholders. Rumors abounded that Germany was about to lend Haiti $2 million in exchange for rights to a coaling station at Mole St. Nicholas. Although the German government denied this, it did state that "no scheme of reorganization or control can be regarded as acceptable unless it is undertaken under international auspices."[7] This was a direct challenge to the new Roosevelt Corollary to the Monroe Doctrine.

On December 17, 1914, U.S. Marines removed $500,000 in bullion from the Haitian *Banque Nationale* which had been pledged toward the redemption of the currency. Bank officials requested the removal out of fear that the Haitian government might seize the money and use it to meet current expenses. While this was transpiring, Franco-German interests demanded access to the custom house receipts.[8]

Virbrun Sam seized power in Haiti in early 1915 and promised to bring stability. This proved to be beyond his power and, within months, Dr. Rosalvo Bobo rebelled, traveled north, and raised an army. In the meantime Bobo's supporters in the south threatened the capital. On June 15 a small number of U.S. and French Marines landed from warships in Port-au-Prince to protect their nations' interests.

To secure his hold over the government, Sam seized 200 Haitian hostages, many of whom were prominent citizens. He ordered their jailer to immediately execute them should his palace be assaulted. The rebels attacked the palace on July 26, and Sam fled to the French Legation seeking sanctuary. Appreciating that matters were disintegrating, additional U.S. Marines landed. On the twenty-seventh, 167 of the 200 hostages were murdered. The next day a mob broke into the French Legation and then tore Sam and Port-au-Prince apart.[9]

As pieces of Sam's corpse were being dragged through the streets in different directions, the U.S. armored cruiser *Washington* entered Port-au-Prince and landed the Marines. The cruiser had hurried under forced draft from Cap Haitien, 195 miles away. Rear Adm. William B. Caperton sent 330 marines and sailors ashore and by nightfall they had restored order. Within twenty-four hours the 24th Marine Company arrived from Guantanamo on board the steamer *Jason*. On July 30 the French cruiser *Descartes* landed additional marines as well. On July 31 the battleship *Connecticut* dropped anchor in Port-au-Prince with a regimental headquarters and five companies of the 2nd Marine Regiment on board, totaling some 600 Marines.[10]

OPPOSING FORCES

By late 1915 approximately 3,000 Marines were in Haiti. And additional Marines were nearby in Santo Domingo, Guantanamo, and Panama. The Marine Corps had recent experience in dealing with semiorganized mob violence in China.[11]

Haiti's large army was an ill-disciplined, rag-tag force and for sale to the highest bidder. In addition, bands of ruffians known as *Cacos* (fiercely independent thieves, bandits, and mercenaries who controlled much of the mountainous interior)[12] abounded in Haiti since it had been in a state of almost constant civil war since independence. The weapons available to both the army and the thugs were a conglomeration, mostly of poor quality. As throughout the Caribbean, gunrunners carried on a brisk trade with the competing factions.

OPENING STRATEGY

U.S. strategy was first to restore order, then take control of the customs house at Port-au-Prince (thereby controlling some 90 percent of Haiti's income), and finally to occupy key cities. The United States would then control the selection of the president, thus guaranteeing an individual friendly toward itself. Once these objectives had been accomplished, the task would become finding those opposed to the United States who were hiding in the hinterland.

The rebels attempted to follow the decades-old strategy for conquering Haiti. They would hasten to the north; win a following of *Cacos* through pay and promises; and proceed along the coast through Gonaives (100 mi NNW of Port-au-Prince) and St. Marc (60 mi NW of Port-au-Prince) to the capital. By the time they reached Port-au-Prince, those supporting the old regime would melt away. Seizing power would not be so simple after the American occupation began.[13]

The principal tactics of rebels were intimidation through violence and attacks from ambush. Due to the poor quality of their weapons and worse marksmanship because of a lack of training, the rebels frequently resorted to hand-to-hand combat. This was costly against the well-disciplined U.S. Marines.[14]

THE OPENING MOVES

The Haitian Congress, dominated by the United States, elected Sudre Dartiguenave president on August 12, 1915, by 94 out of 116 votes. Dartiguenave and the Haitian Congress were then coerced into signing the Haiti Treaty of 1915 which gave the United States more extensive control than it ever held in Cuba or the Dominican Republic. As a consequence of Dartiguenave's election, Bobo's supporters in Port-au-Paix (40 mi W of Cap Haitien) rioted.

However, soon the port was occupied by some of the additional 850 Marines who had arrived on board the armed cruiser *Tennessee*.[15]

While tranquility was being restored in the west and south, the *Cacos* joined forces with Bobo in the north. In the past, the *Cacos* had frequently practiced extortion against those who ruled in Port-au-Prince. A group of *Cacos* attempted to sell protection to the Marine commanding the garrison at Gonaives, Smedley D. Butler. After a brief fight, he put 200 *Cacos* to flight. Not far from Cap Haitien, two Marine patrols were surrounded and attacked. In late September Colonel Eli K. Cole, commanding 130 Marines, drove off the besiegers, thus restoring access to the Cap's food supply. Two marines were killed; eight wounded; and sixty Cacos killed.[16]

Col. Littleton Waller attempted to pacify the north by bribing opposition leaders, sweeping the area with patrols, garrisoning Ouananminthe and Fort Liberté, and seizing all arms. These measures failed. Marines patrolling south from Cap Haitien clashed with *Cacos*. On October 24 a marine patrol was ambushed by 400 *Cacos* while crossing a mountain stream after dark. The Marines fought and gained a good defensive position against continuous but ineffective rifle fire. At daybreak, three squads of Marines attacked and the *Cacos* scattered. The Marine patrol then located the *Cacos* stronghold at Fort Dipitie. In the ensuing fight, eight *Cacos* were killed and ten wounded; one Marine was slightly wounded.[17]

THE DESTRUCTION OF FORT RIVIÈRE

The *Cacos* slowly fell back to the old stronghold Fort Rivière some eight miles from Grande Rivière. Marines, commanded by Colonel Butler, surrounded the old masonry fortress. Butler found a deep ditch concealed by overgrowth which led to a three-foot drain which ran under the walls of the fortress. On the morning of October 18, the Marines attacked the walls while 27 men crawled through the drain.[18] Attacked from both inside and outside, the *Cacos* surrendered. Twenty-seven *Cacos* were killed. The Marines sustained only a few minor wounds. The Marines blew up the fortress, using a ton of dynamite.[19]

THE TRANQUIL EARLY YEARS

From 1916 through early 1918, the United States was busy creating a *gendarmerie* (a national police) and starting public works in spite of sporadic attacks by bandits. The *gendarmerie* replaced the national army which had been disbanded. Major Butler became the "acting" chief of the *Gendarmerie d'Haiti* with the Haitian rank of Major General. By 1921 the *gendarmerie* numbered 2,533 enlisted (all Haitians) and 138 officers (of whom 122 were Americans). Toward the end of the occupation, more Haitians were elevated to officers.[20]

CHARLEMAGNE PERALTE REBELS

In 1918 Charlemagne Massena Peralte led a new *Cacos* revolt in the north, beginning the "*Cacos* War." Perhaps as many as 5,000 *Cacos* united behind Peralte; most were poorly armed carrying only machetes or old muskets. The revolt was sparked by traditional complaints: the brutal and corrupt forced labor system known as the *corvée* used to build roads, and a new one—the continued occupation by the United States. The *Cacos* drove laborers from the fields, many of whom sympathized with their causes. This created food shortages in the towns. Also, an underground sprang up in Port-au-Prince in support of Charlemagne.

The *gendarmerie* were not strong enough to put down the revolt. In March 1919 the 868-man Marine Brigade, reinforced by four companies from Guantanamo, joined the *gerdarmerie* in their fight against the *Cacos*. The opposing forces fought some eighty indecisive skirmishes. On October 7 Charlemagne attacked Port-au-Prince but was repelled. Later that month the *Cacos*' chief was killed in a trap set by Sgt. (acting *Gendarmerie* Captain) Hermann H. Hanneken. The *Cacos*' force disintegrated without Charlemagne's leadership.[21]

BENOÎT BATRAVILLE REBELS

Haiti was not at peace for long. In January 1920 a new rebellious *Cacos* leader emerged. Some 300 followers of Benoît Batraville infiltrated Port-au-Prince and went on a rampage. Marines and *gendarmerie* chased them from the capital. Some 150 Haitians were killed, wounded, or captured; two Marines were wounded. Numerous clashes took place between Marine-*gendarmerie* patrols and the *Cacos* and, although 3,000 *Cacos* surrendered over the next six months, many more remained in the hills. A patrol led by Sgt. (acting *Gendarmerie* Lieutenant) Lawrence Muth was ambushed on Mount Michel. Muth was killed but the patrol escaped. A retaliatory raid killed 25 *Cacos*. In May 1920 a 30-man patrol, led by Capt. Jesse L. Perkins, found Batraville's main camp and killed the *Cacos* chief. This ended the "*Cacos* War."[22]

On February 11, 1922, President Warren G. Harding appointed Marine Brig. Gen. John H. Russell the American High Commissioner and his personal representative to Haiti with the rank of Ambassador Extraordinary. He held the position until November 12, 1930.[23]

By the late 1920s U.S. public support for occupations throughout the Caribbean waned. In Haiti the U.S. military was accused of excesses and outright atrocities by the "Women's International League for Peace and Freedom" in 1927.[24] The United States reduced the strength of the Marine brigade from almost 900 men to about 500. In December 1928 the Haitian President declared martial law due to unrest caused by economic conditions exacerbated by the worldwide depression. In 1929 the *Garde d'Haiti* reverted to the control of the U.S. Marine Corps and several clashes with strikers occurred.

As a result of the Haitian demonstrations against continued American control and increasing U.S. public opinion against the occupation, President Herbert Hoover sent an investigating commission to Haiti in 1930. Haitian President Louis Borno resigned and the first Haitian legislature since 1917 was convened. Numerous services under American control were "Haitianized." In September 1932 a draft treaty was negotiated for the "Haitianization" of the *Garde d'Haiti*; however, American financial control continued. On August 7, 1933, President Franklin D. Roosevelt signed an executive order that provided for the complete "Haitianization" of the *garde* by October 1, 1934, and the withdrawal of the U.S. Marines within thirty days. As a good will gesture, all Marines were withdrawn by August 1934. The United States also gradually loosened its financial control and Haiti regained its independence.

OBSERVATIONS

Although the United States ruled Haiti for nineteen years and practically wrote the Haitian Constitution of 1918, it took no significant steps to reform Haiti's political process. During the occupation, the United States ruled through the presence of the U.S. Marines and they evacuated Haiti as a result of the opposition of American public opinion to their continued occupation.[25]

Casualties are difficult to determine. One author estimates that 50,000 Haitians died as a result of the American occupation. This number obviously includes those individuals who died

Figure 6. The U.S. Intervention in Haiti (1915–34). U.S. Marines follow a locally improvised "armored car" mounted with a Lewis machine gun. The photograph was taken in 1917. *Courtesy of U.S. Marine Corps, Washington, D.C.*

working on the *corvée* and those who died in detention camps established by the United States. Also, some 300,000 persons out of Haiti's population of two million emigrated to Cuba or Santo Domingo.[26] The United States lost a few hundred personnel to all causes.

Following the occupation the *Garde d'Haiti* proved less politically powerful than the U.S. Marine-created *guardia nacional* in the Dominican Republic and in Nicaragua. To prevent the *Garde* from becoming too powerful, Stenio Vincent, the first post-intervention president, exiled the commander of the *Garde d'Haiti*.

Many of the U.S. civilian and military representatives sent to Haiti were chosen from U.S. southern states on the theory that southerners were more accustomed to working with blacks. Many of these individuals, as well as some from the northern states, were blatantly racially prejudiced. Marine Corps hero Smedley Butler, a Pennsylvanian, wrote, "I am reduced to a very humiliating position, am simply the very subservient chief of a nigger police force."[27] This deficiency was not addressed by the United States until numerous complaints had been made by the Haitians.[28]

CHAPTER 7

THE DOMINICAN REPUBLIC, 1916–24

It is with the deepest reluctance that I approve and authorize the course here proposed [the establishment of a U.S. military government in the Dominican Republic], but I am convinced that it is the least of the evils in sight in this very perplexing situation.

—President Woodrow Wilson, November 26, 1916

THE SPARK

In early May 1916 fighting erupted in the city of Santo Domingo between some 800 supporters of President Juan Isidro Jiménez and about 500 followers of Desiderio Arias, the Minister of War and a *caudillo* from the northwest. Arias held the city's fortress, San Gerónimo, and threatened to seize control of the capital. As the crisis worsened, the United States, which maintained control over much of the Dominican government's revenues, demanded that Jiménez appoint a financial advisor, which it had to approve, and suggested that a new military force under American officers be created before it would intervene on his behalf.

Jiménez first agreed and then changed his mind. Notwithstanding, American troops landed in the capital on May 5. Two companies of Marines (totaling 150 men) marched to the American and Haitian legations and 130 sailors seized Fort San Gerónimo. This began eight years of occupation.[1]

BACKGROUND

Following the construction of the Panama Canal (1903–1914), the United States considered peace and tranquility throughout the Caribbean important to the security of the "big ditch." Santo Domingo was no exception. This nation had a turbulent political history and shared the island of Hispañola with Haiti, long its bitter enemy. In the seventy years between 1844 (independence) and 1914, Santo Domingo had had fifty-three presidents (of whom only three had completed their elected terms) and nineteen constitutions. Most came to power through the barrel of a gun and left the same way.[2]

Since independence, the finances of Santo Domingo had been continuously in a state of crisis. Racked by revolutions, both the government and the Revolutionaries borrowed heavily from foreign banks. When the Revolutionaries won, which they frequently did, their debts were added to those of the former government. By the beginning of the twentieth century, the Dominican debt had grown to $32 million, an amount that could not be serviced by national revenues. And Santo Domingo seemingly owed everyone—Belgium, France, Germany, Italy, Great Britain, and the United States (the latter two in particular).

In 1903 and 1904 the United States intervened and placed the Santo Domingo Improvement Company in charge of collecting customs at Puerto Plata and Monte Cristi. This brought a protest from European creditors who claimed that the revenues from these ports had previously been pledged to them. This economic confrontation between the United States and the European nations followed a similar crisis in Venezuela which almost led to war between the United States and Germany in early 1903.[3]

Until 1911, the receivership worked reasonably well for the creditors. In that year President Ramón Cáceres was assassinated, plunging Santo Domingo into yet another civil war. Those attempting to win control incurred new, large debts. U.S. Secretary of State Philander Knox forced the resignation of President Eladio Victoria and the election of his successor, the Archbishop of Santo Domingo, Adolfo A. Nouel. The Archbishop was more interested in the spiritual world than the temporal one and ultimately fled to Europe to escape Dominican politics. In July 1914 President Woodrow Wilson drafted a plan calling for North American supervised elections in exchange for American recognition.[4]

By May 5, 1916, the followers of President Jiménez and General Arias were fighting openly in the streets of Santo Domingo and the U.S. Marines had landed. President Jiménez resigned on May 7 rather than comply with U.S. demands for more political and economic control. On May 12 Rear Adm. William B. Caperton arrived and consulted with the U.S. Minister to the Dominican Republic, W. W. Russell. By that point over 400 U.S. Marines were in the capital. On the thirteenth, Caperton demanded that Arias, who was held up in Fort Ozama, disband his army and surrender his weapons, but Arias and his supporters quit the city rather than comply.[5]

OPPOSING FORCES

Although the number of U.S. Marines stationed in Santo Domingo never exceeded 3,000 men, they could be rapidly reinforced from Port-au-Prince, Haiti, or Guantanamo, Cuba. The Dominican army was corrupt and ineffective. Its chief activity had been deciding who would rule in the capital. The countryside was controlled by *caudillos* and their semidisciplined, armed followers. In particular, these *caudillos* dominated the eastern side of the nation.[6]

OPENING STRATEGY

The initial strategy of the United States was to seize the capital and other ports in order to take control of the custom receipts. The strategy of General Arias was to fall back to his inland Santiago stronghold in the north-central part of the republic and wait out the Americans.

THE MARINES EXTEND THEIR CONTROL

While the Dominican Congress was trying to select a new president, the United States began extending its control over the country. On June 1, following a bombardment, the Marines landed at Monte Cristi (181 mi NW of Santo Domingo) and Puerto Plata (150 mi NNW of Santo Domingo) along the north coast. They were opposed at the second port by some 500 supporters of General Arias and the Marines had to fight their way ashore. On June 21, the 4th Marine Regiment, normally stationed in San Diego, California, also landed at Monte Cristi.[7]

Figure 7. The U.S. Intervention in the Dominican Republic (1916–24). The photograph shows armed Dominican cowboys. They fought as bandits, guerrillas, and soldiers, depending on what their *caudillo* (leader) instructed them to do. Cowboys were known by a variety of names throughout Latin America—*gauchos, llaneros,* and *vaqueros* being the most common—and were numerous in Argentina, southern Brazil, central Cuba, eastern Dominican Republic, Uruguay, and Venezuela. *Courtesy of National Archives, Washington, D.C.*

CAPTURING SANTIAGO

On June 26 Marine Col. Joseph H. "Uncle Joe" Pendleton led a two-pronged advance from the north coast against Santiago, a distance of 75 miles. Some 837 marines, starting from Monte Cristi, closed from the northwest while 135 Marines moved down from the north along the railroad from Puerto Plata. On the twenty-seventh, after marching some twenty miles, the column advancing from Monte Cristi encountered a strong defensive position on Las Trencheras Ridge. Covered by artillery, the Marines attacked and overran the position. The rebels fell back to a second defensive line but could not hold this either.

Pendleton again clashed with the rebels on July 3 at Guayacanas. The two Marine columns united at the railway junction at Navarette. On July 5 a peace delegation from Santiago met the Marines and handed over the city while General Arias surrendered to the Dominican governor of the city of Santiago. Three Marines had been killed and fifteen wounded. The United States then extended the occupation to the inland cities of Moca and La Vega.[8]

THE MELÉE AT *FORTELEZA*

At San Francisco de Macorís (30 mi SE of Santo Domingo), Governor Juan Pérez, a supporter of Arias, refused to recognize the U.S. military government. Using some 1,000 released prisoners, he was preparing to defend the old Spanish colonial structure, the *Forteleza*. On November 29 U.S. Marine Lt. Ernest C. Williams, whose detachment was billeted in San Francisco, charged the closing gates of the fort at nightfall with a dozen Marines. Eight were shot down; the others, including Williams, forced their way in and seized the old structure. Another Marine detachment seized the police station. Reinforcements from nearby detachments soon suppressed the uprising.[9]

THE UNITED STATES SEIZES CONTROL

The United States pressured the Dominican Congress to select a new president who would agree to the proposed treaty.[10] The United States refused both recognition and money (while still controlling the custom houses) until the legislature complied with its wishes. The selection of a new president dragged on for months. When the Congress finally chose Dr. Francisco Henriquez y Carvajal, he refused the American demands. On November 29 Capt. Harry S. Knapp (Admiral Caperton's relief) declared from his flagship, the cruiser *Olympia*:

> I . . . acting under the authority and by the direction of the Government of the United States, declare and announce to all concerned that the Republic of Santo Domingo is hereby placed in a state of military occupation . . . and is subject to military government and the exercise of military law."[11]

Cabinet posts were filled by U.S. military officers.[12]

THE GUARDIA NACIONAL DOMINICANA CREATED

On September 12, 1916, President Francisco Henriquez y Carvajal had signed a decree abolishing the army. Subsequently, the *Guardia Nacional Dominicana* was created on April 7, 1917, by Executive Order of the Chief of the Military Government. Initially, the lone colonel, eight majors, and fourteen captains were U.S. Marines; half of the sixteen first lieutenants were Dominicans as were all of the second lieutenants. On August 15, 1921, the U.S. military government founded the Haina Military Academy.[13]

THE LATER YEARS OF OCCUPATION

Throughout the remaining eight years of the U.S. military government in the Dominican Republic, U.S. marines and naval officers held key political and military positions. Although organized attacks against American strongholds ceased, patrols were ambushed by dissidents and bandits. On August 13, 1918, a five-man Marine patrol was ambushed near Manchado; four Marines were killed and the survivor wounded. And the Marines never controlled most of the rugged eastern half of Santo Domingo. There, some 600 fighters led by a dozen *caudillos* dominated.[14]

GROWING HOSTILITY

Dominican public resentment against the American unilateral decisions increased. Trying to defuse these tensions, in November 1919 the U.S. State Department instructed the Military Governor, Rear Adm. Thomas Snowden, to appoint a consultant committee composed of prominent Dominicans who were selected by the State Department. Rather than increase the civil liberties as recommended by this committee and desired by the State Department, the Military Governor increased the censorship of speech and press. In March 1920 prominent Dominicans formed the Dominican National Union (*Unión Nacional Dominicana*), the purpose of which was to restore Santo Domingo's independence. It refused to cooperate with the U.S. military government and initiated a very successful public affairs campaign throughout Latin America against the American occupation. When the United States attempted to involve more Dominicans within its process, the Dominican National Union prevented this by declaring that anyone who accepted the American invitation would be declared a traitor.[15]

THE U.S. WITHDRAWAL

The Wilson administration attempted to withdraw but could not get the Dominicans to agree to the terms Washington desired. The 1920 remarks by the Democratic vice presidential candidate, Franklin D. Roosevelt, that he had written the Dominican constitution, gave the Republican presidential candidate, Senator William G. Harding, an opening to attack. He declared that his administration would not "empower an Assistant Secretary of the Navy to draft a constitution for helpless neighbors in the West Indies and jam it down their throats . . . at the point of bayonets borne by the United States Marines."[16]

With the election of Harding, the American public expected the immediate withdrawal of U.S. Marines from Santo Domingo and they were not disappointed. In June 1922 they agreed upon the terms of withdrawal. A Dominican provisional government would replace the U.S. military government; the U.S. Marines would withdraw to coastal towns, and a new treaty would validate the acts of the U.S. military government and extend the receivership until the existing bonds were liquidated. Dominican elections were held and the new government installed on July 12, 1924. The last Marine was withdrawn on September 18.[17]

OBSERVATIONS

The U.S. intervention in Santo Domingo demonstrated its preoccupation with political stability within the Caribbean. Imperialistic America of the early twentieth century had no desire to annex the trouble-plagued island-nation, as pointedly stated by Theodore Roosevelt, "I have about the same desire to annex it as a gorged boa constrictor might have to swallow a porcupine wrong-end-to."[18]

The final report of U.S. Marine Maj. Gen. Harry Lee, the last military governor of Santo Domingo, succinctly summarized what the United States believed it had accomplished:

> The occupying forces assumed control of a state rife with revolution, banditry, ungoverned and mismanaged. We left a state enjoying peace, and with a loyal and well-developed military force, with fine roads, many schools, a fine military hospital, and, in short, with every promise for a future of stable government under Dominican rule.[19]

Absent from this statement was any reference to democracy or to whom the new professionalized military created by the U.S. Marine Corps would be loyal. Perhaps the General and others in the United States believed that order and stability were precursors to democracy; if so, they were wrong. Another American legacy was the commissioning of Rafael Leonidas Trujillo Molina as Second Lieutenant on December 18, 1918.[20]

Occupation duty did not sit well with senior military officers. Admiral Caperton wrote, "I really believe these people are worse than the Haitiens, if such a thing be possible, and I am more convinced each day that the only way to handle them is by force and the big stick."[21]

During the occupation, five officers and eleven enlisted Marines were killed in combat. Additionally, fifty-four men died from disease and fifty-five Marines were wounded in action. No one has estimated the number of Dominicans killed as a result of the occupation.[22]

Argentina attempted to lead Latin American political opposition to the U.S. intervention. Symbolically, in 1919 the Argentine cruiser *Nueve de Julio*, under instructions from President Hipólito Yrigoyen, did not salute the U.S. flag flying above the government house in Santo Domingo as was the custom, but rather the cruiser saluted the Dominican flag which was being carried by some citizens ashore.[23]

CHAPTER 8

NICARAGUA, 1927–33

The person and property of a citizen are a part of the general domain of the nation, even when abroad.

—Calvin Coolidge, 1927

THE SPARK

On about May 24, 1927, Augusto César Sandino[1] sent a letter to Liberal Gen. José María Moncada proclaiming, *"I will not sell myself, nor will I surrender. I must be conquered. I must comply with my duty and I hope that my protest will remain for the future written in blood."*[2] Sandino subsequently drew the United States into a five-and-a-half-year guerrilla war.

BACKGROUND

Nicaragua, offering the least geographical barriers to crossing the isthmus that separates the Atlantic and the Pacific, had long attracted the attention of the United States and its citizens. The construction of the Panama Canal (1903–14) did not diminish that interest. Even after the digging of the canal, the United States did not wish another nation to have the possibility of developing an alternate route and it considered political stability throughout the Caribbean, including Nicaragua, to be critical to the protection of the Panama Canal.[3]

The cruel, capricious, and economically exploitive dictator José Santos Zelaya had come to power within Nicaragua in 1893. Over the years he and Yankee businessmen profited handsomely from their schemes. The American decision to build the canal through Panama soured

---

Figure 8 (opposite). The U.S. Intervention in Nicaragua (1927–33). Augusto Sandino is wearing a Stetson hat and his .44-caliber Smith & Wesson, two of his trademarks. Copied from the Victor F. Bleasdale collection—Captain Bleasdale, USMC, served in Nicaragua between 1927 and 1929 and fought against Sandino. The photograph was annotated as follows: "'*Description of Sandino*' speaks some English, Eyes ~~Bluish Green~~ Light Brown (not sure of this), Age About (28) years, Slender about 5'6" high, weight about 140 lbs, well educated, Indian Blood, only characteristic is he likes to speak as a Mexican using Mexican-Spanish words and interjections." *Courtesy U.S. Marine Corps Museum, Washington, D.C.*

55

United States–Nicaraguan relations, particularly since the United States wanted the potentially competitive Nicaragua route to remain undeveloped.[4]

To counterbalance the growing North American influence in Central America, Zelaya negotiated a large loan with British businessmen and approached the Japanese over the possibility of building a canal across Nicaragua. In 1909 disgruntled Liberals revolted against Zelaya. The Taft Administration decided that the Nicaraguan elite should be encouraged to replace the dictator with someone more favorably disposed toward the United States. Nevertheless, Zelaya crushed the rebellion and executed two North American filibusters, Lee Roy Cannon and Leonard Groce. The U.S. Secretary of State denounced Zelaya as a tyrant. The United States encouraged other conspirators to act; however, before they could, Zelaya fled to Mexico and was succeeded by José Madriz. But this did not deter the conspirators and they rebelled against him.[5]

On May 19, 1910, seven hundred U.S. Marines landed at Bluefields (165 mi E of Managua) on the Caribbean coast of Nicaragua to protect U.S. business interests and to prevent the government forces from seizing the port which was held by the rebels. Also, the U.S. gunboat *Paducah* (6 guns) prevented a Nicaraguan gunboat from shelling Bluefields. The rebellion spread through the country and Madriz fled from Nicaragua on August 20. Eventually Adolfo Díaz emerged as the new president in May 1911. A businessman, he disliked the military and wanted law and order. To that end he was willing to compromise Nicaraguan sovereignty by giving the United States powers to intervene. On June 6, 1911, the two nations signed a convention whereby the United States took control of Nicaragua's customs payments.[6]

On July 29, 1912, Gen. Luis Mena, the Secretary of War, rebelled against Díaz in defiance of U.S. wishes. At Díaz' request, U.S. Marines, led by Maj. Smedley Butler, landed to suppress the rebellion. Butler's force was hard pressed to protect the legation and to keep open the railroad running between the port of Corinto and a little beyond the capital of Managua, a distance of 171 miles by rail. Goaded by U.S. financial interests, President Taft dispatched another 800 Marines commanded by Colonel Joseph Pendelton. They advanced along the rail line driving the rebels southward. Finally, the rebels made a stand at Coyotepe Hill near Masaya on October 4. The Marines carried the rebel position in 37 minutes. The Marines lost four dead and fourteen wounded. The rebels lost at least 60 dead. Organized resistance ceased by November and the Nicaraguan government declared an amnesty. General Mena was deported to Panama and a 105-man Marine legation guard remained in Managua to protect U.S. interests.[7]

On August 5, 1914, after considerable delay, the Bryan-Chamorro Treaty was signed whereby the United States paid $3 million (to be applied against a debt or for purposes approved by the United States) for a canal option and other concessions; it was ratified on June 24, 1916.[8]

On February 7, 1923, at the urging of the United States, the Central American governments, including Nicaragua, signed a "General treaty of peace and amity." Each nation agreed to deny recognition to any government which came to power through a coup and that each government should establish a *Guardia Nacional* (national guard) in order to depoliticize the military. To help Nicaragua create a *Guardia Nacional* the U.S. State Department recommended Calvin B. Carter, who had worked for the Philippine Constabulary, as an individual well suited to accomplishing the task. Carter arrived in Nicaragua in July 1925.[9]

In August 1925 the Nicaraguan elite elected an anti-American coalition government of Conservative President Carlos Solorzano and Liberal Vice President Juan Bautista Sacasa. As a consequence, the U.S. legation guard, which had been in Nicaragua since 1912, was withdrawn. On October 25 former Conservation President Emiliano Chamorro Vargas seized La Loma, a fortification dominating Managua, and overthrew the government. Twenty Nicaraguans died. The recently formed *Guardia Nacional*, possessing only thirty rounds per rifle, did not challenge the machine-gun-armed Conservatives. The United States refused to recognize Chamorro's government, which took power on January 17, 1926, and many Liberals rebelled. Both the Conservative army and the new *Guardia Nacional* attempted to subdue the Liberals.[10]

In May Liberal Bertram Sandoval, sailing from Mexico, landed at Bluefields, Nicaragua's principal port on the east coast. After defeating Chamorro's supporters, Sandoval seized $160,000 from the national bank. As a consequence, 213 U.S. Marines and sailors landed from the cruiser *Cleveland* at Bluefields to protect American lives and property. Rear Adm. Julian H. Latimer, Commander of the U.S. Special Service Squadron (the U.S. fleet in the Caribbean), unsuccessfully attempted to negotiate a cease-fire between Liberals and Conservatives. Failing this, he enforced a 9,000-square-mile "neutral zone." Since the Conservatives were the established government, this decision favored their cause. In Managua Chamorro declared a state of war and began to assemble an army.[11]

In an attempt to pacify the Liberals and the United States, Chamorro resigned in favor of his hand-picked successor, Sebastian Uriza. Among other nations, the United States refused to recognize Uriza. The Nicaraguan Congress then elected Conservative Adolfo Díaz as president; an old friend of the United States, his government was promptly recognized by Washington.[12]

The Liberals were not deterred. Gen. José María Moncada captured Puerto Cabezas and drove Díaz' forces inland. On November 15, 1926, Díaz requested U.S. assistance and Marines once more landed at Bluefields and established a neutrality zone. On the thirtieth, exiled Liberal Juan Bautista Sacasa returned from Mexico and landed at Puerto Cabezas, Nicaragua, and claimed the presidency. Among his followers were Mexican officers who had been granted leaves of absence by their military superiors. At least some of the men and arms were delivered by the Mexican-registered boat *Tropical* which sailed from Salina Cruz, Mexico. The ammunition boxes were stamped "F.N.C.," the national cartridge company of Mexico. Although the Mexican government apparently was not directly involved, some Mexicans must have taken pleasure in the opportunity to pay back the "Gringos" for their activities in Texas during the 1830s. Based on this evidence, the Coolidge administration accused Mexico of spreading Communism in Central America.[13]

In late December a Liberal army led by Moncada defeated the Conservative army at Laguna de Perlas, midway between Puerto Cabezas and Bluefields. Casualties were in the hundreds. Despite the recognition and military assistance from the United States in support of the Conservative government, the prominent Liberals—Juan Bautista Sacasa and José María Moncada—continued to fight. The U.S. Marines established additional neutrality zones at Rama (160 mi E of Managua) on January 10, 1927, and at Corinto (140 mi NW of Managua) on January 24.[14]

In January Liberal rebels led by General Moncada moved southward from their strongholds in the north. In an attempt to bolster the Díaz government, the United States sold Nicaragua 3,000 Krag rifles, 200 Browning machine guns, and three million rounds of ammunition. On February 1 it established a 150-man legation guard in Managua whose mission included defending the capital. Marine forces in Nicaragua included an air detachment, although the mission of this force was limited to protecting U.S. citizens and property.[15]

Figure 9. The U.S. Intervention in Nicaragua (1927–33). The Nicaraguan army on the march in 1927. Typical of Central American and Caribbean armies, the men are wearing white cotton clothes and hats, not uniforms. Most wear thongs, some wear sandals, and others are barefooted. The home-made Nicaraguan flag lacks the national emblem. *Author's collection.*

On February 6 some 1,500 Liberals captured the town of Chinandega (180 mi NW of Managua) from 500 Conservatives following a bloody house-to-house fight. The Conservatives retook the town but its center was in ruins. In order to maintain communication between Managua and Cortino, an additional 850 Marines were landed; detachments encamped at strategic points along the rail line that connected the two cities. In March 3,000 Liberals led by Moncada defeated a Conservative army at Muymuy midway between Matagalpa and Managua. The United States realized that even with its assistance the Díaz government was incapable of suppressing the Liberals without its direct involvement in the fighting.[16]

On March 31, 1927, U.S. President Calvin Coolidge sent Henry L. Stimson, former Secretary of War, to restore order through diplomacy, if possible, but he was armed with the threat of open intervention. Stimson concluded that militarily the situation was a stalemate so he met with the Liberal Moncada. Ultimately, Moncada and twelve of his thirteen generals agreed to the terms: Díaz would complete his term; Liberals would be admitted to the Cabinet; the combatants (both Liberal and Conservative) would disarm and receive ten *córdobas* for each rifle surrendered; the United States would maintain order and would train a national security force that would be loyal to the elected president; and the United States would supervise the 1928 election. The one Liberal general who refused to accept the Tipitapa agreement was Augusto César Sandino. On May 27, fifteen days after Moncada sent Stimson the telegram accepting the agreement, Sandino also wrote to Moncada initiating his fight against the U.S. intervention.[17]

OPPOSING FORCES

Nicaragua is the largest Central American republic and is about the size of the state of Alabama. The population of Nicaragua in 1927 was about 800,000 persons. Some 1,000 U.S. citizens lived in Nicaragua, most associated with the $22 million invested in agriculture, mining, timber, and railroads. By comparison, British investments were $3.9 million and French $1 million.[18]

Between 1927 and 1932 U.S. Marine Corps strength in Nicaragua ebbed and flowed between 1,200 and 6,000 men. Also, Marine reinforcements were close at hand in Panama. Many U.S. Marines, who had enhanced their military reputations on Hispañola, came to Nicaragua. The Marines were bravely led, well equipped, and highly motivated.[19]

The *Guardia Nacional* had been created in 1925 as a consequence of the 1923 "General treaty of peace and amity." Initially composed of about 400 men, it was not liked or supported by either the Liberals or the Conservatives. On May 8, 1927, President Díaz requested that the U.S. Marines take charge of the *Guardia*. By December 1927 the *Guardia* was composed of 82 officers and 574 men; by July 1932 its numbers had increased to 267 officers and 2,240 men. Selected Marine officers and sergeants held temporary commissions in the *Guardia* and commanded units down to platoon size.[20]

The Nicaraguan army continued to exist throughout the conflict, although it increasingly became irrelevant. The officers owed their first allegiance to their political party and the men were impressed into service. The army received almost no training and was very poorly equipped. Typically, the enlisted went unpaid because the officers stole their money.

The Marines preferred Thompson submachine guns and other automatic weapons to rifles because of the limited visibility and the suddenness of ambush from close quarters. Fire support was provided by Stokes mortars, 37mm cannon, and aircraft.[21]

Sandino held only nominal leadership over the bands of Liberals who were fighting the government. Sandino attempted to exercise discipline over these, but could only control the band that he led. He wanted to avoid the possibility of irresponsible acts turning the peasants against him.[22]

Sandino drew his fighters from three groups. Foremost, he had a dedicated following among the agrarian working-class Liberals. These men and women were ideologically motivated, making them much more tenacious opponents than those whom the Marines had faced in Haiti and the Dominican Republic. To this nucleus, Sandino could rally at times significant numbers of peasants who had limited combat value, although they were excellent sources for intelligence. The war caused mines and plantations to close down in the north and many of these unemployed workers chose to fight with Sandino.

Additionally, a number of individuals from other Latin American countries joined Sandino's ranks. Among the most noted were Gregorio Gibert of the Dominican Republic, Farabundo Martí of El Salvador, José de Paredes of Mexico, and Jirón Ruano of Guatemala. By July 1927 Sandino commanded about 1,000 followers. Sandino was very charismatic and he strongly believed in a calling to eliminate U.S. influence from Nicaragua. He was most popular in the remote north which held no particular loyalty to the distant government in Managua.[23]

Many of Sandino's followers were mounted on horses and mules. He had three sources of weapons: those captured from the enemy, those purchased from Mexico, and those acquired from gunrunners. Sandino, on occasion, referred to his rifles as "*concones*"; these were rifles purchased in Mexico by the Liberals in 1926 and 1927. They had been carried to Nicaragua on board the steamer *Concón*, hence the origin of their name. His weapons ranged from crude handmade firearms to Browning machine guns. Most of his outside aid passed through the porous Honduran border. Sandino raised considerable amounts of money throughout the Americas, including the United States.[24]

OPENING STRATEGY

Sandino did not articulate his initial strategy. His acts suggest that he planned to expel the U.S. Marines by overwhelming them with numbers, overthrow the government, and seize power.[25] Sandino planned to rebuild the Liberal party following the Mexican model. He also discussed reestablishing the Central American confederation, perhaps under the protection of Mexico. To execute his military strategy, Sandino built a fortified camp on the remote El Chipote Mountain, surrounded by jungle in northwestern Nicaragua, from where he could strike his enemies. El Chipote was located in the Department of Nueva Segovia, about which Sandino noted, "The entire region of Nueva Segovia belongs to us in body and soul."[26]

The U.S. Marines initially employed the strategy that had proved successful in Haiti and the Dominican Republic. The capital and important cities were pacified and garrisoned. Patrols probed the countryside seeking possible opposition. When opposition materialized, it was immediately confronted.

The rough terrain and inadequate infrastructure created logistical problems and limited the scale and speed of Marine Corps operations. Nicaragua had a 159-mile narrow-gauge railroad line between Corinto and Granada with a spur from Masaya to Diriamba. Three "motor roads" existed totaling 126 miles; they were frequently unusable in the rainy season which lasted from May through December. Heat in excess of 100 degrees fahrenheit was common. Cart and burro paths were the main transportation routes. The Marines usually landed their supplies at Corinto.

The supplies were then shipped by rail to Managua or León. From there, they traveled mostly by bull cart (a few trucks, caterpillar tractors, and aircraft were available) to the garrisons in the interior. The 160-mile trip from León to Ocotal required eleven to thirteen days by bull cart. Some supplies—fresh meat, vegetables, forage, and pack animals—were locally purchased.[27]

THE EARLY STRUGGLE

Sandino led some forty followers from the gold-mining area west of Puerto Cabezas on the east coast into the Department of Nuevo Segovia in northwestern Nicaragua. He set up his base camp atop El Chipote Mountain which lies between the Coco River and the Honduran border.

As the U.S. presidential envoy, Henry Stimson was being seen off by the Conservative Díaz and the Liberal Moncada during the early morning of May 16, three hundred Liberal guerrillas ambushed a U.S. Marine patrol in the town of La Paz Centro northwest of the capital where it had gone to investigate reports of gunfire. The fighting lasted two hours and the rebels were readily identified as Liberals by their red headbands. Two Marines were killed, including Capt. Richard B. Buchanan, and two others were wounded; the Liberals lost fourteen dead.[28]

In the weeks that followed the Tipitapa agreement, both Liberals and Conservatives turned in guns for the ten *córdobas* reward; however, most came from the Conservatives. They sold the government 11,000 rifles and 300 machine guns but the Liberals were less forthcoming, turning in only 3,100 rifles and 30 machine guns. While 3,000 U.S. Marines maintained order, Moncada, the Liberal, won the new election but Sandino perceived this to be a sellout to the gringos.[29]

Brig. Gen. Logan Feland, USMC, soon learned the general vicinity of Sandino's mountain stronghold and on May 21 ordered the 5th Regiment, 2nd Brigade north from Managua, to disarm the rebels. Nineteen days later the Marines occupied the nearly deserted provincial capital Ocotal (100 mi N of Managua). A garrison of forty-one Marines under Capt. Gilbert D. Hatfield and forty-eight *Guardia* commanded by Capt. G. C. Darnell was established. In June Sandino seized the American-owned Butter's mine near San Albino in Nuevo Segovia where he had worked. He captured wagons, ammunition, and explosives. For a while his men worked the mine, minting their own money. Late in June, Hatfield and Sandino exchanged increasingly antagonistic telegrams.[30]

THE BATTLE OF OCOTAL

At one o'clock in the morning on July 16, some sixty followers of Sandino, supported by a few hundred peasants armed principally with machetes, attacked the recently established eighty-nine-man garrison at Ocotal. The Marines had become suspicious on the previous day when the townspeople began to hide their valuables. The officers ordered their men to sleep fully clothed next to their weapons. At one o'clock in the morning Sandino and his deputy, Rufo Marín, led three unsuccessful assaults against the Marine position; Marín was killed. Although the Marines and *Guardia* were able to defend themselves, they could not prevent the looting of property belonging to the Conservatives. At 10:15 A.M. two patrolling "DeHavilland DH-4" aircraft flying out of Managua some 80 miles away discovered the attack by reading signal panels laid by Marines in the courtyard of the town's administration building. One aircraft flew the intelligence back to its base to seek help; the second strafed rebel positions with its rear-facing .30-caliber machine gun. At 2:35 P.M. five "DeHavillands" attacked Sandino's force for 45 minutes with machine guns and jury-rigged 17-pound bombs. This proved

Figure 10. The U.S. Intervention in Nicaragua (1927–33). Mounted U.S. Marines in front of the "Pink House" in Ocotal which they defended against attacks led by Augusto Sandino in July 1927. Following this and other head-to-head fights with the Marines, Sandino changed his tactics, appreciating that his inferiorly trained and armed men could not directly confront the Marines. *Courtesy of U.S. Marine Corps, Washington, D.C.*

decisive; by late afternoon the rebels and their supporters melted away. Sandino considered burning out the enemy but the townspeople, many of whom supported him, dissuaded Sandino from this action. The attackers lost more than 50 dead; one Marine was killed, another wounded, three members of the *Guardia* were wounded and one captured.[31]

Rear Adm. David F. Sellers, who had replaced Admiral Latimer, believing that Sandino was a mere bandit and no longer a threat, followed through with plans to reduce the Marine force in Nicaragua in order to meet needs in China and Haiti. In July one of two Marine brigades (the 11th) was withdrawn from Nicaragua except for its 5th Regiment and its air component. The Marines were now commanded by Col. Louis M. Gulick.[32]

Later in July Sandino suffered defeats near the towns of San Fernando and Los Calpules. However, during the pre-dawn darkness of September 19, 1927, some 150 Liberals, led by Carlos Salgado, attacked the 45-man garrison (20 Marines and 25 *Guardia*) at Telpaneca (10 mi SE of Ocotal) on the Coco River. Although the garrison successfully defended itself, the rebels were able to carry off food and supplies. Two Marines died as did about 25 rebels. This attack demonstrated the resilience of Sandino's forces. Clashes continued as Marine-led patrols stumbled into bands of Sandino's followers.[33]

On October 8 the rebels shot down a Marine Corps aircraft with "El Chula," a machine gun mounted on a homemade stand which could elevate and pivot.[34] Some 400 rebels then ambushed an eighteen-man rescue patrol near Las Cruces which escaped without losses. On December 26 a Marine patrol clashed with well-armed Honduran troops. Apparently, someone had strayed across the border.[35]

MARINES ADVANCE ON EL CHIPOTE

On November 23 a reconnaissance aircraft discovered Sandino's camp at El Chipote. Recently arrived Vought 02U-1 Corsairs attacked the camp with 17-pound bombs. It took a month to ready a 174-man (Marines and *Guardia*) force for the arduous trek across swollen steams to the mountain stronghold. The force advanced in two columns, one departing from Jinotega and the other from Telpaneca.[36]

As Marines closed in on El Chipote they were ambushed on December 30 by four mounted bands. The rebels first attacked the column composed of 114 men (mostly Marines) led by Capt. Richard Livingston. The rebels fired small arms and threw dynamite bombs as the Marines advanced along a narrow path on the right bank of the Jicaro River two miles from Quilali. Foretelling the tactics the Marines would employ through the Nicaraguan campaign, the Marines attempted to pin down the enemy with a superior volume of fire and then charged the enemy to defeat them with grenades, small arms, and bayonets. After an hour and a half, the Marines supported by aircraft drove off the attackers. However, their mule pack train had been scattered. Five Marines were killed and 23 wounded during the Battle of Camino Real, including Livingston; and two *Guardia* were killed and two wounded. The rebels sustained perhaps 400 casualties. Just eight days earlier (December 22) the U.S. Congress voted to provide funds for the U.S. expeditionary force in Nicaragua.[37]

On New Year's day the second column (40 Marines and 20 *Guardia*) led by 1st Lt. Merton A. Richal was attacked six miles northwest of Quilali by 50 guerrillas. The Marines dug in and finally beat off the attackers with their Stokes mortar, 37mm field gun, air support, and a 44-man relief column from Livingston's force. The second column had one casualty during the Battle of Sapotilla Ridge. The two shaken columns took refuge in Quilali and awaited reinforcements. Some 400 rebels encircled the village which lay near the junction of the Coco and Jicaro Rivers some 26 miles east of Ocotal. The Marines converted the main street into a 500-foot air strip which ended atop a steep cliff. The landing gear of a Vought 02U-1 Corsair was replaced by the less rigid landing gear of the Dh-4 DeHavilland. Between January 6 and 8, 1928, this aircraft made ten roundtrips carrying in 1,400 pounds of supplies and a relief officer and taking out 18 wounded. The pilot, 1st Lt. Christian F. Schilt, was awarded the Congressional Medal of Honor. The rebels abandoned their siege.[38]

Once the Marines had been resupplied and relieved of their wounded, they attempted to renew their ground assault against El Chipote. Large rebel ambushes were broken up by air attacks. Nonetheless, harassing fire caused the Marines to abandon the advance.[39]

Following the failure to reach El Chipote on the ground, the Marines adopted a new strategy. They aggressively harried Sandino's patrols. Changing his strategy from pitched battles to hit-and-run, Sandino withdrew his patrols into the haven of El Chipote. Once this was accomplished, four Corsairs dropped recently arrived 50-pound bombs as well as 17-pounders on El Chipote where several hundred rebels had taken refuge. The rebels responded with a coordinated hail of small arms fire. On January 26, 1928, Maj. Archibald Young, leading 300 Marines, scaled the heights of El Chipote only to find that Sandino had escaped into Honduras. Marine Corps aircraft successfully drove Sandino from his mountaintop fortress but failed to end his operations. The Marines could not prevent Sandino's escape. He established a new base camp called El Chipotón in the center of the Department of Jinotega which was almost an impenetrable jungle.[40]

General Feland returned to Nicaragua on January 15, 1928, with reinforcements and orders to eliminate the rebels before the end-of-year elections. He commanded 2,500 Marines and some two dozen aircraft (twelve Corsair and Curtiss-Falcon reconnaissance bombers, seven OL-8 Loening amphibians, and five Ford trimotor transports). Although he did not directly command the *Guardia*, most units were commanded by Marines. The Marines immediately intensified their patrols.

BATTLE OF EL BRAMADERO

On February 27, two hundred rebels attacked an empty bull-cart Marine convoy at El Bramadero in the department of Estelí. The rebels besieged the Marines and the fighting raged for over five hours. The Marines sustained thirteen casualties. The following day aircraft drove off the attackers and a Marine relief column rescued the survivors.[41]

Sandino's followers succeeded in harassing the coffee plantations and mining operations just south and east of their stronghold in Nueva Segovia. On April 12, one hundred fifty rebels led by Gen. Manuel Girón seized La Luz mine. They carried off the gold, mules, and the assistant superintendent, George B. Marshall, who later died. In spite of being hunted by seven columns of Marines, Girón escaped into the hinterland. The inexperienced 11th Regiment had trouble forcing the enemy to make a stand. Overland patrols were tied to the dirt roads and paths because of the difficulty of the terrain. However, Marine Corps aircraft attacked numerous bands of suspected rebels forcing them to disperse.[42]

On May 13, one hundred rebels led by Girón ambushed a 36-man Marine-*Guardia* patrol led by Capt. Robert Hunter along the Cúa River 70 miles east of Jinotega. The Marines sustained one dead and three wounded including Hunter.[43]

THE RÍO COCO PATROLS

Marine patrols emanating from Puerto Cabezas on the Caribbean side used native dugouts to transport men and supplies westward along the Río Coco. On occasion patrols going up the river were coordinated with patrols pushing northward along the west coast in an attempt to create a pincer. In July and August, during the height of the rainy season, Capt. Merritt A. Edson, leading 46 men, pushed 140 miles up the Coco River in search of Sandino's base-camp. Skirmishes occurred along the way and he received limited supplies by air drops. On August 7 Sandino and Girón, leading 200 men, attacked the Marines' advanced patrols, which were proceeding up the banks of the river in advance of the dugouts to prevent an ambush. The Battle of Ililihuas lasted three hours. Sandino lost thirteen men and Edison lost three. On August 14 Edson captured the town of Abraham and a supply train. Three days later, he took Poteca at the confluence of the Poteca and Coco Rivers only to find it deserted.[44]

ELECTIONS IN NICARAGUA AND IN THE UNITED STATES

On November 4, 1928, U.S. Marines supervised Nicaraguan national elections. Ninety percent of those registered voted, and Moncada was reelected president. Both the U.S.-supported Nicaraguan government and Sandino sought the backing of the Nicaraguan people. Marine aircraft dropped leaflets on towns in areas traditionally sympathetic to Sandino, while Pedro Altamirano, Sandino's lieutenant, rode from village to village urging the peasants not to vote. The government propaganda included peace terms and letters from Sandino's parents appealing for his surrender.[45]

At this time approximately 6,000 U.S. military personnel were in Nicaragua. After the elections Marine patrols combed the north searching for the rebels. On December 6 a patrol led by Capt. Maurice Holmes cornered a rebel band near the Honduran border. The rebels were completely routed at the Battle of Cuje; the Marine patrol lost one man.[46]

THE REBELS RENEW MILITARY OPERATIONS IN NUEVA SEGOVIA

On January 10, 1929, some one hundred rebels attacked a seventeen-man *Guardia* patrol commanded by a Marine near the hamlet of Guancastilla. Two *Guardia* members were killed and four wounded; the rebels lost seven killed. The rebels had more success against a seven-man patrol led by Marine 1st Lt. Alexander Galt, which they attacked on January 21 near the village of San Antonio. Three Marines were killed and the rebels sustained no casualties. Offsetting this setback, a Marine patrol surreptitiously captured Sandino's close advisor, Gen. Manuel Girón, near San Albino as he was riding alone.[47]

In early 1929 President Moncada recruited 500 *voluntarios* from the northern departments. The *voluntarios* joined the Marine-*Guardia* patrols. They contributed little to military operations and both the Nicaraguan Conservatives and the U.S. diplomats opposed the existence of the *voluntarios*, fearing that the force would become the military arm of the Liberal Party. The United States persuaded President Moncada to disband the *voluntarios*; this was carried out by July.[48]

On March 4, 1929, Herbert Hoover became president of the United States and the new administration accelerated the withdrawal from the expensive and unpopular war. The Marine force was reduced to approximately 1,500—the 11th Regiment was brought home and the 5th restricted to defensive operations. Brigadier General Dion Williams relieved Feland. The *Guardia* was increased to over 2,000 men.[49]

Figure 11. The U.S. Intervention in Nicaragua (1927–33). General Manuel Jirón, one of Augusto Sandino's commanders, poses with his men in 1928. This group hardly gives the impression of being ragtag. The photograph is from the Victor F. Bleasdale collection. *Courtesy U.S. Marine Corps Museum, Washington, D.C.*

During March the U.S. Marines probably violated the ill-defined Nicaraguan-Honduras border on two occasions. On March 17 Marines attacked a rebel force led by Carlos Salgado, killing four and wounding three. Two weeks later Honduran President Mejía Colindres asked the United States to withdraw its forces from his nation. On March 23 Marine Corps aircraft bombed Salgado's forces near Las Limas, again provoking a Honduran complaint.[50]

In June 1929 Sandino with twenty-five armed followers accepted the invitation of Mexico's President Emilío Portes Gil to visit his country allowing a respite from the intensive campaign. Sandino traveled to Veracruz and then Mérida, Mexico, and unsuccessfully waited six months for the audience. The United States pressured Mexico not to permit Sandino to visit Mexico City and to meet with Portes Gil, fearing the internationalizing of the Nicaraguan conflict. Within the United States, some in the press were increasingly sympathetic to Sandino and promoted him as a liberator.[51]

The relations between the *Guardia*'s U.S. Marine officers and its Nicaraguan enlisted became strained at times. Between 1928 and 1932 nine mutinies occurred during which a few Marines were killed. In October 1929 the *Guardia* garrison at Telpaneca mutinied, killed its commander (a Marine sergeant), took his replacement captive, and fled into Honduras.[52]

SANDINO RETURNS FROM MEXICO

On May 16, 1930, Sandino again returned to Nicaragua and rebuilt his following. Helped by the poor economy, he won many new recruits Although most rebels professed a loyalty to Sandino, not all were under his complete control. They operated in units of 50 to 300 men and were armed with rifles and dynamite seized from mining operations. New recruits learned tactics by participating in combat. In June Sandino assembled a 150-man force with the intention of attacking the *Guardia* (65 mi NE of Managua) to the south of his normal area of operation. The gathering on Saraguazca Mountain was discovered by a reconnaissance aircraft. *Guardia* patrols immediately converged on the mountain. Fighting erupted on the nineteenth as the *Guardia* made contact with Sandino's pickets. Marine Corps aircraft attacked and Sandino, wounded in the leg, fled north.[53]

Because of public and congressional pressure to withdraw the Marines, the U.S. administration pressured Moncada to expand the *Guardia*. During 1930 the *Guardia* was enlarged and turned over to native officers. In mid-1930 the *Guardia* penetrated into the department of Nueva Segovia, Sandino's stronghold. In November Sandino attempted to disrupt senatorial elections and stop all commerce flowing into and out of northwestern Nicaragua. Consequentially, Marine garrisons were established on six large coffee plantations to ensure the flow of commerce. The plantation owners told the peasants that the Marines were there to guarantee that they worked.[54]

In November President Moncada told the U.S. Secretary of State, Henry L. Stimson, that Nicaragua could no longer afford the "scientific warfare" being orchestrated by the U.S. Marines to eliminate banditry. On December 31 a ten-man Marine telegraph repair party was almost wiped out north of Ocotal, increasing the U.S. public outcry for withdrawal. On January 17, 1931, three hundred rebels attacked and captured the town of Somoto (80 mi N of Managua) in Nueva Segovia. Their armaments included four machine guns. On February 5 Lt. Col. Calvin B. Matthews was placed in charge of the *Guardia* and later that month all U.S. Marines began withdrawing from the hinterland into Managua.[55]

At 10:20 A.M. on March 31, 1931, a major earthquake shook Managua, killing 1,450 Nicaraguans and four Americans and injuring 4,000 more. Thirty-two city blocks burned to the ground; among the buildings destroyed was the National Palace.

THE REBELS EXPAND INTO THE EAST

Taking advantage of the chaos in Managua caused by the earthquake, four rebel columns attacked American fruit and lumber interests along the Mosquito Coast and mining interests in the mountains. Both sides sustained important casualties. Capt. Harlen Pefley, USMC, was killed while leading a *Guardia* patrol. Pedro Blandón, Sandino's chief lieutenant, was also killed. In mid-April shore parties landed at Puerto Cabezas from the cruiser *Memphis* and the gunboat *Ashville*. A party was also put ashore at Bluefields from the gunboat *Sacramento*. On May 12 Pedro Altamirano, leading 150 men, seized the Neptune Mine and carried off gold, dynamite, and supplies. Other rebel columns attacked the towns of San Pedro del Norte and Rama, both in the vicinity of Bluefields, where North Americans held large financial interests. Throughout the fighting, Marine Corps aircraft harassed suspected rebel bands. On July 23 the rebels shot down an aircraft with small arms fire. The U.S. embassy warned its citizens that they remained in Nicaragua at their own risk.[56]

BACK IN THE DEPARTMENT OF NUEVA SEGOVIA

Sandino led an attack against the hamlet of Palacagüina on May 14. Marine Corps aircraft drove off the attackers after heavy fighting. Sandino was again wounded and Miguel Ortez y Guillén, a trusted lieutenant, was killed. On June 21 Socrates Sandino, Augusto's brother, and José de Paredes, a former officer in the Mexican army and a friend of President Portes Gil, joined Sandino carrying a vague promise of help from Mexico.[57]

SANDINO MOVES SOUTH AND WEST

In the fall of 1931 Sandino invaded the departments of Chontales, León, and Estelí. Rebels tore up recently laid railroad tracks between the towns of León and El Sauce. In response, Marine Corps aircraft carried *Guardia* troops to the most threatened areas. Sandino had been able to expand his operations in part because supporters in Honduras purchased arms used to suppress the 1931 revolt of Gen. Gregorio Ferrera against the government of Vicente Mejía Colindres.[58]

Appreciating that U.S. public support continued to wane, military operations against Sandino took on a sense of urgency in 1932. The United States pressured Honduras to patrol more vigorously its frontier with Nicaragua in an attempt to deprive Sandino of arms and the freedom of sanctuary. The frontier offered no barrier to Sandino—in fact, Honduras was a haven. Honduran peasants were as sympathetic to Sandino as the Nicaraguan peasants. These sympathies were created in part by U.S. Marine Corps aircraft accidently bombing Honduran villages in the border area. Throughout the fighting the Honduran border patrols captured only one of Sandino's supporters and then allowed him to escape! On July 30, 1932, the U.S. chargé in Honduras, Lawrence Higgins, lamented,

> while not the smallest, it [the army] is the weakest of any independent state in the world. In recent years the latter has been reduced to an unusually low strength, and has been incapable of coping with even small group[s] of bandits and desperadoes within the country to say nothing of preventing their incurrsions from outside.[59]

On June 30, 1932, the U.S. Congress specified that "no money appropriated in this [naval appropriation] Act shall be used to defray the expense of sending additional Marines to Nicaragua."[60]

Battlefield successes ebbed and flowed between Sandino's followers and the Marine-led *Guardia*. On April 21 the rebels ambushed a *Guardia* patrol led by Marine Lt. Laurin T. Covington between Apali and Jalapa. The patrol was rescued by a relief patrol commanded by Marine 1st Lt. Laurence C. Brunton. Then the combined patrols were ambushed and routed. Ten *Guardia* (three Americans and seven Nicaraguans) were killed. On April 26 a forty-five-man *Guardia* patrol and rebels fought a three-hour battle. Among the rebel dead was a chief lieutenant, Florencio Silva. On September 26 a *Guardia* patrol, led by Capt. Lewis P. Puller, surprised a 150-man rebel camp and killed sixteen men while sustaining two dead and three wounded.[61]

THE INCURSION FROM COSTA RICA

Liberals launched a small expedition into the southern department of Rivas from Costa Rica with the hope that the force would gain momentum as it advanced north toward Managua. Instead, it disintegrated.[62]

THE NICARAGUAN ELECTION OF 1932

During the height of the rainy season, the government launched an offensive of its own to prevent Sandino from disrupting the presidential elections scheduled for the fall. On July 31 a mobile patrol known as "Company M" began operations. Led by Captain Puller (nicknamed "El Tigre" by the Nicaraguans), it surprised a large band of rebels on September 26. The Liberals lost sixteen men and the *Guardia* lost five.[63]

On November 6 Juan Bautista Sacasa (in whose name the Liberals had launched the 1926 rebellion) was elected president without serious incident. At the same time the U.S. negotiated two agreements with the outgoing Conservatives and the incoming Liberals. First, Sandino would be offered generous terms to surrender so that if he refused he could be branded a bandit. Second, both the Liberals and the Conservatives had to agree that the *Guardia* would remain apolitical.[64]

On November 15 Sacasa named his nephew Anastasio Somoza,[65] who had been Moncada's foreign minister, the first Chief Director of the *Guardia Nacional*. When asked by a Marine officer how he would defeat Sandino, Somoza responded, "Simple, I would declare an armistice, I would invite Sandino in, and we'd have some drinks, a good dinner, and when he went out one of my men would shoot him."[66]

Outgoing President Moncada wanted to dedicate the new rail extension from Léon to El Sauce located in the troubled north. He learned that Sandino planned to disrupt the work. On December 21 Sandino attacked a train with eight automatic weapons a few miles south of El Sauce. To Sandino's surprise, 64 Marine-led *Guardia* burst from the train and charged. Sandino lost 31 dead, 67 horses and mules, and supplies.[67]

On December 26 some 250 rebels led by Juan Umanzor attacked and overran a railroad construction camp just south of El Sauce. While they were preparing to execute the overseers, a train pulled in carrying seven Marines and sixty-four *Guardia* led by Captain Puller. The superior training and firepower of the government's forces took a heavy toll on the rebels. Once

Figure 12. The U.S. Intervention in Nicaragua (1927–33). U.S. Marines escort their dead through the streets of Managua. Forty-seven Marines died while fighting in Nicaragua between 1927 and 1933. This photograph is from the Victor F. Bleasdale collection. *Courtesy U.S. Marine Corps Museum, Washington, D.C.*

again, Sandino escaped across the Honduran border. The inauguration of the new rail line was held on December 28 as scheduled.[68]

Public pressure continued to mount in the United States for the withdrawal of the Marines. On January 1, 1933, Dr. Juan Sacasa was sworn in as the president of Nicaragua and Somoza took command of the 2,650-man, Marine-trained, U.S.-outfitted *Guardia*, which was now entirely composed of Nicaraguans. And on January 2 the last elements of the 5th Marine Regiment sailed from Corinto.[69]

On February 2 Sandino accepted Sacasa's invitation to talk. He flew to Managua, talked with the President, received amnesty, and retired with a few followers to an agricultural collective in the Coco River Valley. Perhaps President Sacasa feared the increasing military power of Somosa and wanted to cultivate Sandino as a possible ally. Except for a 100-man force which was to be maintained at government expense, all of Sandino's followers (about 1,800 men) were to turn in their weapons within three months. Sandino was to maintain order in the Rio Coco area of Nueva Segovia and Jinotega.[70]

On February 21, 1934, Sandino was invited back to the capital to discuss a new mining project. He was wined, dined, and then shot as Somoza had foretold. Sandino, his brother, and two rebel generals were taken to the Managua airport and mowed down by machine guns shortly after midnight. On March 3 Somoza ordered the *Guardia* to destroy the Rio Coco cooperative, accusing the remaining followers of Sandino of having devised a Communist plot. The offensive ended on March 12 when Sandino's children were murdered. Three years later, on May 29, 1936, Somoza's *Guardia* surrounded the new National Palace and forced Sacasa to resign. In December Somoza staged an election in which he was chosen president, beginning four decades of rule by Anastasio Somoza and his two sons.[71]

OBSERVATIONS

The U.S. intervention in Nicaragua was in many respects a crossroads in the relations between the U.S. government and the people of Central America. The peasants were increasingly seeing the United States through Sandino's eyes as an exploiter. For the first time within Central America, an individual, Augusto Sandino, articulated an ideology which had a strong appeal to the peasants. In 1931 an American coffee planter wrote to Secretary of State Henry Lewis Stimson, "Today we are hated and despised. . . . This feeling has been created by employing the American marines to hunt down and kill Nicaraguans in their own country."[72]

Also, the North American people were becoming increasingly concerned about U.S. military intervention in Latin America. It was their growing opposition to the intervention that was the most important catalyst for the removal of the Marines.

Within Nicaragua the United States tried to foster a nonpolitical *Guardia Nacional* and to encourage the drafting of electoral reform. Both of these efforts failed miserably. Instead, the U.S. actions helped create a political-military environment which permitted the rise of the brutal dictator Anastasio Somoza. The conflict between the Liberals and Conservatives within Nicaragua, which began with the declaration of independence, was temporarily extinguished by the iron-handed rule of the Somoza family backed by the U.S.-trained *Guardia Nacional*.[73]

Significant differences existed between the U.S. intervention in Nicaragua and those in Haiti and the Dominican Republic. No U.S. military government was created as it had in the Dominican Republic. The United States undertook few civic improvements within Nicaragua as they had in Haiti. Within Nicaragua national leaders retained more control than in either Haiti or

Santo Domingo. Unlike in Haiti and Santo Domingo, the Marine officer in charge of military operations against Sandino was restrained by the command structure. He commanded the U.S. Marines and indirectly the *Guardia* through the Nicaraguan President. The U.S. Navy, responsible for protecting the Caribbean coast, reported to the Chief of Naval Operations in Washington, D.C.[74]

The Marines aggressively pursued Sandino but failed to capture him. This failure harmed North American military prestige. Sandino learned that it was not to his advantage to stand and fight the Marines. Many of the early Marine victories could be attributed to the fact that Sandino had not yet learned that he could not defeat this better trained, led, and armed enemy in open battle.

Air power in support of antiguerrilla warfare came of age. Although aviation had its limitations (aircraft could fly neither at night nor in bad weather) Marine Corps close-air support frequently proved decisive in defeating Sandino's followers in battle. As the struggle continued the Marines found innovative ways to employ their aircraft to help solve logistical and other problems. However, errors were made in identifying the enemy from the air, thus causing civilian casualties and increasing the number who supported Sandino.

While the Marines and *Guardia* controlled the urban centers, much of the hinterland, particularly in the north, was dominated by Sandino. Typical of a popular insurgency, Sandino received excellent intelligence and frequently was able to plant misleading intelligence with the enemy. As he noted, "Our Army's success is the result of our espionage service. The enemy doesn't carry out a maneuver that we don't know about at once."[75]

Sandino correctly perceived that U.S. forces could not remain in Nicaragua indefinitely, but he underestimated the potential of the *Guardia Nacional*. Sandino's efforts to solicit outside aid was decades ahead of its possibility. He considered recruiting volunteers from Mexico and other Latin American nations.

During the occupation 47 Marines were killed or died of their wounds, 41 more through accidents including air crashes, and 24 from disease and other causes. Also, 66 Marines were wounded. The campaign cost the United States approximately $20 million. The *Guardia Nacional* admitted to 48 killed and 109 wounded. Reportedly, the rebels lost 1,115 killed, 526 wounded, and 76 captured. The ratio of one dead *Guardia Nacional* or Marine for every nine dead rebels can in large part be explained by the better training of the government forces in rifle aiming and better weapons. Most rebel forces did not teach their followers how to aim like a sharpshooter. Civilian casualties must be added to these numbers.[76]

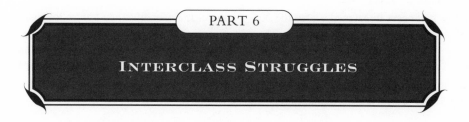

PART 6

INTERCLASS STRUGGLES

CHAPTER 9

NAVAL MUTINIES, 1910–31

Mutiny, armed or otherwise, has always been the gravest of military crimes.
—British Historian J. M. Brereton

THE SPARK

In two unrelated events, the crews of Brazilian and Chilean warships, both of which had recently visited foreign ports, mutinied. The recently completed Brazilian dreadnought *São Paulo*, en route from England to Brazil, stopped at Lisbon, Portugal, in 1910 where it was boarded and searched by leftists. They were seeking King Manuel who was in hiding elsewhere. In 1931 the Chilean dreadnought *Almirante Latorre* underwent overhaul in Great Britain at a time when units of the British fleet were mutinying over pay cuts. Thus, foreign advocates for social, economic, and political change (through violence, if necessary) shared their political beliefs with these sailors.[1]

BACKGROUND

Although these mutinies were spread between two navies and more than two decades in time, they had similar backgrounds and motives. At the time of the mutinies, both Brazil and Chile were struggling through economic crises. Socialists, Anarchists, and Communists were all attempting to exploit the economic circumstance to achieve power.

OPPOSING SIDES

In both cases, the mutineers controlled the most powerful warships in their respective fleets. The governments nominally controlled the remainder of the military which included lesser naval units.

OPENING STRATEGIES

The mutineers threatened to use the heavy guns of the warships they controlled against the government to achieve their demands. The governments first wanted to isolate the mutineers to prevent the revolt from spreading. If negotiations failed, they then planned to use loyal military units to subdue the mutineers. The rebellious units did represent a substantial national investment and were important assets *vis-a-vis* any potential confrontation with neighbors. Therefore, the possible destruction of the mutinous ships could have severe consequences.

BRAZILIAN FLEET MUTINY (THE REVOLT OF THE "WHIP")

On November 21, 1910, crew members of the *Minas Gerais* mutinied, murdering the captain and a few officers, forcing other officers to go ashore, and detaining British engineers who had accompanied the newly completed dreadnought from the builder's yard. The mutiny soon spread to sister ship *São Paulo*, the old coast defense ship *Deodoro*, and the recently completed scout cruiser *Bahia*. A number of men ashore, including those at the barracks on Cobras Island, were in sympathy with the mutineers. The crews of several torpedo boats remained loyal to the government.[2]

A contributing cause to the mutiny was the severe discipline code enforced by the Brazilian navy. A few days earlier a sailor had been flogged—a punishment frequently inflicted for minor offenses—even though it had been legally banned. In addition to corporal punishment, the mutineers complained of overwork and poor pay.[3]

Once in control of the dreadnoughts, the mutineers exercised surprisingly good discipline. In addition to other measures, the leader, João Cándido, ordered all liquor thrown overboard. Moreover, the *Minas Gerais* and *São Paulo* smartly carried out daily drills.[4]

Rio de Janeiro was now held hostage by two of the most powerful warships in the world, manned by crews who were demonstrating their proficiency. Also, the government suspected that many men manning the harbor's defenses were sympathetic to the mutineers' plight. The mutineers sent an ultimatum to the government. If flogging was not abolished, living conditions improved, and an amnesty granted, they would use force. The senate acquiesced to their demands. Notwithstanding, more than one thousand sailors were cashiered from the navy.[5]

CHILEAN FLEET MUTINY

In the early morning of September 1, 1931, crews among the Chilean warships[6] anchored at Coquimbo (254 mi N of Valparaíso) mutinied. Coincidently, the Active Squadron and the Training Squadron, which between them composed the majority of the Chilean navy, met at Coquimbo after the government's announcement of pay cuts. The sailors and officers were demoralized by the unexpected news. During the afternoon of August 31, officers' staterooms were robbed of firearms, and shortly after midnight disgruntled sailors seized their officers; few resisted.[7]

At 4:55 P.M. on September 1, the mutineers radioed twelve demands to the government which were a combination of typical sailors' grievances and those of individuals seeking social changes.[8] The sailors demanded a reply within forty-eight hours, adding that they would not use force to win their demands and that their actions had not been instigated by the Communists or any other political party.[9]

The mutiny provoked a crisis in the government. Acting President Manuel Trucco wanted to negotiate, whereupon his cabinet resigned. The government sent Rear Adm. Edgardo von

Schroeders north by plane to mediate. He was instructed not to concede anything to the mutineers.[10]

On September 2 naval units at Talcahuano, the principal naval base (391 mi S of Valparaíso), also mutinied. Crews seized control of the warships without meeting resistance. The following night small-arms fire was exchanged between loyal troops ashore and those on board the submarine tender *Araucano*. Early on the fourth, the warships not undergoing repairs sailed north to join their comrades.[11]

Meanwhile, Admiral von Schroeders met with the mutineers late in the morning of September 3. He perceived that a split was developing among the mutineers. A small group of assistants to the supply officers, who had joined the navy under contract just a few weeks earlier, argued for sweeping social change, while those from the other ships were only concerned with the sailors' issues. The talks continued through the fourth. Hindering a settlement was the fact that the mutineers sensed growing public support for their actions. The Admiral's arguments did not prevail nor did those of a delegation of students the government sent to parley with the rebels.[12]

With the arrival of the warships from Talcahuano the mutineers gained renewed confidence. On September 4 airmen seized the 2nd Air Group base at Quintero and radioed their demands to the government, which were similar to those listed by the fleet. The naval mutineers promised to send their air force comrades the destroyer *Aldea* for defense if they sabotaged their aircraft so that they could not be used against the fleet. The request was honored.[13]

Figure 13. The Chilean Naval Mutiny (1931). The authenticity of this photograph is suspect. It reportedly shows army aircraft bombing the fleet with misses not too far off the bows of the dreadnought *Almirante Latorre* (left) and the cruiser *O'Higgins* (right). The aircraft and splashes may have been touched into an earlier generation of the photograph showing the fleet at anchor. *Author's collection.*

On the morning of September 5 the government decided to take action against the mutineers. Loyal ground forces attacked and captured the Quintero Air Base and the Talcahuano Naval Base. The loss of Talcahuano was a severe blow to the mutineers. It was the only facility that could repair damage to the ships, Coquimbo being no more than an anchorage.[14]

The government gathered some forty aircraft near Coquimbo, including rebel planes from the 2nd Air Group that could be repaired. Mutinous mechanics had been forced to repair the aircraft and, as a guarantee of their workmanship, were required to accompany the air crews in the attack against the fleet. Early in the morning two aircraft were sent to reconnoiter the fleet. This was easily accomplished but they failed in an attack on the *Araucano*.[15]

Early in the afternoon on September 6, 1931, the government's air squadron took off from the Tuquí Airfield near Ovalle to attack the fleet. The force consisted of nine Curtiss-Falcon observation planes armed with 25-pound bombs, two Vixen bombers armed with 110-pound bombs, two French Wibault-73 pursuit planes with 25-pound bombs, and two Junkers bombers with one 660-pound bomb each. The maximum altitude that the Junkers could fly was 5,000 feet, which constrained the force's tactics.[16]

The aircraft approached from the west, flying out of the sun at about 5,000 feet. One Junker flew a zigzag course over the anchorage and dropped its 660-pound bomb, which fell several hundred yards from any of the ships. Minutes later the second Junker flew a straight course over the ships and dropped its lone bomb; it fell within 50 yards of the *Almirante Latorre*. Then the remaining thirteen aircraft attacked. The ships returned fire, but like most warships in 1931, they had few anti-aircraft guns.[17]

Neither side received much damage. The submarine *H-4* was strafed and two of her crew wounded. Apparently some aircraft were damaged and one may have crashed.[18]

The attack broke the spirit of the mutineers. They offered to send a delegation to Santiago to negotiate a settlement. Flush with victory, the government would have no part of that. A split developed among the mutineers and while they argued, the destroyers *Hyatt* and *Riquelme* slipped out of the bay and sailed to Valparaíso to surrender. They were soon followed by the *Aldea*, *Orella*, *Serrano*, and *Videla*. By the end of September 7, all of the ships had surrendered.[19]

The government initially reacted harshly against those in charge and those involved. The two flag officers afloat, all commanding officers, and all executive officers were relieved. Concerning the mutineers, thirteen were sentenced to death, twelve to life imprisonment, and others to sentences ranging from one hundred days to fifteen years. The severe punishment caused public demonstrations. On October 16 Acting Vice President Manuel Trucco commuted the death sentences and many of the prison terms were shortened. Ultimately, the mutineers were pardoned, given government jobs, and even their time during and after the mutiny was counted toward their retirement.[20]

OBSERVATIONS

Both mutinies were warning alarms of the growing unrest due to political, social, and economic inequities plus the increasing influence of leftist political movements. Although Communists undoubtedly contributed to the unrest that caused the mutinies, they were not among the initial leaders nor were they numerous among the mutineers. In the case of the Chilean mutiny, Communists did eventually gain substantial influence. Neither of these mutinies sought to overthrow their governments; rather, they aimed to redress typical sailor grievances. In both cases the mutineers came from the enlisted ranks.

Within both nations the mutinies had far-reaching consequences. In Brazil the government issued a new code for the punishment of crimes within the navy and reformed naval administration. In addition, the newly elected president, Hermes Rodrigues da Fonseca, reordered the navy's priorities. Instead of money continuing to be spent on buying dreadnoughts, it was reallocated to improve shore facilities and living conditions for the sailors. In Chile, the navy lost its most favored status among the nation's military which it had won during the 1891 Civil War (see companion volume). Much of this prestige was recaptured, however, by its role in the overthrow of Salvador Allende in 1973 (see chapter 34).[21]

CHAPTER 10

INTERNATIONAL COMMUNIST
SUBVERSION, 1928–35

Let the ruling classes tremble at a communistic revolution. The proletarians have nothing to lose but their chains. They have the world to win. Working men of all countries, unite!
— Karl Marx

THE SPARK

The Sixth Congress of the Communist International, held between July 17 and September 2, 1928, in Moscow, abandoned its short-lived policy of cooperation with left of center, non-Communist movements and adopted a policy of armed struggle which required Communist parties throughout the world to launch a final offensive against capitalists.[1] This policy change caused many Latin American Communist parties to engage in subversion.

BACKGROUND

The first Latin American Communist party was established in Argentina in 1918. Within twenty years almost half of the nations within the Western Hemisphere had Communist parties, many legal and a few clandestine.[2]

On December 11, 1927, Communist delegations from Argentina, Brazil, Chile, Colombia, Cuba, Ecuador, Mexico, and Uruguay met in Moscow on the tenth anniversary of the Bolshevik Revolution. This first meeting of Latin American Communist parties "called a rally of the 'working masses' against the 'imperialism of the United States and the aggression of the Latin American bourgeoisie.'"[3]

The first multinational Communist conference held within Latin America took place in Buenos Aires during June 1929. In attendance were delegates from Argentina, Brazil, Colombia, Cuba, Ecuador, El Salvador, Guatemala, Mexico, Panama, Paraguay, Peru, Uruguay, and Venezuela. The proceedings were supervised by André Stepanov, "Comrade Luis." He closely watched Victor Codovilla, the Latin American secretariat of the Comintern. The conference stressed the need for an alliance with workers and peasants in order to create a social revolution and classified the Mexican Revolution "as a merely democratic middle-class affair."[4]

OPPOSING FORCES

The Communist Party preyed upon human hopes. The myth of the Communist Party was that it was the champion of the working class. The reality was that Communism was authoritative, highly centralized, and elitist. The myth provided the bait to attract and hold the people to its cause whereas the reality provided the Communists with the leadership and organization necessary to attempt to create subversion. Latin American Communist parties were small and remained so due to this elitist attitude.

Latin America was undoubtedly vulnerable to the Communist threat. Political immaturity and instability, poor distribution of wealth, and social discrimination were common. By 1920 few Latin American governments represented the majority of their people. Latin American nations had had very modest experience with representative government prior to their declarations of independence. Latin America was the property of kings, and they ruled it as absolute monarchs. And these kings succeeded in preserving loyalty for almost three hundred years when Napoleon Bonaparte upset the *status quo*. Following Napoleon's jailing of the Spanish King, practically all of Spanish America declared its independence not from Ferdinand VII, but from metropolitan Spain which had anointed itself his regent during his captivity.

The sudden change precipitated by the wars for independence without prior conditioning meant that throughout the nineteenth century and well into the twentieth century, most Latin Americans lived in political turbulence. The colonial legacy of placing loyalty to the King above efficiency to those being served left Latin America with the tradition that the first loyalty of the civil servant, whether civilian or military, was to his superior and not the nation.

Many Latin American economies could not (and in some cases still cannot) provide the basic necessities for their people. Wealth was poorly distributed in part due to colonial practices. The Spanish Crown rewarded *conquistadores* with large tracts of land. The King required from his new subjects, the Indians, many days of labor each year in exchange for the "services" he provided. This collectivism of land and labor, reinforcing the preconquest traditions of the Indians, remained unbroken in many areas until well into the twentieth century and proved to be poor breeding ground for a representative government.

Other problems contributed to poor economic development. Many Latin American nations became dependent upon monocrop economies which were susceptible to boom or bust cycles. A high birth rate, particularly in the tropics, outstripped resources. Latin America's infrastructure—challenged by formidable geographical barriers—remained underdeveloped. Many well-intentioned but naive attempts to rectify these imbalances only compounded the problems. Thus, far too many citizens lived on the marginal edge of subsistence; and as a result, the social pyramid within Latin America lacked stability.

The social structure inherited from the colonial era also contributed to unrest. The sixteenth century *conquistadores* were confronted by potentially overwhelming numbers of Indians. To compensate for their own inferior numbers, the *conquistadores* destroyed the Indians' social structure and superimposed their own. This created a rigid class structure that suppressed the majority. It also created a dual culture, thus making it difficult to create a national identity and the modern nation-state.

As elsewhere, the militaries within Latin America existed to defend the *status quo*. They attempted to imitate their wealthier counterparts in Europe. Most Latin American armies had general staffs and aspired to acquire the latest battlefield technologies such as tanks, aircraft, and submarines. Latin American militaries varied significantly in size and capabilities. Without exception they were tailored to oppose threats which mirrored themselves.

OPENING STRATEGIES

Both the myth and the reality of the Communist party made subversion a natural strategy. Although no ideology has a monopoly on the use of subversion for challenging power, the Communist Party had extensively employed it from its inception in 1903 by Vladimir Ilyich Ulyanov, who had assumed the pseudonym N. Lenin at the end of 1901, and subversion became a primary tool which it used from 1928 until 1935 throughout Latin America. For the most part, this was a strategy based upon seizing initiatives begun by others.

The tactical objective was to capture the hearts and minds of the people and to terrorize the opponents. Therefore, success could not be measured in the traditional military terms of conquered territory; rather, success could only be judged by influence.

Access to the hearts and minds of the people became critical. One could gain an appreciation of to what degree Communism had successfully infiltrated the print media by comparing the vocabulary used on the first page in the newspaper, which was read by everyone, to that used in the editorials, which was typically read only by those who supported the government. The adoption of the Communists' lexicon by the populace helped establish a sympathetic mindset.

The tactics used by the Latin American Communists mimicked those employed during the Russian Revolution. The standard operating procedure was to infiltrate existing institutions such as the military, labor unions, the Church, and the professional guilds. Next, cells were created. Ultimately, subversion was fomented. Teachers' guilds, communication workers' unions, and public facility workers' organizations received special attention. With rare exception, guerrilla warfare was not employed.

MEXICO

The young Communist Party of Mexico attracted three prominent artists—José Clemente Orozco, Diego Rivera, and David Alfaro Siqueiros—and through their art won prominence beyond that entitled by their deeds.[5]

The Mexican Communist Party fielded armed units for the first time as a consequence of the 1923 presidential election. Initially, the Communist Party agreed to support Gen. Adolfo de la Huerta, by force if necessary, against Gen. Plutarco Elías Calles. However, by the time de la Huerta began his revolt in late 1923, the party had changed sides and fielded several bands of *campesinos* in the state of Veracruz in support of Calles.[6]

In 1926 Calles recognized the Soviet Union and it dispatched Alexandra Kollontay as its ambassador. This wily zealot organized the "Friends of the Soviet Union" and subsidized trips to Russia for Mexican intellectuals. Later that year, two Soviet diplomats were implicated in a disrupting railroad strike. Relations between the revolutionary Mexican government and the Mexican Communist Party were deteriorating when Soviet Foreign Minister Georgij W. Tchitcherin announced that Mexico would become the center of Communist activities in the New World. President Calles quickly replied that all such actions must comport to international law and respect the sovereignty of Mexico.[7]

The 1928 order by the Communist International to parties throughout the world to overthrow capitalism coincided with another Mexican presidential election. This was handily won by former President Alvaro Obregón, who was assassinated before taking office. At the end of 1928 Gen. Emilio Portes Gil was elected as an interim president. More conservative than his revolutionary predecessors, President Portes Gil launched an anti-Communist campaign. Some three hundred Communists were arrested by the Mexico City Police. The Communist paper, *El Machete*, was shut down and its presses destroyed.[8]

In 1929 President Portes Gil came into possession of confidential Russian documents which contained detailed instructions to Communist agents to foster insurrection in Mexico. The papers also cited the desirability of assassinating Mexican politicians, including the President. Because of these papers and attacks carried out by Communists in foreign countries against Mexican interests, Portes Gil attempted to exterminate the Mexican Communist Party. The Mexican President closed the office of the Mexican Communist Party and in 1930 he broke diplomatic relations with the Soviet Union.[9]

While under attack by the Mexican government, the Mexican Communist Party was chastised by the Communist International for having sided with the Mexican government against a rebellion led by José Escobar in 1929. The Communist International reasoned that since this was a fight between rival capitalists, the Mexican Communist party should have remained neutral. Since the Communist International controlled the purse strings, it ordered the expulsion of those not following the party line, including Diego Rivera and other luminaries.[10]

Portes Gil was succeeded in the presidency by Ortiz Rubio (1930–32) and then Abelardo Rodríguez (1932–34), both of whom continued the anti-Communist program. Strikes by Communist-led unions were broken by federal troops. In 1932 twenty-four Communist leaders were imprisoned on the Islas Tres Marías, a penal colony. Also, the government took few measures to restrain the "Gold Shirts" (a pro-fascist group), who terrorized Communists and Jews alike.[11] The persecution against the Communists ended with the election of the more left-of-center Lázaro Cárdenas in 1934. The following year Cárdenas legalized the Communist Party once again. In spite of their efforts, the Soviet Communists failed to divert the Mexican revolutionary movement from its national agenda and redirect it into those of international Communism.[12]

CHILE

The Chilean Communist Party traced its roots through the Socialist Workers Party (*Partido Socialista Obrero*) which had been founded in 1912. The early Communist Party lacked cohesion and by the early 1930s had split in two. During the 1930s the Chilean Communists attempted to take advantage of the disorder initiated by others.[13]

In the early morning of September 1, 1931, crews of some Chilean warships mutinied (see chapter 9). The underlying cause was demoralization due to a sudden pay cut. At 4:55 P.M. the rebels radioed twelve demands to the government which were a combination of typical sailors' grievances and those of individuals seeking social change. Neither Communist Party had had a hand in planning the mutiny, but both attempted to take advantage of it. The Communists planned a general strike in support of the mutineers but were unable to pull it off. On September 6, fifteen government planes attacked the fleet. Neither side received much damage, but the spirit of the mutineers broke. The fleet surrendered by the end of the seventh.[14] A year later the Communists acknowledged that "the failure to work among the soldiers and sailors constituted a great failure on the part of the party."[15]

On December 24, 1931, Communists seized the barracks of the "Esmeralda" regiment and that of the *Carabineros* (federal police) in Copiapó (482 mi N of Santiago) and held it for three hours in an attempt to spark a revolt within the army and police. The Communists were driven off by soldiers and police. As a result, a number of Communists were shot. Shortly afterward, twenty more Communists were shot in Vallenar (396 mi N of Santiago) for conspiracy.[16]

On June 4, 1932, Socialists seized the University of Chile and declared a "Socialist Republic." The Communists viewed this as being a ploy of the capitalists and hastily organized the "Revolutionary Council of Workers, Peasants, Soldiers and Sailors" as a countermovement, but this attracted little notice. The Socialist Republic was crushed by the military on June 16.[17]

In 1934 Professor Juan Segundo Leiva Tapia declared the highlands of Bío Bío, Ranquil, and Lonquimay to be "free territory." In June the army eliminated the armed bands of Communists.[18] These attempts to spark intraclass struggle stood no chance of success because of the disunity of the party.

EL SALVADOR

The Communist Party of El Salvador was founded in 1925, and due in large measure to the great disparity of wealth and the abominable treatment of the poor within the country, it soon attracted a significant following.[19] The U.S. Army attaché, Maj. Arthur Harris, observed concerning San Salvador:

> There appears to be nothing between these high-priced cars and the oxcart with its barefoot attendant. There is practically no middle class. . . . Thirty or forty families own nearly everything in the country. They live in regal style. . . . The rest of the population has practically nothing. These poor people work for a few cents a day and exist as best they can.[20]

By late 1931 the Communist Party planned to overthrow the government. By mid-December the Communists had infiltrated the 1st Cavalry Regiment and organized barracks committees. This unit was to form the backbone of the insurrection. The rebellion was scheduled for January 22, 1932. The Salvadorian Communists asked for help from parties in Guatemala and Honduras and in return promised to aid them.[21]

The Central Committee of the Salvadorian Communist Party created a Revolutionary Military Committee which was to serve as the general staff for the Salvadorian Red Army. The Military Committee began issuing instructions for the rebellion; however, the Salvadorian government was warned by President Jorge Ubico of Guatemala who had learned of the plot. As a consequence, the Salvadorian government, led by Gen. Maximiliano Hernández Martínez,[22] declared a state of siege on January 18. He arrested suspected army personnel and prominent Communists, including Agustin P. Martí,[23] and shut down the Communist newspaper *Estrella Roja*.[24]

Those Communists still at liberty attempted to cancel the uprising but only caused confusion. As a consequence, uncoordinated uprisings occurred on January 22 and, although serious, they were doomed to failure. The *campesinos* (mostly Indians) went on a rampage in western El Salvador,[25] raping and killing those suspected of being landed oligarchy and members of the defense forces. Some one hundred people were killed.[26]

The government reacted immediately. It sent troops under Gen. José Tomás Calderón into the region and encouraged "responsible" citizens to form militias (*Guardias Civicas*). The government forces, armed with guns against those wheeling machetes, crushed the uprising. President Hernández Martínez then moved to eliminate the potential for future uprisings. Communists were identified from voter rolls and killed. But the reprisals did not stop here. Anyone suspected of having participated or even thought to harbor sympathies for the rebels stood a good chance of being executed. Those who escaped to Guatemala were captured and remained in jail until Ubico was overthrown in 1944. The number of deaths is estimated to be between 8,000 and 25,000 people. The Communist Parties of El Salvador and Guatemala were temporarily destroyed.[27]

BRAZIL

The Communist Party of Brazil traced its roots to the anarchist movement and not that of the socialists as was typical elsewhere in Latin America, and it had strong support among the lower ranks in the military. The latter in large measure could be attributed to conversion of the "living legend," Luis Carlos Prestes, to Communism in the late 1920s (see chapter 14).[28]

By 1935 the Brazilian Communist Party had successfully organized a variety of labor movements under its leadership and created a political union, the National Liberation Alliance. Although Brazilian President Getulio Vargas declared the alliance dissolved on July 12, 1935, it continued to function. In October the workers of the Great Western Railway went on strike and were supported by the alliance. The strike spread, and in Recife (1,160 mi NE of Rio de Janeiro) troops refused to fire on the workers. The Communist leaders of the alliance judged that there was enough unrest throughout the country to forcefully overthrow the government. The Communist-led revolt began prematurely in the northern cities of Natal (1,295 mi NE of Rio de Janeiro) and Recife on November 24. Three days later the army aviation cadets and the 3rd Infantry Regiment (part of Rio de Janeiro's garrison) rebelled and declared Prestes to be the President of Brazil. The fighting in the north was easily suppressed by the government; however, it took some nine hours of severe street fighting in the capital to defeat the rebels.[29]

As a consequence, the Communist Party was driven underground, not to regain its ability to function openly until 1945. Nearly 10,000 Brazilians were arrested, including Prestes, several national deputies, and a number of university professors. The prisoners were judged by special tribunals, and many cases were dismissed for lack of evidence. No death sentences were imposed. The ringleaders' prison sentences were not to exceed twenty seven years.[30]

OBSERVATIONS

The adoption of subversion by various Communist parties within Latin America in 1928 proved disastrous. Those parties that openly opposed their governments—the Mexican, Brazilian, and Salvadorian—were almost exterminated. The Communist parties of Guatemala and Honduras were crushed because of their geographical proximity to the Salvadorian rebellion. And, Communists in Chile were persecuted because of their aggressive activities.

The failures of the Communist parties can be attributed to a number of factors. First, all were attempting to execute a strategy dictated from Moscow which had little appreciation for the realities of Latin America. Second, all were young and had not developed the infrastructure needed for subversive activities. In Chile and Mexico the Communists were split, primarily over ideology, and could not act in unison. In El Salvador the government could resort to a degree of brutality which the Communists could not yet match.

In 1935 the Communist International adopted a new strategy of advocating participation in broadly based, antifascist alliances; and this saved the remaining Communist parties from almost certain decimation. What helped the Latin American Communist parties survive was the emergence of fascism, first in Italy and then in Germany. The Latin American Communist parties recuperated and participated within coalition governments in Chile (1938) and Cuba (1940) as World War II approached.

Although Latin American Communist parties were badly mauled during the late 1920s and early 1930s while carrying out the instructions from the Communist International, they did succeed in winning important converts, particularly among the faculties at the national universities and among the press.

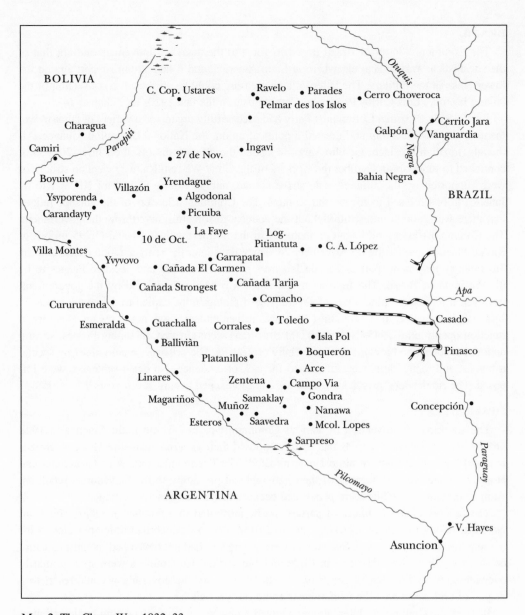

BOLIVIA

C. Cop. Ustares

Ravelo • Parades
Pelmar des los Islos

Cerro Choveroca

Charagua

Parapiti

Camiri

27 de Nov.

Ingavi

Galpón
Cerrito Jara
Vanguardia

Negra

Bahia Negra

Boyuivé

Yrendague

Villazón

Algodonal

Ysyporenda

Picuiba

Carandayty

La Faye

BRAZIL

10 de Oct.

Log.
Pitiantuta

• C. A. López

Villa Montes

Yvyvovo

Garrapatal

Cañada El Carmen

Cañada Tarija

Cañada Strongest

Comacho

Apa

Curururenda

Guachalla

Corrales

Toledo

Casado

Esmeralda

Ballivián

Isla Pol

Platanillos

Boquerón

Pinasco

Linares

Arce

Zentena

Campo Via

Magariños

Samaklay

Gondra

Concepción

Muñoz

Nanawa

Esteros

Saavedra

Mcol. Lopes

Sarpreso

Paraguay

ARGENTINA

Pilcomayo

V. Hayes

Asuncion

Map 2. The Chaco War, 1932–33.

PART 7

CHAPTER 11

THE CHACO WAR, 1932–35

Fortunately, the very territory over which the dispute arises is so difficult that neither nation could invade the other with any large force.
      —U.S. Office of Naval Intelligence, *Monthly Information Bulletin*, 1925

THE SPARK

On April 25, 1932, a Bolivian reconnaissance aircraft discovered the location of a freshwater lake in the central Chaco with some apparently deserted buildings along its eastern shore. A Bolivian eighteen-man military expedition sent to establish a presence on Laguna Chuqisaca (the Bolivian name) found that the small Paraguayan *fortin*[1] Carlos Antonio López had already been built on Lake Pitiantuta (the Paraguayan name). On June 15, 1932, the Bolivians attacked and drove off the six-man Paraguayan garrison, killing one and occupying the *fortin*. Paraguay chose to interpret this clash, one of many in recent years, as a violation of the nonaggression agreement signed in 1931, thus ending ongoing peace talks and creating a state of war.[2]

BACKGROUND

As a result of Paraguay's defeat in the War of the Triple Alliance (see companion volume) and Bolivia's defeat in the War of the Pacific (see companion volume) during the nineteenth century, both nations had lost the opportunity to develop as maritime nations. Increasingly they began to look toward the interior of the continent for development opportunities. Between Bolivia and Paraguay lay the vast, inhospitable, poorly explored, and sparsely populated Chaco. The summer heat (June–November) parched the earth for months on end, while the rainy season (December–May) created vast, shallow, impassable marshes. This huge area, the size of Italy, was an enormous breeding ground for disease-carrying insects. Drinkable water was scarce in the Chaco; therefore, the discovery of fresh water determined the pattern of exploration and settlement. There were no paved roads and only some *picadas* or *sendas*. The best of these were crude, dirt roads, but more typically they were footpaths. Most of the Indians who lived in the Chaco were pro-Paraguayan. In spite of its inhospitality, both Bolivia and Paraguay lay claim to the Chaco.[3]

Following independence, Bolivia claimed the Chaco primarily on the basis that the Audiencia of Charcas, created in 1559, had joined the Gran Chaco with Upper Peru (Bolivia). The Paraguayan claim was based primarily upon exploration and occupation, which had been initiated from Asunción beginning during the colonial era. Paraguay had also encouraged European immigration into the Chaco. Francisco Solano López had arranged for 410 Frenchmen to settle in the Chaco during his 1853 visit to Paris. More recently, in 1929 some 6,000 Canadian and Russian Mennonites established a colony (*Colonia Filadelfia*) near the terminus of the 125-mile-long Casado Railway.[4]

In an attempt to improve its claim through occupation, Bolivia began to build a series of *fortins*, pushing them farther and farther into the Chaco. *Picadas* were hacked between each *fortin*. Beginning in the 1870s, the two nations signed numerous agreements that not only delayed the war, but also complicated the legal situation as each party created new arguments which finally exasperated both sides. Increasingly patrols operating from these outposts clashed.

In spite of the Chaco's inhospitality, in many ways it represented the contemporary wealth of Paraguay and the promise of the future for Bolivia. A third of Paraguay's revenues and most of its foreign exchange came from the harvest of quebracho trees and cattle-raising in the Chaco. Bolivia perceived it to be an avenue to a potential fluvial outlet for its underdeveloped eastern lowlands, an unrealistic dream since Bolivia had neither the technical expertise nor the wealth to finance such an undertaking. The most valuable part of the Chaco belonged to foreign investors, mostly Argentines.[5]

Throughout the 1920s both sides prepared for war—the Bolivians more overtly and the Paraguayans rather covertly. Once the war began in 1932, both nations were subjected to arms embargoes by numerous nations; however, these were ineffectively enforced. Throughout the war Paraguay received substantial support from Argentina.[6]

As a result of its perceived advantage in arms and manpower, the Bolivian politicians and military believed that it could successfully settle the Chaco dispute by force. The Paraguayan leadership had been so successful in secretly building its war machine that not only did the Bolivian military believe itself superior, but also many in the Paraguayan military incorrectly believed that its government was not preparing for the predictable confrontation and thus was acting irresponsibly.[7]

On December 5, 1928, Paraguayan Maj. Rafael Franco, frustrated by his government's apparent lack of concern, disobeyed a standing order and attacked and captured the Bolivian *fortin* Vanguardia on the Rio Negro in the far northeastern corner of the disputed territory. From a Paraguayan point of view, he almost triggered the war prematurely. In retaliation, the Bolivians stormed the Paraguayan *fortin* Boquerón in the central Chaco on December 14. They also conducted an unsuccessful air attack on the fifteenth with one aircraft against the Paraguay River port of Bahia Negra; the four bombs failed to explode.[8]

Both sides immediately began to mobilize; however, neither country was very successful because of a lack of planning, arms, and logistics. War was temporarily averted, primarily because both nations realized how ill-prepared they were and, less significantly, because of the mediation by the United States. As a temporary measure, both sides agreed to reduce the size of their armies. However, both continued to expand their presence in the disputed territory. During the next few years, one clash after another contributed to increasing tensions. In January 1930 Paraguayan cryptographers foiled a Bolivian plan to attack in the central Chaco when the Paraguayan government released copies of intercepted messages to the press. [9]

OPPOSING FORCES

The population of Paraguay in 1932 was 900,000 citizens. In June of that year the Paraguayan army totaled 4,026 men (355 combat officers, 146 surgeons and noncombatant officers, 200 cadets, 690 NCOs, and 2,653 soldiers). It was organized into 8 regiments (5 infantry and 3 cavalry), 2 artillery groups, and a battalion of engineers. Also available were 679 naval personnel and 2,300 armed police and prison guards. On paper, Paraguayans between 18 and 20 years of age served two years on active duty followed by reserve status until the age of 28. Then they served in the National Guard until the age of 39 when they became members of the Territorial Guard until age 45. Racially and culturally, the Paraguayan army was homogeneous. Practically all of the officers and enlisted men were *mestizos* of Spanish-Guarani mix. The army was French indoctrinated and Argentine trained. [10]

A substantial part of the Paraguayan army was stationed in the Chaco. Before June 15, 1932, there were perhaps 3,000 to 3,500 Paraguayans in the Chaco. Mobilization started on August 1, 1932, and by August 28, 18,000 men (17,300 army and 700 navy) were in the Chaco. These forces were outfitted with 56 field pieces, 22 mortars, 38 heavy machine guns, and 375 light machine guns. [11]

In August 1932 Paraguay possessed some 21,450 rifles (7,000 good Belgian Mausers, 10,363 poor Spanish Mausers, and 4,096 old rifles). Some 25 million cartridges were on hand in 1932. Paraguay had 32 new heavy machine guns (Colts), 29 old heavy machine guns (6 Madsen, 11 Vickers, and 12 Maxims), and 406 light machine guns (151 Madsens without tripods, 255 Madsens with tripods). There were also 22 Madsen aircraft machine guns. The heavier weapons were a conglomeration. There were 24 mortars, 24 modern Schneider 75mm mountain guns, 8 modern Schneider 105mm mountain howitzers, and 28 old field pieces. For the old 75 and 76mm guns, some 6,400 shells were available, of which 2,000 had been purchased in 1925. The 24 mortars were delivered with 2,400 shells, and the modern Schneider guns and howitzers with 9,800 shells. Not more than 70 trucks, buses, and cars were available. [12]

In 1932 the Paraguayan air arm was significantly inferior in numbers to its Bolivian counterpart and remained so throughout the war. The Paraguayans began the war with five Wibault 73 C1 fighters (these remained from seven acquired in 1929), seven Potez 25C light reconnaissance bombers, three flying boats (flown by naval pilots), and a dozen other miscellaneous types useful for support and training functions. [13]

The navy consisted of two modern and two old gunboats, two tugs, and some launches. The launches were unarmed and locally built. The navy also controlled one passenger ship, 8 freighters, 22 tugs, 8 large and 16 small *chatas* (barges), and about a dozen motorboats. [14]

The population of Bolivia in 1932 was three million inhabitants, about three times that of Paraguay. Its army was only marginally larger, totaling 5,539 men. Twenty-five regiments (13 infantry, 5 cavalry, 3 artillery, and 4 engineers) existed on paper, but in fact, each was only of battalion strength (typically a few hundred men), and a few (the 1st and 11th) may not have existed at all. These regiments were organized into six divisions, five of which were stationed in the far northern region of the disputed Chaco. On paper all Bolivian males served two years active duty between the ages of 19 and 25. Following this they served in the reserves until age 32. From age 32 to 40 they were in the Second Reserve and from 40 to 49 in the National Guard.[15]

The Bolivian army had many underlying problems, although these were not apparent prior to the war.[16] Its social stratification reflected that of the nation. The officers were mostly Spanish-speaking whites with the wrong kind of training; they had been prepared for a mountain war against Chile to regain "*la salida al mar*" (the outlet to the sea). The troops were largely Aymará-speaking Indians from peasant stock. The bulk of the army spoke only Aymará or Quechua and many of the NCOs could not write Spanish. Ninety percent of the army was native to the highlands, or *altiplano*, with no immunity to tropical diseases. Also, many were addicted to the chewing of the coca leaf which dulls the senses.[17]

The Bolivian army had a veneer of German indoctrination and training with a dash of Chilean influence. When Hans Kundt[18] became Chief of Staff of the Bolivian army on February 10, 1921, former President Eliodoro Villazón said to him, "I entrust you with the best thing the nation owns, its army."[19] For over one hundred years, a military parade highlighted the annual independence day celebration. On August 6, 1925, Kundt organized a 6,000-man, Prussian-style parade complete with German military music. Lt. Col. Angel Rodriguez, Chief of the Operations Section of the Bolivian General Staff observed,

> The Bolivian Army has had a twenty-year propaganda, as a logical consequence of innumerable parades. The people believed in the organization of their military institution, it also knew that it boasted a good contingent of trained reservists; what no one knew was that he who had organized the Army had done so simply to show it in parades. The Army was a political instrument, it was never an instrument of war. The various Presidents of the Republic desired and considered it as such.[20]

Also, the Bolivian president, Daniel Salamanca, had little faith in the military capabilities of his general staff; and they, in turn, had little confidence in his political abilities.[21]

Beginning in the mid-1920s, Bolivia also spent large sums on armaments. Altogether, Bolivia acquired 115 modern Vickers guns and howitzers (65mm, 75mm, and 105mm). They also had about 30 old Krupp and 48 Schneider Field and mountain guns. Bolivia also bought 12 SEMAG 20mm AA guns, 16 Oerlikon 20mm AA twin-guns, and 10 Oerlikon 20mm antitank guns. Not all of these guns had arrived by June 1932. Frequently, the Bolivians had twice or three times as many guns as the Paraguayans and often more shells. The items that had been delivered prior to the outbreak of war included 39,000 modern rifles (mostly Czech Mausers), 750 Vickers medium and light machine guns, 115 modern artillery pieces, 3 Vickers 6-ton tanks, and 2 Carden-Lloyd Mk VIb tanketts. Within a year of the outbreak, Bolivia was able to supply the front lines with some Stokes-Brandt mortars (May 1933), flame-throwers, and hand grenades.[22]

Bolivia had also assembled a numerically respectable air force, with some 80 aircraft. At the outbreak of the war, it possessed on paper 5 Fokker CCV fighters, 15 Breguet 19 A2 reconnaissance bombers, 4 Curtiss Hawk 1A (P-1) fighters, 12 Curtiss-Wright Osprey light reconnaissance bombers, 3 Vendace III trainers, 6 Vespa III bombers, 6 Vickers 143 scout fighters, and some 20 miscellaneous types. However, many of these, including some acquired as recently as 1932, were not airworthy. Also, the government-owned German-managed civil air-

Figure 14. The Chaco War (1932–35). A Bolivian Vickers 6-ton tank, Type "A." The main weapons were two machine guns mounted in twin, side-by-side turrets. The turret on the right is visible but the one on the left is hidden behind the reserve crew. Bolivia possessed five tanks (Paraguay none) and each tank had two crews. Most of the officers were German or Austrian. By the early 1930s the tank had not adequately matured to be reliable in the harsh climate and terrain of the Chaco. *Courtesy Adrian English, Ireland.*

lines, Lloyd Aereo Boliviano, operated a dozen aircraft (including 3 Junker JU 53/3M trimotors, 4 Junker F 13Ls, and 3 Junker W 34s) which could be commandeered if required.[23]

The most significant disparity between the two combatants was their logistical situation. Paraguay's main population and administrative and manufacturing center was its capital, Asunción, which lay opposite the junction of the Pilcomayo and Paraguay Rivers on the southeast edge of the Chaco. Shallow draft steamers and barges could move troops and supplies along the southern and eastern boundaries of the disputed territory. A railroad line 125 miles long penetrated toward the future battlefields from Puerto Casado. It was serviced by three steam locomotives; a fourth was added during the war.[24] From there Paraguayan troops and material could be transported by trucks or the men marched. During the early days of the war, Asunción's buses and sixty trucks were requisitioned to complete this vital link. At the time the war broke out, it typically took three and a half days for a Paraguayan soldier to travel from Asunción to the front.

Figure 15. The Chaco War (1932–35). U.S.-manufactured trucks are being transported to the front on the Paraguayan railroad that began at Puerto Casado on the Paraguay River and ran west for 125 miles into the Chaco. Typically it took less than a day to reach the end of the rail line. Although the Paraguayans never possessed more than four locomotives, this critical transportation link never became a target of Bolivian air attacks. The Paraguayans preferred Chevrolet and Ford trucks; whereas Bolivia favored those manufactured by GMC. However, both sides purchased all three. On the Paraguayan side each driver and his assistant were responsible for maintaining their vehicle and it became a matter of honor to do so well. *Courtesy U.S. National Archives, Washington, D.C.*

On the other side, the Bolivian population and production center lay on the *altiplano* between the eastern and western *cordilleras* of the Andes Mountains. Bolivia had developed three principal routes into the Chaco. The oldest paralleled the Pilcomayo River from Villa Montes and ran toward the southeast. The newest started in the central Chaco on its eastern frontier at *Fortin* Villazon and penetrated toward the southeast. These two routes pinched toward each other. The third route transversed across the northern Chaco.

The Bolivian supplies and personnel using the more heavily traveled central route had to go from La Paz by train to Villazon and from there by truck over 200 miles of *picadas* to *Fortin* Arce which was located within a few miles of Payaguayan *fortins*. At best this took nine days, but usually up to fourteen. Land transport was complicated by the fact that Bolivia was critically short of trucks. On April 25, 1932, Gen. Filisberto Osorio had requested the purchase of 605 trucks and received twenty-five. The President stated that the government could not afford them. Also, Bolivia was accustomed to purchasing its supplies for the Chaco garrison from Argentina bordering on the southeast and Brazil on the northeast. Both sources were ultimately reduced to trickles of contraband.[25]

OPENING STRATEGIES

The Paraguayan strategy, formulated by Lt. Col. Juan B. Ayala, Chief of Staff from 1931 to 1935, envisioned a defensive fight along the Casado railroad, using the cavalry and guerrilla forces for offensive operations. He believed that the enemy could be lured toward the Paraguay River by a slow retreat and then defeated once its supply lines were overextended. The Paraguayans had their misgivings about operating with large forces in the Chaco. Large forces could only be employed if roads, trucks, fortins with barracks to lodge troops, and fresh water existed. All of these depended upon the will of the nation and the amount of money it was prepared to spend.[26]

The Bolivian General Staff had not formulated a detailed war plan. Before the war, the Bolivians were convinced that due to logistics not more than about 6,000 men could operate at the same time in the Chaco and planned to operate with five strong battalions plus five mountain batteries. The generally agreed-upon objective among the military was to dominate the west bank of the Paraguay River, thus gaining control of the entire Chaco. This was to be accomplished by drawing Paraguayan forces into the southwest toward *Fortin* Ballivián and then outflanking them to the north. The Bolivians would make a major drive above Puerto Casado and lesser ones against Bahia Negra and Fuerte Olimpo, all ports on the upper Paraguay River. These vague plans were confused and unrealistic due to a shortage of men, water, and trucks. President Salamanca, who as Captain-General would play a major role in strategic decisions, believed that the military's objective should be the capture of Asunción and that this could be accomplished with 4,000 men! He did not believe that it was necessary to commit all of Bolivia's resources to the war effort and refused to fully mobilize for political reasons.[27]

WAR BEGINS

On July 15, 1932, one month after the Bolivians had stormed *Fortin* Carlos Antonio López, 388 Paraguayans, supported by one of the recently purchased mortars, captured the new Bolivian *Fortin* Mariscal Santa Cruz on Lake Pitiantuta defended by 170 soldiers. The Paraguayans lost eleven men and the Bolivians fourteen. Retaliating, the Bolivians attacked and captured *fortins* Corrales, Toledo, and Boquerón, all in the central Chaco, between July 26 and July 31.

Figure 16. The Chaco War (1932–35). The Paraguayan gunboat *Humaitá* is crowded with troops being carried to Puerto Casado, two hundred miles up the Paraguay River. The *Humaitá* and her sister, the *Paraguay*, could carry 2,000 soldiers (standing room only) in a single trip. The trip typically took less than three days. *Courtesy U.S. National Archives, Washington, D.C.*

Then President Salamanca ordered the suspension of Bolivian military operations fearing an armed intervention by Argentina in favor of Paraguay.[28]

Ultimatums were exchanged and both sides ordered mobilizations. However, Bolivia carried out only a partial mobilization. On the other side, the Paraguayans mobilized some 20,000 reservists, the majority of whom were rapidly transported into the Chaco. The size of the Paraguayan mobilization was governed by the amount of weapons available, mainly rifles. In order to move the force quickly, the Paraguayan army commandeered almost every truck and bus in Asunción (perhaps a hundred) plus hundreds of oxen-drawn carts. Lt. Col. José Félix Estigarribia,[29] Deputy Chief of Staff, was placed in charge of Paraguayan field operations. He was ordered by senior military officials to remain on the defensive, but he disobeyed. Estigarribia was convinced that he could defeat the Bolivians provided he could attack them while he had superior forces.[30]

On August 15 Dr. Eusebio Ayala, a Liberal, was elected president of Paraguay. Estigarribia briefed the new president and convinced him that the Paraguayans, who had mobilized more quickly than the Bolivians, had to strike before the Bolivians could mobilize their greater manpower and war potential.

THE FIRST PARAGUAYAN OFFENSIVE

The Bolivian army was frustrated by President Salamanca's order to cease offensive operations and to only partially mobilize. On the Paraguayan side, Estigarribia, believing it a mistake to concede territory to the Bolivians in the Chaco and hoping to defeat them once overextended, dismissed the prewar strategy conceived by Colonel Ayala and supported by Gen. Manuel Rojas, nominal Commander-in-Chief of the Paraguayan army. Estigarribia simply ignored General Rojas and when Rojas intrigued against him, President Ayala sided with Estigarribia.[31]

Estigarribia believed that Bolivia would attack from *Fortin* Boquerón against *Fortin* Isla Poi and not through *Fortin* Toledo toward the Mennonite colonies. On September 9 Estigarribia began a general offensive with a force of 7,500 men on his own authority and attacked *Fortin* Boquerón, defended by some 448 soldiers. The Bolivians had significantly improved the defenses at Boquerón during the month they had held the *fortin*, and this proved to be an unpleasant surprise for the Paraguayans. The Paraguayans had to deal with many problems. They had only one telephone line to Isla Poi (Villa Militar); they lacked trucks; the shortage of water limited the size of their force and the flexibility of tactics; their inaccurate artillery fire sometimes hit their own troops; and they lacked leadership at the battalion and regiment levels.[32]

The Paraguayans attacked on September 9 without proper reconnaissance and were harshly repulsed. Initially, each Paraguayan soldier had only the water he had carried with him and the nearest source was 30 miles away at Isla Poi, from which it had to be hauled by the few trucks available. As the fighting continued the Bolivians sustained heavy loses from mortar fire. A 3,500-man Bolivian relief column from *Fortin* Arce, which included an old French-Renault Ft-17 tank and some air support, was repulsed on September 12; it lost about 1,500 killed, wounded, or taken prisoner.[33]

The Boquerón defenders were sustained by eating their mules and by infrequent and inaccurate air drops. All the Bolivians could recover from the various air drops were 916 cartridges, 110 pounds of dried meat, and a sack of bread. Soon, their wells became contaminated with dead bodies. Paraguay had its own water problems as the wells at Isla Poi began to fail due to

Figure 17. The Chaco War (1932–35). Paraguayan soldiers march out of Asunción in February 1933. The Paraguayan soldier was nicknamed "Pila" by the Bolivians. This was derived from *pata pilada* (barefoot), because many were without shoes. The Paraguayan soldier was carried up the Paraguay River by rivercraft and then traveled by rail for 125 miles toward the front. Early in the war, it took a Paraguayan soldier 3.5 days to reach the front; whereas a Bolivian soldier, who had to cross the eastern range of the Andes, typically took fourteen days. *Courtesy U.S. National Archives, Washington, D.C.*

the heavy demand. In order to shorten the struggle and ease the demand for water, Estigarribia ordered an all-out attack on September 26. Paraguay committed the majority of its meager air force, three Wibault 73 fighters and three Potez 25 reconnaissance bombers, to the attack; but they had only limited value.[34] Exhausted, the Bolivians ran out of water, food, and ammunition. When they surrendered on the twenty-ninth, only 240 able-bodied men remained.[35] Estigarribia recaptured Boquerón, winning the first battle of the war. The Paraguayan losses were probably about 500 killed or died from their wounds and thirst. Some 1,500 were wounded and 1,000 sick. The Bolivian losses in and around Boquerón were about 2,200 killed, wounded, sick, and captured.[36]

The fall of Boquerón shocked the overconfident Bolivian people. Numerous demonstrations took place in La Paz and many called for the return of Gen. Hans Kundt from exile. Osorio was demoted to Commanding General of the Second Army Corps and Gen. José Leonardo Lanza was made interim Chief of the General Staff pending the arrival of Kundt. The decision by the President, who was unpopular with the military, to replace a native Bolivian with a German-born general caused much dissension in the army.[37]

Meanwhile the Paraguayans, tempered by limited logistical capability, a shortage of water, and the knowledge that a defeat could be disastrous for their cause, continued a conservative offensive. On October 8 Estigarribia began his advance against *Fortin* Arce (30 mi S of Boquerón), the Bolivian headquarters in the south-central Chaco.[38]

Many of the recently arrived Bolivian troops suffered from poor morale caused by dissension in the officer corps and inadequate training and support. Even though some veteran units fought well, they were too few and Arce fell on October 23. The degree to which the Bolivian army had disintegrated might well be judged by an incident at *Fortin* Alihuatá. Col. Enrique Peñaranda,[39] attempting to rally his command, the 4th Division, challenged his officers and men to escape from their encirclement at Alihuatá. He asked, "Who will accompany me?" Only 1,300 out of 3,000 did so. Alihuatá fell to the Paraguayans on October 26.[40]

Estigarribia now turned his attention to his exposed right flank. Toledo was captured on September 27. Between November 7 and 10, the Paraguayans failed to capture the Bolivian positions at *Fortin* Kilometer 7; these were a stretch of field fortifications. Here, on the tenth, the Bolivians won a defensive victory. The Paraguayans continued to attack until the twenty-four-hour armistice arranged by the Pope during December 24–25. They then retreated to *Fortin* Kilometer 12.[41]

KUNDT'S FIRST OFFENSIVE

General Kundt arrived in La Paz on December 6, 1932, and was greeted with a tumultuous welcome. He was the man who had built the army and now he would command it in war with the title of General-in-Chief of the Field Army. He reorganized his 12,000-man force into six divisions. General Kundt immediately began a limited offensive when reinforcements arrived from the *altiplano*. He attacked in the northern Chaco, attempting to force the Paraguayans to spread their forces. On December 28 the Bolivians attacked the Paraguayans at *Fortin* Kilometer 12, hardly more than a clearing on the *picada* between *Fortins* Saavedra and Alihuatá. Two Bolivian divisions were cut to pieces by machine-gun and artillery fire losing about 700 men; Kundt had not ordered this attack and criticized those who had. The Bolivians took *Fortin* Kilometer 9 but soon withdrew to their positions at Kilometer 7.

The Bolivians once again focused their attention against the Boquerón region. Troops were force-marched from the north. On December 31 they attacked *Fortin* Corrales about 65 miles northwest of Boquerón. The defenders, some 300 Paraguayans, fell back to *Fortin* Toledo the following day.

The new year held better promise for success by the Bolivians. Efforts in the northern Chaco had forced the Paraguayans to disperse some of their forces. Kundt changed objectives and attacked *Fortin* Nanawa (60 mi SSE of Boqueron), considered by the Paraguayans to be the backbone of their defenses. This *fortin* had received the extensive attention of fortification specialists Generals Ivan Belaieff and Nicolas Ern, White Russians in the service of the Paraguayans.[42] On the surface a crude outpost, Nanawa was the hardest of all of the Paraguayan *fortins* in the Chaco. Its defenses included zig-zag trenches, miles of barbed wire, and numerous machine-gun nests (some in trees). The Paraguayans had four old Krupp 7.5cm guns and 500 shells at Nanawa in January 1935. However, they could not be used because the Paraguayans did not have any fuses for their shells. They only had six mortars which soon ran out of ammunition.

On January 20, 1933, Kundt, in personal command, launched nine regiments and some unhorsed cavalry (6,000 men), supported by twelve 7.5cm Vickers guns (with up to 6,000 shells available) and six to nine aircraft, against Nanawa. By the beginning of 1933 cavalry units on both sides were on foot; the horses had died from lack of food and water. Three frontal assaults failed. The Bolivians next attempted to cut the *fortin* off from the rear. They dug a trench around the *fortin* which had a twelve-mile diameter. Although the Bolivians succeeded in capturing some of the outer trenches, heavy rains forced them to abandon the attack. The Paraguayans soon reoccupied the entire complex. Four Paraguayan aircraft flew sixteen boxes of cartridges to Nanawa; three of these planes were severely damaged but their contents were saved. By the end of January, the Bolivians had sustained about 2,000 casualities without making any progress. The Paraguayans lost 248 killed, missing, and wounded. This defeat seriously damaged Kundt's prestige. The *fortin* was nicknamed the "Verdun of South America."[43]

Beginning in late February the Bolivians attacked the outer defenses of Toledo and Corrales with 3,618 men. On the twenty-fifth the Bolivian Air Force carried out a dawn raid. In order to attack at first light, the aircraft flew at night over the Chaco by dead reckoning without instruments. One aircraft was shot down by Paraguayan anti-aircraft machine guns. The air attack was followed by successive waves of infantry attacks over the next two days. These broke against the fortifications created by the Russians who specialized in that art. By March 3 the Bolivians had lost 1,216 men and the Paraguayans 241 men. The Paraguayans intercepted intelligence that the enemy's will to fight was ebbing due to poor leadership and support. The Paraguayans tried to envelop the Bolivians but they successfully escaped without much discipline. During the retreat the Bolivian four regiments sustained mutinies. Two regiments, the 9th and 30th, had to be subdued by force; both were dishonorably dissolved.[44]

The Bolivians next focused their efforts against *Fortin* Toledo. First they attacked *Fortin* Alihuatá; the Paraguayan evacuated the *fortin* during the night of March 11–12 and the Bolivians occupied it the following day. Its capture cut off the road to Arce and isolated the 1st Division, Paraguay's most experienced unit. On the sixteenth, the 1st Division retreated in good order, field guns being carried by hand, twenty men to a weapon, until they reached a spot where they could be loaded onto trucks. Bolivian losses were about 150 and the Paraguayans' were lighter. More important, Kundt had lost the opportunity to capture a key Paraguayan unit. This Bolivian victory, which in fact was little more than a tactical retreat by the Paraguayans, bolstered the morale and hardened the Bolivian position in the continuing peace negotiations being pursued by the neutral nations.[45]

The rains continued throughout February and March. In April and May the Bolivians launched another offensive. Paraguayan public opinion reacted with fear to even the smallest tactical retreat by their army. By this time the Bolivian drive was faltering due to heavy casualties, epidemic sickness, and rising desertion. Morale was crumbling. Among the troops attacking Nanawa, some demoralized Bolivian troops turned their guns on their officers, for which many soldiers were court-martialed and shot. On May 10 Kundt ordered 2,000 Bolivians to attack the 1,200 defenders at *Fortin* Herrera but this failed, in part because too few troops were committed to the task. The Bolivians lost 556 dead and 314 wounded.[46]

On May 10, 1933, Paraguay finally declared war on Bolivia, hoping to force the "ABCP" (Argentina, Brazil, Chile, and Peru) nations to close their borders to the passage of Bolivian war material. Chile and Peru sympathized with Bolivia and did not enforce neutrality permitting war materials, trucks, food, and fuel to cross the border. Argentina immediately adopted a position of benevolent neutrality toward Paraguay and closed the Pilcomayo ports to all Bolivian commerce, stating that Bolivia had no civilian population in the Chaco and therefore all trade had to be contraband.[47]

June of 1933 was a particularly unpleasant month for the combatants. The rainy season had not ended in May as was typical, and the winter was intensely cold for the Chaco, dipping below freezing. Malaria was one of the consequences.[48]

On July 4 Kundt began his massive frontal assault against Nanawa. The attack began when a mine exploded in front of Nanawa's strong point, "Fortified Island," at nine o'clock in the morning. Bolivian sappers had dug a tunnel some 400 yards along and packed tons of explosives under the Paraguayan position. This had no tactical effect; the Paraguayans retreated about 30 yards just before the mine was exploded. Twenty-two guns and 12 mortars pounded the Paraguayans until the artillery fired its entire supply of 4,800 shells. The Paraguayans responded with 12 modern guns and a few old ones. Between 10 and 12 aircraft dropped 28.5-pound bombs. Kundt then attacked with some 9,000 men against an equal number of defenders. The Bolivian infantry attacked supported by four flame-throwers. In one section coordination between the artillery and infantry was so poor that Bolivian shells rained down on attacking Bolivian soldiers. Kundt then committed his five tanks which failed to break through the Paraguayan defenses. One of the three 3-ton Vickers tanks was destroyed by Paraguayan gunfire (its turret is now on display in the Army Museum in Asunción.) On the ninth, the Paraguayans counterattacked, but the demoralized Bolivians held their trenches. This battle had cost the Bolivians 1,600 casualties and the Paraguayans 500. Frustrated, Kundt shifted his attention to *Fortin* Gondra, 10 miles north of Nanawa. But again he failed. Kundt had steadfastly stuck to his policy of frontal assaults at Nanawa, Toledo, and Herrera.[49]

On September 15, 1933, the opponents fought the Battle of Pampa Grande. The Bolivians sustained 1,000 killed and wounded and 931 men taken prisoner. Among the casualties was the destruction of the Bolivian elite 16th "Castillo" Regiment, the backbone of which were the *Carabineros* (police) of La Paz.[50]

THE SECOND PARAGUAYAN OFFENSIVE

Estigarribia, now a brigadier general, went on the offensive. He had been hoarding supplies for months in order to sustain his drive. Twenty-two new wells were drilled to assure needed water for the Paraguayan army. By contrast the opposing Bolivians could not concentrate their forces because of a shortage of water. A despondent Kundt returned to La Paz on October 2 to seek additional resources. Col. David Toro Ruilova,[51] left in temporary command, was instructed to prepare defenses but not to reposition any troops. Greeted as a hero, Kundt lost his resolve to plead for additional troops and equipment.[52]

On October 23 Estigarribia launched 26,500 men along a 55-mile front using Nanawa as his primary base. Local Charagua Indians cut narrow *picadas* to gain access to the rear of Bolivian lines. Although discovered by the Bolivian Air Force, Kundt believed that the pilots had exaggerated the extent of the work. As the Paraguayan pressure increased, Kundt assumed personal command at Alihuatá. Typically he refused to yield ground and committed his meager reserves to an overextended line of defenses. The shortage of men was acute since Kundt had granted leave to about 1,500 men, of which practically none returned to the front. Estigarribia unsuccessfully attempted to envelop the enemy; the Bolivians fired on *Fortin* Alihuatá and retreated. Whatever move the Bolivians made, Estigarribia was able to counter it due to superior intelligence gained through tapped phone lines, intercepted radio messages, interrogated prisoners of war, and espionage. On December 11 the Bolivian 4th and 9th Divisions, some 8,000 men, surrendered to the Paraguayans at *Fortin* Campo Via. More importantly, the Paraguayans captured a large quantity of war materials: 20 spiked guns, 25 mortars, 536 Vickers machine guns and automatic rifles, plus 8,000 rifles.[53]

In two months Estigarribia had practically destroyed Kundt's central force; but Bolivia's army and will to fight remained. In addition, Estigarribia did not possess fresh troops to follow up these victories. Kundt was relieved by Enrique Peñaranda, who was promoted to Brigadier General. Both sides took advantage of a truce which lasted from December 19, 1933, to January 7, 1934, to reorganize their armies and to call up additional reservists.[54]

The Bolivian army now consisted of the 1st Army Corps (4th and 7th Divisions plus one reserve regiment) and the 2nd Army Corps (3rd and 8th Divisions plus one infantry regiment), three more regiments as the army reserve, one regiment isolated near *Fortin* Carandayty and another division with two regiments near Puerto Suarez in the northeastern Chaco. The Bolivian forces retreated toward the west, slowly and in good order. As they withdrew, their logistical problems lessened and those of Paraguay increased. Estigarribia's new strategy was to trap the Bolivian army against the Pilcomayo River and force it to surrender or seek asylum in Argentina. Heavy rains brought the Paraguayan drive to a standstill. Some Paraguayan units were isolated on high ground, cut off from their supply lines. The Bolivians attacked these isolated detachments and forced the Paraguayans to garrison strategic locations such as river fords.

The Paraguayan army renewed its offensive on January 7, 1934. Between March 22 and 27, the Paraguayan 6th Division destroyed the Bolivian 18th Division at Tarija, capturing 900 men. On May 25 the Bolivian army achieved its greatest triumph of the war when it enveloped a 1,556-man Paraguayan force at *Fortin* Cañada Esperanza and forced it to surrender.[55]

THE THIRD PARAGUAYAN OFFENSIVE

On June 18 Estigarribia struck at the Bolivian headquarters, *Fortin* Ballivián (120 mi SSE of Villa Montes) on the bank of the Pilcomayo River. On the twenty-sixth a dog fight occurred between the opposing air forces over the battlefield. The Bolivian troops fought well, resulting in heavy Paraguayan casualities. Ballivián, although of no extraordinary military significance, had become the symbol of Bolivia's presence in the southern Chaco. The politicians in La Paz feared that its evacuation would have negative domestic and international implications. Nevertheless, Peñaranda ordered Toro to abandon the *fortin* in order to shorten the Bolivians overextended defenses and to free troops for the offense. Toro refused to obey! Peñaranda acquiesced to his subordinate and Toro, who had under his command the bulk of the Bolivian army (Toro had 16,000 men in the south; Bilbao 9,000 in the north; and Moscoso 6,000 in reserve), became the *de facto* commander of the army.[56]

The Paraguayan offensive during June and July 1934, the so-called *"Battalle general,"* was largely a failure and was later known as *"la batalla de los milimetros"* because of the small gains. Between January and the end of July 1934, the Paraguayans lost about 5,000 men against only 4,000 Bolivians.

Taking advantage of a dispute between Peñaranda and Salamanca, Estigarribia increased the Paraguayan forces in the north-central Chaco to 15,000 men. On August 13, 1934, Col. Rafael Franco's 6th Paraguayan Division of 4,200 men spearheaded the next offensive against the western defenses, achieving complete surprise. The Paraguayan force drove deep into the western Chaco virtually unopposed. On August 27 it reached the Chiriguanos Mountains (in fact, foothills) a few miles east of *Fortin* Carandayty, the geographical limit of the Chaco. This Paraguayan drive outdistanced the capacity of their supply system. Even with the dedication of one hundred new trucks to the drive, the advanced position was too far forward to be maintained. Estigarribia ordered Colonel Franco to retire slowly, holding the enemies attention.[57]

TORO SEIZES THE INITIATIVE

Toro, who ironically was the one who had reassured President Salamanca that all was not lost, attempted to seize the opportunity of cutting off the retreating Paraguayans under Franco. Toro relinquished command of Ballivián and led three divisions, two of dismounted cavalry and one of infantry (12,000 men), north. On September 5 he caught up with the Paraguayans and attempted a double envelopment at Pozo del Burro. The Paraguayans secretly slipped through Toro's trap during the night of September 8, losing perhaps one hundred men and abandoning 14 trucks, seven spiked guns, and 78 automatic weapons. The secrecy of the escape was so complete that on the ninth the Bolivian Air Force was still dropping surrender leaflets on the former Paraguayan position.[58]

More bad news for the Bolivians—in the normally quiet far northeastern sector along the upper Paraguay River, the Paraguayans occupied *Fortins* Vanguardia and Vargas on September 11. It seems that the Bolivians abandoned these *fortins* and the Paraguayans, due to a lack of trucks, boats, and men, were unable to attack the retreating enemy.[59]

In spite of Franco's narrow escape at Pozo del Burro and his severe shortage of water (half a pint per man per day), Estigarribia insisted on executing a slow withdrawal. On September 22 Toro again unsuccessfully attempted to double-envelop Franco's force. After sustaining heavy casualties, the Paraguayans broke through the Bolivian lines the next day. The discovery of unlimited potable water at *Fortin* Yrendagué significantly eased Paraguay's logistical problems. Truck engines were used to pump water from five new wells. Prior to this discovery, the majority of Paraguay's trucks had to be used to transport water from the wells at *Fortin* La Faye (36 mi SE of Yrendagué) to Franco's force. These trucks were now freed for other duties and Franco's long, vulnerable water supply line significantly shortened. Franco continued his slow retreat, luring Toro toward Picuiba.[60]

By September the Bolivian command was ripe with dissension. President Salamanca paid his fourth visit to the Chaco to discuss the reassignment of officers, a contentious issue. A meeting on the twenty-third between the President and the commander of the army, General Peñaranda, almost disintegrated into a gun duel between the President's son Rafael and the General. Salamanca contemplated replacing General Peñaranda primarily because of his inability to control his subordinates, Toro in particular.[61]

Toro, commanding 12,000 men, again tried to double-envelop Franco's force of 5,000, this time at *Fortin* Villazón (7 mi SW of Yrendagué). On November 10 the Paraguayans broke out toward *Fortin* Picuiba, 17 miles southwest of Villazón. The Bolivians did manage to captured 400 Paraguayans and some 50 new trucks. But they lost some 200 to 400 men themselves. Throughout his drive to capture Franco's force, Toro constantly exaggerated the enemy's numbers to the point that the Bolivian command believed that Estigarribia was making his main effort in that area. As a result, the Bolivian forces defending *Fortin* Ballivián in the south were constantly being weakened to send reinforcements north.[62]

In November the Bolivians began carrying out high altitude bombing raids. Prior to this date, bombings had been carried out by dropping relatively light (55-pound and 22-pound) bombs from low-flying aircraft which afforded the Paraguayan infantry the chance to fire back. On November 14, three Junker W34 transport planes, which had been modified with underwing racks, dropped 200-pound bombs from a height at which the Paraguayan small arms could not reach them. This unpleasant surprise inflicted some damage and caused disruption. Usually, these improvised bombers were escorted by some fighters, all of which formed a mixed squadron of some ten planes known as *Punta de Alas* (Point of Wings).[63]

THE BATTLE OF EL CARMEN

While Toro was attacking Franco's reteating command farther to the north, a Paraguayan force of 11,000 men successfully enveloped 9,000 Bolivians at El Carmen some 120 miles northwest of Ballivián in November. The 1st, 2nd, 7th, and 8th Paraguayan Divisions attacked the newly created, so-called Bolivian Infantry Reserve Corps. Bolivian casualities were high— 2,500 died, 4,000 were taken prisoner, and large quantities of arms and munitions were captured, as well as seventeen days' worth of rations. The Bolivians were forced to abandon Ballivián, and on November 17 the Paraguayans entered the *fortin*, the symbol of Bolivian presence in the southern Chaco. Amazingly, Toro continued to attack Franco in the north-central Chaco despite the disaster at El Carmen.[64]

SALAMANCA DEPOSED

President Salamanca naively hurried to the Chaco to dismiss the senior military officers en masse and make new appointments. On November 26 he directed Gen. José Lanza to take command of the army. Col. Felipe Rivera, Peñaranda's Chief of Staff (who was also to be reassigned by the President) hurried to the not-too-distant front and returned with 300 men of the 4th Artillery Group. They seized the President on the morning of the twenty-seventh. Later, Salamanca observed, "This is the only maneuver in which they [the senior officers] have obtained success."[65] A military junta convinced Salamanca to resign and elevate Vice President José Tejada Sorzano in an attempt to give an air of legitimacy to their actions. However, the junta did stipulate that Tejada Sorzano must be accountable to the military. On December 4, 1934, he was the one who *finally* decreed a general mobilization.[66]

TORO'S DEFEAT

All the while Toro persisted in his pursuit of Franco, despite the fact that his right flank was exposed by a 75-mile gap. Toro believed that he could strike south and envelop Estigarribia's main force. This plan was unrealistic. Toro did not have adequate transport and his troops were nearly exhausted. On the Paraguayan side, Estigarribia had reinforced Franco with enough resources to permit him to sustain his orderly withdrawal. Estigarribia now ordered the Paraguayan 8th Division (2,000 men) to hack their way through the brush and seize the wells at *Fortin* Yrendagué, which had previously fallen into Bolivian hands. These wells were Toro's sole source of water. The Paraguayan 8th Division passed between the Bolivian 7th Infantry and 2nd Cavalry Divisions undetected. The Paraguayan "thirst march," over 37 miles, started on December 5 in the early morning hours. Only about 150 men were capable of launching an attack on the wells of Irendaque at 1:00 A.M. on December 8. They were followed hours later by another 140 men, all belonging to the Regiment "Batallion 40" of the 8th Paraguayan Division under Col. Eugenio Garay, then 64 years old. Two other regiments of the division had collapsed en route due to the lack of water, discipline, and leadership.

Finally, Franco's retreating force turned on its pursuers. The Bolivians were still marginally superior in numbers. Toro commanded about 11,300 men against 9,500 Paraguayans. Toro's communications with his leading units broke down. Some could not and others would not obey his orders to retreat to El Cruce. The Bolivian 7th Infantry Division was ordered to retake the lightly defended wells at Yrendagué (9 mi SE of Yrendagué), but failed to obey. Toro's troops were without food or water, in many cases officers were absent, and Toro's headquarters was some 100 miles behind the lines at Carandayty. As a result, discipline broke down. [67]

Sensing the pending disaster, Peñaranda ordered a general retreat on December 9 and for once Toro obeyed. This came too late for many of Toro's troops. Perhaps 3,000 Bolivians died (either in action or of thirst) or were captured; only a few officers were included in this number. On the eleventh a heavy rain temporarily saved the remainder of the force, some 8,000 men, by giving them much-needed water and by slowing the pursuit of Franco's troops. But many of them died of thirst before reaching their own lines. The last remaining Bolivian hold in the central Chaco had been lost. But in spite of this series of disasters—El Carmen, Ballivián, and Yrendagué—Bolivia showed no signs of capitulating.[68]

The Paraguayan army, reequipped with captured booty and financed in secret with a large loan from Argentina,[69] prepared to invade Bolivia. Having failed to completely destroy the Bolivian army in the Chaco, Estigarribia's objectives now became to capture the town of Villa Montes and the oil fields in order to improve Paraguay's negotiating position.[70]

BATTLE OF YBYBOBO

Bolivia tried to establish a new defensive line from Ybybobo (33 mi SE of Villa Montes) on the Pilcomayo River northward to Carandayty (54 mi NE of Villa Montes). In late December 1934 the Paraguayan-reinforced 2nd Cavalry Division, some 2,525 men strong, surrounded the 9th Bolivian Division, some 2,700 men, at Ybybobo with their backs against the river. Following a weak effort to break out, the force surrendered on December 30. At least 300 men were killed or drowned attempting to swim the swollen Pilcomayo River, and 1,717 were taken prisoner. A few hundred Bolivians did escape with some of the artillery to Palo Marcado; after this defeat the 9th Division was disbanded. Paraguayan casualities were 24 killed or missing and 35 wounded. Bolivian defenses fell farther back to a line from Palo Marcado to Capirendá.[71]

Bolivian forces in the far northeast came under increasing pressure as well. On December 20, two Paraguayan naval Macchi M18 flying boats carried out the first night air attack in Latin America when they bombed the *Fortins* Vitriones and San Juan. Estigarribia had vetoed bombing raids against towns because of the risk to the Bolivian civilian population and, probably above all, to the few neutrals living there. Only the summer rains halted the Paraguayan advance. By the close of 1934 Paraguay had almost completely taken control of the Chaco.[72]

DEFENSE OF VILLA MONTES

Beyond Villa Montes lay the Bolivian eastern lowlands and the oil fields. The mood in Paraguay had swung from one of determined resistance to one of conquest. If Villa Montes fell, the eastern Bolivian lowlands would be seriously threatened. Bolivian Colonels Bilbao and Moscoso accepted the task of commanding the defenses of the town after others had refused.

Appreciating the importance of Villa Montes, the Bolivians concentrated 20,000 men in the immediate region (1st, 3rd, 4th, and 8th Infantry Divisions and 2nd Cavalry Division plus 44 guns and some light anti-aircraft) plus most of its surviving air force. The Paraguayans had about 17,740 men, which included the logistical rear echelons, along with 24 guns and 19 mortars but only a few shells.

Estigarribia attempted to bypass Villa Montes. The Paraguayan 3rd Corps (4,500 men) penetrated north of the town on January 23, 1934, and captured Carandayty, taking some prisoners. The Bolivians fell back to the foothill passes in an attempt to defend the Camiri oil fields. The Paraguayan offensive was finally turned away by the more numerous Bolivian troops. One of the reasons for the Paraguayan failure was that they were not used to operating in hilly or mountainous terrain and lost several small detachments surrounded by the mountain-warfare-trained Bolivians.[73]

Having failed to isolate Villa Montes from the north, Estigarribia attacked the outer defenses on February 13 with 5,000 men. The Bolivian air force and artillery brought the attack to a standstill. This Paraguayan failure was followed by an unsuccessful attempt to capture the oil fields at Camiri. Next, a Paraguayan force crossed the Parapiti River into Bolivia and captured Cooper on April 5. The Bolivians fell back to Charagua in hopes of luring the Paraguayans up the road toward Santa Cruz. Lacking transport, the Paraguayans could not be induced even if they had wanted to advance. On April 16 the Bolivians opened a general offensive. They retook Parairi on the nineteenth, Mandyjypecuá on the twentieth, Carandayty on the twenty-first, and kept some pressure on the Paraguayan force besieging Villa Montes.[74]

The tide of war had subtly began to turn. Now it was Paraguay that had the overextended supply lines. The hilly terrain in eastern Bolivia partially nullified Paraguay's greater mobility. The Bolivians were more acclimated to the cooler climate and accustomed to mountains than the Paraguayans. During the last two years of the war, captured equipment had sustained the Paraguayan effort; now it was no longer being taken in large quantities. Also, Paraguay was dependent upon Argentina for its gasoline and all of its artillery shells, a potentially unreliable source. Aircraft were needed to successfully attack Villa Montes, yet these could not be acquired due to the embargo. Most of all, Paraguay suffered from shortages of men. Paraguay had exhausted its manpower and financial resources. Sixteen-year-old boys were being drafted; regiments had shrunk from 1,600 men to typically 350 men. Paraguay was simply running out of everything.[75]

Bolivia, on the other hand, showed some signs of getting its second wind. In spite of its losses, Bolivia was able to rebuild its army to 50,000 by 1935. Also, Bolivia was spending relatively large sums on new armaments. Tin prices were slowly increasing from 191 pounds sterling per ton in 1932 to 226 pounds in 1935, and production rose from 14,956 tons in 1933 to 20,634 tons in 1934.[76] However, Bolivia was not without major problems. It still did not have a general equal to Estigarribia. Bolivia could mount local attacks, but the army was incapable of initiating a major offensive. Also, Paraguayan propaganda had been fanning the flames of separatism in the Bolivian province of Santa Cruz. On June 12, 1935, the negotiators for both sides agreed to a protocol, and on the fourteenth a cease-fire took effect. Although the war did not formally end until 1938, the fighting stopped.

OBSERVATIONS

The war cost Bolivia almost any claim it had to the Chaco, drained the treasury dry, discredited the army, and destroyed the nation's fragile political stability. Under the peace agreement, Bolivia kept about 19,200 square miles, one sixth of Chaco, or one fourth of what La Paz claimed in 1932. Of the 250,000 Bolivians mobilized for the Chaco War, 52,400 died and 24,000 were captured. This catastrophe sowed seeds of social and political discontent which bloomed in the 1952 Bolivian Revolution (see chapter 23).[77]

Paraguay had conquered 90 percent of the Chaco and was awarded 80 percent of the disputed territory for its battlefield successes by the peace process.[78] Before the war, Paraguay controlled about 42,577 square miles of the Chaco and the peace treaty granted Asunción an additional 52,395 square miles. But the war was also too much of a strain for Paraguay's democratic processes. On February 17, 1936, Col. Rafael Franco led a successful coup against President Ayala, which was followed by a coup against Franco led by Col. Ramón L. Paredes on August 15, 1937. Paraguay had mobilized 100,000 men, of which 36,000 died and 4,000 were captured. In spite of the fact that Paraguay had mobilized only half as many soldiers as Bolivia, it was rarely outnumbered at the point of attack, a tribute to General Estigarribia's leadership.[79]

The sharpest contrast between the two sides was in the quality of leadership. The Paraguayan civil-military relationship worked in harmony. General Estigarribia fought to achieve the political goals of President Ayala. On the other side, President Salamanca held the Bolivian high command in contempt. The President and his generals did not even share the same strategic objectives. Also, Salamanca wished to provide his generals with just enough resources to continue fighting. They were constantly working at cross purposes. Salamanca misinterpreted his function as Captain-General. Neither he nor Kundt knew the Chaco and the few Bolivians who had some Chaco experience either died early in the war, were not consulted, or their advice was ignored.

Estigarribia and his Bolivian counterparts did not share the same strategy. For Estigarribia the objective was the destruction of the enemy's army. When this was no longer possible because the enemy had grown stronger and he weaker, the objective became the capture of Villa Montes and the oil fields in order to force Bolivia to quit fighting. The Bolivian commanders— Osorio, Kundt, Peñaranda—believed that the way to win was to capture or hold terrain. They distrusted the abilities of their subordinates. As a result, they destroyed initiative. Ironically, the

Figure 18. The Chaco War (1932–35). Paraguayan Felix Estigarribia (foreground on the right) was the war's most successful general. In 1935 R. W. Thompson, British war correspondent, described him as "a man then in his forties, simple in dress and taste, his uniform unadorned, his voice deep almost to the point of gruffness, but with a fine timbre. He was a handsome man of medium height, about five feet eight or nine inches, thick curly black hair framing a broad square cut forehead over a fine noise and very direct dark eyes, brilliant and intelligent." *Courtesy U.S. National Archives, Washington, D.C.*

individual who made the most of this stagnant intellectual environment was Colonel Toro, who openly disobeyed orders for egotistical, political reasons not fearing the consequences. On the other side, Estigarribia gave his subordinates some freedom of action and he was rewarded with victories. Unlike Peñaranda, Estigarribia knew how to deal with insubordination; it was immediate banishment from the war zone. A shortcoming was his lack of generosity regarding promotions and decorations. But on the whole his leadership, although not faultless, was much superior to the Bolivian performance.[80]

The opening strategies of both sides were unrealistic. The Bolivian army projected operating along the right bank of the Paraguay River without any thought of neutralizing the Paraguayan navy. President Salamanca's plan to take Asunción was sheer nonsense for the same reason. The Paraguayan opening strategy was not much better, as it was particularly based upon extending the railroad for which there was neither time nor money.

The Bolivians persisted in making the same tactical mistakes, which cost them dearly. Bolivian patrols often hid out in remote spots for days and returned reporting no contact; the Paraguayan patrols obtained much better results. The superior Bolivian air reconnaissance could not fully compensate for this shortcoming. Frontal assaults were the order of the day, particularly while Kundt commanded. Bolivian subordinates also inevitably committed all troops available in the first attack wave and held nothing in reserve; frequently they did not protect their flanks; and their command posts were typically too far to the rear.[81]

Mobility and logistics dominated the war and Paraguay was more adept at solving the problems associated with these than was Bolivia. In spite of having three times the manpower of Paraguay, the Bolivian army never exceeded 60,000 men. Never more than two-thirds of the Bolivian army were in the Chaco at any given time. The Paraguayan army reached 50,000 men and its maximum strength in the Chaco was 30,000. Paraguay was much more creative at meeting its logistical needs internally. The naval arsenal at Asunción employed 10,000 workers. Working in two to three shifts, they manufactured hand-grenades, repaired a few mortars, constructed 2,300 truck bodies, numerous canteens, and water tanks. In the area of ordnance, the naval arsenal produced some 300,000 hand-grenades, 2,000 33-pound bombs, and 10,000 mortar shells (admittedly 40 percent of these were duds or fired prematurely). The Paraguayans also produced nearly five million pieces of clothing or equipment but only a half-million pairs of shoes. Paraguayan soldiers were given the nickname "Pata-pilas" because of the noise they made when marching with bare feet.[82] Bolivia, having no equivalent facility, had to import practically all of its war material.

Frequently, the key to winning was supplying enough water, which was dependent upon logistics. The motor truck revolutionized logistics by tremendously increasing flexibility.[83]

In general Bolivia won the international propaganda war. Its diplomats were generally superior to those of Paraguay, particularly at the League of Nations in Geneva. Bolivia was seldom named or treated as the aggressor, and measures such as arms embargoes were often in reality only directed against Paraguay, particularly during the early years of the war. However, Paraguay was the most successful at publicly exaggerating its battlefield successes at times when critical diplomatic negotiations were underway, thereby influencing the world community to its benefit. Outside Latin America the Chaco War provoked hardly any media interest at all and most of what was published was inaccurate.[84]

During the Chaco War Bolivia seldom used its aircraft to attack the Paraguayan logistical system such as the three or four existing locomotives, truck convoys, repair bases, water pumps, communications, or airfields. If such attacks had been carried out early in the war, they might have had devastating effects upon the Paraguayan effort. Bolivian aircraft were never used to bomb strategic targets such as Asunción for fear of international repercussions. Although they could have done little material damage since they could carry only a few small bombs and they would have had to operate at their maximum range, the psychological effect might have been significant.

Instead, the Bolivian air force was used to provide fire support for attacking troops, logistical support, and reconnaissance. Frequently such fire support was totally ineffective because of the difficulty of identifying the target and poor real-time communications with the ground. Reconnaissance was wasted because many ground commanders chose to ignore air intelligence. And the Bolivians had to waste much of their air power providing logistical support because no alternative existed. These missions—combat support, reconnaissance, and logistics—forced the Bolivian Air Force to fly low where its aircraft were vulnerable to ground fire.

The Bolivians lost about thirty-four aircraft of various types by all causes. A British pilot flying for the Bolivians wrote, "I don't think it would be an exaggeration to say that one out of every three flying men—including observers as well as pilots—was either killed or badly injured in flying accidents during my own time at the front."[85] In September 1934 Bolivia still possessed some thirty aircraft, among them six Curtiss Hawks, six Curtiss Ospreys, three JU-34Ws, and three JU-52s. The Paraguayans lost some twenty-four aircraft, at least half of which were destroyed through accidents. Nevertheless, the Paraguayan planes flew some 3,000 sorties in three years and transported over 1,000 wounded.

By the mid-1930s the tank was even less mature than the aircraft. The Bolivians had three tanks and two tankettes, while Paraguay had none. These consisted of three 6-ton Vickers (one armed with a 4.7cm gun and a machine gun, and the other two tanks with two machine guns) and two Carden-Lloyd tankettes which had little fighting value. One tank was destroyed by a direct hit from a 7.5cm Krupp gun and subsequently blown up by the Paraguayans. The Paraguayans captured without a fight the two remaining tanks at the Battle of Campo Via on December 11, 1933, while the crews were resting. The two tankettes were discarded during the war due to mechanical problems. Most of the officers of the Bolivian tank corps were German or Austrian. The Bolivian tank force was hardly adequate to form a shock force. In addition, these tanks were severely hampered by the Chaco's terrain.[86]

Neither side was able to solve their communications problems, a by-product of existing technology. The Paraguayans were able to intercept about 15,000 Bolivian radio messages, 7,000 of which they decoded. By July 1933 the Paraguayans kept a 24-hour vigil on 34 Bolivian radio stations in the field, in the rear, and at La Paz. By contrast, Bolivian efforts at code-breaking were poor.[87]

CHAPTER 12

THE LETICIA DISPUTE, 1932–33

Peace in the interior and war on the frontiers to the end.
—Colombian Senator Laureano Gómez

THE SPARK

At 6 o'clock in the morning on September 1, 1932, two hundred Peruvians (165 civilians and 35 military) armed principally with hunting weapons seized public buildings in the Colombian river port of Leticia (222 mi E of Iquitos, Peru) to prevent the permanent transfer of territory to Colombia under a 1922 treaty settlement. These filibusters ejected the eighteen-man Colombian national police force. The Peruvian government in Lima initially disavowed the action, but Peruvian authorities at Iquitos (612 mi NE of Lima), farther up the Amazon River, provided military support to the filibusters. In response, the Colombian government sent an 800-man "Juanambú" Infantry Battalion and strong riverine reinforcements up the Amazon River, a measure that the Peruvian public viewed as punitive. They demanded action.[1]

BACKGROUND

Slowly improving means of exploration among the Andean nations allowed them to better understand their *selva* areas beginning in the first half of the twentieth century. All confirmed that they had conflicting claims with neighbors. Colombian and Peruvian forces clashed in 1911 at La Pedrera (288 mi NE of Iquitos), a recently established Colombian outpost on the Apaporis River, a tributary of the Amazon. During this conflict Peruvian forces in the *selva* were significantly superior to those of Colombia due to the presence of the recently purchased riverine gunboat *América*. The Peruvians reacted to the Colombian outpost by sending the *América* and the troop-laden launch *Loreto*. The Peruvian force commanded by Lt. Col. Oscar Benavides[2] arrived off La Pedrera at midday on July 10, 1911. An ultimatum was presented to the Colombians demanding that they abandon their position, which they refused to do. Fighting began in the afternoon. The *América* and the *Loreto* steamed toward the Colombians, bypassing some makeshift mines the Colombians had planted. Apparently demoralized by the failure of the mines to stop the Peruvian craft and considerably outnumbered, the Colombians surrendered on the twelfth. On the fifteenth, Colombia and Peru signed an agreement at

Map 3. The Leticia Dispute, 1932–33.

Manaos, Brazil, and four days later a convention in Bogotá, Colombia, ended the fighting. But this was only a respite.[3]

On March 24, 1922, representatives of Colombia and Peru signed the confidential Salomón-Lozano Treaty, which acknowledged the Leticia Trapezium (approximately 2,250 square miles which included 68 miles fronting the north bank of the Amazon River) as belonging to Colombia. In exchange, the Colombian government ceded to Peru its rights to a strip of land south of the Putumayo River, known as the Sucumbios Triangle, to which Ecuador also lay claim. What Colombia gained was a highly prized Amazon port, Leticia. What Peru gained was the simplification of the dispute for the remaining contested territory. Ecuador, a country whose military and economic resources were far less formidable than those of Colombia, was now Peru's sole rival in the remaining disputed territory.[4]

The proposed treaty, which was leaked to the public, was most unpopular in Peru, particularly with those who had invested treasure and talent in the area to be ceded to Colombia. The government of Augusto Leguía after much delay, in part due to Brazilian concerns, ratified the treaty on January 23, 1928, under pressure from the United States. As Leguía had feared, the *Aprista* Party (see chapter 15) immediately used the treaty to create public hostilities toward his government. On August 27, 1930, Col. Luís Sánchez Cerro overthrew Leguía. Key supporters of Sánchez Cerro were members of the *Civilista* Party, who opposed the treaty.[5]

OPPOSING FORCES

In 1932 the population of Colombia was 9 million inhabitants and that of Peru 7.5 million.[6] Both sides possessed potential military advantages. Colombia had recently taken possession of three brand new British-built riverine gunboats—the *Cartagena, Santa Marta*, and *Barranquilla*—although only two were in the Amazon *selva*. The third, the *Barranquilla*, was far away on the Magdalena River which flowed into the Caribbean Sea. In addition, Colombia possessed in the Amazon basin the gunboat *General Nariño* (built unk) and the launch *Huila* (built unk). The principal riverine craft of the Peruvian navy were the gunboats *América* (built 1904) and *Napo* (built 1925); and launches *Iquitos* (built 1875), *Cahuapanas* (built ca. 1880), and *Portillo* (built ca. 1880).[7]

Peru possessed a superior deep-water navy compared to that of Colombia. The Peruvian fleet was built around two light cruisers acquired from Great Britain in 1906 and four submarines purchased from the United States in the late 1920s. At the beginning of the conflict, Colombia possessed no modern blue-water warships. It had the coastal gunboats *Junin* (built 1925) and *Pichincha* (built 1925) in the Caribbean and the *Carabobo* (built 1925) in the Pacific. The commander of the Peruvian fleet was Capt. W. O. Spears, U.S. Navy; this unusual arrangement was a by-product of North America's desire to win influence in Latin American navies through an aggressive program of naval assistance.[8]

On paper, the Peruvian air force was superior to that of Colombia. It possessed about 60 aircraft, the most valuable being Vought 02U-1E reconnaissance aircraft, Corsair 02U-3B light bombers, Curtiss Hawk fighters, Nieuport 121 C1 fighters, and Potez 49A-2 observation aircraft.[9]

The Colombian air force possessed three serviceable Swiss-built Wild X observation planes, three Curtiss Fledgling trainers, and one Curtiss P-1 Hawk. More importantly, Colombia could count on the aircraft and expertise of the commercial firm SCADTA (*Sociedad Colombo-Alemana de Transporte Aéreo*). It possessed two Junkers F-13 float planes, and one Junkers W-33. Immediately after the outbreak of hostilities, SCADTA acquired one Dornier Wall 34 flying boat and one Hamilton float plane from the Andian National Corporation Ltd. SCADTA's chief pilot was Herbert Boy,[10] an influential and experienced German aviator. He was immediately given the rank of major and asked to organize an aerial supply route to the Putumayo River.[11]

Both armies were very far from the theater of operations. The Colombian army possessed 6,200 officers and men and the Peruvian 8,955. The Peruvians were better armed, possessing a hundred machine guns, three times as many as the Colombians. Both sides possessed enough Mauser rifles (models 1912 and 1924) for their standing armies. Colombian Gen. Alfredo Vázquez Cobo,[12] who was the Minister Plenipotentiary in France, was given command of the forces charged with reoccupying the disputed territory. The losing presidential candidate in 1930, his selection was motivated by politics. On November 9 Gen. Fernando Sarmiento was given overall command of Peruvian forces in the *selva*.[13]

Peru possessed the following ground forces within the *selva*: On the Putumayo River, there were 20 soldiers at Puerto Arturo (129 mi N of Iquitos) and 12 men at Güeppi (273 mi NW of Iquitos). On the Amazon River, there were 28 soldiers and two 1905 Krupp 77mm guns at Chimbote and 180 men and five sea planes at Iquitos. On the Napo River there were 16 soldiers at Pantoja. In addition, 92 soldiers protected the frontier with Ecuador. Colombia had even fewer soldiers in the *selva*: 12 soldiers at San Miguel, 39 soldiers at Caucayá, 10 soldiers at La Tagua, and 17 soldiers at El Encanto.[14]

Both sides went on buying frenzies in North America and Europe. Many of the acquisitions were embargoed because the two nations were considered belligerents or the weapons simply did not arrive in time. There were some important exceptions. Colombia was particularly successful in increasing its air power. SCADTA assumed the responsibility for recruiting pilots and technicians and assembling aircraft upon their arrival. SCADTA recruited 36 German pilots, three foreign mechanics, and took deliveries of 26 Curtiss Hawk II fighters, 30 Curtiss Falcon F8C reconnaissance bombers, 10 Curtiss Fledgling J2 trainers, and 16 Consolidated PT-11 trainers. Peru acquired 6 Douglas 0-38P observation aircraft and 10 Curtiss Falcon light bombers shortly after the outbreak of fighting.[15]

Colombia was also more successful at acquiring warships. It purchased the following merchantships and yachts to serve as auxiliary cruisers and transports, primarily in France and the United States: the *Córdoba* (ex-German M-146), *Mosquera* (ex-*Royal Highlander*), *Bogotá* (ex-*Helgoland*), *Mariscal Sucre* (ex-*Flying Fox*), *Boyacá* (ex-*Bridgetown*), *Jamary* (ex-*Nariño*), and *Ciudad de Cúcuta* (merchant name retained). It also bought two new destroyers from Portugal, the *Antiquois* (ex-*Douro*) and the *Caldas* (ex-*Tejo*). Peru purchased two ex-Russian destroyers from Estonia, the *Almirante Guise* (ex-*Lennuk*) and the *Almirante Villar* (ex-*Vambola*).[16]

OPENING STRATEGIES

As with previous encounters in the *selva*, the strategy of both sides was to seize and hold the river ports. Colombia possessed a geographical advantage. The distance by land between Bogotá and Leticia was 620 miles *over* mountains, *across* unmapped savannahs, and *through* almost impenetrable jungles. Since Peru held forts on the upper Putumayo River, Colombia could not use the river to approach Leticia from the west. Leticia, a small village in the midst of the jungle, was not connected by road to any other town in Colombia. The distance by water from the Colombian Caribbean port of Barranquilla through the Atlantic Ocean and up the Amazon River was 2,200 miles. Notwithstanding these geographical challenges, Colombia, a Caribbean nation, lay hundreds of miles closer to Leticia than Peru, a Pacific nation, by sea. The distance from Callao to Leticia via the Panama Canal was 5,500 miles. Plus, Colombia's military reinforcements did not have to pass through the Panama Canal, potentially a politically sensitive passage, where the canal was the most practical sea route for Peru. The pressing operational question for Peru was how to employ its superior fleet to its advantage given the riverine environment of the conflict.[17]

By land, Peru appeared to have an advantage. Lightly armed soldiers could travel from Lima to Iquitos successively by train, automobile, mule, canoe, and launch; it was a trip requiring seventeen days. The exploitation of aviation gave the advantage to Colombia. SCADTA flew 185 tons of material, including light artillery, and 450 Colombian soldiers into the combat area during the first months of the conflict.[18]

THE BATTLE FOR TARAPACÁ

Both nations acted quickly following the incident at Leticia. Peru immediately sent additional lightly armed troops over the Andes, allowing it to act first. In late 1932 Peru reinforced Puerto Arturo and seized the Colombian port of Tarapacá (240 mi NE of Iquitos). These two river towns lay on the Putumayo River, which flowed into the Amazon above Leticia.[19]

In the meantime, on November 30, 1932, the Colombian *Mosquera* and *Córdoba* sailed from Rouen, France, crewed primarily by Frenchmen with General Vázquez on board. They anchored in the Brazilian river port of Pará on December 21. Seven days later they were joined by the "Amazon Detachment" (*Destacmento Amazonas*). The Amazon Detachment had been assembled in the Caribbean and was composed of the riverine gunboat *Barranquilla*, the coastal gunboat *Pichincha*, and the transports *Boyacá* and *Nariño*. The 791-man "Juanambú" Infantry Battalion was on board the two transports.[20]

At this point the Colombians worked out the details of their strategy. Gen. Efraín Rojas,[21] second in command, proposed that the Putumayo River towns of Tarapacá, Güeppi, and Puerto Arturo be captured first. Next the Amazon Detachment in conjunction with the Colombian forces on the Napo River supported by aviation would neutralize the Peruvian stronghold at Iquitos. Then Leticia should be recaptured. General Vázquez favored moving directly against Leticia. However, Gen. Francisco Valderrama Díaz, a Chilean military advisor to the Colombian Minister of War, and Capt. Carlos Uribe Gaviria, Minister of War to the President, supported General Rojas' plan which won out.[22]

Seven weeks elapsed before the Colombian flotilla arrived below Tarapacá. In the meantime, Colonel Boy (recently promoted) commanding seven float planes (one Junkers K43 bomber, two Dornier Wall, one Junker F13, and three Curtiss Hawk fighters) flew over the Andes Mountains and joined the Amazon Detachment. They operated from the river. On February 14 General Vázquez demanded the surrender of Tarapacá but the Peruvian commander refused. Three Peruvian Vought Corsairs, flying from the river port of Iquitos, tried to attack the combined Colombian force. The Colombian Curtiss Hawks, led by Colonel Boy, immediately took off from the river and drove off the Peruvian aircraft before they could inflict any damage. The Colombian aircraft and river craft then bombarded Tarapacá. At 7:30 A.M. on the fifteenth, the Colombians landed 270 men. The 104 defenders, possessing only two 75mm Krupp 1894 guns, abandoned their defenses as instructed when confronted by overwhelming force. Losses were light, if any.[23]

THE BATTLE OF GÜEPPI

The Colombians chose to bypass the heavily fortified river port of Puerto Arturo and steamed farther up the Putumayo River, attacking the Peruvian river port of Güeppi. It was garrisoned by 209 officers and men, their heaviest weapons being machine guns. Although the Peruvian troops were protected by trenches, they suffered badly from tropical diseases and their radio transmitter was unreliable. As the Colombian flotilla proceeded upriver, it was attacked by Peruvian Corsairs and recently arrived Douglas O-38Ps. These aircraft dropped their bombs from above 5,000 feet and missed their targets. On March 25 the gunboats *Santa Marta* and *Barranquilla*, protected by Colombia aircraft, bombarded Güeppi. During that night 150 men disembarked from the Colombian squadron. Supported by covering fire from the *Cartegena* and *Santa Marta* as well as 50-kilo bombs dropped by six Colombian amphibious aircraft, they captured the Peruvian defensive positions. Following a brief defense, the Peruvian troops retired into the jungle. The Colombians sustained 5 dead and 9 wounded; the Peruvians suffered 10 dead, 2 wounded, and 24 captured.[24]

COLOMBIA CHANGES COMMANDERS

On April 3 President Olaya Herrera ordered Gen. Vázquez Cobo to return to Europe to supervise the attempted acquisition of two destroyers from Estonia. Peru acted more swiftly and purchased the destroyers. Efraín Rojas took command of Colombians forces in the *selva*.[25]

PERU COUNTERATTACKS

On April 16 Lt. Col. Oscar Sevilla, leading twenty Peruvian soldiers from Puerto Arturo through mud up to their waists, surprised the fifty-man Colombian garrison at Puerto Calderón some 45 miles above Puerto Arturo on the Putumayo. The Colombian troops found refuge under the guns of the nearby *Santa Marta* and *Cartagena*. The attacking Peruvians fell back to Puerto Arturo. On the twenty-eighth a larger Peruvian force, taking a Krupp cannon, steamed in the launch *San Miguel* some 60 miles up the Campuya River and surprised the Colombian garrison at Yabuyanos. The Colombian gunboats *Santa Marta* and *Cartagena* came to the rescue. During the night, they exchanged fire with the Krupp gun. The *Cartagena* was hit before the Peruvians again withdrew to Puerto Arturo.[26]

PERU MOBILIZES

Finally, Peru began to deploy its superior navy. On April 1 the Peruvian cruiser *Almirante Grau* and two R-class submarines sailed, passing through the Panama Canal on May 3. Four days later Peru replied to an inquiry from the advisory committee of the League of Nations that the warships were bound for the upper Amazon. On May 8 the warships reached Willemstad, Curaçao, took on supplies, then sailed for Port of Spain, Trinidad, and Pará, Brazil, near the mouth of the Amazon River.[27]

To reinforce its defenses at the major river port of Iquitos, Peru ordered the old seagoing gunboat *Lima* and the old torpedo boat *Teniente Rodríguez* from Callao through the Panama Canal and up the Amazon River. Although these two warships were ill-suited to operate in a tropical, riverine environment, they could serve as floating batteries. The depth of the river at Iquitos (200 miles farther up the Amazon from Leticia) was sufficient to permit ocean-going merchantships to operate from the port. The *Almirante Guise* and the *Almirante Villar* were dispatched to the Caribbean to intercept the Colombian warships, a vigil that kept them there for two months, using Martinique and Trinidad as supply bases. Despite their efforts, the two Colombian destroyers arrived without incident.[28]

PERUVIAN PRESIDENT ASSASSINATED

In April 1933 President Luís Sánchez Cerro appointed Gen. Oscar Benavides, the victor at La Pedrera in 1911, as Commander-in-Chief of the Peruvian armed forces. On the thirtieth Sánchez Cerro was gunned down by an *Aprista* assassin as the President was leaving the San Beatriz racetrack where he had just reviewed 25,000 troops. Congress chose General Benavides to succeed to the presidency even though the selection of an active-duty member of the military was a violation of the 1933 Constitution.[29]

THE ADVANCE AGAINST PUERTO ARTURO

Back on the Putumayo River, the Colombian flotilla moved against Puerto Arturo, which it had bypassed. Puerto Arturo was defended by 630 men, possessing two old Krupp mountain guns and two old 37mm cannon. On May 4 Peruvian Corsairs unsuccessfully attacked the approaching Colombian flotilla. Three days later three Peruvian 0-38Ps again attempted to attack the Colombian flotilla and were intercepted by Colombian Hawks. One Peruvian plane was shot down and the others damaged. As both armed forces prepared for the battle, their governments accepted a cease-fire negotiated by the League of Nations which went into effect on May 24. A contingent representing the League occupied and administered Leticia for one year.[30]

OBSERVATIONS

International pressure to end the hostilities increased. Peru, finding itself in the short term at a military disadvantage, backed off its demand that the ownership of the Leticia Trapezium be reexamined. Facilitating the negotiation was the fact that the new Peruvian President was a close friend of the President-elect of Colombia, Alfonso López. On June 19, 1934, Leticia was transferred from a commission representing the League of Nations to Colombia. This was the first time that the League had assumed direct control of disputed territory and had involved itself in the affairs of the Western Hemisphere. The Protocol of Rio de Janeiro, signed on September 27, 1935, ended the disagreement.[31]

This was the first conflict in Latin America where air power played an important role. General Vázquez Cobo's plea to Colonel Boy as the Colombian flotilla approached Puerto Arturo, "For God's sake, don't leave me without air cover,"[32] captures its importance. Colombia began the conflict with 11 aircraft; acquired 55, and lost 6, all due to accidents. But it was Peru that took the lesson concerning air power to heart. As a consequence of the conflict, the Peruvian air force was reorganized with the help of a mission from Italy, modern aircraft purchased, and air bases constructed in the north, close to disputed territory with Ecuador. By the late 1930s Peru was possibly the second leading air power in Latin America, inferior only to Argentina.[33]

Much of Colombia's success was owed to German pilots who flew its aircraft and French sailors who manned its riverine flotilla. Nevertheless, these contributions would have been meaningless without the successful landings effected by the Colombian army.[34]

Peru's mobilization was far less effective than that of Colombia. Symptomatic of this, most of the Peruvian soldiers in the *selva* were short-term conscripts from the highlands who were poorly acclimated to the jungle environment. A secret report by Col. Víctor Ramos informed the Peruvian high command of the many shortcomings that had contributed to the defeat.[35]

Probably less than 200 individuals died in combat. Those who died from sanitation and disease-related problems probably numbered a thousand or so.[36]

CHAPTER 13

ECUADOR AND PERU, 1941, 1981, AND 1995

If there was any region in which boundaries were uncertain, doubtful, and almost
non-existent, it was the jungle.

—Historian Felix Denegri Luna

THE 1941 SPARK

Fighting broke out between Ecuador and Peru on July 5, 1941, at outposts near the Ecuadorian towns of Huaquillas and Chacras along the Zarumilla River. On the sixth, Peru began
large-scale operations which bogged down in a few days. Both contestants accused the other of
aggression.[1]

BACKGROUND

No Latin American border dispute is more complex and no two disputants further apart in
their interpretation of the historical events than Peru and Ecuador. The components that made
up colonial Ecuador—particularly the provinces of Quito, Maynas, Santa Fe, Jaén, and
Guayaquil—were transferred more than once between the Viceroyalties of Nueva Granada and
Peru. In 1534 Sebastián de Benalcázar, a lieutenant of Francisco Pizarro, founded the town of
Quito or San Francisco de Quito which became the seat of a governorship (*gobernación*). In
1562 the Spanish King Carlos I elevated Peru to the status of viceroyalty, and a year later Quito
was made an *audiencia*, subordinate to Peru. In 1717 Quito, along with the *audiencias* of Santa
Fe de Bogotá, Caracas, and Panama, became the new Viceroyalty of Nueva Granada. Six years
later this viceroyalty was dissolved, and Quito once again returned to the jurisdiction of Peru.
In 1739 the Viceroyalty of Nueva Granada was reinstated, and Quito was once again removed
from Peru. Ecuadorians argue that the *Cedula* of 1740 (only part of which has been found) designated the Tumbes River as the boundary between the Viceroyalties of Nueva Granada and
Peru.[2]

While Spain was administratively realigning its empire, the Portuguese were expanding
westward from the Atlantic Ocean. In an attempt to halt this incursion into what it perceived to
be its territory, Spain recognized that Portugal occupied substantial amounts of the Amazon
Basin by the Treaties of Madrid (1750) and San Ildefonso (1777) in hopes of protecting that
which remained.[3]

This strategy was not successful, and the Portuguese continued to penetrate up the Amazon River. In an attempt to militarily strengthen the Spanish hold in the *selva*, Col. Francisco de Requena,[4] the Spanish Commissioner of the Fourth Border Commission, recommended to the Crown that the provinces of Maynas and Quijos be transferred from the Viceroyalty of Nueva Granada to that of Peru. According to Peruvians, this was accomplished by the *Real Cédula* (Royal Order) of 1802. Ecuadorian authors argue that this *cédula* only gave Peru administrative authority over the religious missions and the responsibility for defense, but no territorial rights. In 1803 another royal *cédula* separated the province of Guayaquil from Nueva Granada and placed it under the jurisdiction of Lima, in part to improve the seaward defenses of the west coast of South America.[5]

The *Audiencia* of Quito unsuccessfully rebelled against Spain in 1809 and again in 1810 (see companion volume). In December 1819 the revolutionary Colombian Congress of Angostura unilaterally declared Quito (the future Ecuador) a part of Gran Colombia (the union of Colombia, Venezuela, and Ecuador). On October 9, 1820, the province of Guayaquil declared its independence from Spain and declared itself at liberty to unite with any nation of its choice. Gen. José de San Martín, then in Peru, dispatched Gen. Tomás Guido to persuade the Guayaquilans to join with Peru. They only conceded to place themselves under San Martín's protection. Simón Bolívar sent Gen. José Mires on a similar mission, and he received a similar answer.[6]

On May 21, 1821, revolutionary Gen. Antonio José de Sucre, a lieutenant of Simón Bolívar, disembarked at the port of Guayaquil with 650 Gran Colombian soldiers in order to aid the Ecuadorian Revolutionaries and to prepare Guayaquil for incorporation into Colombia. Ultimately, Sucre, aided by soldiers from San Martín's army, defeated the Royalists at the Battle of Pichincha on May 24, 1822, winning independence for Ecuador.

While Sucre and Santa Cruz were advancing from the southwest into the highlands of Ecuador, Bolívar was advancing overland from the northeast through Colombia. Bolívar entered Quito on June 16, 1822. There he wrote to San Martín explaining his decision to incorporate Ecuador into Gran Colombia. Bolívar then marched to Guayaquil, arriving on July 2. Two days later he declared the province in a state of anarchy and under the protection of Colombia. On July 26, 1822, Simón Bolívar and José de San Martín met in the port of Guayaquil. Their personalties and political philosophies were sufficiently different to cause San Martín to retire from public life and leave the final destruction of the Spanish Empire in South America to Simón Bolívar unchallenged by his presence (see companion volume).

Events in the province of Jaén paralleled those along the coast. This province had been made part of the *Audiencia* of Quito by the *Cédula Real* of 1563. On June 4, 1821, the province of Jaén, following a plebiscite among the influential *criollos*, declared its independence from Spain and sought to become part of Peru. Although Bolívar privately recognized the probable *de facto* loss of the province of Jaén to his confidants, he hoped to retain parts of Jaén—the territory of Quijos and parts of Maynas—for Gran Colombia.[7]

Publicly, Bolívar refused to recognize the *de facto* incorporation of the province of Jaén into Peru since the province had been part of the Viceroyalty of Nueva Granada to which Gran Colombia claimed to be heir. Following Bolívar's successful military campaign in Peru, the wars for independence, and his return to Gran Colombia, he sent Joaquín Mosquera to Peru in October 1825 as Gran Colombia's Minister Plenipotentiary with orders to negotiate boundaries based upon those that existed between the Viceroyalties of Nueva Granada and Peru in 1810, the principle of *Uti Possidetis* ("as ye possess, continue to possess"). If this were agreed to, the province of Quijos would revert to Gran Colombia. No agreement was reached. Peruvian politicians chaffed under the presence of the Gran Colombian garrison left behind in Peru following the wars for independence by Bolívar. They successfully intrigued for its peaceful removal, along with another Gran Colombian garrison stationed in Bolivia (see companion volume).[8]

A war ensued in 1828 between Gran Colombia and Peru, in which the latter was defeated. Peruvian President La Mar signed the Treaty of Girón (February 2, 1829) which agreed to the boundaries that existed between the Viceroyalties of Nueva Granada and Peru in 1809, and it established a commission to work out the details. Back in Lima, the new Peruvian President, Agustín Gamarra, rejected the terms, arguing that La Mar had signed the document under duress. However, on September 29, 1829, both nations signed the Treaty of Guayaquil in which Peru conceded much of the disputed territory, although the boundaries were not precisely defined. On August 11, 1830, the Protocol of Pedemonte-Mosquera delineated the boundaries in the *selva* between Gran Colombia and Peru as the banks of the Marañón or Amazon, the Macará, and the Tumbes Rivers. Gran Colombia would govern the territory on the left bank of the Marañón River and Peru on the right.[9] However, Peruvians questioned the authenticity of the document. On the date it was supposedly signed (August 11, 1830), Mosquera was at sea on his way home and Pedemonte was ill. The original document has never been found—only a copy—and no reference was made to the document prior to 1892. Additionally, Gran Colombia had already dissolved when Venezuela withdrew in April and Ecuador in May; the Gran Colombian negotiator, Mosquera, knew this. Also, the Peruvian Congress never ratified the agreement. Peru therefore, claimed that the agreement, if it ever existed, was invalid.[10]

The dispute continued to simmer. In 1840 Ecuador unsuccessfully raised the border dispute with Peru, attempting to take advantage of Peru's recent defeat at the hands of Chile in the War of the Confederation (see companion volume). On September 21, 1857, Ecuador attempted to use the disputed territory to pay a debt to British creditors. Peru protested and on October 26, 1858, blockaded Ecuadorian ports, which continued for more than a year. This contributed to the disintegration of the Ecuadorian political system which devolved into a state of near anarchy. A Peruvian 4,000-man expeditionary force carried in thirteen ships captured Guayaquil on November 21, 1859, without resistance. There, Peru signed the Treaty of Mapasingue on November 25, 1860, with the local *caudillo* Gen. Guillermo Franco. This document annulled the use of the disputed territory as payment to Ecuadorian creditors and restated the borders as established by the disputed *Real Cédula* of 1802. Once the Ecuadorian central government was reestablished, it denounced the treaty as illegal on the basis that General Franco possessed no authority to act for the central government.[11]

During the mid-1880s, both Peru and Ecuador attempted unsuccessfully to use disputed land in the *selva* to pay international debts, generating complaints from the injured party. In 1887 Ecuador and Peru asked the King of Spain to arbitrate the dispute; he never rendered a verdict. At the same time, the two nations began direct negotiations which resulted in the proposed García-Herrera Treaty. This was ratified by the Ecuadorian Congress but rejected by that of Peru.[12]

In 1901 Ecuador established outposts on the Napo and Aguarico Rivers in the disputed area, in part attempting to replace Jesuit missionaries who had been expelled from the country in 1896. When Peruvian troops, ravaged by illness, were withdrawn from the vicinity, Ecuadorian soldiers advanced down the Napo River as far as the trading post at Angosteros. In reaction, the Peruvian launch *Cahuapanas*, commanded by Midshipman Oscar Mavila, transported twenty soldiers commanded by Maj. Chávez Valdivia from the river port of Iquitos (612 mi NE of Lima) to the vicinity of Angosteros (172 mi NW of Iquitos). The soldiers were secretly landed below the Ecuadorian position. The launch then moved upriver opposite Angosteros. On July 26, 1903, shots were exchanged between the launch and the Ecuadorians. The Peruvians soldiers ashore surprised the Ecuadorians and drove them from Angosteros. The Ecuadorians' losses were two dead, three wounded, and five captured. One year later, on July 28, 1904, a 180-man Ecuadorian force, led by Lt. Col. Carlos A. Rivadeneira, surprised a Peruvian detachment commanded by Maj. Chávez Valdivia at Torres Causana, a trading post. In spite of the Ecuadorians' stealth, they were defeated, sustaining twenty deaths and numerous captives, including Rivadeneira.[13]

Once again the King of Spain was asked to arbitrate the dispute. The Spanish Consul of State recommended to the King that with minor exceptions the decision be based upon the Royal Cédula of 1802. This would give almost the entire disputed territory to Peru. When this secret leaked out, both sides prepared for war. At this point, the United States, Brazil, and Argentina offered to mediate, and this was accepted by both disputants. In November 1910 the King of Spain declared that he had insufficient information to make a decision. For the next three decades, Washington attempted to negotiate a solution. Finally, on September 28, 1938, Peru withdrew from the negotiations.[14]

An uneasy truce was maintained throughout the 1920s and 1930s. Then, in spite of their military inferiority, Ecuadorian field commanders pushed their positions forward. They argued that this was necessary to improve their defensive positions. In July 1939 Lt. Col. Segundo Ortíz occupied Noblecilla Island in the Zarumilla River without orders. When ordered to withdraw by the Ecuadorian General Staff, he initially refused. In May 1940 Ecuadorian troops occupied a forward position at Casitas and yet another at Meseta (also called Cerro del Caucho). These activities disrupted the *status quo* under a 1936 agreement as defined by Peru. As tensions continued to build, Ecuadorian officials attempted to mobilize the public, ordering all men between 18 and 35 years of age to report for training on January 12, 1941. Rather than a display of patriotism, the 20,000 citizens who gathered at Quito's football stadium errupted into an antigovernment riot. As a consequence of these events, Peruvian President Manuel Prado ordered the creation of the Northern Army Group (*Agrupamiento del Norte*—AN) and reinforced the Peruvian forces in the *selva* in January 1941.[15]

OPPOSING FORCES

Following the Leticia Conflict in 1932 (see chapter 12), Peru began a significant increase in the size of its army. The army grew from 8,000 men in 1933 to 9,318 in 1934; to 10,233 in 1936; to 13,452 in 1939; to 16,705 in 1940; and to 25,864 by 1941. By contrast, the Ecuadorian army numbered 4,000 men on July 20, 1941. Ecuadorian President Carlos Alberto Arroyo del Río, who had won a hotly disputed election on September 1, 1940, retained a significant portion of the army in Quito and other major towns in order to deal with potential unrest. At the same time, he strengthened the Federal Police (the *Carabineros*) at the expense of the army.[16]

Due to its improving economy, Peru was also able to both improve training and infrastructure and buy new weapons. Peru had had a French army mission in the country since 1896 with but brief interruption. Practically all Peruvian generals during their younger days had spent some time training in France. In 1937 President Oscar Benavides contracted Italian air force and police missions. Peru sent aviation cadets to train at the aviation academy at Caserta, Italy. The Italian air mission was ended in March 1940 and replaced by a U.S. naval air mission on July 31. In 1938 the President renewed the contract with a U.S. naval mission which had expired in 1933.[17]

In spite of the gathering of war clouds throughout the industrial world during the 1930s, Peru successfully purchased a small quantity of modern military hardware. Among the most important acquisitions were 24 LTP Czech-made light tanks and 26 Italian Caproni Ca 135 bombers. Additionally, Peru improved its roads, barracks, and airfields along its norther border with Ecuador during the 1930s.[18] Although Ecuador made some post-World War I purchases following the advice of its Italian mission, these were not particularly useful. Also, Ecuador reduced its military budget by ten percent in 1941.[19]

The Ecuadorians were clearly aware of their material shortcomings. On December 23, 1940, Chancellor Julio Tobar Donoso reported to the Council of State:

> Peru, over the last few days, has accumulated on the southern border the following elements . . . : sixty planes at the Talara base and a cruiser, and destroyer, and several smaller vessels at Puerto Pizarro. Peru also has motorized forces and even parachutists. . . . In contrast . . . in material aspects there is absolute and humiliating inequality.[20]

OPENING STRATEGIES

The international situation precluded that the United States would endeavor to end any conflict as soon as possible through diplomatic means only. In July of 1941, the Third Reich's *Panzer* divisions were rolling toward Moscow, the Japanese were defeating the Chinese in Asia, and the neutral United States was frantically rearming. A conflict in the Americas would be a most unwelcome distraction for the United States. Peru accurately perceived this and knew that their best opportunity consisted of striking decisively, occupying the disputed territory, seizing undisputed lands as a negotiating tool, and then waiting for the pressure from Washington to freeze the situation.[21]

On March 7, 1941, the War Staff (*Estado Mayor de Guerra*) of the Peruvian army ordered the Northern Army Group to expel the Ecuadorians from Casitas, Cerro del Caucho, and other sites; plus the Division of the *Selva* (V Division) was charged to defend Peru's claims in Amazonia.[22] Brig. Gen. Eloy Ureta,[23] who commanded the Northern Army Group, did not confine himself to the objectives in the orders. He wrote:

> In case of an offensive reaction by the enemy [to his capturing Casitas and other sites as ordered] he [the Ecuadorians] should be pushed out of Peruvian territory and, if circumstances are favorable, he [the Ecuadorians] should be pursued into his own territory, in order to reach and hold bases of strategic value which would facilitate future operations.[24]

Given the fact that the Peruvian President was the son of President Mariano Ignacio Prado, who had fled the country during the War of the Pacific in 1879–83 (see companion volume), it should not be surprising that Manuel Prado did not restrain Ureta's liberal interpretation of his orders. Also, Ureta threatened to march south against his own government if not allowed to march north.[25]

Figure 19. The Ecuador-Peru War (1941). Mariscal del Peru Eloy Ureta, a Peruvian leader (general).
Ureta planned and executed Peru's successful campaign. He graduated from the Chorrillos Military
School for Officers in 1913 and received additional training in France and Italy during the 1920s
and 1930s. The sword and marshal's baton shown in the painting are in the Collection of Arms in
the Museum of Gold in Lima. *Courtesy Eloy A. Ureta y Ureta, Spain.*

By mid-1941 the Northern Army Group was composed of two light divisions (each possessing three infantry battalions and some artillery), four independent infantry battalions, two
groups of artillery (one equipped with 75mm mountain guns and the other with one 105mm
gun), two cavalry regiments, a parachute company, a detachment of twelve LTP light tanks, and
a signal company. The Northern Army Group also directly controlled five English Fairey fighters, a squadron of Caproni bombers, and a squadron of single-engine Caproni transports plus a
small fleet of patrol launches. This force totaled 9,827 men.[26]

Col. Octavio Ochoa commanded the Ecuadorian forces along the Zarumilla frontier while
Col. Luis Rodríguez commanded the troops behind the frontier in El Oro Province. These two
commands were designated the Fifth Military Zone with its headquarters located in Zaruma.
Ochoa's and Rodríguez' forces were composed of two battalions of infantry, a police battalion,
an artillery group, a squadron of cavalry, an anti-aircraft battery, and a battalion of engineers.
These units totaled only some 2,000 men. In addition, two reserve infantry battalions were assigned to Loja; both units were merely skeleton forces. Most of these soldiers were used to
garrison towns. The commanders within the Fifth Military Zone had no aviation or riverine
forces at their disposal.[27]

The Amazonian or *selva* front spanned a distance of some 312 miles, from the Putumayo
River in the east to the Cenepa River in the west. When fighting began, the Peruvian Division
of the *Selva* was composed of 64 officers and 1,755 soldiers; by November it had increased to
189 officers and 3,722 soldiers. The Division was under the command of Brig. Gen. Antonio
Silva Santisteban. The troops manned 32 garrisons and 5 lookout posts. General Silva controlled five riverine gunboats and could call for air support. The 1,800-man Ecuadorian force
in the *selva* manned 35 garrisons but had neither aviation support nor armed riverine craft.[28]

THE ZARUMILLA CAMPAIGN

The Zarumilla River separated the Peruvians from the Ecuadorians; the river flows almost
due north as it approaches the Pacific Ocean. During July 1941 it was three feet deep and ford-
able. East of the river (the Ecuadorian side), the land was flat and covered with forests, which
became more dense to the south and east, and ultimately became jungle. Few roads penetrated
the region. Ecuador could supply the Zarumilla front via two routes. The most convenient was
to carry supplies by sea to Puerto Bolívar. A rail line began at the port and ran a few miles
westward to Machala, then twelve miles to Santa Rosa, and then six miles southwest to
Arenillas, where it ended. Alternatively, supplies could be brought by dirt road from Cuenca to
the eastern spur of the rail line at Pasaje. From there it could be carried through Machala to
Arenillas.[29]

Fighting began with serious skirmishes in early July during which the Peruvians employed
both artillery and fighter-bombers. On July 22 the Peruvian 1st Light Division seized Noblecilla
Island and crossed the Zarumilla River, attacking across a 19-mile-wide front. Apparently, the
force included twelve LTP light tanks.[30] The Peruvian navy blockaded the Jambeli Channel
which gave Puerto Bolívar access to the Pacific Ocean. On the twenty-third the Peruvian air
force lost a Northrop NA-50A fighter-bomber to ground fire due to the low operating ceiling
caused by poor flying weather. The tanks were employed in support of the infantry in World
War I fashion. Within two days the Peruvians overran the Ecuadorian outposts at Huaquillas,
Chacras, Quebrada Seca, and Rancho Chico. In large measure this success was due to the coordination of aerial bombardment and ground attacks. General Ureta wanted to isolate the Ecua-

dorian railhead at Arenillas which supplied the Zarumilla sector; this lay at the southern end of his advance. At the northern end of the advance, Peruvian troops penetrated seven miles eastward to the vicinity of Cayancas by the twenty-eighth. Colonel Rodríguez, in charge of Ecuadorian defenses in the Zarumilla sector, was unable to form a defensive line.[31]

THE PERUVIAN BLITZKRIEG

In the early morning of July 31, the Northern Army Group, using trucks to transport infantry, attacked the railhead at Arenillas. The Ecuadorian defenders, after a stout defense, retreated into the jungle. The Peruvians endeavored to follow them but they fell victim to ambush. At 11:45 A.M. Northrop fighter-bombers strafed and bombed the town of Santa Rosa as five Caproni Ca 111 transports landed at the town's airport and discharged Peruvian infantry. There was little resistance. Santa Rosa lay 32 miles northeast of the site where the Peruvian forces had crossed the Zarumilla River. At 3 P.M. Caproni transports landed on a dry lake bed and discharged infantry which captured Machala. The Peruvians sustained only one casualty in these operations.[32]

Next, three paratroopers dropped on Puerto Bolívar a few miles west of Machala at about 5:30 P.M., marking the first time in Latin America that paratroopers were employed in combat.[33] This success permitted naval troops to come ashore at that Pacific Ocean port unopposed. The capture of Machala closed Ecuadorian road and rail access to El Oro Province and the capture of Puerto Bolívar closed access by sea. The Ecuadorian defenders were stunned by the rapidity of the attacks, and Peru conquered almost the entire El Oro Province in only one day through the coordinated use of air, land, and sea power.[34]

WAR IN THE *SELVA*

A week after Peruvian forces crossed the Zarumilla River, General Silva launched attacks from Peruvian garrisons in the *selva* on August 1 against Ecuadorian garrisons. The rivers penetrated through Peru and into Ecuador like parallel fingers; they provided the most accessible avenues of advance. Land communications required cutting narrow paths which took enormous effort to keep clear. During the first week the Peruvians captured the settlements of Corrientes, Cuyaray, and Tarqui. For the most part the garrisons on both sides were left to their own devices to sustain themselves.[35]

On August 11, the most important fighting in the *selva* took place at the Ecuadorian post of Rocafuerte (243 mi NW of Iquitos) which the Peruvians captured. Only here did the numbers engaged by both belligerents reach company strength. The Peruvians continued to advance unopposed up the Pastaza River and captured Sihuín on August 16 and up the Morona River and captured Cashuime on September 6. By early September the Peruvians had occupied some 15,385 square miles of territory.[36]

By mid-August the Ecuadorian army had disintegrated. Both officers and men were deserting their posts in Guayaquil and elsewhere. Sporadic fighting continued throughout August and September. On October 2, 1941, the two nations signed a cease-fire in the Peruvian port of Talara which left Peru in control of the disputed lands plus the Ecuadorian province of El Oro but halted its advance against Guayaquil. By November the Ecuadorian army had increased on paper to 12,013 men, though it was hardly an effective fighting force.[37]

OBSERVATIONS CONCERNING 1941

Peru was victorious and Ecuador lost most of the disputed territory. The land lost equaled the size of Ecuador that remained. In addition, Ecuador lost access of the headwaters of the Amazon when it lost the land bordering the navigable part of the Marañón River.[38]

In January 1942 the third meeting of the foreign ministers of the American republics took place in Rio de Janeiro. On the twenty-ninth, the last day of the meeting, the Peruvian and Ecuadorian Chancellors, Dr. Alfredo Solf y Muro and Dr. Julio Tobar Donoso, respectively, plus the representatives of Argentina, Brazil, Chile, and the United States, signed the Peruvian-Ecuadorian Protocol of Peace, Friendship, and Limits. The Protocol of Rio de Janeiro confirmed Peruvian rights to the provinces of Tumbes, Jaén, and Maynas. Peru evacuated El Oro Province and recognized Ecuador's sovereignty to Quijos and its access to the Putumayo River.

Blitzkrieg had come to Latin America, admittedly on a miniscule scale. Ecuador had been completely defeated in one lightning blow. And although the great powers of the Western Hemisphere had interceded, they came too late to save Ecuador from a disastrous defeat.[39]

A factor contributing to Ecuador's defeat was its underestimation of Peru's soldiers. Ecuadorian Col. Francisco Urrutia reported to the nation's leaders just before the war:

> With all this [Peru's significant numerical superiority], I should affirm that Ecuador is superior to Peru in terms of race; the Ecuadorians have a warring nature, while the Peruvians are pacifists. Peruvian officers are good because regular contingents of young men study in military schools abroad. Consequently, the Peruvian General Staff is efficient and well-trained, but the troops are inferior to those of Ecuador.[40]

Peru's Northern Army Group sustained 84 dead (which included four aviators) and 72 wounded in combat.[41] To this must be added Peruvian losses in the *selva* plus Ecuadorian loses in the two areas of operations.

Eloy Ureta, then Peru's youngest general, became a national hero. He was promoted to division general and appointed inspector general of the army. Eighty officers who served under Ureta were also promoted.[42]

THE 1981 SPARK

On January 22, 1981, a Peruvian helicopter, flying over observation posts in the Condor mountains previously abandoned by the army, discovered soldiers flying the Ecuadorian flag. Attempting a second overflight, the Peruvian helicopter was hit by machine-gun fire. The following day a Peruvian helicopter made a second reconnaissance flight and was also fired on.[43]

BACKGROUND

The demarcation required under the 1942 protocol was never completed. In 1946 Ecuadorians discovered an inaccuracy in the geographical assumptions in the upper Cenepa Valley upon which the agreement was based and claimed that the protocol was not executable. In 1960 Ecuadorian President José María Velasco Ibarra declared the 1941 protocol as invalid. Ecuador unsuccessfully sought to have the dispute reviewed by one or another of the international forums. This left Ecuador in a difficult position. The only way to reopen the issue was through military action.[44]

OPPOSING SIDES

Peru retained over Ecuador its military superiority in all categories. In the combat area Peru possessed significant advantages in air power, both fixed-wing and helicopters. Each side employed no more than a few hundred men within the area of conflict.

OPENING STRATEGIES

Ecuador planned to occupy and fortify some advanced bases that Peru had abandoned. It would then announce a *fait accompli* and fight defensively if challenged. Peru's strategy was to regain the lost bases as rapidly as possible and to confine any fighting to the disputed area.

THE FIGHTING

On January 28, 1981, the Peruvians attacked the Ecuadorian-occupied outpost known as PV-22. Sixty-eight soldiers landed from helicopters about 300 yards from the outpost. Approaching the objective they discovered that they were outnumbered two-to-one. Peruvian MI-8 helicopters attacked the outpost with rockets and machine guns but were driven off by a quad .50 cal. machine gun and small arms fire. The 68-man force withdrew without being detected.[45] On the twenty-ninth, the Peruvians launched a second attempt against PV-22. Some 150 men landed from helicopters, scattered on a nearby river beach. The terrain prevented them from uniting so they withdrew. The following day a Peruvian helicopter attacked PV-22 with rockets and machine-gun fire. One of the rockets flipped the defenders' .50 cal machine gun over. Peruvian soldiers landed, and after a brief but intense fight the Ecuadorian soldiers hastily withdrew, leaving most of their equipment. On January 31 Peruvian President Belaúnde Terry visited the battle site. Shortly after his departure, two Ecuadorian Jaguar aircraft ineffectively bombed the outpost.

That same day, the Peruvians attacked Ecuadorian outpost PV-3. Six Mirage, an A-37B, an Antonov, and two MI-8 helicopters bombarded the outpost. Then three MI-8 and two Bell helicopters landed Peruvian troops south of the outpost. These soldiers captured PV-3 after a brief fight. The next day the Peruvians made a similar successful assault against PV-4.

Some two weeks later the Peruvians discovered three more Ecuadorian outposts. The Peruvians successfully attacked these on February 19 using similar tactics and captured the border hamlets of Paquicha, Mayaycu, and Macinaya.[46]

OBSERVATIONS CONCERNING 1981

Peru was the clear victor of the "Paquicha Incident." Air superiority determined that it held the initiative. Without helicopter support the Ecuadorians were forced to abandon much of their equipment, the capture of which proved to be a significant propaganda victory for the Peruvians. Casualties for both sides were about a dozen killed and twice that number wounded. The Peruvians lost one helicopter to ground fire. The 49-mile unmarked stretch of the border remained unresolved.

THE 1995 SPARK

Once again Ecuador initiated a confrontation near the anniversary of the 1942 Rio Protocol to draw attention to its renunciation of that document.[47]

BACKGROUND

Following the 1981 conflict, Peru increasingly had significant demands against its military resources. It had to maintain most of its heavy armor and aircraft plus thirty percent of its infantry near the border with Chile, a residue of the 1879–83 War of the Pacific (see companion volume). Although the Leftist guerrillas, *Sendero Lumioso*, sustained a crushing loss on September 12, 1992, with the capture of its messianic leader Abímeal Guzmán, these and other Leftist guerrillas still tied down many of the best-trained, mobile forces in the southern highlands. Also, some military assets were devoted to the fight against drug traffickers in the Upper Huallaga Valley and elsewhere. This left about forty percent of the army and a small percentage of Peru's aircraft near the frontier with Ecuador.[48]

Also, Peru's economy was near chaos having sustained a two million percent inflation rate between 1985 and 1990. The new Fujimori administration judged that Peru was in no position to fight a border war with anyone.[49]

Ecuador, on the other hand, perceived Peru to be its most important threat. But, as in 1941, a significant part of the Ecuadorian army was stationed near Quito, the capital, to deal with internal security. The Ecuadorian air force was divided equally among Guayaquil, Quito, and the northwestern littoral—the disputed area.[50]

Concerning morale, the advantage shifted to the Ecuadorians. The Peruvian military had been worn down by its fifteen-year fight with Leftist guerrillas. At one time the Peruvian navy even had to use its highly trained submariners for shore duty against the guerrillas. Frequently, Peruvian conscripts were sporadically paid and poorly armed and equipped.[51]

Access to the disputed jungle area, which was about the size of the District of Columbia, had improved little over the centuries. Few roads existed and many outposts were sustained by aircraft using airstrips hacked out of the jungle and helicopters.

OPPOSING SIDES

Peru retained significant numerical superiority which could be exploited given time. The Peruvian armed forces totaled 115,000 personnel compared to 57,000 for Ecuador. The Peruvians possessed 95 combat aircraft, 150 helicopters, and 70 transports, whereas the Ecuadorians had 57 combat aircraft, 95 helicopters, and 30 transports. The Peruvian navy outnumbered that of Ecuador at least three-to-one in almost all categories.[52]

OPENING STRATEGIES

Once again, Ecuador's strategy was to establish bases in the disputed territory and then defend the sites. It chose to establish these in a salient of the Cenepa River Valley (220 mi S of Quito and 590 mi N of Lima) which was surrounded on three sides by high ground of undisputed Ecuadorian territory. Peru, satisfied with the 1941 Protocol and not wanting to appear to be the aggressor, was forced to concede the initiative to Ecuador. Earlier clashes had demonstrated that the conflict could be limited to the disputed area and that seizing and holding terrain as soon as possible was important, for typically the arbitrators (Argentina, Brazil, Chile, and the United States) called for a cease-fire.[53]

THE FIGHTING

Opposing forces began shooting at each other in January 1995. On the twenty-sixth, helicopters on the opposing sides began firing on enemy positions. The Ecuadorians captured a Peruvian helopad. Retaliating, the Peruvians forced the Ecuadorians to abandon the position. The Ecuadorians avoided direct encounters and fought from ambush.[54]

The air war intensified. During the first two days, Ecuadorian French-built Mirage F1JE fighters, flying from the Taura Air Base six minutes' flying time from the disputed area, shot down two Peruvian Soviet-built Su-22 Fitter attack aircraft, while an Ecuadorian Israeli-built Kfir C.2 fighter shot down a U.S.-built A-37 attack aircraft. All three Peruvian aircraft were shot down with air-to-air missiles. On the twenty-ninth the Ecuadorians shot down an Mi-8T helicopter with a ground-to-air missile. Taking advantage of its local air superiority, Ecuadorian A-37Bs based at the Manta Air Base attacked Peruvian ground positions.[55]

Meanwhile, Peru assembled a 2,500-man force and on February 1 launched an offensive supported by Soviet-manufactured T-55 tanks at El Alto. Some 1,000 Ecuadorians, employing ambush and hit-and-run tactics, opposed the Peruvians. On February 14 the Peruvians shot down an A-37B with a surface-to-air missile. The Peruvians captured the outposts of Cueva de los Tayos and Base Sur. The United Nations brokered a cease-fire on the seventeenth, but it broke down. On February 22 the Peruvians attacked Tiwinza, which was strongly fortified. Both sides called in significant air support. The Ecuadorians, employing artillery mounted on surrounding hilltops, stubbornly defended Tiwinza.[56]

OBSERVATIONS CONCERNING 1995

On March 1 the United Nations brokered another cease-fire and this one held. Ecuador and Peru signed the Declaration of Itamaray on March 17, 1995. The declaration provided for a separation of the combatants, a demobilization by each side, the return of normal relations, and the initiation of substantive talks.[57]

Unlike earlier fights, Ecuador got the best of this one. The victory may be attributed to carefully choosing where to fight and improved tactics and logistics.[58]

Some 5,000 troops from both sides had been interjected into a disputed area the size of which was less than 60 square miles of jungle. During the nineteen days of fighting, the Ecuadorians lost about 100 personnel and the Peruvians about 400. The Peruvians also lost two Sukhoi SU-22 attack aircraft, a Canberra bomber, two Cessna A-37B light attack aircraft, two Mi-8 helicopters, and a third unidentified helicopter. The Ecuadorians lost one 1A1 Kfir fighter and one A-37B light strike aircraft. Most of the losses on both sides were caused by ground fire. Costs for the war were estimated at nearly one billion dollars.[59]

The prospect for a solution to the dispute had significantly improved by important shifts in positions by both sides. Ecuador announced its willingness to work within the framework of the 1942 Rio Protocol and Peru acknowledged that a territorial dispute did exist. Both nations are currently engaged in direct diplomacy concerning the issue.[60]

PART 8

CHAPTER 14

FORGING MODERN BRAZIL, 1922–32

What we attempted, principally, was to arouse the masses of the interior, shaking them from the apathy in which they were living, indifferent to the fate of the nation, hopeless of any remedy for their difficulties and sufferings.

—Luís Carlos Prestes

THE SPARK

The unexpected emergence of a group of junior officers known as the *"tenentes"* (lieutenants), who sought social, political, and economic reform, sparked uprisings against those who governed.

BACKGROUND

Brazil emerged from its Wars for Independence (1821–23) as an Empire which lasted until 1889. As the result of an almost bloodless coup d'etat, Brazil then became a republic which was controlled by an elite, an important element of which was the senior military officers. Republican Brazil of the early twentieth century was a confederation of states dominated by Minas Gerais and São Paulo. The economies of these two states dwarfed all others.[1]

OPPOSING SIDES

Brazil of the 1920s possessed many armed forces. The federal troops were the best armed and trained. The vast majority of the officers came from the Federal District, the northeast, or the south. Each state had two types of uniform police—a paramilitary force which was militarily trained, used the same small arms, and possessed the same ratings and ranks (up to colonel) as the federal army. These troops lived in barracks. In the interior, they were used as police and in the state capitals they were held in abeyance for use in case of political upheavals. The other police organization, although uniformed, was civilian and was used in the capitals and larger cities for daily police duties, such as traffic control and crime prevention and investigation. São Paulo possessed the largest of these paramilitary police forces. In 1932 it had 9,000 paramilitary police called the *Força Pública*. Other states with large paramilitary police were Minas Gerais (7,494 men), Federal District (5,248 men), Rio Grande do Sul (4,404 men), Pernambuco (2,415 men), and Bahia (2,276 men). The remaining states each possessed less than 2,000 paramilitary police. Also some of the wealthier ranchers, miners, farmers and politicians possessed small but loyal private forces for their own protection and to implement their will.

OPENING STRATEGIES

The traditional strategy for both loyalists and rebels alike was to seize the opponent's capital; if successful, this almost always resulted in a capitulation. Beginning in 1924 the leader of the "*tenentes*" by acclamation, Luís Prestes[2], professed a new dimension to the strategy for seizing power. Finding that his forces were inadequate to capture the capital, he argued "war in Brazil whatever be the terrain, is a war of movement. The war of position is more convenient for the government, which has munitions factories, money factories, and enough illiterates to throw against our machine guns."[3]

THE "TENENTE" REBELLION 1922

Former president Marshal Hermes Rodrigues da Fonseca (not to be confused with his uncle, former president Marshal Deodoro da Fonseca), now the head of the powerful Military Club,[4] led disgruntled army officers as he championed the presidential candidacy of former president Nilo Procópio Peçanha against the choice of President Epitácio da Silva Pessoa, Artur da Silva Bernardes. When Peçanha lost to Bernardes, Hemes da Fonseca demanded a recount and encouraged disloyalty among the officer corps. Finally on June 28, 1922 Hermes da Fonseca sent an inflammatory telegram to the military commander in the state of Pernambuco. President Pessoa ordered the Marshal reprimanded which he rejected! As a consequence, the President placed Hermes da Fonseca under arrest for 24 hours and ordered the Military Club closed for six months.[5]

During the early morning of July 5, a revolt erupted at the Igejinha fortress at Copacabana in the harbor of Rio de Janeiro; it had been instigated by those at the Military Club. Most other military bases failed to follow suit and by the following day only some 200 individuals at the fort still held out. On the sixth the huge 12-inch guns of the two Brazilian dreadnoughts drove the defenders from the fort. Some of the mutineers made a suicide stand on the beach; sixteen were killed and eighteen survived. As a result, the government declared a state of siege (martial law) in the federal district and state of Rio de Janeiro. Although the mutineers utterly failed in their immediate political objectives, their dedication to their cause catapulted them into national heroes. As a consequence of the rebellion, a thousand cadets were expelled from the Army School and many officers were posted to remote garrisons.[6]

THE "TENENTES" REBELLION OF 1924

On July 5, 1924, the second anniversary of the uprising in Rio, a group of officers, many of whom were lieutenants (*tenentes*), revolted in the city of São Paulo (230 mi SW of Rio de Janeiro). The original plan called for simultaneous rebellions in the states of São Paulo, Paraná, Santa Catarina, Rio Grande do Sul, Minas Gerais, and Mato Grosso. Because of poor communications and defections, only those in São Paulo acted. Led by retired Col. Isidoro Dias Lopes, they won the support of recently inducted army specialists and the São Paulo state police under the command of Maj. Miguel Costa. Within three days the 3,500 rebels forced the governor, Carlos de Campos, and those loyal to the federal government, mostly police and firemen, to evacuate the city.[7]

Lopes armed migrant workers, some of whom had had experience on the European battlefields of World War I. However, he would not create "peoples'" battalions, nor did he initiate guerrilla warfare as desired by the Anarchists and Communists. The rebels remained in control of the city for three weeks. When superior government forces approached, 3,000 rebels retreated westward on July 27 in good order to the state of Mato Grosso and then southward to Paraná. In February 1925 they made a successful stand at the Iguaçu Falls (740 mi SW of Rio de Janeiro). The 1,000 remaining rebels controlled a triangular area bordered by Argentina, Paraguay, and the Sierra do Medeiros.[8]

Sporadically, numerous other rebellions did occur, but these were uncoordinated and easily suppressed by the government with the exception of the one in the state of Rio Grande do Sul.[9] There, on October 28, a captain in charge of a construction section in a railroad engineering battalion, Luís Carlos Prestes, rebelled and was joined by some *gauchos* from the plains. During November Prestes fought skirmishes with federal forces which continually grew stronger. Outnumbered, Prestes marched 2,000 rebels northward through the backlands of Rio Grande do Sul to join with the São Paulo insurrectionists. In January 1925 Prestes was surrounded at Palmeira, Rio Grande do Sul. On the thirtieth he fought his way through the encirclement and retreated northward through Santa Catarina and into western Paraná. While this was transpiring, the rebel column from São Paulo suffered a serious defeat at Catanduvas (700 mi W of Rio de Janeiro) on March 25, 1925. Lopes, believing that the fight was lost, stepped down and Major Costa took command.[10]

Finally, Prestes and Costa met in April near the Iguaçu Falls. Costa took command of the 1,500 well-armed and well-mounted followers and Prestes became Chief of Staff. The force had a large number of camp followers and soon became know as "Prestes' Column." The command of the government's forces was entrusted to Gen. Candido Mariano da Silva Rondon, who had won notoriety as Theodore Roosevelt's guide during a hunting trip by the former president. He did not satisfy expectations.[11]

Back in the harbor of Rio de Janeiro, 1st Lt. Hercolino Cascardo[12] and seven second lieutenants, helped by sailors and civilians, seized the powerful dreadnought *São Paulo* on November 4, 1924. Steam was raised and the *São Paulo* menacingly circled her sister ship, the *Minas Gerais*. Frustrated because the mutiny did not spread, the rebels fired a six-pounder shot into the *Minas Gerais*, wounding one sailor, and then sailed out of the harbor, exchanging ineffective gunfire with the forts protecting the entrance. The mutineers, appreciating that most on board the *São Paulo* were at best reluctant supporters, sailed to Montevideo, Uruguay, where they obtained asylum.[13]

"THE LONG MARCH," 1925-27

Prestes escaped from Rondon by commandeering the riverboat *Bell* and crossing the Paraná River into Paraguay on April 26. Unopposed by the Paraguayans, he marched north and recrossed back into Brazil on May 3 into Mato Grosso at Ponta Porã. In early May Prestes fought an indecisive engagement at Catanduvas and then crossed into the state of Goiás ever marching northward. Finding inadequate support for his cause in the east and because his enemy was growing stronger, Prestes shifted his objective from capturing the capital of Rio de Janeiro to inspiring revolution in the backlands of Brazil. In July and August Prestes crossed the plains of Minas Gerais and then turned back into Goiás. This constant crossing of state borders allowed Prestes to shake off state troops who would not cross boundaries even when in hot pursuit due to strong federalist sensitivities.[14]

By December 1925 Prestes had led his column to the extreme northeast where he and 400 followers contracted malaria in the swamp lands of Paraíba. Additionally, the hoped-for uprisings never occurred so in January 1926 Prestes turned southward. The column crossed Paraíba and Pernambuco. In April he forded the São Francisco River into Bahia. There he ran into the private army of Horácio Mattos, a local "colonel."[15] Although poorly equipped, their knowledge of the terrain gave Mattos' men an advantage and their rate of march was equal to that of Prestes'. The column was constantly harrassed. By the beginning of July, Prestes reforded the São Francisco River and reentered Pernambuco. As the government showed no signs of clemency, Prestes turned westward and marched toward Bolivia, attempting to avoid all combat. His 600 men and women reached the Bolivian border town of Gaiba (975 mi WNW of Rio de Janeiro) on February 3.[16]

Between April 1925 and February 1927, Prestes had led his small band on a 14,000-mile trek throughout the interior of Brazil. His strategy evolved into one of constant movement in order to avoid being trapped by the superior numbers that hunted him. His pursuers had included federal troops, state police, and mercenaries. During the march Prestes burned debt records and tax lists and freed political prisoners.[17]

Although militarily defeated, Prestes and his men, like the "*tenentes*" of 1922, emerged as national heroes. They were admired for their dedication to their political, social, and economic principals, their aggressive strategy, and their fighting spirit.[18]

THE REVOLUTION OF 1930

Prior to 1930 the political "golden rule" of Brazil was that the "power-house" states of São Paulo and Minas Gerais alternately support each other's candidates for the presidency, guaranteeing their election. This unwritten agreement fell apart in 1930. Outgoing Paulista President Washington Luís Pereira de Souza gave his endorsement (tantamount to a guarantee of election since he controlled the counting of the votes) to fellow Paulista, Governor Júlio Prestes (no relation to Luís Carlos Prestes). The Governor of Minas Gerais, Antonio Carlos de Andrada, who had expected to be the next president, helped create an opposition coalition which selected the Governor of Rio Grande do Sul, Getúlio Dorneles Vargas, as its candidate. Júlio Prestes was declared the winner amid charges of widespread fraud.[19]

The "*tenentes*" became the most visible proponents for revolution and helped convince Vargas that the use of force was necessary. The true military leader of the revolution was Lt. Col. Pedro Aurélio de Góis Monteiro; he devised the strategy. The colonel had campaigned against Luís Carlos Prestes in 1927; he had become a Vargas supporter following his transfer to Rio Grande do Sul in 1930. Monteiro created an army composed of police and private forces belonging to ranchers. Although some regular army officers and units joined the movement, they were not heavily recruited nor did they do much of the fighting.[20]

Following months of preparations, the revolt began on October 3. Within forty-eight hours the rebels won control of the state of Rio Grande do Sul; most garrisons declared for the rebels without fighting. The next day, October 5, the majority of the federal troops in the neighboring state of Santa Catarina joined the rebellion. On the sixth the state of Paraná also declared for the cause. By now the rebel army had swelled to between twenty and thirty thousand men. Next, the rebels marched northward through Santa Catarina and Paraná. Finally, their path was blocked by federal forces near the town of Itararé (428 mi SW of Rio de Janeiro) in northern Paraná.[21]

In mid-October both sides prepared for a show-down at Itararé. The government readied barbed wire, machine guns, and artillery for the attempt to hold the town, which lay on the strategic north-south railway line. Bad weather interrupted preparations. Elsewhere, rebels in Minas Gerais seized control of that state, thus opening a second front. Rebel soldiers from Minas Gerais successfully invaded the states of Espírito Santo, Bahia, and Goiás. Further north, rebels in the states of Rio Grande do Norte and Recife seized their capitals.[22]

At this point outgoing President Júlio Prestes agreed to resign. Now, the old elite within the army attempted to preempt the rebels. On October 24 it surrounded the Presidential Palace, forced the president to vacate his office, and set up a three-man junta (*Junta Pacificadora*) as the chief executive. For ten days the junta and Vargas supporters argued over who would govern Brazil. Finally, as troops loyal to Vargas occupied the national capital, the junta had no choice but to accept Vargas as "interim" president.[23]

Vargas now forged a new army, retaining most of the old army, including the senior officers, and at the same time returning the "*tenentes*" to service, many of whom were rewarded with jumps in rank and important political assignments. Vargas proved particularly adept at defusing the tensions between the two groups.[24]

THE SÃO PAULO REVOLUTION OF 1932

Those in São Paulo were not pleased with their loss of power as a result of the Revolution of 1930; Washington Souza, a native son, had been ousted from the presidency. Also, Vargas worked to curb the independence of São Paulo. A military governor was appointed, political leaders jailed, and paramilitary forces disbanded. Many non-Paulistas and "*tenentes*" were appointed to important positions within the state.[25]

On July 9, 1932, the Paulista leadership, incorrectly believing it had the support of Minas Gerais and Rio Grande do Sul, proclaimed a revolution, professing as their goal a return to constitutional rule. The rebels, calling themselves "*Constitucionalistas*," continued to fly the national flag and named volunteer battalions after other states to emphasize the nonseparatist character of the rebellion.[26]

The *Constitucionalistas* immediately raised an army of 10,000 regular army troops and some 8,000 paramilitary police. In addition, some 180,000 untrained men volunteered for service. Also, these *Constitucionalistas* were able to scrap together an air squadron of six attack aircraft, one makeshift bomber, and a handful of miscellaneous civilian types. In spite of the fact that factories were hastily converted to the production of munitions, São Paulo lacked practically all the weapons and munitions of war.[27]

The federal army was composed of some 40,000 men and the navy approximately 7,000. The Brazilian army and navy possessed about thirty operational attack aircraft; the government immediately placed orders in the United States and Europe for more aircraft. The Brazilian navy possessed two dreadnoughts, two light cruisers, about ten modern destroyers and a collection of older ships. Collectively the government's forces were known as the "*Legalistas*."[28]

The *Constitucionalistas* seized control of the state of São Paul within twenty-four hours and took up defensive positions along the frontiers. The government acted immediately to isolate

São Paulo. The navy blockaded the coast and loyal forces assembled along the borders of São Paulo. The *Legalistas* attacked along three fronts. One force drove northward from the state of Paraná and two columns pushed southward from the states of Minas Gerais and Rio de Janeiro. In mid-July the *Legalistas*, approaching from the south, captured the fortified town of Itararé. Short of ammunition, the *Constitucionalistas* retreated toward their capital.

Throughout the fighting, both sides carried out frequent but indecisive air attacks. *Constitucionalista* aircraft attacked enemy ground forces and dropped leaflets over the federal capital, Rio de Janeiro. *Legalista* aircraft attacked Campo Domarte, an airfield on the outskirts of São Paulo, with little effect. On September 24 a rebel air squadron composed of two Curtiss O-1E "Falcons" and a Waco CSO, all armed with 30-pound bombs, attacked the blockading ships. At the very least, they hoped to distract the attention of the navy in order to permit the merchantship *Ruth* to run the blockade. The bombs missed their target and one Falcon was shot down.[29]

The end of the fighting came unexpectedly when the commander of the *Constitucionalista* forces, Gen. Bertoldo Klinger, asked for an armistice on September 29. The rebellion failed for numerous reasons. First, it began before the political alliances with other states had been forged, thus isolating São Paulo. Second, this allowed Vargas to paint the insurrection as a separatist movement. Third, the rebels did not wait for the delivery of arms they had purchased outside the country. As a consequence of the rebellion, thirty-eight civilians and forty military officers were exiled. Only those federal units assigned to São Paulo prior to the rebellion were used to garrison the city following its surrender.[30]

OBSERVATIONS

The "*tenentes*" had a profound influence on the political, social, and economic evolution of Brazil beginning in the 1920s. They were not a homogeneous group nor did they coalesce seeking collectively to impose their ideas upon the nation. Rather, they worked within various movements, principally that of Vargas, which they profoundly influenced and which significantly altered them. A major defection from their ranks was Luís Prestes who in 1931 became a Communist (see chapter 10).[31]

Many years later Prestes wrote about the futility of his strategy:

> I also defended the Column's march tactics, claiming that they presented opportunities for recruiting new fighters. This however, was not the case. The farmers sympathized with us for the simple reason that we were against the oppressors, they admired our heroism and devotion, but had no intention (with rare exceptions of some young people) of committing themselves to a struggle in whose success they could not believe.[32]

Concerning military tactics, Prestes concluded, "the tactics of swift marches, evasion as far as possible of contact with superior enemy forces, and surprise attacks aimed at demoralizing the enemy and capturing arms and ammunition, demonstrated that in Brazilian conditions it was possible to stage a protracted struggle."[33]

With the help of the *tenentes* Getulio Vargas forged a highly personalized dictatorship. Vargas prevented the development of a viable coalition against him as he won control over diverse elements of power within a confederated Brazil. The military was neutralized by winning over the most dynamic officers, including the *tenentes*, through influential assignments and promotions.

CHAPTER 15

THE PERUVIAN SENIOR MILITARY
VERSUS THE *APRISTAS*, 1930–68

It is this middle group [class] that is being pushed towards ruination by the process of imperialism. . . . This, then, is the abused class that will lead the revolution.
—Politician Victor Raúl Haya de la Torre

THE SPARK

On August 27, 1930, the charismatic Lt. Col. Luís Sánchez Cerro[1] overthrew President
Augusto Leguía in the "Revolution of Arequipa." His immediate motivation was to forestall the
implementation of a boundary treaty with Colombia and to prevent the newly created *Aprista*
Party from exploiting the issue to its advantage (see chapter 12). The dark-skinned Sánchez
Cerro, who was popular with the masses, soon found himself opposed by many, including the
old oligarchy on the political right and the *Aprista* Party on the left, both of which were suspi-
cious of his personal ambitions. When these elements failed to support his agenda, Sánchez
Cerro chose to go into voluntary exile in Europe.[2]

Due to popular demand, both Sánchez Cerro and the youthful activist Victor Raúl Haya de
la Torre,[3] founder of the *Aprista* Party, were permitted to return from exile and to compete in
the violently contested presidential election of October 1931. In Lima alone, twenty of Sánchez
Cerro's followers were gunned down. The results of the election were 49.1 percent for Sánchez
Cerro, 34.2 percent for Haya de la Torre, and the remainder scattered among minor candidates.
This bitterly fought election sparked a thirty-eight year struggle between the *Apristas* and the
senior Peruvian military.[4]

BACKGROUND

On May 24, 1924, while in exile in Mexico City, Haya de la Torre cofounded the worker-
based, populist party, the Popular Alliance of Revolutionary America (*Alizanza Popular
Revolucionaria Americana*—APRA), more commonly called in Peru the *Aprista* Party. It was
conceived to be a Latin America-wide, indigenous, anti-imperialist union. The *Aprista* Party
was formally established in Peru on September 20, 1930. Its objective was to redistribute
wealth in order to eliminate the sharp economic disparities within Peruvian Society.[5]

OPPOSING SIDES

Although its international following was modest, within Peru the *Apristas* rapidly became the single most important political party. *Apristas* were anti-imperialists who professed the political unity of "Indo-America," the control of foreign capital, the redistribution of wealth, agrarian reform, industrialization, and the internationalization of the Panama Canal. Initially, *Apristas*, including Haya de la Torre, were vehemently anti-United States. Principally their leaders came from the universities and labor movements and the rank and file of the working class, especially the sugar workers in the northwest. The members were concentrated in the cities of Trujillo in the northwest and to a lesser degree Lima in the central west.[6]

Initially, the *Apristas* could count on the support of the Civil Guard (*Guardia Civil*), the national police. President Augusto Leguía (1919–30) had enlarged the police, attempting to counterbalance the army. Also, some junior officers and senior enlisted men within the traditional armed services—the army and navy (the air force would be created in 1929)—increasingly sympathized with the *Apristas*.[7]

Opposed to the *Apristas* was the leadership of the Peruvian army. The army was preeminent among its sister services. In 1930 the Peruvian military drew its officers primarily from the upper class and conscripted its men from the poorer classes. During subsequent decades, the officers increasingly came from the middle class and some were even from the lower economic tiers. By the early 1940s, most officers were graduates of the Military Academy at Chorrillos (*Escuela Militar de Chorrillos*).[8]

OPENING STRATEGIES

The responsibility of the Peruvian military to safeguard the existing political system was unambiguously laid out in the Constitution of 1933, which stated that the purpose of the Armed Forces was to assure "compliance with the Constitution and the laws and the preservation of public order."[9] The strategy for implementing this responsibility had been time-tested, and that was to seize and control the capital; typically, the remainder of the nation acquiesced. Initially, the *Apristas*, in their quest for power, resorted to intimidation, subversion, and assassination.

INAUGURATION DAY

On December 8, 1931, the *Apristas* supported by the *Guardia Civil* executed a poorly coordinated rebellion in an attempt to prevent Sánchez Cerro's inauguration. On that day, Haya de la Torre declared before a mass meeting in Trujillo, "Companions, today begins for the *Apristas* a new chapter in the history of their party. The pages will be of glory or of shame. We will write them with blood or with mud."[10] This rebellion was easily suppressed by the army. Sánchez Cerro reacted immediately. He cut the size of the *Guardia Civil* and changed its leaders. He also changed the leadership within the navy. In late December the *Guardia Civil*, now loyal to Sánchez Cerro, seized *Aprista* headquarters in Trujillo, wounding some party members. In January 1932 the President forced through Congress a law giving him emergency powers.[11]

The *Aprista* delegates to the recently elected national Congress became obstructionists. Sánchez Cerro showed little patience with them. In February 1932 he ordered all twenty-three *Aprista* delegates arrested and expelled from Peru. Some sought asylum in Panama. Lt. Col. Gustavo Jiménez, Sánchez Cerro's chief protagonist within the army, was also deported to Chile. *Apristas* in turn orchestrated street violence throughout Lima.[12]

THE FAILED ASSASSINATION ATTEMPT

On March 6, 1932, an eighteen-year-old *Aprista* severely wounded President Sánchez Cerro in the Church of Miraflores. Haya de la Torre claimed that the man had separated himself from the party before the act so as not to violate the party's policy against violence. On May 6 Haya de la Torre was arrested. He used the trial to publicize his ideology. He was convicted and sentenced to a lengthy jail term.[13]

THE 1932 FLEET MUTINY

In the meantime, at 9:30 P.M. on May 7, 1932, the crew of the Peruvian cruiser *Coronel Bolognesi*, inspired by *Apristas*, mutinied in Callao Harbor (3 mi W of Lima). Apparently only the lowest grades supported the mutiny. The mutineers locked the officers in their cabins and then moved onto the cruiser's sister ship, the *Almirante Grau*, where they overpowered those on watch at about 11:30 that night. Soon after, the mutineers seized the destroyer *Teniente Rodríguez*.[14]

While the mutineers were occupied securing the *Almirante Grau*, a loyal sailor slipped down the anchor chain and swam to the submarine *R-3*, warning it of the uprising. In an attempt to gather more support for the mutiny, the mutineers sent emissaries to the submarines. The men were greeted and their leaders escorted below decks, expecting to read a manifesto to the crew. But the lights were turned out and loyal submariners arrested them. Then the submarine started to submerge, forcing those on deck to retreat to their boats.[15]

The sailor who had escaped from the *Almirante Grau* had been sent ashore to spread the alarm. Capt. Carlos Rotalbe, commander of the squadron, and Capt. Juan Althaus, his executive officer, gathered loyal sailors, police, and soldiers. They captured two of the leaders of the mutiny who had come ashore to coordinate their actions with a police sergeant who was also a conspirator. The two senior officers then embarked on a submarine and moved the flotilla to the San Lorenzo Island Naval Base, where the boats were armed with torpedoes and munitions. A command post was set up at the naval academy in Callao and the two were soon joined by the Minister of the Navy, Alfredo Benavides, and others.[16]

When news of the mutiny reached the presidential palace, the president's naval aid and former commander of the *Coronel Bolognesi*, Cmdr. Félix Vargas Prada, volunteered to go to Callao and negotiate with the mutineers. At about 1:30 in the morning, Vargas approached the cruiser in a longboat. He was met by rifle fire; one of his party was wounded and later died. Finally, at 3 A.M. the mutineers opened negotiations with the *Almirante Grau*'s executive officer, but these made no progress.[17]

At 2:30 that same morning, President Sánchez Cerro told the Minister of the Navy to order the rebels on the cruiser to surrender at 5:00 A.M. If they refused, aircraft and the submarine flotilla were to attack them. At 4:00 A.M. the *Coronel Bolognesi* began to raise steam. Responding, the government issued the following communiqué:

> Last night at 11 P.M., a mutiny broke out on board the cruisers *Grau* and *Bolognesi*. The movement is of a Communist character and surely forms part of a revolutionary social plan prepared for execution yesterday. Similar acts ought to be occurring throughout South America. The government was informed of this plan some five days ago in a telegraph received from Europe.[18]

The communiqué went on to describe the events of the mutiny and warned all others to remain loyal. The President declared a state of siege, claiming that "communists in the squadron had produced a mutiny that endangered the social order and peace of the republic."[19]

At 5:30 A.M. the government by radio ordered the mutineers to surrender unconditionally or the ships would be sunk. The *Almirante Grau* and the *Teniente Rodríguez* agreed but the *Coronel Bolognesi* refused. Shortly afterward, three planes dropped bombs near the rebellious ships. At about 7:30 in the morning the submarine *R-4*, Captain Rotalbe on board, opened fire with its deck gun. One shot passed through an oil tank on the *Coronel Bolognesi* and started a fire and a second shot hit her waterline, whereupon the mutineers surrendered. By 8:00 A.M. Sunday morning the mutiny was crushed.[20]

The trial of the 160 alleged mutineers began that same day at 3:00 in the afternoon! After a fifteen-hour trial which ended on May 11, eight sailors (one of whom was a minor) were condemned to death and shot, fifteen others received ten to fourteen years' imprisonment, and the remainder were exonerated. Although the court testimony showed that members of the cruisers' crews had had contact with *Apristas* during a recent visit to Balboa, Panamá, no direct tie to the Communist Party has ever been proven.[21]

THE TRUJILLO "MASSACRE"

At 2 A.M. on July 7, 1932, "masses" of *Apristas* (primarily sugar workers and students from the National College of San Juan) attacked the "O'Donovan" army garrison in the city of Trujillo (288 mi NNW of Lima). The garrison housed the 1st Artillery Regiment and a company of the 1st Infantry Regiment and contained significant quantities of arms and munitions. Following four hours of hard fighting, the *Apristas* captured the garrison, both sides having sustained significant casualties. Three hours later, the *Apristas* captured police headquarters. The captured government officials, civilian and military, were taken to the city jail where the common criminals were freed. Agustín Haya de la Torre, Raúl's brother, was named the Prefect of Trujillo by the *Apristas*. The rebellion spread into the communities surrounding Trujillo, including the port of Salaverry (9 mi SE of Trujillo).[22]

Reportedly Sánchez Cerro said, "I want to see the point of each bayonet red with the blood of *apristas*."[23] The government ordered the cruiser *Almirante Grau* from Callao to Salaverry. On board were two rifle companies and a machine gun section from the 7th Infantry Regiment, which were landed at Chimbote, a port south of Salaverry. The troops, marching by land and supported by the cruiser, recaptured Salaverry on the ninth. Next, the government soldiers marched toward Trujillo but met stiff resistance and fell back to Salaverry. Both sides lost lives and many of the undisciplined *Apristas* celebrated their victory by getting drunk.[24]

The government now ordered Col. Manuel Ruíz Bravo, the regional military commander, to retake Trujillo. He commanded the 7th Infantry Regiment, a machine-gun section, and various smaller units. In addition, Colonel Ruíz was supported by two squadrons of aircraft, one being attack planes stationed in the north and the other being seaplanes that had accompanied the cruiser *Almirante Grau* from Callao. Colonel Ruíz attacked from two directions. The government troops from Lima once again advanced northward from Salaverry while Ruíz' troops moved southward to Cajamarca (276 mi N of Lima). The government troops launched their attack in the early morning hours on July 10; it was preceded by an indiscriminate aerial bombing. The *Apristas* resisted house by house. Regardless, at one o'clock in the afternoon, the government troops captured the central plaza.[25]

Upon entering the city's jail, the army discovered that some fifty captive army and *Guardia Civil* personnel, both officers and conscripts, had been executed and that some of the bodies were also mutilated. The army retaliated by executing about 1,000 males which it guessed had participated in the fighting against them. Although other *Aprista*-sponsored rebellions occurred throughout the north, these all failed. The events at Trujillo elevated the animosity between the senior army officers and the *Apristas* into a blood feud.[26]

JIMÉNEZ RETURNS

Exiled Lieutenant Colonel Jiménez, allying himself with the *Apristas*, secretly returned to Peru and on March 11, 1933, declared a rebellion from the northern city of Cajamarca. Without firing a shot, he raised 300 men (some from the army regiment stationed in the city). They commandeered a train and steamed toward Pacasmayo. However, *Guardia Civil* troops loyal to the government destroyed the railroad bridge at Quebrada Honda, delaying their advance. During the early hours of the fourteenth, government troops defeated the rebels at Malabrigo (327 mi NW of Lima). Jiménez was among those who died. The anticipated *Aprista* support never materialized.[27]

SÁNCHEZ CERRO IS ASSASSINATED

During the following month, on April 30 President Sánchez Cerro was shot to death by a seventeen-year-old *Aprista* assassin. Oscar R. Benavides succeeded Sánchez Cerro. Those *Aprista* leaders still at liberty were jailed and some were tortured.[28]

Benavides soon moderated his policies and released Haya de la Torre and other *Aprista* leaders. They were even permitted to hold political rallies, and the universities, hot beds of the *Apristas*, were reopened. This rapprochement, however, was short-lived and the *Apristas*, arguing that the government had not lived up to its promise to hold Congressional elections, returned to violence. Once again, the party was outlawed and its leadership jailed. However, Haya de la Torre escaped capture and remained in hiding for over a decade.[29]

MIRÓ ASSASSINATED

On May 15, 1935, Antonio Miró Quesada, the director of the newspaper *El Comercio*, and his wife were assassinated by an *Aprista*. This act further enraged those opposed to the *Apristas*. The lenient sentence (twenty-five years in prison versus death) also set some of the extreme right against Benavides.[30]

VOIDING THE 1936 ELECTION

Four candidates ran for the presidency in 1936. Haya de la Torre was the standard-bearer for the *Apristas* although he remained in hiding. Anticipating that the elections would not be honestly conducted, *Aprista* leader Manuel Seoane convinced the Bolivian president, David Toro, to provide arms to be used in the overthrow of the Peruvian government. In turn, the *Apristas* would support Bolivia in its quest to gain the Pacific coast port of Arica from Chile. Benavides learned of the plot and forced Toro to recant the offer. On September 5 the Peruvian National Election Board banned Haya de la Torre from the election and barred the *Aprista* Party. The *Apristas* threw their support to Luís Antonio Eguiguren. When it appeared that he would win, Benavides suspended the election on October 21 and retained power. Late in the month, *Apristas* and air force personnel failed in an attempt to seize a Lima police barracks and the air force base at Ancón (21 mi NW of Lima). Benavides cracked down, imprisoning and exiling the most radical of those opposed to his policies.[31]

THE FAILED RODRÍGUEZ *COUP*

On February 19, 1939, General Antonio Rodríguez Ramírez, the Minister of Government and Police (*Ministerio de Gobierno y Policía*), attempted a coup with the support of the *Apristas*. Once again, the rebellious element within the military and the *Apristas* poorly coordinated their actions. Within six hours Rodríguez was shot dead by troops loyal to Benavides. The coup attempt collapsed; twenty-four military personnel were arrested, tried, and sentenced to prison terms. Benavides harassed the *Apristas* until they lost their effectiveness.[32]

In December 1939 civilian Manuel Prado, who was from a prominent banking family, was elected president and served until 1945. The senior military, held in high esteem because of its recent victory over Ecuador (see chapter 13), worked closely with this aristocratic administration. However, many junior officers and senior enlisted men sympathized with the *Aprista* movement.[33]

THE FIRST FAILED ANCÓN COUP

As the 1944 presidential election approached, some one hundred militant junior officers clandestinely organized the "Revolutionary Committee of Army Officers" (*Comité Revolucionaro de Oficiales del Ejército*—CROE). Its leader was Maj. Victor Villanueva. In early 1944 Villanueva, with the knowledge of Haya de la Torre, planned a coup. Villanueva feared that Prado would either cancel the election or impose the hero of the 1941 war with Ecuador, General Ureta. Although Villanueva was arrested in February 1944, the plotting continued. On March 18 Sgt. Claudio López Lavalle and some twelve noncommissioned officers and sergeants seized the air base at Ancón. The *Apristas*, at the last minute, backed out of the conspiracy and within a few hours the coup collapsed. Eighteen military personnel were court-martialed and others were transferred to remote posts. Haya de la Torre was not tried.[34]

President Prado's successor, José Luís Bustamante, an attorney and university professor from the middle class, won the 1944 election in large measure due to the support of the *Apristas*, and he developed a cordial relationship with the party. Initially, he saw in the party the solution to Peru's social problems and began laying the groundwork to permit an *Aprista* to succeed him. Among other steps, he allowed exiled *Apristas* to return to Peru, and permitted Haya de la Torre to come out of hiding. However, his policies did not go far enough to satisfy the *Apristas* and went too far for the military. As a consequence, the *Apristas*, who held the largest bloc in Congress (18 of 45 seats in the senate and 55 of 139 seats in the House of Deputies), worked to strip Bustamante of his power and renewed acts of violence.[35]

Also, the *Aprista*-dominated Congress directly challenged the authority of the military. In 1945 it passed an amnesty law which freed from jail and restored ranks to military officers (primarily *Apristas*) who had engaged in political activism. Major Villanueva was among those released. The CROE began recruiting new members, issuing manifestos, and developing tactics. The most violent members were the "*los Definistas*" (the Defenders). Many had participated in previous attacks against the government, served prison terms, and endured torture.[36]

In August 1945 the *Aprista*-dominated Congress had the remains of the executed 1932 mutineers exhumed and reinterred with honors in a Lima cemetery. Congress also passed legislation that increased the pay of the conscripts and junior officers while forcing some senior officers to retire. Also, the *Apristas* tried unsuccessfully to force the immediate retirement of 240 senior military officers. Some senior military officers began plotting Bustamante's removal because of his inability to control the *Apristas*.[37]

GRAÑA ASSASSINATED

On January 7, 1947, Francisco Graña Garland, the editor of *La Prensa*, was gunned down in Lima by *Apristas*. This newspaper had been very critical of *Aprista* policies and this assassination helped galvanize those opposed to the *Apristas*.[38]

At the opening of the 1947 Congress, senators and deputies opposed to the *Aprista* agenda refused to take their seats. This denied the Congress a quorum and forced the suspension of the session. Bustamante was now constitutionally empowered to govern by decree. Although the President was willing to discuss a compromise with the *Apristas*, his cabinet unanimously informed Bustamante on July 9, 1948, that it would resign if he allowed the Congress to meet.[39]

THE SECOND FAILED ANCÓN COUP

On February 6, 1948, Villanueva ordered the rebellion to begin at Ancón but the *Aprista* leadership (Haya de la Torre was absent on a lecture tour to the United States) countermanded the order. The uprising was suppressed before its potential magnitude was fully understood by the government. The event, nonetheless, continued to polarize the actors. The President chose a new, all-military, anti-*Aprista* cabinet. The *Definistas* became bolder. And, the *Aprista* leadership became more timid.[40]

A FAILED MILITARY COUP

The senior military plotted against the Bustamante government. During the night of July 4 the impetuous Lt. Col. Alfonso Llosa, commander of the garrison at Juliaca in southern Peru, prematurely declared rebellion against the government but failed to win the support of the garrison. General Odría was unable to quickly organize support for the uprising in Lima. By the afternoon of the sixth, the effort collapsed and the conspirators fled to Bolivia where they were given asylum. Senior military officers, including General Odría, were involved in the plot. However, the government took little action against these senior conspirators. Only Gen. Alejandro Villalobos, the commander of the armored division, was removed from command. General Odría was permitted to retire and others were reassigned. He reportedly declared, "I do not support revolutions, I start them. Llosa acted prematurely."[41]

Following his removal from the cabinet on February 27, 1947, Gen. José del Carmen Marín Arista,[42] a former Minister of War, approached Haya de la Torre with the proposal that if the *Aprista* leader would abort the party's efforts to subvert junior members of the armed forces and support a military coup, anticipated to be bloodless, that del Carmen Marín would permit the *Apristas* to take part in the elections which would follow. Apparently Haya de la Torre agreed, but del Carmen Marín failed to act expeditiously so Haya de la Torre did not reign in the *Definistas*.[43]

THE 1948 FLEET MUTINY

On Sunday, October 3, 1948, the *Definistas* surprised the *Aprista* leadership when these militants led a naval mutiny in Callao Harbor. At 1 A.M. Cmdr. Enrique Aguila Pardo and six sailors seized control of the cruiser *Almirante Grau* and confined its officers to their cabins. Mutineers then gained control of the frigates *Ferré*, *Palacios*, and *Villars* plus six small craft which composed the Division of Submarine Hunters. Mutineers ashore captured the Naval Academy at La Punta and the Naval Station on San Lorenzo Island.[44]

At 2 A.M. the *Almirante Grau* opened fire on the barracks of Infantry Battalion No. 39 with its 4-inch guns (the cruiser had no ammunition on board for the main battery of 6-inch guns) without knowing that the *Aprista* leadership had sent contradictory orders to its followers. As a result, the rebels failed to capture the Air Force Base at Las Palmas. More critically, the success of the plan depended upon large numbers of *Apristas* flooding the streets of Lima in order to block the movement of government reinforcements and to demonstrate widespread support of the mutiny. The *Apristas* did not turn out! Nevertheless, at 6 A.M. some 400 rebels, principally sailors and armed civilians, captured the fortification Real Felipe.[45]

In the meantime, the government rushed reinforcements to support Infantry Battalion No. 39 which was still under fire from the cruiser. At first light, government forces attacked the rebel-held *Real Felipe*. A unit of tanks drove off ships' launches which were attempting to land reinforcements for the rebels in the fortress. The fighting lasted for hours but the government prevailed and 250 defenders were captured at about 2:45 in the afternoon. Next, the government forces concentrated on the naval arsenal. Tanks advanced against the facility but the first two were destroyed by 90mm guns from the Coastal Artillery (*Defensa de Costa*). The government troops renewed their attack and by 8 P.M. controlled most of the arsenal. Soldiers from the Military Infantry School (*Escuela Militar de Infantería*) retook the Naval Academy at 3 P.M.[46]

Also at dawn on the third, Major Villanueva led an attack by *Definistas* and armed civilians against the Central Telephone Exchange of Lima in an attempt to support the mutineers. However, the *Aprista* leadership failed to mobilize its followers or to persuade General Marín and his conspirators to support the mutiny. The attack foundered.[47]

While these events were transpiring, the frigates had steamed out into Miraflores Bay where they were attacked by loyal aircraft. Those on board appreciated that the rebellion had failed and returned to Callao. The rebels on board the *Almirante Grau* learned of the surrender of the naval arsenal a little before nightfall. On the morning of the fourth, the mutinous sailors, who had gathered on board the *Palacios*, surrendered to their former captives. During the process, Commander Aguila Pardo was shot dead. The naval mutiny had been crushed.[48]

About 1,500 sailors and a few hundred civilians had participated in the mutiny. Some 250 of these individuals died and over 1,000 others were arrested. About sixty government troops were killed. The senior naval leadership was forced into retirement because of its ineffectiveness. The day after the mutiny Bustamante outlawed the *Aprista* Party, but most of its leadership eluded arrest and they continued to plot against the government. President Bustamante's inability to decisively eliminate the *Aprista* movement spurred the senior military to action.[49]

"THE RESTORATIVE REVOLUTION"

Within three weeks of the failed mutiny, on October 27, retired Gen. Manuel A. Odría[50] proclaimed a coup d'etat which was supported by the garrison at Arequipa (465 mi SE of Lima). Two days later, senior military officers met in Lima and they chose to support Odría over the President. The two most important votes against Bustamante were Marshal Ureta, the patriarch of the army, and Gen. Zenon Noriega, the commander of the 2nd Light Division which controlled Lima. The leaders of the armed forces ordered Bustamante to resign. He refused, and the President was put on a plane for Argentina. On October 30 Odría seized the presidency without firing a shot.[51]

Odría's most immediate problem was restoring control over and discipline within the military. Odría increased the pay of junior officers, purchased modern weapons, and, finally, created new educational institutions. The Center of Military Instruction (*Centro de Instrucción Militar*—CIMP) was established in 1949 and the Center for High Military Studies (*Centro de*

Altos Estudios Militares—CAEM) the following year. Those officers who reached the middle and upper grades (major through general) received additional training at these schools. The charter for CAEM professed that "national defense and social development are one and the same."[52] Therefore, students of this school were exposed to a broader interpretation of the military's role to include economic and social development than was found in the school's counterparts throughout Latin America.[53]

Odría prosecuted the *Aprista* Party. It (for a second time within two months) and the Communist Party were outlawed on November 21. He closed the *Aprista* national headquarters. Odría forced *Apristas* from influential positions in labor unions, universities, and secondary schools. By mid-November more than one thousand *Apristas* had been jailed and many more had fled the country. However, Odría failed to catch Haya de la Torre, who in January 1949 slipped from hiding into the Colombian Embassy. Odría encircled the embassy with a moat, barricades, and troops and Haya de la Torre was contained therein for five years! Colombia was forced to rent another facility from which to conduct routine business, leaving Haya de la Torre and one embassy official to inhabit the old building.[54]

Some 250 civilians and naval personnel were tried for their complicity in the failed naval mutiny. The civilians receiving the longest sentences were two members of the triumvirate to whom Haya de la Torre had temporarily empowered to lead the *Aprista* Party, Senator Cirilo Cornejo (who received five years in prison) and Congressional Deputy Luís Felipe de las Casas (who received six years). The third member of the triumvirate, Luís Negreiros, was killed in a shootout with Lima police. The *Apristas* went underground. Among the naval conspirators, a noncommissioned officer, Domingo Castañan Rivera, was convicted of murdering a superior officer and sentenced to death, and two others received life sentences. Other punishments ranged between one and fourteen years in prison.[55]

For the first two years, Odría ruled by decree. A "Military Board of Government" replaced the cabinet. Its members included General Noriega (who had refused to act against Odría) and Lt. Gen. Alfonso Llosa (who had led a failed revolt at Juliaca in July 1948). Numerous political uprisings occurred during Odría's six-year rule. In 1952 university students rioted. In February of the following year, Communists and other leftists rebelled in Arequipa.[56]

THE FAILED NORIEGA COUP

On August 10, 1954, at 2:30 in the morning, soldiers loyal to President Odría's closest military ally, Minister of War Noriega, seized the Central Telephone Exchange and Radio Magdellena in Lima. Rebellious soldiers from the 7th Artillery Unit positioned themselves in strategic sites throughout the city. There, the coup foundered and troops loyal to Odría retook the city. Thirteen army officers, many of them senior grade, were implicated. General Noriega was put on a navy destroyer the following day and deported to San Francisco, California. Noriega planned a second coup from exile but this was detected and the conspirators were arrested on December 19. Protests against Odría continued. In May and June 1955, the students at the University of San Marcos refused to attend classes.[57]

By late 1955 Odría relaxed his policies. Exiled *Apristas* (but not Haya de la Torre) were permitted to return. In 1956 Odría promised free elections for the presidency but few of his opponents believed him. On February 16, 1956, Gen. Marcial Merino Pereyra revolted at Iquitos (612 mi NE of Lima). Isolated in the Amazon *selva*, this fizzled. This was followed by a ninety-day boycott of the University of San Marcos.[58]

"LA CONVIVENCIA" ("LIVING TOGETHER")

Civilian Manuel Prado y Ugarteche won the June 16, 1956, presidential election with *Aprista* support. The party had agreed to back Prado in exchange for its legalization. Haya de la Torre, who was permitted to return to Peru in mid-1956, negotiated an agreement ("La Convivencia") with Prado whereby the *Aprista* Party agreed to moderate its ideology and to continue to support Prado in order to safeguard its right to run its own candidate in the June 1962 presidential election. Many young, radical members of the party perceived this to be a sellout of principals. Although there were some political disturbances during Prado's tenure, the military backed his government until its closing days.[59]

Not surprisingly, Haya de la Torre was the *Aprista* candidate in the 1962 election and was endorsed by President Prado. *Apristas* and supporters of the other major candidates frequently came to blows. The army had to use machine guns in Huancayo to restore order between *Apristas* and the followers of Fernando Belaúnde Terry and in Cuzco to separate *Apristas* and Communists. Haya de la Torre received the most votes in the presidential election, although that accomplishment was tainted by some degree of fraud. Haya de la Torre received 32.99 percent; former President Belaúnde 32.14 percent; former President Odría 28 percent; and the remainder was scattered among four other candidates. However, the Peruvian Constitution required that to be elected president the candidate must receive 33.3 percent of the vote. If no one received this percentage, Congress would choose the president.[60]

THE 1962 COUP

Beginning on June 28 the military issued a series of communiqués which challenged the honesty of the election and declared that Haya de la Torre must withdraw. Finally, on July 17 he did withdraw but asked his supporters to vote for former President (and retired General) Odría, who in earlier years had spilled *Aprista* blood! However, the senior military would also not permit Haya de la Torre to dictate who would become president—not even a former general! And an Odría presidency would have been a return to the old aristocracy and he was only the third most popular candidate. At 3:20 A.M. on July 18, the day that Congress was to vote for the president, Army Chief of Staff Gen. Ricardo Pérez Godoy sent tanks crashing through the gates at the Presidential Palace. The army arrested President Prado, who had but ten days remaining on his term, and he was exiled to Paris, France. No lives were lost in the coup and only minor street fighting took place. The *Aprista* leadership called a general strike but the membership did not respond. The United States and nine Latin American nations broke diplomatic relations with Peru.[61]

A four-man junta—Army Chief of Staff General Pérez, Air Force Cmdr. Pedro Vargas Prada, Army Gen. Nicolas Lindley López, and Vice Adm. Juan Francisco Torres Matos—imposed a state of siege although initially their policies were moderate. On July 24, 1961, General Pérez took the office of president; and the junta assumed all executive and legislative powers as outlined in the 1933 Constitution. The junta did announce that elections would be held in June 1963 and that none of the junta would be a candidate. Businessmen, church leaders, and the Supreme Court all endorsed the military action. President Pérez initiated some social and economic reforms. In January 1961 General Pérez cracked down on the political opposition, jailing many of its members. In March 1963 the military junta replaced Pérez with General Lindey due to internal dissension.[62]

As promised by the junta, elections were held on June 9, 1963. Belaúnde, who had the tacit endorsement of the military, received over 708,000 votes; Haya de la Torre 632,000, and Odría 463,000. Following the election, the *Apristas* joined forces with their old enemy Odría to block reform legislation put forward by Belaúnde's Popular Action Party (*Acción Popular*). This decision alienated some of the more of the liberal members of the party who now perceived the actions of the *Aprista* leadership as obstructionist. The more radical members formed the Communist-oriented APRA *Rebelde* and chose to follow the Fidel Castro model for acquiring power through guerrilla warfare (see chapter 29).[63]

Belaúnde's social and economic program proved disastrous. His party, the Popular Action (*Acción Popular*), lacked a majority in either house of Congress and Belaúnde's initiates were opposed by both the *Apristas* and Odría's followers. Belaúnde was forced to create six different cabinets and made 94 changes in their memberships. The president's inability to solve the crisis surrounding the negotiations with the American-owned International Petroleum Company concerning subsoil rights proved his undoing.[64]

THE 1968 COUP

Gen. Juan Velasco Alvardo,[65] Commander-in-Chief of the Army, began plotting against Belaúnde in June 1968. He positioned loyal followers in key commands such as the Lima Military District and the Lima Armored Division. At 2 A.M. on October 3, troops seized the capital in a bloodless coup. President Belaúnde was whisked away to exile in Buenos Aires, Argentina. The heads of the air force and navy, who had not been conspirators, were asked to support the coup. Air Force Lt. Gen. Alberto López Causillas agreed and was named Minister of Aviation. Vice Adm. Mario Castro de Mendoza refused and was replaced by Vice Adm. Raul Ríos Pardo de Zela. A few senior officers who did not support the coup were placed under house arrest. Less than three weeks after the coup, General López resigned from the cabinet; this was probably caused by Velasco promoting air force officers loyal to himself without consulting López.[66]

A junta composed of the commanders of the army, navy, and air force named General Velasco president and he formed a cabinet composed exclusively of senior military officers. Initially the populace protested the coup although their actions were disorganized. Students poured into the streets and *Apristas* denounced the military. On October 9 the Velasco government annulled the unpopular Act of Talara. By this act the International Petroleum Company (IPC) agreed to give up title to the oil-rich La Brea y Pariñas fields in exchange for the cancellation of the $144 million debt incurred through unpaid taxes. The Velasco government expropriated these properties. These actions won immediate spontaneous endorsement across a wide spectrum of the populace—unionists, businessmen, peasants, and even *Apristas*, including Haya de la Torre who was then in Europe.[67]

Soon the *Apristas* worked to separate their approval of the expropriation from any implicit endorsement of the military government. Returning to Peru on February 22, 1969, following an eleven-month absence, Haya de la Torre declared, "We have always been opposed to any kind of dictatorship, and we are calling now for free elections as soon as possible. We don't like the dictatorship of Communism or the dictatorship of the military. But we have to be flexible."[68] Ironically, the military government led by General Velasco implemented many political, social, and economic reforms that had long been championed by the *Aprista* Party.[69] The military was motivated by the fact that the old political, economic, and social structures of Peru prevented it from being able to deal with external threats. These reforms were so radical that Fidel Castro declared that it was as if the firemen (the military) had "started a fire to the firehouse [Peru]."[70]

In 1979 Haya de la Torre, at the age of seventy-nine, was elected president of the Constituent Assembly charged with writing a new constitution. This was largely an honorary post. He fell ill and died before the work was complete.

OBSERVATIONS

This conflict had pitted an old institution, the Peruvian senior officers, against a new institution, the *Aprista* Party. Although this was apparent, what was less oblivious was that following the 1948 fleet mutiny the senior military was transfiguring itself from the "enforcer" for the upper-class oligarchy into a political activist with its own political, social, and economic agendas. In large measure that transition was caused by the realization that if Peru did not become socially and economically modern, it would never be able to effectively deal with its national security threats, both internal and external. Therefore, the military was not the dinosaur many perceived it to be.[71]

Even Haya de la Torre recognized the change that had taken place in the Peruvian army. In a February 1969 interview he stated, "The officers who run the Peruvian army are middle-class people, and ours is a middle-class party. None of us can hate each other, in view of that."[72]

On the other hand, the *Aprista* Party lost its appeal to many within the working class between 1924 and 1968. As the economic reality of Peru had evolved from foreign subservience in the 1930s to a more symbiotic relationship in the 1960s, the party had not kept in touch.

Perhaps Haya de la Torre had the last word. As the President of the Constitutional Assembly, he helped craft the 1979 Constitution which, at least on paper, limited the military's responsibility "to guarantee independence, sovereignty and territorial integrity of the Republic" but makes no mention of "compliance with the Constitution and the laws and the preservation of public order" as did the Constitution of 1933.[73]

CHAPTER 16

THE ARGENTINE SENIOR MILITARY VERSUS *PERÓNISMO*, 1951-66

Thief or not, we want Perón.
— a ditty sung by *Perónistas*

THE SPARK

On September 16, 1955, Rear Adm. Isaac F. Rojas,[1] having broad support within the navy, and retired Gen. Eduardo Lonardi,[2] supported by some army officers in Córdoba, successfully overthrew the charismatic Juan Perón.[3]

BACKGROUND

By mid-1945 Juan Perón stood out from among the military junta that had ruled Argentina since 1943. Senior officers and wealthy landowners feared Perón's growing popularity among the working class and his ambition. As a consequence, Gen. Eduardo Avalos, commanding the *Campo de Mayo* Base (the nation's most important military base, 15 miles WNW of the center of Buenos Aires), forced Perón to resign as Vice President on October 9, 1945. Four days later Perón was sent to the island prison of Martín García and was placed under naval guard.

On October 17,[4] Evita Perón,[5] supported by Cipriano Reyes, a leader of the meat-packing workers' union, mobilized a mob in the southern suburbs of Buenos Aires. The press named its members the *descamisados* (shirtless ones), since many of the workers were naked to the waist. They marched on the *Plaza de Mayo*, the capital's central plaza, and demanded Perón's release. The government acceded to the mob, and Perón returned politically stronger than before his detainment. Within five months Perón was elected president by an overwhelming majority.[6]

Perón built a new political power base in Argentina. He courted the senior military, while at the same time attempting to reduce its influence. Perón increased officers' pay to the highest in the world. In 1948, for example, an Argentine lieutenant general earned $11,250 U.S. whereas his North American counterpart earned $8,800. All Argentine ranks between first lieutenant and lieutenant general earned more than their American equivalent. Perón purchased modern weapons and improved the military's facilities. He won the loyalty of the new air force by championing the research and development of a world-class jet fighter.[7]

To undermine the strength of the senior officers, Perón encouraged interservice rivalries. He is reported to have said, "So long as their surplus energies are used up in fighting one another, they won't have the strength to bother me much."[8] Perón increased the strength of the various national police forces to offset the power of the army. He courted the junior officers and senior enlisted men. Perón took the control of appointments to the military academy away from the senior officers and gave it to Congress, dominated by the *Peronista* Party. As early as July 1951, Perón began threatening the senior military that he would arm the *descamisados* should they misbehave. At the same time, Perón cultivated the labor movement by passing legislation favorable to workers, regardless of its long-term economic consequences on Argentina.[9]

OPPOSING FORCES

By the mid-1940s, the Argentine armed forces numbered some 200,000 men—100,000 in the army, 22,000 in the navy, 15,000 in the air force, and the remainder in national police forces. By 1945 military expenditures accounted for over half of the national budget. But within five years the Argentine economy staggered under the weight of Perón's spending sprees. This severely impacted military expenditures and began to undermine the military's loyalty to Perón. By the early 1950s perhaps a fifth of the army officer corps became increasingly skeptical concerning Perón's rule; two-fifths remained loyal; and the remainder were neutral. Perón's popularity within the air force waned slightly.[10]

The most persistent opposition to Perón came from naval officers, who initially stood almost alone in opposition during the early days of Perón's presidency. From his ascent to power, Perón's relationship with the navy was manifestly cool. Rarely did the President have a naval official sitting in the place of honor next to him at public gatherings, and seldom did the navy enthusiastically receive Perón at naval-sponsored events. Unlike the army where Perón could use the service's intelligence branch to report on the political loyalty of its members, the Naval Intelligence Service (*Servicio de Informaciones Navales*—SIN) was primarily oriented toward collecting external intelligence and therefore of little use to Perón.[11]

Civilians were also divided in their loyalty to Perón. Ardent unionists supported Perón. Their leadership had the potential to rally 100,000 followers, or more, in Buenos Aires on very short notice. Some influential civilians within Argentina became increasingly dissatisfied with Perón's rule. Most important among these were devout Roman Catholics. In 1954 Perón would campaign to undermine the influence of the Church. The struggle became increasingly bitter and violent. Retaliating, the Church would excommunicate Perón in June 1955.[12]

OPENING STRATEGIES

Both sides perceived control of the seat of government (the "Pink House"—*Casa Rosada*) and the personal safety of Juan Perón to be the keys to victory. Perón confided to close associates:

> In order to sustain myself in power, I need "insurance" of one million workers to obey me blindly and with whom I will be able to defend myself from whatever action by the military; and "reassurance" of one hundred thousand bayonets to impede excessive advances by the popular masses.[13]

Increasingly, some opposed to Perón saw his death as the only real measure of victory.

THE FAILED COUP OF SEPTEMBER 1951

The first serious attempt to overthrow Perón occurred on September 28. Gen. Benjamín Menéndez, commanding some 200 army troops, revolted at *Campo de Mayo*. He attempted to gain control over thirty Sherman tanks, but noncommissioned officers loyal to Perón thwarted his efforts. All Menéndez could muster was two tanks, three armored cars, and some cavalry. *Perónista* artillery stopped the rebels at El Palomar Air Force Base near Campo de Mayo. Cmdr. Vincente M. V. Baroja, commandant of the naval air unit at Punta Indio (60 mi SE of Buenos Aires), who supported Menéndez, ordered twenty naval planes to drop manifestos and "buzz" Buenos Aires in a show of support. However, the rebels were few and in disarray, plus the *Perónistas* were well organized and able to isolate the rebels within a day.[14]

As a result of this failed coup, Perón implemented the Special Law for the armed forces which empowered the President to transfer, promote, or retire any armed forces personnel at his discretion. Some 300 officers were imprisoned. Pensions were denied to the families of those imprisoned. The government asked for a death sentence for General Menéndez; instead, a military court condemned him to fifteen years in prison. Nine generals and thirty admirals were retired. And the *Prefectura* (the Argentine coast guard) was taken from naval control and placed under the Ministry of the Interior.[15]

THE FAILED COUP OF JUNE 1955

The second serious attempt to overthrow Perón occurred in June 1955 and was led by Rear Adm. Samuel Toranzo Calderón,[16] Chief of Staff of the Marine Corps. The conspirators included some army officers and opposition party leaders but lacked any support among senior army officers who commanded combat troops. The only notable exception was Brig. Gen. León Bengoa, who commanded the Third Infantry Division. The division's headquarters was in Paraná, Entre Ríos (358 mi NW of Buenos Aires). On June 14 Admiral Toranzo believed that the plot had been discovered and decided to act in spite of the lack of support from the army. The coup was scheduled for June 16, but Admiral Toranzo then changed his mind and decided to postpone the uprising.[17]

The aviators at the naval air base at Punta Indio, marines commanded by Cmdr. Juan C. Argerich, and Cmdr. Antonio H. Rivolta, a member of the navy's General Staff, never received word of the delay and carried out their operations as originally scheduled. On the evening of June 15, Rivolta informed his colleagues at the Non-Commissioned Officers School (*Escuela de Mecánica*) that the revolt would begin at ten o'clock the next morning. The plan called for the seizure of public broadcasting stations and the bombing of the *Casa Rosada* (government house) by naval aircraft. Those at the school were to commandeer transport and proceed with the troops—the naval students at the school—to the naval headquarters, which was only two blocks from the *Casa Rosada*. There they were to join forces with marines commanded by Commander Argerich. This combined force would move against the government house and take Perón prisoner if he were not killed by the air attack.[18]

At seven o'clock in the morning on June 16 the conspirators at the *Escuela de Mecánica* canceled daily classes, sent civilians home, and called naval personnel to general quarters. They then proceeded to commandeer local buses passing in front of the complex. The weather was foul and rainy. By ten o'clock no radio stations had been seized and no bombing had occurred. At this point the superintendent of the school, who was not one of the conspirators, reacted. He countermanded the orders given by the conspirators, put them under arrest, and tried to contact naval headquarters.

Perón reacted at 11 A.M.; he announced that he was going to the school to investigate. Instead, acting on the advice of his Army Minister, Gen. Franklin Lucero, he took refuge in the subbasement of army headquarters. A rebel force of Beechcraft AT-11 trainer/bombers and Douglas C-47 transports flew low over the center of Buenos Aires in hopes of intimidating the *Perónistas*, but the populace had expected to see a scheduled air show on this day, and the demonstration did not produce the desired effect. (The sixteenth of June was the date that naval aviation annually paid homage to "the Liberator," Gen. José de San Martín.) At 12:40 P.M. pandemonium broke loose. Naval aircraft belatedly bombed the *Casa Rosada* in spite of a ceiling of less than one hundred feet. Many of the bombs dropped did not explode because they were released from too low an altitude to permit their fuses to arm.[19]

The 4th Marine Battalion seized the naval headquarters and then moved against the *Casa Rosada*. En route they encountered army troops loyal to Perón and fighting broke out. Within a short time the loyal army troops were reinforced. As a consequence, the marines fell back to naval headquarters, a distance of four blocks. In the meantime, the pro-Perón General Confederation of Labor (*Confederación General del Trabajo*—CGT) called out the workers to oppose the navy. The opposing forces fought for three hours before the marines surrendered at 4 P.M.[20]

In the meantime, those servicing rebel aircraft at Punta Indio Naval Air Station, some sixty miles from Buenos Aires, found their location untenable as loyal army troops approached. Quickly improvising, at 3:15 P.M. a wave of naval aircraft landed marines at the Ezeiza airfield on the outskirts of Buenos Aires. They captured the field and naval transport aircraft airlifted aircraft-maintenance crews to the site. There, the detachment was fueling and arming aircraft within the hour. The air force base at Morón (12 mi SW of Buenos Aires) also fell to marine assault, allowing a rebel logistics detachment to begin servicing planes at that airfield as well. However, bad weather began closing in once again and limited the usefulness of naval aviation.[21]

A few retired officers and civilians finally seized a radio broadcasting station at around noon and broadcast a few revolutionary communiqués before being cut off. However, after the surrender of the marines at naval headquarters the rebellion ultimately collapsed, and by 6 P.M. most of the rebels had quit fighting. Many of the sixty-eight officers assigned to the Punta Indio Naval Air Station fled to Uruguay. Enraged *Perónistas* burned some of the oldest and richest Catholic churches in Buenos Aires.[22]

One hundred six officers were charged with conspiracy, eighty-one of whom were from the navy. The Perón-controlled press tried to reassure the populace that "the principle nucleus of the navy constituted by the High Seas Fleet and forces of the Naval Bases . . . as well as the Naval Academy . . . remain loyal to the government without exception."[23] In total, about a thousand casualties, mostly civilian, were sustained by the two sides. In fact, the fleet had been awaiting the successful completion of the first phase before joining the rebellion.[24]

The revolt failed principally because of poor coordination. Almost the entire burden of fighting fell on naval aviation and the marine corps, though modest support had come from army, air force, and the fleet. Junior officers had led the revolt; however, they found that many of the enlisted men would not follow orders without the involvement of admirals and captains. Senior officers either were pro-Perón, held positions of little use in the coup attempt, or were timid.

Rear Adm. Benjamín Gargiulo, director of the marines on the Naval Staff, learned of the coup a few hours before the attempt and did nothing to stop it. Rear Adm. Aníbal Osvaldo Olivieri, Minister of the Navy, had been taken to the naval hospital with chest pains on June 15. When the coup started, he returned to the navy building in an attempt to regain control of the navy. These two officers and Admiral Toranzo Calderón were arrested by army troops, and on the morning of the seventeenth were "advised" by the commanding officer of the troops occupying the navy building to commit suicide. Admiral Gargiulo did so.[25]

Following the failed coup, naval officers were singled out for punishment. Even though he had not been a conspirator, Admiral Olivieri accepted responsibility for everything done by his subordinates and received eighteen months of minimum-security imprisonment and destitution. Admiral Toranzo Calderón was sentenced to indefinite confinement and public degradation. Many other admirals and captains, although they had no connection with the event, were retired because Perón lacked confidence in them.[26]

Numerous officers of the lower rank received punishment, but many others implicated in the action were not indicted, possibly because General Lucero urged Perón to act in a conciliatory manner and Perón did not want to reveal the magnitude of the plot. In fact, the proceedings against the conspirators brought them together and gave them the opportunity to win new converts to their cause, primarily their defense counsels.[27]

Perón attempted to extract a heavy price from the navy for the June coup attempt. On June 19 the Perón government issued a decree, the purpose of which was to eliminate the navy's ability to militarily act against the government. Article 1 removed naval aviation and the marine corps from the Ministry of the Navy; Article 2 placed the dispersed units of these two bodies under the authority of various naval zone commanders; and Article 3 distributed the control of logistics activities to naval zone commanders. Instructions for the implementation of the new system were listed in Article 4. A Senate resolution on the same date gave Perón the power to promote or retire any military officer without his complying with established regulations.[28]

Additional steps were underway to render the navy impotent. All bomb fuses in naval custody were collected and dropped into the ocean, and *Perónistas* confiscated ordnance that had been gathered at Ezeiza Airfield during the revolt. Most naval aircraft were grounded and were being made inoperable. The marine corps was to be cut in half, from 5,000 men to 2,500 men. The ammunition used for training by the marine corps was closely guarded and issued sparingly.[29]

In order to intimidate the senior officers in the army who might be contemplating a coup, Perón once again threatened to create labor militias. However, he appreciated that such a move might make him the servant of labor and not its master.[30]

THE COUP OF SEPTEMBER 1955

The naval conspirators were not deterred. Rear Adm. Isaac F. Rojas, Director of the Naval Academy, emerged as the head of the anti-Perón naval forces; he had not taken part in the earlier conspiracies. The naval conspirators appreciated that they must have some participation by the army in order to prevent the perception that they were acting alone. They were able to establish contact with Gen. Pedro Aramburu,[31] the leader of but one group.[32]

Coincident with the navy's activity, high-ranking officers in the army were attempting to forge their own conspiracies against Perón. The most important leaders were Gen. Dalmiro Videla Balaguer, commander of Military Region No.4 (which encompassed the western provinces of La Rioja, Mendoza, San Juan, and San Luis); retired General Lonardi who was well known for his anti-Perón activities prior to the failed September 1951 coup; and Maj. Gen. Pedro Aramburu, the Director of the National War College.

General Videla acted first; on September 1 troops in Río Cuarto, Córdoba, pronounced against Perón. Ironically, the government refused to believe that this modest event had any real significance. General Lucero, Minister of War, proclaimed "those who suppose there is a conspiracy under way are completely mistaken."[33] However, this premature act convinced General Aramburu that any future action was doomed to failure, and he withdrew from participation.[34]

On September 14 retired General Lonardi surprised Videla with a visit and told him of his own plan to oust Perón. Terminally ill with cancer, Lonardi had begun planning the coup while a patient at the Buenos Aires military hospital. General Videla chose to subordinate his efforts to those of the senior Lonardi, provided that the retired general accept Videla's military and political strategies, to which Lonardi agreed.[35]

The rebels potentially controlled the entire navy, a few army units at Córdoba, and a few air force planes. The most important naval assets were forty naval AT-6 trainers, which could be used as attack aircraft, located at Comandante Espora Naval Air Base; the amphibious element of the marine corps which had not yet been reduced as planned by Perón; and the three 6-inch-gun cruisers and two 7.5-inch-gun cruisers in the fleet.

In the center of the country, the principal army units loyal to the rebellion (in major part) were the Infantry School (*Escuela de Infantería*), the Artillery School (*Escuela de Artillería*), and the Córdoba police. The rebels also controlled ten air force Gloster Meteor jets and three Avro Lincoln bombers at Córdoba Air Force Base (434 mi NW of Buenos Aires) and ten miscellaneous aircraft at El Plumerillo Air Force Base (600 mi W of Buenos Aires). Brig. Gen. León Bengoa, who commanded the 3rd Infantry Brigade located at Curuzú-Cuatiá in Corrientes Province (340 mi N of Buenos Aires), also supported the rebellion as did the Deputy Chief of the Army General Staff, Col. Eduardo Señorans.[36]

Since the *Perónistas* had seized much of the navy's munitions following the June coup attempt, the navy needed to rearm. Trusted junior officers were charged with the replacement of necessary hardware and munitions by whatever means necessary—stealing, bribing, or manufacturing. Ingenuity was the order of the day. Ordnance experts provided drawings for fuses and disseminated them to the various machine shops at Puerto Belgrano Naval Base for manufacture. The dental laboratory, manned after regular work hours by junior officers and their wives, was used to work over the small pieces with dental drills and to assemble the fuses one by one. By September 16 those working in the dental laboratory had reached a capacity of five hundred fuses a day. Bombs were rigged from torpedo warheads and depth charges, and naval air strength was reforged.

Practically the entire air force sided with Perón. On paper its combat strength was 28 four-engine, Avro Lincoln heavy bombers; 78 twin-engine Calquín I.Ae.24 medium bombers; and 90 single-seat, jet-propelled Gloster Meteor fighters. Perhaps as few as ten percent of these aircraft were in flying condition. The only totally loyal army units were those stationed around the city of Buenos Aires. The remainder of the army paid "lip-service" to Perón but, in fact, were not ready to commit to combat.

Both the conspirators and those supporting Perón accurately perceived that the capital was firmly controlled by Perón, due in large measure to the support organized labor gave him. General Videla's strategy (which General Lonardi had agreed to adopt) was to turn the city of

Córdoba into a fortress and defeat the *Perónista* forces sent against it. Admiral Rojas' strategy was to isolate Buenos Aires by seizing control of the sea lanes entering the port and threatening the port with a bombardment.

General Lucero, who planned Perón's strategy, wanted to swiftly attack the rebels in Córdoba while holding the fleet at bay by capturing the naval base at Puerto Belgrano and attacking the ships at sea with the loyal air force.

In September 1955 the Argentine navy's major fleet element, the High Seas Fleet, was scheduled to sail for its yearly exercise. On the fifteenth, Admiral Rojas had five senior captains present themselves to the fleet headquarters with fictitious orders, allegedly from Secretary of the Navy Luis J. Cornes. Ostensibly they were replacing officers of questionable loyalty; but after securing command, the new arrivals informed Vice Adm. Juan B. Basso, Commander-in-Chief, and Rear Adm. Nestor P. Gabrielli, Commander of Cruisers, that a rebellion was imminent and gave them fifteen minutes to state their position. Admiral Basso declared his loyalty to the constitutional process, Gabrielli remained loyal to President Perón, and both were placed under arrest. Other key Perón supporters then arrested were Vice Adm. Ignacio C. Chamorro, the commander of the Maritime Naval Zone, and Rear Adm. Hector W. Fidanza, the commandant of Puerto Belgrano. The ships' crews, when mustered and given the same choice, overwhelmingly gave their support to the rebellion. A similar farce was executed at Comandante Espora Air Station. Of approximately four thousand naval personnel asked to join the revolution, only ninety-three refused to do so. By the close of the day the rebels controlled key sea- and shore-based units.[37]

Meanwhile, at the Naval Academy, Admiral Rojas ordered third- and fourth-year cadets to fill out the crews of the destroyers *Cervantes* and *La Rioja* and get them ready for sea. The remainder of the cadets prepared to defend the academy; they were armed with rifles and supported by the 40mm guns from the corvettes *King* and *Murature*. The *King's* diesel engines were being repaired, so it could not get underway.

Early in the morning hours of September 16, Admiral Rojas proclaimed the revolt. At 8 A.M. the destroyers *Cervantes* and *La Rioja* sailed from Rio Santiago with orders to blockade access to the ports of La Plata, Buenos Aires, and the interior rivers. At about 10 A.M. air force Gloster Meteor aircraft loyal to Perón attacked the destroyers; these warships sustained numerous casualties and the *Cervantes* received engine damage. At about midday the commanding officers of the destroyers requested permission to retire to the mouth of the Plate River, owing to the air attacks. The *Cervantes* entered Montevideo, off-loaded her dead and wounded, and, as a consequence, was interned. Sister ship *La Rioja* avoided the same fate by transferring her casualties to tugs outside the harbor.[38]

Realizing that the Naval Academy could not be defended, Admiral Rojas and most of his supporters embarked on two personnel landing craft (*Buques Desembarco Infantería*) at 9 o'clock that evening. The next day, the seventeenth, he declared a blockade of Rio de la Plata and its tributaries but stopped short of declaring a total blockade. He was aware that, as yet, he did not have the ships to enforce it, an important consideration under international law. The cruisers *17 de Octubre* and *La Argentina* joined the Admiral's forces near the Pontón lighthouse at midday on Sunday the eighteenth, whereupon he declared a total blockade.

The *9 de Julio* was the only commissioned major unit not with the High Seas Fleet when the conspirators seized the fleet. At the time, the *9 de Julio* was having her turbines repaired at Puerto Belgrano Naval Base (380 mi SW of Buenos Aires). Her crew, when they heard the news of the revolt, worked around the clock to prepare her for sea. Forty-eight hours after the fleet had been commandeered, the *9 de Julio* sailed to join her sister units off Rio de la Plata. The quick action of the *9 de Julio*'s crew indicated the degree of solidarity within the navy. Even the naval attaché to Washington, Vice Adm. Jorge P. Ibarborde, acted on instructions from the rebels when he requested that the United States recognize a state of belligerency. The United States refused to do so.[39]

Also on September 16, General Lonardi declared against Perón. However, his staff was almost immediately captured due to the carelessness of the civilians involved in the plot. As planned, Lonardi's forces nevertheless won control of the army and air force units around Córdoba but only after some brief but fierce fighting. At Curuzú Cuatiá the conspirators failed to win over armored units. Army units loyal to Perón immediately advanced against these Lonardi supporters. On the eighteenth, General Lonardi radioed Admiral Rojas that his position in Córdoba was precarious and requested a demonstration of force by the navy.[40]

In the meantime, General Lucero dispatched army units against the Puerto Belgrano Naval Base. Artillery Regiment No. 2 approached from Azul, cavalry and artillery units from Neuquén, and Motorized Infantry Regiments 1 and 2 from Buenos Aires. However, they halted when attacked by naval aircraft, offering no more than symbolic resistance.[41]

While these events were transpiring, the rebels waged intensive propaganda campaigns over radio. The rebels wanted to convince the populace that the entire navy had revolted and that it had the support of substantial elements of the army and air force. The rebels also used the radio to convince workers to remain off the streets. On Saturday evening, September 17, the rebel radio said the 5th Infantry Regiment in Bahia Blanca (398 mi SW of Buenos Aires) had surrendered, and troops in Mendoza and San Luis had defected. The rebel radio demanded that Perón surrender by 6 A.M. Sunday, a deadline later postponed to noon; failure to comply would result in the bombardment of Buenos Aires. The radio described in full detail the capabilities of the fleet's guns, which was substantial. The government radio declared Buenos Aires an "open city" and requested that no bombardment be made. This implicit admission that the rebels could actually execute their threat contrasted with the boastful broadcasts the government had made earlier, declaring that only a small portion of the fleet was discontent and that the loyal air force could defend the city.

Weather conditions, which had helped foil the June attempt to oust Perón, now worked against the loyal air force. There was a thousand-foot ceiling and one mile or less visibility.

Monday at 7 A.M. the cruiser *9 de Julio*, escorted by two destroyers, bombarded the oil storage tanks near the submarine base at Mar del Plata, which the navy had been forced to evacuate earlier.[42] The first salvo of shells fell near the tank farm and the second hit the target. The frigates then landed a force of about 350 marines and sailors; they captured Mar del Plata after meeting only light resistance. The three warships then shifted fire to the antiaircraft school, which surrendered and joined the revolt after only a few rounds had been fired. Various ground forces coming under fire either surrendered or retreated. The ease with which the attack was accomplished lent credence to the navy's threat that it could bombard Buenos Aires at will. This would serve as the demonstration of strength that General Lonardi had requested.[43]

Finally, on September 19 General Lonardi was able to win control of Córdoba at about the same time that Juan Perón renounced the presidency of Argentina. Possibly contributing to his downfall was a lack of self-confidence following the death of his wife Evita. In a communiqué issued at 1 P.M., Gen. Franklin Lucero, the Minister of Defense, announced the resignation and stated that the government was in the hands of the military junta.[44]

Immediately afterward Admiral Rojas received a dispatch inviting the revolutionary chiefs to Buenos Aires to negotiate. The Admiral immediately responded: "Your invitation to travel to Buenos Aires is an imposition; the meeting will take place on board the flagship of the operational fleet, the cruiser *17 de Octubre*, Tuesday the twentieth, at 1700 hours."[45] The Admiral gave the military junta a few hours to respond favorably, which it did.

The junta delegates arrived at the appointed hour and, after an all-night session, tentatively agreed to the terms of Act No.1:

1. The President, Vice President, and cabinet will resign.
2. The Chief of the Revolution, Division General Eduardo A. Lonardi, will head a provisional government, Thursday, September 22, at 1200.
3. All necessary steps will be taken immediately to implement conditions 1 and 2.
4. All military units will be ordered immediately to return to their normal peacetime duties and status with the exception of those assigned to the Capital which will be evacuated before 1200 on the 22nd.

Figure 20. The Argentine Senior Military versus *Peronismo* (1951-63). The reading of "Action No. 1 the Capitulation" on board the cruiser *17 de Octobre,* flagship of the rebel fleet, at 8 P.M. on September 20, 1955, while docked at La Plata. Left to right are Lt. Gen. Emilio Forcher, Commander Alberto Tarelli (reading), Rear Adm. Isaac Rojas, Gen. Juan Jose Uranga, and Capt. Mario Robbio Pacheco. Ironically, the name of the cruiser—*17 de Octobre*—commemorated Perón's rise to power. In retribution, the navy renamed the warship the *General Belgrano*. The cruiser was sunk on May 2, 1982, by the British during the Malvinas War. *Courtesy Adm. Isaac Rojas.*

5. All military aircraft will be ordered immediately to fly to the Comandante Espora Naval
    Air Base and will remain at the orders of the Revolutionary Government.[46]

The members of the junta delegation stated that they were not empowered to accept the terms but had to report back to Buenos Aires. They departed.

At 8 A.M. on September 21, Admiral Rojas received a dispatch from head of the junta asking whether he would allow one or two tankers to enter Buenos Aires because the city was running out of oil.[47] He responded, "When you accept the terms of Act No. 1 signed yesterday, the blockade will be lifted and all the necessary ships may enter."[48] At 9:30 A.M. the Admiral received a dispatch accepting the terms.[49]

Perón, either informed of the terms or fearful of his fate, fled to the Paraguayan Embassy and thence to the Paraguayan gunboat *Paraguay*. On October 2 he sailed to Asunción and into exile. The coup, which became known as the "Liberating Revolution" [*Revolución Liberatadora*], had succeeded within six days! Perón now began seventeen years in exile while remaining Argentina's most dominant politician.[50]

On September 23 Gen. Eduardo Lonardi was sworn in as provisional president, and Rear Adm. Isaac F. Rojas as provisional vice president.[51] The naval air arm and the marine corps were returned to their former strengths. In Buenos Aires the navy's school for noncommissioned officers (*Escuela de Mecánica*), which had been closed for its part in the revolt of June 16, was reopened on its former site.[52]

The turbulent political era that Perón gave to Argentina in 1946 did not end with the coup of September 1955. The senior officers of the new government had had little opportunity to agree upon a political agenda prior to the rebellion due to the need to hide their activities from the surveillance of Perón's security forces. Now the rebel leaders discovered that they held very divergent views.

A special revolutionary advisory board recommended the retirement of 114 senior officers. These included 63 out of 86 generals and every admiral, except for Rojas. This allowed the victors to promote themselves and their followers. By early 1956 some 1,000 midlevel and junior officers plus large numbers of senior enlisted men were purged from the armed forces. Two factions began to coalesce among the recently promoted senior officers—those adamantly opposed to *Perónismo* and those willing to reach some compromise.[53]

THE BLOODLESS COUP OF NOVEMBER 1955

On November 13 a four-man junta of anti-*Perónistas* led by Maj. Gen. Pedro Eugenio Aramburu, Chief of the General Staff, forced terminally ill Lonardi to resign. The following day the pro-Perón General Confederation of Labor called a general strike for the fifteenth. Aramburu acted immediately. He seized CGT headquarters, arrested its leadership, and on November 30 dissolved the *Perónista* Party. Many of the labor leaders were jailed for as much as six months. Government decrees of December 23, 1955, and March 7, 1956, barred from office any civilian who had held office under Perón. Then on May 1, 1956, Aramburu abrogated Perón's 1949 constitution and reinstated the 1853 constitution.[54]

THE FAILED *PERÓNISTA* UPRISING OF JUNE 1956

On June 9 purged Generals Raúl Tanco and Juan José Valle led the *Perónistas* into rebellion. Mostly composed of senior enlisted men and unionists, they won control of the 7th Infantry headquarters in La Plata (35 mi S of Buenos Aires) and the sergeants school at *Campo de*

Mayo. In Buenos Aires the rebels intended to subvert the army's noncommissioned officers school and the barracks at Palermo. The unionists gathered at the city's arsenal waiting to be armed. Rebellion also broke out in Santa Rosa (350 mi WSW of Buenos Aires). In the absence of Aramburu, Admiral Rojas—the Vice President—used the naval aviation to bomb the rebels into submission. Aramburu declared martial law and 38 civilian and military rebels, including General Valle, were shot on June 11 and 12. These were the first twentieth-century Argentine executions for rebellion. Some 2,500 citizens were arrested and many were exiled to Patagonia.[55]

Soon Aramburu eliminated opposition to his rule from among the senior military. In November 1956 he removed Maj. Gen. Francisco Zerda, the Commander-in-Chief of the Army, and seventeen other generals. In March Rear Adm. Arturo Rial was arrested for criticizing those making economic decisions and forced to retire. Air force Commodore Ricardo Krause was also forced into retirement. Rial and Krause had been prominent leaders in the "Liberating Revolution."[56]

Aramburu continued to take strong measures against any potential opposition from either the political left or the right. In April the government arrested 300 members of the Communist Party. Then 119 former members of the legislature of the province of Buenos Aires were jailed. Ten generals were retired for protesting government actions. In May twenty-one more officers, including the Commander-in-Chief, Gen. Luis Bussetti, were dismissed for protesting the promotion of Gen. Víctor Jaime Majó to Army Minister. In July Perón announced that he would return if Aramburu were overthrown and on the seventh of that month Argentina severed relations with Venezuela when it refused to expel Perón. In September Aramburu arrested some 300 labor leaders. In early October the government imposed a state of siege which lasted for a month. To forestall a strike by petroleum workers, Aramburu temporarily conscripted them into the army.[57]

FRONDIZI'S GOVERNMENT

Amazingly, the February 23, 1958, presidential election was peaceful and fair. Political acrobat Professor Arturo Frondizi won by promising something to everyone. He promised the *Perónistas* a general amnesty, the return of confiscated property, and the restoration of political rights sometime in the future; Perón was sufficiently pleased to endorse Frondizi from exile. Frondizi won the backing of the senior military officers by promising that they had the right to approve the appointments of the ministers in charge of the armed services. He took office on May 1, 1958. At the inaugural parade the chiefs of the military services passed in review without saluting the new President, setting the tone for their relationship.[58]

Frondizi's first military challenge came from the navy. In July 1958 Adm. Arturo Rial orchestrated anti-Frondizi agitation within the navy and gave an inflammatory speech. Rial was placed under disciplinary arrest for eight days. The senior naval officers did not come to Rial's rescue and he was forced to retire.[59]

Next, air force officers refused to obey Air Force Minister Commodore Roberto Huerta. The reinstating of the controversial Commodore Krause on September 1 by the President sparked the uproar. The mutineers isolated Huerta by depriving him of access to the air force communications network. Finally, after a week of mounting insubordination, the President rescinded Krause's recall and replaced Huerta.[60]

In June 1959 rumors spread concerning a pact between Fondizi and Perón. Generals Raúl Poggi, Commander of the 3rd Army Division, and Florencio Yornet, Commander of the 3rd Motorized Division, both headquartered in Córdoba, championed a protest. The War Minister, Gen. Hector Solanas Pacheco, ordered their arrest. No one within the military would enforce the warrant and on June 22 the entire cabinet resigned.[61]

TORANZO MONTERO FACES DOWN THE PRESIDENT

Frondizi continued to struggle with severe economic difficulties and the increasingly rebellious senior army officers. Many of the officers openly opposed any reintegration of *Perónistas* into political life. In an attempt to restore discipline, Frondizi appointed retired Gen. Elbio Anaya as Army Minister. A traditionalist, he appointed the senior major general, Carlos Toranzo Montero,[62] as commander-in-chief. Toranzo Montero was the leader of the anti-*Perónistas*.

The two generals soon clashed over the assignments of subordinate officers. On September 2, 1959, Anaya removed Toranzo Montero as commander-in-chief. However, fourteen generals in Buenos Aires declared their support for Toranzo Montero and were immediately arrested. Encouraged by this show of loyalty, Toranzo Montero set up a rebel headquarters at the army's Non-commissioned Officers School in Buenos Aires. Armored units loyal to Frondizi rolled out of *Campo de Mayo* for the school in the center of the capital. The loyalty of the air force was split but the navy was solidly behind Toranzo Montero. The rebellious 4th Division in Córdoba mustered 10,000 troops and prepared to march to Toranzo Montero's rescue. Frondizi gave in to General Toranzo Montero in order to avoid fighting and Anaya, finding himself without presidential support, quit on September 5. General Toranzo Montero now assigned anti-*Perónistas* to important commands.[63]

While the *Perónistas* and *anti-Perónistas* struggled for dominance, the Communist Party overtly and covertly attempted to exploit their discord. On February 17, 1960, a bomb in Córdoba killed thirteen persons. On March 12 another bomb destroyed the house of an army intelligence officer, killing his daughter. As a consequence, the Argentine government ordered Nikolai Belous, Counselor of the Soviet Embassy, to leave Argentina on April 7. The next day Argentina declared four East-Bloc diplomats *personae non gratae*. At the end of the month, Frondizi closed all Communist Party offices and banned party activities. Frondizi gave control of the police and courts to the army. Some 500 suspects were arrested. However, two civilian courts in the province of Córdoba refused to comply. The provincial governor supported the civilian courts. On May 12 General Toranzo Montero accused the Governor of clandestinely supplying weapons to the *Perónistas* and the National Chamber of Deputies removed the Governor on June 11. In mid-August Frondizi announced that Communists and *Perónistas* would not be permitted to take part in the 1960 elections.

In October 1960 the relations between the President and the Commander-in-Chief of the army Toranzo Montero took a turn for the worse. Toranzo Montero proclaimed a doctrine of military vigilance over civilian rule and demanded that the President replace numerous senior politicians whom he declared were soft on *Perónismo*. In a radio address, Minister of War Gen. Rodolfo Larcher defended the President and accused Toranzo Montero of wanting to seize power. President Frondizi did not back his Minister of War and Larcher resigned. However, President Frondizi refused to accept it. In protest to Larcher's retention, eighteen senior officers resigned, forcing the Minister to submit another resignation which was accepted. On October 15 Frondizi made Gen. Rosendo Fraga, one of those who had resigned in protest, as the new minister of War.[64]

On November 10, 1960, *Perónistas* rebelled in Rosario (188 mi NW of Buenos Aires). The rebels captured the 11th Infantry's garrison but their attack on the arsenal failed. Ten were killed and 50 wounded. The leaders of the rebellion, *Perónista* Gen. Miguel Ángel Iñíguez, who had been expelled from the army in 1959, and labor leader Dante Viel, fled to Asunción, Paraguay.[65]

Finally in March 1961 President Frondizi was afforded the opportunity to remove Toranzo Montero. Argentina offered to mediate the United States-Cuban differences. Toranzo Montero, who opposed such a policy, was unable to muster support for a coup from among the senior military officers. As a consequence, he was forced to retire.[66]

THE MEETING WITH CHE

On August 18, 1961, Frondizi shocked Argentina's senior officers by secretly meeting with Cuba's Argentine-born, Minister of Finance, Ernesto Guevara in Buenos Aires. Che had been to the Inter-American Economic and Social Conference meeting in Punta del Este, Uruguay. The Argentine armed forces, led by the navy, reacted strongly to this meeting with a communist and accused Minister of Foreign Affairs Adolfo Mújica of having made the secret arrangements. The military forced Frondizi to give a national broadcast explaining his actions, to fire Mújica, and on February 8, 1962, to sever relations with Cuba.[67]

THE BLOODLESS COUP OF MARCH 1962

Labor strikes continued to plague Frondizi. Underestimating the strength of the *Perónistas*, Frondizi permitted them to participate in the congressional and provincial elections on March 18, 1962. *Perónistas* parties won 35 percent of the popular vote, far outdistancing the second highest total. This gave them control of ten provincial legislatures, nine governorships, and the right to 46 seats in the national Chamber of Duties, placing third. The military demanded that Frondizi nullify the election and carry out numerous political changes which he failed to achieve. On March 29 Gen. Raúl Poggi, Commander-in-Chief of the army, declared martial law; he arrested Frondizi and imprisoned him on the island of Martín García.[68]

GUIDO'S GOVERNMENT

In the confusion surrounding the fall of the Frondizi government, an officer faction favoring continued civilian rule supported the immediate swearing-in of Senate President José María Guido as the new Argentine president. This was in accordance with the 1853 Constitution. Guido's ascendancy was accomplished before a military junta could claim control. The anti-*Perónistas* were forced to accept the *fait accompli*.[69]

By now the army, the most powerful armed service, was split into two factions. The *Golpistas*, led by retired Gen. León Justo Bengoa, were moderates, having supported Lonardi, Frondizi, and now Guido. Their military power was centered in the *Campo de Mayo* garrison and among the cavalry (which included the armor and mechanized troops). The *Gorilas-democráticos*, led by retired General Toranzo Montero, were violently anti-Perón. Their military power was centered in the interior garrisons (particularly that at Córdoba) and the navy. Guido chose a hard-line position, setting aside the *Perónista*-won elections, and set October 27, 1963, as the date for national elections.[70]

The first confrontation between the *Golpistas* and the *Gorilas* occurred on Good Friday, April 20, 1962. Gen. Enrique Rauch, Commander of the Cavalry Corps, demanded the resignation of the anti-*Perónista* War Minister, Gen. Marino Carreras, and the Commander-in-Chief of the army, General Poggi. Poggi took control of the center of Buenos Aires and the *Golpistas* set up their headquarters at the Military Academy in *Campo de Mayo* (15 miles WNW of Buenos Aires). The *Golpistas* dispatched a tank column from *Campo de Mayo* against the positions held by troops loyal to Poggi. To avoid a bloody confrontation, President Guido agreed to most of Rauch's demands. At Rauch's suggestion, the President chose Gen. Juan Bautista Loza to become both the Minister of War and the Commander-in-Chief. No shots had been fired.[71]

The *Gorilas* struck back. On August 8, 1962, Gen. Federico Toranzo Montero, Carlos' younger brother and Commander of the 4th army Corps at Salta, demanded the resignation of Minister of War Loza. Failing to win support to arrest Toranzo, Loza resigned. Guido named another *Golpista*, retired Gen. Eduardo Señoráns, as Minister of War. Señoráns stated that he would arrest the younger Toranzo Montero but President Guido did not endorse such action. *Gorilas* prevented Señorans from entering the Ministry of War so he took the oath of office in the *Casa Rosada*. Both military factions rushed troops in the capital. President Guido proposed a truce with Toranzo Montero in a cabinet meeting, and as a consequence, Señorans resigned. The navy blocked the routes from *Campo de Mayo* on the outskirts of Buenos Aires, where the *Golpistas* had gathered, thus giving control of the capital to the *Gorilas*. Guido conceded to the *Gorilas* and named Gen. José Octavio Cornejo Saravia as Minister of War, Gen. Juan Carlos Lorio as Commander-in-Chief, and Gen. Bernardino Labayru as Chief of Staff of the army. Within days *Gorilas* began to fill key commands and many *Golpistas* were forced to retire.[72]

Col. Juan Francisco Guevara, the former Chief of Operations of the *Campo de Mayo* base, emerged as the elusive spokesman for the *Golpistas*, mysteriously appearing, granting interviews with the press, and then disappearing again. On September 18, 1962, the *Gorilas* attempted to replace the three *Golpistas* who commanded the troops at the *Campo de Mayo* base. *Gorila* Gen. Juan Onganía, who was without assignment for having criticized General Cornejo Saravia, declared himself the commander of the camp and the Cavalry Corps. His supporters seized the radio station at nearby Morón Air Base and issued a manifesto emphasizing professionalism, and began broadcasting demands.[73]

The *Golpistas* and *Gorilas* prepared for a showdown. Army units throughout the country began to choose sides; the *Golpistas* donned blue arm bands and the *Gorilas* red ones. On the twentieth, forty *Golpistas*' Sherman tanks broke out of *Campo de Mayo* and advanced on the capital, while rebel aircraft flew menacingly low over *Gorilas*' positions. That night Guido offered to resign to avert a civil war. The cabinet, including the military members, tendered their resignations. The next day Guido accepted these resignations and proposed a truce. The *Golpistas* agreed but the *Gorilas* did not; however, the leadership of the *Gorilas* was in disarray, having just submitted resignations. The air force intimidated the movement of *Gorilas* forces. However, the navy announced its support for the *Gorilas* during the night of September 21 but took no action. Skirmishes took place on the twenty-second. Fourteen were killed and 54 wounded. The *Golpistas* "rescued" President Guido from the *Gorilas*. Guido appointed General Onganía as Commander-in-Chief of the army and he placed *Golpistas* in key positions.[74]

As a consequence, the *Golpistas* issued Communiqué No. 150. This document declared,

> Our objective . . . is to maintain the existing executive power. . . . In the military field we
> seek the reestablishment of justice and discipline. . . . We believe, above all, that the nation
> should return as soon as possible to the full reign of the constitution. . . . We believe that the
> Armed Forces should not govern.[75]

The *Golpistas* immediately attempted to purge the army of the *Gorilas*. One hundred sixty five officers were required to retire—17 generals, 42 colonels, 64 lieutenant colonels, 32 majors, 8 captains, and 2 first lieutenants. Some 280 officers were detained and interrogated but soon released.[76]

THE FAILED COUP OF APRIL 1963

The key political question remained: Would Guido's government permit the participation of a *Perónista* party in the 1963 elections? Increasingly, the answer appeared to be, yes. On April 2, 1963, retired Admirals Isaac Rojas, Arturo Rial, and Carlos Sánchez Sañudo led naval personnel at several shore stations into revolt; the fleet, which was at sea, remained loyal. The rebels were supported by retired army Generals Benjamín Menéndez and Federico Toranzo Montero plus retired air force Commodore Osvaldo Lentino. Most army units around the capital remained loyal and opposed the rebels. After some skirmishes, the rebels boarded ships at Río Santiago Naval Base (36 miles SE of Buenos Aires) and retreated south for Puerto Belgrano.[77]

In the meantime, rebellious marines and sailors occupied a number of coastal ports. Naval aircraft from Punta Indio attacked the army base at Magdalena (60 mi SE of Buenos Aires). The air force retaliated on the third, attacking the rebel naval air base and destroying five aircraft on the ground. With the approach of the loyal 8th Tank Regiment, which had sustained casualties at the hands of the naval aircraft, the naval aviators flew off to Uruguay.

The active-duty naval leadership, which had been aware of the plot but not involved, realized the hopelessness of the fight and endeavored to salvage the situation. It would surrender the fleet and naval forces ashore, over which it now had control, provided that the victors (the army and the air force) agreed not to cut the navy's budget, naval aviation, or the marine corps. Some senior army and air force officers agreed. Apparently 23 men were killed and 87 wounded in the failed revolt. The government arrested 662 officers and 1,200 enlisted men; eventually all were released. All but two admirals were forced to retire and the size of the marine corps was reduced from 8,000 men to 2,500. This poorly led failed coup destroyed the navy's political influence which it had gained by its leading role in the "Liberating Revolution" in 1955.[78]

However, the navy's anti-Perón sentiment and a resurgence of *Gorilas* within the army were not lost upon Guido, who closed many political avenues for *Perónista* participation in the election process. As a consequence, once again from exile, Perón instructed his followers to cast blank ballots in the 1965 national elections. Out of some 600,000 voters, 18 percent did so. Although this was the second largest voting bloc, it was significantly less than the 25 percent who cast blank ballots in 1957. Nevertheless, the vote demonstrated that the *Perónistas* had not been absorbed into the body politic and remained a force with which to be reckoned. Arturo Illía with 25 percent of the popular vote won a plurality but had to strike compromises to acquire the necessary electoral votes to become president. He took office on October 12, 1963.[79]

ILLÍA'S GOVERNMENT

President Illía, a small-town physician from the interior of the country, almost immediately took sides in the *Golpistas-Gorilas* contest. He promoted mostly *Golpistas* to important command vacancies. In December 1964 Perón attempted to fly to Argentina but his airplane was turned back in Rio de Janeiro and he returned to Spain. Having promised to return that year, this was possibly a token attempt. In the March 1965 congressional elections, a combination of *Perónista* parties won 38 percent of the vote, the largest percent for the *Perónistas* since the 1951 elections. This worried the senior military officers and caused a rapprochment between the *Golpistas* and the *Gorilas*.[80]

THE BLOODLESS COUP OF JUNE 1966

By November 1965 an open breach developed between Illía and the senior military officers over the issue of how to deal with the *Perónistas* and the increasing urban violence. The Commander-in-Chief of the army, Gen. Juan Onganía, chose to retire and work behind the scenes to orchestrate Illía's overthrow. On June 27 the army arrested Gen. Carlos A. Caro, the Commander of the 2nd Army Corps, for having taken part in a political meeting in violation of army orders. The charge was probably contrived in order to place the 2nd Corps under the command of an officer committed to the conspiracy. The next day, the Commander-in-Chief of the army, Gen. Pascual Angel Pistarini, demanded the resignation of President Illía. Pistarini controlled all the major army commands in Buenos Aires except those at *Campo de Mayo* and had the backing of the air force and the navy. Illía complied. The heads of the three armed forces installed retired General Onganía as president (see chapter 31).[81]

OBSERVATIONS

Argentina's most controversial twentieth-century leader, Juan Perón, was overthrown by the navy, a small number of army officers, and some devout Catholics in 1955. Admiral Rojas and General Lonardi, each acting almost independently, had forged a loose coalition which successfully overthrew Juan Perón. Many army officers, who professed loyalty to the government, had lost confidence in Perón and showed little enthusiasm for defending his regime. The rebels won because of the leadership provided by the navy; it is difficult to conceive how General Videla's strategy could achieve success. Luck was also on the rebel's side as the *Perónista* air force was frequently grounded by bad weather.

All said and done, the navy was the heart of the "Liberating Revolution." Could it have succeeded without the uprising of the army units in Córdoba? Possibly not, but those in Córdoba were surely doomed to failure without the navy. An amphibious-capable marine corps and naval attack aircraft (fighters and bombers), combined with the age-old firepower of the fleet's guns, permitted the navy to successfully influence events ashore. To symbolize its victory, the navy renamed the *17 de Octubre* the *General Belgrano*. The name *17 de Octubre* had commemorated Perón's coming to power.[82]

Nevertheless, Juan Perón remained Argentina's most popular political figure throughout the late 1950s and into the 1970s. The senior military opposed to Perón were unable to permanently undermine his popularity and they always had to resort to extralegal means to prevent the *Perónistas* from winning significant political power or Perón from returning from exile. Opposition to *Perónismo* was the most important factor that caused the senior officers to attack civilian governance. For a few, personal ambition and interservice rivalry were more important.

Perón accelerated social discontent within Argentina. He gave the improvised working class a voice in the future of Argentina. True, Perón bought their loyalty at a cost that stagnated Argentina's economic development for decades. Nonetheless, he created a cohesion among the disadvantaged that would leave an indelible imprint on Argentine society.[83]

By the mid-1960s, subversion from the extreme left and right was emerging as Argentina's primary threat, complicating the senior officers' struggle against *Perónismo* (see chapter 31).

PART 9

ANOTHER EXTRAHEMISPHERIC WAR

CHAPTER 17

WORLD WAR II, BRAZIL AND MEXICO, 1942–45

Although this [the declaration of war] altered nothing in our existing relationships with Brazil, which had already taken part in hostile acts against us, it was undoubtedly a mistake to have driven Brazil to an official declaration.

—German Admiral Karl Donitz

THE SPARK

German U-boat attacks against Brazilian and Mexican shipping drove both nations to war. On August 14, 1942, Germany began a U-boat *blitzkrieg* against Brazilian coastal shipping. On that date the *U-507* sank the *Baependi* which was carrying pilgrims to the São Paulo Eucharistic Congress; 270 lives were lost. Also on the fourteenth, the *U-507* torpedoed the *Araraquara*, causing another 131 deaths. The following day this U-boat sank the *Anibal Benévolo*, killing 150 people including 120 soldiers. On the seventeenth, it sank the *Itagiba* and the *Arará* followed by the *Jacira* two days later. The *U-507*'s activities off northeastern Brazil accounted for over six hundred lives.[1] On August 21 Brazil declared war on Germany and Italy to take effect on the thirty-first.

Mexico was also driven to war by U-boat attacks. On April 11, 1942, the *U-552* torpedoed the U.S. flag tanker *Tamaulipas*, owned by a subsidiary of Petroleos Mexicanos, off Cape Hatteras. On May 13 the *U-564* torpedoed the tanker *Potrero del Llano* in the Florida Keys; fourteen people died. Seven days later, The *U-106* sank the tanker *Faja de Oro* in the Keys; ten died. On June 1 Mexico declared war on Germany, Italy, and Japan, making the state of war retroactive to May 22.

BACKGROUND

When global war began on September 1, 1939, for the second time within the century, the Western Hemisphere was politically divided. Argentina championed strict diplomatic neutrality, favoring neither Allies nor Axis, whereas the United States argued for a noncombatant position that favored the Allies. Many Latin American nations supported the position of the United States, principally Brazil, Uruguay, and the Caribbean nations.

Three weeks after the invasion of Poland, the United States called a foreign ministers' meeting. Held in Panama in September 1939, the U.S.-driven agenda included neutrality, protection of peace in the Western Hemisphere, and economic cooperation. The conference adopted a general declaration establishing a neutrality zone around all of North and South America, except for Canada, which was at war.

Following the fall of France, a second wartime meeting of American foreign ministers was held in Havana in July 1940. A primary concern for the United States was the status of American colonies belonging to European countries that had been occupied by Germany. Argentina led the opposition to the U.S. position, arguing that taking any action toward these colonies was provocative and threatened neutrality. Besides, if the matter of colonies were addressed, the goal should be to end colonialism in the Americas altogether, not to protect the *status quo*. The objective of Argentine diplomacy was to focus attention on the Malvinas (Falklands) dispute. The United States prevailed, and the conference issued the following statement: "An attack on one American state is considered as an attack on all American states."[2] The conference provided the diplomatic basis for bilateral defense commissions between the United States and most Latin American nations.[3]

Following the Japanese attack on Pearl Harbor, the United States requested a third foreign ministers' conference of Latin American nations. This was held at Petrópolis, a summer resort in the mountains near Rio de Janeiro. The United States sought the adoption of a resolution whereby all the American republics would break diplomatic relations with the Axis powers.[4]

The response of the American republics was divided geographically. Nine Central American and Caribbean nations—Costa Rica, Cuba, the Dominican Republic, Guatemala, Haiti, Honduras, Nicaragua, Panama, and El Salvador—had already declared war on the Axis powers, and three countries in the same region—Colombia, Mexico, and Venezuela—had severed diplomatic relations. The eleven remaining nations had proclaimed their status as nonbelligerents. At the conference, Chile asked for guarantees of economic and military aid from the United States as a condition for breaking relations, but agreement on terms could not be reached. Argentina held to her position of neutrality. Thus, by the end of the meeting all the Latin American republics except Argentina and Chile had broken diplomatic relations with the Axis powers.

BRAZIL GOES TO WAR

As World War II erupted in Europe, Brazil was in the middle of a revolution which was to transform the nation from a rural-agrarian society to the early stages of an industrialized nation. Brazil's traditional threats had been its Spanish-speaking neighbors and intervention by the industrial powers. Between 1935 and 1940, Brazil played American and German interests off against one another. By 1940 Brazil sided with the United States for pragmatic as well as idealistic reasons.[5]

Brazil's most important military asset was its strategic location. Jutting far into the Atlantic Ocean, the country lay just eighteen hundred nautical miles from the African coast. Due to the limited range of aircraft in 1941, most planes that flew across the Atlantic had to hop across using either the northern route via Iceland (which could not be used during the winter months) or the southern route via Brazil.[6] All ships transiting between the North and South Atlantic had to pass through these waters, and thus they were ideal hunting grounds for the U-boat. But for the Axis they were also a bottleneck, being the only practical route for blockade runners and raiders traveling to and from the South Atlantic, Indian, and Pacific Oceans.

Across the Atlantic from Brazil lay French West Africa, controlled by the Vichy government after the fall of France in May–June 1940. There, in the port of Dakar, were important French naval units, including the new but damaged battleship *Richelieu*, two light cruisers, four destroyers, three submarines, and some smaller warships.[7] Between September 23 and 25, 1940, Free French and British forces attempted unsuccessfully to capture the port by amphibious assault. This failure further increased Brazil's strategic importance.

Brazil's attitude toward the world conflict was not readily apparent. Brazilians greatly admired French culture, and the years of service performed by the U.S. naval mission since 1918 with but brief interruption had resulted in many friendships between North American and Brazilian officers.[8] But relations between Brazil and Great Britain were strained. As in World War I, Great Britain had commandeered warships under construction for Brazil in British yards. And British warships frequently violated the Pan American security zone, leading to diplomatic confrontations.[9] Germany violated the Brazilian neutrality, less frequently at first, in hopes of keeping the Latin American countries out of the war.[10]

If Brazil were to join the Allies, it would take courage. A prime concern, which had caused national leaders worry during World War I, was first- and second-generation immigrants from Axis countries living in Brazil. Their numbers had increased dramatically following World War I. Germany in particular was making a special effort to win the loyalty of these individuals in cultural clubs, in schools, and by covert means. Although fears of the possibility of a German invasion of Brazil in 1941 may seem incredible today, they did not appear unreasonable at that time.

When Brazil entered World War II, it was an "archipelago" which depended almost entirely on sea transportation. The major urban "islands" along the coast were not linked by adequate ground transportation; roads were scarce and of very poor quality. The railroads were export corridors which did not connect the cities, but rather linked the countryside with the major seaports. Most of the track was narrow-gauge, and train engines burned wood. Air France, the German Condor, and Italy's Lati Airlines controlled air traffic, internal and external. Additionally, these airlines controlled a number of radio transmitters in Brazil.[11] Brazil needed airlines and could not suppress the Axis activity without replacing them. Brazil made a secret agreement with the United States government and Airport Development Project, a subsidiary of Pan American Airlines, to displace the influential Axis companies, but this took time. On January 27, 1942, Brazil broke diplomatic relations with Germany after that nation declared war against the United States.

Between February and April, U-boats torpedoed five Brazilian merchantships, causing 109 deaths.[12] On May 16 the German high command issued orders that all armed ships belonging to South American nations, except those of Argentina and Chile, could be attacked without warning.[13] Two days later, off Cape São Roque, the Italian submarine *Barbarigo* torpedoed the Lloyd Brasileiro ship *Comandante Lira* and attacked her with gunfire. The U.S. cruiser *Omaha* picked up survivors from two lifeboats; the third lifeboat reached the coast. Two lives were lost. In retaliation the Brazilian Ministry of Aeronautics announced that Brazilian aircraft would attack any U-boat sighted.[14]

Following these incidents, Rear Adm. Jonas H. Ingram, U.S. Navy, brought to Brazilian waters elements of his Task Force 3, which consisted of four old cruisers and five destroyers. It patrolled a triangular area formed by Trinidad, Cape São Roque, and the Cape Verde Islands. Admiral Ingram developed a plan dividing responsibilities between the Brazilian and U.S. forces. The joint operations began before the end of April 1942.

In response to the announcement that Brazil's Air Force would attack U-boats on sight, and to an encounter between the armed merchantship *Goncalves Dias* and the *U-502* on May 24, Adolf Hitler ordered his submarine command to prepare a plan for a concentrated attack off the Brazilian coast. Initially he approved the resulting plan, but fear that the attack would drive not only Brazil but Argentina and Chile to war as well drove him to cancel it. He changed his mind again, and on June 29, U-boats were diverted from other areas to attack ships in Brazilian waters.[15] As in World War I, the German U-boat offensive drove Brazil to action. On August 21, 1942, Brazil declared war on Germany and Italy to take effect on the thirty-first.

BRAZIL'S FORCES

When Brazil entered the war, her armed forces possessed only a few modern weapons. The Brazilian army was very weak. In 1939 it numbered some 66,000 men and was organized into five infantry divisions. Although a number of programs had been initiated to modernize the ground forces, they were not followed through because of a shortage of resources. Brazil did not have an indigenous arms industry and suffered from a shortage of hard currency. Therefore, it had to find suppliers willing to barter arms for agricultural products and raw materials. Only Germany would enter into such an agreement. In 1938 Brazil sent a large military mission to Germany and placed a substantial order for arms with Krupp. Only three shiploads reached Brazil before the war interrupted the supply.[16]

An independent Brazilian air force had been carved out of the army and the navy in 1941. In that year the air force had 430 aircraft of 35 different types. Of these, 99 aircraft (of 15 types) were ex-navy and 331 machines (of 25 types) were ex-army. Prior to the 1941 amalgamation, the two services had only five types of aircraft in common.[17]

The Brazilian navy had few warships of value. The two battleships *São Paulo* and *Minas Gerais* were long out of their prime, their only real value being to function as harbor defense ships. The two light cruisers *Bahia* and *Rio Grande do Sul*, workhorses of the earlier world war, were thirty years old and "in reality little more than oversized destroyers and relatively slow."[18] The submarines *Tupi*, *Tamoio*, and *Timbira*, completed in 1937, and the mine-laying submarine *Humaitá*, completed a decade earlier, were of limited operational value. Being Italian built, however, and nearly identical to some submarines used against Brazil, these craft were valuable for antisubmarine training. The remainder of the fleet were pre-World War I relics.

As had been the case in World War I, the new core of the Brazilian navy was in the process of being built. Brazil had nine destroyers under construction, perfect ships for the pending conflict. Following the World War I pattern, Great Britain appropriated Brazil's six *Juruena*-class destroyers for her own need in late 1939.[19] The war also delayed completion of the *Marcílio Dias* class destroyers, which were being built in Brazil. These destroyers were based on North American drawings.[20]

The Brazilian merchant marine was perhaps a more important asset than its navy to the Allies. Brazil had 485,000 gross registered tons of shipping. It was the fourth largest in the

Americas, behind only the merchant marines of the United States (11,363,000 tons), Canada (1,224,000 tons), and Panama (717,500 tons). By 1940 there were 376 ships in the fleet including some small river types.[21]

BRAZIL'S STRATEGY

Brazil's primary asset to the Allied cause was its strategic location and second its vast raw materials. The initial strategy was to protect Brazil from invasion and fifth-column activities. Prior to the war the Brazilian army had been concentrated along its southern borders with Argentina, Paraguay, and Uruguay. As the war expanded to north Africa, the U.S. Army perceived a threat of a German drive through west Africa and an airborne assault across the South Atlantic, thus threatening the Panama Canal.[22] Neither the Brazilian armed forces nor the U.S. Navy shared this view. They believed that the initial task confronting the Brazilian military was to safeguard merchantships in contiguous waters from U-boat attacks.

To meet the U-boat threat, Brazil moved air units, which included most of its tactical aircraft, to the northeast, placing them under the command of Brig. Gen. Eduardo Gomes. A dispute arose between the Brazilian and American militaries concerning the use of aircraft. The United States wanted to deploy its own aircraft to Brazil and the Brazilians wanted these planes transferred to them so they could be flown by Brazilian pilots. Ultimately, the United States had its way, in part because the infrastructure did not exist to train the Brazilian pilots in a timely manner.[23] The first Maritime Patrol Squadron, VP-52 with six PBY-5 Catalina flying boats, arrived at Natal on December 11, 1941. By June of the following year three U.S. Navy squadrons were operating from Brazil.[24]

Next came the task of organizing the naval forces. The Commander-in-Chief of the Brazilian navy, Adm. Jorge Dodsworth Martins, divided the fleet in two; they were the South Patrol Group commanded by Capt. Ernesto de Araujo and the Northeast Naval Force commanded by Rear Adm. Alfredo Carlos Soares Dutra. Admiral Dutra was placed under the operational command of Vice Admiral Ingram, U.S. Navy. Ingram also had the frontline aircraft of the Brazilian air force under his command as well.[25]

Antisubmarine warfare required the most technologically advanced equipment available. The Allies could not spare from the North Atlantic the amount of assistance needed. The poor sound conditions that prevailed off the Amazon River further complicated the task. The large amount of fresh water flowing into the ocean created temperature layers that reflected sound and made submarine detection difficult.[26]

As elsewhere, a convoy system was created to counter the U-boat threat. However, creating such a system was difficult and took time. In the interim, from August through mid-December 1942, antisubmarine groups patrolled Brazilian waters. Initially, the convoy system operated between Trinidad and Bahia. Brazilian warships escorted merchantships between Bahia and Recife, and U.S. warships took them from Recife to Trinidad. The first southbound convoy (TB-1) sailed on December 15, 1942, and the first northbound (BT-1) on January 6, 1943. Once additional escorts became available on July 3, the convoy system was extended to Rio de Janeiro (TJ-1). South Atlantic convoys sailed every ten days until December 1944, then every five days beginning with JT-54 and TJ-54. The convoys' assigned speed was eight knots, but strong westward currents across the north coast of Brazil usually affected speed by two knots.

THE BRAZILIAN NAVY'S WAR

By early 1943 merchantships escorted by the Brazilian navy were attacked. The merchantship *Brasilóide*, en route to join BT-6, was sunk on February 18 by the *U-518* off Bahia. This U-boat then sank the American Liberty Ship *Fitz-John Porter*, being escorted by the corvettes *Carioca*, *Caravelas*, and *Rio Branco*, part of BT-6.[27]

July 1943 was the turning point in the Battle of the North Atlantic, that critical corridor between the United States and Great Britain. The increasing quantity and quality of Allied anti-submarine forces were taking an increasingly heavy toll on German U-boats. In order to give its forces relief from the Allies ASW forces and yet still have valuable targets to attack, the German high command diverted the U-boats south to the Brazilian littoral. Twelve U-boats began operating off the Brazilian coast. Between June 21 and August 17, 1943, they torpedoed twenty ships, sinking seventeen. But the price proved high here as well—six U-boats were sunk in July, two in August, and one in December.[28]

Although the back of the underwater blitz against Brazil was broken by 1944, U-boat attacks continued. Near midnight on July 19, 1944, the *U-861* torpedoed the naval auxiliary *Vital de Oliveira*, under the escort of the subchaser *Javari*. The auxiliary sank on the twentieth. The next day the Brazilian corvette *Camaquã* capsized in heavy seas off Recife after her group had been relieved by U.S. warships escorting a JT convoy.[29]

The Brazilian navy also had to deal with the problem of neutral merchantships, commanded by Axis sympathizers, radioing information concerning convoys and stragglers to the enemy. The Brazilian navy believed the practice to be common among Spanish captains and to a lesser degree Argentine captains.[30]

PREPARING THE BRAZILIAN ARMY TO FIGHT IN EUROPE

During the late months of 1942 some Brazilian officers suggested that the army take independent action against either French Guiana or Dakar in French West Africa, but these suggestions were never followed through, in part due to a lack of resources.[31]

On December 31, 1942, President Vargas suggested that Brazilian troops actively fight in the war and not merely as a "simple expedition of symbolic contingents."[32] During a January 28, 1943, meeting between Presidents Franklin Roosevelt and Getulio Vargas in Natal, the latter formally requested that Brazil be given a combat role in the war. Drawing upon Brazil's World War I experience, the Brazilian believed that only a combat role would win the nation the postwar influence it sought.[33] As a result, Roosevelt agreed to help equip and train Brazilian troops for fighting in Europe.

In April 1943 the Brazilian army outlined plans for a four-division expeditionary force to General George Marshall, Chief of Staff, U.S. Army. The plan was accepted in principle and Major Gen. J. Ord was sent to Brazil to work out the details.[34] However, due to the lack of resources only one was formed—the 1st Expeditionary Infantry Division of the Brazilian Expeditionary Force (BEF). The Brazilian army had to be completely restructured. It had been modeled after that of France, down to its 75mm French artillery.[35] Officers needed to be schooled, manuals needed to be translated, and troops needed to be trained on an entirely new set of weapons from the rifle to the largest cannon.[36]

The Brazilian division was organized and equipped as a standard U.S. Infantry Division. The BEF was supplemented by two Brazilian Air Force units. The 1st Liason-Observation Flight was equipped with Piper L-4 Grasshopper light aircraft, operated by air force pilots and army artillery observers, and was under the divisional artillery command of the BEF. The 1st Brazilian Fighter Squadron, equipped with Republic P-47 Thunderbolt aircraft, was part of the 350th Fighter Group, U.S. Army Air Forces. This fighter-bomber outfit was itself subordinated to the XXII Tactical Air Command.[37]

By October 1943 the division began to take shape under Maj. Gen. João Batista Mascarenhas de Morais. Training was hampered by the fact that the units of the division were scattered throughout the states of São Paulo, Minas Gerais, and Rio de Janeiro. They could not be united at Vila Militar in Rio until March 1944.[38]

The first of five contingents of the Brazilian Expeditionary Force sailed from Rio de Janeiro in the U.S. transport *General W.H. Mann* on July 2, escorted by Brazilian destroyers and warships from the U.S. 4th Fleet; it arrived at Naples, Italy, on the sixteenth. On September 22 the largest contingent of Brazilian troops embarked in two transports at Rio de Janeiro.

FIGHTING IN ITALY

The Brazilian Division arrived in Italy at the time that theater was being drained of experienced units for the offensive in southern France. As a result, the date for the BEF to be sent into combat was moved up. Gen. Mark Clark, Commander of the Allied Forces, decided that the Brazilian 6th Infantry Regiment should form a Regimental Combat Team under the command of Brig. Gen. Zenóbio da Costa and be sent to the front as soon as possible. Some 270 battle-experienced U.S. Army officers and noncommissioned officers joined the Combat Team to provide instructions.[39]

On September 15 the combat team was assigned to the U.S. 4th Corps which had been reduced to the size of a reinforced division because numerous units were detached for the invasion of southern France. The U.S. Army was responsible for the western half of Italy and the British the eastern half. By late 1944 the Italian front was returning to static warfare. In May the Allies had finally broken through the formidable German "Gustav Line" but the Germans had subsequently established the "Gothic Line" which ran roughly from Pisa to Rimini. Fighting had been heavy throughout 1944. Therefore, the Brazilian combat team was one of the few fresh and conversely inexperienced units in the Italian theater.[40]

The Brazilian combat team reinforced by three U.S. tank companies entered the front on September 15, 1944, at Vecchiano, north of Pisa, and manned a six-mile front. Brazilian patrols failed to make contact with the enemy, so the combat team pursued the retreating Germans as they fell back to the new Gothic Line along some high ground. The German tactical retreat allowed the Brazilians to liberate the villages of Massarosa, Bozzano, and Chiesa. The combat team's first action occurred on September 18 when it captured a communications center at Camaiore; this forced the Germans to abandon Monte Prano on the twenty-sixth. The Brazilians lost four dead and seven wounded; 23 Germans were captured.[41]

THE SERCHIO VALLEY OFFENSIVE

On September 28, the 4th Corps ordered the Brazilians to move eastward into the Serchio River Valley and to advance northward along the river. The advance was delayed by rain and mud. The towns of Fornaci and Antelminelli were captured on October 6, but the operation was suspended when 4th Corps borrowed the 1st Battalion, 6th Regiment and some of the team's artillery. The advance could not be renewed until the fourteenth.[42]

In the meantime, the Brazilian Air Force's 1st Fighter Squadron, outfitted with U.S.-built P-47 Thunderbolts and under the command of the U.S. Army Air Corps XXII Tactical Air Command bombed, strafed, and flew reconnaissance.[43]

By October the Combat team returned to full strength and prepared to attack Castelnuovo di Garfagnana, an important German communications center. Reinforced with two U.S. field artillery battalions, the attack began on October 21 and by the thirtieth the combat team was only four kilometers from its objective. On October 31 the Germans counterattacked; they took the Brazilians by surprise and the combat team fell back to Sommocolonia. The Allied command decided that the Serchio Valley route could not be used to break through the Gothic Line so the Brazilian combat team was relocated to the Reno River Valley, 120 kilometers to the northeast.[44]

ASSAULTING MONTE CASTELLO

In November the entire Brazilian Division deployed to the Reno River Valley near Bologna. The strong German position at Monte Castello dominated the valley. The U.S. command created Task Force 45, which included elements of the BEF,[45] which was assigned the task of driving the Germans off the mountain. The attack was launched on November 24 and the fighting raged for three days. The offensive was a complete failure. The Brazilians lost 34 dead and 153 wounded. The remainder of the BEF division was thrown into the fight with orders to capture the ridge including Monte Castello. On the twenty-ninth, three infantry battalions supported by tanks and artillery attacked unsuccessfully.[46] For the next six days, artillery and aircraft pounded the Germans. On December 12 the BEF attempted a surprise attack which was compromised by American artillery. The attack immediately bogged down and failed.[47]

Throughout the end of the winter, both sides remained on the defensive as heavy snows fell. In February 1945, the recently arrived U.S. 10th Mountain Division, supported by the 1st Fighter Squadron Brazilian Air Force and artillery from the BEF, seized outer defenses of Monte Castello. On February 21 the Brazilians attacked and carried the German stronghold. This was a moral victory for the Brazilian force; it demonstrated their ability to defeat the Germans even when the enemy occupied strong defensive positions.[48]

PO VALLEY OFFENSIVE

The Brazilian Division now attacked eastward liberating Roncovecchio on February 25 and Seneveglio the following day. The Brazilian Expeditionary Force then formed two battle groups. The western, commanded by Gen. Zenóbio da Costa, protected the U.S. 10th Mountain Division's lines of communications, while the eastern battle group, commanded by Gen. Mascarenhas de Morais, attacked Castelnuovo which fell in early March. The Brazilians sustained some 70 casualties and took 98 Germans as prisoners. On April 16 the Brazilian Division captured Montese following a difficult four-day battle; it sustained 426 casualties.[49]

The 1st Brazilian Fighter Squadron began its operations on October 31, 1944, from Targuinia Airfield, and was moved to Pisa in December. By the end of the war, it destroyed 2 aircraft and damaged 9 others (while on the ground), as well as destroying 1,304 vehicles, 250 railway cars (including fuel tank cars), 25 bridges, 31 fuel and ammunition depots, 85 artillery positions, and other targets.

The Brazilian squadron suffered from a chronic shortage of pilots because there was no system for replacements. The squadron's hardest day was April 22, 1945, during the Po Valley offensive, when it flew eleven, four-plane missions with only twenty-two pilots. According to the 350th Fighter Group's operations report, during the period from April 6 to 29, the Brazilian Fighter Squadron flew 5 percent of the sorties generated by the XXII Tactical Air Command, but it destroyed 15 percent of the vehicles and 28 percent of the bridges plus damaged 36 percent of the fuel dumps and 85 percent of the ammunition depots claimed by the command.[50]

On April 18 and 19, 1945, the Brazilians were redeployed to the north and by the twenty-second had fought their way into the Po Valley. Other Allied forces had also reached the valley floor and broken into the north Italian plain. The Germans were in full retreat. The BEF, pursuing toward the northwest, captured hundreds of Axis troops daily. To speed the pursuit, the Brazilian commander stripped ten of his twelve artillery batteries of their vehicles and created several motorized columns. The troops were transported in 606 jeeps and 676 assorted trucks. The German 148th Infantry Division made a stand at Fornovo. On April 28 the Brazilian 6th Regiment supported by American tanks attacked. The next day Gen. Otto Fretter Pico surrendered his command of 14,779 German and Italian troops, 80 guns, and 1,500 vehicles. The 148th Division was the only German division to surrender intact in the Italian theater. On May 2 all Axis forces in Italy capitulated. During the campaign the BEF lost 13 officers, 105 noncommissioned officers, and 339 privates.[51]

BRAZIL'S ROLE IN THE PACIFIC WAR

On June 6, 1945, Brazil declared war on Japan and planned to send air force units into the Pacific theater. Brazilian and other Allied warships were stationed in the Atlantic as potential rescue craft for U.S. Army transport planes carrying personnel from the European to the Pacific theaters. The Brazilian light cruiser *Bahia* sank, probably through an accident, while serving on plane-guard duty before the war ended in the Pacific.[52]

MEXICO GOES TO WAR

Similar to Brazil's circumstance, Mexico was acting out the effects of a great revolution that had occurred between 1910 and 1920 (see chapter 3). Relations with the United States and Great Britain were particularly strained.

During the 1930s, Mexico showed interest in European affairs. Mexico was one of the most ardent supporters of Republican Spain when it was at war against Gen. Francisco Franco's Nationalists.[53] Mexico also became one of the most important havens for Spanish refugees, the first of whom arrived on April 20, 1939. Although relations with Great Britain and the United States remained uncertain, Mexico's position vis-a-vis developments in Europe was quite clear. On May 12, 1940, the country sent a note to Germany protesting the invasions of France and the Netherlands. Mexican President Cárdenas denounced the Italian declaration of war against France on June 11, one day after the event. And on the following day, the head of German legation was asked to leave Mexico.[54]

In early June 1940, Mexico and the United States held a series of meetings which addressed the problems of hemispheric defense. Mexico needed equipment and munitions, the United States air and naval bases. President Cárdenas intimated that his country was prepared to develop the bases "at places to be chosen strategically, not only from the purely national point of view but from the broader point of view of hemisphere defense."[55] Thereafter the government of Mexico had to move cautiously.

Avila Camacho was elected president, and followers of the losing candidate threatened re-volt. Any rapprochement with the United States would probably be denounced by the opposi-tion as a sellout to the gringos. Complicating matters was a controversy over the expropriation of the petroleum industry, an issue that had plagued relations between the two countries for some time. The day following the attack on Pearl Harbor, Mexico broke off relations with Ja-pan, freezing its assets, and on December 11 severed all relations with Germany and Italy. A month later Mexico declared that ships and aircraft of American republics at war would not be treated as belligerents. This meant that their stay in Mexico would be immune to the provisions of international treaties limiting the activities of belligerents.[56]

MEXICO'S FORCES

Like Brazil, Mexico's most important asset was its geographical location; aircraft operating from its airfields could dominate the western half of the Gulf of Mexico. Militarily, Mexico had little to offer. Its army and navy were ill-suited to all but indigenous duties. The Mexican mer-chant marine did possess a few tankers, a type of vessel in critically short supply early in the war.[57]

MEXICO'S STRATEGY

Naval officers took command of Mexico's tanker fleet, which was manned by merchant sea-men, in order to better control the movement of oil.

MEXICO AT WAR

Mexico's newly created tanker fleet proved to be easy prey during the 1942 U-boat blitz off the coast of North America. On June 26 the tanker *Tuxpan* was sunk by the *U-129* near the Tecolutla Bar; four men died. The next day the same U-boat sank the tanker *Las Choapas* be-tween Tecolutla and Tuxpan, killing three men. And the *U-171* torpedoed the steamer *Oaxaca* near Matagorda, Texas, killing six.[58] As a result of these U-boat successes, Mexico authorized the use of Cozumel Airfield by U.S. aircraft for antisubmarine patrols—an extraordinary con-cession, considering the animosity that had divided the two nations a few years earlier. At this time the United States was also establishing a convoy system on the western side of the Atlan-tic, thus ending the extreme vulnerability of the Mexican merchant marine to U-boats. The Mexican navy had no antisubmarine capability, so up to this point merchantships had to trust their own skills and luck.

The merchant marine acquired additional ships as U-boat successes began to abate. Mexico's government seized the French tanker *Merope*, interned at Tampico, and renamed her the *Potrero del Llano II* on August 21, 1942. On September 4 the tanker *Amatlan* became the last Mexican merchantship to fall victim to a U-boat. The *U-171* torpedoed and sank her off Tordo Bar; five died.[59]

From mid-1942 to early 1943, Mexico permitted the United States to use Cozumel Airfield and two other airfields in the Yucatan, as well as a bomber base at Tehuantepec, for flight op-erations. With the decline of U-boat activity in the waters off the Americas, the United States' use of the airfields wound down at the request of Mexico.[60] On October 2, 1942, Mexico and Cuba signed a covenant for the joint surveillance of the Gulf of Mexico.

MEXICAN AIR FORCE ACTIVITY

On May 8, 1944, President Camacho announced that a unit of the Mexican air force would be sent overseas to fight. Ultimately named the Mexican Expeditionary Air Force, the 300-man unit was trained at numerous bases throughout the United States. The unit outfitted with 25 P-47s was declared operational on June 3, 1945, at Porac Airfield in the Philippines. The Mexican force was used to attack Japanese forces on Luzon Island which were endeavoring to block the U.S. ground advance into the Cagayan Valley. Once the valley was secured, the Mexican unit flew long-range fighter sweeps and bombing missions over Formosa (Taiwan). The unit returned to Mexico in November.[61]

OBSERVATIONS

Brazilian and Mexican military entries into World War II were most timely, coming in the bleak summer of 1942 when U-boats ravaged the North Atlantic and the Japanese were capturing one colony after another. The most important military contribution of both nations was the permission to use strategically located airfields. Thousands of U.S.-built aircraft flew across the South Atlantic allowing them to arrive in Africa and Europe during the critical months of late 1942 and throughout 1943. Additionally, aircraft flying from Brazil sank eleven Axis submarines and those flying from Mexico controlled the western Caribbean.[62]

Brazil sent 25,000 men to fight in Italy. Although they were members of only one out of seventeen Allied divisions fighting in that theater during late 1944 and early 1945, the Brazilian Expeditionary Force was one of the few fresh units.[63] Brazil lost some 1,942 men due to enemy activity. The Brazilian Expeditionary Force lost 457 men and the Brazilian air force lost eight pilots in Italy; the navy lost 492 against the U-boats; and the merchant marine lost 470 crewmen and 502 passengers, many of whom were military.[64] Three Brazilian warships were sunk—the old cruiser *Bahia* (by an accident), the corvette *Camaquã*, and the auxiliary *Vital de Oliveira*—and 32 merchantships. The air force lost 22 aircraft and the war cost Brazil 21 million *cruzeiros*.[65]

Mexican losses were significantly less. Sixty-three naval and merchant marine personnel died while serving on board seven merchantships. The Mexican air force lost seven pilots.[66]

Brazil in particular believed that its contribution went unrecognized. Twenty-five thousand troops committed to the Italian theater did not gain Brazil the post-World War II dividend it had sought—a permanent seat on the Security Council of the United Nations.[67] Expressing this frustration, President Vargas wrote, "We fought in the last war and were entirely forgotten and rejected in the division of the spoils."[68]

Mexico also contributed its vast natural resources and manpower as well as a quiet, friendly border. It had more experience in dealing with the "gringo" and it did not have the same post-war frustrations as did Brazil.

Political and economic changes wrought as a result of the war altered the balance of power within the Western Hemisphere. Prior to the war, Great Britain, France, Germany, and Italy shared with the United States in the political and economic influence. As war drew nearer during the 1930s, the European powers withdrew in order to invest their time and treasure in strategically more important regions and the United States became more aggressive in developing its influence. Therefore, by the time the war had ended, the United States had emerged as the world's greatest power and the preeminent nation in the Western Hemisphere.

External to the region, the outcome of the war caused a polarization of world power between the United States and the Soviet Union. Latin America, now well under the influence of the United States, was soon drawn into this contest and frequently became the battleground of the emerging cold war.

Within South America, the traditional balance of power between Argentina and Peru on one hand, and Brazil and Chile on the other, had been upset. Due to its role in World War II and the military aid it had received, Brazil was now the dominant Latin American power. Argentina lost considerable political stature and economic well-being due to its sometimes neutral, sometimes pro-Axis positions which lasted until the "eleventh hour" of the war.

Also, Brazil's participation in the war altered internal Brazilian politics. Much as the War of the Triple Alliance had done, World War II significantly increased the competence and confidence of the Brazilian army's officer corps. Even though the expeditionary force was immediately disbanded upon its return to Brazil, its veterans became a political force. On October 29, 1945, Gen. Pedro Monteiro, now the Minister of War, overthrew the fifteen-year-old Vargas regime. Former Minister of War Eurico Dutra was elected president on December 2, beginning nineteen years of elected governments.

PART 10

CHAPTER 18

CENTRAL AMERICA AND
THE CARIBBEAN, 1944–54

The last such government [dictatorship], that of Ubico, was overthrown in the latter part of World War II by a group of people who when they came in were primarily idealists and had no particular ideology other than to try to establish a democratic form of government in Guatemala.

—Edward G. Miller, Assistant Secretary for Inter-American Affairs

THE SPARK

Continuous repression ignited fighting first in Central America and then in the Caribbean in the closing years of World War II. In El Salvador, air force and army personnel led by Col. Tito Calvo revolted against the dictator Maximiliano Hernández Martínez on April 3, 1944. In Guatemala, the death of secondary-school teacher María Chinchilla Vega on June 25, 1944, during a series of street clashes between the followers of Jorge Ubico[1] and reformers solidified national anger against the long-abusive regime. In the Caribbean, exiles prepared to attack Rafael Trujillo of the Dominican Republic in 1947. In Nicaragua, Leonardo Argüello chose not to be the puppet of Anastasio Somoza in 1947 and caused the presidential palace to be attacked. In Costa Rica, the 1948 disputed presidential election erupted into civil war.

BACKGROUND

By the closing years of World War II, the distribution of power and wealth throughout Central America and the Caribbean had changed little since the colonial days. The King's appointees had been replaced by homegrown dictators, whose rule was even more repressive than their predecessors. Foreigners, particularly North Americans, controlled much of the wealth. The army was the guarantor of the status quo and the conservative leadership of the Roman

Figure 21. Central America and the Caribbean (1944–54). The "Caribbean Legion" ready for inspection on a coffee-bean drying field at "Pepe" Figueres' *finca* (farm) at Río Conejo, Costa Rica, in 1948. One can readily see this is not a ragtag outfit. The men are all uniformed, armed, and well fed. They are possibly armed with Mauser rifles acquired through Guatemalan President Juan Arévalo from Argentine President Juan Perón. *Courtesy anonymous.*

Catholic Church anesthetized the Indians. The exploitation of the masses was the foundation of the political, social, and economic order.[2]

Central American society began to change through the exposure of the very small but growing middle class to new ideas, in part fostered by economic opportunities created by World War II. Professional and merchant groups increasingly demanded freedoms, better working conditions, and changes in the government; junior officers wanted their militaries professionalized.[3]

OPPOSING FORCES

The ruling elites depended upon their militaries to maintain the status quo and chose senior officers based on their loyalty to the regime. El Salvador possessed a 1,855-man army (1944); Guatemala a 5,967-man army (1944); the Dominican Republic an estimated 3,750-man army (1947); Nicaragua a 3,538-man national guard plus a 4,000-man reserve (1948); and Costa Rica a 330-man army supported by some 1,600 members of police forces (1948). By far the strongest among these, in quality as well as quantity, were the armies of the Dominican Republic and Nicaragua. In the Dominican Repulic the arsenal at San Cristóbal produced rifles, machine guns, and ammunition. Nicaragua possessed the best air force in the region.[4]

Within each country, there were many oppositions typically composed of professionals, union leaders, professors, students, shopkeepers, and junior officers of the armies. Beginning in the 1920s, the Communist Party had infiltrated some of these groups (see chapter 10).

Externally, a fighting force, which by April 1948 had become known as the "Caribbean Legion," emerged. Exiles from Central American and Caribbean nations met in Guatemala and on December 16, 1947, their leaders signed a secret pact to cooperate, through sharing resources (primarily weapons), in the overthrow of regional dictators. As created in 1947, this was no more than a skeleton general staff—all "generals" without any "privates." These exiles were supported and protected by Guatemalan President Juan José Arévalo.[5]

Although the leaders who signed the secret pact came from three nations, the Dominican Juan Rodríguez García[6] controlled the purse strings and therefore the use of the weapons. He had been his nation's second richest man before fleeing Anastasio Somoza. Others signing the pact were the Costa Rican José Figueres Ferrer[7] and the Nicaraguans Emiliano Chamorro, Gustavo Manzanares, Pedro José Zepeda, and Rosendo Arguello (Sr.).[8]

OPENING STRATEGIES

To varying degrees the dictators who ruled these countries won control through the use of bribery, brutality, and assassination—"plata, palo, y plomo" [money, the stick, and lead]. Their strategies in the 1940s were to rely once again upon brutality to deal with these uprisings. The opposition was neither homogeneous nor united. Therefore, elements opposing each dictator perused their own strategies. Typically, the young military officers thought in terms of coup d'etats and the civilians relied on demonstrations of public support such as strikes to force the dictator to change. Since those who wanted to overthrow the governments of the Dominican Republic and Costa Rica organized themselves outside their country, they planned traditional military invasions on very modest scales.

EL SALVADOR

Maximiliano Hernández Martínez had ruled El Salvador since December 1931. In December of that year he executed a coup d'etat against the recently elected president Arturo Araujo.

In 1932 Martínez suppressed a Communist conspiracy with blood-chilling brutality (see chapter 10). He was an eccentric who believed in the occult; once Martínez ordered the San Salvador hospital to hang green lights to ward off a smallpox epidemic.[9]

In February 1944 Martínez made Congress "elect" him to another six-year term. On April 2 army and air force personnel, led by Col. Tito Calvo, seized two radio stations in San Salvador and broadcast the misinformation that Martínez had been overthrown and that he had fled the country. The rebels won control over San Miguel and Santa Ana Provinces. Rebels in the air force bombed the army barracks in the capital, setting fires in the center of the city.[10]

As these events were transpiring, Martínez went to the National Police Headquarters at El Zapote Barracks in the capital, rallied his followers, and recaptured the radio stations. Within forty-eight hours the dictator had regained complete control. About 250 died in the fighting. Colonel Calvo and ten other officers were shot. Martínez continued to exterminate the opposition and perhaps 3,000 were murdered.[11]

On April 27 those opposed to Martínez began a nationwide strike which dragged on through early May. On May 9 Martínez resigned and fled to exile on the eleventh; the dictator's rapid fall surprised many. The Congress, which represented the elite, chose the Defense Minister, Gen. Andrés Ignacio Menéndez, as the provisional president. On May 18 the opposition threatened to call another general strike if elections were not held immediately. On October 21 General Mendéndez resigned for "reasons of health." Col. Osmín Aguirre y Salinas, Chief of Police under Martínez, became provisional president.[12]

Gen. Salvador Castañeda Castro, whom Aguirre hand-picked, opposed Dr. Arturo Romero in the presidential elections of January 1945. Those believing that little change was taking place called for another general strike. In response, the Aguirre government deported hundreds. The Supreme Court declared the Aguirre government as illegal, and as a consequence, its judges were arrested.[13]

On December 9 another revolt broke out. It appeared that the rebels might win when Honduras intervened with planes and troops in support of the Salvadoran government. Aguirre controlled the vote counting and General Castañeda won the January 1945 election receiving practically every vote cast. During the summer, Aguirre, disappointed by his inability to control Castañeda, led an unsuccessful coup. In December 1948 Castañeda told "his" Congress that his presidential term should be for six years and not four as stipulated at the time of the election, and that Congress should address the issue. Congress called for a constituent assembly to determine the length of a presidential term.[14]

At 2 P.M. on December 14, 1948, military forces, led by a few civilians and a group of junior officers, fired on the presidential palace. Castañeda attempted to rally followers but found himself deserted. He resigned at 5 P.M. and was arrested. One person died and eighteen were wounded. A junta headed by Col. Manuel de Jesús Córdoba took power. Martial law was lifted and public confidence in the government increased. On March 25, 1950, Col. Oscar Osorio, the real leader of the coup, was elected president. After a turbulent political campaign, he was succeeded through the electoral process by Lt. Col. José María Lemus.[15]

These various attempts to interject moderate reforms into the Salvadoran political system were initiated by the fledgling middle class, including younger military officers. However, President Lemus was deposed by a military junta in October 1960. And for the next thirty years, the military remained the dominant political power in El Salvador.

GUATEMALA

Gen. Jorge Ubico Castañeda had ruled Guatemala since February 1931. Typical of Guatemala's past, he acquired the presidency through political manipulation and held it by force.[16]

On June 22, 1944, students demanded that Ubico give the national university almost complete autonomy. He refused and suspended several constitutional guarantees. Ubico accused the students of being "Nazi-Fascist agitators," an accusation which was losing its terror for Washington.[17]

On June 24, a group of 311 prominent citizens submitted a petition to the government explaining the cause for the unrest and requested that constitutional guarantees be restored. That night Ubico's agents brutally dispersed a crowd at the National University, killing twenty-five. The following day, June 25, Ubico's enforcers fired on a mourning procession, killing fourteen women and five children including María Chinchilla Vega. Fighting broke out and continued throughout the night; many were killed and hundreds arrested.[18]

By the twenty-seventh the strike had spread to all elements of the society. The outraged citizens broke off negotiations with the government which were being conducted through the U.S. Embassy. The protesters grew in number to include many government workers. Ubico placed railway and public utility employees under martial law. In spite of this, opposition continued to grow. Finally on July 1, Ubico succumbed to the flood of petitions asking for his resignation and the weight of the general strike and surrendered authority to a military triumvirate. Gen. Federico Ponce Valdes emerged as the acting president.[19]

Initially General Ponce attempted to win support among the middle class by granting concessions such as permission to organize labor unions and political parties; he also abolished the monopolies on sugar, meat, and tobacco. Soon, Ponce perceived these concessions to be counterproductive to retaining power so he stopped granting them.

In order to circumvent an election, General Ponce had the Congress declare that he remain provisional president without elections. The Guatemalan Constitution allowed for changes in the fundamental law with a two-thirds congressional vote and this procedure had been used repeatedly by past dictators to broaden their powers. Opposition leaders were arrested; those who escaped sought asylum in foreign embassies. The owner of the newspaper *El Imparcial*, Alejandro Córdova, was assassinated.[20]

Next, Ponce attempted to sow fear among his adversaries by bringing groups of Indians into Guatemala City and arming them. Many in the army had taken the side of the popular movement. Ponce hoped that the middle-class shopkeepers would feel threatened by the presence of the Indians and seek his protection. The attempted intimidation failed.

The primary strategy of the reformers was to organize in order to present a united front. The most important junta was composed of Capt. Jacobo Arbenz Guzmán,[21] businessman Jorge Toriello, Maj. Francisco Javier Arana,[22] and university professor Juan José Arévalo.[23] On October 16 the professor and other civilians issued a manifesto calling for a political strike, which was followed on the eighteenth by a strike at the National University.[24]

During the early morning hours of October 20, 1944, rebellious army officers smuggled seventy students and workers into the *Guardia de Honor* fortress in the capital. This facility was serving as a barracks, arsenal, and prison. The commanding officer was killed and weapons, acquired under the U.S. Lend Lease Program, were distributed to supporters. An artillery duel then broke out between the opposing forces. Ponce supporters in Fortress Matamoros fired on and destroyed Fort San José. A counterbarrage from the *Guardia de Honor* fortress silenced Fortress Matamoros. The rebels, supported by tanks, armored cars, and troops from the *Guardia de Honor*, laid siege to the national palace and within a few hours Ponce unconditionally surrendered. The entire operation had taken less than twelve hours and had cost somewhat less than 1,000 lives. By the twenty-second, General Ponce and his closest supporters flew into exile.[25]

The middle class led by shopkeepers, young professionals, and midlevel army officers won a revolution that offered the hope of profoundly altering the political, social, and economic structure of Guatemala. In large measure, it was possible for this event to occur without U.S. intervention because the United States did not feel its interests threatened.[26]

However, the new government of President Juan José Arévalo almost immediately came under suspicion by the United States. Exiles were permitted to return, including Communists. The most important was Carlos Manuel Pellecer who arrived from Mexico on December 1, 1944. In 1945 Guatemala severed diplomatic relations with Spain and established them with the Soviet Union. Arévalo soon began championing the left in its quest to overthrow regional dictators.[27]

DOMINICAN REPUBLIC

The leading candidate for the most despicable dictator of his era was Rafael Leonidas Trujillo y Molina. Coming to power in 1930 through the army, thanks to its upgrading by the United States, he was a megalomaniac. Trujillo stole a fortune by treating the nation he ruled as his private property. The man's ego knew no bounds. He renamed the capital, Santo Domingo, for himself, Ciudad Trujillo. And half of the six largest ships in his navy were named for him—the *Trujillo*, the *Presidente Trujillo*, and the *Generalisimo*—all existing at the same time.[28]

Over the years many of those exiled from the Dominican Republic concentrated in Cuba. In 1946 exiles "Juancito" Rodríguez, Juan Bosch,[29] and Angel Morales planned an assault on their homeland. Through the help of Guatemalan President Arévalo, the conspirators acquired some one thousand Mauser rifles plus one million rounds of ammunition. These came from Juan Perón's Argentina; however, Perón believed they were for the use of the Guatemalan army. The conspirators initially purchased three aircraft—a DC3 transport, a Cessna, and an AT-13 trainer—which allowed them to transport the additional weapons they purchased in the United States to Cuba, their base of operations. In early 1947 two small ships loaded with World War II veterans plus weapons and munitions, which had been clandestinely stored in the greater New York City area, sailed from New York to Cuba.[30]

The assault force, which was in place by August 1947, was impressive. The "navy" was composed of seven ships: the *Aurora* (a "landing craft, tank"—LCT); the *Berta* (a former U.S. army, 100-foot air-sea rescue boat); the *Máximo Gómez*, also called *Fantasma* (a "landing craft, infantry"—LCI); the *Maceo* (a 120-foot steel-hulled schooner, formerly the *Angelita*); the *La Victoria* (a 75-foot schooner); and the *R-41* and *R-42* (patrol torpedo boats belonging to the Cuban navy). Additionally, the rebels had purchased the *Patria* (another LCI) but it had been seized in Baltimore by U.S. Customs officials. The rebel "air force" was composed of some sophiscated warplanes—six P-38 fighters, one B-24 bomber, two B-25 bombers, two Vega Ventura bombers, one C-46 transport, two C-78 transports, and two C-47 transports.[31]

The black market was awash with small arms to outfit the 1,100-man force. In addition to the Mauser rifles acquired from Perón, the rebels purchased 50 Argentine-manufactured, Madsen-design light machine guns; some 200 Thompson submachine guns; 15 bazookas with 300 rockets; three 81mm mortars; three 37mm antitank guns; 2,000 hand grenades, plus all kinds of support equipment. The rebels called themselves the "Liberation Army of America."[32]

Cuban President Ramón Grau enthusiastically supported the planned attack on Trujillo. Cuba's Minister of Education, José Alemán, reportedly used ministry money to support the military build-up and used his own *finca* (ranch) to clandestinely store the materials. Cuba's director of the national sports program, Manolo Castro, recruited hundreds of Cubans for the expedition; they included idealistic youth and hardened criminals. Cuban navy Captain Jorge Felipe Agostini served as liaison between President Grau and the rebels. Many of the clandestine arms shipments entered Cuba through the Mariel Naval Base where the rebels parked their P-38s. Obviously, Trujillo's diplomatic representatives in Cuba, the United Nations, and the United States protested these activities but the Cuban government denied any knowledge.[33]

To do a better job of hiding its presence, President Grau ordered the "Liberation Army of America" moved from Holguín (400 mi E of Havana) to Cayo Confites, a tiny island off the eastern end of Cuba near the port of Nuevitas, where it arrived on July 28. Life on this remote, inhospitable, barren island required that the "Liberation Army of America" be employed soon or it would disintegrate. The leadership on the island slipped away from the Dominicans into the hands of the more numerous Cubans. The move to Cayo Confites and the seizure of the *Patria* by U.S. officials caused the invasion to be delayed.[34]

Things continued to go wrong. By early August the United States discovered the rebel hideaway and began daily reconnaissance flights from Guantanamo. In mid-September Cayo Confites was hit by a severe tropical storm. Then on September 15 police representing two rival Cuban political factions fought a two-and-a-half-hour gun battle in Havana, leaving six dead and eleven wounded. More assassinations occurred the next day. President Grau ordered his army chief of staff, Gen. Genovevo Pérez Dámera, home from Washington to deal with the internal crisis. Trujillo bribed General Pérez with $2 million to be sure that the elimination of the threatened invasion was part of the solution. The General seized the opportunity to decrease the power of the national police (including the elimination of some gangsters), which was a rival of the army. Those discredited by the army included Alemán and Manolo Castro who were deeply involved with the planned invasion of the Dominican Republic. On September 20 army troops raided Alemán's ranch. They seized thirteen truckloads of weapons and made the cache public. Grau, embarrassed by the exposure of his government's complicity in the plot against Trujillo, ordered Rodríguez to leave Cuba within twenty-four hours.[35]

The would-be invaders on Cayo Confites followed these events on their radio and feared that the Cuban government would now take action against them. On September 22 the *Aurora*, *Angelita*, and *Máximo Gómez* sailed west, stopping at Cayo Santa María where Rodríguez joined them on the twenty-fifth. They were also joined by their other ships. President Grau, in radio contact with the vessels, agreed to provide food, water, and fuel but outside Cuban waters. A Cuban patrol boat escorted the ships to Cayo Güinchos in the Bahamas. The expedition then fell apart and the adventurers were ultimately taken to Camp Columbia, the Cuban army's principal base outside Havana. One individual did manage to escape by jumping ship and swimming ashore; he was Fidel Castro.[36]

Surprisingly, the people of Havana gave the captives heroes' welcomes. On October 3 the Cuban Supreme Court ordered their release. General Pérez was discredited for having accepted a bribe from Trujillo and for having arrested these "freedom fighters" and seizing their property. The military leaders of the expedition—Rodríguez and Miguel Angel Ramírez[37]—successfully moved their operation to Guatemala, taking many of their small arms with them. The weapons were flown in Guatemalan air force planes and stored in secret locations near Guatemala City. Men and weapons came under the protection of President Arévalo. The "common soldiers" were left in Cuba to fend for themselves.[38]

NICARAGUA

To say that Anastasio Somoza was less despicable than Rafael Trujillo is splitting hairs. Anastasio Somoza had come to power on January 1, 1937, through assassination and intrigue. Like Trujillo, his manipulation of the U.S.-trained army made this possible. Somoza systematically made the nation his personal political and economic domain. Throughout the World War II era, he crushed his opposition by claiming that they were Nazis and putting those he did not kill into concentration camps.[39]

In 1947 Somoza chose to step behind the presidential chair and run the government through a puppet due to internal opposition and pressure from many in the United States. The Nicaraguan opposition took heart from the changing attitude in the United States as well as the overthrow of the Martínez regime in El Salvador and the Ubico regime in Guatemala by Liberals. Somoza picked Leonardo Argüello, then seventy-five years old, as his successor; Somoza did retain command of the national guard. All, including Somoza, expected Argüello to be a dutiful puppet. On May 1, 1947, Argüello stated in his inaugural address, "I will not—you can be sure of that—be a mere figurehead President."[40] Practically all believed this to be only rhetoric. Argüello acted quickly. He removed the chief of police in the capital; transferred Somoza's son, Maj. Tachito Somoza, from Managua to the garrison in Léon; gave the national university autonomy; and recalled Somoza's son-in-law, Guillermo Sevilla Sacasa, from his ambassadorship to the United States.[41]

All of this was too much for Somoza. He called each regional commander, got his backing, and then acted. Somoza ordered the military commanders to disregard orders from the president. Somoza offered opposition leaders a "role" in his projected new government. They refused to become involved with Somoza but they failed to warn Argüello of his projected removal. On May 26, twenty-five days after Argüello had taken office, Somoza seized the national communications building and ordered the national guard to attack the presidential palace. Within a few hours Argüello fled to the Mexican Embassy. Those loyal to Argüello were arrested. Somoza's handpicked Congress deposed Argüello and chose Víctor Román y Reyes, Somoza's uncle, as president. At first the United States withheld recognition of the Román y Reyes government but it finally did so in early 1948. In 1950 Somoza, once again through a sham election, made himself president.[42]

COSTA RICA

Not even Costa Rica escaped the post–World War II turbulence. The February 8, 1948, presidential election between former President Rafael Calderón Guardia, the mentor and patron of current President Teodoro Picado Michalski, and Otilio Ulate, a newspaper publisher, was particularly violent. Both sides charged the other with voting irregularities and riots occurred. On

February 28 the national election board ruled in favor of Ulate. However, the very next day the pro-Calderón Congress voted 27-to-10 to nullify the election and set April as the time period for a new election.[43]

On March 1 Ulate was arrested and one of his chief supporters assassinated, but Archbishop Victor Sanabria won the release of Ulate. Ulate called and then postponed a general strike. President Picado declared a "state of siege." At 5 A.M. on March 12, thirty followers of Costa Rican farmer José Figueres, who supported Ulate, seized the town of San Isidro del General (85 mi SE of San José). During the morning three commercial Costa Rican DC-3 airliners landed at the town's airport and were captured by Figueres. Two of the aircraft were sent to pick up the Rodríguez-owned arms from Guatemala City to San Isidro. Figueres later stated, "Many of our boys had never flown solo before."[44] The aircraft returned the next day carrying weapons, munitions, and seven volunteers, all Dominicans.[45]

Figueres established a defense position at Santa María de Dota. Surrounded by mountains, it was about midway between San Isidro and the capital. A government force of 180 men tried to advance along the Pan-American Highway to attack the stronghold but could not break through the rebels' defenses. On March 20, the government tried a different approach. A 300-man conscript force drawn from banana workers and led by Nicaraguan Gen. Enrique Somarribas Tijerino and Costa Rican Communist Carlos Luis Fallas landed at Dominical on the Pacific coast. They advanced inland for 41 miles to the edge of San Isidro. There on the twenty-first, Miguel Angel Ramírez, reputed to be a dead shot, led a counterattack against this government force and routed it during a two-day battle.[46]

Also in mid-March, Anastasio Somoza sent Nicaraguan National Guard troops into Costa Rica as "volunteers." Somoza offered to airlift one thousand guardsmen to the Costa Rican capital. Picado declined this offer. President Enrique Jiménez of Panama led the international protests against Somoza's actions. On March 31 Somoza withdrew the guardsmen from Costa Rica.[47]

By early April the "Army of National Liberation" had swelled to some 700 men and Figueres initiated an air-ground offensive. A rebel DC-3 dropped a homemade aerial bomb on the presidential compound. On April 11 Figueres used two of his DC-3s to airlift 65 fighters to Puerto Limón (102 mi E of San José), which they captured. *Time* reporter Jerry Hannifin named this unit "*La Legión Caribe*" (the Caribbean Legion), and the term was soon loosely applied to the "Army of National Liberation" and those fighting dictatorial regimes in the Caribbean.[48] Puerto Limón was connected to Cartago (14 mi SE of San José) by a railroad line, the objective of Figueres' ground attack. In the meantime, Costa Rican President Picado gathered a hodgepodge of aircraft to fight the rebels. However, two Vultee BT-13As and a DC-3 were lost in crashes.[49]

Using burro trails, Figueres' 600-man ground force passed undetected through the government troops confronting his stronghold and captured Cartago at 6 A.M. on the twelfth, threatening the capital. The government troops soon realized that they had been outmaneuvered and followed after Figueres. The rebel "Empalme" Battalion decisively defeated the government troops near the town of El Tejar.[50]

President Picado asked the diplomatic corps to assume the protection of the capital. The corps created a committee headed by the Papal Nuncio, Luigi Centoz, and composed of representatives from Chile, Mexico, Panama, and the United States. By April 13, Figueres controlled most of Costa Rica with the primary exception of the capital, San José, and negotiations between the opposing sides began. The primary obstacle was the "labor brigades" controlled by Manuel Mora, the head of the Communist Popular Vanguard Party (*Partido Vanguardia Popular*). Mora threatened a house-by-house fight. Figueres bought Mora's neutrality by promising not to interfere with existing labor laws and practices. As a consequence, the Costa Rican Communist Party lost all influence.[51]

On April 17 some 500 Nicaraguan guardsmen occupied three Costa Rican border towns. A unit was also airlifted to Villa Quesada, over 100 miles inside Costa Rica. The previous day, Francisco Calderón (Rafael's brother), representing Picado, had signed an agreement which permitted Somoza to do this should he believe his border threatened. Somoza, attempting to pacify the United States which was bringing substantial pressure against him, gave Washington a copy of the secret agreement. Agreeing to such an infringement on national sovereignty caused Pico's dwindling numbers of supporters to desert him even faster.[52]

On April 19 Pico signed the "Pact of the Mexican Embassy" and fled from Costa Rica to Nicaragua, taking the national arsenal and treasury with him. Figueres entered San José on April 24 and the Nicaraguan guardsmen soon returned to their homeland. A junta, which included Figueres, governed Costa Rica until November 8, 1948, when Ulate was inaugurated for a three-year presidential term. Two thousand individuals died during this "War of National Liberation."[53]

Figueres was indebted to Rodríguez and Arévalo. To the first, he agreed to return twice as many rifles as those he had used and to quarter the Caribbean Legion in Costa Rica. To the President of Guatemala he reaffirmed his commitment to the anti-dictator pact but without specifying any actions to be taken.

Somoza knew he was the next target of the Caribbean Legion and he was not ready to accept the fall of his ally in Costa Rica as a *fait accompli*. He began training Costa Rican exiles who supported Calderón; assembled a 1,000-man national guard strike force; and sent agents into Costa Rica to organize resistance against the new government. Back in Costa Rica Figueres, surprisingly, disbanded the Costa Rican army on December 1 and relied on the thirty-man Caribbean Legion to train a 1,000-man voluntary reserve at his ranch.[54]

On December 9, some 150 Calderón supporters invaded Costa Rica from Nicaragua and captured the town of La Cruz in the northwestern corner. Others captured the undefended hamlets of Puerto Soley, El Amo, and Murcielago during the next two days. Other émigrés landed near the town of Liberia and captured it. Although the Nicaraguan national guard had helped the émigrés to invaded Costa Rica, the guard stopped at Santa Rosa. Figueres publicly accused Somoza of complicity in the attacks. However, he did not call on the Caribbean Legion to oppose the invasion, fearing this would promote an all-out attack on Costa Rica by the Nicaraguan national guard. At the urging of the United States, Figueres appealed to the Organization of American States (OAS) under the Inter-American Treaty of Reciprocal Assistance for help.[55]

Guatemalan President Arévalo immediately offered help to Costa Rica. In large measure Somoza withdrew his support for the adventure due to intense international scrunity and it collapsed. The OAS mediated a truce which was signed on February 21, 1949. The OAS investigation did publicly expose Costa Rica's assistance to the Caribbean Legion and caused it to leave and relocate in Guatemala.[56]

DOMINICAN REPUBLIC (AGAIN)

The Caribbean Legion, still led by Rodríguez, changed its primary target from Somoza to Trujillo with the support of Guatemalan President Arévalo. The strategy this time was to airlift a small force to the Dominican Republic. It would be equipped to train and to arm volunteers. This coincided with the plans of a group of exiled Dominicans living in Puerto Rico led by Tulio Arvelo, a veteran of the 1947 aborted invasion. Rodríguez and Arvelo decided to work together.[57]

Aircraft were purchased in Mexico and the United States with Spanish Civil War refugees playing a prominent role. Among them was Alberto Bayo, Fidel Castro's future instructor in guerrilla warfare. They acquired seven transport aircraft: a C-46 Curtiss Commando; two Douglas C-47s; two PBY Catalina amphibians; a Lockheed Hudson; and an Avro Anson V. They could not hire enough aviators to fly all the aircraft, so the last two were left in Mexico.[58]

On June 18, 1949, D-Day, the mercenary pilots (two North Americans and two Mexicans) flying a C-47 and a Catalina, fled to Mexico. The Mexican pilot of the other C-47 was stopped from deserting at gunpoint. Amazingly, in very short order two Guatemalan air force C-47 transports flown by Guatemalan air force personnel took their place and the invasion proceeded.[59]

At 4 o'clock on June 18 a four-plane invasion air fleet took off from San José, Guatemala. The planes landed on Cozumel Island, Mexico, to refuel. The occupants believed that permission for refueling had been clandestinely arranged. The Mexican authorities seized the expedition. Back in Guatemala, the expedition's remaining Catalina unsuccessfully tried to take off from Lake Ornes but was delayed until the next day because it was overloaded. Unaware that the other planes had been seized, the Catalina flew to Luperón Bay on the northern coast of the Dominican Republic. There the three aviators (North Americans) and twelve invaders (eight Dominicans, three Nicaraguans, and one Costa Rican) failed to inspire a following and soon fled for their lives on foot. Ten were killed and five were captured. Diplomatic charges and countercharges flew across the Caribbean and the Caribbean Legion collapsed.[60]

COSTA RICA (AGAIN)

The demise of the Caribbean Legion did not end the feud between Somoza and Figueres. In 1954 Nicaraguan Emiliano Chamorro plotted the assassination of Somoza with the help of "Don Pepe" Figueres. Somoza discovered the plot; he shot many of the conspirators, and others fled into exile. Somoza rejuvenated the Costa Rican exiles under West Point-trained Teodoro Picado (a classmate of Tachito Somoza), the former President's son. On January 11, 1955, some 500 émigrés supported by the Nicaraguan national guard invaded Costa Rica and occupied the border town of La Cruz. An unmarked C-47 transport aircraft dropped arms and supplies to the invaders while two unmarked T-6 trainers strafed Costa Rican cities including San José. A second group of invaders captured the town of Villa Quesada (42 miles NW of San José).[61]

For a second time, Figueres invoked the Rio Treaty. On January 15 an Nicaraguan F-47 attacked an observer aicraft belonging to the Organization of American States and then attacked Liberia. This introduction of a fighter aircraft was a serious escalation. The United States sold Costa Rica four P-51D fighters for one dollar each from its active inventory; they arrived one day later on January 16. Somoza declared that this was "putting dangerous toys in the hands of a lunatic." These planes, which outclassed any planes in the Nicaraguan inventory, immediately scared their opponents from the sky (supposedly while being flown by Costa Rican pilots). Somoza had purchased 26 F-51s from Sweden in late 1954 but they did not arrive in crates until January 17, 1955. It took two months to make twenty-two of them operational, but even then few Nicaraguan pilots were trained to fly them.[62]

Figueres once again mobilized the Costa Rican people (called "Ticos"). The invaders were pushed out of Costa Rica by January 18 and young Picado was killed during the fighting. Once again Somoza professed his innocence. The United States, facing what it perceived to be a significant Communist threat in Central America, chose not to press its most vocal anticommunist ally, Anastasio Somoza. Some fifteen years earlier, President Franklin Roosevelt reportedly had questioned Secretary of State Cordell Hull, "Isn't that man [Somoza] supposed to be a son of a bitch?" The secretary reportedly replied, "He sure is but he is *our* son of a bitch."[63]

OBSERVATIONS

Prior to World War II, the United States had dominated Central American and Caribbean politics *when it chose to*. The 1907 Washington Treaty and the 1923 Washington Treaty, both of which it helped broker, offered the promise for a more democratic future for at least the Central American isthmus. Citing this second treaty (which the United States did not sign), the United States had delayed the recognition of Central American dictators for as much as two years. In 1933 Secretary of State Cordell Hull stated at the Seventh Inter-American Conference in Montevideo, "no government need fear any intervention on the part of the United States under the Roosevelt Administration."[64]

However, the perceived threat of fascism and communism caused the United States to emphasize insuring political stability even when it meant abandoning the promotion of democracy. A clear example of the United States caving in to such pressure was the recognition of Anastasio Somoza on May 5, 1948, in spite of the fact that it knew he had overthrown President Argüello and that Somoza's past actions offered no hope that he would honor any promises he might make toward creating a more democratic environment. In the eyes of many Latin American liberals, such decisions by the United States demonstrated that nation's condonation of the likes of Anastasio Somoza and Trafael Trujillo.[65]

The upheavals in El Salvador, Guatemala, the Dominican Republic, Nicaragua, and Costa Rica continued a long pattern of violence in Central America and the Caribbean and were nothing new. What was new was that these events were initiated by leftists, some of whom possessed democratic ideologies. This offered the United States the opportunity to change its policy of maintaining the status quo to promoting democratic values. This opportunity was appreciated by the Assistant Secretary of State for Inter-American Affairs, Spruille Braden.[66] He and others tried to take advantage of it. But as the cold war intensified throughout the late 1940s and early 1950s, anticommunist zealots like John Foster Dulles (Secretary of State between 1953 and 1959) dominated the direction of U.S. policy in the Americas. They judged men like Arévalo of Guatemala and Figueres of Costa Rica as being at best anti-*Yanqui* and at worst dupes of the Communists.[67]

Also, these opportunities in Central America and the Caribbean could not compete for America's attention with the threats that occurred in Europe, the Middle East, and Asia, where the United States believed the stakes to be much higher.

CHAPTER 19

PARAGUAY, 1947

Given the state of rebellion provoked by the leadership of the *Febrerista* of Concepción—in criminal complicity with the Communist Party and the *Concentración Revolucionaria Febrerista* [the Revolutionary *Febrerista* Party]—it is the imperative duty of all of the honest and working people fond of peace and respectful of the law to cooperate with the government in order to extinguish this criminal element.

—Government Proclamation of March 10, 1947

THE SPARK

On March 7, 1947, conspirators rebelled against the iron rule of President Higinio Morínigo. They attacked police headquarters, the military academy, the Interior Ministry, and the office of the President. Although these rebels were easily dealt with, nonetheless the rebellion spread.[1]

BACKGROUND

President Morínigo assumed power in September 1940 when President José Estigarribia was killed in a plane crash. Morínigo quickly evolved into a dictator who maintained power through shifting coalitions which included the senior military officers and the most conservative members of the *Colorado* Party. These *Colorados* wielded significant influence; they controlled the paramilitary band, the Red Standard (*Guión Rojo*).[2]

In late 1946 Col. Rafael Franco,[3] a nationalist and popular hero of the Chaco War, was permitted to return to Paraguay after many years of exile. Morínigo unsuccessfully attempted to incorporate Franco's supporters, the *Febreristas*, into his government. This failed and the Cabinet resigned in January 1947.[4]

In the meantime, Franco orchestrated an unlikely coalition of *Febreristas*, Liberals, and Communists; their goal was the overthrow of Morínigo. Although the March 7, 1947, coup attempt in Asunción failed, the 2nd Infantry Division in the river port of Concepción (134 mi N of Asunción) revolted and was joined by other army units, including most of the troops garrisoning the Chaco (the sparsely populated western half of Paraguay). On March 23 four rebel aircraft bombed Asunción but caused little damage and no casualties. The stalemate persisted for a month with the loyalists holding Asunción and the rebels Concepción.[5]

Apparently, the Paraguayan navy was protecting some fugitive conspirators at the Asunción Navy Yard. When President Morínigo ordered the Commander-in-Chief of the navy, Capt.

Sindulfo Gill, to surrender the conspirators, he refused. During the evening of April 26 the majority of the navy joined the rebellion.

OPPOSING FORCES

The principal military strength of the rebels was the army's Chaco garrison and the navy. The Chaco garrison was about 3,000 men, many of them conscripts. In general, most Paraguayan officers and noncommissioned officers supported the rebellion, although many could not directly aid in the cause because they either held unimportant positions or were far from the sites of conflict.[6]

The navy possessed two river-gunboats, the *Paraguay* and *Humaitá* (launched in the early 1930s), and an assortment of armed river craft, most of which had been constructed for commerce. The *Paraguay* and *Humaitá* were not immediately available since they lay in Buenos Aires (570 mi S of Asunción) undergoing repair.

The loyalists commanded some 2,000 soldiers who garrisoned or were near the capital; most were veterans of the Chaco War (see chapter 11). Importantly, practically all of the air force remained loyal. It had perhaps thirty planes.[7]

OPENING STRATEGIES

The rebels had two strategic problems. First, the loyalists controlled the capital, Asunción, which was the seat of political and economic power. Second, the rebel's principal forces were geographically split at two extremes. The Chaco garrison and the less potent naval craft were at Concepción some 134 miles north of Asunción up the Paraguay River (which flowed into the Plate River) and the gunboats *Paraguay* and *Humaitá* were some 570 miles to the south of Asunción at Buenos Aires, Argentina, on the Plate River.

Given the spontaneous nature of the rebellion, the rebels did not develop an offensive strategy until late in July, three months after the navy had joined the rebellion and four months after the Chaco garrison had rebelled. Finally, the rebels at Concepción planned to sail down the Paraguay River and take the capital by riverine assault while the two gunboats attempted to sail up the river and attack from the south.

The loyalists planned to dispatch a force over land to recapture Concepción. If successful, this would leave the rebels without a base of operation.

INITIAL FIGHTING AROUND THE CAPITAL

On April 27, loyal army troops attacked the Asunción Naval Yard. After a few hours of fighting, the commanding officer of the loyalists, Col. Federico W. Smith,[8] pretended to negotiate an armistice and then joined the rebels. In spite of this loyalist defection, the navy and its supporters were badly outnumbered and faced ultimate defeat. The loyalists renewed the attack on the naval yard which was located in an important working-class neighborhood, a stronghold of the Communists. Some naval personnel attempted to flee to Argentina in the steamer *Pratt Gill*, while others, supported by the Communist workers at the naval yard, fought on. Finally, the army overwhelmed the defenders on the twenty-ninth. A few days later two government aircraft attacked the fleeing *Pratt Gill*. The steamer was forced to beach near the mouth of the Pilcomayo River, and the fugitives were interned in Argentina.[9]

THE NAVAL ASSAULT FROM THE SOUTH

On May 6 the crews of the *Paraguay* and *Humaitá*, which were still at Buenos Aires, called a political meeting to air a number of grievances. Some wanted a more democratic government at home, some wished to show support for their rebellious naval comrades, and a few were Communists who supported world revolution. The officers, for the most part, remained loyal to the Morínigo government. The rift between officers and crew ended in a fight in which four men were wounded and ten officers arrested. On May 7 rebellious crew members seized the *Paraguay* and the *Humaitá* and joined the rebellion.[10]

Two days later the gunboats sailed up the Plate River, leaving behind their machine guns, ammunition, and fuses, which had been put ashore when the ships entered dry dock. Some ten officers who remained loyal to the government were also left behind. The two ships reached the Canal Guazú, opposite the Uruguayan port of Carmelo, on May 9 and remained there until July 5. Those on board discovered that most of their rifles were unserviceable and that they had only fifteen hundred pesos with which to pay the ships' expenses. On July 1, with the help of Paraguayan navy Capt. José A. Bozzano,[11] who was then living in Uruguay, the crews acquired rifles and ammunition: eight shells for the 4.7-inch main battery, seven machine guns, three heavy and four light, and more than two hundred rifles, some in very bad condition. Not one centavo of money remained, and there was only enough food and fuel for eight to ten days.[12]

During the morning of July 10, the gunboats, accompanied by three steamers, passed Paso de la Patria and entered Paraguayan waters. Lt. Col. Alfredo Stroessner,[13] commanding loyalist forces in the south, asked the air force to attack the gunboats. In the ensuing attack at least one bomb hit the *Humaitá* in the fire control center. On the twelfth aerial reconnaissance revealed that one gunboat was beached some three miles above Ituzaingó (125 mi S of Asunción). Four sorties were flown that afternoon, and at least one 210-pound bomb scored a hit. Stroessner moved troops and ordnance downriver in the steamers *Tirador*, *Hellen Gunther*, and *Mariscal Estigarribia* and the armed tug *Capitán Cabral*. On July 18 he landed 180 men and five guns on Cerrito Island, from which his ordnance fired on the beached gunboat. The rebel ships were also attacked from the air between July 15 and 21. Between July 24 and 29, Stroessner's forces captured the Coratei Islands from the rebels. The gunboats had been halted.[14]

THE FLOTILLA ASSAULT FROM THE NORTH

As the loyalist ground force approached Concepción, the rebels decided to evacuate the port on July 29 and advanced against the capital. In twenty-four hours Lt. Cmdr. Néstor Martínez Fretes organized a flotilla capable of transporting 3,000 men. He armed three steamers, ten large river boats, and 24 lesser craft with field pieces, heavy and light machine guns, and mortars. All rebel troops were embarked by late afternoon on the thirty-first, the very day the loyalist troops entered the port.[15]

The rebels' plan called for Infantry Regiment No.1 to attack Puerto Milagro at 1 P.M. and then march upon Ybapobó. Meanwhile, the flotilla would force passage through the river port of La Caida and, while steaming to Ybapobó, defeat en route the loyal gunboat *Coronel Martinez* and the armed tug *Ñeembucú*, lying between La Caida and Puerto Milagro. Overcoming these difficulties, the flotilla would then make the best possible speed toward Asunción.

The initial assault went well. Infantry Regiment No.1 successfully attacked La Caida and the flotilla reached Puerto Milagro on August 1, dispersing government forces there. After heavy fighting at Puerto Milagro, the rebels captured the *Coronel Martinez* and the *Ñeembucú* as well as two shore-based guns. The flotilla then continued down the Paraguay River and was attacked by loyal aircraft.

On August 2 the rebels attacked Puerto Ybapobó after the garrison there fled. Fire from a river battery hit a large river boat that was carrying many of the rebels' provisions; it exploded. On the third the flotilla joined forces with a rebellious cavalry unit at San Pedro and Rosario but halted its push toward Asunción. It disbarked 2,700 men at Arecutacuá (32 mi N of Asunción). At first, the rebels successfully rolled back the army units that opposed them, but soon the rebels were running short of munitions and supplies. A Sikorsky S-44 seaplane, belonging to the Uruguayan TAG II Society, crashed while attempting to fly munitions from Uruguay to the rebels. The flotilla had lost much time landing small attachments in villages without military significance.[16]

THE LAST REBEL PUSH

Back in the south, the rebel gunboats *Paraguay* and *Humaitá* renewed their efforts to force passage up the Paraguay River on August 4. As they attempted to advance, Stroessner's guns hit one of the gunboats in heavy fighting, whereupon both boats retired.[17]

The rebellion began to falter. Stroessner's guns beat back the *Paraguay* and the *Humaitá* at Punta Jacquet Island. The gunboats retreated down the river and asked the Argentine authorities at Itá Ybaté for interment on August 15. In the north government troops recaptured Cuatro Mojones from the rebels. On the 18th the rebels abandoned the thirty-six surviving ships and craft of the flotilla at Puerto Copacar. They were immediately taken over by loyal naval personnel under the command of Captain Pedro Meyer and brought to Asunción on August 19. The next day the rebellion collapsed. Rebellious officers and political leaders fled by plane and boat to Argentina while soldiers and sailors surrendered.[18]

OBSERVATIONS

Although Paraguay had suffered numerous rebellions from the close of the Chaco War in 1935 until 1947, none were of the magnitude or had the far-reaching consequence of the 1947 rebellion. First, following the failed rebellion, Paraguay returned to single-party rule by the *Colorados*, a dominance it had not enjoyed since 1904. Second, the rebellion propelled Alfredo Stroessner into national prominence, a status that allowed him to seize and hold the government for 35 years (1954–89). Third, since the majority of the military officers had supported the rebellion, their defeat allowed Morínigo to significantly reduce the influence and reshape the military.[19]

Notwithstanding Communist participation on the side of the rebels, the 1947 rebellion was an intraclass fight principally between *Febreristas*, Liberals, junior army officers, and most of the navy on one side, and *Colorados*, the army establishment, and the air force on the other. On the losing side, the enlisted men were granted amnesty; however, about thirty officers were purged and *Febreristas*, Liberals, and Communists were chased into hiding or exile. Once again, Rafael Franco returned to exile.[20]

No casualty figures have ever been released for the 1947 rebellion, but they must have been at least several hundred. Much of the fighting was fierce, particularly the bloody boarding of the *Coronel Martínez* and the *Ñeembucú*. The strategy of a riverine assault from Concepción upon Asunción was brilliant and well organized but poorly executed. This force was too easily diverted from its primary goal, the capture of Asunción. Moreover, the loyal air force played an important role, helping to halt the upriver progress of the *Paraguay* and the *Humaitá* and slowing the downriver assault of the Concepción river flotilla. The rebels had no effective means of opposing these air attacks.[21]

CHAPTER 20

COLOMBIA, *LA VIOLENCIA*, 1948–64

The *"Bogotazo"* of 1948 was . . . the most impressive spontaneous insurrection of the urban poor.

—E. J. Hobsbawn

THE SPARK

On April 9, 1948, Jorge Eliecer Gaitán, the messianic leader of the Liberal party, was mortally wounded two blocks from the capitol building in Bogotá. His assassin was beaten to death by bystanders. As news of the event spread, a mob formed and began attacking members of the government, clergy, and public property.[1]

BACKGROUND

The Conservative victory in the "Thousand Days War" at the turn of the century began an era of relative peace in Colombia that had not been experienced since colonial times (see companion volume). Some fighting did occur between 1902 and 1947. These disturbances were caused by the elections of 1910, the "banana strike" of 1928, the elections of 1930, and the Leticia border war with Peru in 1932 (see chapter 12). In general, however, the country was relatively at peace, when compared to its nineteenth-century history.[2]

In 1930 the Liberals won the elections on an economic reform platform and returned to power following an absence of forty-six years. However, they failed to improve economic conditions for many reasons. Foremost, they, like the Conservatives, represented the interests of the elites of society and not the increasingly large labor movement. Thus, labor and land reforms were half-hearted and did not satisfy the urban and rural masses. Secondarily, world depression stagnated the economy; and new taxes on income, inheritance, and excess profits alienated the rich.[3]

In 1946 Jorge Eliécer Gaitán, a persuasive orator, proposed significant change to benefit the masses and as a consequence split the Liberal party between the old-line elite and the recently organized labor movement. This permitted Conservative Mariano Ospina Pérez to win the presidency that year with a 42 percent plurality. However, the Liberals won a majority in Congress and Gaitán emerged as the leader of the reunited Liberal party. President Ospina formed a coalition cabinet hoping to head off violence, which it failed to do. In Congress Gaitán proposed changes so radical that not even his own party was willing to fully support him. The newspapers of each party viciously attacked the opposition. The Conservatives accused the Liberals in Congress of converting the capital's police force into their private army. Clashes occurred between mobs representing the opposing parties.[4]

Conditions worsened throughout 1947 and early 1948. Strikes occurred in Bogotá and Cali. The department (equivalent to a state) of Tolima (the area surrounding Bogotá) revolted, apparently with the support of its Liberal governor. Gaitán, in a memorandum to the President, accused the Conservatives of persecuting organized labor, wrecking the coalition, and encouraging violence. The President rejected the changes and refused to aid thousands of destitute refugees in the capital. As a consequence, the Liberals within the coalition cabinet withdrew in March 1948. Tensions ran high as the Ninth International Conference of American States opened in Bogotá on March 30. Ten days later, Gaitán was shot and soon would die.

OPPOSING SIDES

At the time of *La Violencia*, Colombia's population was 17,298,000 individuals, making it the third most populous Spanish-speaking nation in Latin America (only Mexico and Argentina had larger populations). Its people were 68 percent *mestizo*, 20 percent white, 7 percent pure Indian, and 5 percent black. It was 90 percent Roman Catholic, and the Catholic Church was particularly influential in the rural areas. Some 90 percent of the population lived in the river valleys nestled among the three mountain ranges of the Andes in the western one-third of the nation. Much of the eastern two-thirds of the nation was a sparsely populated plain known as the *llanos*.[5]

Politically, Colombia was divided between Liberals and Conservatives. An individual's affiliation could be determined by many factors other than political ideology, such as religion, family traditions, or those of the city, town, or village in which he resided. For example, Bogotá was overwhelmingly Liberal whereas Medellín (337 mi NW of Bogotá) was strongly Conservative. Party affiliation caused by regional loyalty was exacerbated by Colombia's rugged terrain and inadequate transportation and communication networks. Each party possessed members from all social classes.

Three armed groups fought each other—the army (including the national police), the partisans, and the bandits. And frequently, individuals and even groups would change loyalties, particularly among the partisans and the bandits.

In 1948 army officers were predominantly Conservative although some junior officers were Liberals. The army as an institution had not played a significant role in Colombian politics since independence. Its prime mission had been defending Colombia's disputed borders, and it was configured to fight a conventional war. The army was untrained and ill-equipped for guerrilla operations in the rugged and forested mountain country.

Partisans were, for the most part, individuals who were fighting for either the Liberal or Conservative party, although some may have had little understanding of ideology. Initially, the Liberals, many of whom were city laborers, acquired their arms from the capital's police and later the flourishing black market. The Conservatives received theirs mostly from the national police and the army.

Bandits had ravaged rural Colombia since independence and flourished during the era of *La Violencia*. They armed themselves by thievery from army and police stations, by ambushing small patrols, and by smuggling, which was a serious problem along the coasts and across the borders. They also developed the ability to manufacture crude but effective small arms.

OPENING STRATEGIES

Apparently, neither political party had planned to seize power in April 1948; however, during their decades of feuding they must have produced contingency plans. This observation is supported by the fact that radio stations were systematically seized shortly after the riots began and broadcast the recipe for "Molotov cocktails."[6]

Once the melee began on April 9, 1948, strategies were ill-defined and almost impossible to enforce. Controlling the hearts and minds, or at least the actions, of the people became more important than controlling territory. The Liberals attempted to convert the younger army officers and the capital's police to their cause. The Conservatives worked to increase their influence among the national police and the senior army officers. The bandits intuitively knew that sustaining chaos was to their advantage. In this environment, the bandits held tactical advantage. They were able to strike without warning and disappear before the army or national police could react because of the small size, mobility, and familiarity with the terrain of the bandit forces.[7]

THE *BOGOTAZO* (RIOTS IN THE CAPITAL)

Following the shooting of Gaitán, an enraged mob attempted to storm the presidential palace but was repulsed by its guard. Next, it attacked the nearby Capitol where arch-Conservative Laureano Gómez was presiding over the Conference of American States. Gómez and the delegates escaped but the mob succeeded in seriously damaging the building. The capital's police, who sympathized with the mob, turned over arms and ammunition, and some even joined in the rampage. The mob became further enraged when it learned that Gaitán had died. Thousands from all over the city swelled its ranks. Looting, murder, dynamiting, and arson spread. Radio stations were seized and used to direct the mobs. The only means of communications available to the military were the telegraph lines.[8]

The violence spread to other cities. A mob fleetingly took over Barranquilla (950 mi N of Bogotá) and flew the red flag from the city hall for much of the day. Churches, convents, and schools were looted and burned, and priests were beaten to death. Serious riots also occurred in Bucaramanga (280 mi NE of Bogotá).[9]

The government declared a "state of siege" and suspended many civil liberties. Troops supported by a few M3A1 tanks were brought into the capital from outlying garrisons, and they forcefully dispersed the mobs. But this took several days, and in the meantime, central Bogotá was severely damaged. Perhaps 10,000 people were killed in the capital. Once order had been restored in the capital, President Ospina again brought Liberals into the government in an attempt to form a new coalition acceptable to all. Liberals filled half of the cabinet posts, including those of Minister of Government and Minister of War. A fragile political stability was created in the capital and the major cities, and the state of siege was lifted.[10]

THE "FIRST WAVE," 1948–53

The violence returned and spread from the cities, through the western coffee-producing area, to the eastern plains. In the countryside, Conservative and Liberal villages attacked each other. The national police, primarily loyal to the Conservatives, did not protect Liberal villages and even aided in the attacks upon them. Liberal villages retaliated by attacking the national police.

As the chaos spread, the army became increasingly loyal to the Conservatives as Liberal officers deserted under pressure, some taking entire units with them into the mountains and the *llanos* (the eastern plains).[11]

THE PRESIDENTIAL ELECTION OF 1949

The violence again increased as the 1949 elections approached, and in early November the President reinstated the state of siege.[12] The violence spread to the floor of the House of Representatives where Conservative legislators opened fire at their Liberal counterparts who returned fire. One deputy was killed, and several wounded.

The Conservatives intensified their efforts to suppress the Liberals as arch-Conservative Laureano Gómez returned from self-imposed exile in Spain to run as the Conservative candidate. In the countryside, the Conservatives used their control of the national police and the army to intimidate Liberals. Conservative deputies, accompanied by police and the army, rounded up liberal peasants, took away their voter registration papers, and forced them to sign a document stating that they did not belong to the Liberal party. Two days before the election, someone shot at Dario Echandia, the Liberal presidential candidate. The Liberals withdrew his candidacy and boycotted the election. Murder and fraudulent vote counting were common.[13]

Gómez, in his inaugural address on August 7, 1950, stated that law and order would prevail. He perceived those opposed to his programs to be Communists, Liberals, and bandits, all subject to summary execution for violating the smallest infraction such as not obeying the curfew, carrying of firearms without a permit, and evading military service. Violence again increased. Initially it was principally politically motivated with outbursts of religious prejudice. As the government took increasingly drastic steps to keep order, the violence continued to escalate. Bandit gangs terrorized the countryside and the villages—trains were attacked, banks were robbed, and crops were held for ransom.[14]

A military expedition was sent to pacify the *llanos*, a Liberal stronghold. Military aircraft dropped leaflets ordering residents to depart and troops followed, burning the vacated villages. Many of the men escaped into the brushland and joined the partisan bands. The government tactic created mass migration and vast refugee problems. Many of the hastily recruited national police committed atrocities. Since most Protestants were Liberals, their clergy and property became targets, particularly on the *llanos* and in the department of Valle del Cauca in southwestern Colombia.[15]

By 1949 the violence had spread throughout the country. It was the worst on the *llanos*, in the highlands from the departments of Santander through Valle del Cauca, and in the upper Magdalena Valley. The destruction of cattle, crops, and infrastructure was so severe that food shortages occurred in the cities. As anarchy took hold in the countryside, Liberals created "independent peasant republics," which challenged government authority and control.[16]

In 1953 Gómez announced his desire to change the constitution to permit a Falangist state to be created. This plus his condoning acts of violence caused the defection of moderate Conservatives and much of the Catholic Church from his support base. Gómez, realizing his increasing dependency upon the army, attempted to oust its commander, Gen. Gustavo Rojas Pinilla,[17] and replace him with a crony. However, the army remained loyal to its commander and Rojas seized the government in a bloodless coup d'état on June 13, 1953 (see chapter 21).[18]

THE ROJAS REGIME

The new military government was at first welcomed with relief by most. Amnesty for partisan bands and the release of political prisoners immediately reduced the violence. A few days after the announcement, some 600 partisans surrendered in Medellín. By July 4,000 Liberals had surrendered. And by the end of 1953, most of the 20,000 partisans and some of the bandits had laid down their weapons. Peace was temporarily restored on the *llanos* when Rojas traveled to the region and appealed to the dissidents to lay down their arms. He began a pacification program which included the construction of roads, schools, and health clinics. Displaced Colombians were helped to reestablish their homes. Taxes were reformed and the government established corporations to reconstruct the badly damaged infrastructure and provide electrical power, transportation, and low-cost housing.[19]

General Rojas' initiatives caused the moderate Liberals and Conservatives to begin to work together with the prospect of power sharing (*convivencia*). However, Rojas undermined the thought of a coalition replacing his regime.[20] Rojas endeavored to create a new political base patterned after that of Juan Perón of Argentina. This lost him the support of moderates among the Liberals and Conservatives. As a consequence, Rojas formed his own political party, ruling as a *caudillo*, and individual liberties were drastically reduced.[21]

THE "SECOND WAVE," 1953–57

By the end of 1953 violence was again on the rise in spite of the doubling of the army and the absorption of the national police into the army. The violence once again returned to its point of origin, the western cities. Liberal and Conservative parties' newspapers began to brutally attack the opposing party. On June 8, 1954, the police fired on student demonstrators in Bogotá, killing one student. The following day army discipline broke down as troops confronted a large demonstration. They fired into the crowd, killing nine and seriously wounding thirty. During 1954 and 1955 the army used bomber aircraft against one partisan band that was estimated to be 2,000 members strong.[22]

Within Rojas' politically narrow-based government, corruption became common. Also, coffee prices, which earned over 75 percent of Colombia's foreign exchange, dropped in 1954, and the following year's crop was poor. By 1956 the government could not meet its short-term foreign loans. Also, Rojas' pacification program broke down. He failed to insure the impartiality of the administrating officials, coordination among government agencies, and a long-term strategy. In his 1956 New Year's address, Rojas blamed the Protestants and the Communists for supporting those committing the violence.[23]

Opposition to Rojas began to come together. In 1956, Liberals began working toward a new *convivencia* at Benidorm, Spain, where the "Civil Front" (later renamed the "National Front") was created by Conservative Laureano Gómez and Liberal Alberto Lleras Camargo. During the year the Roman Catholic Church withdrew its support for Rojas. Finally, in May 1957, a thoroughly disillusioned military forced Rojas to designate a junta of five officers to replace himself as head of state and to go into exile on May 10.[24]

THE JUNTA RULES

Once again the change in regimes initially proved popular and political violence subsided. However, banditry flourished as gangs exerted territorial domain. A favorite target was coffee plantation owners who were subjected to extortion at harvest time. The military junta then began working closely with the "National Front" to facilitate a return to civilian rule.

CREATION OF THE "NATIONAL FRONT"

On July 20, 1957, President Lleras and former President Gómez, meeting at Sitges, Spain, defined in greater detail the joint platform of the "National Front." The agreement provided: (1) equal representation by the Liberals and the Conservatives in all representative bodies, in the cabinet, and in the civil administration; (2) proportional allocation of each party's quota among the factions of the party in legislatures and the cabinet; (3) that in Congress, decisions should be made on the basis of an absolute majority;[25] (4) that the arrangement should remain in force through three presidential terms (of four years each) beginning with the 1958 election; and finally, (5) that a plebiscite should formally ratify the agreement, which occurred on December 1.[26]

In a compromise suggested by Gómez, Lleras became the National Front's candidate and, in return, the Liberals agreed that the coalition government would prevail until 1974. The presidential terms were to alternate between the two parties over a sixteen-year period, thus giving each party two terms and allowing the Conservatives to serve last.

The return to democratic rule was reasonably free of violence. One of the first acts of President Lleras was to raise the national state of siege which had been in effect since November 1949. The only areas excluded from the declaration were the departments of Caldas, Valle del Cauca, Tolima, and Huila (the central and south-central highlands). He reinforced rural garrisons and established a rehabilitation prison for captured partisans and bandits on Gorgona Island, some 100 miles southwest of Buenaventura in the Pacific Ocean. Although lawlessness had not been eliminated, it had become manageable, and normal administrative and judicial procedures returned.[27]

"INDEPENDENT REPUBLICS" DECLARED

A few Liberal leaders had enough local control to declare "independent republics." The most prominent of these was the Dominican Father Camilo Torres Restrepo, who established the lower-class movement *Frente Unido del Pueblo* (People's United Front—FUP) at the peasants' republic of "Marquetalia" in the department of Tolima (120 mi WSW of Bogotá). Shortly, the army seized control of Marquetalia in 1964 inflicting numerous casualties. Ironically, this bloody event is considered the end of *La Violencia*.[28]

OBSERVATIONS

La Violencia was in part a continuation of the Liberal-Conservative, intraclass struggle between elites which had raged in Colombia throughout the nineteenth century; in part an interclass revolution by laborers seeking significant political, social, and economic change; and in part rural banditry which had existed since the colonial era due to the government's inability to govern the countryside. Throughout much of this era, constitutionally elected, narrowly based governments were able to govern because the army remained loyal to the constitution. But the National Front only fleetingly reduced the violence.[29]

La Violencia increased the fragmentation of society that was taking place in Colombia. Frustrated, young Liberals increasingly sought a solution among the radicals of the Communist Party championed by the charismatic Fidel Castro. And the radical Catholics (violent Liberation Theologians) looked to Father Camilo for leadership.

The tradition of violence gave the Castro-inspired, radical Communists of the 1960s an opportunity to begin their operations in an environment where some Colombian fighters were willing to swear allegiance to its cause to bring about political, social, and economic change and others simply to perpetuate the violence that had become their way of life (see chapter 29).[30]

La Violencia forced much of the rural population to seek haven in the unfamiliar, sprawling *barrios* of the city, thus destroying their ties to the land and the Church.

Accurate casualty numbers are not available. Monsignor Germán Guzmán Campos believes that at least 200,000 deaths occurred due to *La Violencia* and guerrilla activities between 1949 and 1962. Germán Arciniegas states that between 1948 and 1951 some 200,000 inhabitants fled to the cities or across the borders into Venezuela and Ecuador.[31]

PART 11

THE EARLY COLD WAR STRUGGLES

CHAPTER 21

COLOMBIA IN KOREA, 1950–53

No cannon fodder for Yanqui imperialists.

—slogan of Cuban Communists opposed to sending troops to Korea

THE SPARK

What motivated Conservative President Laureano Gómez to send Colombian troops to Korea in 1951 is still being argued. Some suggested that the decision was made in order to get weapons from the United States to suppress the Liberals at home. Others said that the participation allowed Gómez to send potentially dangerous Liberal officers far away. Some argued that he had changed his hostile attitude toward the United States and wanted to demonstrate his solidarity.[1]

BACKGROUND

Immediately following World War II, the United States policy toward Latin American nations was in disarray as a new Democratic president and a Republican Congress struggled for dominance. In September 1945 the United States stopped providing new lend-lease aid to Latin American nations; only those items previously agreed to were provided. In late 1945 and again in 1946, the Truman administration requested from Congress the authority to continue military cooperation with Latin America as recommended by the Inter-American Defense Board,[2] but this was ignored. The Mutual Defense Assistance Act of 1949 was the first post-World War II U.S. legislation that made arms available to Latin American nations. However, this act required Latin American nations to pay for the weapons.[3]

At the outbreak of the Korean War in 1950, the Truman administration sought Latin American military participation and closer military cooperation between the American republics to help the United States meet the threat of what some in his administration believed to be the beginning of World War III. Only Colombia sent combat forces to Korea.[4]

In 1950 the rule of law within Colombia was disintegrating due to a civil war known as *La Violencia* (see chapter 20). Although many of the senior military officers were Conservatives and many of the junior officers Liberals, the army, as an institution, had remained neutral. In his August 1950 inaugural speech, Conservative Gómez, who had won the presidency in a controversial election, took a strong pro-U.S. position and in November volunteered to send troops to Korea.[5]

OPPOSING FORCES

In 1950 there were about 15,000 men in the Colombian army. The army had served as a constabulary since being professionalized at the turn of the century. It was armed with obsolete weapons—Mauser rifles (models 1912 and 1924) and pre-World War II, Belgian-manufactured artillery.[6]

The navy possessed a small number of obsolete ships, the sole exception being the frigate *Almirante Padilla* which had been purchased from the United States in 1947. And the air force flew obsolete aircraft. The enemy in the Korean War, the Communist North Koreans and Chinese, posed no direct threat to Colombia.[7]

OPENING STRATEGIES

Colombia's goal was to fulfill its treaty obligations *and* to modernize its armed forces. Colombia probably hoped that its participation in the "police action" would result in the United States significantly upgrading its armed forces.[8]

THE WAR AT SEA

On September 18, 1950, Colombia announced that it was offering its only frigate, the *Almirante Padilla*, to the United Nations for service in Korea. On November 1 the frigate sailed for Long Beach, California, under the command of Lt. Cmdr. Julio César Reyes Canal, who had served a year on the old U.S. destroyer *Roper* as an exchange officer. After an extensive overhaul, the *Almirante Padilla* sailed from San Diego, California, on March 14, 1951, and on May 8 the *Almirante Padilla* arrived in Sasebo, Japan, to join Task Force 95. On May 20, newly assigned to South Korea's West Coast Support Group, the frigate started operating in Korean waters.[9]

Between mid-May and mid-June the frigate, whose presence was important due to the shortage of shallow-draft warships, operated off the west coast in various patrolling, escorting, and bombarding missions. It fired 686 rounds of 3-inch ammunition while bombarding enemy positions and sailed 5,182 miles.[10]

The *Almirante Padilla* then shifted its operations to the east coast and was placed under the command of Korea's East Coast Support Group. Between mid-June and September 9, 1951, the frigate operated off Wonsan and Songjin, being used extensively for bombardment and in-shore patrols and, on a number of occasions, for landing special agents behind enemy lines. The frigate returned to Cartagena, Colombia, on March 21, having steamed 48,000 nautical miles.[11]

In the meantime, Colombia acquired a second frigate to take the place of the *Almirante Padilla* in the war zone. Lt. Cmdr. Hernando Beron Victoria, together with seven officers and 114 enlisted men, sailed to Korea, where they took over the recently acquired U.S. frigate *Bisbee*, which was renamed the *Capitán Tono* on February 22. The entire crew of the *Almirante Padilla* volunteered to join the *Capitán Tono*; of them, four officers and sixty-two enlisted men were chosen to remain in the war zone.[12]

For two months the *Capitán Tono* patrolled the east coast of Korea, on May 23 participating in the bombardment of Wonsan. There it shelled road and rail communications day and night, an activity that frequently provoked duels with shore batteries. This lasted until the end of August. After a brief rest, the frigate escorted major U.S. units, then returned to Colombia. In all, the *Capitán Tono* steamed 50,000 nautical miles.[13]

Colombia began negotiations for a third frigate to relieve the *Capitán Tono*. On June 26, 1953, the nation took over the USS *Burlington* at Yokosuka Naval Base and renamed the frigate *Almirante Brion*. Lt. Cmdr. Carlos Prieto Silva commanded a crew composed primarily of veterans from the *Capitán Tono*. The *Almirante Brion* was only in Korean waters a few days before the armistice was signed on July 27, 1953.[14]

THE WAR ON LAND

In mid-November 1950 Colombia's ambassador to the United Nations, Zuleta Angel, offered a 1,060-man infantry battalion for service in Korea. Training began in Colombia on February 5, 1951, based on American military doctrine and using American rifles and artillery. On May 21, 1951, the battalion sailed for Korea on board the U.S. transport *Aiken Victory* and arrived on June 16.[15]

Following a six-week acclimation period, the Colombian battalion, commanded by Lt. Col. Jaime Polanía Puyo, was assigned to the 21st Infantry Regiment of the 24th U.S. Infantry Division. It entered the fighting on August 7. Between October 12 and 30, 1951, the battalion took part in the "Fall Offensive." It held the flank position of the division and on the thirteenth attacked "Hill 561" near Kumsong. The Colombians lost 6 dead and 23 wounded, including the battalion commander.[16]

On February 29, 1952, the Colombian battalion was transferred to the 31st Infantry Regiment, 7th U.S. Infantry Division. It, like other units serving in Korea, was routinely transferred in and out of the front lines. Most of the Colombian casualties occurred while conducting small patrols into enemy-held territory. Replacements for rotations and casualties periodically arrived from Colombia. On June 21 the battalion captured "Hill 400" and the following month, on July 4, Lt. Col. Alberto Ruiz Novoa took over command of the unit.[17]

During mid-March 1953 the Colombian battalion took part in the attack on "Hill 180." Between March 13 and 23, the battalion was subjected to an intense artillery barrage. The Chinese counterattacked during the night of the twenty-third and captured the hill "Old Baldy." The Colombians lost 33 dead, 97 wounded, 92 missing, and 30 prisoners. The Chinese losses were much more numerous. The Colombian battalion was withdrawn from the front line and reorganized. It returned to the fighting on March 26.[18]

On May 18 the Colombian battalion was transferred to the 17th Infantry Regiment, 7th U.S. Division. In July 1953 its combat role ended with the signing of the Panmunjom Armistice; Lt. Col. Carlos Ortiz Torres took command of the battalion at this time.[19]

OBSERVATIONS

At least in the short term, Colombia's participation in the Korean War significantly improved its relations with the United States. Edward G. Miller, the Assistant Secretary of State for Inter-American Affairs, testified before Congress on February 20, 1952, "The record between the United States and Colombia could not be better. They sent troops to Korea and they negotiated an economic treaty with us."[20]

Admittedly, other Latin American nations made token contributions of food, medicine, and miscellaneous materials. This lack of military participation was very disappointing to the United States. After all, the Latin American recipients of aid provided under the Mutual Security Act of 1951 had reaffirmed their intention "to give their full cooperation to the efforts to provide the United Nations with armed forces as contemplated by the Charter."[21]

Colombian participation in the Korean Conflict did ultimately produce the first Colombian military dictator in many decades. Gen. Gustavo Rojas Pinilla, a Conservative, had been sent to Korea to serve on the United Nations' general staff. President Laureano Gómez, fearing Rojas' increasing popularity, next sent him to serve on the Inter-American Defense Board in Washington. Returning to Colombia in early 1953, Rojas overthrew the government on June 13. The battalion returned from Korea in December 1954. It was stationed in Bogotá and was used to create an elite unit and as a cadre to raise the performance of the army in general.[22]

The three Colombian frigates had served five tours of duty in support of U.N. forces in Korea, a contribution from which the Colombian navy also benefited. At a time when the United States was eager to obtain the support of as many U.N. members as possible, Colombia stepped forward, receiving in turn ships, training, and equipment that would not otherwise have been available.

The Colombian army lost 131 men in combat, 10 from other causes, and 60 missing in action. Those wounded in combat were 448 men, and 162 were injured due to other causes. The Colombian battalion was awarded the U.S. Presidential Unit Citation and the U.N. Service Medal for valor. Colombians won 18 U.S. Silver Stars and 25 U.S. Bronze Stars for valor.[23]

CHAPTER 22

THE GUATEMALAN REVOLUTION, 1954

> The history of guerrilla movements in Latin America, indeed the contemporary history of Latin America itself, cannot be understood without reference to this cardinal event.
>
> —Richard Gott

THE SPARK

Procommunist Guatemalans, anticommunist Guatemalans, and the United States would each consider different events as sparking the 1954 revolution. The Communists might choose the first broadcast of the "Voice of Liberation" on May 1. For the United States, the event would probably be the election of Arbenz as president in late 1950. For the anticommunist Guatemalans, the event would be the assassination of Col. Francisco Arana on July 18, 1949.

BACKGROUND

In 1944 Guatemala experienced a revolution, the ideological roots of which were progressive and democratic. Following the revolution a junta composed of Arana, Arbenz, and Toriello acted as an interim government. Arévalo was elected president by a large majority and took office on March 15, 1945. A new, very liberal constitution was promulgated. The Arévalo government worked on rebuilding the nation's infrastructure.[1]

The Arévalo government attempted to restructure land tenure, labor laws, education, and the military. Military installations were modernized, emphasis was placed on professionalism and pay, and benefits were substantially increased. Arévalo tried to win the support of young army officers for their participation in civic and social activities. However, the military was split as to the appropriate degree of its involvement in nontraditional duties. The military academy graduates were led by Colonel Arbenz, then the Minister of Defense, and the "mustangs" (those who became officers without going to the academy) by Colonel Arana, the Chief of Staff. The issue was temporarily extinguished when Colonel Arana was assassinated in 1949.[2]

Many of Arévalo's programs threatened U.S. commercial domination of the Guatemalan economy. The U.S.-owned United Fruit Company was virtually sovereign within Guatemala. It owned the telephone and telegraph companies; administered the only Caribbean port; held a majority share in the stock of the railroad company; held a monopoly on electricity; and monopolized banana exports. United Fruit exploited its Guatemalan employees, but it also provided thousands of jobs as well as education and medical help to them. A peasant working for United Fruit was exponentially better off than his typical fellow countryman.

Arévalo placed the Guatemalan government in direct economic competition with the United Fruit Company. He constructed a new port facility in the Caribbean, built a highway giving access to the interior, and constructed a hydroelectric plant.

These commercial irritations to the U.S.-owned firm were aggravated by the increasingly important roles being played by Communists within the Guatemalan government. Communists were able to penetrate the Libertarian Popular Front and National Renovation (*Frente Libertario Popular Renovacion Nacional*) and thus gain key positions throughout the Arévalo government.[3]

U.S. political sensitivities against Communism were becoming more acute each day as Senator Joseph McCarthy convinced many in the United States that it was losing the cold war. By the time Arévalo left office in 1950, the U.S. State Department believed that he was under the influence of the Communists.[4]

In late 1950 Arbenz was elected president and took office in March 1951. He was not a Communist,[5] nor did he appoint Communists to his cabinet or subcabinet. The Communists held only four seats in Congress and it was the smallest component of Arbenz' ruling coalition which controlled 51 seats out of 65 in the 1953–54 legislature.[6] However, Communists did hold important lesser positions within the government. They were particularly influential in the implementation of land reform and the formation of labor unions. Arbenz relied heavily upon their organizational skills. In 1951 the Communist Party was legalized and changed its name to the Guatemalan Workers Party *(Partido Guatemalteco de Trabajo*—PGT). By August 1953 its membership had increased by a modest two or three thousand members.[7]

The Guatemalan foreign ministry was significantly infiltrated by Communists. As a result, many of the positions taken by the foreign ministry gave the perception that the Communists had substantial influence throughout the country. For example, Guatemala was the only country at the Tenth International Conference of American States held in Caracas to vote against the U.S.-sponsored resolution condemning international Communism.[8]

In 1952 U.S. President Harry Truman approved a plan to topple the Arbenz administration, but Secretary of State Dean Acheson convinced Truman to cancel it.[9]

On June 17, 1952, a new Guatemalan law authorized the expropriation of large land estates. In February 1953 the United Fruit Company was notified that it had to sell its fallowed land for redistribution; the company farmed perhaps 15 percent of the land it owned. Arbenz offered double the tax value of the land. Admittedly, the land was grossly underassessed; however, the company had never complained about the underassessment when it was the basis for taxation. The company demanded twenty-five times the assessed value as compensation. The land was expropriated. The land belonging to the International Railway of Central America, whose largest shareholder was the United Fruit Company, was also expropriated on October 10, 1953.

In January 1953 the Eisenhower Administration resurrected the plan to overthrow the Arbenz administration. In March the Central Intelligence Agency provided weapons, which were paid for by the United Fruit Company, to Guatemalan officers who opposed the Arbenz administration. The officers rebelled in April, but this was crushed by troops loyal to Arbenz. In the subsequent trial, the role of the United Fruit Company was exposed but not that of the Central Intelligence Agency.[10] Following this failure, the CIA began a more serious effort to overthrow Arbenz.

OPPOSING FORCES

The forces employed were unique in the annals of Latin American military history. The United States chose to rely on agents from the recently created (1947) Central Intelligence Agency, dissident Guatemalans, and mercenaries. Headquarters for the operation was set up at Opa Locka, Florida. The Nicaraguan dictator Anastasio Somoza provided a site for a training camp and an airfield. The Honduran dictator Andino Carías made a Caribbean island available for a radio station. In addition to small arms, the United States supplied thirty aircraft.

Arbenz had lost the support of much of the military following the assassination of Colonel Arana. Therefore, he tried to curry support among the recently created labor unions, many of which were dominated by Communists; however, they had few weapons.

OPENING STRATEGIES

The United States chose to employ the Central Intelligence Agency to topple the Arbenz government. The Eisenhower Administration had developed a global strategy of the "New Look" which placed reliance upon nuclear weapons versus conventional arms. Where possible, "brush fires," such as the crisis in Guatemala, were to be solved by covert means. The Arbenz government had not developed a strategy. Too late it would attempt to mobilize world opinion and arm workers.

Several influential members of the Eisenhower administration had or previously had significant finanial interests in Guatemala. How much this bore upon the decision to intervene is unclear. Secretary of State John Foster Dulles (whose brother Allen was the director of the Central Intelligence Agency) had been the legal representative of the United Fruit Company in 1936 when it had negotiated the concession agreements for land with the Guatemalan government. The brother of John M. Cabot, the Assistant Secretary of State for Latin American Affairs, had been a director and president of the United Fruit Company. And Anne Whitman, the wife of the public relations director of the United Fruit Company, was President Eisenhower's personal secretary.

THE WAR OF WORDS

On January 26, 1954, the U.S. Ambassador to Guatemala, John E. Peurifoy, testified before the U.S. Congress, "the situation is so critical that I am afraid if we let this situation continue for another six months without doing something, then I tell you I believe we will have a Soviet satellite between the oil fields of Texas and the Panama Canal."[11]

In January Arbenz received incriminating letters between Castillo Armas and Miguel Ydígoras Fuentes who had lost the 1950 election to Arbenz. They were living in Nicaragua under the protection of Somoza, whom, along with the United States, Arbenz accused of plotting against his regime. Although Arbenz publicized the letters, the conspirators denied their authenticity.[12]

On March 17 the U.S. State Department announced that "an important shipment of arms from Communist-controlled territory" had arrived at Puerto Barrios, Guatemala, on board the merchantship *Alfhem*. The United States argued that this 2,000-ton shipment was far in excess of the needs of the 6,000-man Guatemalan army.[13]

THE CIA'S FIRST COUP

The CIA established a clandestine radio station, supposedly broadcasting from within Guatemala but in fact doing so from an island off Honduras. The radio station was to undermine the confidence of the Guatemalan people in the Arbenz government and to coordinate opposition. The first broadcast of the "Voice of Liberation" was on May 1, Labor Day and a holiday.

The Voice of Liberation claimed that the arms delivered from the *Alfhem* were to be distributed to the militia, controlled by the labor federation and not the army because Arbenz distrusted his senior military officers. The Voice of Liberation called on the military to rebel against the government which it argued was planning its destruction. Castillo Armas' air force, which had been supplied by the CIA, complemented the propaganda effort by dropping thousands of leaflets on the capital and other towns.

On May 24 the U.S. Department of State announced that U.S. arms and munitions were being flown to Honduras and Nicaragua under the Military Assistance Program, concluded with those two countries on April 23 and May 20 respectively.[14]

On June 8 Arbenz announced the suspension of civil liberties for thirty days. In a few days, a Guatemalan Air Force pilot defected to a neighboring country. He broadcast an appeal over the Voice of Liberation to fellow aviators urging them to follow his example. Fearing that some might do so, the Arbenz government grounded its planes.[15]

In the capital, the Arbenz government cut electricity at night, ostensibly to enforce an ordered blackout but more likely to deny the populace the opportunity to listen to the Voice of Liberation. Tensions increased. The blackout did not inhibit rebel cargo aircraft, two C-46s, from dropping supplies to supporters in the hills surrounding Guatemala City. The Voice of Liberation successfully appealed to the people of the capital to light candles to help guide the planes.

The Voice of Liberation consolidated the belief that it was operating from within Guatemala by fabricating an on-the-air government raid against the station. Government-controlled radio stations believed the ploy and eagerly reported the rebel-fabricated story. When the Voice of Liberation reemerged on the air the next day and detailed its fictitious, harrowing escape from government forces, who would doubt that the rebel radio station was truly operating from within Guatemala in the midst of the enemy?[16]

THE INVASION

On June 18 the Voice of Liberation broadcast that Col. Carlos Castillo Armas and his supporters had invaded Guatemala. The announcement stated, "At our command post here in the jungle we are unable to confirm or deny the report that Castillo Armas has an army of five thousand men." In fact, the Colonel led 150 poorly trained and poorly armed men across the border from Nicaragua. The rebel air force of World War II vintage fighters and B-26 bombers flew low, noisy sorties, dropping a few homemade bombs and doing a little strafing. The aircraft earned the nickname *Sulfatos* (laxatives), allegedly because of the effect they had on the opposition.[17]

In fact the situation was a stalemate. Neither side could attack—the insurgents were far too weak and the government was not sure of the loyalty of the army. On June 25 a rebel aircraft dropped a single bomb in the middle of the empty military parade ground in Guatemala City. Two days later the Voice of Liberation broadcast that two rebel columns were approaching the capital. These events successfully created the elusion that Guatemala City was soon to become the center of the fighting.

In the meantime, U.S. Ambassador Peurifoy had been carrying on secret talks with Col. Carlos Díaz, a high-ranking army officer. Díaz persuaded Arbenz to resign the night of June 27.[18] Arbenz and six hundred supporters sought asylum in foreign embassies.[19]

AN AFTERSHOCK

Shortly after coming to power Arbenz ordered a victory parade in Guatemala City during which the participating military units (which had not taken sides in the conflict) were ordered to salute the "liberation army." This did not sit well with the military, particularly the cadets from the academy. During the night of August 2 some drunken members of the "liberation army" forced two cadets to strip and sent them back to the academy naked. That night, the cadets locked up their officers, won the support of the nearby *Guardia de Honor* (presidential guard), and attacked the "liberation army" at Roosevelt Camp outside Guatemala City. The American ambassador and church officers helped end the fighting. Lives were lost on both sides.

The senior cadets (some twenty-five) were sent outside Guatemala to finish their military education. The junior cadets (some fifty-five) continued their normal program. The "liberation army" was disbanded but many of its leaders became politicians helping to create the new political party, the National Liberation Movement (*Moviemento de la Liberacion Nacional*). Others were taken into the Guatemalan army (see chapter 18).

OBSERVATIONS

The Guatemala Revolution of 1954 was of cardinal significance for many reasons. First, the actions of the United States convinced the Latin American radical left, Che Guevara among them, that the United States would resort to covert means to prevent Communists from coming to power by whatever means within the Western Hemisphere. This drew the battle lines.

Second, the outcome indebted the winners in Guatemala to the United States for the very existence of their government. The United States would collect this debt by using Guatemala during 1960 and 1961 as one of the training sites for the Bay of Pigs invasion, a fact never forgotten by Fidel Castro. Third, the Eisenhower administration viewed the outcome of the revolution as proof that its strategy of using covert actions against "brush wars" worked. Fourth, Latin American governments failed to evolve and articulate a coordinated response, the necessary first step if they had any hope of influencing future events.[20]

Tactically, the prime lesson of the 1954 revolution was the impact of the communication revolution and the power of propaganda. Allen Dulles, the director of the Central Intelligence Agency, reported to President Eisenhower,

> The use of a small number of airplanes and the massive use of radio broadcasting are designed to build up and give main support to the impression of Castillo Armas' strength as to spread the impression of the regime's weakness. . . . From the foregoing description of the effort it will be seen how important are the aspects of deception and timing.[21]

One did not have to have "sensitive" sources to come to this conclusion. A British diplomat noted, "The soldiers had nothing to do with it. The war was won by that radio station."[22] Although both sides sustained casualties during an engagement at Guabán, nonetheless, the overthrow of Arbenz was accomplished with a minimum of bloodshed.

Figure 22. The Guatemalan Revolution (1954). Carlos Castillo Armas' bodyguard at the time of the CIA-funded overthrow of the Arbenz government. *Courtesy Dell C. Toedt, United States*

The prime unanswered question concerning the Guatemalan revolution was how "red" was the Arbenz government. The 1944 revolution started Guatemala on a path which by the early 1950s increasing numbers of influential Americans believed was leading to Communism. When Tracy Barnes, a senior CIA official, was questioned by agent David Atlee Phillips, why it was necessary to depose the freely elected Arbenz government, Barnes replied,

> It's not just a question of Arbenz. . . . Nor Guatemala. We have solid intelligence that the Soviets intend to throw substantial support to Arbenz. Weapons. There are six thousand soldiers in the Guatemalan Army, twenty-five hundred constabulary, and several government-organized paramilitary units. Given Soviet backing, that spells trouble in all of Central America. An easily expandable beachhead.[23]

Following the fall of the Arbenz government, CIA agent Phillips concluded,

> After reviewing the documents left behind by Arbenz and his collaborators, I am more inclined to agree with those who saw the endeavor as a justifiable act of American foreign policy. The documents revealed a paradigm of Soviet Cold War expansionism, a program clearly intended to establish a power base in the Western Hemisphere.[24]

Although Phillips addressed the perceived intentions of the Soviet government, he did not speculate on those of the Arbenz government.

Communist or not, the Arbenz government made two political blunders. The first was the purchase of arms from the East Bloc and the second was the attempt to arm unionists. The first drove the United States to action and the second lost Arbenz what support he had within the Guatemalan army. A key lesson was that a government that does not have support of its military can be easily toppled.

PART 12

MID-TWENTIETH-CENTURY INTERCLASS REVOLUTIONS

CHAPTER 23

BOLIVIAN REVOLUTION, 1952

Land to the people, mines to the state.

—Bolivian Marxist-Leninist Gustavo Navarro, 1926

THE SPARK

Defeat during the Chaco War between 1932 and 1935 (see chapter 11) shocked many Bolivians into the belief that the political, social, and economic direction which the nation had followed during the past hundred years was leading to its destruction.[1]

BACKGROUND

Throughout much of the nineteenth century, *caudillos* supported by feudal-like followings had misruled Bolivia (see companion volume). Significant political and economic changes occurred by the turn of the century which altered that paradigm. Following the War of the Pacific (1879–83), Indian communal lands (*ayllus*) were forcefully swallowed by the large estate owners, a tin boom created a super wealthy absentee elite but none of this wealth trickled down, and a professional military system was begun with the establishment of an officer's corps and the standardization of conscription. One task exercised by this military was guaranteeing the new political, economic, and social status quo which benefited the wealthy ranchers and the mining magnates who now controlled the government. Those who represented this elite became known derogatorily as the "*rosca*".[2]

The Chaco War laid bear inequities within Bolivian society. In many cases, Bolivian officers, who were mostly Spanish-speaking *cholos*, could not even talk to their own soldiers, who were Quechua- or Aymará-speaking Indians. Frequently the officers and enlisted needed the intercession of the bilingual, *cholo* noncommissioned officers.[3]

Those who survived fighting the war wanted to change Bolivia. Thousands of Indian soldiers shunned the return to servitude under the estate owners and immigrated to the towns and cities looking for work. Many young officers, while being held captive in Paraguayan prisoner-of-war camps, formed a secret lodge called the "Fatherland's Cause" (*Razón de Patria*—*Radépa*), whose goal was to transform Bolivia into a modern nation. Some of its leading members showed fascist tendencies. Also, young intellectuals created the National Revolutionary Movement (*Movimiento Nacionalista Revolucionario*—MNR) which espoused the emancipation of the poor. In 1941 the MNR evolved into a political party which was a coalition of middle-class intellectuals, peasants, and miners. The MNR was pronationalism, pro-Germany, anti-United States, antisemite, and would become Pro-Perón.[4]

In addition to the MNR, a myriad of other political parties burst onto the scene during the late 1930s and early 1940s. These included the Trotskyite Revolutionary Workers Party (*Partido Obrero Revolucionario*—POR), the Bolivian Socialist Falange[5] (*Falange Socialista Boliviana*—FSB), and the Leftist Revolutionary Party (*Partido de Izquierda Revolucionaria*—PIR). Although these movements encompassed political ideologies ranging from fascism to Communism, they shared the goal of destroying the old power elite that governed Bolivia.[6]

The years between the Chaco War and the 1952 revolution were turbulent. One of the numerous casualties of the Chaco War was the fledgling Bolivian democracy. President Daniel Salamaca was overthrown on November 27, 1934, and replaced by Vice President José Luis Tejada, a puppet of the military. On May 17, 1936, Col. David Toro Ruilova overthrew Tejada. Toro, a member of the National Socialist Party, declared, "The social doctrine [of his government] has been born in the sands of the Chaco, in the trenches where the civilians and military men have shed their blood for the *Patria*."[7] He established the first Ministry of Labor and the *Banco Minero* which promoted small and mid-size exploitations. Toro also nationalized the holdings of the Standard Oil Company; this was the first confiscation of a major multinational company in Latin America. Standard Oil was held in contempt because it had delivered oil to Paraguay clandestinely through Argentina during the Chaco War.[8]

During the night of July 14, 1937, Col. Germán Busch,[9] representing more radical officers, overthrew Toro in a bloodless coup d'etat. The new constitution of 1938 stressed common good over private property. Busch created a Ministry of Public Health and championed women's suffrage and education. In April 1939 Busch dissolved Congress and proclaimed himself a dictator. He directly challenged the *rosca* by decreeing that mining companies could not remove capital from the country. Busch only succeeded in uniting his enemies and on August 20, 1939, he died under mysterious circumstances. A month after Busch's death, all his major initiatives were annulled. Although the Toro and Busch regimes produced few political, social, and economic changes, they did raise expectations among the masses.[10]

By the spring of 1940, Gen. Enrique Peñaranda was elected President. The commander of the army during the latter stages of the Chaco War, he was supported by the Conservatives and less radical members of Congress who formed the *Concordancia*. By now, the MNR led the opposition to the government. After some hesitation, the Peñaranda regime supported the Allies in World War II. Between 1940 and 1944 Bolivian mines produced more than 40,000 tons of tin. The United States, which controlled transportation to and from Latin America, set the price of tin at 52 cents per pound. Many Bolivians believed that fair market value was $4.50 per pound. The MNR denounced Peñaranda's cooperation with the United States and his agreement to compensate Standard Oil with $200 million for the nationalization of its holdings.[11]

In December 1942, some 8,000 miners went on strike at the Patiño mines in Catavi (60 mi SE of Oruro). Patiño refused their demands and the government sent in the army. On December 21 the miners, their wives, and their children formed three columns and advanced toward the 700 troops. At 1,000 yards the troops fired over their heads but the strikers continued to advance. Then the soldiers fired into the protesters. Government accounts place the casualties at nineteen men, women, and children dead and thirty wounded; the opposition said that 700 had been killed and 400 wounded. The MNR used this tragedy to win miners to its cause. This disaster led to the *Radépa* and the MNR joining forces.[12]

In the early morning of December 20, 1943, the *Radépa* and the MNR overthrew Peñaranda in a bloodless coup d'etat. Maj. Alberto Taborga, leading some 600 men, arrested the President and other key officials. Members of the *Radépa* persuaded the troops to remain in their barracks. Maj. Gualberto Villarroel,[13] a member of the *Radépa*, became president and Víctor Paz Estenssoro,[14] the leader of the MNR, became Minister of Finance. All the countries within the hemisphere, except Argentina, refused to recognize the new government charging that there were ties between the new government and Nazi Germany. Numerous leaders, both allied to and opposed to Villarroel, were assassinated. The Villarroel regime supported a strong union movement in the mines. In 1944 the MNR won the majority in the elections, the United States recognized the government, and MNR members returned to the cabinet. The regime assembled over one thousand Indian chiefs (*caciques*) in the first National Indian Congress during May 1945.[15]

Finally, the opposition coalesced against Villarroel's use of violence, his hostility toward Marxism, and his suppression of the old elite. In June and early July 1946, unsuccessful revolts occurred. On July 20 a gathering of some fifty students swelled into an enormous crowd of 150,000 people. Troops fired on the people and dispersed them. On Sunday, July 21, the people burst into the streets. Mobs of teachers, students, and marketplace women seized arms from the arsenal and stormed the presidential palace, capturing it following an hour of fighting. They captured and shot President Villarroel and then hung his body from a lamppost, perhaps inspired by a recently shown newsreel of Benito Mussolini's end.[16]

Some 250 people died during the four-day rampage. Paz Estenssoro fled to the Paraguayan Embassy, where he remained for four months before being allowed to go to Argentina and the protection of Juan Perón. Some 5,000 Bolivians fled to Argentina and a lesser number to Uruguay. The army did nothing to control the violence.[17]

The military purged itself of the *Radépa* and supported the old elite. Social unrest continued between 1946 and 1952. Also, the state of the economy worsened; the world price of tin fell following World War II and the quality of ore declined as the richer veins were exhausted. The labor sector became more radical and the government more repressive. In 1947, some 7,000 miners at the Patiño Mines were dismissed and only those considered loyal were rehired.[18]

On August 27, 1949, the MNR, led by Hernán Siles Zuazo,[19] seized control of the department of Santa Cruz and part of Cochabamba to the east of La Paz. The bloodiest fighting occurred in Catavi. The government used aircraft against the rebels which caused numerous casualties among the population at large. After two months of fighting, the army, remaining united, overwhelmed the MNR. Some 1,200 persons died and few of these were among the government's forces. The government arrested Senator Juan Lechín,[20] a popular labor leader, among others. A protest strike broke out in Catavi and two American engineers were killed. The army reacted harshly, thus winning sympathy for the strikers. In May 1950 a factory strike in

La Paz evolved into an MNR-led insurrection. The army used planes and artillery to destroy the worker's headquarters and break the rebellion. Weary and ill, President Enrique Hertzog resigned.[21]

On May 6, 1951, Paz Estenssoro apparently won the presidential election from exile in Argentina. However, President Mamerto Urriolagoitia, who had been jailed during the Villarroel-Paz Estenssoro government, refused to accept the results and would not turn the matter over to the Congress as required by the constitution. Rather, he encouraged the military to seize the government and this *auto-golpe* became known as the "Mamertazo." Gen. Antonio Seleme was a vocal opponent of the MNR. A military junta assumed power on May 16 and Gen. Hugo Ballivián Rojas became president. Senior military officers, perceiving Ballivián to be inept, jockeyed to become the next president.[22]

OPPOSING FORCES

Bolivia is the third largest country in South America (Argentina and Brazil are bigger) and according to the 1950 census the population was only 2,704,000 people. The actual population, including many uncounted Indians, may have been closer to 3,500,000 inhabitants. The Bolivian army was composed of about 18,000 men. Some 3,000 troops were stationed in or near the capital.[23]

Miners composed a major element of the rebel forces. Nowhere in the hemisphere was there a more exploited group of workers. Foster Hailey, a New York *Times* correspondent, wrote in June 1951:

> Indians clad only in G-string and rubber boots hack at the precious rock. . . . The temperature varies from 120 to 150 degrees. The humidity is 90 to 95 percent. Rock dust fills the air and the lungs. Carbon dioxide bubbles from freezing water. . . .
>
> For eight hours a day, or longer, six days a week, 3,000 to 4,000 men, women and children ranging in age from 10 to 35 labor at cutting out the ore. For this they receive wages that reach a peak, for the men, at 135 bolivianos a day (about 68 cents). These miners are the highest paid workers in Bolivia. . . .
>
> Sixty percent of the miners, it is estimated, have tuberculosis. Half are syphilitic . . . half the babies born die in the first year. Those who live have a life expectancy of 35.[24]

Unbeknownst to the government, the rebels could also count on the lightly armed 3,000 *Carabineros* (national police), many of whom were stationed in the capital. Additionally, there were many militant miners and MNR members; however, like the miners, their participation was limited by the number of rifles available.[25]

OPENING STRATEGY

By the late nineteenth century, La Paz had evolved into the political power center of Bolivia. Therefore, like so many of its Latin American sister republics, whoever controlled the capital in all probability controlled the nation.

In late 1951 Siles Zuazo, former MNR vice-presidential candidate, clandestinely returned from exile to organize a rebellion. He chose to rebel on a Sunday late in March 1952 because the President would be traveling to southern Bolivia and many of the military would be on leave.[26]

At this point Gen. Antonio Seleme, who was the junta member responsible for internal affairs (his portfolio included the command of the *carabineros*), offered to participate in the rebellion. In return, he wanted to be the next president. Siles Zuaza mistrusted Seleme but was not sufficiently confident in his own potential for victory to refuse the offer. Zuaza stated, "we must cross a river, and it doesn't matter if we cross with the hand of the devil."[27] Seleme was required to formally join the MNR and swear his allegiance on a Bible in front of a recorder. The rebellion was rescheduled for April 9, Easter weekend.[28]

The government's strategy was to maintain sufficient forces near La Paz to guarantee its control. The danger of this strategy for those in power could come from the officer who controlled the troops in the capital. Therefore, it was essential that he be loyal to those who ruled. The military government of General Ballivián chose Gen. Humberto Torres[29] to command the army because he had opposed the military seizing the government. The thinking was that Torres had demonstrated that he had no designs of making himself president.[30]

PREPARATIONS

General Seleme convinced General Ballivián that General Torres was unreliable and that the troops he commanded should be posted outside La Paz. Seleme suggested that the *carabineros* (whom he controlled) and the Presidential Guard would be adequate to maintain control. Accordingly, in late March the "Sucre" and "Andino" regiments were removed to the *altipano*. General Seleme then concentrated the *carabineros* in the capital. Without revealing its conspiracy, the MNR contacted General Torres and urged him to support early elections. Jorge del Solar, an MNR leader, attempted to recruit army officers.[31]

REVOLUTION

At about 11 P.M. on April 8, members of the MNR clandestinely gathered at a few locations in La Paz where they were to receive arms from General Seleme. The weapons did not arrive and one group of 140 persons was arrested by *carabineros*. Other members of the MNR were rounded up and detained. Some MNR leaders incorrectly concluded that Seleme had betrayed them. In fact, the General was playing it "close to the vest" and had not told his subordinates involved in the plot that civilians would also be participating. Seleme immediately ordered the civilians released and provided weapons.[32]

At 5 A.M. on April 9, Holy Wednesday, *carabineros* and militant MNR members seized government buildings and the Illimani radio station. The confused Presidential Guard offered little resistance. The *carabineros* distributed weapons from the arsenals in La Paz to MNR supporters who streamed into the city; their numbers grew to 1,000 or more. For a moment, it appeared that the coup d'etat might be bloodless.[33]

Then at 3 o'clock in the afternoon General Torres ordered his troops to fight. The MNR had hoped that Torres would not react to their actions. Army reinforcements were rushed from the countryside and along with the cadets from the military academy they fought their way almost to the center of the city. As night fell the position of the rebels became increasingly difficult. General Seleme, who had assured Solar that "I will fight to the death,"[34] fled to the Chilean embassy.[35]

By the afternoon of April 10, miners led by Juan Lechín, who emerged from hiding, began pouring into La Paz from Oruro (146 mi SSE of La Paz) and prevented additional troops from entering the capital. Women from the Indian markets, who supported the MNR, simply went up to the Indian soldiers and grabbed their weapons. Also, there were some serious defections from the government's forces. The air force refused to bomb the capital, and the troops in

Viacha (26 mi SW of La Paz) refused to fight. During the early evening government troops began using artillery and mortars against rebel positions. Some forty miners attacked and silenced the guns. By the afternoon of April 11, Good Friday, the fighting was over and the MNR had won. Paz Estenssoro, 1,400 miles away in Buenos Aires, became president on April 16, 1952.[36]

OBSERVATIONS

The brevity of the fighting that achieved a true "revolution" may be explained by the social changes which had been accelerated in Bolivia by the Chaco War. By 1952 many Bolivians, including some within the army, saw the MNR assuming power as being inevitable.[37] Robert Alexander wrote, "The Bolivian National Revolution is the most profound movement of social change in America since the beginning of the Mexican Revolution of 1910."[38]

Also, like the Mexican Revolution of 1910, the military amateurs won in Bolivia. Although many of the members of MNR had served in the Chaco War and were supported by some officers within the *Radépa*, none of the leaders had served in the middle or senior levels of command; none were educated at the military academy.

The revolutionary government introduced many reforms. First, universal suffrage for men and women replaced a system under which an individual had to possess wealth and be able to read and write. Almost one million persons voted in the 1956 election whereas only 200,000 had voted prior to the revolution. Second, the mines were nationalized, but the "tin barons" received huge compensation settlements. Third, land ownership was reformed resulting in the expropriation of many large *haciendas* and the creation of landed peasantry. And, the army was transformed from an instrument of old elite to one that supported the new revolutionary government.[39]

Initially, the army was abolished; however, the MNR soon recognized the need for an army and it was reestablished on July 24, 1953. Numerous measures were taken to constrain the army's ability to play a political role. All top military officers were either imprisoned or exiled. Other officers associated with the old elite were purged. Remaining officers were required to take a loyalty oath to the MNR. The Military Academy (*Colegio Militar*) was closed. The manpower of the army was cut from some 20,000 to about 5,000 soldiers. The military budget was significantly reduced. The government created an MNR party militia and a miners' militia.[40]

In an attempt to keep the military from reverting to their old ways, its budget was kept low, but the militias retained their arms. The 1963 editions of the U.S. Army-produced Area Handbook for Bolivia observed,

> The civilian militias are considerably more dangerous and effective than appearances indicate. What they lack in professional polish they more than made up for in reckless abandon. The record shows that on every occasion when their services were required to protect national security, they performed successfully and well.[41]

Swearing allegiance to the MNR became a requisite for military service. An MNR political cell was established within the army. Much of the army was stationed away from the capital. The *carabineros*, although significantly reduced in number, were given better weapons. And the MNR created a "political police" (*Control Político*) whose task it was to seek out the opposition.[42] The military academy was reopened in 1953. Twenty percent of the cadets were to be sons of peasants; 30 percent sons of miners and city workers; and 50 percent sons of the middle class who could prove six years of standing in the MNR.

The MNR would spin apart in 1962. However, the major political, economic, and social changes it wrought have never been reversed.[43]

Estimates of the number of lives lost during the fighting on April 9–11, 1952, range between 300 and 3,000 persons.[44]

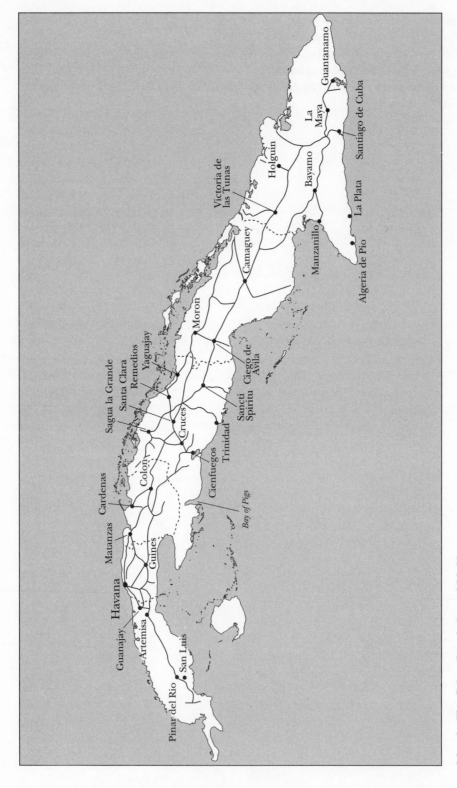

Map 4. The Cuban Revolution, 1956–59.

CHAPTER 24

THE CUBAN REVOLUTION, 1956–59

A civil war was won against a large army by a small group of amateurs.
—Hugh Thomas

THE SPARK

On July 26, 1953, Fidel Castro[1] led 164 followers, many of whom were or had been students at the University of Havana, in an attempt to seize the Moncada Barracks in Santiago de Cuba (604 mi ESE of Havana) and a smaller army base at Bayamo. Castro's plan was to capture arms and a radio station. He would then broadcast a manifesto declaring an uprising against the Batista regime and arm the new recruits who, he believed, would flock to his call.

Initially the attack succeeded. A military hospital was seized to care for the wounded. Raúl Castro,[2] Fidel's brother, captured the Palace of Justice in order to cover the main assault against the barracks from the rooftop of the palace. However, almost half of the main force lost its way (or courage). Fidel attempted to seize the barracks with about fifty men, but they were driven off by superior fire power. The attack on Bayamo also failed.[3]

Fidel Castro and the survivors retreated into the hills. The Archbishop of Santiago negotiated their surrender. About sixty-five rebels were summarily executed. A small number, including the Castro brothers, were saved when an army officer refused to obey orders to execute them upon capture.[4]

The July 26 attack was ill-conceived. The attackers were poorly trained, outnumbered, and outgunned. This seemingly catastrophic failure would inspire the Cuban Revolution and the date of the event, July 26 (26 de Julio), became the battle cry for the ultra-left throughout Latin America.[5]

BACKGROUND

The underlying cause for the Cuban Revolution was the increasing frustrations of the middle class with the excesses of the Batista government. Cuba hardly seemed ripe for Communist exploitation in 1956. It was perceived to have a large middle class for Latin America, seemingly infertile ground for ideological exploitation.[6] Cuba had been ruled directly or indirectly by Fulencio Batista[7] since 1933 with but brief interruptions. Cast from the same mold as Rafael

Figure 23. The Cuban Revolution (1956–59). Fidel Castro poses in the Sierra Maestra Mountains. Individuals who were vehemently anti-Castro claim that this widely published photograph, where he is cradling a rifle with a telescopic sight, is evidence that he would only fight from a distance. The other individual with a scope-mounted rife is his brother Rául. *Courtesy Library of Congress*

Trujillo of the Dominican Republic and Anastasio Somoza of Nicaragua, Batista was corrupt and brutal.

Castro and the others who attacked the Moncada Barracks were put on trial. No defense witnesses were permitted and the press coverage was limited. During this trial, Castro conducted his own defense. He was sentenced to fifteen years in prison and sent to Isla de Pinos Prison.[8]

In May 1955 Castro and his followers were released from jail under a general amnesty on the condition that they accept exile. Before departing for Mexico, Castro began to organize an underground movement headed by Frank País in Santiago de Cuba. In July, Fidel, Raúl, and several other veterans of the Moncada assault traveled to Mexico where they continued to plan for another uprising. There they met Ernesto "Che" Guevara,[9] who had worked as a minor bureaucrat within the Arbenz government.[10]

In Mexico, Fidel Castro enlisted Col. Alberto Bayo,[11] a Spanish socialist living in exile, to train himself and his followers in guerrilla tactics. Bayo started the training in Mexico City but it was soon moved to a ranch called "Santa Rosa" some 20 miles from Mexico City. These activities were twice interrupted by Mexican authorities (helped by Batista's spies) who confiscated the munitions. During this time Castro traveled to New York, Florida, and Texas and gained the financial support of influential exiled Cubans. In addition to money, they gave him the old yacht *Granma*.[12]

In November País met Fidel Castro in Mexico City and set November 30 as the date for a uprising in Santiago and a simultaneous landing by Castro at Niquero in western Oriente Province. Castro was to be met by hundreds of sympathizers with trucks and together they would seize Manzanillo and Bayamo.[13]

OPPOSING FORCES

Initially, Castro was supported by a few dedicated ultra-leftists and others seeking serious social, economic, and political reform. They were willing to make extreme sacrifices for their beliefs.[14] The leadership and approximately half of the rank and file of the rural guerrillas who would fight in the Sierra Maestra were city-bred members of the middle class. Most of the urban guerrillas were also from Cuba's middle class. One-tenth of the force was non-Cuban—Argentine, Dominican, Mexican, Nicaraguan, and Venezuelan.

In the beginning, one became a rural guerrilla by taking a weapon away from a Batista soldier either through bribery or force and joining Castro in the mountains. The number desiring to be rural guerrillas exceeded the need during the second half of 1957 and the early months of 1958. Thus, Castro could be selective as to who fought with him in the mountains.[15]

Most of the arms used by the guerrillas were captured from government forces. It is estimated that more than half the weapons sent to Castro from outside Cuba were intercepted by the Batista government, and those that got through accounted for no more than about 15 percent of the guerrilla arsenal. The .30-caliber Garand rifle was the most common weapon used by both sides. The guerrillas also had a large assortment of shotguns, old Springfields, and hunting rifles. Sixteen-gauge shotguns were modified to hurl "Molotov Cocktails" although these were almost as dangerous to the user as to the intended victim. The shortage of ammunition was a severe problem until the closing months of the struggle. Weapons training was normally conducted without ammunition.[16]

Fidel Castro was the maximum leader. He appointed front commanders and assigned them their operational territory and objectives. Each front commander appointed the several column commanders who were responsible to him. The column commander, in turn, appointed his captains and lieutenants. The only grade below lieutenant was soldier. The ideal size of a column while in the countryside was one hundred guerrillas.[17] The column was divided into platoons of thirty to forty men each headed by a captain, and the platoon was divided into squads of eight to ten men headed by a lieutenant.[18]

The Cuban army was composed of about 29,000 men. Much of the army was stationed near Havana to discourage coup. The countryside was primarily the responsibility of the Rural Guard (*Guardia Rural*). It maintained at least one company in each provincial capital to deal with uprisings.[19]

In theory, the army had been configured and trained by its American advisors to fight a World War II-type conflict. It had no training in counterguerrilla operations. In fact, the army was ill-prepared to fight in any environment. At the top were a large number of generals who owed their position to Batista's favoritism. The few professional officers, most of whom were graduates of the military academies, were not trusted with command positions. Many nonacademy junior officers served for forty years without receiving one promotion. They were not required to advance or retire. The enlisted ranks came from the poor and uneducated and received almost no training.

The air force possessed some forty-five planes—B-26 bombers, T-33 fighter trainers, F-47 fighters, and C-46 and C-47 transports.[20] The navy had four frigates and twenty-eight patrol craft. Most were stationed in the Havana area. The number of vessels available was too small to patrol the entire coast.[21]

OPENING STRATEGIES

Castro's planned strategy in 1955 was to lead Oriente Province into revolt. His landing party, linking up with hundreds of waiting followers, would then proceed to Manzanillo and along with others attack the barracks. At the same time, urban guerrillas in Santiago, Holguín, and other cities would create diversions through shootings and bombings.

Batista's strategy was to prevent Castro from landing and to terrorize his followers and sympathizers in Cuba (and those his secret police could reach outside the island).

Later, both sides would recognize that the 600-mile-long nation was fragilely held together by the Central Highway and its control was essential. And in the mountainous regions, particularly the eastern third of the nations, mules remained the most reliable means of transportation.

CASTRO'S DISASTROUS LANDING

On November 25, 1956, eighty-three Revolutionaries embarked on the overloaded and ill-provisioned *Granma* at Tuxpan, Mexico, and sailed for Cuba.[22] Of the eighty-three men on board, twenty-two were veterans of the attack on Moncada barracks and five were foreigners, one each from Argentina, the Dominican Republic, Italy, Mexico, and Spain. Before sailing, Castro left a manifesto with the United Press International in Mexico City announcing his return to Cuba to fight Batista. Release of the manifesto probably alerted Cuban reconnaissance.[23]

The *Granma* was delayed at sea because of rough weather. Due to poor communications, some of the planned urban actions against the Batista government were carried out on November 30 as scheduled while others were delayed. Those who went into action were crushed.[24]

Two days later, on December 2, Castro's yacht foundered near the shore of Cuba, and much of the food and munitions were lost. The guerrillas staggered ashore on the southeastern tip of Oriente Province at Belic, east of the intended landing site near Niquero and two days late. As they waded ashore, the guerrillas were attacked by a Cuban coast guard cutter and air force planes that had been alerted by a coast watcher.[25]

On the fifth, members of the Cuban army and navy intercepted the guerrillas at Algería del Pío as they walked toward the Sierra Maestra. Twenty-one guerrillas were killed and twenty-six captured. By the time they reached the mountains, only seventeen of the guerrillas remained. They had lost most of their weapons and supplies.[26]

The Sierra Maestra had traditionally been the refuge of Cuban dissidents and were well suited to rural guerrilla activities. The mountains peak at 8,000 feet and drop to heavily wooded foothills surrounded by thick brush and lowland jungle. Peasants engaged in subsistence farming on the fertile northern slopes. They were the source of food, intelligence, and recruits. The guerrillas courted peasant favor by paying fair prices for food, giving medical aid, and offering instructions on a wide variety of subjects.[27]

Attempting to isolate the survivors, Batista evacuated 400 families from the foothills and established a "zone of death." Unauthorized personnel found in the zone were shot. The Castro-led group excited little interest in Havana, where it was viewed as another harebrained scheme like the suicidal attack on the Moncada Barracks.[28]

OPENING SKIRMISHES

On January 17, 1957, the guerrillas carried out their first attack, this against the small naval barracks at La Plata at night. The government lost two sailors killed and eight captured of whom five were wounded. The rebels did not sustain any casualties. The attack succeeded, in part, because the local peasants had provided the guerrillas with information, desiring to punish the military for past atrocities. The Batista regime continued to use brutality, attempting to intimidate the population while hunting for the guerrillas. These acts won additional sympathizers for Castro's cause.[29]

THE WORLD'S PRESS COMES TO CASTRO

On February 24 the New York *Times* published the first of three articles by correspondent Herbert Matthews based on interviews with Fidel Castro in the Sierra Maestra. A stream of international journalists visited Castro in the mountains and helped created a "Robinhood" image.[30]

THE EVOLUTION OF TACTICS

During the early days of the fighting, the guerrillas ambushed small patrols and attacked remote barracks. This was repeated over and over. When government troops pursued the guerrillas, they in turn were ambushed, frequently sustaining heavy casualties. For the first six months, the army initiated no attacks against the rural guerrillas, who in the beginning were less than two dozen. Batista did order his air force to strafe and bomb suspected rebel strongholds and remote villages. By April, the number of guerrillas had increased to some eighty men.[31]

ATTACK AND COUNTERATTACK

Finally, in June 1957, the army launched an offensive. Some 4,000 troops attempted to hunt down the now less than 200 guerrillas. However, the various army columns did not coordinate their movements. The troops were used to living in barracks and were unaccustomed to rugged life. Their large patrols were slow moving and the local populace would not give them useful intelligence. The army also tried to establish a cordon around the Sierra Maestra during the summer of 1957. The guerrillas attacked the outposts, and the military found pursuit into the guerrilla stronghold to be very costly.[32]

From May to November 1957, the guerrillas ambushed army patrols and attacked small garrisons in the area bordered by Pilon, Niquero, Manzanillo, and Bayamo. The guerrillas attacked at night and retreated deep into the Sierra Maestra by dawn. By November the guerrillas were attacking during daylight as well.[33] The guerrillas continued to win small encounters from which they gained more weapons, recruits, experience, and a growing reputation. Enemy patrols were provoked into an attack and shepherded into a trap. If the soldiers did not respond to the bait, they were encircled and attacked from the rear. One tactic was to ambush the vanguard of a patrol trying to intimidate those who followed. Against barracks, the guerrillas divided into three units. Two groups attacked the flanks and the third guarded against reinforcements. Typically the battle was over within a few hours.[34] In almost every instance the guerrillas were numerically superior to the enemy at the point of attack and had the element of surprise. On occasion, government soldiers fought well in defense, at times sustaining significant casualties before surrendering or fleeing, but had no desire to take the initiative.

By August 1957 the guerrillas had established a safe haven (later called a *foco*) in the Sierra Maestra.[35] The mountain stronghold was secure enough to permit the basic training of recruits, the establishment of a field hospital, and the small-scale manufacture of leather goods and gunsmithing. An adequate supply of boots and shoes for pack mules was essential. The primary goal of recruit training was to determine who could withstand the hardships of being a rural guerrilla, such as hunger, and not to teach weapon proficiency.[36]

URBAN GUERRILLA ATTACKS

During the two years Castro was in the mountains, numerous groups, some of which were politically aligned with Castro, carried out acts of urban violence. The 26th of July Movement was Castro's primary urban arm. It dealt mostly in sabotage and other subversive activities within the cities. The urban guerrillas virtually ended tourism to the island, thus crippling the economy. Although successes were numerous, the casualties were high. The 26th of July Movement also organized an armed militia which grew to about 2,000 strong by the time of the abortive strike in April 1958.[37]

One such attack occurred on March 13, 1957, when the Revolutionary Directorate (*Directorio Revolucionario*), composed primarily of students and alumni of the University of Havana and other groups not associated with the 26th of July Movement, attacked the presidential palace in a bloody and unsuccessful attempt to assassinate Batista. Other students seized *Radio Reloj* and broadcast Batista's death, unaware that the assassination had failed. Within minutes Batista's police killed those who had captured the radio station. Suspects (primarily students) were arrested, tortured, and killed throughout the island.[38]

On July 30 the Revolutionaries sustained another defeat when Frank País, the head of the 26th of July Movement's urban guerrillas, was shot and killed in Santiago. Thousands marched at his funeral.[39]

DISSIDENT OFFICERS ATTEMPT A COUP

On September 25, 1957, some cashiered naval officers (members of Castro's 26th of July Movement) and supporters of exiled Carlos Prio Socarras (who had been overthrown by Batista in 1952) planned a coup involving individuals from the army and navy. On September 4 the naval conspirators attempted to postpone the uprising; however, the naval station at Cayo Loco, Cienfuegos (121 mi ESE of Havana), did not receive the message. On the morning of September 5 the local conspirators seized the station. Some 2,000 sympathizers joined them, armed with captured weapons. Word of the rebellion did not spread due to the censorship in force throughout the island.[40]

Within six hours a government column from Santa Clara (187 mi ESE of Havana) counter-attacked. After a day of fierce fighting, the rebels surrendered at 8 A.M. on September 26. Those rebels caught were shot without a trial. Some were protected by the naval commander who had remained loyal to Batista. They were tried and sentenced to prison on Isla de Pinos. Others escaped into the Escambray Mountains and formed the Second Front of Escambray [*Segundo Frente Nacional del Escambray*]. As a consequence, Batista instituted loyalty checks on some officers and placed others under surveillance. Also, Batista increased the practice of appointing people to important command positions based on loyalty and not competency.[41]

THE ARMY'S MORALE WANES

By the end of 1957 the deterioration of the Cuban military became evident. Snipers, hiding in the hillsides, picked off the Cuban soldiers as they emerged from their military posts. Those wishing to join Castro in the mountains ambushed army patrols as evidence of their prowess and dedication to the cause.[42]

POPULAR SUPPORT

Many Cubans wanted to support the struggle against Batista. Most could not or would not join the rural guerrillas or commit urban violence. These people expressed themselves through the Civic Resistance Movement. The movement transported supplies, gathered intelligence, and raised money. The propaganda section printed and distributed materials. By the early spring of 1958, 65,000 copies of three bulletins a week were published. "Freedom bonds" were sold. The Cuban underground had sixty-two foreign cells in Costa Rica, Mexico, the United States, and Venezuela distributing propaganda and collecting money.[43]

However, not all was bleak for Batista. The economy was growing stronger. The various rural guerrilla groups had been semicontained in the Escambray, Sierra Maestra, and Cordilla de los Organos Mountains. The various rebel factions had not coalesced and were arguing among themselves.[44]

BATISTA INTENSIFIES INTIMIDATION

Batista attempted to increase the pressure upon his opponents by additional torture and murder. A typical tactic was to leave the tortured corpse of a suspected guerrilla or sympathizer at some prominent intersection in a city. This did much to alienate the public as well as the few professional soldiers in the Cuban military.[45]

THE BEGINNING OF THE END

By early 1958 the rural guerrillas were principally operating in three areas. Some 100 guerrillas were in the Sierra de los Organos at the western end of the island; they were members of the *26 de Julio* Movement. Some 100 guerrillas operated in the Escambray range located in south-central Cuba; their loyalty was split among the *26 de Julio*, the Authentic Party [*Partido Autentico*], and the Second Front of Escambray. Some 900 guerrillas (including many women) were operating in the Sierra Maestra in the far east of the island; these were directly under Castro. Castro's force was divided into six columns, each composed of 50 to 100 men. His headquarters was at La Plata, near Pico Turquino. On March 12, Castro declared that beginning April 1 total war would be waged, and a general strike would take place on April 9.[46]

THE UNITED STATES DESERTS BATISTA

After much public debate, the United States placed an arms embargo on the Batista government on March 18, 1958. The embargo was a psychological blow to the Batista military. Batista was able to replace some of the lost hardware through purchases from the Dominican Republic and Great Britain, but these nations could not replace the moral support of the United States.[47]

CASTRO GAINS MOMENTUM

On March 28 a DC-3 aircraft landed at a rebel-controlled airstrip in the Sierra Maestra carrying a considerable load of small arms and ammunition. This permitted Castro to increase the size of his force.[48]

On April 1 Raúl Castro led a sixty-five-man guerrilla column to the Sierra del Cristal on the northern side of the Central Highway, establishing another front. By now the guerrillas could manufacture land mines. They blew up railroad bridges, trails, roads, and finally the Central Highway across Cuba. The guerrillas gradually stopped all movement except that escorted by armor and aircraft. The use of aircraft by Batista demoralized the guerrillas in spite of their poor performance.[49]

The guerrillas treated captured government troops well and gave first aid to the wounded. Before turning them over to the Red Cross, the prisoners were lectured on the goals of the revolution.[50]

Under considerable international pressure in March, the Batista regime called for elections to be held in June. Under pressure from the United States, the elections were rescheduled for November to allow the opposition time to prepare.[51] Several opposition parties and revolutionary organizations fighting against Batista announced candidates, but not Castro. On February 21, he stated that his forces would execute anyone who participated in this government farce.

CASTRO CALLS A GENERAL STRIKE

Castro also called for a general strike over *Radio Rebelde* to take place on April 9, 1958; the transmitter had been smuggled into the Sierra Maestra and began broadcasting in February. The strike failed due to lack of support by key labor officials, whose loyalty had been purchased by Batista, and by that of the Communist Party from which Castro had not sought cooperation.[52]

BATISTA'S LAST OFFENSIVE

Inspired by the failure of the strike, Batista launched an offensive in May against the guerrillas in the Sierra Maestra. Some 15,000 troops supported by tanks and aircraft surrounded the mountains. The troops were under the titular command of Gen. Alberto del Río Chaviano. The actual commander of the offensive was Gen. Eulogio Cantillo, a career soldier and one of the most respected professionals in the Cuban army. The force was divided into thirteen combat battalions of about 900 men each. Each was equipped with bazookas, mortars, and automatic weapons. On May 24 the army advanced from the north and northwest against Santo Domingo. On June 5 the guerrillas captured a code book and short-wave radio equipment. From that date until July 25, the guerrillas were able to monitor government communications and anticipate troop movements. As the army battalions advanced they were ambushed. Finally, in late June, the demoralized units withdrew. The government lost 36 killed, 50 wounded, and 28 captured, plus quantities of small arms and munitions. The guerrillas lost two killed and one wounded.[53]

On July 11 the Cuban army launched another attack into the Sierra Maestra, this time against Castro's column at La Plata. While army forces to the north of Castro held his attention, a naval battalion commanded by Maj. José Quevedo made an amphibious landing on the southern coast at Las Cuervas in the vicinity of La Plata on July 11. The sailors advanced to the junction of the Río Jigue and Río La Plata where they encountered guerrilla resistance and sustained significant casualties. The wounded were evacuated; however, the sailors' route back to the beach was soon cut off. For three days the sailors unsuccessfully endeavored to break through the encirclement. Then, the air force began dropping 500-pound fragmentation and napalm bombs on suspected guerrilla positions. These killed peasants and destroyed their homes but failed to dislodge the guerrillas.

While the aircraft continued their attacks, a second battalion landed. On July 19 the newcomers started to move inland, but within twenty-four hours they were driven back to the beach. During the fighting Castro learned that the commander of the surrounded naval battalion had been a classmate of his at the University of Havana. By loudspeaker, Castro asked for a parley. After the meeting, the battalion commander joined the guerrillas. His men were given a choice between joining Castro or being returned to Batista's army as prisoners of war. The sailors sustained 41 killed and 30 wounded. The guerrillas captured 249 assorted arms including mortars, bazookas, and machine guns, as well as 31,000 rounds of ammunition.[54]

While the sailors were being defeated, an army battalion moved into position to continue the offensive against the guerrillas in the Sierra Maestra. The battalion began to advance on July 28. After three days of fighting, it reached the vicinity of Las Vegas de Jibacoa but was surrounded. On August 1 a reserve force fought its way through to the battalion but sustained severe casualties. The army force withdrew to Estrada Palma while continuing to take heavy casualties.[55]

The torrential rains of the hurricane season significantly influenced the government's decision to end the offensive in August. On the seventh the troops were ordered back to their barracks. The government had sustained 207 dead, hundreds wounded, 423 prisoners, and lost thousands of weapons plus hundreds of mules. The guerrillas lost 27 dead and 31 wounded. General Cantillo opened a dialog with Castro, reinforcing Batista's belief that field commanders were not to be trusted. By now all important command positions within the Cuban military had been given to those politically loyal, most of whom were militarily incompetent. Senior officers remained in headquarters distant from the fighting, and the soldiers showed little enthusiasm to seek out the enemy.[56]

The government forces withdrew to the edges of the Sierra Maestra and established garrisons in major towns and conducted daylight patrols along the major roads.[57]

Also in July 1958, Castro gained the status as political leader of the prominent resistance movement when the various dissident factions agreed to a unity pact, the Civilian Revolutionary Front, which he had proposed.[58]

RAÚL'S OFFENSIVE

While Fidel had been under attack during June and July, Raúl launched an offensive to relieve the pressure on his brother. Organizing his men into small units, these began hit and run raids against neighboring towns. The raids were followed by ambushes against the counterattacking army units. By mid-July Raúl had created an active front within an arc bordered by Mayari, Baracoa, and Guantanamo.[59]

Raúl found that his columns were vulnerable to air attack given the more open terrain in which he now operated. As a consequence, he issued an order for his commanders to capture foreigners, particularly targeting Americans, as hostages. Between June 26 and July 1, three Canadians and forty-five Americans (including thirty sailors and Marines from the U.S. Guantanamo Naval Base) were held at the rebel headquarters in the Sierra del Cristal. The plan worked. While negotiations were being conducted, the Cuban air force stopped its attacks. Fidel announced that his brother had acted without authority. Nonetheless, Raúl forced the United States to negotiate with the rebels and demonstrated the weakness of the Batista regime.[60]

CASTRO EXPANDS THE RURAL WAR

In mid-August Fidel began his own offensive. The arrival of a planeload of weapons from Costa Rica, added to those recently captured from the government, permitted the opening of two new guerrilla fronts.[61] A new column under Che Guevara was to establish itself in the Escambray Mountains. Its objective was to tie down government forces in central Cuba and prevent the egress of troops from Havana to Oriente Province. The second new column under Camilo Cienfuegos[62] was to set up camp near Yaguajay in northern Las Villas and then move on to Pinar del Río. Thus, four fronts would be in existence at the same time—two in Oriente (Fidel's and Raúl's), one in Las Villas (Che's), and one in Pinar del Rio (Camilo's).[63]

On August 23 Guevara and his column rendezvoused with a DC-3 transport near Las Mercedes which was carrying arms and munitions from the United States. The two columns, Cienfuegos' of 82 men followed by Guevara's of 150 men, then moved west. The march was very arduous over difficult terrain.[64]

Batista had learned of the guerrilla strategy and attempted to intercept them. Guevara's column was ambushed near Cuatros Compañeros and then attacked by aircraft. Near Ciego de Avila, Guevara found troops deployed along a railroad embankment directly in his path. He and his column skirted the army by wading through water that was up to their armpits.[65]

Cienfuego's column turned north and avoided the government ambush. It destroyed the water plant at Ciego de Avila. After commandeering trucks near Marroqui, they were attacked by the air force. Abandoning their vehicles near Yaguajay, they reached their area of operations. Cienfuegos reported to Castro, "During the trip through Camagüey [268 mi ESE of Havana] that was delayed for thirty-one days, we ate only eleven times, this being the cattle zone of Cuba. After four days without tasting any food, we had to eat a mare, she being the best of our poor cavalry."[66]

Figure 24. The Cuban Revolution (1956–59). A group of revolutionaries. Ernesto "Che" Guevara is sixth from the left among this group. This charismatic individual analyzed the fighting and formulated the "*foco*" theory of guerrilla warfare. This became the radical left's dominant strategy from 1960 through the early 1970s. *Courtesy Library of Congress*

By mid-October both Cienfuegos and Guevara had reached their operational areas. Cienfuegos was ordered to abandon his mission in Las Villas and to aid Guevara. Castro believed that the Batista regime was crumbling and he wanted to enter Havana as soon as possible to prevent the military from seizing power.[67]

By October 1958 the rural guerrilla force under Castro's control had grown to seven fronts composed of twenty columns representing perhaps 7,000 men in four provinces—Camagüey, Las Villas, Oriente, and Pinar del Río.[68] A column led by Maj. Huber Matos conducted a hit-and-run raid out of the Sierra Maestra against the town of Palma Soriano. This demonstrated the inability of the government to seriously contest guerrilla initiatives in the east. Raúl's front attacked Victoria de las Tunas and Sagua de Tanamo. His patrols closed the Central Highway and operated on the outskirts of Guantanamo, 40 miles east of Santiago.[69]

By now most of Batista's troops had been driven into larger *cuarteles*, or barracks. Movement between these could be guaranteed only by armor and air escort. Many garrisons were abandoned, and others received no air or armor support. Guerrilla platoons attacked the *cuartels*. They struck at night and at close range. The guerrillas sustained a heavy small arms fire until the enemy either evacuated or surrendered, or until the guerrillas ammunition ran low.[70]

In a meaningless act, the Batista-backed presidential candidate, Andrés Rivero Agüero, was declared the winner of the November election. The inauguration was to take place in February 1959 but most foreign nations, including the United States, refused to recognize the results of the election. In fact, Cuba's future was being decided elsewhere.[71]

THE FINAL OFFENSIVE

On November 17, 1958, Fidel Castro began a general offensive. Commanding Column Number 1, he seized Bueycito while Columns 3 and 9 protected his flanks. The garrison had abandoned the town when it learned that the reinforcements requested from Bayamo were not being sent. Next, Castro moved against Guisa. There the government committed significant reinforcements, including armor, but to no avail. After a stubborn fight, the garrison fled on November 30. The army sustained 200 casualties; the guerrillas had eight killed and seven wounded.[72]

Next, Fidel marched north capturing Jiguani. This cut the Central Highway between Bayamo and Santiago. At about the same time, Column 4 under Matos took El Cristo on November 26. Raúl marched south, seized Alto Songo, and linked up with Maj. Juan Almeida who had captured San Luis. Fidel now moved down the Central Highway through Baire toward Palma Soriano. By now, Santiago was encircled, as was Guantanamo. The remainder of the east was in guerrilla hands.[73]

With the east under control, Castro now directed his attention to the central plains. The offensive in Las Villas was divided into three sectors. Cienfuegos would attack in the north at Yaguajay. In the center, Guevara would seize Sancti Spiritus and then threaten Santa Clara, the provincial capital. In the south Revolutionary Directorate supporters under Faure Chomon would seize Trinidad and Second Front of Escambray supporters under Eloy Gutiérrez Menoyo would seize Cienfuegos.[74]

Toward the end of December, the guerrilla columns captured the cities of Sancti Spiritus, Cienfuegos, and Yaguajay and swelled with new recruits. From these points the columns under the overall command of Che converged on Santa Clara. The provincial commander, Gen. Alberto del Río Chaviano,[75] informed Batista that he could not stop the guerrillas; he was replaced.[76]

In mid-December the Cuban "Congress" granted Batista emergency powers. Special repair units were created in an unsuccessful attempt to keep communications open between Havana and the central plain. An armored train was readied to carry troops and supplies from Havana to Santa Clara. The army's chief engineer, who was to command the train, traveled to Santa Clara. After seeing the state of affairs, he fled to Miami in his private yacht.[77]

He was not the only member of the military to lose his nerve. On December 28 General Cantillo, commanding the army troops in Santiago, met with Castro in an attempt to curry favor before the inevitable happened. He promised to turn against Batista if Castro would leave the army intact. Castro would not agree and Batista learned of the meeting. He called Cantillo to Havana and questioned his actions. Cantillo argued that he was acting on Batista's behalf. Not privy to what actually happened and afraid to take action against Cantillo, who held the confidence of many in the officer's corps, Batista ordered him to return to Santiago and defend the city.[78]

BATTLE OF SANTA CLARA

The fight for Santa Clara was Batista's last chance to turn the war around. The city of about 150,000 persons was defended by a substantial number of infantry, supported by several armored vehicles. By December 29 Guevara was fighting in the city using "elite"[79] rural guerrillas, urban guerrillas, and recent volunteers.[80]

On December 31 the guerrillas captured Yaguajay just east of Santa Clara. Batista met that night with his key advisors who told him all was lost. The old elite tried to save the situation through a military coup. Cantillo, who had returned from Santiago to Havana, was to become the Chief of the Army. Castro learned of the plot. He ordered preparation for an immediate attack on Santiago, told Guevara and Cienfuegos to march on Havana, and began preparations for a general strike. This was too much for the opposition, which collapsed.[81]

During the morning of January 1, 1959, Batista, his family, and a few close supporters fled to the Dominican Republic, seeking asylum from Batista's old enemy Rafael Trujillo. On January 8 Fidel Castro entered Havana to a tumultuous welcome.[82]

OBSERVATIONS

Fidel Castro's campaign was the most influential military victory within Latin America since the wars for independence that had occurred more than 130 years earlier. It gave the radical left a legitimate seat of power (the Cuban government) from which to project violent revolution. Individuals dedicated to change through the use of force had overthrown the American-endorsed "status quo."

Fidel Castro won in the mountains because his small, mobile units were highly motivated, disciplined, and willing to fight until killed. But these battlefield successes were but one contributor to the downfall of Fulgencio Batista.

The Cuban Revolution was in large measure a middle-class revolution. Decades of political and economic corruption caused many Cubans to support and transform a violent movement led by Fidel Castro, possessing limited military and political potential, into the centerpiece of a national revolution. The overwhelming majority of the Cuban people grew to oppose Fulgencio Batista, in large measure due to the atrocities he committed during his struggle against the guerrillas. Conversely, many Cubans grew to support Fidel Castro because he appeared to be the one leader who was willing to take decisive action against an increasingly repressive regime.[83]

Fidel Castro defeated the Cuban military after only two years of guerrilla warfare. During the summer of 1957, he had been outnumbered perhaps a hundred to one; the guerrilla force probably numbered less than 400 persons. By late 1958 the rural guerrilla force had grown to over 7,000 persons. Thus, by December, the ratio of government forces to rural guerrillas had shrunk to less that seven to one fighters. Apparently, Castro lost 1,000 rural guerrillas during the struggle and the Batista military perhaps double that number. More significantly, between 1956 and 1959, perhaps 10,000 Cubans died due to urban guerrilla warfare and Batista's intimidation campaign. To this must be added over one thousand Cubans who were executed by Castro.[84]

Throughout the struggle Castro's political ideology was sufficiently ambiguous to permit many with anti-Batista sentiments to unite behind Castro.[85] The fact that Castro was generally opposed by the Soviet-sponsored Communist Party led many, including the U.S. Central Intelligence Agency, to conclude that Fidel Castro was not a Communist.

Internationally, the one potentially dominant force, the United States, acted indecisively.[86]

Castro's military tactics evolved as he sought to oust Batista. In 1953 Castro had attempted to execute a classic coup d'etat or *golpe de estado*,[87] when he attacked the Moncada Barracks. Three years later he landed at Belic, probably hoping for a coup but prepared for a longer struggle in the mountains if necessary.[88] Failing to achieve a coup and initially badly beaten, Castro developed a rural and urban guerrilla strategy. The rural guerrilla tactics matured from ambushing enemy units of ever-increasing size, to isolating Batista's troops which sought haven in *cuartels*, to forcing those in *cuartels* to flee or surrender by subjecting them to heavy and persistent small arms fire. This tactic exploited a major weakness of the enemy, a lack of motivation to fight.

Also, the corruption within the Batista military was a significant contributor to its defeat. Many of the senior officers got rich on graft. Some of Batista's cronies believed that they were once again dealing with a conflict among the elite, and that no drastic changes within the system would take place even if they were defeated. So, they viewed the Castro threat as one more opportunity to enrich themselves. Since the nonacademy junior officers and the senior enlisted men possessed few opportunities to advance, many supplemented their incomes by intimidation and extortion. As a consequence, they were fat, old, and lazy! Notwithstanding the better moral character of the few dedicated professionals within the army, the entire military became increasingly despised by the Cuban public.

Many may be credited with playing important roles in the defeat of the Batista regime. The guerrilla force in the Sierra Maestra was a symbol of resistance, but by itself it initially did not pose a serious military threat to the Batista regime. Many Cubans, both loyal to and opposed to Castro, sacrificed more than he did. Castro himself estimated that the urban guerrillas fighting in the cities sustained nineteen times the casualties of those in the mountains.[89] Also if one analyzes the guerrilla operations in the mountains, Raúl Castro and then Che Guevara emerged as the most dynamic strategists and executioners of rural guerrilla warfare and not Fidel. But, all said and done, "[Fidel] Castro and his cohorts created and believed in the Mystique of the Victorious Guerrilla."[90]

The war of words, initiated by the Communists during the years of subversion (1928–35) were further perfected by the Cuban Revolution. In the cities propaganda was spread by illegal presses, telephones, and word of mouth. It was sufficiently effective to cause a run on the national banks. In the countryside, *Radio Rebelde* emphasized rebel successes and the illegality of the Batista regime. The rebel radio broadcast select, accurate military information to counter the blatantly false communiqués of the Batista regime.[91]

CHAPTER 25

THE VENEZUELA REVOLUTION, 1958

[The Venezuelans] were disturbed because the U.S. Government had decorated and praised the Dictator Perez Jimenez. . . . they did not understand our great concern over communism and our apparent lack of concern over their social and economic problems.
—John F. Gallagher, Vice President, Sears, Roebuck & Co., 1960

THE SPARK

On December 15, 1957, Marcos Pérez Jiménez declared that a plebiscite (which he had manipulated) confirmed that he should continue as President of Venezuela. This declaration eventually caused those opposed to Pérez Jiménez to unite and to work toward his overthrow.

BACKGROUND

October 18, 1945, marked the beginning of the end of an era in Venezuelan history known as the "Andean Hegemony."[1] On that day a coup, lasting twenty-four hours, overthrew the democratic government of Gen. Isaías Medina Angarita.[2] Maj. Marcos Pérez Jiménez,[3] a thirty-one-year-old artillery officer, was one of the leaders of the movement. Nevertheless, Pérez Jiménez was not part of the new governing junta which was presided over by Rómulo Betancourt,[4] leader of the Democratic Action Party (*Acción Democrática*). He had opportunely supported the coup in its last hours of planning. The governing junta was composed of five civilians from the Democratic Action Party and two military officers—Majors Carlos Delgado-Chalbaud Gómez[5] and Mario Vargas. They became respectively the Minister of War and Navy and the Minister of the Interior. Major Pérez Jiménez was appointed the Chief of Staff of the Army which was second in seniority to the Minister of War and Navy. From this moment, an animosity developed between Pérez Jiménez and Betencourt that would persist for decades.

Rómulo Gallegos, an educator, was elected President in 1947 with the support of the Democratic Action Party. He was overthrown by a bloodless coup on November 24, 1948. The new military junta was composed of Lieutenant Colonels Delgado-Chalbaud Gómez, who presided; Pérez Jiménez, who served as Minister of War (formerly Minister of War and Navy); and Luís Felipe Llovera Páez,[6] who became Minister of the Interior. Two years later, on November 13, 1950, the president of the ruling junta, Delgado-Chalbaud, was assassinated. The remaining

junta members chose diplomat Germán Suárez Flemerich to preside over the junta; nevertheless, Pérez Jiménez exercised the real power.[7]

Soon, numerous junior officers attempted coups but they all failed. On November 30, 1952,
the military junta orchestrated the election of the National Constitutional Assembly. Although
the Democratic Republican Union (*Unión Republicana Democrática*) appeared to have won, on
December 2 the electoral authorities proclaimed the National Independent Front (*Frente
Nacional Independiente*), Pérez Jiménez' party, as the winner. On that day the armed forces renounced their rule and Pérez Jiménez became the provisional president. The Congress wrote a
new constitution under which Pérez Jiménez became the President of Venezuela for a five-year
period.

Financed through revenues by oil exports, Pérez Jiménez initiated a massive public works
program that included superhighways, airports, the most modern aircraft for the national airlines (*Aeropostal*), port improvements, modern merchantships, a merchant marine academy,
hospitals, and sports stadiums. Education was given special priority. Hundreds of schools were
constructed. The United States donated a small nuclear reactor to the Institute for Scientific Investigation.[8]

At the same time the Venezuelan military was being built into a regional power through the
modernization of its hardware and the professionalization of its personnel. The army increased
from 15,000 soldiers to 125,000. During the 1950s the army acquired the Belgian-manufactured
F.N. *FAL* automatic rifles; 40 French-built AMX-13 light tanks; Swiss-built 20mm antiaircraft
guns; U.S.-built M-18 tank hunters, M-8 armored cars, 155mm, 105mm, and 40mm cannons;
and French- and Italian-built trucks.[9]

The navy purchased three British-built *Nueva Esparta* class destroyers; six Italian-built
Almirante Clemente class frigates; a French-built transport; and numerous secondhand U.S.
warships. Also, new naval bases were constructed that included technical training facilities.[10]

The Venezuelan air force became the strongest in Latin America. Venezuela purchased British-built Canberra jet bombers, Havilland Vampire and Venom jet fighters, and Dove light
transports. In 1955 the United States transferred 22 North American F-86F Sabre jet fighters to
Venezuela, the first Latin American country to receive that warplane. These aircraft were added
to a large inventory of older but useful planes. Like the navy, the air force built new bases and
technical schools.[11]

The national guard, the fourth armed service, was also restructured. It was given new equipment and technical training.[12] And a strategic goal became the recovery of 61,500 square miles
of disputed territory known as British Guiana.

The beginning of the end of the Pérez Jiménez regime occurred on May 1, 1957, when the
Archbishop of Caracas, Monsenor Rafael Arias Blanco, published a pastoral letter in the daily
Roman Catholic newspaper *La Religión* which denounced the inhuman conditions under which
a large part of the Venezuelan population lived. The Catholic Church now became a center of
social discontent. Pérez Jiménez unsuccessfully attempted to suppress the Church's activities by
arresting and detaining numerous priests.[13]

In June 1957 representatives of numerous political parties, including the Communist Party,
secretly formed the "Patriotic Junta" (*Junta Patriótia*) to work for the overthrow of Pérez
Jiménez. It immediately created regional and professional cells.[14]

On November 4 Pérez Jiménez announced that the presidential election scheduled for late that year would not be held but rather a plebiscite would be held to see if he should remain in office. Numerous protests occurred; police and demonstrators clashed in the *barrios* of Caracas and at the national university.

At this time groups throughout the armed forces began to conspire against Pérez Jiménez. The center of the activity was at the joint Military Academy (*Escuela Básica de la Fuerzas Armadas*).[15] In October 1957 the Patriotic Junta created the "Civilian-Military Committee" (*Comité Cívico Militar*) whose mission was to organize the dissidents within the military. However, Pérez Jiménez rapidly executed the plebiscite and arrested a group of officers thereby undermining the work of the "Committee."

OPPOSING FORCES

Pérez Jiménez' power rested upon the loyalty of the senior military officers, all of whom he had handpicked. The Patriotic Junta was composed of businessmen, intellectuals, students, priests, journalists, and midlevel and junior military officers who were fed up with Pérez Jiménez' corruption and wastefulness.

OPENING STRATEGIES

Drawing upon past experience, Pérez Jiménez perceived the greatest danger to be from a "rogue" member of the senior military and, therefore, focused many of his intelligence assets to spying upon his handpicked military leaders. The Patriotic Junta concentrated on broadening its base of support. Its goal was to involve so many that the coup would succeed because of its overwhelming support. The danger was that the plot would be discovered as more and more people were included.

THE UNSUCCESSFUL COUP OF JANUARY 1, 1958

On the last day of 1957, Pérez Jiménez received an intelligence report stating that an army officer by the name of "Hugo" was conspiring against him. Assuming that his source was referring to the Commander-in-Chief of the army, Brigade Gen. Hugo Fuentes, Pérez Jiménez ordered his arrest. In fact, the head of the conspiracy was army Lt. Col. Hugo Trejo,[16] who was assigned to the Armed Forces Superior Staff and Command School and had no association with General Fuentes at all. Pérez Jiménez also ordered the arrest of air force Col. Jesús María Castro León,[17] Chief of the Air General Staff and second in command of the air force.[18]

The arrest of Castro León required the air force conspirators to advance their plans. During the early hours of January 1, 1958, groups of officers successfully seized the Boca de Río Air Base, the Palo Negro Air Base, and other air force facilities near the city of Maracay.[19] Minutes later rebel aircraft flew over the city as a prearranged signal to army conspirators. Immediately, airmen from the Parachute Detachment School occupied strategic cites throughout Maracay. Numerous army units in Maracay joined the rebellion—the Army Transport School, the *Bravos de Apures* (the 2nd) Armored Battalion,[20] the *General Bartolome Salom* Field Artillery Group, and the *General Francisco Avendaño* Combat Engineers Battalion.[21]

To gain more information concerning the air force rebellion, Pérez Jiménez ordered air force Lt. Col. Martín Parada, his personal pilot, to fly to Maracay and acquire firsthand information. Instead, when Parada landed at Maracay at nine o'clock in the morning, he assumed command of the rebellion.[22]

At 6:30 A.M. Pérez Jiménez ordered a state of alert for the *General Bermúdez* (the 1st) Armored Battalion and the *Ayacucho* Field Artillery Group stationed in a western *barrio* of Caracas at the *Urdaneta* Barracks. They were to prepare to advance against Maracay and crush the rebellion. In fact, the army officers at the barracks were sympathetic to the rebellion but unprepared to participate. Earlier, Pérez Jiménez, suspicious of their loyalty, had ordered their munitions retired to the central arsenal which was under the control of the Ministry of Defense. The acting commanding officer, Maj. Evelio José Gilmond Báez, responded to Pérez Jiménez that they could not enter combat for lack of munitions. Nevertheless, Pérez Jiménez insisted that the units go on alert and begin preparations. He also ordered that they be sent munitions.[23]

On the rebel side, air force Maj. Edgar Suárez Mier y Terán, commander of Fighter Squadron 35, overflew Caracas in a Vampire jet fighter to assure those conspirators below that the revolt in Maracay had succeeded. An hour and a half later, rebel planes began reconnaissance flights over the capital. Back in Maracay, chaos developed due to the lack of coordination among the rebel units. At 1:05 P.M. rebel Vampire, Venom, and Sabre jet fighters and Canberra jet bombers attacked Miraflores Palace (where the President had his office), the defense ministry, and other military targets in the Caracas area. Although the attacks continued throughout the day, they produced poor results.[24]

In late afternoon, navy Capt. Ricardo Sosa Ríos, Director of the Naval Education Center at Catia La Mar and chief of La Guaira Zone Joint Garrison, called a meeting of his senior and some junior officers to analyze the situation.[25] They decided to support the rebellion and ordered the warships anchored near La Guaira to put to sea without the normal authorization from Caracas.[26]

In the meantime, the Pérez Jiménez government began assembling four powerful columns to recapture Maracay and its vicinity. Three columns consisted of loyal army troops, while the fourth, which would come from the north, was composed of Marines.[27]

Also late in the afternoon, the rebel command at Maracay sent a message to the army officers at the *Urdaneta* Barrack imploring them to join the rebellion. At 6:30 P.M. Maj. Gilmond Báez, commanding the rebels, ordered the barracks seized and officers loyal to Pérez Jiménez arrested. Now, Lt. Col. Hugo Trejo—the officer who had been confused with the commander-in-chief of the army on December 31—returned to the barracks and assumed command of the rebel forces. The munitions, which Pérez Jiménez had ordered sent to the *Urdaneta* Barrack, arrived at 7 P.M. Báez suggested to Trejo that he place his artillery in a position that would force the surrender of those in the Ministry of Defense building. Instead, Trejo chose to retire to Maracay to support the rebellion there. Before the trek to Maracay had begun, Maj. Edgar Trujillo Echeverría asked Trejo for three M-18 armored cars in order to attack the presidential palace. However, Trejo refused the request, apparently believing that he did not have enough ammunition to carry out the attack. Instead, a rebel column composed of ten M-18 armored cars and two 155mm towed cannons set out for Maracay via Los Teques (19 mi SW of Caracas).[28]

Pérez Jiménez, an artillery officer, appreciated the potential of the units stationed at the *Urdaneta* Barrack and feared their advance into the heart of Caracas. He ordered Col. Victor Maldonado Michelena to prepare to defend the presidential palace. The Colonel commanded 400 men, four M-18 and a few M-8 armored cars, six 40mm anti-aircraft guns, and some heavily armed police. To the surprise of the palace defenders, Trejo chose to attack Los Teques instead of the palace. The National Guard troops school was the only military objective there.[29]

At about this time, late on January 1 and early the following day, government forces reached Maracay. The rebel forces dispersed, their leaders escaping to Colombia in an air force C-54. Sosa Ríos, informed of the surrender, ordered the naval ships that had sailed from La Guaira to return. The commander-in-chief of the navy, Capt. Oscar Ghersi Gómez, asked why the ships had sailed from La Guaira without his authorization, to which Sosa Ríos responded that with an air force rebellion it was wise to disperse the ships. Captain Ghersi accepted this and did not inquire further.[30]

Trejo departed Los Teques for Maracay, leaving Major Trujillo Echeverría in command. By the time he arrived in Maracay, the rebel leadership had fled to Colombia and troops loyal to Pérez Jiménez were in the process of recapturing the city. During the early morning of January 2, Trejo returned to Los Teques where he was captured by a column commanded by Col. Marco Aurelio Moros Angulo.[31] The rebellion collapsed, and in early January the government arrested numerous military, political, religious, and media personalities. However, neither the air force-led Maracay rebellion nor the one led by Lieutenant Colonel Trejo had had any contact with the "Civilian-Military Committee," so most of its members escaped the arrests and continued to work for the downfall of Pérez Jiménez.

Unrest continued. On January 9 five warships sailed from La Guaira (14 mi NE of Caracas) without the authorization of the naval command. Army Brigade Gen. Rómulo Fernández, the chief of staff of the armed forces, negotiated with the commanders of the rebellious ships, promising that no retaliation would be taken if the warships quietly returned to port, which they did. Notwithstanding, Brigade Gen. Luís Felipe Llovera Páez, commanding a column of armored cars, occupied the naval base, seized the ships' ammunition, and arrested the commanding officers of the warships.[32]

THE COUP OF JANUARY 22, 1958

On January 10, 1958, the Civil-Military Committee contacted marine Ens. Haroldo Rodríguez Figueroa of Marine Battalion No. 1 and won him over to the cause.[33] That same day General Rómulo Fernández, representing some senior officers, presented Pérez Jiménez an ultimatum which demanded changes in the armed forces high command; the reconstitution of the cabinet with all military members; and the deportation of the Minister of the Interior (Laureano Vallenilla Lanz) and the head of the political police (Pedro Estrada). In order to win time and discover the names of those who supported Rómulo Fernández, Pérez Jiménez agreed in principal and designated Rómulo Fernández the new Minister of Defense and made numerous other appointments as required by Rómulo Fernández.[34]

On January 13 Pérez Jiménez had General Rómulo Fernández arrested in the presidential office by General Llovera Páez. Subsequently, Rómulo Fernández was transported to the La Carlota Airport in an eastern *barrio* of Caracas and then flown in a civilian government plane to the Dominican Republic. While Rómulo Fernández was being exiled, General Llovera Páez led a force to the Ministry of Defense and arrested numerous senior officers. Pérez Jiménez again reorganized the government and the armed forces. He assumed direct control over the Ministry of Defense.[35]

On January 14 the Civil-Military Committee learned of a navy plan to rebel the following day under the leadership of Capt. Miguel Rodríguez Olivares.[36] Air force Lt. José Luis Fernández immediately contacted Cmdr. José Vicente Azopardo, one of the naval dissidents, and the naval officers agreed to join forces with the civil-military movement.[37]

Two days later Captain Rodríguez Olivares asked Adm. Wolfgang Larrazábal[38] to join the plot, which he did. On January 20 the principal members of the Civilian-Military Committee met, and Commander Azopardo and Cmdr. Carbonell Izquierdo proposed that Adm. Wolfgang Larrazábal be selected to head the ruling junta after the deposition of Pérez Jiménez. This met with approval.[39]

Throughout the crisis the United States expressed concern for the stability of the Pérez Jiménez government, to which it had given substantial military aid. The destroyer *Allen M. Sumner* was dispatched to watch over U.S. national interests. U.S. companies had invested heavily in the Venezuelan petroleum industry, and an estimated forty thousand U.S. citizens resided in Venezuela, most of whom were oil industry workers and their families.

The Patriotic Junta proclaimed a general strike at noon on January 21. Strikers and police clashed; people were killed and property destroyed. At 6 P.M. the government imposed a curfew. For various reasons, Capt. Italo Brett Smith of the national guard failed to instigate a planned uprising at the various military schools. Civil disturbances continued the following day, ending in more street fighting and additional deaths.

According to the plan, at 4 P.M. on January 22 the frigate *General José de Austria* and Marine Battalion No. 2 rebelled at Puerto Cabello Naval Base. The Marines took over the base and the munitions in the arsenal. These were immediately conveyed to La Guaira, where the destroyer *Nueva Esparta* and the frigates *Almirante Brión* and *Almirante José García* awaited them. The transport *Dos de Diciembre*, also at La Guaira, joined the rebellion.[40]

Two hours later, at 6 P.M., Adm. Wolfgang Larrazábal ordered the destroyers *Nueva Esparta*, *Zulia*, and *Aragua*, which were in La Guaira, to steam to Puerto Cabello to find munitions. Pérez Jiménez ordered the air force to find and attack the warships. The aircraft intercepted the warships at sea but did not fire on them. At Puerto Cabello the destroyers received the munitions along with Marine Battalion No. 1 and transported both to the vicinity of La Guaira. The marines waited to march on Caracas and unite with national guard troops. This force would then reinforce the rebels at the military and armed forces academies.[41]

At 10 P.M. Col. Pedro Quevedo,[42] Director of the Military Academy, informed Pérez Jiménez that subversives had infiltrated the school system, whereupon the President ordered the *Bolívar* (No. 3) Infantry Battalion, commanded by Lt. Col. Simón Medina Sánchez who was loyal to Pérez Jiménez, to regain control. During the night a patrol from the battalion, commanded by 1st Lt. Sergio David Camargo, arrived at the academy and demanded its surrender. Camargo was shot dead in the pursuing exchange of gunfire and the patrol withdrew.[43]

Also during the night, Pérez Jiménez ordered Rear Adm. Wolfgang Larrazábal to attack the rebels, who rather than comply presented the dictator with an ultimatum to resign. Pérez Jiménez now realized that it was impossible to suppress the insurrection. His naval aide negotiated his surrender through Cmdr. José Vicente Azopardo, a member of the Civilian-Military Committee, and Pérez Jiménez was guaranteed safe passage from the country. On January 23 Pérez Jiménez boarded an Air Force C-54 transport with his family and flew to the Dominican Republic, where *Generalísimo* Rafael Leonidas Trujillo received him.[44]

At 1:00 A.M. on January 23, the rebellion officers asked Rear Adm. Wolfgang Larrazábal, the senior military officer who had plotted against Pérez Jiménez, to form and preside over a military junta. Initially the junta was composed of Adm. Wolfgang Larrazábal, army Col. Roberto Casanova and air force Col. Abél Romero Villate. Within hours this junta was replaced by one composed of civilians as well as military.[45]

AFTERSHOCKS

The overthrow of Pérez Jiménez magnified the political divisions within the armed forces, particularly the army, national guard, and air force. The navy remained united behind Adm. Wolfgang Larrazábal, the president of the junta. Groups of officers expressed their dissatisfaction with the junta and sought to increase their influence. The two most vocal groups were those headed by air force Col. Jesús María Castro León (the Minister of Defense) and army Lt. Col. Hugo Trejo (Vice Chief of the Armed Forces General Staff).

The junta was challenged by minor crisis. Trejo emerged as the vocal popular hero of the younger officers in the army and national guard. He demanded social and economic changes. Finally, he was given a comfortable political exile by making him the Ambassador to Costa Rica on April 27.[46]

A major crisis was created by the visit of U.S. Vice President Richard Nixon on May 13. The Vice President and his entourage were greeted at the Maiquetia international airport by thousands of anti-American protestors. An hour later when Nixon arrived at the National Pantheon to pay homage to Simón Bolívar, a mob attacked his car and almost overturned it. The Vice President was rescued by Venezuelan soldiers. Learning of the incident, President Dwight Eisenhower sent elements of the 101st Airborne Division and marines to the Caribbean, should the Venezuelan government "need help." The following day, army armored cars escorted Nixon to the airport.[47]

On July 5, the day that army Gen. Jesús María Castro León ascended to the position of Minister of Defense, he presented Adm. Wolfgang Larrazábal with a personal note that complained about inequities of the governing junta. This was received as an ultimatum. Tensions built. On July 23 the government discovered a plot to seize Adm. Wolfgang Larrazábal. The Admiral, along with the commanders of the national guard, the air force, and other senior officers escaped to the coast in order to come under the protection of the head of the navy, Adm. Carlos Larrazábal,[48] Wolfgang's brother. General Castro León remained in the Ministry of Defense while large public demonstrations supporting Wolfgang Larrazábal and the junta occurred throughout the capital. On the following day, July 24, General Castro León relented to public pressure. He and six other officers were expelled from Venezuela to Curaçao.[49]

Lt. Col. Juan de Dios Moncada Vidal and Maj. Hely Mendoza Méndez, both of whom had been expelled with General Castro León in July, clandestinely returned to Venezuela and at dawn on September 7 subverted the 2nd Armored Military Police Detachment. It was stationed at the Miraflores Barrack and functioned as a presidential guard. Adm. Wolfgang Larrazábal and the majority of the junta took refuge in La Guaira under the protection of the navy.

Major Mendoza attempted to capture the presidential palace. He was confronted by Col. Pedro José Quevedo and Dr. Arturo Sosa, the only two members of the junta who remained in Caracas. Supported by loyal marines and army troops, Quevedo and Sosa persuaded the rebels to surrender. Notwithstanding, fighting broke out between the rebels and a mob that had surrounded their barrack. Twenty people were killed and more than one hundred hurt before order was restored. The 2nd Armored Military Police Detachment was disbanded and naval police and marines took over the responsibility of presidential guard until 1959 when the Guard of Honor (*Guardia de Honor*) was created out of personnel from all four armed services.[50]

As promised, the junta held free elections on December 7, 1958. Wolfgang Larrazábal ran as the Democratic Republican Union and Communist Party candidate and won a substantial majority of the Caracas vote. However, the rural electorate gave victory to Rómulo Betancourt of the Social Democratic Party. Rómulo Betancourt received 49 percent of the vote, Wolfgang Larrazábal 35 percent, and Rafael Caldera 16 percent. The reins of government passed to the newly elected president on February 13, 1959.[51]

OBSERVATIONS

A cursory analysis of past coups in Venezuela, and for that matter throughout Latin America, suggested that this intraclass struggle had little potential to lead to a prolonged period of democratic rule. What was not readily appreciated was the breadth of support for democracy among the middle class, including the officer corps.

Many in the United States were very uneasy with the consequences of this Venezuelan intraclass struggle. Pérez Jiménez, a faithful supporter of U.S. policy against international Communism (albeit an unscrupulous dictator), had been replaced with a caretaker government under Admiral Larrazábal which received the endorsement of the Venezuelan Communist Party.

Politically and militarily, Larrazábal supported the Revolutionaries in Cuba. During "Operation Condor," Larrazábal clandestinely flew some ten planeloads of weapons and munitions into Cuba and flew wounded guerrillas to Caracas hospitals! On January 23, 1959, just a few weeks after Castro's triumph in Cuba, a Venezuelan national airliner flew Castro to Caracas so that he could participate in the first anniversary of the overthrow of Pérez Jiménez. And the new Betancourt government supplied arms through Cuba during the summer of 1959 to those trying to oust Dominican dictator Rafael Trujillo.[52]

Internally, the Venezuelan navy played an important role in the removal of Pérez Jiménez. Militarily, its actions on January 22, 1958, were much more united than those of the other services, which undoubtedly gave confidence to those supporting the revolt in the army, air force, and national guard. The participation of the Venezuelan marines, a part of the navy, proved to be decisive.

Politically, the navy contributed to the junta an individual who did not threaten to become a military strongman like Pérez Jiménez. As a naval officer, Rear Adm. Wolfgang Larrazábal would have to rule by compromise, in absence of the military base to do otherwise. Admiral Larrazábal must be credited with wisely leading his nation during the politically volatile year of 1958 and helping to create a democracy that has endured for more than four decades.

Between 161 and 472 people lost their lives and between 300 and 1,000 were wounded during the overthrow of Pérez Jiménez in January 1958. These figures do not include those killed or wounded before or after the overthrow.[53]

PART 13

CHAPTER 26

THE YEAR OF THE PRE-*FOCO* FOLLIES, 1959

I knew he [Fidel Castro] was not a Communist [in 1959] but I believe I knew also that he would become a Communist.

—Che Guevara

THE SPARK

A Cuba under "revolutionary" control attracted the "outs" primarily from the political left of Central American and Caribbean nations. They wanted to use the island as a launching pad for the conquests of their homelands.

BACKGROUND

Aside from being committed to "revolution," it was unclear in early 1959 exactly for what Fidel Castro and the Cuban Revolution stood. After all, Castro repeatedly denied being a Communist. All that was readily apparent was that a group of fatigue-wearing women and bearded men had overthrown one of Latin America's most corrupt dictators, Fulgencio Batista.

And hot on the heels of this event, yet another of these brutal totalitarians, Marcos Pérez Jiménez of Venezuela, was overthrown by a coalition of civilian and military leaders (see chapter 25). Some in Latin America interpreted these two events, occurring only a few years after the reordering of world power caused by World War II, as signaling the rebirth (and many would argue the birth) of democracy within the region.

Seemingly, the hour had arrived for the Liberals in the region to rise up against their nemesis, the Conservatives. Generally, the Liberals had been on the losing end of the feuds that dated from the wars for independence.

OPPOSING FORCES

The entrenched dictators of the Caribbean became the targets for revolutionary attacks—the "first families" (the ruling elite) of Panama, the Somoza family of Nicaragua, Rafael Trujillo of

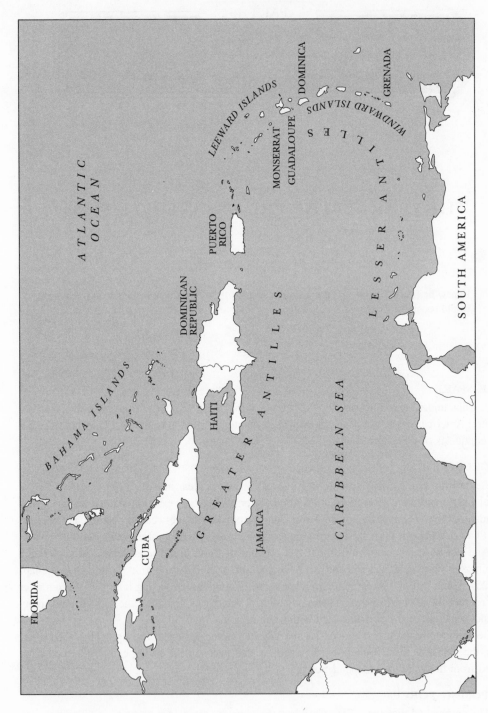

Map 5. The Era of the Pre-*Foco* Follies, 1959.

the Dominican Republic, and "recently elected" François ("Papa Doc") Duvalier of Haiti. Although each had a sizeable military, the poor performance of the Batista army raised doubts as to the capabilities of the militaries serving these other dictators.

The revolutionary forces were a mixed bag. Some of the people who flocked to Cuba were motivated by high ideals and others by pure greediness. In addition to the guerrilla fighters that could be forged from this very raw material, significant aid could be expected from revolutionary Cuba and Venezuela, and to a lesser degree Costa Rica with the emergence of José Figueres in 1948.[1]

OPENING STRATEGIES

The strategy used by the Cuban Revolutionaries had evolved by trial-and-error throughout their struggle from 1953 to early 1959. By early 1959 no one had yet articulated how the guerrillas won. The symbols were easily seen—jungle fatigues and beards—and those wishing to duplicate the Cuban success adopted these. The old-line dictators relied on a well-tested strategy—catch anyone suspected of sympathizing, aiding, or being with your enemy and brutally kill him in order to intimidate others.

DOMINICAN REPUBLIC, ATTACK AND COUNTERATTACK

The hatred between Dominican strongman Rafael Trujillo and Fidel Castro predated Castro's rise to power. As early as January 2, 1959, Rafael Trujillo sponsored a mercenary band known as the "Foreign Legion," which was dedicated to the overthrow of Castro. The legion attracted to the Dominican Republic 200 exiled Cubans, including those wanting to reestablish the old oppressive order as well as those seeking to create a democracy. In addition, there were mercenaries from the four corners of the world. These included some 400 Spanish "volunteers," reportedly from the "Blue Division" (which had fought for Germany on the Eastern Front during World War II) during May.[2]

Anti-Castro conspirators operating from the Dominican Republic clandestinely contacted Majors William Morgan and Eloy Gutiérrez Menoyo, now members of Cuba's new Revolutionary army, and asked them to lead the attack against Castro. Both had served in the anti-Batista (and anti-Communist) Second Front of Escambray guerrilla band, which had not been under Castro's direct control during the Cuban Revolution.

Sources are contradictory as to whether Morgan and Gutiérrez Menoyo joined the plot against Castro as a ploy to expose those opposed to the Cuban Revolution or whether they were really trying to oust Castro. On April 15 Morgan, a former U.S. Army enlisted man, met the Dominican consul in Miami, Florida, and agreed to lead the assault for $1 million. Following a number of planning meetings in Miami, the majors informed Fidel of the plot. Castro instructed Morgan and Gutiérrez Menoyo to go along with the conspiracy and report all the details.[3]

The conspiracy plan called for Morgan and Gutiérrez Menoyo to cause a rebellion in the Sierra del Escambray and for others to sabotage the Cuban air force. After these were accomplished, the 3,000-man "Foreign Legion" would sail from the Dominican Republic and land in Las Villas Province.[4]

On August 6 Morgan sailed from Florida with fifty men, some forty machine guns, and ammunition, all of which he turned over to Castro. Morgan and Gutiérrez Menoyo then entered the Sierra del Escambray and radioed Trujillo that the rebellion in the mountains had begun. In order to encourage Trujillo to commit the "Foreign Legion," Castro made it appear that the

capture of the city of Trinidad, some 40 miles northeast of Cienfuegos, was imminent. However, in August 1959 the international press, which still operated with some freedom within
Cuba, began to release information concerning Castro's crackdown on possible conspirators.
This news made Trujillo suspicious. Morgan assured Trujillo by radio that all was going well
and that the news releases coming from Cuba were no more than propaganda created by Castro.
Morgan concluded by telling Trujillo that Trinidad had just fallen and that the airport was available to the Dominican dictator. On August 12 a C-47 transport flying from the Dominican Republic landed. Trujillo's personal representative, Father Ricardo Velazco Ordóñez, was tricked
into believing that Morgan had captured Trinidad! Flying back to the Dominican Republic, he
personally reported the good news to Trujillo.[5]

On the 13th Castro ordered Morgan to send the following message to Trujillo: "The
troops . . . advanced on Manicaragua and later fell on Santa Clara. . . . We must take advantage
of the state of demoralization to land our foreign legion which will give them the final kick."[6]

Although Trujillo was still reluctant to commit the Foreign Legion, he did dispatch another
plane carrying a personal emissary, military advisors, and supplies. The C-47, piloted by the
individual who had flown Fulencio Batista into exile, landed at 8:15 P.M. on the thirteenth.
Castro, believing that no more could be gained by continuing the deception, seized the aircraft
and the ten occupants. At the same time, Castro arrested some 4,000 suspects throughout the
island.[7]

In spite of this fiasco, Trujillo persisted in his effort to overthrow Castro. For some time he
supported former Batista Gen. José Eleuterio Pedraza's attempt to use the Dominican Republic
as a staging area for an attack against Castro.[8]

While Trujillo was plotting Castro's overthrow, Castro permitted Cuba to be used to prepare
an invasion of the Dominican Republic. As Fidel toured Caracas, Venezuela, following the Cuban Revolution, he told a cheering crowd, "Everywhere I hear the chant 'Trujillo next.'"[9] He
then tossed the first coin into a hat for a projected fund of $300,000 to support an invasion of
the Dominican Republic.

In early 1959, two hundred men, many veterans of the Cuban Revolution, including a Dominican leader, assembled in Cuba and trained for the invasion of the neighboring island. On
June 11 a Venezuelan plane flew to Cuba where it was repainted in the colors and markings of
the Dominican air force. On the fourteenth, fifty-six men (Dominicans, Cubans, Venezuelans,
Puerto Ricans, and Guatemalans), armed principally with Belgian-manufactured automatic
rifles supplied by Venezuela, flew to Constanza, Dominican Republic. The Dominican pilot,
Juan Ventura Simó, had been planted by Trujillo among the rebels, and he landed them in a trap
where most were massacred.[10]

Meanwhile, a second group of 140 invaders sailed from Cuba in two dilapidated yachts flying U.S. flags. They were escorted by three Cuban frigates, holdovers from the Batista navy, to
within 70 miles of the northern coast of the Dominican Republic. On June 20 the yachts were
attacked and sunk by the Dominican navy. The guerrillas who escaped ashore were killed by
the Dominican army.[11]

HAITI INVADED

The losers of the 1957 presidential elections—Louis Dejoie, Daniel Fignolé, and Clément
Jumelle—created the Haitian Revolutionary Front (*Front Révoltionnaire Haitien*) in Cuba during early 1959 to overthrow François Duvalier. A large number of Haitians (perhaps 100,000

individuals) were working on sugar and coffee plantations in Oriente Province during the Cuban Revolution and many supported Castro's effort. From these, some 500 persons now actively backed the new Haitian Revolutionary Front.[12]

Some thirty armed men sailed from Cuba and landed on Haiti's southwest coast on August 13. They briefly seized control of the hamlet of Les Irois (168 mi WSW of Port-au-Prince) at the western tip of Haiti and then retreated on to Caracasse Mountain. However, by the twenty-fifth most of the invaders had been killed and four captured. The captured were Cubans except for Louis Dejoie, who was a Haitian.[13]

Some speculated that Castro supported these activities as part of a strategy to put added pressure on Trujillo in the Dominican Republic.[14]

PANAMA INVADED

In early April Dr. Roberto Arias, a member of a family that had been extremely influential in Panama during much of the 1930s and 1940s, purchased a yacht in Miami and sailed to Cuba. There, he recruited some eighty experienced guerrillas, mostly Cubans. Led by three Panamanians, they sailed on board the *Majaré* from Puerto Surgerido, Cuba, on April 19 and landed near the town of Nombre de Díos (75 mi N of Panama City) on the twenty-fifth. Apparently, the Panamanian leadership was washed overboard and drowned. Maj. Cesar Vega, a Cuban, took command. As planned, some one hundred Arias' supporters in Panama rose up, but they were quickly wiped out by the Panamanian *Guardia Nacional* (the army in all but name). Reinforcements expected from Cuba never sailed, so most of the invaders surrendered on May 1 to a fact-finding team sent to Panama by the Organization of American States. Arias, who had returned to Panama before the uprising, sought refuge in the Brazilian Embassy and ultimately fled to Brazil. Castro's role in this adventure is still unclear.[15]

NICARAGUA INVADED

Apparently, competing factions of Liberals invaded Nicaragua with the hope of ousting Luis Somoza. On May 31 and June 1, some 110 Nicaraguans flew from Punta Llorona, Costa Rica, to two mountainous sites in Nicaragua in a C-46 aircraft of Costa Rican registry. A leader, Pedro Joaquín Chamorro, claimed that the invasion was an attempt to preempt a planned invasion from Cuba. Gen. Anastasio "Tachito" Somoza Jr. (the President's brother and heir to the dynasty) mobilized 2,000 *Guardia Nacional* (the army). Unable to inspire an uprising among the peasants, the invaders surrendered without a fight.[16]

On June 13, thirty-one Cubans led by a Nicaraguan exile sailed from La Coloma, Cuba, on a Cuban-registered fishing vessel and landed on the Yucatan Peninsula of Mexico. The Mexicans captured sixteen of the men and they were deported back to Cuba. On June 16 the Costa Rican government dispersed some 160 armed men who were preparing to invade Nicaragua. One week later the Honduran army had a fire fight with forty-two armed men who were trying to enter Nicaragua; seven Nicaraguan exiles were killed. Captured documents revealed that the leader had received $2,400 and logistical support from Che Guevara.[17]

On July 3, nineteen more armed men on their way to Nicaragua were captured by Honduran authorities disembarking from two barges at the mouth of the Patuca River.[18]

The Somoza family, sometimes aided by their neighbors, easily thwarted these attempts to create a Cuban-style revolution.

In October rebels calling themselves the September 15 Column (*Columna 15 de Septiembre*) invaded Nicaragua from Honduras. Led by Julio Alonzo Leclaire, they attacked the town of Santa Clara (100 mi N of Managua). After a few minor successes, the guerrillas were dispersed by the *Guardia Nacional* and their base camp destroyed. Eleven members who fled to Honduras were arrested.[19]

By the end of 1959, a rebel group headed by Indalecio Pastora was conducting raids from Costa Rica into Nicaragua. The guerrillas raided the towns of Cardenas, El Castillo, Tiruli, and Sabalos. Apparently, the *Guardia Nacional* lost thirty killed and twenty-two wounded; the guerrillas lost two missing and five wounded.[20]

Exactly what role Fidel Castro played in these events is unclear. Fidel was no friend of the Somozas. Among other irritants, the Somoza regime had sold armored cars to Batista after the U.S. arms embargo of March 18, 1958. The amount of Che's donation (if accurate) suggests that he was probably acting on his own.[21]

In spite of the abuses by the Somozas and the air of uncertainty caused by the guerrillas, the United States did not wain in its openly expressed support of the regime. The journal *Latin American Review* reported in December 1959:

> In Managua, the Somozas forgot the rebel threat long enough to celebrate the birthday of General Anastasio Somoza Debayle, commander of the National Guard, at a banquet given by the U.S. Military Mission. Ambassador [Thomas] Whelan and Colonel [fnu] Reynolds, chief of the U.S. Military Mission, joined in singing "Happy Birthday" to the guest of honor.[22]

OBSERVATIONS

By early 1959 Fidel Castro was a dedicated "revolutionary" but no convincing evidence existed that he was a Communist. Castro's power at that time was virtually absolute. If he had not fully encouraged these exports of revolution, they would have been halted immediately. Subversion had already become a basic policy of the Guevara-Castro-Castro triumvirate. Che was the strategist; Raúl provided the resources; and Fidel gave the undertaking legitimacy.

The fact that these ill-conceived and poorly executed invasions were supported by officials in Venezuela and Costa Rica demonstrated their desire to change the political status quo in the Caribbean. This was possible because the U.S. cold war strategy of "Containment," which required all nations to choose sides between the United States and the Soviet Union, had not been entirely effective.

In response to the threats to the status quo posed from Cuba, the United States acted primarily through the CIA. Its activities were clandestine, and in all probability much remains secret. Nevertheless, the actions of the United States demonstrated that it would stand behind those Latin American dictators who had supported first its antifascist policy and then its anti-Communist policy, regardless of how despicable those individuals might be.

CHAPTER 27

MILITARY OPERATIONS BY
CUBAN EXILES, 1960–65

How could I have been so stupid to let them go ahead [with the Bay of Pigs invasion]?
—U.S. President John F. Kennedy

THE SPARK

On May 17, 1960, President Dwight D. Eisenhower approved a National Security Council directive entitled "A Program of Covert Action Against the Castro Regime." Although a North American initiative, this decision made it possible for Cuban exiles, who had already begun to attack the Castro regime, to escalate operations to a scale they could not achieve on their own.[1]

BACKGROUND

Following the Cuban Revolution, which ended on January 1, 1959, United States relations with the new Cuban government deteriorated from cautiously optimistic to openly hostile. The two issues through which one could most accurately measure the deterioration in Cuban-American relations were American property rights in Cuba and the quota the United States allocated to Cuban-grown sugar for entry into the U.S. market. Also during 1959, Castro facilitated revolutionary violence against the Dominican Republic, Haiti, Nicaragua, and Panama (see chapter 26). In February 1960 Havana and Moscow agreed to a sugar-for-oil swap.[2]

It wasn't long before those who fled Cuba to the United States were carrying out clandestine attacks against the Castro regime. Between October 11 and 22, 1959, Cuban émigrés flying light aircraft from the United States bombed with incendiaries sugar mills in Pinar del Río and Camagüey Provinces, strafed a train in Las Villas Province, and bombed Havana. The bombings continued into 1960, a favorite target being sugar cane fields. On March 4, 1960, Cuban émigrés blew up the French ship *La Coubre* in the Bay of Havana, killing one hundred and injuring many more; the ship was carrying weapons from Belgium.[3]

Reacting to Castro's increasing hostility toward American investment in Cuba, his aid to leftist Revolutionaries, and his courtship of the Soviet Union, President Eisenhower reduced the Cuban sugar quota by 700,000 tons on July 6, 1960. This in effect eliminated the quota for the remainder of that year and it was never reinstated. In retaliation, Cuba seized more American property, and on September 17 Cuba nationalized all remaining U.S. private interests on the island.[4]

On January 2, 1961, Castro demanded that the United States reduce its embassy staff in Havana from sixty-seven persons to twelve. As a consequence of the accumulation of these and other events, President Eisenhower broke diplomatic relations with Cuba the following day. To implement President Eisenhower's decision of May 17 to overthrow Fidel Castro, the National Security Council assigned the Central Intelligence Agency the task of recruiting, organizing, training, and supporting a force of Cuban exiles. This effort was to be clandestine and no conventional U.S. forces were to be employed.[5]

As these events were transpiring, a number of prominent Cubans defected from the Revolutionary movement as Castro became increasingly entangled with Communism. The most prominent of these was Maj. Huber Matos,[6] who resigned as the Commander of the Revolutionary army in Camaguey Province on October 19, 1959, in protest of the Communist takeover of the Revolutionary army. Others who abandoned the cause were Humberto Sorí Marín, Pedro Díaz Lanz,and Manuel Artime.[7] Castro accused them of treason. Matos was arrested and jailed; Sorí Martín went underground (only to by caught and executed at the time of the Bay of Pigs); and Díaz Lanz and Artime escaped to the United States.[8]

OPPOSING FORCES

As Fidel Castro rapidly assimilated power, many Cubans fled their homeland. By early 1961 the number exceeded 100,000 persons. Many were from the professional, mercantile, and upper classes. Most settled in the Miami, Florida, area. The Cuban Revolutionary Council (*Consejo Revolucionario Cubano*), headed by José Miro Candona, emerged as the unifying anti-Castro movement. Miro had served as Castro's prime minister in 1959 before Fidel directly assumed power.[9]

The young sons of these middle- and upper-class émigré families became the recruits for the Bay of Pigs and later military adventures against Castro. Prior to the death of President John Kennedy on November 22, 1963, the United States recruited, organized, trained, and equipped the Cuban exiles. Materially, they lacked only that which the United States did not wish to give them.[10]

Although many of Fidel Castro's followers had become disenchanted shortly after his rise to national power on January 1, 1959, he easily made up for their defections by assimilating to his cause members of the lower class who, under the U.S.-supported Batista regime, had been ignored at best and exploited at worst.

In March 1959 Raúl Castro and Che Guevara began organizing a militia to defend the island against any American-sponsored intervention. The Batista army was disbanded on August 9 and a new Revolutionary militia was created. By early 1961 the Cuban militia had grown to between 200,000 and 300,000 men. Few of these individuals had military experience.[11]

Immediately following the revolution the Cuban militia had to rely upon weapons left over from the Batista regime. Soon Raúl dispatched an emissary to Moscow to request arms and advisors. The Soviets sent two Spanish Civil War émigrés and fifteen Soviet officers of Spanish descent to Cuba. On February 13, 1960, Cuba and the Soviet Union signed a major trade agreement and on May 7 they reestablished diplomatic relations, which had been broken in

April 1952 following the coup by Batista. By April 1961 over 30,000 tons of military hardware and supplies had arrived from Eastern Europe and the Soviet Union.[12]

Fidel Castro inherited a Cuban air force possessing thirty-six aircraft. Of these probably twelve combat planes were operational—six B-26 light bombers, four T-33 jet trainers, and two "Sea Fury" attack aircraft. The CIA incorrectly believed the T-33s were unarmed. Some fifty Cuban pilots were training in Czechoslovakia and MiG-15 interceptors could be expected in Cuba sometime after April 1962. The pilots remaining in Cuba were not well trained.[13]

The Cuban navy possessed a few dilapidated patrol ships and craft. These had little military value and Castro did not trust many serving in the navy.[14]

Just as important as the militia, Castro created a secret police. "Committees for the Defense of the Revolution" (*Comités de Defensa de la Revolución*—CDRs) were formed, seemingly on every city block. Their members kept a twenty-four-hour watch, recording movements and looking for suspicious activity. This drove organized anti-Castro activity underground.[15]

OPENING STRATEGIES

The CIA dominated the early military planning against Castro. Its initial plan called for an operation modeled after the 1954 Guatemalan experience (see chapter 22). Castro would be brought down through propaganda and covert operations.[16]

Che Guevara and Raúl Castro appreciated that the most immediate threat to Fidel's regime was a U.S.-supported uprising. To prevent this, they planned to control the cities through the "Committees for the Defense of the Revolution" so that they could preempt any fifth-column movement. Any invasion was to be overwhelmed by the new militia. The strategy for dealing with the raids being carried out against the island from the United States was to create an air force and navy based on the Soviet models of coastal defense. The navy in particular would take years to develop.

THE BAY OF PIGS

Contingency planning for the overthrow of Fidel Castro began in the spring of 1960. By summer the plan evolved from inserting guerrillas into Cuba to landing a paramilitary force. Initially 200 to 300 Cuban exiles were recruited and began training. Over the next year this force incrementally escalated to 1,500 men who were trained principally in conventional tactics.[17]

The émigré recruits received preliminary training in Florida and Louisiana. The United States arranged for the émigrés to lease a larger training site on the Pacific coast of Guatemala with the tacit approval of President Miguel Ydígoras. This was on a large coffee plantation known as Helvetia belonging to Roberto Alejos, the brother of the Guatemalan ambassador to the United States. The camp became known as *Base Trax*. The tank crews were trained at Fort Knox, Kentucky, and sixty men were sent to Panama to receive guerrilla training. Also, Anastasio Somoza agreed to permit a Nicaraguan airfield and port facilities to be used against Fidel Castro. The airfield was 500 miles from central Cuba. This was within the range of the aircraft to be employed but far from ideal.[18]

Those who instructed the exiled Cubans came from a variety of backgrounds. Some had fought in World War II and others for and against Fidel Castro during the Cuban Revolution. The brigade was organized into five battalions—one paratrooper, two infantry, one armor, and one heavy weapons. In addition, a number of special units were created including those for infiltration. They were to assist the underground with sabotage in order to divert attention away from the landing site.

The CIA provided an "air force" and a "navy" for the invasion. Twenty B-26 light bombers were given to the rebels. This type of aircraft was chosen because some of the exiled Cuban recruits had experience in the B-26. Also, the choice of this aircraft helped obscure the origin of the operation since a number of Caribbean air forces, including that of Cuba, flew this model. Some of the "navy" was purchased and some chartered. The ships were crewed primarily by former Cuban naval personnel who had fled Cuba. In total, two LCIs (landing craft, infantry), three LCUs (landing craft, utility), and six small freighters (each about 1,500 tons) were provided.[19]

The invasion plan called for two successive days of preemptive air strikes against Castro's air force and armor followed by an amphibious landing at Trinidad on the southern coast of Cuba. The air strikes were to destroy Castro's air force on the ground so that Brigade 2506[20] could land under friendly skies.

The CIA had acquired and installed a 50-kilowatt, medium-wave transmitter on Swan Island midway between Cuba and the United States. U.S. Seabees (naval construction battalion) had to construct a pier on the island in order to accommodate the landing of the radio gear. It began broadcasting on May 17, 1960. Radio Swan was operated under a commercial guise. To supplement Radio Swan, the CIA bought air time on commercial stations throughout the Caribbean. Their broadcasts were kept low key and were to intensify after the invasion. Beginning in September CIA-sponsored aircraft began dropping weapons to sites in the Escambray Mountains. And on October 27 President Eisenhower ordered the first reconnaissance flight over Cuba.[21]

The plan was not well integrated. Exiled political leaders argued among themselves and with the CIA; the members of Brigade 2506 were becoming increasingly restless, believing that they were overtrained; American government agencies not "in the know" innocently interfered with preparations.[22]

In late 1960 President Eisenhower, believing that more time was needed for planning, postponed the invasion until the new Kennedy administration had an opportunity to review the plan. This decision fueled the existing frictions. President Kennedy asked the Joint Chiefs of Staff to review the plan. They did so and gave it a lukewarm, but favorable endorsement.[23] The first of March, 1961, was selected as D-Day. Radio Swan intensified its broadcasts. Also, infiltration teams were dropped into Cuba to organize those opposed to Castro. Féliz Rodríguez,[24] who would emerge as an anti-Castro leader, was among them. The invasion date slipped to April 17 in order to enlarge the brigade by 400 men.

In April the landing site was changed from Trinidad (272 mi ESE of Havana) to the Bay of Pigs (*Bahia de Cochinos*[25]—173 mi SE of Havana), one hundred miles to the west, but the invasion date held fast at the seventeenth. Apparently, Secretary of State Dean Rusk persuaded the President that landing near a population center might involve civilian casualties. Also, Rusk argued that since the runway at Trinidad was too short to accommodate B-26s, it would be difficult to explain the B-26 flights since the new plan called for the insurgent B-26s to behave as if they were defecting Cuban aircraft. So the landing was moved to the swampy, sparsely inhabited Zapata Peninsula because of the 4,500-foot airstrip suitable for B-26s at Girón.[26]

From a tactical point of view, the new landing site had numerous disadvantages; it was not near mountains into which the invaders could flee if disaster befell them. The name of the new landing site—the Bay of Pigs—had little appeal to the propaganda section. Also, the number of preinvasion air strikes was reduced. Now only two air sorties were approved, one just before D-Day and the other on that morning. Also, propaganda leaflets would not be dropped prior to the invasion as previously scheduled.

Between April 8 and 11, Brigade 2506 flew from the training camp in Guatemala to Puerto Cabezas, Nicaragua, where it boarded the small merchantships which sailed between the ninth and the eleventh. A U.S. Navy LSD (landing ship, dock) rendezvoused with the Cuban flotilla at sea and offloaded three LCUs and two LCIs which were then manned by Cuban crews. The invasion force consisted of 1,500 men supported by five M-41 "Walker" tanks, ten 2.5-ton trucks mounting 12.7mm machine guns, three quarter-ton jeeps, four 106.7mm mortars; fifteen 81mm mortars, three 75mm recoiless rifles, fifteen 57mm recoiless rifles, and three 12.7mm machine guns.[27]

The invaders had suffered a major blow on March 18 when the leader of the anti-Castro movement in Cuba, Rafael Díaz Hanscom, and eight of his confederates, were arrested while meeting. On April 12 Castro's agents began arresting thousands of people throughout the island, many simply for being well dressed. Within three days some 250,000 people were being held. The backbone of the underground was broken.[28]

A diversionary landing at Baracoa (641 mi ESE of Havana) of 160 men scheduled for the night of April 14–15 failed to take place. The Cuban émigré in charge did not carry out his orders.[29]

At dawn on April 15, eight B-26 aircraft flying from Puerto Cabezas, Nicaragua, attacked the military airfields at San Antonio de Los Baños, Ciudad Libertad (formerly Camp Columbia) in Havana, Pinar del Río (106 mi SW of Havana), and Santiago de Cuba (580 mi ESE of Havana). The air strikes destroyed five aircraft and damaged an indeterminable number. President Kennedy ordered that the scale of the attack be reduced; therefore, only eight aircraft were employed and not the sixteen or seventeen available. Overly enthusiastic estimates claimed that more than half of Castro's air force had been destroyed. One attacking B-26 was lost. Anticipating an air strike, Castro ordered the inoperative aircraft to be displayed on the airfields and the serviceable planes to be dispersed and camouflaged.[30]

Following this initial air strike a B-26, riddled with bullet holes, was flown to Miami and the crew claimed to be defectors who had just bombed the remainder of Castro's air force. U.S. Ambassador to the United Nations Adlai Stevenson, who was not privy to the hoax, adamantly denied the Cuban Ambassador's charges of American complicity. Instead of scattering his remaining aircraft, Castro gathered them at a field near Havana. Not far from this site was the majority of his armored force. While Brigade 2506 was at sea, President Kennedy canceled the second air strike against Castro's bases, thus leaving the remainder of the Cuban air force superior to that of the insurgents and Castro's armor in tact.[31]

At about midday on April 16, President Kennedy approved the landing. However, at 9:30 P.M. McGeorge Bundy, Special Assistant to the President, ordered Gen. Charles Cabell at the CIA to cancel future air strikes. Offensive air operations would not be renewed until the airfield at the Bay of Pigs was secured and operational.[32]

CIA officials tried to compensate for the cancellation of air operations by advising the invasion fleet to offload and withdraw before dawn. Given the speed of the ships and the poor training of the crews, this was impossible to achieve. A plan was also devised whereby continuous air cover over the beachhead was to be provided by the B-26s flying in rotation. This plan permitted only two aircraft to be on station during daylight hours. Each aircraft would have thirty minutes over the landing site. Five-and-one-half hours were required to fly to and from the air base in Nicaragua, and an additional two hours were needed on the ground to refuel and rearm. A U.S. task force clustered around the carrier *Essex*, then off the coast of southern Cuba, was alerted of the possible requirement to give early warning and to provide air cover to the invasion. At 4:30 A.M. on the seventeenth, President Kennedy approved providing early warning to the invaders but disapproved the air protection.[33]

The Bay of Pigs was shaped like a very narrow bottle. Just inside the mouth of the bay on the east side lay the small town of Girón with an airstrip. The town was being developed as a resort and only a few roads served the area. Once away from the town and roads, the ground became very swampy. The landing was to occur on three beaches. "Red Beach" lay at the top of the narrow neck some 20 miles northwest of Girón. "Blue Beach" lay just south of Girón where the bay joined the ocean. "Green Beach" lay about 15 miles to the east of Girón away from the bay. The distance from Red Beach at the extreme east and Green Beach at the extreme west was 36 miles.[34]

Frogmen went ashore late Sunday, April 16, to mark the beaches for the invaders. A Cuban militia patrol discovered them and surprise was lost.[35]

José Pérez San Román, a former officer in Batista's army, led the first elements of Brigade 2506 ashore at Blue Beach at 1:15 A.M. on April 17. Their immediate objective was to capture the nearby airstrip. Because surprise had been lost, the landing at Green Beach was canceled and these men also landed on Blue Beach. In spite of air attacks by the Cuban air force, the vehicles and tanks assigned to Blue Beach were successfully offloaded from the three LCUs by 7:30 A.M. and all troops destined for this beach were ashore by 8:25 A.M. However, due to the depth of the water through which the invaders waded, their radio equipment got wet and they were unable to communicate with those offshore.[36]

Also at 7:30 A.M., five C-46s and one C-54 dropped the 172-man paratroop battalion behind the Cuban militia defending the beach. The paratroopers who fell north of Red Beach were captured. Those who fell to the east seized San Blas, an important crossroads 10 miles northeast of Blue Beach. The paratroopers at San Blas were soon reinforced by a heavy-weapons detachment from the Third Battalion.[37]

The landing at Red Beach did not go well from the beginning. The 2nd and 5th Battalions were embarked in the freighter *Houston*. Because of the shallow depth of the water at the top of the bay, the *Houston* had to remain a considerable distance off the beach. The invaders were required to transfer to aluminum boats for a twenty-minute run into the beach. Out of the nine boats on the *Houston*, only two proved to be operational. The 5th Battalion never got ashore due to the boat problem and the lack of initiative by its commander. Practically the only supplies to get ashore at Red Beach were those carried on the backs of the 2nd Battalion. At about 6:30 A.M. the *Houston* and the LCI *Barbara J* were damaged by attacking aircraft. After a short time the *Houston* grounded about five miles south of Red Beach. Some 130 men of the 5th Battalion were still on board, and at least 28 died attempting to get ashore.[38]

The 270 men of the 2nd Battalion who had landed at Red Beach pushed inland for about four miles. There, the battalion's advance was blocked by 800 Cuban militiamen. The battalion failed to achieve its objective of cutting the road that crossed the swamp east and west. By noon twelve tanks joined the Cuban militia and by 6 P.M. they received artillery support.[39]

At about 7:00 A.M. on April 17, a Cuban air force "Sea Fury" jet fighter flown by Capt. Enrique Carreras Rojas, a holdover from the Batista air force, sank the freighter *Río Escondido* which was carrying ten days' reserve of ammunition, communications equipment, and other vital supplies. At 10:00 A.M. the contract employee in charge of the invasion flotilla radioed CIA headquarters that if air cover was not provided, he would pull out. CIA headquarters advised him to pull back some 50 miles offshore. The freighters *Atlántico* and *Caribe* led the flight followed by the slower LCIs and the three LCUs.[40]

What percentage of Brigade 2506 and its equipment had been landed is unclear. In spite of these setbacks, the invaders overpowered the militia defending the beach, killing 40 and taking about 100 prisoners.[41]

The nearest Cuban regular-army unit to the Bay of Pigs was a 900-man battalion commanded by Osmani Cienfuegos (brother of Camilo Cienfuegos) at the sugar mill Central Australia, 15 miles to the northeast. Also, militia platoons dotted the region. These and other units scattered throughout Matanzas Province were ordered to converge on the invaders. Castro also ordered his air force to attack.[42]

Castro traveled to the invasion site; however once he arrived, he was told that another landing was taking place near Havana so he hurried back to the capital. Castro soon discovered that this was a ruse so he returned to the Bay of Pigs and established his headquarters at Central Australia because it had the only phone in the area.[43]

The invaders were supported by the B-26s, flying in pairs, after President Kennedy reauthorized flights during the morning. A little after 3 P.M., the invaders established radio contact with two of the supporting B-26s. Those on the ground ordered the aircraft to attack a column of seventy vehicles and 700 men advancing toward the beachhead. The B-26s decimated the column. The tables turned against the Brigade's B-26s when a T-33 jet trainer and a "Sea Fury" jet fighter from Castro's air force shot down two of the light bombers. The air combat during the day was intense. The rebel B-26s flew thirteen missions, during which time Cuban T-33 aircraft shot down four of the light bombers. Castro lost two "Sea Furies" and two B-26s to antiaircraft fire.[44]

Late on D-Day, the CIA decided to attack the San Antonio de los Baños airfield in an attempt to destroy the T-33s on the ground. Two strikes, each by three B-26s, attempted the mission. Two aircraft aborted the mission and the others could not attack due to thick haze and clouds.[45]

Due to the shortage of ammunition on the beachhead, four C-54s and two C-46s made emergency airdrops during the evening. Some of the supplies were successfully recovered by those on the beach.[46]

Meanwhile, the invasion flotilla reached its pull-back position 50 miles to the south. The two LCIs and the three LCUs awaited further instructions; however, the freighters *Atlántico* and *Caribe* kept going. The *Atlántico*, loaded with ammunition, was intercepted by the U.S. Navy 110 miles south of Cuba and the *Caribe* was caught 218 miles to the south. Both were persuaded to return to the rendezvous site. The *Atlántico* arrived at 4:45 P.M. on the eighteenth and the *Caribe* did not return in time to participate in future operations. The *Caribe* was carrying equipment and supplies to be used to service rebel aircraft landing at the Girón airstrip.[47]

The fighting on the seventeenth, the day of the landing, decidedly favored Brigade 2506. Castro committed his militiamen piecemeal as they arrived, perhaps fearing that this was a prelude to a larger invasion. He kept the regular army units in reserve, perhaps fearing that they might be less motivated. During the first day Brigade 2506 lost less than 100 men and Castro had more than 300 casualties plus 100 of his troops had been captured.[48]

During the early morning of the eighteenth, the tide turned. The brigade members, who had landed on Red Beach and pushed northward, were attacked by tanks. As their ammunition ran low, they began pulling back to Blue Beach at 9 A.M., an operation which took one-and-a-half hours to complete. In the meantime Castro's forces continually increased. After being resupplied during a two-hour rest, the Red Beach force was ordered to return to Red Beach and block the enemy's advance. They briefly did so but were overwhelmed by the Cuban militia.[49]

At about 4 A.M. on the eighteenth, the defenders at San Blas came under an increasingly intensive barrage from 122mm howitzers recently acquired from the Soviet Union as well as other ordnance. Over 3,000 shells rained down on the brigade's positions in a matter of hours. Although those at San Blas tenaciously held their position, they were increasingly constricted and their counterattack to the north failed. An assortment of Soviet-, American-, and British-manufactured tanks and self-propelled guns attacked over the three roads leading into the defended area. Brigade 2506 inflicted heavy casualties, knocking out some of the armor with the 57mm recoilless rifles and their own tanks. That evening CIA headquarters communicating through the LCI *Blagar* asked Brigade Commander San Román if he wanted to withdraw his force. He replied, "I will not evacuate. We will fight to the end here if we have to."[50]

By the eighteenth some 20,000 Cuban troops, mostly militia, and twenty tanks surrounded the invaders. Brigade 2506 was being constantly pounded by artillery and constricted by advancing tanks. The pilots of Brigade 2506 were exhausted and many had lost heart, so American civilian-contracted pilots took their place. Beginning in the afternoon they flew six sorties, attacking a column of tanks approaching the beachhead from the north.[51]

Meanwhile, at sea, the *Atlántico*, which had returned to the rendezvous site 50 miles south of Cuba, offloaded ammunition into the three LCUs. The transfer was completed at 11:00 P.M. on the eighteenth. The LCI *Blagar* escorted the LCUs toward the Bay of Pigs, with the estimated arrival time to be 6:30 A.M. on April 19. The captain of the LCI radioed CIA headquarters that if he could not get a U.S. escort he believed the crews would mutiny. The CIA ordered the resupply flotilla to abort the mission. Also, four C-46s attempted to deliver supplies to the encircled Brigade. Three turned back due to enemy air activity but the fourth landed and then escaped from the captured airfield.[52]

During the eighteenth the CIA sought presidential permission to have the U.S. military fly combat air patrol over the beachhead in order to allow Brigade 2506's B-26s to close air support. Permission was granted for one hour—six unmarked U.S. aircraft, from the carrier *Essex*, protected the skies between 6:30 A.M. and 7:30 A.M. on the morning of the nineteenth but were prohibited from attacking ground targets. However, the Brigade's B-26s, again flown by CIA-contracted pilots, arrived early and two were shot down by Cuban T-33s.[53]

All of these measures were too little, too late. By the morning of the nineteenth the Brigade members at San Blas began to retreat. The last message from the Brigade commander at Blue Beach, received at 2:32 P.M., read: "Am destroying all equipment and communications. Tanks are in sight." The communiqué went on to say: "I have nothing left to fight with. Am taking to the woods. I cannot wait for you."[54] The fighting ended shortly after 5 P.M. on April 19— Castro captured 1,122 invaders.[55]

By the nineteenth all of the B-26s were out of action. Eight had been lost in combat: five shot down by T-33s, two by "Sea Furies," and one by antiaircraft fire. Rafael del Pino[56] emerged as a hero of the Cuban air force. Among the attacking aviators who were killed were four CIA-contracted personnel who had volunteered to relieve the exhausted Cuban exiles.

Brigade 2506 still had twenty-one aircraft operational but these were not combat types. The Cuban air force lost five aircraft on the ground the day before the invasion and four more to anti-aircraft fire over the beach. Nonetheless, by the nineteenth the Cuban air force completely controlled the skies. On April 24, President Kennedy publicly accepted the responsibility for the failed invasion and the following day he declared a total trade embargo against Cuba.[57]

On December 2, 1961, Castro stated, "I am a Marxist-Leninist and will be a Marxist-Leninist until the last day of my life."[58]

ANTI-CASTRO FREELANCE OPERATIONS

Immediately following the Bay of Pigs fiasco, the Kennedy administration reduced the visibility of its support for clandestine operations as it negotiated for the release of the members of Brigade 2506. It did, however, smuggle a large quantity of weapons into Cuba between the fall of 1961 and the summer of 1962. As a consequence of the apparent inaction of the United States, anti-Castro Cubans, on and off the island, carried out hundreds of acts of sabotage. Aircraft dropped homemade incendiary bombs on sugar-cane fields and propaganda leaflets on cities. Small boats, also operating from the United States, raided the Cuban coast. Most of these efforts were uncoordinated and short-lived. However, a few individuals persisted in their struggle against Castro.[59]

"ALPHA 66"

Eloy Gutiérrez Menoyo,[60] the leader of the "Second Front of Escambray" during the Cuban Revolution, organized and led a group known as "Alpha 66"[61] which specialized in harassing Cuban waterborne commerce from small craft. The operation was financed through private donations and not the CIA. On May 12, 1962, the group attacked a Cuban patrol boat and killed three of the five-man crew. On September 10 an Alpha 66 armed boat machine-gunned the Cuban freighter *San Pascual* and the British freighter *New Orleans* off Cayo Francés. They were carrying Cuban sugar to Eastern Europe. On March 17, 1963, another Alpha 66 boat attacked the Soviet freighter *Lgov* while docked in Sagua de Tanamo (610 mi ESE of Havana), wounding twelve sailors.[62]

Cuba retaliated. On March 18 two Cuban jets fired on the U.S. merchantship *Floridian*; Cuba quickly apologized, describing the attack as an error. On the twenty-sixth an émigré boat sank the Soviet freighter *Baku* loaded with sugar at Caribarièn (210 mi ESE of Havana). Two days later a Cuban jet fired on a boat flying the U.S. flag 50 miles north of Cuba; again the Cubans apologized for the mistake. On March 29 President Kennedy ordered U.S. agencies to stop the raids by Alpha 66; they were only partially successful.[63]

In 1964 Gutiérrez Menoyo set up a guerrilla training camp in the Dominican Republic and then clandestinely entered Cuba in an attempt to establish a base camp in the Escambray Mountains. He and three followers landed in eastern Cuba on December 28. Within four weeks he was hunted down. Following Gutiérrez Menoyo's capture on January 26, 1965, Tony Cuesta led Alpha 66. Although he was later severely injured and captured while attempting a mission, the Alpha 66 organization continued to carry out attacks.[64]

OTHER FREELANCERS

On August 24, 1962, Manuel Salvat, head of the university students in exile (and calling themselves the Revolutionary Student Directorate, or *Directorio Revolucionario Estudiantiles*—DRE), and some six other young exiles machine-gunned the Rosita de Hornedo

Hotel, where Russian advisors were residing, from a 31-foot pleasure craft. The Russians and their Cuban hosts sustained some twenty casualties; the attackers escaped without a scratch. This amateurish yet successful raid was carried out without the knowledge of the U.S. government and caused considerable political embarrassment.[65]

One of the more bizarre incursions into Cuba occurred after the Cuban Missile Crisis (October 1962). An odd collection of individuals attempted to spirit two defecting Soviet colonels from Cuba to prove that Soviet offensive missiles were still on the island. Known as "Operation Red Cross," the eight-man team that landed in Cuba was never heard from again.[66]

On the phony side, individuals, who wished to exploit the Cuban exiles, conducted countless training exercises in the Florida Everglades but then would abort their expeditions for one reason or another. These were schemes to raise money and win political influence.[67]

RAIDS FINANCED UNDER "OPERATION MONGOOSE"

While these freelance endeavors were playing out, the CIA with Kennedy's approval began a new initiative to overthrow Fidel Castro. Known as "Operation Mongoose," it had many facets, one of which was the financial underwriting of raids against the island orchestrated by Manuel Artime. The CIA's involvement was limited to providing funds and intelligence; all of the raiders were exiled Cubans. They adopted the name "Comandos Mambises" (the name given to the Cubans who had fought against the Spaniards for independence). The objective of Operation Mongoose was "to build toward an eventual internal revolt."[68]

Artime established a complex system of bases—an operational headquarters, a communications base, and a commando base in Nicaragua; a commercial front in Miami; an arms depot hidden on a barge up a river in Costa Rica; and a resupply site in the Dominican Republic. Artime operated an impressive amount of equipment. He had two 250 foot freighters, two 50 foot Swift boats, an assortment of small craft, a C-47 transport aircraft, two Cessna aircraft, and a small Beaver amphibious aircraft.[69]

CUBAN MISSILE CRISIS

The agreement between the Soviet Union and the United States ending the Cuban Missile Crisis of October 1962 directly impacted on the operations of the Cuban émigrés. As part of the arrangement, the United States agreed not to invade Cuba in exchange for a United Nations' on-site inspection to confirm that the missiles had been withdrawn. The inspection never took place because of Castro's opposition. Kennedy had also conditioned his pledge against invasion upon Castro's commitment not to conduct "aggressive acts" in the hemisphere. In spite of the fact that the other side did not live up to the agreement, Kennedy gave up the thought of invading and waned in his support of the émigrés.[70]

RAIDS FOLLOWING OPERATION MONGOOSE

Although Operation Mongoose was disbanded following the Cuban Missile Crisis in October 1962, the CIA continued to support clandestine raids by Artime and others against Cuba. Also, arms continued to be delivered to dissidents on the island. The political objective of these raids became more limited. They were "to nourish a spirit of resistance and disaffection which could lead to significant defections and other byproducts of unrest."[71]

Following John Kennedy's assassination on November 22, 1963, CIA support of these operations waned. In fact, on April 17, 1964, President Lyndon Johnson decided to stop the CIA-supported raids against Cuba and to abandon the idea of overthrowing Castro. Nevertheless, on

May 13 Artime's group attacked the Cabo Cruz sugar refinery on the south coast of Oriente Province. A small landing team blew up water-cooling pipes and a pump house while a fast boat fired recoilless rifles and machine guns at warehouses and holding tanks. Ten commandos were involved in the operation.[72]

In August 1964 Artime launched an operation directly against the north coast of Cuba. The raiders spent forty-five days plowing through heavy seas before reaching the Cuban coast. There they found that the intelligence they had received, apparently from the CIA, was outdated and that the beach was well guarded. Then, by chance, on September 24 they saw a large merchantship and mistook it for the Cuban merchantship *Sierra Maestra*. They attacked the Spanish *Sierra Aránzazu*, killing its captain, injuring others, and setting the ship afire. This catastrophy spelled the end of the U.S.-supported raids. From late 1961 through late 1964, Artime had launched fourteen missions, of which only four achieved their objectives.[73]

Diehard anti-Castro groups continued to harass Cuba into the 1990s. Most active among these was Alpha 66. Regardless, by the mid-1960s, the U.S. government had lost the zeal for these operations.[74]

OBSERVATIONS

What went wrong at the Bay of Pigs and subsequent operations? Overconfidence permeated American plans; this was due in part to the ease of the CIA-engineered Guatemalan Revolution of 1954. Given the number of participants in the Bay of Pigs operation, it was impossible to keep anything other than when and where a secret.[75] The invading force did not establish air superiority due to political indecision. The landing site was a poor choice and the invaders were ignorant of beach conditions and local defenses. The Bay of Pigs was easily accessible from Havana where Castro's most reliable units were concentrated.

The United States included some Batista cronies among the invading force; this compromised the integrity of the invaders. The leaders of the invasion were sons of the rich upper class, contributing to the perception that the objective of the landing was to restore the old aristocracy. Castro's secret service neutralized the underground. The United States perceived the Cuban Brigade as a catalyst for an uprising against Fidel Castro; the Cuban exiles viewed the operation as a liberating force which the United States would not permit to fail. The CIA underestimated the efficiency of the Cuban militia; it judged the militiamen by their recent performance in the Escambray Mountains which, unknown to the CIA, was a ruse (see chapter 26).[76]

David Atlee Phillips, a member of the CIA invasion team, concluded,

> Two mistakes eclipsed all others. The first was the decision to cancel the air strike on D-Day. . . . The second, . . . At some time we should have cried, "enough." When told the plan was to be changed from a classic guerrilla landing at Trinidad to a military operation we should have protested individually to the point of refusing to obey.[77]

The unsuccessful amphibious assault of Cuba had severe repercussions throughout the World. The Soviet Union concluded that it was only a matter of time before the United States got its act together and did the job right. Therefore, the Bay of Pigs significantly contributed to the Soviet decision to base missiles in Cuba, which led to the missile crisis of October 1962.[78]

The failure also significantly damaged U.S. prestige throughout the world, and Latin America in particular. The operation was a military and propaganda victory for Fidel Castro.

The failed landing was such an embarrassment to the United States that it felt compelled to ransom the survivors, who were sentenced by a Revolutionary tribunal to thirty years in prison.[79]

Although the Kennedy administration did an after-action report following the Bay of Pigs fiasco, it persisted in the belief that Fidel Castro's regime was teetering on the brink of collapse and that all it needed was a good push. Therefore, Kennedy initiated Operation Mongoose, which in some respects was less in touch with reality than its failed predecessor.

The anti-Castro freelance operations and those financed by Operation Mongoose did cause Castro concern for several years. The Cuban military even organized special units (Fighting Against Bandits—*Lucha Contra Bandidos*, LCB) to combat the problem. However, by the end of the 1960s over 500,000 persons, mostly white, educated individuals had emigrated from Cuba to the United States to escape Castro's revolution. This exodus doomed any counterrevolution from taking place on the island because most of the dissidents were now in the United States. And those who weren't, some 20,000 persons, were in Cuban jails and workcamps by 1965.[80]

Much mistrust existed between the American administration and the Cuban exiles. Many on both sides were suspicious of the other side's motives. Many Cuban exiles believed that the Americans' only interest in Cuba was its significance in the East-West struggle and not Cuban democracy. Many American officials believed that the exiles wanted to turn back the hands of the clock to elitism. These mistrusts contributed to the failure of operations against Castro.[81]

Also, by the mid-1960s the Cuban air force and navy had been sufficiently strengthened through Soviet aid that, without significant U.S. help, raids against the island by Cuban dissidents were becoming prohibitively costly.[82]

CHAPTER 28

VENEZUELA—REACTIONARY RIGHT
AND RADICAL LEFT, 1960–62

He [President Betancourt] is beset by extreme rightists, fidelists, and Communists intent on frightening private capital and hampering constitutional democracy to the point where he in desperation must rule by decree.

—*Christian Science Monitor,* March 16, 1962

THE SPARK

The election of Rómulo Betancourt as President of Venezuela on December 7, 1958, sparked numerous coup attempts. He was inaugurated on February 13, 1959.

BACKGROUND

Betancourt's new government was caught between the radical left and the reactionary right. The radical left felt unrewarded for its role in the overthrow of Marcos Pérez Jiménez, and the reactionary right felt dispossessed since it had ruled Venezuela for decades by controlling the military (see chapter 25). Externally, Rafael Trujillo, the long-lived dictator of the Dominican Republic, looked to take revenge upon Venezuela for its aid to those seeking his overthrow in 1959 (see chapter 25). And, initially, the United States government feared that Betancourt's government was unduly influenced by Communists.

OPPOSING SIDES

In 1959 it was unclear who would defend the recently elected government. Some senior military officers wished to return to the privileged positions they had enjoyed under Pérez Jiménez; and, at the opposite end of the political spectrum, some young radical Communists and Socialists wanted to overthrow the democratic government and establish a socialist state. Trujillo could be counted on to support those from the reactionary right and Castro those from the radical left.

OPENING STRATEGIES

The reactionary senior military officers relied on the old strategy of a coup d'état. They intended to subvert military units through demagoguery and intimidation and then seize the seat of government before forces loyal to the newly elected president could react.

Much of the radical left also wanted to use military units to seize power. They appealed to the "social conscience" of the junior officers and senior enlisted; and these military people, in turn, would provide the loyalty of their men. Others of the radical left preferred to follow the example of the Cuban Revolution and fight a guerrilla war (see chapter 29).

The Betancourt government had little choice but to place its fate in the hands of the moderate officers and civilians who had played a critical role in the overthrow of Pérez Jiménez.

INITIAL VIOLENCE

The new government was almost immediately attacked diplomatically and militarily from both the right and the left. On March 22 the Venezuelan chargé d'affaires to the Dominican Republic was declared *persona non grata*. On June 11 Venezuela retaliated against the Dominican chargé d'affaires in Caracas and on the following day Venezuela severed diplomatic relations with the Trujillo government. On August 4 antigovernment demonstrations broke out in Caracas. Four people were killed and forty-six injured as Betancourt suspended some constitutional rights. Between October 9 and 15, numerous bombs exploded in Caracas and on the sixteenth the Ministry of the Interior accused the Dominican Republic of conspiring with antigovernment forces.

On the ideological left, Cuba recalled its ambassador to Venezuela on November 7 after Venezuela objected to a visit to Caracas by Raúl Castro, head of the Cuban armed forces, and Ernesto Guevara. Between January 1 and 5, 1960, bomb explosions again rocked Caracas; nineteen people died including four policemen.[1]

BIRTH OF THE REVOLUTIONARY LEFT MOVEMENT

At the beginning of April 1960, militant and young activists, expelled from the governing Democratic Action Party, formed the Revolutionary Left Movement (*Movimiento de Izquierda Revolucionaria*—MIR). Led by Domingo Alberto Rangel, Simón Sáez Mérida, and Américo Martín, it proclaimed a Marxist ideology.[2]

A COUP ATTEMPT FROM THE RIGHT

On April 19, 1960, retired air force Brig. Gen. Jesús María Castro León, former Minister of Defense, revolted again and subverted the army garrison at San Cristóbal in the Andes. However, without the hoped-for support of air force, army, and national guard units, his movement foundered. The following day, loyal army troops supported by the national guard and air force "Canberra" bombers overpowered the rebels.[3]

AN ASSASSINATION ATTEMPT FROM THE RIGHT

On July 24, 1960, as President Betancourt was motoring to a ceremony honoring the Venezuelan army, dynamite planted in a parked car exploded, wounding him and his Minister of Defense, air force Brig. Gen. Josué López Henriquez. Additionally, his Chief of Aides-de-Camp, air force Col. Romón Armas Pérez, and one policeman were killed. A Venezuelan investigation concluded that Dominican dictator Rafael Trujillo was behind the conspiracy. Venezuela placed its military on alert, denounced Trujillo, and asked the Organization of American States (OAS) to apply sanctions against the Dominican Republic. Finally, in August the OAS voted unanimously to condemn the Dominican Republic for its aggression and embargoed arms shipments to the island nation. This was the first time that collective sanctions were recommended under the Rio Treaty of 1947.[4]

THE INSURRECTION OF LIEUTENANT SALDIVIA

At dawn on September 21, 1960, national guard Lt. Exio de Jesus Saldivia, leading forty guardsmen, seized a radio transmitter and began broadcasting subversive messages against the Betancourt government. Shortly, they were arrested by troops from their own unit, the 56th Detachment.[5]

CASTROITES (CASTISTAS) TAKE THE OFFENSIVE

On July 26, 1960, the Cuban chargé d'affaires to Venezuela, León Antich, led a group of Venezuelans, who sympathized with the Cuban Revolution, to the Catholic Cathedral in Caracas and they stoned the building. During October and November the followers of Fidel Castro ignited riots in Caracas. Thirteen were killed and a hundred were wounded. On November 2 Venezuela recalled its ambassador to Cuba. On the twenty-eighth Betancourt ordered the military to restore order and suspended constitutional guarantees. On the thirtieth the radical left barricaded themselves in the University of Caracas. By December 2 the military had restored order and evicted the leftists from the university.[6]

THE TURBULENT TWENTIETH OF FEBRUARY

At dawn on February 20, 1961, army Col. Edito José Ramírez, supported by a group of civilians, attempted to subvert the Army Command and General Staff School (*Escuela Superior de Ejército*) where he was the director. Neither the officers nor cadets would support his actions and he was arrested. Almost at the same time, a group of junior officers attempted to subvert the presidential guard. Among its leaders was the chaplain of the army, Father Simón Salvatierra. The rebels soon surrendered to government forces.[7]

YET ANOTHER ATTEMPT BY TRUJILLO

On May 31, 1961, Venezuela arrested twenty-one individuals who were conspiring to overthrow the government. They were armed with weapons traced to the Dominican Republic. Trujillo's assassination the day before (the thirtieth) eliminated this external threat.

EL BARCELONAZO—AN ATTACK FROM THE RIGHT

At 4 A.M. on June 26, 1961, army Capt. Tesalio Murillo Fierro, second in command of the army barrack in Barcelona (470 mi E of Caracas), subverted two companies of the "General Santiago Mariño" (9th) Infantry Battalion. After Murillo had gained control, the leaders of the rebellion—air force Lt. Col. Martín Parada, army Maj. Luís Alberto Vivas Ramírez, army Capt. Rubén Massó Perdomo, and army Capt. Enrique José Olaizola Rodríguez (all retired) entered the barrack and took command of the subverted troops. Joined by civilians, the rebels seized the airport, the police station, the radio station, and the state capitol. The governor, Rafael Solorzano Bruce, was detained. The rebels hoped that other units in the armed forces would join them but only one minor element did so. A national guard detachment at the Caracas International Airport, commanded by 2nd Lt. Elonis López Curra, rebelled. López' men were easily overcome by loyal marines.

At 7 A.M. on the twenty-sixth, North American B-25J "Mitchell" bombers began dropping pamphlets of the rebellious barrack in Barcelona, calling for its occupants to surrender. Two hours later the Minister of Defense, air force Brigade Gen. Antonio Briceño Linares[8] spoke to Major Vivas by phone and warned that if the rebels did not surrender immediately, the B-25s would drop bombs. In Barcelona, street demonstrations broke out in support of the government and the discipline of the rebels began to break down.

While these events were occurring, army 2nd Lt. Ramón Carrasquel and other loyal officers began fighting to recapture the barrack for the government. Between the opposing sides, forty men died and fifty were wounded. When the B-25s reappeared over the barrack, they observed white sheets on the roof, indicating that the rebels had surrendered.[9]

Following "El Barcelonazo," relations between Venezuela and Cuba declined rapidly. On July 26 Venezuela withdrew its chargé d'affairs from Havana at the request of the Cubans. He was accused of serving as a middleman between anti-Castro Cubans. On November 11 Venezuela broke diplomatic relations with Cuba.[10] On the twenty-seventh, leftist students hijacked a Venezuelan passenger plane and forced it to drop antigovernment leaflets on Caracas. Two days later government troops closed Communist Party headquarters and the newspaper *Clarin*. Two policemen were killed and dozens of leftists arrested.

EL GUAIRAZO—AN ATTACK FROM THE LEFT

On January 22, 1962, a wave of street violence began in Caracas. On the twenty-eighth, hundreds of youths—many of them students of Central University—rampaged through the streets of La Guaira, ostensibly in support of a transportation strike. They confronted the barracks of the marines' "Simón Bolívar" (No. 1) Battalion in hopes of arming themselves for an uprising. The action had been instigated by the Communist Party, which may have wanted a massacre to create instant martyrs. The leader of the battalion, marine Lt. Cmdr. Victor Hugo Morales Monasterios, exercised restraint and called the police, who detained more than two hundred youths. Two ensigns assigned to the battalion were implicated in the subversive action, but Morales Monasterios and later the Commander of the Navy, Vice Adm. Carlos Larrazábal, defended their activities.[11]

EL CARUPANAZO—AN ATTACK FROM THE LEFT

On February 9 President Betancourt summoned Rear Admiral Sosa Ríos, who had recently taken over command of the navy from Vice Adm. Carlos Larrazábal, to an urgent meeting at the Palacio de Miraflores with the Minister of Defense and the director of the armed forces intelligence service. The Admiral was informed of a plot against the government instigated by the Communist Party and the Leftist Revolutionary Movement. Among the alleged conspirators were Morales Monasterios, as well as the commander of the army's "General José Francisco Bermúdez" (No. 8) Armored Battalion in Caracas and the commander of national guard Detachment No. 99 in Maiquetía. President Betancourt ordered Sosa Ríos to replace Morales Monasterios immediately as commanding officer of the Marine battalion. To expedite the order, Sosa Ríos accompanied Cmdr. Gómez Muñoz to the seat of the marine corps "Simón Bolívar" Battalion at Maiquetía, some fifteen miles to the north of Caracas. There the battalion was assembled and the command changed, after which the Admiral returned to Caracas with Morales Monasterios in custody. With the other military services also replacing accused conspirators, this subversive movement failed. Remaining within the navy, however, and especially the marine corps, were those who did not support the new regime. Their continued efforts to conspire eventually came to a head in May.[12]

In the meantime, the extreme left attempted to assassinate President Betancourt on February 13 at an anti-Castro rally in Caracas but only succeeded in wounding him.

On April 1, 1962, a leftist uprising occurred at the Turiamo Naval Station but it was immediately suppressed.[13] Twenty days later, a group of armed civilians invaded the Venezuelan Merchant Marine Academy (*Escuela Náutica de Venezuela*) near Puerto de la Guaira and made off with 127 Mauser Model 1924/30 rifles and four cases of ammunition. At the same time, on April 20, army troops of the "Mariscal Antonio José de Sucre" (No. 51) Infantry Battalion stationed in the city of Maturín (310 mi E of Caracas) rebelled against their officers and began to shoot at them. A number were wounded before Maj. Félix González González, the commander of the battalion, could restore order.[14]

At 2:00 A.M. on May 4, the marines' "Mariscal Antonio José de Sucre" (No. 3) Infantry Battalion (not to be confused with the army unit of the same name), stationed in the coastal city of Carúpano (367 mi E of Caracas), revolted. Lt. Cmdr. Jesús Teodoro Molina Villegas, commanding officer of the battalion, was supported by the majority of his officers, a group of citizens, some army and national guard officers, and prominent members of the Communist Party and Leftist Revolutionary Movement. After forming a Revolutionary militia, they discussed the possibility of advancing against the national guard unit in Caripito but decided against it because of a shortage of men, munitions, and transport.[15]

Within half an hour of the commencement of the revolt, President Betancourt placed the armed services on alert. Admiral Sosa Ríos ordered the frigate *General Morán* to patrol off Carúpano and instructed navy Capt. José C. Seijas Villalobos,[16] Commander of the Fleet, to establish a naval command post at Cumaná, a port about 87 miles west of Carúpano. At 7:00 A.M. air force "Canberras" attacked rebel positions in Carúpano. The navy began planning for an amphibious assault in support of government forces that were to advance toward the city. Immediately available in Cumaná were the destroyer *Nueva Esparta*, the medium landing ships *Los Monjes* and *Los Roques*, plus the marines' "General Rafael Urdaneta" (No. 2) Battalion.

The Minister of Defense, General Briceño, organized a 3,000-man force made up of army, national guard, and marine corps personnel. Three columns advanced against the rebels. One column composed of the army's "General Santiago Mariño" (No. 52) Infantry Battalion, reinforced by a battery of howitzers, started from Cumaná. A second column made up of the "Mariscal Sucre" (No. 51) Infantry Battalion and reinforced by a section of recoilless rifles mounted on jeeps and by a company of national guard, started from Maturín. The third column composed of the "General Rafael Urdaneta" (No. 61) Infantry Battalion started from Ciudad Bolívar.

Sosa Ríos petitioned the President and the operational commander to allow marine corps personnel to be included in the land force so they would be in a position to accept the surrender of their rebellious colleagues and arrest those responsible. The request was granted, so a reinforced company from the marines' "Simon Bolivar" (No. 1) Battalion was airlifted from Maiquetía to Cumaná by air force transport planes and included in the attack force.[17]

On May 5, one day after the revolt, the three motorized columns advanced on Carúpano. Meanwhile, constant harassment by air force aircraft forced Molina Villegas to transfer the seat of rebel command away from the marine barracks.[18]

At dawn the next day, the government and rebel forces clashed as the former approached Carúpano. Rebel mines planted along roads into the city did little to deter the advancing columns. Throughout the day army field pieces and the battery of the naval frigate *General Morán* joined air force aircraft in attacks against rebel positions.

Under cover of mortar fire, the government column from Maturín approached the Carúpano airport. It was defended by thirty men under Lt. Octavio Acosta Bello. During the fighting a warrant officer in charge of a .50-caliber machine-gun post retired from his rear guard position. He informed marine Lt. Cmdr. Molina Villegas that he was not going to continue fighting because marines from the "Simón Bolívar" Battalion were leading the government's advance, and he did not wish to kill fellow marines. After a token demonstration of force, the rebels retired from the airport, and government forces occupied the position. At this point Molina Villegas began negotiations with Lt. Col. Sánchez Olivares to surrender. Finally, at evening the rebel forces capitulated; and, as previously arranged, the loyal marines from "Simón Bolívar" Battalion occupied the barracks of the rebellious marine "Sucre" Battalion. Within thirty-six hours government forces had eliminated remaining pockets of resistance.[19]

Meanwhile, in Caracas, police raided Communist headquarters, arrested over 100 people, and seized weapons. Eloy Torres, a member of the national Chamber of Deputies, was arrested while attempting to escape on a boat bound for Trinidad and Tobago for having participated in the plot. He was sentenced to eight years in prison. On May 10 the government banned the Communist Party and the Marxist's Revolutionary Left Movement.[20]

EL PORTEÑAZO—AN ATTACK FROM THE LEFT

The most serious military revolt against the Betancourt government occurred a month later. At 3 P.M. on June 1, Rear Admiral Sosa Ríos called Capt. Jesús Carbonell Izquierdo,[21] Commander of the Fleet, to headquarters in Caracas and informed him that marine corps and national guard units at La Guaira, Maiquetía, and Puerto Cabello might rebel. Sosa Ríos ordered him to go to Puerto Cabello. There military and civilian authorities met with him and discussed the possibility of a rebellion.[22]

Upon arrival at the naval base, Carbonell Izquierdo called together the commander of Puerto Cabello Naval Base and Capt. Andrés Oswaldo Moreno Piña, commander of Destroyer Division No. 1, to inform them of his conversation with Sosa Ríos. As a result, the warships at Puerto Cabello and the destroyer *Aragua*, then at La Guaira, were placed on alert. These ships were about the only units then operational.[23]

At 6:50 P.M. Admiral Sosa Ríos ordered all naval personnel to their quarters, and less than two hours later ordered the *Aragua* and the ships at Puerto Cabello to prepare themselves against air attack. Late that night Carbonell Izquierdo and Moreno Piña, inspecting the naval base and the marine barracks, found nothing out of the ordinary. Just before midnight Carbonell Izquierdo met with senior naval commanders and told them that he expected a rebellion at 4:00 A.M. the next day, June 2.[24]

A few minutes after midnight on the second, Carbonell Izquierdo informed the naval command in Caracas that all was normal. At 4:30 A.M. he and senior officials decided once again to tour the facility to see firsthand that nothing was irregular. At the same moment a group of middle-grade officers and warrant officers subverted marine corps "Urdaneta" Battalion numbering about a thousand men and arrested those officers who would not join the rebellion, including the commanding and executive officers of the battalion. Members of the naval security police swelled the rebel ranks to about fifteen hundred. They began attacks on the naval base and the adjacent military establishments and seized Castle Liberator, which guarded the entrance to the port and Fort Solano, located on a hill overlooking the town. At 5:40 A.M. the leaders of the rebellion—Capt. Manuel Ponte Rodríguez, the commander; Cmdr. Pedro Medina

Silva, the chief of naval operations; and Lt. Cmdr. Victor Hugo Morales Monasterios, the chief of land operations—clandestinely entered the naval base.[25]

At 6:15 A.M. the head of national guard Detachment No. 55 notified his command in Caracas that a rebellion had taken place at Puerto Cabello. Carbonell Izquierdo, asleep in the Admiral's residence, was awakened by a posse of men, including some naval police, armed with submachine guns. They arrested him in the name of "a nationalist movement to correct social injustice." The other senior officers were also arrested and escorted to the officers' quarters. Taking advantage of the confusion, Lt. (j.g.) Justo Pastor Fernández Márquez hid in a closet to avoid arrest, a fact that would later assist government forces recapturing the base.[26]

The rebel command began organizing its forces to capture Puerto Cabello and adjacent strategic sites such as the airport, railroad station, and radio station. Morales Monasterios freed a group of Marxist guerrillas being held by the government in Castle Liberator, who, along with militants from the Communist Party and the Leftist Revolutionary Movement, helped rebellious marines, naval security police, and sailors take the city.

At 7 A.M. Lt. Col. Juan Ramón Zerpa Tovar, commander of the army's "Carabobo" (No. 41) Infantry Battalion quartered in Valencia some 35 miles from Puerto Cabello, sent an advanced patrol supported by an M-8 armored car to reconnoiter the rebels. At the same time, the air force began reconnaissance flights. At 7:20 A.M. Lt. Col. Zerpa Tovar started from Valencia with the main body of his battalion to attack the rebels.[27]

Back in Caracas the government of President Betancourt, seeing the magnitude of the insurrection, ordered a full military alert. The Minister of Defense, General Briceño, appointed Col. Alfredo Mönch Siegert, commander of the Fourth Army Division, to be chief of the Puerto Cabello operational theater and gave him a force of 3,000 men drawn from diverse army, air force, and national guard units.[28]

Betancourt rejected a plan of operation presented by the armed forces Chief of Joint Staff, which called for a siege of the city. The President ordered an immediate attack on the rebels—a decision to which the Minister of Defense agreed.[29]

The rebels took the center of Puerto Cabello in the morning (June 2) and overpowered the civilian police. But when the attacking force arrived at the airport, it discovered that the advanced elements of the army's "Carabobo" Battalion were already there. In the meantime Zerpa Tovar, advancing along the highway with the main body of the battalion, established an advanced post in the railway station. There and at the airport, rebel and government forces clashed, resulting in the death of a marine. Commander Medina Silva, after broadcasting a revolutionary proclamation over the city's captured radio station, ordered the rebellious forces to fall back from the airport and rail station and establish defensive positions closer to the port. At 10 A.M. Morales Monasterios asked Carbonell Izquierdo to join the movement. The latter refused and also withheld orders to his warships not to bombard the rebels.

Meanwhile, the fleet lying in the naval base remained quiet. At 10:05 A.M. a task group made up of the frigate *General Morán* and a sister, the *Almirante Clemente*, took up position in front of the naval base while it was under fire from an air force "Vampire" fighter. Ten minutes later the commanding officer of the destroyer *Zulia* ordered the gunners of a 40mm mount to fire on a group of rebellious marines that had approached to within 300 feet of the ships, which were docked inside the naval base. The gunners disobeyed the order and fired into the water. This action resulted in the arrest of the officer in charge of the gun. Within minutes a group of rebellious officers and chiefs from the crew took control of the *Zulia* and freed him.

At 10:20 A.M. the government-controlled *Almirante Clemente* and *General Morán* began firing their 40mm cannon into the marine barracks, destroying the building. Three marines were killed and ten injured; the rebel leader, Capt. Ponte Rodríguez, was wounded. At this point the insurgents decided to evacuate the barracks and move to Castle Liberator before any more bombardments took place.[30]

The only land communication between Puerto Cabello, on a strip of land bordered on the north by the Caribbean and on the south by coastal mountains, and the rest of the country was provided by a highway and rail line that entered the city from the west. To the east were some small towns, the port and its facilities, and the naval base. To confront the rebels at the naval base, government forces first had to pass through the port city. There Medina Silva remained in charge of the rebel defenses. At approximately 11 A.M. the army's "General Juan Carlos Piar" (No. 31) Battalion began to advance on the rebels and came under fire.

To prevent the rebels from capturing inactive warships, sailors loyal to the government anchored the medium landing ship *Los Roques* in front of the drydock to block in the destroyer *Nueva Esparta*, which needed repairs, and about that time the destroyer *Zulia* and frigate *General Flores* were moved to the outer roadstead with the aid of tugs. At noon government reinforcements began to arrive. A company from the air force's "José Leonardo Chirino" (No. 1) Parachute Battalion appeared at the airport. On the northern outskirts, intense fighting broke out and continued for hours between the rebellious marines and the army's "Carabobo" Battalion.

Fernández Márquez, the lieutenant who had hidden himself in a closet at the officers' residence, found a cassock in the chaplain's room and disguised himself as a priest. He went to the quarters of the sailors who worked at the base headquarters and convinced some twenty of them to help him recapture the quarters where Carbonell Izquierdo and the other loyal officers were being held.[31]

Fighting broke out within the naval base. In the patrol craft *Mejillon*, an ensign took control of a .50-caliber machine gun and opened fire on a group of rebellious marines. They, in turn, attacked the craft with antitank grenades. After an hour of fighting, those in the *Mejillon* surrendered and the craft fell to the rebels.

Heavy fighting continued throughout June 2. At 3 P.M. the 1st Company of the army's "Carabobo" Battalion tried to attack the city from the south. Insurgent marines turned them back, killing nine men. The rebels also captured a national guard patrol boat that had entered the naval base. At 3:30 P.M. the frigate *Almirante Clemente* once again fired on the rebels in the naval base with her 40mm cannon. Morales Monasterios, who had boarded the destroyer *Zulia*, radioed that if the frigate did not cease fire the *Zulia* would respond with her 4.5-inch guns. Within a few minutes the frigate's guns fell silent. Government reinforcements, including the army's "General Piar" Infantry Battalion and a company of national guard from Detachment No. 57, continued to arrive.

By 5 P.M. Fernández Márquez and his group of loyal sailors had freed all of the senior officers at the naval base and had gained control over the operations building. Naval Captain Carbonell Izquierdo telephoned Sosa Ríos in Caracas and solicited orders. Two rebel officers were arrested when they entered the operations building unaware that it had been recaptured.

At 5:30 P.M. a patrol from the army's "Carabobo" Battalion, supported by an M-8 "Greyhound" armored car, advanced into the city and took the firehouse, capturing the ensign in charge of rebel forces there. Within half an hour the army's "Colonel Atansio Girardot" (No. 32) Infantry Battalion arrived in Puerto Cabello. At 6:15 P.M. Captain Moreno Piña and

Fernández Márquez, accompanied by ten sailors, captured Morales Monasterios in the vicinity of the operations building. An army artillery battery of Field Artillery Group "General Bartolome Salon" (No. 41), with six 105mm howitzers, arrived in Puerto Cabello at 7 P.M. as the government's strength continued to swell.

In the evening the rebels used the national guard patrol craft that they had captured earlier in the day to harass government troops that had taken up positions along the beach. Ens. Jaime Penso Nebrús was in command of the craft, manned by twenty rebellious sailors and marines armed with two .50-caliber machine guns, hand grenades, and FAL 7.62mm automatic rifles. They attacked and dispersed the government forces. At 8 P.M. a company from the army's "Bravos de Apure" (No. 4) Armored Battalion arrived at Puerto Cabello with sixteen AMX-13 light tanks.

By 8:30 P.M. Carbonell Izquierdo had assembled a force of some fifty loyal sailors at the operations building. He ordered the occupation of all adjacent buildings and sent patrols to determine rebel positions. The majority of insurgents had retired to Castle Liberator. They controlled the main gate of the naval base, which was protected by two .50-caliber machine guns and one 81mm mortar.[32]

At 2 A.M. on Sunday morning, June 3, Carbonell Izquierdo sought permission from the Commander of the Navy for the frigates *Almirante Clemente* and *General Morán* to fire on Castle Liberator. Only two hours earlier the Captain had learned that the rebels controlled the destroyer *Zulia*. At 4:05 A.M. sailors loyal to the government captured Castle Liberator and arrested key leaders of the rebellion, specifically Captain Ponte Rodríguez and Ensigns Penso Nebrús and Sierra Acosta. During the fighting a lieutenant loyal to the government was killed. By 5:30 A.M. a group of loyal sailors recaptured the main gate to the naval base and minutes later another loyal force recaptured the *Mejillon*. Within half an hour Col. Mönch Siegert's forces broke through the rebel defenses around Puerto Cabello.

Street fighting between roughly one thousand marines and government forces remained heavy throughout the day. Government troops employed artillery, light tanks, and aircraft, while the marines had to rely on bazookas, mortars, and heavy machine guns for support. The tactics Siegert used to retake the city were later criticized by many. He had soldiers position themselves behind each tank as it entered the disputed area, and as a result, about thirty soldiers from the "Piar" Infantry Battalion were killed or wounded in what became known as "the Butchery of the Sewer" (*La Carniceria de la Alcantarilla*).

At 6:30 A.M., while loyal army troops were making slow progress through the streets, air force aircraft attacked the rebels at "Fortress Solano" with rockets and machine guns. At 8 A.M. loyal sailors surrounded the *Zulia*, which was still docked, and Carbonell Izquierdo demanded the destroyer's unconditional surrender. An hour and a half later, Lt. (j.g.) Antonio Picardo, leader of the rebels in the destroyer, surrendered. After two hours of fighting, the rebels defending the southern sector had almost depleted their ammunition, so they fell back to Rancho Grande.

The *Almirante Clemente* was ordered at 9:22 A.M. to bombard Fort Solano in support of the advancing army troops. In the northern sector, the 1st Company of Battalion No. 41 and national guard Detachment No. 55 successfully attacked the rebels after an intense bombardment by 106mm recoilless rifles. A group of rebellious marines was captured. At 11 A.M. Carbonell Izquierdo informed Admiral Sosa Ríos in Caracas that the naval base and insurgent ships had been captured. By noon government forces had resumed control of 60 percent of the city.

Nevertheless, resistance continued throughout the day and well into Monday. Small pockets of marines fought in *barrios* in the city and in the mountains to the south. Resistance did not stop until the night of June 4.

No one knows the total number of casualties resulting from the "El Porteñazo." Among government forces, twenty men were killed and seventy men wounded. Sosa Ríos estimated that in all some 200 to 300 men died. Sixteen naval officers, seven naval warrant officers, and thirty-four civilians were tried and condemned to prison for their participation in the rebellion.[33]

OBSERVATIONS

Neither the reactionary right nor the radical left within the military could subvert the majority within the armed forces, and therefore failed to overthrow the government of Rómulo Betancourt. The loyalty of senior and midlevel officers (as examplified by General Briceño) and senior enlisted men proved to be the key. Should they have turned against the government, these officers and senior sergeants could have, in most cases, carried the loyalty of their men with them. However, most of the midlevel officers and senior enlisted men remained loyal to the new democratic government.

While these coup d'etats against the Venezuelan government were failing, it was also under attack by elements of the extreme left which chose the *foco* or rural strategy (see chapter 29).

CHAPTER 29

THE ERA OF THE EARLY *FOCO* WARS, 1962–65

> When we took to the mountains for the first time we were more than a little taken with the idea that our war was going to be a Cuban-style war. . . . We thought that the solution to our problems was no more than two or three years away.
>
> —Luben Petkoff, Venezuelan leftist guerrilla

THE SPARK

The surprising success of the atypical Communists in Cuba inspired many in the radical left of other Latin American nations to copy their rural guerrilla tactics and to seek help from the Cuban Revolutionaries. The most appealing perceived lessons from the Cuban Revolution were that amateurs could defeat the established militaries and that victory could take but a few short years.

BACKGROUND

Prior to the Cuban Revolution, most Latin American Communist parties subordinated themselves to the Soviet-dominated Communist International and these parties were old, legal, and lethargic. In fact, many nations had more than one Communist party, and at times these were more content with arguing with each other than fighting the Capitalists. Within these Communist parties existed young, frustrated radicals who increasingly believed that the only way to achieve power was through violence. They grew to believe that the tactics of the Cuban Revolution could be successfully copied in their countries.

OPPOSING FORCES

Typically, the rural guerrilla was a young, frustrated middle-class student or graduate of the national university. He or she was a member of a Communist or Socialist party. Notable exceptions did exist. Only in Colombia did the rural peasantry become guerrillas in significant numbers; these rural guerrillas were dependent upon Cuba for doctrine, training, and logistics, which proved to be erratic. And in Guatemala, the dissidents came from the army.

Cuba endeavored to control these guerrillas through its Directorate General of Intelligence (*Dirección General de Inteligencia*—DGI). DGI activities included training future guerrillas at special Cuban schools. Apparently, the first formal training of guerrillas in Cuba began in July

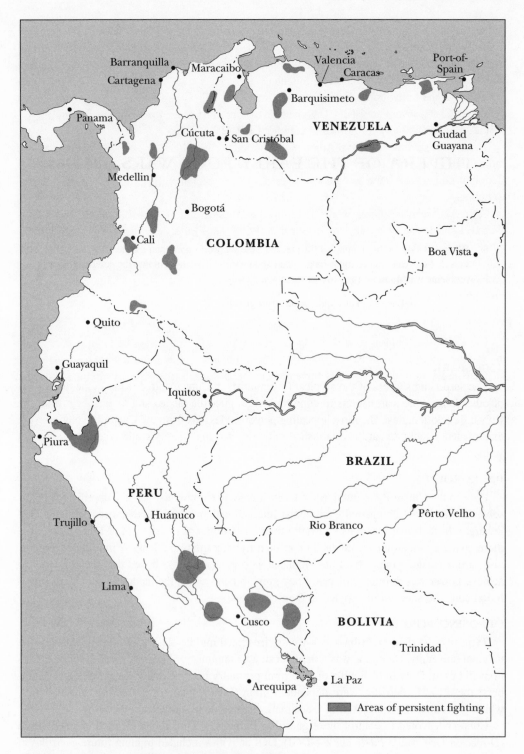

Map 6. The Early *Foco* Wars in South America, 1962–65.

1960. Spanish Communists, Gen. Enrique Lister and Col. Alberto Bayo (Fidel's instructor in 1955), were in charge. By early 1963 possibly ten training camps existed, and by 1966 the number had increased to more than forty camps. By the mid-1960s, some 5,000 young radicals had graduated from guerrilla training in Cuba.[1]

Although the leftist guerrillas did receive arms from Cuba, the flow was sporadic and undependable. Che Guevara advised, "The guerrilla soldier must never forget that the enemy should be the sources of supply for arms and equipment."[2]

Those who governed in Latin America, supported by the United States, were opposed to the radical left. This was a very heterogeneous mix. Latin American governments ranged from fledgling democracy, such as Venezuela, to despicable dictatorships, such as the Dominican Republic.

Latin American militaries were ill-equipped to fight the rural guerrillas. Following World War II, Lend Lease from the United States to Latin America ended. Beginning in mid-1952, numerous Latin American governments began purchasing U.S. weapons under the 1949 Mutual Defense Act. However, the types of weapons supplied demonstrated that both U.S. and Latin American military leaders were thinking in terms of World War II battlefields and not rural guerrilla warfare.[3]

OPENING STRATEGIES

The Cuban Revolution provided a home-grown guerrilla strategist, Che Guevara.[4] According to Guevara, the Cuban Revolution made three fundamental contributions to the mechanics of guerrilla warfare. First, guerrilla forces can defeat a regular army; they were more than just irregulars whose mission it was to harass an enemy's rear. Second, it is not always necessary to wait for all the conditions for revolution to exist; at times, they can be created. Third, in underdeveloped Latin America, the revolutionary struggle should be principally in the countryside.[5]

The United States global strategy of "containment" assigned a low priority to Latin America. As a consequence, the United States chose a defensive strategy within the hemisphere and continued to supply its regional allies with conventional military hardware regardless of their commitment to democratic values or human rights. Among the Latin American militaries, only that of Peru developed a strategy for combating rural guerrillas. This was to eliminate the safe haven (the *foco*) and tenaciously hound the guerrillas to ground.

VENEZUELA, 1962–65

By the end of the 1950s, leftists (some moderates and others radicals) had overthrown a number of right-wing dictators. Among these was Pérez Jiménez of oil-rich Venezuela. The ideological differences between Rómulo Betancourt, the new Venezuelan president, and Fidel Castro were exposed in January 1959 when the two met in Caracas, for the first and only time, during the first anniversary of the overthrow of Pérez Jiménez.[6]

During 1959 Castroites (*Castristas*) began to secretly prepare to overthrow Betancourt's government. This was misinterpreted by Venezuela's twenty-some intelligence gathering agencies which did not coordinate their efforts. Also, these agencies were distracted by the clandestine activities of the extreme right (see chapter 28).[7]

Finally, in October 1960, the Castroites began a wave of violence, attempting to spark a popular uprising. The Movement of the Revolutionary Left (*Movimiento de Izquienda Revolucionaria*—MIR) was the prime instigator. Ironically, the Communist Party of Venezuela

(*Partido Comunista de Venezuela*—PCV), which followed Soviet doctrine, initially was opposed to armed struggle as a means for coming to power, but being afraid of becoming irrelevant, reluctantly joined the fight.[8]

The years 1960 and 1961 were characterized by "popular insurrection" through student demonstrations and street riots, primarily in the capital. These actions were supported and applauded by the Cuban Embassy in Caracas until diplomatic relations between the two nations were broken in December 1961. The violence became so pervasive that the government reinforced the capital's police with military units from outside the city.

"University City," the seat of the Central University of Venezuela located in the southern part of Caracas, became the bastion of the radical left. They were protected by the university's autonomy. This privilege, which had been granted by the King of Spain during the colonial era, prohibited government officials (including the police and military) from entering the campus of this vast installation without the permission of the appropriate university authorities, who were controlled by the radical leftists. Within the university the leftists planned attacks, trained combatants, and provided medical treatment to those injured while fighting the police. At the end of 1961, the government seized control of University City. During the assault by army, national guard, and police forces, the extremists shot down an air force helicopter, demonstrating the extent of the firepower they had acquired. These urban disturbances continued through 1961 when they were finally extinguished by the police and the armed forces. At this point the radical left transferred the majority of its operations to the countryside.[9]

Back in Cuba, Castro began training Latin American leftists in the art of guerrilla warfare. During 1960, he created the School for the Special Preparation of Irregular Troops (*Escuela de Preparación Especial de Tropas Irregulares*—PETI). PETI operated at two sites: one in the Cordillera de los Organos in Pinar del Río Province and the other in Guanabo east of Havana. Apparently some 500 Venezuelans were among those trained.[10]

On December 10, 1961, armed men attacked a police station at Urachiche (200 mi W of Caracas) and killed three policemen. The government considered this a local incident and not an attack by leftist guerrillas. Not until January 1962 did the Venezuelan intelligence agencies suspect that ideologically motivated guerrilla bands were spreading throughout the countryside. By then Venezuela had become the linchpin of leftist guerrilla activities in the Western Hemisphere.[11]

In the countryside, the Castroite MIR took the initiative. Once again, members of the PCV reluctantly supported their more violence-prone compatriots. Initially, guerrilla operations were limited to attacking national guard outposts in small hamlets. The guerrillas would flee into hiding at the approach of the more heavily armed army units. In January 1962 the foreign affairs ministers of the Organization of American States met at San José, Costa Rica, and expelled Cuba from their meeting.[12]

Although the extreme left had moved the majority of its effort into the countryside, it continued some activity in the cities, particularly Caracas. On January 22, 1962, a bomb exploded in the U.S. Embassy. Over the next four days, some forty people were killed and 280 injured during riots before troops restored order in the capital. By March more than 600 leftists (principally members of the MIR and the PCV) were jailed by the Betancourt government.[13]

Back in the countryside, the guerrillas established numerous fronts or *focos*. Among the most active fronts were the "José Leonardo Chirinos" front (commanded by Douglas Bravo) in Falcón State; the "José Antonio Páez" front in Portuguesa State; the "Simón Bolívar" front in

Lara State; the "Ezequiel Zamora" front in the Bachiller Mountains in Miranda State; and the "Antonio José de Sucre" front in the eastern part of the country. Typically a front would have sixty to ninety guerrillas.[14]

On March 29, 1962, the guerrillas attacked the Venezuelan air force's base, "Mariscal Sucre," at Boca de Río (72 mi W of Caracas) but were driven off. Three weeks later Fidel Castro, speaking in Havana, expressed the opinion that President Rómulo Betancourt would be toppled by revolutionary forces within a year. As a consequence of these events and a revolt by Venezuelan marines at Puerto Cabello in May (see chapter 28), the government suspended constitutional guarantees. These were reinstated in August but again suspended in October when violence increased again.[15]

On October 13 the government raided hundreds of locations rounding up and jailing leftists. Coincidently, within two weeks the United States quarantined Cuba, initiating the "Cuban Missile Crisis." As a consequence, on the twenty-seventh, President Betancourt mobilized the Venezuelan armed forces and dispatched the destroyers *Nueva Esparta* and *Zulia* to form part of "Task Force 137" in support of the United States. During the crisis Havana urged "Castroite" guerrillas in Venezuela to increase their attacks. Accordingly, on the twenty-seventh the MIR destroyed four electric power stations belonging to the Creole Petroleum Company (an Esso subsidiary) at Maracaibo. A week later, guerrillas blew up four oil pipelines 160 miles east of Caracas. As a consequence, Venezuela called up 5,000 reservists for internal security. By the end of 1962, the attacks from the radical left subsided and as a consequence the government released the mobilized reservists and restored the constitutional guarantees that had been suspended on October 27.[16]

The new year brought on another wave of violence. On January 16, 1963, guerrillas stole five paintings on loan from France; these were subsequently recovered. Bombings and shootings once again rocked Caracas. During January and February a Sears Robuck warehouse was destroyed; a U.S. Rubber Company warehouse was burned; and a Shell Oil Company installation in Maracaibo was bombed. On February 14 the merchantship *Anzoátegui* was hijacked and five highway bridges damaged or destroyed.[17]

The Venezuelan Supreme Electoral Council voted seven-to-five on March 15 to exclude the Venezuelan Communist Party (*Partido Comunista de Venezuela*—PCV) and the Movement of the Revolutionary Left (*Movimiento de la Izquierda Revolucionaria*—MIR) from the elections scheduled for December 1963. The MIR retaliated. It bombed the Creole Oil Company pipelines near Maracaibo as well as forty government cars. On June 5 MIR guerrillas set fire to the U.S. military mission headquarters in Caracas and forced its members to publicly strip. Ten days later the home of a U.S. Embassy official was vandalized.[18]

Gustavo Machado, head of the now illegal PCV, stated on June 10 that the Communists accepted responsibility for the acts of violence and were "proud of them."[19] As a consequence, President Betancourt arrested some 300 Communists but then released them due to political pressure. Two days later Betancourt revealed that an assassination plot on his life had been foiled.[20]

On August 24 the famous Spanish soccer player Antonio Di Stefano was abducted from his hotel in Caracas. Two days later, he was rescued by police. Beginning in September, the military became the favored target of the radical left. On the sixteenth leftists attacked the jail at Trujillo (345 mi SW of Caracas) and freed nine of their comrades. On the twenty-ninth guerrillas killed five unarmed national guardsmen on an excursion train called *El Encanto* ("the enchantment"). This stupid act helped turn public opinion against the guerrillas. As a consequence of these and other acts, twenty-three members of the PCV and MIR, all members of the national congress, were arrested. Among them were the brothers Gustavo and Eduardo Machado.[21]

By late 1963 the guerrillas were carrying out attacks almost daily and Caracas became a besieged city. The MIR killed police, robbed banks, burned stores and factories, kidnapped hostages, and sprayed crowded streets with machine-gun fire. The government closed the Central University in October and thousands of troops and police patrolled the streets of the capital. The MIR targeted American-owned companies. During 1963 each of the eleven Sears Roebuck retail stores was bombed.[22]

The MIR called a general strike; it hijacked a Venezuelan airliner; and it kidnapped the deputy chief of the U.S. military mission, Col. James E. Chenault. The guerrillas were also active throughout the countryside: in the west in the states of Falcón, Lara, and Portuguesa; in the east in the mountains between Sucre and Monagas; in the south in Trujillo, Merida, and Barinas; and in the center in Miranda and Anzoátegui.[23]

On November 2, 1963, the Venezuelan government discovered three tons of arms of Cuban origin buried on the Paraguaná Peninsula.[24] Venezuela placed the matter before the Organization of American States (OAS). On December 3, the OAS Council of Ministers voted sixteen-to-zero (Mexico abstaining) to investigate the charges. Also in December, the MIR tried desperately to disrupt the general elections by terrorist attacks. These failed; almost 92 percent of the registered voters turned out and Raul Leoni, the governing Democratic Action Party's candidate, was elected president. The success of the election was a defeat for the guerrillas.[25]

In February 1964 the OAS committee unanimously declared that Cuba had conducted a policy of aggression against Venezuela. As a consequence, the OAS recommended that its members take the following actions against Cuba: (1) break diplomatic and consular relations; (2) suspend all trade; and (3) suspend sea communications. However, most nations chose not to do so.[26]

During the first six months of 1964, the MIR refrained from urban attacks. Their rural compatriots did attack a few villages. A government patrol discovered a large food cache in Lara. In July the urban attacks began once more. Between July 17 and 24, the MIR killed four Caracas policemen. The rural guerrillas blew up highway bridges and attacked military outposts. The government reacted forcefully. The military discovered two training camps in the state of Miranda. Government patrols killed some sixty guerrillas and sixty were captured during the second half of 1964.[27]

On November 9, 1964, the urban guerrillas kidnapped U.S. Air Force Lt. Col. Michell Smollen, a member of the U.S. air mission to Venezuela; the guerrilla's stated purpose was to exchange Smollen for the Vietnam Communist Nyen Vantroy who was scheduled to be shot by the South Vietnamese government. However, within a few days Venezuelan police rescued Swollen.[28]

In the countryside, the guerrillas were operating in ten of Venezuela's twenty-two states and controlled significant territory. Typical guerrilla raids were carried out by thirty-man detachments. In late January 1965 the guerrillas started a huge oil fire in the Mene Grande and Mobil Oil Company complex in the state of Anzoátegui. In June guerrillas blew up pipelines and clashed with government forces in the mountains of the states of Lara and Falcón. On August

12, twenty guerrillas raided the village of Cantaura (240 miles SE of Caracas) in Anzoátegui State. In September 1965 guerrillas seized villages in the states of Sucre and Barinas.[29]

Slowly and then more rapidly, however, government forces began defeating the guerrillas in these rural regions. These successes were the result of the training of "Hunter" (*Cazador*) battalions by the United States, which aggressively sought out the guerrillas; by the closer cooperation among the various armed forces; and by the cultivation of the friendship of the peasantry by the military. In August the government captured José Díaz ("El Gavilan"), a guerrilla leader. In January 1966 "Comandant Madero" (Antonio Ortíz), in charge of guerrilla operations in the east, defected to the government.[30]

In March 1966 the MIR called for a rededication to the armed struggle; however, the PCV opposed the continuation of the guerrilla war. On the thirteenth Fidel Castro bitterly accused the orthodox PCV of the error of trying to direct guerrilla warfare from the cities and declared that only Revolutionary fighters would get his support in Latin America. Toeing the Soviet position, in April the PCV condemned armed struggle. As a consequence, Castro extended full recognition to the MIR and accused the PCV of being a pawn of the capitalists. This in-house Communist feud temporarily stagnated organized terrorism although random acts of violence continued.[31]

COLOMBIA, 1962–65

The first Communist guerrilla force, the Revolutionary Armed Forces of Colombia (*Fuerzas Armadas Revolucionarias de Colombia–Ejército del Pueblo*—FARC-EP), commonly called the FARC, began operations in 1962. The FARC evolved out of the Liberal guerrilla group known as the "Southern Bloc," which fought in *La Violencia* (see chapter 20) and grew into the militant arm of the orthodox Colombian Communist Party (*Partido Comunista de Colombia*—PCC).[32] The FARC was led by Manuel Marulanda Vélez (alias "Tirofijo"—"sure shot").[33] It attracted many followers in the departments (states) of Arauca, Caquetá, Huila, Meta, Quindio, Santander, Tolima, and Valle del Cauca (mostly southern and central Colombia).

In 1961 President Alberto Lleras Camargo (1960–62) began a counterinsurgency strategy that combined aggressive military strikes against the "independent republics" (self-declared autonomous enclaves) with limited agrarian reforms. However, Lleras' reforms proved too liberal for his successor, President Guillermo León Valencia (1962–66), and he suspended them, thus alienating the peasants. In August 1962 the Colombian Congress granted President León extraordinary powers to deal with the increasing banditry and violence. The penal code was modified and the courts and jails reorganized. Many of the safeguards, provided by a presumption of innocence, were suspended.[34]

In September 1963, forty-one bombs exploded in five Colombian cities causing considerable damage but no casualties. President León asserted that Fidel Castro was responsible. Strikes, sabotage, and bombs exploding in automobiles, oil pipelines, and even Congress terrified the nation.

The guerrillas were operating almost with impunity in five isolated regions scattered throughout Colombia—El Pato, Guayabero, Rio Chiquito, Sumapaz, and Marquetalia. On March 17, 1963, Tirofijo raided the hamlet of Inza (450 mi S of Bogotá) in the southeast, killing nineteen people and sacking the village.

After the 1964 Havana meeting of Communists, the PCC endorsed a pro-Castro policy. The guerrillas increased their terrorism—robbing trains and attacking foreign-owned oil installations. They seized isolated towns and held them for a few hours while stripping them of food, medicine, and the assets of the local bank. On March 20, 1965, Harold J. Eder, one of Colombia's most important industrialists, was kidnapped from his estate near Cali after a gun battle, and the bandits demanded a $200,000 ransom. On April 12 Eder was found dead. But the guerrillas, lacking weapons and supplies and confronted by an increasingly effective Colombian army thanks to U.S. aid, found it impossible to maintain the intensity of their operations. By the end of 1965, the Colombian army, closely supported by the air force, regained nominal control over many of the more populated areas. However, Leftist guerrillas and bandits moved freely through remote areas.[35]

GUATEMALA, 1962–65

The *foco* war was sparked by a failed coup d'etat. During the night of November 13, 1960, Col. Rafael Sessan Pereira, supported by 100 soldiers, including Lieutenants Marco Antonio Yon Sosa[36] and Luis Augusto Turcios Lima,[37] rebelled against the government of Gen. Miguel Ydígoras Fuentes and seized Fort Matamoros outside of Guatemala City.[38]

There were many underlying causes. Foremost was the political, economic, and social inequities within Guatemala. Next, was the blatant corruption of the Fuentes government. Then there was the dissension within the army officer corps caused by the numerous factions that had evolved since the 1954 revolution. There were the "mustang" officers (called *oficiales de linea*); the academy officers trained in Guatemala; the academy officers trained in Argentina, Chile, France, Spain, and the United States following the *2 de Augusto* fight (see chapter 22); and those from the "Liberation Army," who were made officers following the 1954 revolution. To these groups Fuentes added older officers whom he brought back from retirement in an attempt to assure the loyalty of the army.

Luis Augusto Turcios Lima would claim that in addition to altruism, he wanted to end the practice by the U.S. Central Intelligence Agency of training Cuban exiles at Retalhulen Air Base (110 mi NW of Guatemala City). He may have been "playing" to Fidel Castro who was aware that Guatemalan facilities were being used to train those who wanted to overthrow his government by force.[39]

When Fort Matamoros was captured, a second rebellious group seized the military bases at Zacapa (90 mi NE of Guatemala City) and Puerto Barrios (145 mi NE of Guatemala City), the nation's principal port on the Caribbean. The United States became concerned that the presence of the CIA supported anti-Castro Cubans might inspire Cuba to directly intervene. Five U.S. warships were sent to patrol the Guatemalan coast to prevent any such intervention. The exiled Cuban pilots bombed the rebels and flew logistic missions in support of loyal Guatemalan troops. Failing to win adequate support, the rebels fled into the Zacapa Mountains. The rebels reluctantly conceded that the government was in firm control of the country, so their leaders fled to Honduras and El Salvador.[40]

Within a few months Yon Sosa and Turcios Lima slipped back into Guatemala and formed the Revolutionary Movement of the 13th of November (*Movimiento Revolucionario 13 de Noviembre*—MR13). At first, they unsuccessfully endeavored to forge an alliance among the leftist labor and political organizations in order to attempt another coup. When this failed, they resorted to *foco* guerrilla tactics.[41]

Yon Sosa and Turcios Lima now attracted young intellectuals, many of whom were not members of the Guatemalan Communist Party (*Partido Guatemalteco de Trabajo*—PGT).

Initially, Yon Sosa and Turcios Lima collaborated but eventually could not agree on an ideology. Yon Sosa gained control of the MR13 and Turcios Lima created the Rebel Armed Forces (*Fuerzas Armadas Rebeldes*—FAR).

The first guerrilla attack occurred on February 6, 1962, when two army posts were overrun and a United Fruit Company office robbed. The guerrillas operated principally in the remote regions of the nation, occasionally appearing in urban areas to carry out assassinations, rob banks, and attack military posts. During February and March 1962, the guerrillas collaborated with students who were rioting in the capital. Twenty rioters were killed and 200 wounded. The government regained control and the guerrillas retreated into the mountains. The Kennedy administration immediately came to Ydígoras' aid. Aircraft were sent to the Guatemalan air force, counterinsurgency instructors to the army, and a civic action program developed in the departments of Zacapa and Izabal, near the border with Honduras.[42]

In November 1962 the guerrillas attempted to open a front in the Huehuetenango Region, northwest of Guatemala City. Ill prepared, those who entered the region were captured and shot. And in July 1963, a twenty-one-man *foco* was wiped out in the Izabal Region due to poor security.[43]

Throughout this time Ydígoras' hold on the reigns of government weakened. On November 25, 1962, conservative elements of the air force tried an unsuccessful coup. Coincidentally, on that same day, former President Arévalo announced from Venezuela that he would be a candidate in the presidential elections scheduled for December 1963. The U.S. Ambassador to Guatemala, John O. Bell, told an American newspaper that Arévalo was a Communist and unworthy of the presidency. Reneging on an earlier promise, Ydígoras announced on March 21, 1963, that since Arévalo was a known Communist, he would not be allowed to reenter Guatemala. Riots broke out in the north and east. Ydígoras declared a state of siege on March 25 and used the army to suppress the rioters. However, relenting under pressure from the mob, Ydígoras agreed to allow Arévalo to return to Guatemala City on the thirtieth. Within hours of his scheduled arrival, Minister of Defense Col. Enrique Peralta Azurdía, supported by conservative elements, overthrew Ydígoras.[44]

Peralta immediately began to professionalize the officer corps. The "mustang" officers, Ydígoras' cronies, and those from the "liberation army" were retired. This increased the effectiveness of the army against the guerrillas.[45]

On the other side, Yon Sosa and Turcios Lima repeatedly tried without success to persuade the orthodox Communist Party and other leftist political and labor organizations to actively support them throughout 1963 and 1964. Also, the guerrillas moved away from nationalistic and anti-imperialistic rhetoric toward espousing Marxist ideology. During 1964, Yon Sosa became a convert to Trotskyism, which provided him ideological support. Yon Sosa stated, "Our struggle is not primarily military, but social. It's not our intention to destroy the government by military means; we intend to dissolve it through social action."[46]

In 1965 the guerrillas intensified their campaign of kidnapping and assassination. On February 9, 1965, the MR13 assassinated the Chief of the U.S. Military Mission, Col. Harold Houser. In May the Deputy Minister of Defense, Col. Ernesto Molina Arrega, was assassinated. Wealthy Guatemalans were kidnapped. As a consequence, the Peralta government imposed a state of siege.

Turcios Lima and his FAR had won the favor of Fidel Castro and were invited to the Tricontinental Conference in Havana during January 1966. Castro ignored Yon Sosa and his Trotskyite MR13.

In addition to being anti-Communist, Peralta was an outspoken nationalist. He broke diplomatic relations with Great Britain over Belize and refused the United States' offer to send Special Forces to Guatemala. He intensified the campaign against the guerrillas; tactics included assassinating suspected leftists and imposing states of siege. Although the Peralta government met with some economic success by being more financially responsible than its predecessor, it did not promote democracy or improve Guatemala's human rights policy.

In March 1966 President Lyndon Johnson indicated that he wanted the return to civilian control. To protect the interests of the Guatemalan army, Peralta required the major candidates to sign a pact which, if elected, required them to: (1) always comply with the conditions of the pact; (2) remain anti-Communist; (3) continue the fight against subversive factions and support the army; (4) exclude Communistic elements from the government; (5) protect the lives and property of those of the current regime; and (6) respect the autonomy of the army. Some requirements were placed on the army and Congress as well.[47]

Julio César Méndez Montenegro, from the moderate left, won the presidency in a reasonably fair election. This, coupled with the fact that Guatemala was receiving more U.S. military aid than any other country in Central America, offered hope that the radical left could be defeated.[48]

PERU, 1962–63

In Peru, Castro first helped a group of university students who came to Cuba to learn revolutionary warfare. As the Trotskyte Hugo Blanco[49] was being hunted down by the Peruvian military, thirty-five Cuban-trained guerrillas, long on political theory and short on guerrilla training, were entering Peru from the southwest. They were coming to rescue Blanco even though he was probably ignorant of their efforts. The guerrillas flew to La Paz and then trekked 400 miles across the Bolivian highlands and jungle. An advanced party of six reached Puerto Maldonado, Peru (525 mi E of Lima), on May 14. The police, who were on the alert, discovered them the following day and the six guerrillas were all killed, including the twenty-one-year-old poet Javier Heraud,[50] in a one-sided shoot-out. Those not in the advanced party hid in Bolivia.[51]

Coinciding with the destruction of the Cuban-trained guerrillas and the capture of Blanco, a new guerrilla force began to take shape within Peru. These future guerrillas were the more radical members of the socialistic *Aprista* Party who had been expelled in 1959. Initially, they adopted the name APRA *Rebelde*, but by June 1962 they felt that the association with the old party was a liability, so they changed their name to the Movement of the Revolutionary Left (*Movimiento de Izquierda Revolucionaria*—MIR). Their leader, Luis de la Puente,[52] did meet with the Trotskyte Hugo Blanco in October 1962, but their philosophical differences were too great to permit a combined effort.

From May 1963 through early 1965, these city-bred guerrillas vainly tried to establish a rapport with the Indian peasants in the vicinity of their preselected *focos* (base camps) in the Andes. In part their failure was due to the fact that the Peruvian government had already enacted some land reforms.[53]

The guerrillas projected three areas of operation. The Túpac Amaru *foco*, led by Guillermo Lobatón, was to operate due east of Lima, centered around the town of Satipo (168 mi E of Lima). The Javier Heraud *foco*, led by Héctor Béjar, was to concentrate southeast of the capital in the vicinity of Ayacucho (207 mi SE of Lima). The Pachacutec *foco*, led by Luis de la Puente and Rubin Tupayachi, was to operate south of Lima, near Cuzco (348 mi SE of Lima). A fourth *foco* was to be established on the Ecuadorian border, but it never materialized.

Apparently, the guerrillas were to begin operations in the northern regions and, once army troops had been drawn into that area, those to the south would attack. In May 1965 the leaders of the various *focos* met at de la Puente's camp near the village of Maranura and drew up a fifteen-page "Revolutionary Proclamation." This document outlined their goals but alerted the government to the immediacy of guerrilla operations.

The Túpac Amaru *foco* was the first to go into action. It began operations in the vicinity of the Andamarca River Valley, almost due east of Lima. On June 9, 1965, the guerrillas raided a powder storage depot at the Santa Rosa mine and escaped with large quantities of dynamite. Over the next few months the guerrillas blew up bridges, attacked civil guard (national police) posts, raided haciendas, and destroyed electric power plants. On July 27 the guerrillas successfully ambushed an army patrol, killing seven. The army launched a major counterattack, transporting soldiers to inaccessible areas by helicopters. The army and civil guard pursued the guerrillas, forcing them to keep continuously on the move. On January 7, 1966, the few survivors, including Lobatón, were killed in a battle with government forces. Within six months the Túpac Amaru *foco* had been destroyed.

The Pachacutec *foco* chose as its base camp the inhospitable 12,000-foot plateau, the Mesa Pelada, which was surrounded by valleys descending to 3,000 feet. However, these guerrillas did not begin operations until the Túpac Amaru *foco* had been destroyed. Since the army generally knew where the Pachacutec *foco* had chosen to operate, they were able to pre-position troops before the guerrillas launched their attacks. The operations occurred north of Cuzco and to the south of the Valley of La Convención. The first clash took place on September 9. By late in the month the army had captured the base camp of the guerrillas. During the final clash on October 23, 1965, the remaining guerrillas were killed or captured, including de la Puente.

The Javier Heraud *foco* was located in the department of Ayacucho between the two other guerrilla forces. This *foco* was an outgrowth of the National Liberation Army (*Ejército de Liberación Nacional*) which had been responsible for the Puerto Maldonado episode in May 1963. Although not prepared to act when the Pachacutec *foco* began its operations, the Javier Heraud *foco*, nevertheless, believed that it was essential to show unity with the Movement of the Revolutionary Left. The Javier Heraud *foco* prematurely began its attacks on September 25 by killing two hacienda owners who had been accused of "capital crimes" and exploitation. Apparently the guerrillas caught the army off guard. For the next two months this force operated without opposition as the army concentrated on the Pachacutec *foco*. Then on December 6, 1965, the army began a campaign against the Javier Heraud *foco*. On December 17 the army made its first contact, killing the *foco's* deputy commander in a skirmish. The army tenaciously pursed the guerrillas and they dwindled in number. In late December the guerrilla force broke up after a defeat. Béjar was captured in January 1966.[54]

De la Puente failed for many reasons. First, he did not gain the support of the Peruvian Communist Party, in part because it refused to accept Guevara's thesis that a revolution could be artificially stimulated. Second, de la Puente unnecessarily alerted the army to his intentions before it was necessary, thereby conceding surprise. Third, his poor coordination allowed the Peruvian army to deal with the three *focos* one at a time.[55]

DOMINICAN REPUBLIC

By April 1965 the United States feared that Cuban-inspired Communists were about to take over the Dominican Republic. Following the assassination of Rafael Trujillo on May 30, 1961, that country had elected the Liberal Party's Juan Bosch as president, but he was overthrown by a military coup in September 1963 and the country suffered a second military coup on April 25, 1965.

Bosch supporters attempted to use the confusion caused by the second coup to restore their leader to the presidency. They were joined by two U.S.-trained battalions of the Dominican army and by leftist political parties, including the Communists. Within twenty-four hours, the *Constitucionalistas* (the name they adopted) won control of most of the capital, Santo Domingo. After much delay, the opposing *Leales*, led by Conservative Gen. Elias Wessin y Wessin, made a halfhearted attempt to retake the city, managing to win control of only two small areas.[56]

In the meantime, U.S. President Lyndon Johnson ordered a carrier task force to Dominican waters. As the fighting in Santo Domingo intensified, the U.S. Navy began evacuating U.S. nationals on April 27. Within two days more than 2,000 Americans had been carried by helicopters to the amphibious assault ship *Boxer*. When the U.S. Embassy reported that "collective madness" reigned in the city, Johnson ordered 1,700 Marines into the capital to protect the U.S. Embassy.[57]

These initial steps were soon followed by a full-scale U.S. invasion. At 2 A.M. on April 30, two battalions of the U.S. 82nd Airborne Division landed at the San Isidro airfield some 10 miles to the east of Santo Domingo. The 82nd had planned to conduct a combat parachute drop to seize the San Isidro base, but when they got there, they found it firmly in the hands of the *Leal* Dominican air force. Instead of an airborne assault, the planes landed and quickly discharged their passengers. Over the next few days, U.S. forces flooded into the airfield. Some 14,600 soldiers and 17,000 tons of equipment and supplies were delivered by 1,500 flights.[58]

A few hours after the initial landing, troops from the 82nd Division punched their way across the Duarte Bridge which spanned the Ozama River and connected the capital with San Isidro. These troops were to link up with the *Leales* who in turn were to provide a continuous, secure corridor for the Marines guarding the Embassy in the western part of the city. However, the spearhead of the U.S. advance was ambushed and the 82nd Airborne began to suffer casualties. The situation was very confused. Since elements of the Dominican army were fighting on both sides, word was passed to the *Leales* to wear their hats sideways or backwards so that the American troops could identify them in the link-up operations.[59]

Instead of serving as the center link in the chain between the 82nd Division and the Marines, however, the *Leales* withdrew eastward across the bridge to the San Isidro airfield. Maj. Gen. Robert York, commanding the 82nd Division, requested permission to move on to the embassy, but the politician leadership in Washington refused the request, believing that it might jeopardize negotiations in the OAS. Finally on May 2, Lt. Gen. Bruce Palmer Jr. (who was now in command) was given permission to make the first link-up. Faced with superior U.S. forces, the *Constitucionalistas* withdrew to the southeastern part of the city.[60]

Belatedly, on May 6 U.S. diplomats persuaded the OAS to create an Inter-American Peace Force to supplement the American troops who after their arrival would be reduced in number. The following countries ultimately volunteered a total of some 1,600 soldiers and police: Brazil (1,250 soldiers), Costa Rica (25 police), Honduras (250 soldiers), Nicaragua (164 soldiers), and Paraguay (286 soldiers). Brazilian Gen. Hugo Panasco Alvim was placed in overall command.[61]

The withdrawal of the *Constitucionalistas* to San Isidro on April 30 had serendipitously isolated them from the *Leales*. On August 31 representatives from the two sides signed the OAS-sponsored "Reconciliation and Institutional Act." Hector Garcia-Godoy was chosen interim president; more than once he called upon U.S. troops to restore order.[62]

On September 6, Dominican General Wessin y Wessin attempted a coup against the provisional government but was foiled by American troops. As "punishment," the general was forcibly whisked away to become the Dominican Consul General to the United States. Col. Francisco Caamaño, the leader of the *Constitucionalistas*, was also removed from the scene by making him the Dominican Military Attaché to Great Britain.[63]

In the June 1966 election, the moderate Joaquin Balaguer defeated Juan Bosch, who chose to remain in exile during the campaign for the presidency. Like the U.S. intervention in Guatemala in 1954, the United States acted precipitously in the Dominican Republic because it feared a Communist takeover. Latin American reaction to the U.S. intervention reverted to the usual ideological pattern.

OBSERVATIONS

The Cuban leadership attributed these failures of the early 1960s in large measure to the lack of support from the Latin American orthodox Communist parties and the Soviet Union. As the decade wore on, Castro increasingly chose to promote rural guerrilla warfare in spite of increasing opposition from Moscow. This departure from Soviet desires was institutionalized by the Frenchman Jules Régis Debray[64] in his *Revolution in the Revolution?* published in 1967. Debray, who had Fidel's endorsement, concluded that: (1) a revolution requires a political vanguard but the vanguard need not be the Communist party; (2) the guerrilla struggle will create the revolutionary party and not the reverse; (3) the political and military leadership of the revolutionary movement will have to be controlled by the guerrilla movement; and (4) the rural guerrillas are the vanguard of the revolution and, as such, control the revolutionary activities in the cities.[65]

On the other side, the U.S. military was fixated on Vietnam and did not perceive the riff between Cuba and the Soviet Union and was as a consequence unable to take advantage of the situation.

CHAPTER 30

THE ERA OF THE LATE *FOCO* WARS, 1965–74

If those who call themselves Communists will not do their duty, then we will support those
who in the struggle act as Communists.

—Fidel Castro, March 1967

THE SPARK

By early 1966 Fidel Castro believed that the Soviet Union had betrayed Cuba by the accommodation reached with the United States to end the Cuban Missile Crisis and that the orthodox
Communist parties throughout Latin America had become the "dupes" of the Capitalists. Therefore, he attempted to reinvigorate the Latin American radical left in spite of the lack of support
from the Moscow-controlled parties.[1]

BACKGROUND

Castro's influence among the radical left reached new heights at the Tricontinental Conference, the first African-Asian-Latin American People's Solidarity Conference in Havana, January 3–15, 1966. The Conference adopted a platform that attempted to force the Soviet Union to
champion liberation movements, created a committee to aid such activities, selected Havana as
the site for a tricontinental school to train insurgents, and established the Latin American Solidarity Organization (*Organizacion Latinoamericana de Solidaridad*—LASO) with its headquarters in Havana. In spite of the fact that the Soviets disassociated themselves officially from
the meeting, their delegation did approve the final declaration.

Castro encouraged the radical left to fight on in spite of the Soviet position. In July 1967 he
stated, "a guerrilla never accepts defeat. . . . As long as there is one man with a gun, the seed of
a guerrilla army remains. The phrase 'cease fire' . . . will never be uttered by this country as
long as one single inch of our territory is occupied by any invader."[2] Fidel named 1968 the
"Year of the Heroic Guerrilla."[3]

OPPOSING FORCES

The opposing armed forces remained the radical left increasingly aided by Cuba and the established Latin American militaries increasingly helped by the United States.[4]

OPENING STRATEGIES

The radical left did not believe that the *foco* strategy had been discredited by the failures of the earlier wars and, therefore, it persisted with the strategy.

A few Latin American officers and their U.S. advisors, particularly the on-scene officers, believed that creating small, light infantry units to eliminate the guerrillas' safe havens and then run them to ground was the best strategy. These tactics were increasingly taught at institutions like the School of the Americas.[5] Nevertheless, many senior Latin American and North American officials persisted in the belief that heavy military hardware—artillery, tanks, and attack aircraft—was needed to fight the guerrillas. The shortage of these weapons caused by the Vietnam War worked against the implementation of this strategy.[6]

Another victim of Vietnam was the U.S. Military Assistance Program (MAP), which had been started in 1961 to provide military hardware and training to friendly nations. Frequently that training had taken place inside the recipient country. The U.S. Congress feared that such an arrangement could lead to Vietnam-like escalations. The MAP program was replaced in 1976 by the International Military Education and Training (IMET) Program where the training took place in a U.S. facility, which included those in the Canal Zone.[7]

VENEZUELA, 1966–69

Shortly after the PCV decided to abandon the armed struggle, expelled member Luben Petkoff traveled to Cuba to solicit Fidel Castro's help to continue the fight (see chapter 29). Petkoff sought a contingent of Cuban fighters, modern weapons, and logistical support. He proposed to land in the state of Falcón and join up with Douglas Bravo and other expelled members of the PCV who had created the "José Leonardo Chirinos" *foco*.[8]

At the same time, a delegation from the MIR, headed by Héctor Pérez Marcano and Moisés Moleiro, arrived in Havana. They sought similar help for their two active *focos*. They were the "Ezequiel Zamora" *foco* (commanded by Américo Martín) in the Bachiller Mountains some 100 miles west of Caracas and the "Antonio José de Sucre" *foco* (commanded by Carlos Betancourt and Gabriel Puerta) in the eastern region of Venezuela. Initially, Castro hesitated giving the requested aid, appreciating that providing the help would escalate Cuba's involvement. Finally, he agreed to send fourteen Cubans to Venezuela as instructors in guerrilla warfare. Petkoff unsuccessfully tried to get Che Guevara to head this Cuban group. Once it was decided that Cubans would go, Castro sent Petkoff and the MIR members to the same training camp in Cuba to prepare them for *foco* warfare but in May 1966 he separated them.[9]

The Cuban-Venezuelan group embarked on a fishing vessel on July 17, 1966, in Santiago, Cuba; Fidel saw them off. Known as "Operation Simón Bolívar," the group was commanded by the Cuban *Comandante* Arnaldo Ochoa.[10] Other Cubans included Captains Leopoldo Cintra Frías[11] (second in command), Mario Bouza, and Angel Frías. The Venezuelans included members of the MIR and individuals expelled from the PCV. They sailed on the eighteenth and landed at midnight on the twenty-third on the east coast of Falcón State.

Following a rough landing, the expedition trekked toward the mountains searching for Bravo who was ignorant of its approach. The day after the landing, the guerrillas were detected by Venezuelan forces and attacked by army and marine troops while subjected to aerial assault by the air force.[12] Escaping these pursuers, the guerrillas walked along the bank of the Tocuyo River when they were attacked and mauled by a national guard patrol. The shaken force finally made contact with a guerrilla band headed by *Comandante Magoya* (Elegido Sibada) and former army Lt. Nicolás Hurtado.[13]

At the end of 1966, Petkoff and Ochoa, having built their following to about one hundred men, finally made contact with Douglas Bravo. By January 1967 Petkoff and Bravo argued over leadership and tactics. Finally, Petkoff decided to move toward the Andes to form a new western front while Ochoa remained in the state of Falcón to hold the attention of the Venezuelan armed forces which were increasingly aggressive.[14]

In September 1966 radical leftists began a new urban offensive. On the thirteenth, thirty guerrillas attacked the mayor's office in El Guapo (81 mi SE of Caracas). They bombed a Sears Roebuck store and a supermarket owned by Americans. In October they robbed homes principally of military officers in Caracas. On November 27 the FALN sprayed the U.S. Trade Fair exhibit with machine-gun fire. On December 15 the FALN assassinated Maj. Francisco Astudillo, a member of the highest military court, on a street in Caracas, and wounded the Army Chief of Staff, Gen. Roberto Moreán Soto.[15]

On the night of December 15, President Leoni declared martial law. The next morning the military seized "University City" for a second time. Some 300 persons were arrested, including fifteen leaders of the Communist youth organization. A huge cache of arms was discovered as well as lists naming those to be assassinated and future infrastructure targets.[16]

On May 4, 1967, a second Cuban expedition sailed from Santiago on the fishing boat *Sierra*. On board were four members of the Cuban revolutionary army (Ulises Rosales del Toro[17] and Raúl Menéndez Tomassevich[18] among them) and five members of the Venezuelan MIR plus the boat's crew. The boat also carried Soviet-manufactured AK-47 assault rifles, munitions, radio transmitters, medicine, and supplies. At 2 A.M. on the eighth, the nine guerrillas and material were disembarked at a beach called Cocal de los Muertos east of Machurucuto (93 mi E of Caracas). Their objective was to unite with the "Ezequiel Zamora" front commanded by Américo Martín in the El Bachiller Mountains. But as the two zodiac craft returned to the *Sierra*, a large wave threw those crewing the craft into the water. One was drowned and the other three swam to shore. The Venezuelan army discovered the remains of the zodiacs and debris and began a search for the guerrillas. The three were captured and one revealed the details of the operation.[19]

The Venezuelan army and marines began to hunt for the guerrillas. They were discovered within forty-eight hours of their landing and subjected to air and ground attacks. The guerrillas managed to reach an old campsite of Martín but found it deserted. The "Ezequiel Zamora" front had in fact dissolved due to the constant air attacks initiated by the Venezuelan air force beginning in November 1966. Américo Martín had been taken to Caracas gravely ill, and his successor, Fernando Soto Rojas, and his followers had sought refuge in the vast Guatopo National Park.

One hundred days after landing, the Cuban-sponsored group finally united with those of the "Ezequiel Zamora" front. The morale of the group was shattered and its ailing leader, Raúl Menéndez Tomassevich, was sick and evacuated back to Cuba. He related,

> I became gravely ill. My weight dropped to 100 pounds. I practically could not walk. . . .
> We had bought some chickens. We salted them and put them in our backpacks. They rotted.
> And with mine I made soup. Instead of chicken, what I ate was worms. I caught a tremendous infection.[20]

In the meantime, the Venezuelan military accelerated its attacks against the guerrillas throughout Venezuela. The MIR unsuccessfully tried to unite its *foco* in the east with that from the El Bachiller Mountains. This failed because the leadership of each front wanted to be in charge. In spite of these catastrophic setbacks, the guerrillas under Douglas Bravo fought on and Castro continued to support him.

Late at night on November 12, 1968, the Venezuelan patrol boat *Calamar*, commanded by Lt. Bernardo Jurado Toro, discovered the Cuban fishing boats *Alecrín*, *Sierra Maestra*, and *Róbalo* navigating eight miles off the Venezuelan archipelago of Los Testigos. The fishing craft immediately turned north and ran while their crews threw their cargoes overboard. After a long chase, during which the Venezuelan patrol boat endeavored to stop the fleeing craft without using force, the *Calamar* fired on and hit the nearest target, the *Alecrín*; the other two escaped. The captain of the *Alecrín* declared his boat a stateless craft and demanded the protection of the Red Cross. The *Alecrín* was taken to the Venezuelan port of Carúpano and later to Puerto Cabello. After weeks of diplomatic discord between Venezuela and Cuba, the *Alecrín* was allowed to return to Cuba where the crew was received as "Heroes of the Revolution."[21]

Although the violence initiated by the radical left continued into the 1970s, it no longer represented a threat to the stability of the Venezuelan government.[22] When Luben Petkoff returned to Havana seeking aid for a second time, he was turned away. The radical left's rural guerrillas had been defeated. In December 1968 Rafael Caldera of the Christian Democrats, the opposition, won the presidential election and took office in March 1969. He initiated a political pacification program to reintegrate the guerrillas into the social mainstream.

COLOMBIA, 1965–74

During 1965 and 1966 Communist-instigated violence increased while banditry, particularly north of Bogotá, decreased (see chapter 29). The second Communist guerrilla force in Colombia, the National Liberation Army (*Ejército de Liberación Nacional*—ELN) began operating in the department of Santander (northeastern Colombia) in January 1965. The ELN's ideology was heavily influenced by radical liberation theology and its military strategy was based on Che's *foco* theory. Its founders included Camilo Torres and Father Manuel Pérez. The ELN attacked isolated police stations and government outposts while at the same time preaching to the peasantry. Its early rank and file were mostly peasants. On February 15, 1966, the ELN attempted to ambush an army patrol in the department of Santander. Four soldiers were killed and three wounded. The guerrillas lost thirteen dead, including Father Torres. [23]

Back in the capital some 200 students attacked former President Lleras and John D. Rockefeller, who were attempting to open in October an agriculture course at the national university in Bogotá financed by the Rockefeller Institute. As a consequence of this and Cuban-inspired violence, the Colombian government forbade travel to Cuba, limited street demonstrations, banned the carrying of firearms, abolished the autonomy of the universities, and outlawed the Colombian National Federation of Students (*Federacion Colombiana de Estudiantes*), which was under the influence of the Colombian Communist Youth organization (*Juventud Comunista de Colombia*—JUCO).

The FARC became more aggressive in mid-1966. In August "Tirofijo" ambushed an army patrol killing 15 soldiers and wounding 15 others. The guerrillas lost 17 of their own. On March 3, 1967, FARC guerrillas ambushed an army patrol about 150 miles southwest of Bogotá and killed 20 soldiers. On the ninth, 80 guerrillas held up a pay train, killing ten persons. On March 10 the government responded by arresting 24 leaders of the Communist Party, including 17 of the 18 members of the Central Committee and Gilberto Vieira, Secretary General of the party. The only member to escape was "Tirofijo" who was with his guerillas in the interior. In June the government sent troops into the national university in violation of the Spanish tradition of autonomy. They discovered both FARC and ELN propaganda and weapons.

On August 1, 1967, the ELN broke its ties with the PCC when the pro-Soviet party renounced guerrilla warfare. The PCC and the Venezuelan Communist Party issued a joint communiqué calling for the noninterference in the affairs of other parties.

Yet a third guerrilla force, the People's Liberation Army (*Ejército Popular de Liberación*— EPL), began operations in January 1968. It was the military arm of the Communist Party of Colombia, Marxist-Leninist (*Partido Comunista Colombiana-Marxista/Leninista*—PCC-ML), which was pro-Chinese and illegal. During the late 1960s and early 1970s, the EPL operated in the remote Alto Sinú and Alto San Jorge regions in northern Colombia.

Also, in the late 1960s and early 1970s the ELN operated the "Jose Galan" and "Camilo Torres" fronts in the countryside as well as urban cells. On July 9, 1970, the ELN kidnapped Fernando Londono y Londono, former Foreign Minister; he was released on the eighteenth after his family paid a $100,000 ransom.[24]

Beginning in 1972 the guerrillas began a large-scale kidnapping campaign which netted them large sums of ransom money. The ELN attempted to create a "liberated zone" in northeastern Antioquia. In July 1973 the government began an all-out campaign to eliminate the guerrillas. The Colombian army almost destroyed the ELN in eastern Antioquia. By the mid-1970s the government had reduced the threat from the Communist guerrillas, although violence continued, particularly around Santander.[25]

GUATEMALA 1965–74

Julio César Méndez Montenegro, inaugurated on July 1, 1966, achieved the presidency through the sufferance of the army and the support of the United States (see chapter 29). As a consequence, the United States was able to introduce Special Forces into Guatemala. Their missions were to train the Guatemalan army and encourage it to undertake civic improvements in order to improve its relations with the populace.[26]

President Méndez Montenegro made attempts to broker a compromise between the leftist guerrillas and the army but to no avail. On October 2 the guerrillas suffered a severe blow when Turcios Lima was killed in an automobile accident in Guatemala City. César Montes[27] became the leader of the FAR. At the age of 24, he lacked the military contacts and training of Turcios Lima.[28]

Montes initiated a new campaign of assassinations and kidnappings. The army reacted aggressively. U.S.-trained troops forsook the comfort of their barracks and began hunting down the guerrillas in the Sierra de las Minas in eastern Guatemala. The local commander, Col. Carlos Araña Osorio, armed civilian landholders in order to help root out the guerrillas. Nicknamed the "Butcher of Zacapa" by the radical left, Araña employed U.S.-supplied helicopters and observer aircraft to relentlessly hound the guerrillas as they tried to escape deeper into the jungle or to flee into Guatemala City. The killing at times was indiscriminate; some 8,000 people died.[29]

Also, right-wing death squads began kidnapping and assassinating those they did not like. The three most notorious groups were the White Hand (*Mano Blanca*—MB), the Secret Anti-Communist Army (*El Ejército Secreto Anti-comunista*—ESA), and the Death Squad (*Escuadron de la Muerte*—EM). These reactionaries killed over 2,800 persons, some merely on suspicion. In March 1968 they kidnapped Archbishop Mario Casariego; he was accused of being a Communist sympathizer. The Archbishop was released after a few days. As a consequence, President Méndez Montenegro dismissed a number of high-ranking army officers, but the violence from the right continued.[30]

Late in 1967 Yon Sosa and the FAR reconciled their differences. Yon Sosa had forsaken Trotskyism the year before and Turcios Lima was now dead. The guerrilla cause was not going well. César Montes stepped down to the number two position and Yon Sosa became the leader of the FAR. By 1968 the remaining guerrillas again attempted to create chaos through kidnappings and assassinations. On January 16 the FAR killed the head of the U.S. Military Mission, Col. John O. Webber, and the U.S. Naval Attaché, Lt. Cmdr. Ernest A. Munro, in Guatemala City.[31]

In late August the army captured Camilo Sánchez, one of the leaders of the FAR, in Guatemala City. In order to effect an exchange, the FAR attempted to kidnap the American Ambassador, John Gordon Mein, on August 29; he was killed while resisting. Between December 1969 and February 1970 the FAR killed more than twenty prominent citizens. On March 31 the FAR kidnapped the West German Ambassador, Count Karl von Sprett, and demanded as ransom $700,000 and the release of seventeen political prisoners. When the Guatemalan government refused, the guerrillas murdered the ambassador on April 5. These assassinations contributed to Col. Carlos Araña Osorio being selected by the right-wing Movement of National Liberation (*Movimiento de Liberación Nacional*—MLN) party as their presidential candidate for the 1970 election.[32]

The election of Colonel Araña to the presidency on March 1, 1970, further polarized the struggle. The leading opponent of reconciliation, he intensified the war against the guerrillas and did little to control the violence of the reactionary right. The government relentlessly hounded the guerrillas. Yon Sosa was surprised and killed by Mexican soldiers at a base camp just over the border in the Mexican state of Tabasco on May 16, 1970. The fighting continued to degenerate into a mutual campaign of assassination carried out by small cells of urban guerrillas and right-wing death squads. Torture and mutilation were common. Estimates on the number killed between 1970 and 1973 range from 3,500 to 15,000 dead.[33]

BRAZIL, 1965–72

In 1964 the military seized power and suppressed all opposition. Political parties were outlawed in 1966 and replaced by the military-controlled National Renewal Alliance *(Aliança Renovadora Nacional)* to support the government and the Brazilian Democratic Movement *(Movimento Democrático Brasileiro)* to be the "legal" opposition. A new federal police force was created.[34] These circumstances sparked both rural and urban guerrilla warfare (see chapter 31).

As elsewhere in Latin America, a few among the radical left within Brazil believed that it could create a rural haven *(foco)* and draw support from the cities. Various factions among the radical left turned to both Cuba and China for inspiration and help.

Rural guerrilla warfare began with a sortie in the southwest of Paraná State against the Brazilian President who was then visiting the Iguacu Falls (740 mi SW of Rio de Janeiro). Twenty-one guerrillas belonging to the National Revolutionary Movement (*Movimento Nacional Revolucionario*) and led by a colonel who had been expelled from the Brazilian army, Jefferson Cardin, and a former sergeant of the Rio Grande do Sul State Military Brigade, Albery Vieira dos Santos, occupied the village of Tres Passos, Rio Grande do Sul, without firing a shot. Then they took over Tenente Portela and Santo Antonio do Sudoeste, Paraná. After a brief exchange of gunfire on the outskirts of Leonidas Marques, Paraná, on March 27, 1965, the guerrillas disbanded leaving a former sergeant, Argemiro Camargo, dead. The following day, government forces captured the leader, Jefferson Osório. The objective of the group had been to reach the Iguacu Falls on the border with Paraguay. It would then have sought the opportunity to attack Brazil's President, Marshal Castello Branco, during a meeting with Paraguay's president, Gen. Alfredo Stroessner.[35]

In November 1966 fourteen members of the National Revolutionary Movement (*Movimento Nacionalista Revolucionário*) attempted to establish a combatant nucleus in a high, remote location within the Serra do Caparaó, between the states of Espírito Santo and Minas Gerais. Most were former enlisted men from the Brazilian army. The guerrillas were soon discovered by the Minas Gerais state military police, and after five deserted, the remainder were captured on April 3, 1967. Four days later, five more would-be guerrillas led by Amadeu Rocha departed Rio de Janeiro to join the group, unaware of its capture. These were also captured. Not a shot was fired during any of the captures. Both the guerrillas led by Osório and those led by Ferreira had been sanctioned by the former Governor of Rio Grande do Sul, Leonel de Moura Brizola. After these failures he lost the confidence of his Cuban supporters.

Beginning in 1967 a group of militants from the Chinese-inspired Communist Party of Brazil (*Partido Comunista do Brasil*—PC do B)[36] organized a base camp in the southern part of the state of Pará. Beginning in 1970, sixty-nine guerrillas were dispersed along a 150-mile arc from Xambioá, Goiás (now in the state of Tocantins) to Marabá, Pará. Following Mao's teachings, they integrated into the local population, teaching and providing medical aid. Through an informer, the Brazilian army learned of the presence of the guerrillas. Some 3,000 soldiers, mostly conscripts, unsuccessfully searched for the guerrillas.

Finally, the army employed a new strategy. Intelligence agents infiltrated the region, the government initiated a civic action program (*Ação Civico Social*), and the Parachute Brigade was given jungle training. On December 24, 1972, the PC do B guerrillas carried out an attack near the town of Xambioá (1,180 mi N of Rio de Janeiro), approaching Marabá on the left bank on the Araguaia River. At noon during a light rain, the guerrillas ambushed an army patrol of three soldiers and two civilian pathfinders. The soldiers won, killing four guerrillas including the leader, Mauricio Grabio. In October 1973 the army launched an attack against the guerrillas and by April 1974 the remaining thirty-some guerrillas disbanded.[37]

Beginning in November 1969 the new Popular Revolutionary Vanguard (*Vanquarda Popular Revolutionária*—VPR)[38] led by Carlos Lamarca established a guerrilla school at a hacienda near Jacupiranga in the Ribeira Valley, São Paulo. Located within the rain forest, the region was sparsely populated by peasants who were primarily engaged in growing bananas. Twenty individuals underwent training by some five instructors for five months. In April the Brazilian army detained Celso Lungaretti in Rio de Janeiro. He had dropped out of the guerrilla school and gave the army the precise location of the camp. Learning of the breach in security, Lamarca closed the camp on April 18, 1970. A combined Brazilian army and São Paulo state military police force attacked on the twenty-first. Seventeen of the guerrillas were trapped before they could disperse. The VPR fought on until 1973.[39]

The various Brazilian rural guerrilla movements failed to find locations that offered a combination of the safety of rugged terrain and the proximity to an urban area from which they could draw support. They were never a serious threat to the Brazilian government. But the Brazilian rural guerrillas did further strain a government that was under a more serious attack by urban guerrillas (see chapter 31).

BOLIVIA, 1966–67

The last attempt to initiate the *foco* strategy occurred in Bolivia, and fittingly was led by its primary proponent, Che Guevara. He chose Bolivia as the site to begin his efforts to win control of South America because of its heartland location, its terrain that was suited to rural guerrilla warfare, and his belief that the political, social, and economic conditions were favorable to success. Also, seemingly, Bolivia was far from the power of the United States.[40]

During 1966 agents purchased hacienda *Casa Calamina* in the rugged southeastern foothills of the Andes Mountains near Camiri, Bolivia. Che arrived in Bolivia in November as Dr. Adolfo Mena González. Once there, he chose the *nom de guerre* (war name or pseudonym) "Ramón." Most of the sixty-some assembled fighters were from the middle class—students, tin miners, engineers, and taxi drivers, among others. Some had been recruited by "Tania" (Haydee Tamara Bunke[41]), an Argentine. Sixteen of the guerrillas were Cubans and many of the others had been trained in Cuba. Not surprisingly, the guerrillas chose Che as their leader.[42]

During early 1967 the guerrillas trained to toughen themselves and accumulated supplies. In February Che led thirty guerrillas north of the Rio Grande. The leader of the advanced guard entered the hamlet of Vallegrande and attempted to obtain food. This alerted the Bolivian army to the presence of the guerrillas. An army unit unsuccessfully attempted to follow the advanced guard back to the main body of the guerrillas. On March 11 two guerrillas deserted and surrendered at the 4th Division headquarters in Camiri. They revealed the location of the guerrilla camp at Nancahuazú. Soldiers were dispatched from Vallegrande, Camiri, and Gutierrez in an attempt to encircle the guerrillas. Che, arriving back at Nancahuazú, set a trap. On March 23, 1967, the trap was sprung and the guerrillas ambushed an army patrol. Five soldiers and a civilian guide were killed and fourteen others wounded; the guerrillas sustained no casualties.[43]

Che then invited two journalists to the camp at Nancahuazú—Frenchman Jules Régis Debray, a favorite of Castro, and the Argentine Roberto Bustos. They were ask to spread the news of the revolution and warned to leave Bolivia. The guerrillas escorted the journalists to the outskirts of Muyupampa. However, when they entered the town, they were identified by a deserter and captured. The government extracted valuable information from the pair.[44]

The Bolivian government immediately requested help from the United States. In April, fifteen U.S. Green Berets commanded by Maj. Ralph "Pappy" Shelton set up a training camp on the site of an abandoned sugar mill at La Esperanza, just north of the area in which the guerrillas were operating. Over the next few months, U.S. Air Force C-130s flew in tons of supplies. Also, the U.S. Central Intelligence Agency recruited and trained operatives who began gathering intelligence.[45]

While Che was absent, the camp at Nancahuazú was abandoned and the guerrilla lost many of their supplies. The force divided into fifteen men units and scattered into the countryside.

The Bolivian army began to close in on the guerrillas. On April 4 the army discovered the abandoned camp at Nancahuazú. Six days later the guerrillas successfully ambushed another army patrol at Iripiti. Eleven Bolivian soldiers and two guerrillas were killed. On the following day, the eleventh, the guerrillas captured a twenty-man patrol. In spite of these setbacks, the Bolivian army pressed on throughout the month of May.

In early June Che led the main guerrilla force north of the Río Grande near Abapo in an attempt to locate the rear guard and escape from the patrols of the 8th Division, and to establish a new area of operation. He chose the sparsely populated, inhospitable region where the Andean foothills meet the Amazon basin. On July 3, the 8th Division learned of Che's general location. On the sixth, Che and a small band entered the village of Las Cuevas. They commandeered a truck and a school bus and used these to surprise the garrison at Samiapata. The town was captured after a brief fight. News of Che's success filled newspaper headlines in Bolivia, and the borders with Argentina and Peru were closed.[46]

On July 30 Che's force fought a skirmish with Bolivian troops. Although the losses were light on both sides, the army captured documents and unprocessed film that permitted the government to identify and take action against those in the cities who were supporting the guerrillas.[47]

While Che was operating north of the Río Grande, Col. Reque Terán, commanding the 4th Division based at Camiri, launched an offensive against the guerrillas operating south of the river, which proved to be Che's "lost" rear guard. The guerrillas were chased north of the river. They captured the hamlet of Puerto Mauricio; however, the army immediately learned of their whereabouts. During the evening of August 30, soldiers of the 4th Division ambushed the guerrillas fording the Masicuri River at Vado del Yeso and killed all ten.[48]

Despite their initial successes, the guerrillas failed to gain any momentum. The army had a big reservoir of men and Guevara had no reserves. The peasants showed no interest in aiding the Cuban, Spanish-speaking guerrillas and frequently betrayed their presence to the military. The Bolivian Communist Party (*Partido Comunista Boliviano*) refused to support the guerrillas. In addition, Guevara suffered from asthma and could not treat it because his medicine had been captured. Frequently, Che was unable to walk and had to ride a horse or be helped by others.[49]

During early September Che operated between La Laja and Pucara, north of Río Grande. Late that month another deserter provided Che's precise location to the 8th Division, which now included 800 Bolivian rangers who had completed a nineteen-week course in anti-guerrilla warfare taught by U.S. Special Forces instructors at Guabira, north of Santa Cruz. On September 26 the two forces collided near the village of La Higueras. Three guerrillas were killed and a chase ensued. At 1:30 P.M. on October 8 the army trapped the guerrillas in a narrow defile near La Higueras. Che was wounded in the leg and captured along with two others. Four guerrillas were killed and ten escaped. The government suffered ten dead and some twenty wounded. Che and the two others were taken to La Higueras, a distance of two miles. Che was executed by Sgt. Mario Terán around noon on October 9.[50]

By October 14 all but six of Che's group had been hunted down. Those escaping claimed to have trekked across 260 miles and climbed over the 11,000-foot-high Andes into Chile. During an October 15 speech delivered on radio and television, Fidel Castro said, "Who could deny the significance to the revolutionary movement of the blow of Che's death? . . . It is a fierce blow, a very hard one."[51]

OBSERVATIONS

Naive invasions launched from Cuba into Caribbean nations opened the *foco* wars in 1959, and an ill-conceived invasion into Bolivia closed them in 1968. In between, Cuba courted radical leftists who were shunned by their national Communist parties. During the 1960s and early 1970s, these Cuban-supported, rural guerrillas failed to bring a Marxist government to power anywhere in Latin America. Of the five major conflicts, the *foco* strategy failed outright in Venezuela, Brazil, and Bolivia, while it just stumbled along in Colombia and Guatemala. These attempts to imitate the Cuban success failed for many reasons.

First, and most important, the Cubans themselves failed to appreciate the multitude of factors that had contributed to their unique victory in Cuba. They came to believe that the rural guerrilla as personified by Che Guevara was the key to winning. A terse review of the writings that poured from the revolution reveals that the exploits of the rural guerrilla dominated the literature.

Second, Cuba was not a reliable source of military aid. It had not yet developed the doctrine or logistics necessary to support such operations, near or far.

Third, the United States initiated the Alliance for Progress, admittedly only a marginal success, but nonetheless an attack on the underlying cause for revolution—the political, economic, and social ills of Latin America.

Fourth, in all cases, the armies confronting the rural guerrillas were superior to that of Fulgencio Batista. This can be attributed in Venezuela to public support for a popularly elected, democratic government; in Peru, to a realistic preparation to fight the rural guerrilla; and in Bolivia, to direct American aid.[52] The Peruvian armed forces began teaching courses in antisubversive tactics at the *Escuela Superior de Guerra* in the 1950s prior to the attacks by the ultra-left. Che wrote in his diary, "They [the Bolivians] are good fighters. How they have pursued us. They do not fear death, their chiefs coolly command. I never thought the Bolivian army was so stubborn."[53]

Fifth, in most cases the rural guerrillas remained elitist and were unable to attract the masses. In the case of Che's operations in Bolivia, and to a lesser degree those of Ochoa in Venezuela, this was compounded by the fact that Cubans overshadowed the participation of local nationals.[54]

Sixth, without exception, the orthodox Communist parties failed to support the guerrilla undertakings and frequently worked against them. In January 1968 a frustrated Guatemalan guerrilla wrote, "After four years of fighting this is the balance sheet: 300 Revolutionaries fallen in combat, 3,000 men of the people murdered by Julio César Méndez Montenegro's regime. The [Communist] PGT [*Partido Guatemalteco del Trabajo*] supplied ideas and the FAR the dead."[55]

Seventh, the overwhelming majority of the rural people within the targeted countries would not support revolution. Che's fundamental tenant that revolution could be fostered from the countryside before winning the hearts and minds of the people proved wrong.[56]

Eighth, too many radical leftists wanted to be in charge. For example, cooperation among the leaders of the Venezuelan MIR was problematic and between the MIR and the PCV even more difficult.

Cuban-Soviet relations began to thaw on August 24, 1968, when Castro expressed understanding concerning the need for the Soviet Union to invade Czechoslovakia.[57] The era of rural guerrilla warfare was not a total disaster for the radical left. All of these causes for failure were exposed by *Comandante* Arnaldo Ochoa and other guerrillas who returned from Venezuela and elsewhere to Cuba. The radical left learned that their leaders had the courage to fight for their convictions. Some of these individuals survived the defeats and were available to fight another day. Also, a martyred Che became a powerful symbol.

Many years later Fidel Castro stated, "subjective conditions [in Latin America], many times superior to those in Cuba [existed] to make revolution. . . . [These failed because of a] tragic division between China and the USSR that simply divided the forces of the left."[58]

CHAPTER 31

URBAN GUERRILLA WARS, 1963–76

Take the initiative, assume the responsibility, do something. It is better to make mistakes doing something, even if it results in death.

—Carlos Marighela

THE SPARK

No single event sparked urban guerrilla warfare. Rather, it took root in Latin America during the 1960s and 1970s due to the failure of the *foco* strategy.

BACKGROUND

Three important changes took place between the early 1960s and 1970s that caused some among the radical left in Latin America to abandon the Cuban-inspired *foco* theory of guerrilla warfare and adopt an urban guerrilla strategy.

First, the *foco* strategy had been crushed throughout the region in remote parts of Bolivia, Guatemala, Peru, and elsewhere.

Second, the radical left discovered that they could handsomely finance their operations through kidnapping, extortion, and robberies and that they were not dependent upon Cuban material aid, which had its price. Admittedly, however, Cuba remained important for training, arms, and sanctuary.

Finally, unique windows of opportunity occurred within the more industrialized countries of Latin America, inspiring the radical left to attempt to seize power. In Argentina, the decades-old Perónist versus anti-Perónist struggle was coming to a head. Within Uruguay social programs outstripped the financial capacity of the nation. And in Brazil, urbanization strained the fabric of society. The military overthrew the government of João Goulart in a bloodless coup d'etat in April 1964 and retained power.

OPPOSING FORCES

Like the rural guerrillas, the core of the urban guerrilla membership was the university student. He or she was better educated and more affluent than the average citizen. Many had acquired an anticapitalist philosophy through their university studies, and thousands had received doctrinal and subversive training in Cuba.[1] Also, urban guerrilla movements appealed to

289

relatively small, but important groups outside the universities. In Argentina, about one-third of the guerrillas came from the working class.[2] In Uruguay, numerous professionals and technicians became *Tupamaros*. Also, the ultraliberal members of the clergy provided shelter and communications in a number of countries.[3]

Typically, the urban guerrilla was organized into small cells, or "firing groups," of four or five persons. The cells were relatively isolated from each other in order to ensure security. Operating outside an established political party, a small number of urban guerrillas could make a big impact on the national scene.

Opposing the guerrillas were civilian governments in Argentina and Uruguay and a recently established military government in Brazil. None had foreseen the threat of urban guerrilla violence, nor had they developed any capabilities outside of their existing police forces.

OPENING STRATEGIES

The strategy of the urban guerrilla was to attack the *status quo*, and many guerrilla leaders advocated action even when it lacked clear objectives.[4]

No pan-national theoretician emerged from among the urban guerrillas to inspire an international brotherhood as Che Guevara had done for the rural guerrillas. But there were prominent national theoreticians. Among the most important was Carlos Marighela,[5] a Brazilian, and to a lesser degree Abraham Guillen,[6] a naturalized Argentine.

Urban guerrillas attempted to create the mystique that they were acting as the vanguard of the people. The guerrillas wanted to undermine democratic proponents within the weak democracies of Argentina and Uruguay, plus those within Brazil. The guerrillas were committed to violence and, therefore, determined to discredit any peaceful solution. The guerrillas did this through robberies, kidnappings, murders, and other acts of violence in order to cause the declaration of martial law. The urban guerrilla believed that if the common man were given a choice between a military government and the guerrillas, he would choose the latter.[7]

Initially, the city offered advantages over the country for the radical left. Latin American cities were growing faster than those in any other world region. Montevideo accounted for more than half of Uruguay's population. Brazil's industrial triangle of São Paulo–Rio de Janeiro–Belo Horizonte had a population of some 20 million during the 1960s. One-third of all Argentines lived in the greater Buenos Aires region. In addition, urbanization was moving faster than social services, creating large slums surrounding these megalopolises. These slums were full of potential recruits and hiding places. Operating in the city also offered better access to the media.

On the other side, the governments of Argentina, Brazil, and Uruguay had not developed any strategy outside the traditional judicial system to deal with the urban guerrillas.

URUGUAY 1963–72

This small nation is considered by many as the birthplace of urban guerrilla warfare. In 1963 Raúl Sendic[8] founded the National Liberation Movement (*Movimiento de Liberación Nacional*—MLN). It was a confederation of extremist organizations which chose the motto, "words divide us, actions unite us."[9] The MLN was composed of a few intellectuals, labor leaders, and peasants from the northern frontier, and its goal was the overthrow of the government. The MLN chose to call itself the *Tupamaros* to take advantage of the symbolism of the name.[10]

The name grew to have so much popular appeal that the government banned its use by the media. The *Tupamaros* publicly became "the nameless ones," "bandits," or "criminals."

The *Tupamaros* spent their first four years preparing for the struggle. At first the Uruguayan guerrillas looked to create a rural movement but by the mid-1960s had adopted an urban strategy. During their first six years, the *Tupamaros* carried out sporadic attacks as the movement gathered strength. Between 1963 and 1969 the *Tupamaros* staged 126 robberies, netting $1.7 million, in addition to a large sum extorted by ransom.[11]

By 1969 the *Tupamaros* had increased from about twenty members to approximately 500 active members and some 5,000 supporters.[12] Many of the new recruits came from the universities and the professions, such as doctors, nurses, communication technicians, police, and firefighters. The recruitment of skilled individuals allowed the *Tupamaros* to infiltrate many aspects of society, including the government, banking, medicine, and communications. Members had access to sensitive information. Some cased banks, others monitored communications for intelligence, while others collected information concerning public and private corruption for propaganda exploitation. The revelation in 1969 that the corporate leader Juan Almiratti was a *Tupamaro* leader shocked the nation.

The *Tupamaros* were organized into cells normally composed of five members. These members knew few colleagues outside their own cell, and the cell leader typically knew only his immediate superior in the chain of command. The *Tupamaros* built an elaborate infrastructure. Within Montevideo's massive underground sewage system, the *Tupamaros* established hospitals and prisons. They used the tunnels as avenues of attack and escape. Above ground, scores of "safe houses" were acquired to serve as hiding places.

The *Tupamaros* attempted to foster a positive public image. Ten youths hijacked a truck carrying cakes and other sweets and distributed the goods in the slums of Montevideo (*cantegiles*) during Christmas Day 1963. On occasion they would donate to charities part of their booty stolen during robberies. They also sought to build their image through muckraking. Through their clandestine intelligence network and stolen documents, they gathered sensitive and embarrassing information concerning the government and business community. This was then released to the press.[13]

The *Tupamaros* also had a flare for the dramatic. On February 7, 1969, they left 280 pounds of gelignite in front of the house of an army explosives expert with the attached note:

> Capt Manzino: this material has decomposed and is therefore dangerous to handle, and so we decided to destroy it. We know of your technical ability and believe there is no one better than you to do it.[14]

Beginning in 1968, the *Tupamaros* intensified their activities. In August the *Tupamaros* kidnapped Ulises Pereyra Reverbel, the head of the national telephone and electric combine and a close friend of the President. This was done to humiliate the President; Pereyra was released within a few days. On September 9 the *Tupamaros* kidnapped Gaetano Pellegrini Giampetro, a banker and publisher, during a bitter bank strike. The *Tupamaros* used this kidnapping to show their support for the strikers. Pellegrini was released following the payment of a $70,000 ransom.

A decisive event occurred in late 1969. On October 8, the second anniversary of Che's death, some forty guerrillas, disguised as a funeral cortege, seized control of the town of Pando

(40 mi E Of Montevideo). They looted three banks, humiliated the police, lectured the locals concerning the virtues of their cause, and fled back to Montevideo in a simulated funeral caravan. However, the police intercepted them; three were killed and sixteen captured at Toledo Chico before they could reach the capital. Those captured were tortured. This drew the guerrillas into a war of vengeance with the government's security forces.

Beginning in early 1970, the *Tupamaros* launched a ferocious attack against the police. They assassinated a police official, Carlos Ruben Zambrano, who allegedly had had a role in the events of Toledo Chico. In addition, a number of policemen were ambushed. As a result, some policemen struck for "danger-money" and the right to wear civilian clothes to reduce their visibility. Sixty-six policemen were charged with insubordination.

On March 8, 1970, approximately twenty *Tupamaros* freed thirteen female compatriots from a prison located in Montevideo. On April 4, the *Tupamaros* robbed the Mailhos family of some $400,000. Nine days later, they assassinated Police Inspector Héctor Morán Charquero, allegedly for his role in the torturing of prisoners. In May approximately forty guerrillas stripped the armory at a naval center of 700 rifles, thousands of rounds of ammunition, and numerous other munitions. In June the guerrillas kidnapped Judge Daniel Pereira Manelli, who had sentenced many of their colleagues.

On July 31 the bold *Tupamaros* simultaneously kidnapped three foreign diplomats: Dan A. Mitrione, Chief of the U.S. team advising the Uruguayans concerning counterinsurgency; Nathan Rosenfeld, U.S. cultural attaché; and Aloysio Mares Diás Gomide, Consul and First Secretary of the Brazilian Embassy. They also momentarily held U.S. secondary secretary Gordon Jones, but he escaped.[15]

These abductions were the *Tupamaros'* first attempt to exploit a diplomatic hostage. In exchange for the Brazilian, the guerrillas demanded the release of all political prisoners. When the Uruguayan government refused, the *Tupamaros* executed Mitrione. Although the intensive search did not find Gomide, security forces did net seventy alleged *Tupamaros*, including Raúl Sendic, who was captured on August 7.[16] Gomide was released after 206 days following a ransom payment alleged to be $250,000.

On August 8 the *Tupamaros* seized Dr. Claude L. Fly, a U.S. agronomist working under contract with the Ministry of Agriculture. After suffering a heart attack, he was dropped at the entrance of the British hospital in Montevideo in February 1971.[17]

Between January and August 1971, the *Tupamaros* carried out a series of spectacular kidnappings, the most publicized being that of the British ambassador, Geoffrey Jackson.[18] Also, two precision-planned prison breaks were executed. On July 17, 1971, thirty-eight women were freed by tunneling between the city's sewers and the women's prison. On September 6 the *Tupamaros* dug a 120-foot tunnel into Punta Carreta, Uruguay's maximum security prison located in Montevideo, freeing 106 prisoners, including the founder of the *Tupamaros*, Raúl Sendic.

In late 1971 the *Tupamaros* unsuccessfully endeavored to extend their operations to the countryside. However, most *Tupamaros* were city dwellers and out of their element. Also, the country folk were not interested in revolution and refused to help.[19]

The guerrillas suspended their activities during the national elections in November 1971. The Broad Front, supported by the *Tupamaros*, won eighteen percent of the vote. The lull was short. In January 1972 the *Tupamaros* assassinated the chief warden of the Punta Carreta Prison, Rodolfo Leoncin. On February 12 they kidnapped Homer Farine, editor of *Acción*, a government newspaper. On February 14 the guerrillas attempted to seize control of the hamlet of Soca but were only partially successful.

On February 29, 1972, the guerrillas abducted an organizer of the right-wing death squad, Nelson Bardesio, and extracted details of its membership. Beginning on April 14, the *Tupamaros* killed four and wounded three alleged members of the death squad.

As a result of these attacks, the new government of President Juan María Bordaberry declared (with Parliament's permission) a "state of internal war." This permitted the military and police to conduct searches and make arrests without warrants. Suspects could be held indefinitely and were brought before military and civil judges. Previously, captured *Tupamaros* had acted defiantly because they knew that the police and civil judges were intimidated.[20]

The President mobilized 12,000 troops and 20,000 policemen in an all-out campaign to eliminate the *Tupamaros*.[21] The Uruguayan army, which had been gathering intelligence on the guerrillas, was now committed to counterinsurgency. The government was also aided by the information supplied by a defector, Héctor Amodio Pérez. Over the next few weeks, one hundred *Tupamaros* died, seven hundred more were arrested, and seventy "safe" houses were seized.[22]

The government learned that the *Tupamaros* had a "people's jail" at Juan Paullier Street No 1192, and at 4 A.M. on May 27 its forces descended on the house. They discovered a secret entrance in the garage leading to an underground chamber. After an hour of negotiation, the four guards surrendered. The soldiers freed Carlos Frick Davie, the former Minister of Cattle and Agriculture, and Ulises Pereyra Reverbel, president of the Uruguayan Telephone Company. Davie had been a hostage for twelve months and Pereira Reverbel for thirteen and a half.[23]

Success bred success as the public lost its fear of *Tupamaro* reprisals and increasingly reported suspicious activities. On September 1, 1972, Sendic was captured for a third time following a shootout in which he was wounded. Then additional members of the *Tupamaro* leadership were captured or killed.

By the end of the year, the *Tupamaros* made a desperate attempt to retreat into the countryside, but it was too late. They had been defeated and were no longer a viable fighting force. The few survivors fled to Argentina or went underground.[24]

The *Tupamaros* had miscalculated the actions of the Uruguayan army. They accurately perceived that the government would seek outside help but believed that the aid would come in the form of Brazilian troops patrolling Uruguayan streets. The *Tupamaros* believed that such an event would allow them to turn the struggle into one of national liberation against a foreign invader. Instead, help came in the form of counterinsurgency training and material provided to the security forces from Brazil and the United States. This aid proved decisive.

BRAZIL, 1968–71

While some leftists were attempting to foster revolution in Brazil through the *foco* strategy (see chapter 30), others chose a strategy more in concert with Brazil's demographic and geographical reality by adopting urban guerrilla warfare. They operated principally in Rio de Janeiro and São Paulo, and occasionally in Belo Horizonte, Recife, and Porto Alegre.

Initially, the radical left distributed pamphlets, started a clandestine press, and wrote propaganda on walls. Next, they bombed, kidnapped foreign diplomats, robbed banks, government offices, jewelry and arms shops, and killed law agents.

Many members of the Brazilian guerrillas were frustrated members of the Communist Party (*Partido Comunista*—PC). They formed numerous combat organizations, the most active being the National Liberation Alliance (*Aliança Libertadora Nacional*—ALN) headed by Carlos Marighela, and the Popular Revolutionary Vanguard (*Vanguarda Popular Revolucionária*— VPR) led by Carlos Lamarca, an army captain who had defected to the guerrillas.

Carlos Marighela, Brazil's principal guerrilla theoretician, adopted a philosophy that came close to endorsing spontaneity. He advocated the creation of tiny "firing groups" composed of four to five fighters. Membership was open to all who accepted the organization's principles and each was free to act as he saw fit. Such a philosophy promoted anarchy within the guerrilla movement, making coordination almost impossible. This fragmentation also frustrated the task of the security forces, particularly during the early stages of guerrilla activity. Also, the guerrilla leadership placed no premium on their own security. In order to merit the support of their followers, leaders took part in dangerous operations.[25]

During 1968 and 1969 the guerrillas developed their tactics and built their war chests through kidnappings and robberies. By the 1970s the guerrillas had robbed some 200 banks of more than $2 million and had extracted a $2.4 million ransom from the former Governor of São Paulo, Laudo Natel. By this time there were perhaps 400 guerrillas spread over ten organizations.[26]

In October 1968 a new phase opened with the assassination of U.S. Army Capt. Charles Chandler. This was followed by a series of spectacular kidnappings of diplomats, the purpose of which was to trade the hostages for the release of political prisoners. Between September 4, 1969, and December 7, 1970, the abductions of the United States, German, and Swiss ambassadors and the Japanese consul were rewarded by the release of dozens of detainees.[27]

However, each abduction led to the arrests of more guerrillas than it freed, in part due to the difficulty of security inherent in the guerrilla structure, and in part due to the brute force used by the security forces. The principal guerrilla leader, Marighela, was killed in an ambush by the police on November 4, 1969. Ten months later, his successor, Joaquim Câmara Ferreira, died in a São Paulo prison following his capture. On September 17, 1971, Lamarca, leader of the Popular Revolutionary Vanguard, was killed in the interior of the state of Bahia. By the end of 1971 the urban guerrilla movement had been crushed. At its peak, the ALN had 100 "fighters." Of these, 72 had been trained in Cuba but only 20 of these indiviuals ever entered the fight. These fighters were supported by 300 individuals many of whom came from labor unions, professions, and the Catholic Church. In the end, 64 guerrillas were killed and about 1,000 imprisoned for terms ranging from six months to ten and a half years.[28]

The Brazilian urban guerrilla movement did cause serious disruptions within Brazilian society but never posed a serious threat to the government. The campaign lasted four years and failed in large measure because of its inability to win support outside the student body, particularly among the lower middle class.[29]

ARGENTINA 1966–76

Urban guerrilla movements in Argentina had their roots in the 1960s and gained protection under the umbrella of *Perónismo* during the 1970s.[30] Beginning with Juan Perón's exile in 1955 and until his return in 1973, this charismatic, proletarian-messiah encouraged all to oppose the Argentine government, whether it be democratic or military. To win Perón's blessing, it mattered not how far to the left or right of the political spectrum you might be, as long as you opposed in the name of Perón those who ruled.

Many were dissatisfied with the governing of Argentina and were potential recruits for urban guerrilla warfare. The disfranchising of the *Perónistas* in 1955, who represented one-third of the voting-age population, created an element of extreme nationalists who were openly antagonistic toward those in power. Eleven years later, on June 29, 1966, the government of Gen. Juan Carlos Onganía outlawed the Communist Party (*Partido Comunista Argentino*), making another 60,000 Argentines potential recruits for subversive organizations. Those in the party's youth movement, the Young Communist Federation (*Federación Juvenil Comunista*), were particularly militant. Also on the twenty-ninth, the military government withdrew the autonomy of the eight national universities and one technical school, alienating tens of thousands of students, many of whom were sympathetic to the ultraleft.

Beginning in the mid-1960s, a climate of hostility grew between the extremists within these factions and the government. The Army of National Liberation (*Ejército de Liberación Nacional*) was formed from members of several radical groups to support Che Guevara's activities in Bolivia. They operated in rural, northern Argentina near the Bolivian border; however, their effort was short-lived, for with Che's death, the group dissolved.

Urban violence began during the late 1960s and early 1970s; throughout this period the guerrillas were extremely fragmented. In 1969 the Argentine government attempted to deal with the increasing guerrilla problem by passing counterinsurgency legislation and establishing special civilian courts. Numerous guerillas were captured and prosecuted. In May 1969 some students and workers were killed and scores injured in Córdoba and Rosario during political demonstrations. This event, known as the *Cordobazo*, brought down the Onganía government.

Two urban guerrilla groups exploded onto the national scene during 1970 and would ultimately dominate national attention. The first to emerge was the *Ejército Revolucionario del Pueblo*, which was known by its acronym ERP (frequently cited in English as *Guevaristas* to honor Che who, after all, was an Argentine). The ERP was a Trotskyite movement that had ties with Cuba. The second was the *Montoneros*, who chose this name in an attempt to identify with the legendary plainsmen who defended Argentina's northern border by hit-and-run tactics during the War for Independence following the battle of Sipe Sipe (November 29, 1815). The *Montoneros* received support from Cuba in spite of the fact that some of their roots could be traced to a nationalistic Catholic organization with links to the *Tacuara*, neo-Nazis, and others of the extreme right.

The ERP carried out its first action on September 18, 1970, when members attacked a police station in Rosario (150 mi NW of Buenos Aires), killing two policemen. Five months later they robbed a bank in Córdoba (434 mi NW of Buenos Aires) for $300,000, the largest haul in Argentine history to that date.[31] In August 1972 twenty-five guerrillas, including Mario Roberto Santucho, leader of the ERP, broke jail in Rawson, Patagonia (700 mi SSW of Buenos Aires). Santucho and five others hijacked an airplane to Chile and eventually made their way to Cuba. The others were recaptured after they had held the airport for five hours. Ten days later, sixteen of those captured were killed while trying to escape, including Santucho's wife. The revolutionary press knighted them "the heroes of Trelew." The guerrillas accused the military of having executed the sixteen and carried out a series of assassinations including retired Rear Adm. Emilio Berisso, former Chief of Naval Intelligence, on December 28, 1972, and Adm. Hermes

Quijada, former head of the Joint Chiefs of Staff, on April 30, 1973, who was machine-gunned in the center of Buenos Aires during broad daylight.[32]

The *Montoneros* burst onto the national political scene when they kidnapped, tortured, and executed former president Gen. Pedro Aramburu in late May 1970. The General had conspired against Perón in 1955 and had subsequently become a provisional president.[33]

Also during this period, the guerrillas attacked military installations to capture arms, and they robbed to finance their operations. In February 1972 Perón, who was still in exile, asked his supporters, including the *Montoneros*, not to use violence against the government. Beginning in late 1972, the *Montoneros* subordinated guerrilla warfare to political activity. They formed the *Montonero* Perónist Movement (*Movimiento Perónista Montoneros*) as their political arm. The *Montoneros* promoted the Perónist youth movement and worked for the return of Juan Perón from exile and then for his election as president.

The military government complied with popular demand for elections, and on March 11, 1973 a political coalition orchestrated by Perónists won the victory for Héctor J. Cámpora. The election of Cámpora, who sympathized with the extreme left, substantially boosted the guerrilla cause. There was an immediate flurry of guerrilla activity. Less than a month after the elections, the guerrillas kidnapped Adm. Francisco Agustín Alemán and Antony Da Cruz, a Kodak executive. The *Montoneros* broke their self-imposed restraint, and on April 4 assassinated Héctor Alberto Iribarren, an army intelligence officer for the Córdoba region.[34]

The new President was inaugurated on May 25 and adopted three critical measures his first day in office: Cámpora annulled all antiterrorist legislation; he dismissed the special courts; and he freed 500 accused and condemned prisoners, 400 of whom were guerrillas and the others mostly common criminals. Within a short period of time the guerrillas assassinated several former judges of the dissolved special courts, thus voiding any possibility of effective civil judicial intervention.

Also on May 25, the ERP turned to philanthropy as a means of winning support. It announced that the Ford Motor Company had agreed to contribute one million dollars to children's hospitals and schools throughout the country rather than make an annual "donation" to the guerrilla cause.[35]

On numerous occasions, the guerrillas demonstrated their appreciation for the power of the media. On January 11, 1973, guerrillas held up a train and distributed leaflets. The next month they seized and forcibly renamed a railway station in Rosario to honor a fallen comrade.[36] On April 21 the ERP seized a small town near Buenos Aires. They held it long enough to publicize the act, after which they set fire to the police station and withdrew. Typically armed ERP guerrillas would take over a factory for an hour or so and force the workers to listen to speeches.

Foretelling the future, the right and the left within *Perónismo* clashed during a ceremony on June 8 to honor Gen. Juan José Valle, who had led an unsuccessful attempt to restore Perón to power in 1956. Near anarchy reigned. Cámpora tried to placate everyone. He even had lunch in the *Casa Rosada* (the presidential house) with the ERP and the *Montoneros*, giving the guerrillas *de facto* legitimacy. The President of Argentina, probably glad to escape his problems, then flew to Madrid to escort Juan Perón home.

On June 20, 1973, Juan Perón returned from eighteen years of exile and the airport mob, estimated at over one million, erupted into violence. Those representing the extreme right and extreme left within *Perónismo* confronted each other face to face for the second time. The clashes on the eighth and again on the twentieth attested to the extremes of the views held by those who claimed to be Perónists.

On June 27 the ERP dramatically broke with the government. Buenos Aires' television channels 11 and 13 broadcast a taped, secret press conference with the titular head of the guerrilla movement, Mario Roberto Santucho. He condemned the government of Cámpora and stated that Perón's most intimate advisor, José López Rega, had created a right-wing death squad under the protection of the Social Welfare Ministry which he headed. Santucho declared war on the government but stopped short of attacking Perón.

On September 6 the EPR attacked the Army Medical Command (*Comando de Sanidad del Ejército*).[37] To take direct control, Perón ordered the President and Vice President to resign, clearing the way for himself to be elected President and his third wife, María Isabel Martínez de Perón, Vice President on September 12, 1973; they were inaugurated on October 12. Due to the increasing violence, the government issued Decree 1453/73 on September 23, outlawing the ERP. On September 25 the *Montoneros* assassinated José Rucci, Secretary General of the Trade Union (*Confederacion General del Trabajo*—CGT) and close personal friend of Perón.[38] During the election Perón exhorted the *Montoneros* to remain within *Perónismo*, while he refrained from defining his political position. Shortly after being inaugurated, Perón began to work for legislation to deal with the guerrillas.

In October 1973 the *Montoneros* and the Armed Revolutionary Forces (*Fuerzas Armadas Revolucionarias*—FAR) agreed to coordinate their actions in order to present an armed left wing within *Perónismo* in order to challenge the right. By late 1973 the guerillas began to polarize around the *Montoneros* and the ERP.

On January 19, 1974, eighty-six men from the ERP, disguised as soldiers, entered the compound of the Tenth Regiment of Hussars in Azul (145 mi SW of Buenos Aires), and attempted to kidnap Col. Camilo Gay and his wife. The alarm was sounded and the Colonel was shot in the pursuing struggle. The guerrillas held the compound for seven hours. They escaped with hostages whom they were forced to abandon. As a result of this and other acts, Congress amended the penal codes on January 28, 1974, increasing the penalties for subversive offenses.[39]

To compensate for their decreased popularity caused by Perón's return, the ERP moved their operations from the major cities to the rural province of Tucumán. They hoped to win control of the rural, mountainous area in order to be able to declare a liberated zone. The ERP wanted to win support among the sugar workers in that region. Although it did succeed in temporarily dominating much of Tucumán, this relocation isolated the ERP from the universities and labor unions in the large cities of Buenos Aires, Rosario, and Córdoba, which had previously provided many of the ERP's recruits. In February 1974 the ERP held a clandestine press conference which demonstrated the sophistication of its organization and it continued sensitivity to the power of the press.[40]

The *Montoneros*, becoming increasingly frustrated by the confines of *Perónismo*, began to increase their guerrilla activities. Finally, at a mass meeting on May Day, 1974, Perón accused the *Montoneros* of subversion, so they walked out. The *ERP*, which had continued its guerrilla activities during the strained "honeymoon" between Perón and the *Montoneros*, had accounted for most of the forty or so assassinations committed since Perón's return.[41]

On July 1, 1974, Juan Perón died, leaving his wife, the Vice President, in power. Isabel Martínez de Perón immediately declared a state of siege. The guerrillas exploited the predictable weakness of a government led by a novice of political affairs and governmental administration. During September more than four hundred bombs exploded in Buenos Aires, sixty in one night. The ERP renewed its efforts to win Tucumán Province. As a result, in December 1974 Isabel Martínez de Perón signed a secret decree placing Tucumán under martial law. The resulting military operation, *"Independencia,"* would require a full brigade. By the end of the first year, guerrilla activity would be significantly reduced, although it would take the army almost two full years to regain complete control of the area.

Following Perón's death, secret right-wing groups collectively known as the Argentine Anti-Communist Action (*Accion Anticomunista Argentina*—AAA) and supported by powerful elements within the government, became active. It issued death lists that included not only guerrillas but sympathizers such as actors, artists, deputies, and other public figures. The AAA assassinated scores of leftists, principally in the provinces of Buenos Aires and Tucumán.[42]

In January 1975 right-wing terrorists surrounded an entire city block in Córdoba during daylight and blew up the offices of the newspaper *La Voz del Interior* without police interference.[43]

As a result of their defeats in Tucumán, the ERP shifted the center of their activity back to the province of Buenos Aires. On December 23, 1975, about 270 ERP guerrillas attacked the army garrison in Monte Chingolo (10 mi SE of Buenos Aires). The army had been forewarned and annihilated the attackers. Six months later, in July 1976, Mario Roberto Santucho and other leaders of the ERP were killed in a shootout, but the movement was already in shambles.[44]

While the ERP was being crushed, the *Montoneros* were evolving into the strongest urban guerrilla force yet created in Latin America. They secretly carried out acts of violence. On July 15, 1974, they assassinated Dr. Auturo Mor Roig, the former Minister of the Interior, in a restaurant outside of Buenos Aires.[45]

On September 3 the leftist *Perónista* magazine *La Causa Perónista* published an article by Mario Firmenich and Norma Arrostito outlining how they had kidnapped and killed General Aramburu. The article included correspondence from Juan Perón approving the act. Aramburu supporters were incensed by the vivid description of the cold-blooded assassination; the extreme right was outraged by the attention given to Peron's courtship of the left while he was in exile. *La Causa Perónista* was closed and its property confiscated.

Three days later, on September 6, the *Montoneros* formally declared war against the regime of Isabel Martínez de Perón. Juan Pablo Ventura, a member of the Perónist youth, issued a declaration in the auditorium of the Law Faculty of the University of Buenos Aires. The *Montoneros* declared that those in power had betrayed *Perónismo*. Since *Perónismo* could be almost anything and the only authoritative interpreter was now dead, who was to argue? The *Montoneros* felt that it was necessary to maintain the link between the mysticism of "the Conductor" (Perón) and themselves in spite of the fact that Juan Perón had evicted them from his movement. The *Montoneros* declared that they would go underground and join the ERP in their people's war.

The *Montoneros* had a flair for the spectacular, which constantly won them the attention of the media. On September 19, they kidnapped business magnates Juan and Jorge Born, earning a ransom of $60 million.[46] On October 16 the *Montoneros* stole Aramburu's coffin from Recoleta Cemetery. It was returned one month later when the embalmed body of Eva Perón had been secured by President Isabel Martínez de Perón from its hiding place in Italy. The abduction of Aramburu's remains and their return called attention to the *Montoneros'* claim that they were responsible for Evita's final return to Argentina.

Early in November 1974 the *Montoneros* blew up the federal police chief, Alberto Villar, with an underwater mine while he was boating on the Paraná River. Isabel Martínez de Perón declared a state of siege and asked Congress for emergency powers. Newspapers were closed and journalists arrested. The Martínez de Perón administration was accused of using the crisis to silence those who accused her regime of corruption and incompetence.

The *Montoneros* stepped up urban guerilla attacks in early 1975, leaving the ERP to operate in the countryside. Greater cooperation between the movements became evident. Military targets held special appeal for the guerrillas. On February 5 Martínez de Perón ordered the military "to neutralize and/or annihilate the action of the subversive elements operating in the Province of Tucumán."[47] Four days later, the army began operation "Independence" against the guerrillas. Although operation "Independence" produced local success, the guerrillas were extremely aggressive elsewhere.

On August 22, 1975, a guerrilla scuba diving team exploded a charge against the hull of the destroyer *Santísima Trinidad* while under construction, causing serious damage. On the twenty-eighth, the ERP blew up the runway as an air force C-130 Hercules aircraft was taking off from the Benjamin Mattienzo Airport in Tucumán Province—six military were killed and twelve seriously wounded. And on October 5 *Montoneros* attacked the city of Formosa (841 mi N of Buenos Aires). The army garrison repelled the attackers, leaving twenty-six dead. Another group of guerrillas tried to free prisoners from the local penitentiary but failed. The guerrillas made their escape in a hijacked civilian airliner.[48]

By late 1975 law enforcement agencies had been completely overwhelmed by the chaos imposed by the reign of terror. On October 6 three secret presidential decrees extended martial law to the entire nation.[49] Since Juan Perón's death, the guerrillas had committed 300 murders, to which must be added those of the reactionary right AAA.[50]

On March 24, 1976, the military seized the government from Isabel Martínez de Perón, who had been ineffective in dealing with the ever-increasing violence. In the subsequent war of attrition, the guerrillas proved no match for the military. Once the *Montoneros* had resumed their attacks, particularly bombings against security forces and assassinations, they lost most of the popular support they had won before 1974.[51] Although a few hundred security force personnel were killed, during the same period the *Montoneros* lost about 4,500 persons. Although the *Montoneros* continued isolated killings through 1982, they were effectively crushed.[52]

OBSERVATIONS

The urban guerrillas failed to bring any radical governments to power. They did not develop a strategy that could lead to victory. The guerrillas seemed to assume that a series of successful terrorist acts would cause the downfall of a weak democracy without much consideration as to how then to mobilize popular support against the subsequent military government.

The urban guerrillas could easily goad the large number of underprivileged city dwellers into participating in activities against the government, but the antiestablishment feelings of these disenfranchised people could not be transformed into loyalty for the guerrilla cause.

The guerrillas put little effort into soliciting support from existing popular organizations such as labor unions, political parties, and peasant associations. The guerrillas viewed the possibilities of such interactions as being a possible contaminant. So, they ignored and on occasion even attacked such organizations.

As in the case of the *foco* wars, the urban guerrillas isolated themselves from the population in order to maintain their secrecy. When the guerrillas did attempt to increase their membership, as was the case in Uruguay between 1970 and 1972, they quickly became vulnerable to government countermeasures because of the huge, visible infrastructure they had built.

Also, the guerrillas alienated foreigners by their acts of terrorism against them and their property, thus eliminating any possible international sympathy.

The urban guerrillas were reckless. They believed that they were on the verge of victory; consequently, the guerrillas frequently abandoned safety precautions.

The urban guerrillas also made the mistake of assuming that if the weak democratic government was indecisive in acting against them, the military would be as well. Even Uruguay, which in 1968 possessed 12,000 poorly trained and poorly equipped soldiers and double that number of police, was able to sufficiently improve its forces with outside aid in enough time to defeat the *Tupamaros*.

Once the military took charge, their most serious problem became determining the identity of the enemy. In order to solve this problem, the government (whether civilian or military) used the mass media to urge the populace to report any suspicious activity. The public response was substantial and teams of officers from various military services aided by the police investigated the reports. Once a guerrilla was discovered, information concerning his contacts had to be extracted within twenty-four hours. Once a cell lost contact with a member for twenty-four hours, it had to dissolve and its members go into hiding. Regardless, the urban guerrillas found that once their identities were known they had no place to hide. They could either stand, fight, and die, or they could flee the country.

Some individuals within the military abused the extensive powers granted to them under martial law by civilian authority. In Argentina their acts caused deep national wounds which were painfully exposed in public trials during the 1980s.

The guerrillas also failed to perceive that terrorism from the left would be met by equal violence from the ultraright, which, at the least, was tacitly protected by some in the government and, at the most, actively supported.

When the urban guerrillas attempted to expand their operations into the countryside, they met with disaster because their city-bred members were out of their element and because they could not garner the support of the rural populations.[53]

The urban guerrilla wars were fought and won by the Latin American militaries with little support and frequent criticism from the United States. The United States did not perceive the new urban conflicts to be part of the cold war. America's attitude was heavily influenced by its preoccupation with the Vietnam legacy. Following that war, the Carter administration was particularly unsympathetic to those who had turned the brutal tactics of the urban guerrillas against the guerrillas.

The annihilation of the Latin American urban guerrillas and most of its leadership during the 1960s and 1970s, preceded by the defeat of Che Guevara and his *foco* theory, and concurrent with the overthrow of the Allende government, left those on the ultraleft of the political spectrum without a strategy for winning power.

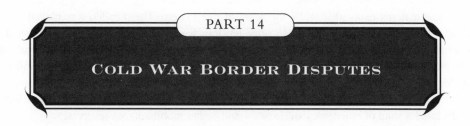

PART 14

COLD WAR BORDER DISPUTES

CHAPTER 32

THE "SOCCER WAR," 1969

It hurts us in El Salvador that now you [the Organization of American States] want to watch the clock, when during the time when Salvadorans were persecuted and insulted, the OAS did not want to see the calendar, much less the clock.
                              —Francisco José Guerrero, Salvador's Foreign Minister

THE SPARK

On June 28, 1969, El Salvador, by a score of three to two, won the third and deciding soccer playoff match in the World Cup tournament against Honduras in Mexico City. Tensions between El Salvador and Honduras mounted as new wrongs compounded old ones. On July 14 El Salvador bombed and invaded Honduras, and what the international press dubbed the "Soccer War" began.[1]

BACKGROUND

Numerous historical animosities contributed to the outbreak of the Soccer War. As throughout Latin America, boundaries between these neighbors were ill-defined. And for more than seventy-five years, Central American nations fought off-and-on over union-versus-separation (see companion volume); at times, Salvadorans and Hondurans were allies and other times enemies. Also, refugees from El Salvador, the smallest yet most densely populated nation in Central America, frequently spilled over into Honduras.[2]

Between 1920 and 1969, some 300,000 Salvadoran *campesinos* crossed into Honduras seeking work; this was equivalent to more than 12 percent of the Honduran population. As is frequently the case, these migrants were hard-working and their success became resented by some Hondurans. The two nations signed numerous bilateral agreements attempting to restrict the movement across the border. These were not successful. Also, in early 1969 Honduras passed an agrarian reform law depriving most illegal Salvadoran settlers of the land they were homesteading.[3]

On June 8, 1969, the Salvadoran national soccer team lost a game in Tegucigalpa, Honduras, to that nation's national team by the score of one to zero. The rematch was played in San Salvador on June 15. In spite of tight security, tensions were so high that three Salvadorans died in rioting prior to the game. The Salvadorans won three to zero. Homeward-bound Hondurans were attacked as they passed through Salvadoran villages. These events were exaggerated by the Honduran press. Hoodlums in Honduras attacked Salvadorans and those selling items produced in El Salvador. The hoodlums stole, raped, and murdered. As a consequence, El Salvador declared a state of emergency on June 24 and began mobilizing its reserves.[4]

On June 25 both nations asked the OAS to investigate the situation. The next day El Salvador broke diplomatic relations with Honduras which reciprocated on the twenty-seventh. On July 3 two Honduran T-28 aircraft forced down a Salvadoran Piper PA-28 Cherokee private aircraft which they suspected of being a reconnaissance flight. Five days later border clashes began which ultimately escalated into the exchange of machine-gun and mortar fire across the border. On July 8 Salvadoran soldiers penetrated Honduras and set fire to dwellings in the village of Colomoncagua.

As these events were transpiring, Salvadoran migrants fled back to their country at a rate that reached 1,400 refugees a day. Over 17,000 persons recrossed into El Salvador. On July 12 the Honduran air force relocated its aircraft from its main base at Toncontin to *Aeropuerto de la Mesa* in San Pedro Sula, farther from the frontier. On the thirteenth, Salvadoran and Honduran ground patrols clashed near El Poy.[5]

OPPOSING FORCES

In 1969 El Salvador's population of some 3,380,000 inhabitants occupied 8,236 square miles (approximately the size of Massachusetts), giving it roughly the same population density as Italy. Honduras' population of 2,333,000 citizens occupied 42,300 square miles (approximately the size of Ohio), giving it a population density less than that of Afghanistan. The two nations share a 130-mile border which has a right angle. The capitals of the two nations lie only 140 miles apart.[6]

The Salvadoran army was composed of 4,500 men; it was based on a twelve-month selective conscription.[7] In theory, some 25,000 army reservists could be called upon. The national guard, national police, and interior police totaled 2,500 men. Front-line infantrymen were armed with modern, German-manufactured G-3 rifles; reservists were armed with a mix of American World War II M-1 Garand and German World War I Mauser bolt-action rifles. El Salvador possessed an overwhelming superiority in artillery—105mm howitzers plus 75mm and 57mm recoilless rifles.[8]

The Salvadorans possessed a small number of M-3 "Stuart" tanks and improvised additional vehicles. Two-and-a-half-ton trucks, designated "*Rayos*," were armor-plated and some were fitted with mortars. Also, armored cars used by banks were requisitioned and designated "*ninas*."[9]

The Salvadoran air force possessed six F-4U "Corsair" fighter-bombers, six F-51D "Mustang" fighter-bombers, two recently acquired B-26B "Invader" light bombers (probably not operational), four C-47 transports, and thirty trainers (which included a total of ten T-6 "Texans" and T-11 "Kansans").[10]

The Honduran army had 3,500 volunteers. The army possessed one detached motorized unit, one artillery battery, and a few light armored cars. There was a 2,500-man civil guard. Front-line infantrymen were armed with the World War II M-1 Garand rifle; reservists were equipped with British Enfield and German Mauser rifles.

The Honduran air force had twelve F-4U "Corsair" fighter-bombers, seven transports (three of which were C-47s), twenty-five trainers (a few T-28s "Trojan" but mostly T-6 "Texans"), and three H-19 helicopters. Honduran pilots were, on average, better trained than their Salvadoran opponents.[11]

OPENING STRATEGIES

El Salvador's objective was to overthrow Honduran President Oswaldo López Arellano within 72 hours by seizing the capital. El Salvador planned a three-pronged attack. A motorized force under Gen. Segundo Martínez was to advance along the Pan American Highway, which exited El Salvador in an easterly direction and then swung north to the Honduran capital, Tegucigalpa, 150 miles from the border. The Salvadorans designated this the "Eastern Theater of Operations" (*Teatro de Operaciones Oriente*—TOO). A force under Col. Mario de Jesús Velásquez was to advance north-northeast toward Honduras' second-largest city, San Pedro Sula, 225 miles across the border. Just south of that city, a road intersected the invasion route and led back southeast toward Tegucigalpa. Using this road would permit Colonel Velásquez to approach the Honduran capital from the north while General Martínez advanced from the south. The Salvadorans designated this the "Northern Theater of Operations" (*Teatro de Operaciones del Norte*—TON). A 300-man force commanded by Lt. Col. Manuel Antonio Nuñez was to attack along the border between these two principal thrusts in order to prevent the Hondurans from concentrating their forces. The Salvadorans designated this the "Northeastern Theater of Operations" (*Teatro de Operaciones Nororiental*—TONO).[12] Apparently, Honduras chose a defensive strategy.

THE SALVADORAN AIR ATTACK

El Salvador launched a preemptive air strike, attempting to reduce the superiority of the Honduran air force. At 5:19 P.M. on July 14, three bombs were rolled out of an unescorted Salvadoran C-47 transport over Tegucigalpa's Toncontin Airport, causing little damage. Other Salvadoran planes attacked ten villages throughout Honduras.[13]

These air attacks were carried out at dusk to limit the possibility of the surviving Honduran warplanes following the attackers to their airfield and counterattacking. This plan almost proved disastrous. While the Salvadoran aircraft were attacking Honduras, the Salvadoran government enforced a blackout on the capital. A pilot described the consequences:

> The blackout meant that there were no landing lights and since all the radios were also run on electricity, there was no radio communication either. We were totally in the dark. We had to find the runway by using the few terrain features we could see and then one of us would swoop down close to see if that was the landing strip, and then the rest of the planes landed by following the landing lights of the proceeding plane.[14]

At about the same time as the air attacks, Salvadoran artillery began firing onto Honduras.

THE "NORTHERN THEATER"

At dawn on July 15, Salvadoran troops crossed the border at El Poy. They were ineffectively strafed by Honduran warplanes and discovered that the Honduran troops had abandoned their defensive positions. Not surprisingly, the Salvadoran communication system broke down and the field commanders had to resort to using runners.[15]

During the night of July 12, some 1,000 Honduran soldiers had fallen back to the Ticante Stream near a hill called "El Quebrachal," a natural defensive position. As the Salvadorans approached a few days later, the Hondurans opened fire. The Hondurans had mined the bridge across the stream but their explosives failed to detonate. Honduran Corsairs bombed the Salvadorans but their marksmanship was poor. At this point, the Salvadorans attacked up the road with two M-3 Stuart tanks, supported by advancing infantry. A Honduran 57mm recoilless rifle and a 3.5-inch bazooka put both tanks out of action. Seeing that they were making no progress, the Salvadorans reoriented their attack. They opened an accurate artillery fire on the Hondurans entrenched on El Quebrachal and silenced their fire. Next, the Salvadoran 8th Battalion stormed the hill. From this high ground, the Salvadorans were able to fire down into the Hondurans along the stream. The Hondurans fell back, trying to delay the Salvadorans by fighting from behind low stone walls that criss-crossed the countryside. The retreat soon turned into a disorganized route.[16]

The Hondurans attempted to make a stand at a hill called "Chicotera" to the east of Nueva Ocotepeque. Once again the defenders were sporadically supported by Corsairs. Combat devolved into small units fighting each other. On the morning of the sixteenth, an M-3 tank led the Salvadoran advance. It ran out of gas and was abandoned. Nonetheless, once again Salvadoran superior numbers and weapons won out and Nueva Ocotepeque fell under their control.[17]

As planned, the Salvadorans advanced along the road toward San Pedro Sula in trucks and buses. When they reached the narrow mountain pass at El Portillo, Salvadoran scouts assured them that it was clear and they could proceed. As they entered the pass an undetected Honduran ranger battalion opened fire with mortars, machine guns, and small arms. Throughout the day the Salvadorans unsuccessfully tried to outflank the defenders. As night approached the Salvadorans fell back and caused confusion among other units that were still advancing deeper into Honduras. A small number of Salvadorans were killed and wounded. More importantly, the repulse stagnated their northern advance.[18]

THE "EASTERN THEATER"

The Salvadoran units, which were to protect the flanks of the main thrust up the Pan American Highway, clandestinely crossed the Río Goascorán into Honduras during the night of July 14. On the morning of the fifteenth, five "*Rayos*" armored trucks drove across the narrow bridge spanning the river and successfully attacked the fortified customs house. The Salvadorans then used bulldozers as improvised tanks to win control of the border town of El Amatillo. The 11th Battalion had advanced about 3.5 miles into Honduras by nightfall.[19]

At dawn on July 16, the Hondurans, supported by aircraft, counterattacked but were beaten back. Two days later, the Salvadorans attacked the town of Nacaome on the Pan American Highway 15 miles from the border. The Salvadorans made little headway. At midnight on July 18, a cease-fire arranged by the Organization of American States went into effect.[20]

THE "NORTHEASTERN THEATER"

As planned, the Salvadorans launched an attack between the two major thrusts. This force rapidly captured a number of small hamlets. It was preparing to advance against La Esperanza (65 mi W of Tegucigalpa) when the cease fire went into effect.[21]

THE HONDURAN AIR FORCE COUNTERATTACKS

On July 15, while the Salvadoran ground forces were advancing, the Honduran air force struck three targets. At 3:18 A.M. a C-47 transport dropped eighteen 100-pound bombs on the Ilopango Airport at San Salvador; it caused little damage. An hour later four Honduran Corsair fighter-bombers attacked the Ilopango airfield with bombs and rockets; most of the bombs failed to explode. The aircraft then attacked industrial targets at Acajutla, Salvador's principal seaport; oil storage tanks were set on fire. This forced the Salvadoran government to ration gasoline. Also, the Honduran aircraft attacked the El Cutuco petroleum facility at La Union, another seaport; five out of seventeen storage tanks were destroyed. Three days later one of the burning tanks exploded, setting five more on fire.[22]

During that same evening, July 15, the Salvadoran aircraft again attacked Tegucigalpa but were no more effective than their first attack on the twelfth. They were chased off by Honduran T-28s.

On July 17 the Honduran air force won control of the skies when Maj. Fernando Soto shot down three Salvadoran fighters. Additional Salvadoran aircraft were downed by another pilot. The Hondurans in turn lost an F-4U Corsair which had to make an emergency landing in Guatemala; the aircraft was interned.[23]

THE BEGINNING OF THE END

Numerous factors now converged to end the fighting. Internally, both sides were running short of ammunition. The Salvadorans were beginning to feel the effects of the air raids against their petroleum facilities; it would not be long before these shortages impacted on military operations. Externally, the United States and the Organization of American States were bringing intense diplomatic pressure against both governments to effect a cease-fire.[24]

A four-point truce was agreed to by Honduras and reluctantly by El Salvador: (1) fighting should stop; (2) all troops should be withdrawn to their respective countries; (3) each country should protect the rights of citizens from their neighbors; and (4) the OAS should monitor compliance. Since only El Salvador had successfully crossed the opponent's border, that nation's "hawks" believed that the agreement was unfair. They wanted Honduras to pay reparations to the Salvadoran migrants who had been mistreated prior to the outbreak of the war. As a consequence, El Salvador dragged its feet concerning troop withdrawal. Salvadoran President Fidel Sánchez Hernández, speaking to the nation, said, "How is it that a man can walk with safety on the moon [which had occurred on July 20, 1969] and cannot do so, because of his nationality, on the prairies of Honduras?"[25]

OBSERVATIONS

The cease-fire went into effect at 10 P.M. on July 18. The war had lasted five days and four hours. Sporadic fighting continued until July 29 when the OAS accused El Salvador of being the aggressor and threatened economic sanctions if it did not immediately withdraw from Honduras. The pullback began on July 30 and was completed on August 5.[26]

The Hondurans were victorious in the air and the Salvadorans on the ground. The rugged, mountainous terrain of western Honduras favored the Salvadoran ground forces because it provided ample places to hide from the Honduran air force. The failure of the dominant Honduran air force to influence ground operations demonstrated a lack of coordination between that service and the Honduran army.[27]

Several thousand civilians are estimated to have died, although this seems quite high given the duration of the fighting and the limited firepower of both belligerents. Salvadoran military casualties were under 300 persons and those of the Honduran military somewhat less. The war displaced between 30,000 and 100,000 refugees, most of whom were Salvadorans who had fled from Honduras.[28]

As a consequence of the war, both sides expanded their armed forces. Over the next two decades, the Honduran army tripled in size to some 10,000 men. El Salvador increased its army to some 15,000 men. El Salvador purchased arms from France, Germany, Israel, and Yugoslavia.[29]

CHAPTER 33

THE MALVINAS (FALKLAND) ISLANDS, 1982

> Don't you [Admiral Lombardo] worry about that [what will happen after Argentina recaptures the islands], because that's not your responsibility. Limit yourself to working on the plan to take the islands; the rest will come later.
> —Adm. Jorge Anaya, Commander-in-Chief, Argentine Navy, December 20, 1981

THE SPARK

The Argentines and the British would probably choose different events as the spark that started the war. The Argentines might choose March 23, 1982, when the British government told the Argentines to remove the workers sent to South Georgia Island (770 mi E of Port Stanley) to scrap an old whaling station or else it would do so. The British might choose December 15, 1981, when Adm. Jorge Anaya ordered Vice Adm. Juan José Lombardo to prepare a contingency plan to recapture the Malvinas Islands.[1]

BACKGROUND

Many factors contributed to the Argentine military's decision to recover the Malvinas in 1982. The underlying factor was the frustration of decades of fruitless negotiations with the British. The more immediate factors were the need of the junta to defuse domestic pressures caused by a poor economy; Adm. Jorge Anaya's desire to be the individual responsible for the recovery of the islands; and the desire of the military junta to leave a legacy.

While it is certainly open to endless argument who discovered these islands, France, Great Britain, and Spain did establish colonies during the eighteenth century and for a while each chose to ignore the presence of the others. At the beginning of the independence movement, the Spanish evacuated the islands. Between 1811 and 1820 the Malvinas were ungoverned. Beginning on November 6, 1920, Buenos Aires sent a number of small detachments to the island; however, the the United Provinces were almost constantly in turmoil (see companion volume) and these were impossible to sustain without interruptions. In December 1831 Master Commandant Silas Duncan of the U.S. sloop-of-war *Lexington* (24 guns) forcefully removed the small Argentine government outpost from the Malvinas as a consequence of a fishing dispute. In 1832 Buenos Aires sent a new governor; however, he was soon killed by mutineers. The administration of the islands then fell on Lt. Col. José María Pinedo, commanding officer of the schooner *Sarandí* (3 guns). On January 2, 1833, the British sloop-of-war *Clio* (18 guns), commanded by Capt. John James Onslow, arrived and evicted the acting governor and most of the Argentine inhabitants, and reoccupied the islands. From that time forward the British maintained a small garrison of a few sappers (engineer troops) and later twenty-five married marines on the islands. For the next 150 years, Great Britain refused to discuss the matter with Buenos Aires. [2]

On December 15, 1981, Adm. Jorge Anaya, the Commander-in-Chief of the navy and a member of the ruling junta, ordered the Commander of Naval Operations, Vice Adm. Juan José Lombardo, to devise a contingency plan to retake the Malvinas; no date was given for its execution.[3] On December 20 Admiral Lombardo presented the plan to Admiral Anaya. By January 6, 1982, the junta had decided that if the negotiations with Great Britain, scheduled for February 27–28 in New York, failed, it would pursue the military option; the negotiations did go poorly. May 15, 1982, was set as the date for the planning to be finalized.[4]

Meanwhile, an incident occurred on South Georgia Island, which lies 800 miles east of the Malvinas, that caused the Argentine junta to accelerate their plans. In 1979 Constantino Davidoff, an Argentine civilian, signed a contract with Christian Salvesen, a Scottish company, to scrap four abandoned whaling stations on the South Georgias Island. The forty-one-man working party arrived at the island on March 16, 1982, on board the naval auxiliary *Bahía Buen Suceso*, which was manned by merchant mariners. A few days later a member of the British Antarctic Survey team, then on a field trip to the island, reported the flying of the Argentine flag and that shots were heard. Unknown to Davidoff, some Argentine naval personnel were among the workers, and these individuals evidently were accountable only to Admiral Anaya; what role they played in these events is unclear. On the twenty-third, the British Foreign Minister, Lord Carrington, informed the Argentine government that unless it removed the workers, British marines would do so. On this date the Argentine junta decided to defend the working party and preparations began to execute the plan to invade the Malvinas, if necessary.[5]

Argentine naval forces began assembling in late March 1982 for the invasion. An amphibious task force and a supporting task force were created.[6] The Argentine ships sailed singly and in small groups to avoid arousing suspicion. The preparations were, however, discovered by the Argentine press and the British government. As the ships sailed south, the weather deteriorated during the twenty-ninth and some units had difficultly keeping station. Hence, a direct route sailing north of the islands was chosen and the sites and times of the landings were changed.

The landing force arrived off the Malvinas Islands during the evening of April 1. The first commando unit went ashore at 9:15 P.M. It was followed by frogmen (*Buzos Tácticos*) at 11 P.M. and the main 600-man force from the landing ship *Cabo San Antonio* at 6:20 A.M. on the second. The Argentine marines captured Port Stanley (1,000 mi S of Buenos Aires—soon to be renamed Puerto Argentino by the Argentines) after a brief fight. True to their orders, the marines had inflicted no casualties upon the British forces. They in turn suffered one dead, plus two severely wounded and one slightly wounded. At 9:15 A.M. on April 2 the British Governor surrendered.[7]

While these events were transpiring, the Argentine junta decided to also capture South Georgia Island. The tensions concerning the fate of the scrap workers on South Georgia had continued to escalate. The Argentine naval auxiliary *Bahía Paraíso*, which was in the area, was joined by the corvette *Guerrico*. On the morning of April 3, a day after the recapture of the Malvinas, a detachment of Argentine marines captured the normally unpopulated South Georgia Island, from a small detachment of British marines.[8]

OPPOSING SIDES

The geography of the South Atlantic dictated that the conflict should be dominated by naval operations. The Argentine navy had one small aircraft carrier, the *25 de Mayo*, and supporting surface units; sixteen attack aircraft; four submarines; and four marine battalions. Due to size and age, the carrier was marginally capable of operating the ten older attack aircraft under ideal weather conditions. The six modern attack aircraft, the French-built Super Etendard, were in crates as late as January 1982, could not operate from the carrier, and their pilots had on average only forty hours of flight training. The ten older attack aircraft, U.S.-built A-4Q Skyhawks, were 1950s-vintage planes without radar. One old submarine was useless; the second old submarine was limited to 6 knots underwater and a diving depth of 300 feet; one modern German-built Type 209 submarine, the *Salta*, was undergoing a major overhaul trying to correct a noise problem; and the other Type 209, the *San Luis*, was operational with a new crew possessing only a few months of experience working together. Two of the four marine battalions were at full strength (approximately 600 men each) and the other two at about half strength.[9]

The Argentine air force had 180 combat aircraft, the most important being eleven French-built Mirage III interceptors, thirty-four Israeli-built Mirage V Dagger attack aircraft, forty-six U.S.-built A4B and A4C Skyhawk attack aircraft, six British-built Mk. 62 Canberra bombers, and twenty-five Argentine-built IA-58 Pucará ground-support aircraft. The Canberras, Skyhawks, and Pucarás were obsolescent. The Argentine air force had only two tanker aircraft (KC-130s) and many of its attack planes were not fitted with air-to-air refueling equipment; it had never contemplated fighting a powerful enemy 400 miles offshore. Adding to the problems of distance and refueling were the air force's air-to-air missiles, which were decidedly inferior to those possessed by the British.[10]

The Argentine army numbered 130,000 men, of which, 90,000 were conscripts. The number of troops that could be usefully deployed to the Malvinas was limited by the army's logistics capacity, fresh water, shelter, and wood for fuel. The army possessed many helicopters, the only practical means of rapid transportation in the islands. By May 1 approximately 11,000 troops had been transported to the islands.[11]

The British armed forces were significantly stronger than those of Argentina but had their own problems. They were "down-sizing" rapidly; had numerous worldwide commitments, NATO being the most important; and did not possess adequate logistics to support an operation in the South Atlantic, 8,000 miles from the British Isles. In large measure, this last problem was solved by the United States when it granted Great Britain access to Ascension Island airfield, thus shortening the British supply line to 3,340 miles. The United States also supplied critical equipment and munitions, such as the top-of-the-line Sidewinder-L air-to-air missiles.[12]

The British navy was responsible for getting an expeditionary force to the South Atlantic and keeping it there. It had two VSTOL (vertical or short takeoff and landing) carriers, the *Invincible* and the *Hermes*. The navy possessed twenty Sea Harrier attack aircraft (to which must be added those of the air force). Supporting the two carriers were some one hundred warships including five nuclear submarines.[13]

The British army possessed some 176,000 men, of whom about 10,000 men were sent to the South Atlantic. Those sent included elite units such as the 40th, 42nd, and 45th Marine

Commandos; the 2nd and 3rd Battalions of the Parachute Regiment; the Special Air Service (SAS); the Special Boat Service (SBS); the 5th Brigade's Welsh Guards and Scots Guards; and the Gurkha mercenaries from Nepal. The army possessed about 120 helicopters.[14]

The British air force possessed some 700 aircraft. Those of greatest utility for a campaign in the South Atlantic were forty-eight Harrier attack aircraft, sixteen Victor K-2 tankers, eleven VC Mk. 1 transports, forty-five C-130H transports, and twenty-eight Nimrod Mk. 2 patrol aircraft. Obviously, not all could be committed to the Malvinas operations.[15]

OPENING STRATEGY

Until April 2, all had gone according to plan for the Argentine junta. They had captured both the Malvinas and South Georgia with a minimal loss of life to themselves, and what they believed to be politically more important, no loss of life to the British. Here, the military clock was supposed to have stopped running.[16] Two weeks passed before the junta could agree that the British would fight, and, as a consequence, only a "jury-rigged" strategy could hastily be formulated. The islands would be defended principally by air power flying from the mainland. British strategy was to immediately recapture the islands by amphibious assault. Nuclear submarines were to drive the Argentine fleet from the seas and the British carriers were to provide local air superiority.[17]

PREPARING TO FIGHT

The Argentine island defenders began arriving the day the Malvinas had been captured. Mistakenly, the junta initially believed that the troops were needed only as a garrison, so political rather than military considerations determined their selection. Argentine merchantships and naval auxiliaries began carrying war materials to the islands. Nonetheless, practically all troops were flown into the islands as were many high-value cargoes because of the threat British nuclear submarines posed to shipping. The vanguard of the British task force sailed from Portsmouth, England, on April 5. On the twelfth the British declared a 200-mile Total Exclusion Zone around the Malvinas.

THE BRITISH RETAKE SOUTH GEORGIA

As the British task force sailed south, the Argentine command appreciated the exposed position of their men on South Georgia. It was aware that militarily the islands could not be defended since they were too far from the mainland (1,200 miles). And yet, politically neither could they be abandoned. Some Argentine decision-makers still believed that South Georgia might be an important bargaining chip in a political settlement. The decision was made that if the islands were attacked, those on them were to offer only a token defense. In the short term, those on the islands required some logistical support. The old submarine *Santa Fé* was ordered to transport necessary personnel and equipment to the islands. Just before midnight on the twenty-fourth, the *Santa Fé* surfaced in Cumberland Bay off Grytviken, the "capital" of South Georgia. During the early morning hours of April 25, the passengers and supplies were offloaded. The *Santa Fé* then departed Grytviken looking for a favorable place to submerge when she was successfully attacked by two British helicopters. The *Santa Fé*, in sinking condition, returned to Grytviken where she was abandoned. The same day, 120 British marines from the 42nd Commando landed and captured the small Argentine garrison.[18]

THE ARGENTINE CARRIER TRIES TO LAUNCH A STRIKE

As the threat of war increased, the Argentine surface fleet sailed from Puerto Belgrano on April 27 and took up position to counter any British move against the islands. The surface fleet was designated Task Force 79 and was commanded by Rear Adm. Gualter Allara. After some reshuffling, the fleet was divided into three task groups by May 1. Northwest of the Malvinas were TG 79.1 and TG 79.2, the first being made up of the carrier *25 de Mayo* and the Type 42 destroyer *Santísima Trinidad*. The old U.S.-built destroyer *Py*, the Type 42 *Hercules*, and three French-built A-69 corvettes composed TG 79.2. Southwest of the islands was TG 79.3, made up of the cruiser *General Belgrano* and the old U.S.-built destroyers *Bouchard* and *Piedrabuena*. All three task groups were supported by an oiler.

At 4:46 A.M. on May 1, the Argentine command in the Malvinas radioed Admiral Allara that the British had attacked the islands. TG 79.1 and TG 79.2 steamed east-southeast, while S2E Tracker aircraft flew from the *25 de Mayo* searching for the British. Finally at 3:30 P.M. a Tracker radioed, "One large, six medium sized warships bearing 031, Puerto Argentino [Port Stanley] 120 miles"; this placed the British force at 49°34' south latitude and 57°10' west longitude, some 250 to 300 miles from the Argentine carrier. Throughout May 1, Admiral Allara steamed toward the enemy. At 10:13 P.M. Admiral Allara received a message erroneously

Figure 25. The Malvinas (Falkland) Islands (1982). Four A-4Q Skyhawks line the flight deck of the *25 de Mayo* on May 1, 1982, as the Argentine task force tries to close the British. The aircraft are fitted with fuel drop tanks. Four additional A-4s are below in the hangar deck. Barely visible on the fantail is an AI-03 Alouette III helicopter, waiting to serve as a plane guard. *Courtesy Argentine Navy*

Figure 26. The Malvinas (Falkland) Islands (1982). The Argentine cruiser *General Belgrano* shortly after having been torpedoed by the British nuclear submarine *Conqueror* on May 2, 1982. Of the crew members, 321 died and 819 survived. Amazingly, 95 percent of those who abandoned the cruiser into the inhospitable sea lived. When power failed, the gun crew of "B" turret manually swung it to starboard to be sure they could make it function without electricity. *Courtesy Martín E. Sgut, Argentina.*

stating that an amphibious assault was taking place southeast of Port Stanley. The Admiral detached the three A-69 corvettes from the main group. Their assignment was to reach the British force immediately after the air strike and attack. During the night six A-4Q Skyhawks were armed with six 500-pound bombs each. The Admiral wanted to launch his attack some 240 miles from the British force; he wished to take advantage of the fact that the Skyhawk had a longer range than that of the Harrier. During the night, the carrier closed to within 200 miles of the enemy. At dawn there was no wind, almost unheard of in these latitudes! In order to catapult the bomb-laden Skyhawks from the *25 de Mayo*, a 35-knot wind along the flight deck was needed. The carrier could only steam at 20 knots. If launched under these conditions the Skyhawks would have less than a 100-mile radius. The unusually light wind conditions were forecast to continue throughout the day.

At about 2 A.M. on May 2, Admiral Allara, also knowing that he had been located by the British, temporarily gave up the idea of attacking and turned north-northeast, waiting for the wind to improve. Although the decision to withdraw the fleet was taken later, this was the last chance that Task Force 79 had to attack the British fleet.

THE TORPEDOING OF THE *GENERAL BELGRANO*

Just before 4 P.M. on May 2, two torpedoes slammed into the port side of the light cruiser *General Belgrano* in rapid succession. The cruiser and two destroyers were patrolling between Isla de los Estados and Burwood Bank off the tip of the continent. The ship raised up in the water and settled with a shudder. The explosion sent a heat wave through the ship, which accounted for most of the casualties, and tore the emergency generators from their foundations. When torpedoed, the cruiser was sailing west toward South America at 10 knots in moderate seas. She was some 150 miles from Isla de los Estados, some 35 miles outside the British-declared exclusion zone, and approximately 250 miles southwest of British surface forces operating against the Malvinas Islands.[19] The cruiser had been torpedoed by the British nuclear-powered submarine *Conqueror* which had been stalking the Argentine warship for hours. The cruiser fell into darkness. The crew, some 300 of whom were conscripts, worked their way up to the main deck, maintaining good discipline. The crew abandoned the *General Belgrano* forty-five minutes after the attack, and it sank at approximately 5 P.M.[20]

At about 9 P.M. on May 2, the naval command ordered Admiral Allara to withdraw to protected waters, deciding that it was too risky to expose the carrier. Argentine relations with Chile had been particularly strained for almost a decade. The navy viewed the *25 de Mayo* as its primary advantage over the Chilean navy. Also, the navy feared that the *25 de Mayo* might be led into a submarine trap; the Argentine navy had few modern ASW ships and aircraft and considered its ability to deal with a nuclear submarine very marginal. So, the carrier was retired to port for the duration of the conflict and the Skyhawks sent south to operate from the airfield at Naval Air Station Río Grande (380 mi WSW of Puerto Argentino).[21]

DEFENDING PORT STANLEY AGAINST AIR ATTACKS

The Argentine navy chose not to challenge the British nuclear submarine blockade, thereby making the Port Stanley airfield the only practical avenue to supply the islands from the mainland. The air defenses of the airport were the best the Argentine armed forces had to offer: The air force contributed the radar, the army the AA guns and Roland missiles, and the navy the means of communication and the trained plotting and direction personnel.[22]

On May 1 a lone British Vulcan bomber flying from Ascension Island dropped twenty-one 1,000-pound bombs on the Port Stanley airfield which caused only modest damage. Later that day Harriers flying from the *Hermes* attacked the airfields at Port Stanley and Goose Green. Following these attacks, the British altered their air tactics against the Port Stanley airfield from close-in bombing to bomb lobbing. This change was probably due to the effectiveness of the Argentine antiaircraft fire.[23]

Later on the first, the Argentine air force counterattacked the British warships off Port Stanley with virtually every attack plane in its inventory. It lost two Mirage interceptors, one Dagger attack aircraft, one Pucará ground-support plane, and a Canberra bomber, and succeeded in only slightly damaging two warships. The air force learned that it was at a significant disadvantage against British Harriers due to its short time over the combat zone and its inferior air-to-air missiles, but that British ships' defenses were not as formidable as believed. As a consequence, the Argentine air force abandoned attacking the Harriers and adopted diversionary tactics attempting to decoy them away from Argentine attack aircraft.[24]

THE SAN LUIS ATTACKS

Some time in early April as the diplomatic situation deteriorated, the submarine *San Luis* took up station in a free-fire zone (any target may be assumed to be British) north of the Malvinas Islands inside the British Exclusion Zone. While in transit to the patrol area, the submarine commander discovered that his main fire-control computer was inoperative. This greatly limited the potential of the boat. Now, the SST-4 wire-guided torpedo, the principal torpedo carried, could only be fired and manually guided to the target, one at a time. This greatly reduced the strike capability and increased the boat's exposure to counterattack.

The *San Luis* was the first Argentine unit to attempt to strike back at the British following their May 1 air raids against the Port Stanley airport. At about 8 A.M. that day, the boat made contact with an enemy force northeast of the Malvinas. The enemy could not be observed through the periscope due to poor visibility. The classification of the targets was incomplete, but they were medium-sized warships. The *San Luis* closed to within 10,000 yards and fired one SST-4. After about three minutes, the wire guiding the SST-4 broke and the submarine lost control of the torpedo. The *San Luis* was then subjected to a twenty-hour attack, principally carried out by ASW helicopters. The submarine was finally able to make good her escape without receiving any damage.[25]

THE SINKING OF THE *SHEFFIELD*

On April 4 an Argentine Neptune patrol aircraft detected a target believed to be a Type 42 destroyer at about 100 miles south of Port Stanley and 380 miles east of the Rio Grande Naval Air Base. Two Super Etendard aircraft took off at 9:45 A.M. They successfully refueled from an Air Force KC-130 some 250 miles from the target. They approached at high speed, flying very low, about 50 feet above the water. The Neptune identified two medium-size warships and one large one some 115 miles from the Malvinas. Just after 11 A.M., the pilots fired their missiles at approximately 27 miles' distance. One slammed into the side of the Type 42 destroyer *Sheffield*. Shortly after 3 P.M., the *Sheffield* was abandoned. Twenty British sailors were killed and many injured. The *Sheffield* foundered while under tow six days later and sank. Apparently, the carrier *Hermes*, a far "juicier" target, was within 30 miles of the *Sheffield's* position when she was hit.

THE LOSS OF BORBON

Shortly after 4 A.M. on May 15, the first clear night in many, forty-eight British commandos attacked the Borbon airstrip located on the westerly main island, some 40 miles northwest of Port Stanley. First, the field was illuminated by flares, and then the aircraft were destroyed by commandos armed with phosphorous charges. The site was turned into an inferno when the rocket pods on the Pucarás exploded. Following the withdrawal of the commandos, the field was subjected to attack from the air. The Argentines lost four T-34 naval trainers as well as six Air Force Pucarás and one *Prefectura* (Coast Guard) Skyvan.[26]

THE LOSS OF THE NEPTUNES

Operationally, the losses on Borbon Island paled by comparison next to that of the two P-2 Neptune patrol aircraft. On May 15, the last Neptunes died from wear and tear. Now the long range targeting information for the Super Etendards would have to be provided by the much less reliable projections from the radar at Port Stanley.[27]

THE LANDING AT SAN CARLOS

By mid-May the British controlled the seas and air around the Malvinas. At 4 A.M. on May 20, some 4,500 British soldiers landed at four beaches near San Carlos (45 mi WNW of Puerto Argentino). The forty-three Argentine defenders offered a brief resistance and then fled. The only British losses were two helicopters and their crews.[28]

THE ARGENTINE AIR ATTACKS BETWEEN MAY 21 AND 25

Beginning early on the twenty-first, Argentine air power, principally flying from the mainland, attempted to drive the British back into the sea. The frigates *Ardent* and *Antelope* were sunk on the twenty-first and twenty-third and six other ships damaged; however, the success of the Argentine attacks was significantly reduced because of a bomb-fusing problem. In spite of these attacks, the British secured a ten-square-mile area by the end of the twenty-first and immediately began sending out raiding parties.[29]

On May 25 (Argentina's National Day), the Argentine air force renewed its efforts. Skyhawks overwhelmed the defenses of the destroyer *Coventry* and it capsized. These "courageous and persistent" attacks cost the Argentine air force 9 Daggers, 7 Skyhawks, and 2 Pucarás and the navy 3 Skyhawks.[30]

THE SINKING OF THE *ATLANTIC CONVEYOR*

Following the operational loss of the Neptune aircraft, Argentine long-range tactical data was provided by the Westinghouse radar located at Port Stanley. Once a Harrier appeared on the radar screen, the Argentine radar operators would project its course beyond the range of the radar in an attempt to fix the location of the British carriers. The British had anticipated this development and had instructed the Harrier pilots to descend below Port Stanley's radar horizon while within 50 miles of the carriers. However, Argentine persistence was rewarded.

On May 25, the Port Stanley radar fixed the general location of the British fleet, approximately 100 miles east-northeast of the port and some 500 miles from the Super Etendard base at Rio Grande. Two Super Etendards took off at 2:28 P.M. and flew north-northwest and refueled about 185 miles out to sea off Puerto Deseado. They then turned due east until they were well beyond the Malvinas and then they turned south. They continued until one picked up a radar emission on its receiving equipment. The attack aircraft turned toward the emissions and descended to the target-approach altitude of 50 feet. Closing at a speed of 630 mph, the pilots switched on their radar, then eased the aircraft into a climb to begin a target search. Almost immediately, a cluster of ships appeared on their radar screens. Both aircraft launched their Exocets and returned to base after having again refueled in the same general location as they had on their way out. The missiles hit the merchantship *Atlantic Conveyor*, which was packed with supplies, including ten helicopters and many tents. The ship was abandoned and twelve lives were lost.[31]

THE ATTACK AGAINST THE *INVINCIBLE*

On May 30, the radar at Port Stanley placed the general location of the British fleet some 100 miles southeast of Port Stanley. In order to reach the target and approach from the east, a distance of more than 500 miles from the Rio Grande naval air base, the aircraft would have to refuel twice on the way out and once on the return in order to sweep around the radar coverage of the British picket ships. During the final planning stages, the Argentine air force requested that four A-4C Skyhawks be permitted to accompany the Super Etendards.

The attack force was composed of four air force A-4C Skyhawks and two naval Super Etendards, one of which was armed with the last air-to-surface Exocet missile. The second Super Etendard was navigational insurance in case the aircraft armed with the missile experienced problems. The first refueling took place southeast of Isla de los Estados and the second south of Soledad Island. When about 300 miles southwest of the position provided by the radar operators on the Malvinas, the aircraft swept northeast looking for targets. At 2:20 P.M. a radar emission was picked up and the aircraft turned toward the source. Ten minutes later the aircraft, armed with the Exocet, launched the missile. The Skyhawks followed the missile's exhaust. Two of the A-4Cs were shot down, possibly by Sea Dart missiles, as they approached. The others pressed home the attack, each carrying two 500-pound bombs. Both air force pilots observed a ship shrouded in black smoke, which they believed to be the *Invincible*. In fact, the attack had been launched against the destroyer *Exeter* and the frigate *Avenger*. Both ships escaped damage.[32]

THE BATTLE FOR DARWIN AND GOOSE GREEN

On May 27 British ground forces broke out of San Carlos. The 45th Royal Marine Commando and the 3rd Paratroop Battalion began the arduous sixty-mile march westward toward Port Stanley while 650 men of the 2nd Paratroop Battalion moved south against Darwin (43 mi WSW of Puerto Argentino) and Goose Green. Here the 642 men principally from the Argentine 12th Regiment had created two defensive lines across the narrow Darwin Isthmus. On May 28 the British attacked and defeated the Argentine forces during a nine-hour battle. The British lost 17 killed (including Col. Herbert Jones) and 31 wounded. The Argentines lost about 50 killed, 121 wounded, and some 600 prisoners (which included support personnel from the Air Force).[33]

THE GROUND ASSAULT ON PORT STANLEY

About 8,400 Argentine troops defended Port Stanley. They were supported by thirty 105mm guns and four 150mm guns, twelve armored cars, and antiaircraft guns. The Argentines did not fortify the rough terrain to the west of Port Stanley and chose to abandon the Fitzroy settlement and Mount Kent because of the shortage of helicopters. The troops pulled from Fitzroy were sent to reinforce Darwin and Goose Green. So the advancing British troops had only the weather and terrain with which to contend. On May 31 British artillery was airlifted to Mount Kent, which overlooked Port Stanley.

In order to expedite the advance on Port Stanley, some British troops were carried by sea because of the shortage of helicopters caused by the loss of the *Atlantic Conveyor*. On June 8, sixteen Argentine air force Skyhawk and Mirage aircraft caught the landing ships *Sir Galahad* and *Sir Tristram* off-loading the two last companies of the "Welsh Guards" at Bluff Cove, 14 miles northwest of Port Stanley. Sixty-three British died and 146 were wounded. The Argentine air force lost three Skyhawks.[34]

In spite of these losses, the British advance continued. Late on the eleventh, the British attacked Port Stanley's defense perimeter. British warships, Harriers, and some forty-five artillery pieces bombarded Argentine positions. The British 3rd Paratroop Battalion captured the hill Two Sisters and the 42nd Commandos took Mount Harriet.

At 3 A.M. on June 12, a land-based Exocet slammed into the British destroyer *Glamorgan* while she was retiring from in front of Port Stanley where she had carried out a bombardment. The missile had been removed from the destroyer *Seguí* and a jury-rigged firing system devised. This was only a momentary setback for the British.[35]

During June 12, the British consolidated their positions and the Argentine marines, which held Tumbledown Mountain, picked up some added strength from army troops who were retreating. Once again the Argentine position came under heavy bombardment. After dark on the thirteenth, the Scots Guards captured Tumbledown Mountain following a hard fight with Argentine marines, and the Gurkhas took Mount Williams. With the exception of the marines, who had regrouped and were preparing a counterattack, the Argentine troops were demoralized and fled back to Port Stanley. Brig. Gen. Marío Menendez surrendered at 9:10 P.M. on June 14, and the fight for the Malvinas ended.[36]

OBSERVATIONS

The Argentine military junta became swept along by a minor political crisis in South Georgia and chose to execute a contingency plan which had been formulated upon events that were yet to occur. These included the down-sizing of the British military. Although the junta had some ability to speed Argentine preparations to recapture the islands, it could only negatively influence British preparations by causing them to reverse their scheduled down-sizing. The junta chose a military solution, namely recapturing the islands, blindly believing that the problem would be solved politically. The root of this naivety was the junta's lack of understanding of both Great Britain and the United States.

If fighting Great Britain aided by the United States were not enough, Argentina failed to neutralize Chile as a potential combatant, so some of Argentina's better air, ground, and sea units had to be husbanded to meet this contingency.

The distances and weather within the theater of operations made a "come as you are" long-distance air defense strategy almost impossible to win. Of the forty-four days of combat (May 1 to June 14), weather precluded operations from the mainland on seventeen days. And on many of the remaining days, Argentine air power attacked with poor or no intelligence. As a consequence, Argentina lost over 120 aircraft and helicopters—89 belonging to the air force, 16 to the navy, and 15 to the army. This included those destroyed on the ground and the ones that fell into British hands after the Argentine capitulation. Also, four Mirage and some ten Skyhawks were so severely damaged that they were written off, and at least one Puma and one Pucará were lost through accidents in Argentina. During the seventy-five days of operations beginning when the Argentines seized the islands, 649 Argentines died as well as 255 British.[37]

Throughout the fighting, the Argentine armed forces rarely fought together. In truth, the Argentine lack of "jointness" was the rule among world militaries and not the exception. "Jointness" was especially difficult for the Argentina armed forces, for they had found themselves on opposite sides in the occasional intraclass feuds that arose following World War II (see chapter 16). Therefore, each Argentine armed service fought its own war against a more unified British military machine.[38]

For the Argentines, some of the most important lessons were the lack of cooperation among the armed forces, inadequate tactical intelligence, inadequate mobility for troops, inadequate logistics, inferior maintenance, and inferior training. For the British, the lessons were the inability to prevent Argentine air power from saturating its air defenses and flying under its radar cover; the inability of its aircraft to penetrate the modern antiaircraft gun defenses around Port Stanley airfield; and the inability of its ASW-oriented navy to find and destroy a Type 209 submarine. Also, the British suffered from the fact that their ships were too small to carry all the modern weapons needed to detect and fight threats from above, upon, and below the water at the same time. This was a consequence of financial constraints at the time when the ships were built.

CHAPTER 34

CHILE AND THE OVERTHROW OF ALLENDE, 1973

> Mission accomplished, the *Moneda* taken, president found dead.
> —Brig. Gen. Javier Palacios, September 11, 1973

THE SPARK

Adm. José Merino believed that the only solution to Chile's political, social, and economic problems was military intervention. The inability of President Allende to dissuade him led to the Admiral setting a coup in motion on September 9, 1973.[1]

BACKGROUND

Shortly before the presidential election on September 4, 1970, in which Salvador Allende, representing a coalition of leftist parties known as the Popular Unity *(Unidad Popular*—UP), won a 36-percent plurality, Gen. René Schneider, Commander-in-Chief of the Chilean army, declared, "The Army is the guarantee that the next election will be legal and normal and that whoever is elected by the people will assume power in Chile."[2] This reaffirmed that the Chilean armed services, which had not attempted a coup since 1931, would refrain from doing so.

Schneider's declaration did not please the Nixon administration in Washington, D.C. Allende was an old nemesis of the United States. The Eisenhower administration in 1958 and the Kennedy administration in 1964 had covertly worked to prevent Allende's election as president.[3]

When Allende received the plurality in the 1970 election, the United States clandestinely worked to dissuade the Chilean Congress from selecting him as president. The Chilean Constitution provided that if no candidate received a majority, then the Congress must choose from between the top two candidates. The United States began a propaganda campaign to influence the legislators against Allende's selection, and attempted to prod General Schneider into executing a coup should Allende be selected. When Schneider refused to cooperate, the United States began conspiring with other Chilean military officers. Nonetheless, as Commander-in-Chief of the army, Schneider's presence presented a stumbling block to any coup attempt. On October 22, the CIA gave arms to the conspirators. General Schneider was murdered during what probably was a poorly executed kidnapping attempt.[4]

Notwithstanding the covert actions of the United States, Allende was confirmed by the Congress on October 24 and inaugurated on November 3. Many Chilean professionals and business people, in part influenced by American propaganda, had feared the election of Allende because of his ultraleft rhetoric. They and others were pleasantly surprised by the moderation and generosity he demonstrated during his first year in office. Business, which had taken a sharp downturn in anticipation of his election, significantly rebounded. The new Allende administration immediately increased the amount of money in circulation, causing an artificial abundance which would eventually lead to high inflation. Serendipitously, copper, Chile's chief export, began selling at record high prices. In July, Allende, with the unanimous approval of Congress, expropriated American-owned mines throughout the nation. Also, the violence perpetrated primarily by the ultraleft, which had plagued Chile since the mid-1960s, significantly declined.

Attempting to improve his image within the military, Allende went out of his way to court those in uniform. Rarely did he miss attending a significant military ceremony or social event. He sponsored a bill to increase military salaries by almost 49 percent and to authorize increases in the size of the air force and navy.[5] Trying to find favor with the navy, Allende purchased a Swedish cruiser that was totally unsuited to the needs of that service.

From the beginning, Allende's actions seemed to confirm U.S. suspicions that he was trying to convert Chile into a Marxist state from within. Allende pardoned over forty members of the Movement of the Revolutionary Left (*Movimiento Izquierda Revolucionaria*—MIR) who had been imprisoned for various acts of violence, including bank robbery, kidnapping, and murder. Peasants led by the radical left, in particular the pro-Castro MIR, illegally seized 1,458 farms in the south during Allende's first year in power.[6]

At the international level, Allende quickly recognized Castro's Cuba. On March 25, 1971, North Vietnam, a country with which the United States was fighting an undeclared war, opened a commercial mission in Chile. In November of that year Fidel Castro, America's nemesis within the hemisphere, paid a state visit to Chile. Initially scheduled for ten days, Castro stayed for three and a half weeks. On December 27, a Soviet delegation, which included a member of the Politburo, arrived in Santiago to celebrate the fiftieth anniversary of the Chilean Communist Party. And a year later, the Soviet Union extended a $30 million credit to Chile.[7]

As a consequence of Allende's actions, the United States began working harder for the downfall of his administration. The United States gave money to political rivals and covertly manipulated the Chilean press. The United States prevented loans to Chile from the U.S. Export-Import Bank, the Inter-American Development Bank, and the World Bank. The Nixon administration also discouraged American private businesses from investing in Chile. The detrimental consequences of these actions upon the Chilean economy were significant.[8]

While undermining the Chilean economy, the United States attempted to court the Chilean officer corps through its military assistance program. U.S. military aid to Chile grew from $800,000 in fiscal year 1970 to $12.3 million by 1972. Allende, not wanting to alienate the Chilean military, permitted the training to take place.[9]

In addition to the growing problems with the United States, the economic euphoria of Allende's first year in office was followed by a rapid economic decline. Many factors contributed to the downward slide. The radical left within Allende's coalition organized extralegal seizures of agricultural lands and industrial plants. Only a few large farms were free from MIR-supported squatters. These seizures resulted in decreased productivity and alienated the middle class within the cities which had broadly supported Allende. Allende's popularity in part was purchased with lavish expenditures during the first year in office which completely drained the nation's foreign reserves. The United States' efforts to economically isolate the Allende administration were increasingly effective. By the end of 1971, the Allende administration had nationalized some 200 firms, including most of the banks.[10]

On December 1, 1971, some 5,000 women, mainly from the middle and upper classes, protested food shortages in Santiago in what became known as "the March of the Empty Pots" (*La Marcha de las Ollas Vacías*). The women were attacked by members of the MIR and dispersed by tear gas. This was followed by the first major rioting against the Allende government. Gen. Augusto Pinochet Ugarte,[11] the military commander of the province of Santiago, took immediate action to restore order. The next day Allende declared a state of emergency and within a week, the government had to assume control of all food distribution.[12]

As a consequence of the 1970 Congressional elections, three parties each had won roughly one-third of the seats—Allende's Popular Unity coalition, the moderate Christian Democrats (*Partido Democrata Cristiano*), and the Conservative National Party (*Partido Nacional*). During Allende's first year in office, the Popular Unity coalition had been able to work with the Christian Democrats. That now ended. On September 9, 1971, Allende announced that the UP coalition would sponsor a plebiscite for a new "workers constitution" which would be unicameral. Within two weeks the Christian Democrats withdrew their support for the Allende government. Also, Congress refused to change the tax structure to increase the burden on the more productive elements within society.[13]

On October 10, 1972, the Allende administration's dispute with small independent truckers, who organized themselves into the Confederation of Truck Owners (*Confederación de Sindicatos de Dueños de Camiones de Chile*), grew into a nationwide strike. Eventually, the strike cut off the flow of food from the countryside into the cities. Clandestinely, the CIA indirectly provided money to the truckers. Soon, professionals and shopkeepers who opposed the government's price controls joined the truckers in the strike. The work stoppage dragged on for twenty-six days and the government had to place twenty-one of twenty-five provinces under martial law.[14]

In addition to supporting the truckers, the CIA provided money and training for members of the Fatherland and Liberty Movement *(Movimiento Patria y Libertad)*. It was a reactionary right-wing group that created disorder and carried out acts of violence against the Allende government. The movement called for Allende's overthrow.[15]

By October 1972 the confidence of the middle and upper classes in Allende's administration had deteriorated so much that he had to ask the heads of the military services to serve within a restructured cabinet in order to restore confidence. Thus, Allende himself introduced the military back into politics after an absence of almost fifty years. Gen. Carlos Prats Gonzales, Commander-in-Chief of the army, became Minister of the Interior on November 2. In the cases of the air force and navy, their commanders-in-chief, demonstrating significant independence, sent subordinates to fill the cabinet positions assigned to them. Air force Gen. Claudio Sepúlveda

Donoso became the Minister of Mines and Rear Adm. Ismael Huerta became Minister of Public Works.[16]

The immediate crisis of the food shortage caused by the truckers' strike was solved by appointing air force Gen. Alberto Bachelet Martínez to head the newly established, cabinet-level national Secretariat of Distribution (*Junta de Abastecimientos y Precios*—JAP). The selection of a military officer meant that the distribution of food would not be controlled by politicians. Also, the Congress passed an arms control law that gave the military the right to search public and private property for arms. This was an attempt to reduce the threat from the extremists, particularly the MIR.[17]

The March 4, 1973, midterm congressional elections offered those opposed to Allende an opportunity to derail his leftist agenda. Inflation was triple digit, food was scarce, and productivity was down. Also, historically the party of the President had never improved its numbers within Congress during midterm elections. The moderate Christian Democrats and the Conservative National Party formed the Democratic Confederation in opposition to Popular Unity coalition.

In contradiction to historical trends, the Popular Unity coalition won 43 percent of the vote in the congressional elections; this was an increase of 8 percent over its 1970 congressional returns. Impeaching Allende, which had been openly talked of by some in the opposition, was now impossible because to do so required a two-thirds majority; the results of the 1973 election eliminated this possibility. However, the election gave the armed forces an opportunity to distance itself from the Allende administration and the military men resigned from the cabinet on March 27.[18]

Following the congressional elections, elements within the Popular Unity coalition more aggressively pursued their radical left agenda. In April the MIR seized government factories; however, the *carabineros* (national police) forcefully evicted them. Then, Allende announced that he wanted to change the national education system. Many interpreted this, probably accurately, as an attempt to institutionalize the teaching of Marx and other socialists. Many, including the Roman Catholic Church and the military, viewed this as a violation of the Statute of Guarantees (*Estatuto de Garantías*)—an amendment to the Constitution. In late April, when over 100,000 high school students marched in protest of the proposed educational changes, they were attacked by pro-Allende supporters and a destructive riot ensued. Allende was forced to postpone his educational proposals.[19]

In mid-April the workers at the El Teniente copper mine, the largest in the world, went on strike over wages. This soon escalated into a measure of strength between the Popular Unity coalition and the Democratic Confederation. Street fights broke out in cities located near the mine. The provinces of Santiago and O'Higgins were placed under states of emergency law. On June 20 thousands of professionals joined the strike. The following day, street fights broke out in Santiago between pro- and anti-Allende followers. As a show of support for the administration, Allende authorized government-controlled labor, the Only Center for Workers (*Central Unica de Trabajadores*—CUT) to stage a twenty-four-hour walkout, climaxed by a pro-Allende march in Santiago. This work stoppage shut down social services to the capital. The anti-Allende forces raised the stakes by organizing a protest by 30,000 high school students and a 500-woman (wives of striking miners), 50-mile march from Rancagua to Santiago. The miners' strike dragged on until July 1 and cost the nation about $1 million a day. Evidence suggests that the CIA may have clandestinely subsidized the copper strikers.[20]

A bizarre incident occurred on June 27. A middle-aged housewife stuck out her tongue at General Prats' chauffeur-driven car in downtown Santiago. The General fired his revolver in the direction of the woman, hitting his car door. The Allende administration defended the actions of the General (alleging another Schneider-style kidnapping) while the opposition called for the General's resignation.[21]

On June 28 the officers of the 2nd Armored Regiment, whose barrack was in Santiago, convinced their commanding officer, Col. Roberto Souper, that the mere appearance of their tanks on the streets of the capital would cause the collapse of the Allende government. A secondary objective became freeing one of the regiment's officers who had been charged with conspiracy and was being held in the Defense Ministry. The tanks reached the *Moneda* and the Ministry of Defense without opposition. A few shots into the door of the ministry secured the officer's release. Soon afterward, however, snipers loyal to Allende began appearing on the rooftops surrounding the *Moneda* and began firing upon the tanks. Also, Allende ordered loyal workers to occupy their factories where they received weapons from members of the radical left. General Prats rushed to the *Moneda* and convinced the rebellious tankers to return to their barracks. The "tanquetazo" rebellion ended.[22]

The senior military officers became concerned that they might not be able to regain control over another spontaneous rebellion in the future. Thus, the armed services created the Committee of Fifteen—five flag officers each from the army, the navy, and the air force. The committee recommended that the military present twenty-nine demands to Allende. Adm. Raúl Montero, the Commander-in-Chief of the navy, and General César Ruiz, the Commander-in-Chief of the air force, carried the demands to the *Moneda* only to find that General Prats had already given and discussed a preliminary draft of the demands with the President. Montero and Ruiz felt compelled to return without confronting Allende.

As a consequence, Adm. José Toribio Merino,[23] the second most senior naval officer, and Adm. Sergio Huidoboro, Commandant of the marine corps, demanded Montero's resignation. Allende called Montero, Merino, and Huidoboro to his residence. The President lectured Merino and Huidoboro that they had no authority to demand Montero's resignation. The meeting ended in discord and Montero remained the Commander-in-Chief of the navy.[24]

Meanwhile, the domestic situation continued to deteriorate. A second truckers' strike began on July 26 when the Allende administration failed to live up to the agreement made at the end the first strike. The following day, Allende's naval aide, Capt. Arturo Araya Peters, was assassinated—both the left and the right accused each other. The Catholic University of Chile published a report claiming significant fraud by the Popular Unity coalition in the last congressional elections. Allende unsuccessfully attempted to reopen a dialogue with the Christian Democrat Party which had ruptured during the 1972 congressional elections.[25]

By early August Chile was dividing into two armed camps. Acts of violence were becoming increasingly common. On August 9 Allende informed the commanders-in-chief of the armed forces that they had to return to the cabinet. The Committee of Fifteen counseled the three chiefs that they should condition their return upon the President's acceptance of the twenty-nine points in the memorandum. Allende agreed. Except for Prats, the commanders-in-chief did not readily return to the cabinet. Montero procrastinated and sought consultation within the navy; Ruiz refused. Finally they agreed. Prats became Minister of Defense (traditionally held by a civilian); Montero became Minister of Finance; and Ruiz became Minister of Public Works.[26]

However, on August 17 Ruiz resigned from the cabinet after discovering that civilian subordinates in the Ministry of Public Works were undermining his efforts to end the truckers' strike. Allende took Ruiz' resignation from the cabinet to include resigning as Commander-in-Chief of the air force as well and replaced him in that position with the second most senior air force officer, Gen. Gustavo Leigh. Ruiz threatened not to obey; he sought and received support from fellow air force officers; however, Prats threatened to use the army against the air force. Prats' unwillingness to support Ruiz' move to retain his position as Commander-in-Chief of the air force further undermined Prats' popularity among his military colleagues.[27]

Leigh reluctantly accepted the appointment as Commander-in-Chief of the air force but refused to join the cabinet. Instead, he sent Gen. Humberto Magliochetti to become the Minister of Public Works. Allende, desperately trying to keep the military within the cabinet, accepted this circumstance.[28]

On August 21, in an unprecedented event, some 300 wives of military officers went to Prats' house and presented the General with a letter demanding an explanation of his actions in support of the Popular Unity coalition. Furious, Prats ordered the *Carabineros* to disperse the women; they used tear gas to do so. Realizing that he had lost the support of the officer corps, Prats resigned. With Prats' resignation as Commander-in-Chief of the army, Allende lost his only control over the military.[29]

Allende was now faced with yet another crisis, finding a replacement for Prats. On August 23 the President appointed Gen. Augusto Pinochet as Commander-in-Chief of the army. The next day, Admiral Montero resigned from the cabinet but agreed to remain as the head of the navy; once again, an admiral (Daniel Arellano) other than the commander-in-chief became the Minister of Finance. However, like Prats, Montero could not repair his lagging support within this armed service and resigned as Commander-in-Chief of the navy under pressure from his fellow admirals.[30]

Strikes, demonstrations, and violence were becoming daily events; the nation appeared on the brink of anarchy. In the meantime, the navy had been conducting an investigation of illegal leftist activities. It concluded that Senator Carlos Altamirano, from Allende's own Socialist Party, was a leader of the ultraleft and demanded that he be arrested and turned over to the navy on charges of conspiracy. Allende refused. On September 7 President Allende summoned Merino to the *Moneda* and told the Admiral to drop the charges against the senator or Allende would not elevate Merino to be the next Commander-in-Chief of the navy. The two men reached no accord during a six-hour meeting.[31] The stage was set for a coup.

OPPOSING FORCES

The Chilean armed forces totaled some 75,000 men and were the best in Latin America. The army possessed five divisions and enough miscellaneous components to put together a sixth. The navy had a small but highly trained fleet with a very modest amphibious capacity. The air force possessed 41 combat aircraft, 90 transports, and 30 helicopters.[32]

The most radical elements of the Popular Unity coalition, the Castroite Movement of the Revolutionary Left (*Movimiento de Izquierda Revolucionario*—MIR) and Allende's own Socialist Party (*Partido Socialista*), believed violence was inevitable and had been preparing to fight. The orthodox Communist Party, loyal to Moscow, counseled against becoming too extreme. They, however, were a minority within the leftist coalition and went unheeded.[33]

Following the reestablishing of diplomatic relations with Cuba by Allende, Cuba opened a large embassy in Chile. Among its personnel were Allende's Cuban son-in-law and numerous Cuban military experts. They trained Allende, his personal bodyguard (the Group of Personal Friends—*Grupo Amigos Persones*—GAP), and many in the radical left to use weapons.[34]

The MIR had been smuggling weapons into Chile for decades, and this accelerated following Allende's election. Members sympathetic to the radical left had been appointed to important government positions, making it much easier to clandestinely import the weapons. In March 1972 thirteen large wooden crates packed with small arms from Cuba bypassed customs inspection on the orders of the interior ministry.[35]

OPENING STRATEGIES

Given the disparity in strength, the radical left knew that it had to reduce the effectiveness of the military before any armed conflict took place. It identified senior officers who needed to be removed through political action or assassination. Allende used his personal bodyguards, the GAP, to spy on the senior officers.[36]

PREPARATIONS

Merino decided to propose a coup to the senior naval officers following his September 7 meeting with Allende. The navy leadership met at a private house for Mass on Sunday, September 9, and agreed to overthrow the government on the eleventh. Admiral Huidobro was sent to Santiago to inform Generals Pinochet (army) and Leigh (air force) of the navy's decision and ask for their help. In fact, both were in the process of planning a coup; the army's was tentatively scheduled for September 14. Both Pinochet and Leigh agreed to adopt the navy's schedule.[37]

During the afternoon of Saturday, September 8, Senator Altamirano had delivered an inflammatory speech calling for the workers to arm themselves. General Pinochet used it as an excuse to inform the Minister of Defense that he was going to carry out exercises on the eleventh, the alleged purpose of which was to train the troops in maintaining domestic order.[38]

During the early morning of September 10, the naval squadron lying off Valparaíso sailed as scheduled to join American warships and to begin the Chilean participation in the joint naval exercises known as Unitas.[39] During that afternoon, General Pinochet informed his generals that the coup would take place the next day.[40]

THE COUP

During the early morning hours of September 11, President Allende was awakened and told that the Yungay Regiment at San Felipe (80 mi N of Santiago) was making preparations to move out. His Minister of Defense told the President not to be concerned; the Minister had been informed of these maneuvers by General Pinochet.[41]

At 5 A.M. the crews of the Chilean naval squadron were awakened. They were told that a coup was to take place and that the fleet was returning to Valparaíso to participate. By 7 A.M. the navy had seized control of Valparaíso by landing armed sailors.[42]

At 6:30 in the morning, army headquarters notified all units to execute the plan to overthrow Allende. Military units seized all television and radio stations and took them off the air. The *Carabineros*, who were guarding the *Moneda*, were ordered to withdraw. Since the air force was delayed, an artillery barrage began the attack against the presidential residence. Army

Puma helicopters attempted to clear snipers from the rooftops of the Ministry of Public Works and the State Bank. At about 2 P.M., two Hawker Hunter aircraft fired rockets at the *Moneda*.

From time to time, the military paused in their attack to permit Allende to surrender. The President had been informed that his life would be spared but that he must immediately leave the country. Following the air attack, the troops, led by General Palacios, advanced under sporadic sniper fire and entered the building about 2 P.M. They found the Red Room, the presidential office, in flames. Allende was found dead in the Independence Room, the President's private room. Apparently, Allende had committed suicide with an AK-47 automatic rifle, a gift of Fidel Castro.[43]

Although the MIR continued to fight throughout the day, the much anticipated workers' uprising never materialized. Over the next few months, the radical left attacked military patrols with decreasing frequency. The coup had succeeded.

OBSERVATIONS

Within the context of the cold war, the overthrow of the Allende government allowed Fidel Castro to berate his Soviet ally that its strategy of achieving power through subverting the democratic process was a failure. Castro argued that the Chilean coup proved the United States would always intervene before the Soviet strategy could reach its fruition.[44]

The meddling of the United States was not the cause of the coup. Given the independence and institutional strength of the Chilean armed services, it is highly unlikely that the covert actions of the United States could motivate the Chilean military to overthrow the Allende government. Notwithstanding this fact, the clandestine activities of the United States carried a very high moral price. The United States demonstrated that it was willing to clandestinely work for the destruction of the longest existing democracy in Latin America in order to achieve a victory in the cold war. The coup succeeded because of the cohesiveness within Chilean military. It acted decisively as an institution.

The military sustained 162 dead as a result of the coup. Concerning civilians, most sources range between 122 and 750 dead.[45] General Pinochet wrote, "numerous encounters caused many casualties on both sides. Many more casualties were the result of these encounters than the fighting on September 11. Armed encounters only began to decrease gradually after the fourth month."[46] To these casualties must be added the thousands of victims of both the radical left and the reactionary right in the decades before and after the coup.

CHAPTER 35

CUBAN TROOPS IN AFRICA, 1960–91

[Africa is] one of the most important, if not the most important, battlefield against all the
forms of exploitation in the world, against imperialism, colonialism, and neocolonialism.
—Che Guevara

THE SPARK

Fidel Castro, believing that the Soviet Union was not adequately supporting the radical left
throughout the Third World, began championing its cause, particularly in Africa.[1]

GENERAL BACKGROUND

Fidel Castro's desire to take the offensive against capitalism and spread revolution ultimately led to the Cuban army fighting in Africa. His aim was to create many Vietnams, reason-
ing that U.S. troops bogged down throughout the world could not fight any single insurgency
effectively.[2] Africa was still emerging from colonialism when Castro came to power, thus pre-
senting him many opportunities.

The Cuban presence in Africa evolved through many phases before leading to the introduction of combat troops. The first phase, guerrilla training, began in 1960 when arms and medical personnel were sent to the Algerian National Liberation Army (*Armée de Libération
Nationale*). This was followed by the first permanent military mission which arrived in Ghana
the following year when a few instructors set up a training camp near the border with Upper
Volta. Guerrilla training expanded and continued until the early 1990s.[3]

In the second phase, Cuba attempted to militarily bolster a friendly nation. In October 1963
Cuba supplied Algeria with forty Russian-built T-34 tanks and some fifty Cuban technicians
who were at sea on board the *Aracelio Iglesias* when a border conflict erupted between Algeria
and Morocco. This equipment was followed within the same month by perhaps three other
shipments (two by sea, one by air), raising Cuban strength to approximately 300 men, plus artillery, mortars, and tanks. Apparently the Cubans did not participate in combat and they were
withdrawn by the end of the year after training Algerians in the use of the hardware.[4]

During the third phase, Cuba attempted to influence the outcome of tribal rivalries, siding
with groups whose ideologies were most compatible with that of Cuba. This phase opened with
high-level delegation visits to Africa. In October 1964, Cuban President Osvaldo Dorticos went

327

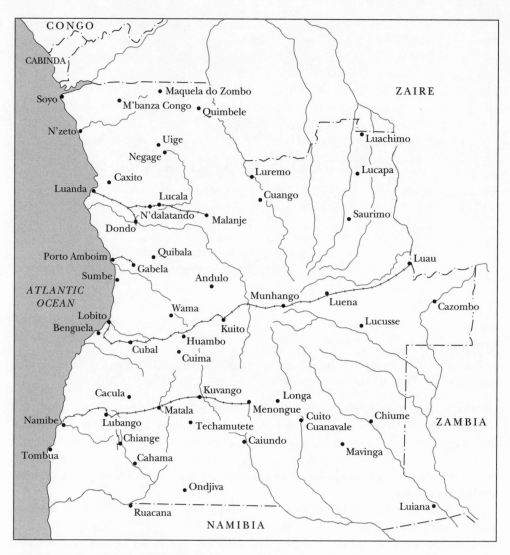

Map 7. Cuban Operations in Angola, 1976.

to the Second Conference of Non-Aligned Nations, meeting in Cairo, and declared that Cuba could not be passive "toward mankind's greatest problems."[5]

In December, Che Guevara traveled to Algeria, Mali, Congo-Leopoldville (soon to become Zaire), Ghana, Guinea, Dahomey, Tanzania, and Egypt. Che was empowered by Castro to offer material aid to those who shared Castro's ideology. By mid-1965 the Popular Movement for the Liberation of Angola (MPLA) received weapons from Cuba. Arms for the Guinea rebels, the African Party for the Liberation of Portuguese Guinea and the Cape Verde Islands, arrived in 1966. And apparently, Cuban instructors were training members of the Front for the Liberation of Mozambique in Tanzania by the late 1960s.[6]

Che returned to Africa to lead guerrilla fighters in Zaire, which he entered through Tanzania with a small band of Cubans in the spring of 1965. They were joined by several hundred more Cubans who entered through Congo-Brazzaville. However, Che found the rebels unwilling to fight; and after Joseph Mobutu seized power in November 1965, most of the Cuban fighters withdrew. Che remained behind in neighboring Congo-Brazzaville until March 1966 organizing the Cuban mission that had been sent there.[7]

Adding to the Zaire setback, two of Castro's closest allies were toppled by military coups—Ahmed Ben Bella in Algeria (1965) and Dr. Kwame Nkrumah in Ghana (1966). Thus, Cuba lost both of its African training bases. Following these experiences Cuba paid more attention to protecting its hosts. New training bases were established in Congo-Brazzaville and former French Guinea. In Brazzaville, Cubans formed part of the presidential guard, and they also trained a militia from the ruling party as a counterbalance to the national army.[8] The Cuban mission to Congo-Brazzaville grew to nearly one-half the size of the entire Congolese army. On June 27, 1966, that army attempted to overthrow President Massamba Debat. Cuban troops and the party militia protected the political leaders for three days. Capt. (later Brig. Gen.) Rolando Kindelán Bles stated, "We Cubans opposed the coup. We took the entrance to the airport, the main radio station; we controlled the road intersections; the nerve centers; and in that way we were able to impede it."[9] The coup collapsed when the Congolese army refused to fight the Cubans. In August 1968 Marien Ngouabi did overthrow the Cuban-supported government. Notwithstanding, Ngouabi permitted the Cubans to continue to operate in the Congo.[10]

Cuba continued to send military help to leftist regimes in African nations, and additionally focused upon liberating Portuguese colonies, thus beginning phase four.[11] Cuban aid to former French Guinea (independent since 1958) was directed in part to the guerrillas fighting the Portuguese in bordering Portuguese Guinea (today Guinea-Bissau). Cuban advisors began operating with the guerrillas in February 1967, and in November 1969 the Portuguese captured Cuban Capt. Pedro Rodriguez Peralta.[12]

Between the late 1960s and the early 1970s, Cuban activity in Africa subsided. However, it soon increased again with missions being sent to ex-Spanish Equatorial Guinea, Somalia, Algeria, Mozambique, and Sierra Leone—plus to the Middle East, South Yemen, Syria, and Iraq.[13]

ANGOLA BACKGROUND

Angola was strategically important because of the petroleum exports from the Cabinda enclave and because the Benguela Railroad, the major transportation link for landlocked Zaire and Zambia, ran through it.

The war for the liberation of Portuguese West Africa (the future Angola) from colonial rule began in February 1961 when the Marxist-oriented Popular Movement for the Liberation of Angola (MPLA) attacked the colonial headquarters in the capital of Luanda. The Portuguese had occupied some coastal regions since the end of the fifteenth century, although modern Angola became Portuguese only after the Conference and Treaty of Berlin in 1885.

Between 1961 and 1975 an estimated 20,000 Africans died in the fighting, and by the late 1960s perhaps half of the Portuguese national budget was spent on the war in Angola. By the mid-1970s, Angola was the last Portuguese colony in Africa. On April 25, 1974, junior Portuguese officers overthrew Dr. Marcelo Gaetano, who had succeeded the long-serving dictator Antonio de Oliveira Salazar. The new, leftist Portuguese government invited the principal

Angolan guerrilla organizations to participate in the transition from colonial rule to independence. As a consequence, fighting broke out among the competing guerrilla factions in March 1975 to see who would win control of the country from the Portuguese.[14]

OPPOSING FORCES IN ANGOLA

Five "armies" were fighting for control of Angola—three from disparate revolutionary factions plus those of Portugal and the Union of South Africa. In addition, the Zairean army operated openly in the northern region of Angola.

The National Front for the Liberation of Angola (FNLA), which fielded about 5,000 fighters, dominated the northwestern section of Angola. Led by Holden Roberto, the Bakongos tribe provided its popular base. It was considered pro-West and was supported by Mobutu Sese Seko of Zaire. The Zairean army even operated within the area controlled by Roberto. Despite his pro-West affiliations, Roberto secured help from Peking in December 1973. Between June and August 1974, China sent 450 tons of military material to the FNLA via Zaire and began training its soldiers.[15]

Just below that area was the region dominated by the Popular Movement of Liberation of Angola (MPLA) led by Agostinho Neto. The MPLA had about 2,000 fighters and its support base was among the Mbundu Tribe. During the mid-1960s, fighters from the MPLA trained in Cuba and a Cuban-operated base in the Congo.[16]

The MPLA received most of its arms from the Soviet Union; these weapons were shipped through the People's Republic of the Congo-Brazzaville. During one week in October 1975, the MPLA received twelve MiG aircraft, twenty-one tanks, thirty armored cars, 200 rocket launchers, plus small arms.[17] By the spring of 1975, Neto appreciated that his MPLA guerrillas could not effectively use the advanced Soviet weapons being provided; hence he turned to Castro for advanced training, which began in June 1975, one month after the request. This significantly changed the balance of power among the rival Angolan factions. Because of Cuban and Soviet help, the MPLA grew in military prowess and, as a consequence, attracted many new recruits.[18]

South of the territory dominated by the MPLA lay the area controlled by the National Union for the Total Independence of Angola (UNITA), led by Jonas Savimbi. The Benguela Railroad passed through this area. The movement had splintered from the FNLA in 1966 over tribal differences and objections to clandestine support from the United States. The UNITA fielded 1,000 men and its tribal support came from the Ovimbundu in the south.[19]

The Portuguese government had about 55,000 troops in Angola but by mid-1974 was committed to withdrawing. To the south was the well-equipped, well-trained 50,000-man South African army.[20]

OPENING STRATEGIES IN ANGOLA

The Cuban-supported MPLA wanted to seize control of most of Angola's provincial capitals prior to November 11, 1975, the date set by the Portuguese for Angolan independence. In response, the FNLA and the UNITA sought aid from the Union of South Africa. South Africa, for its part, wanted to prevent the MPLA from winning control of Angola.[21]

ANGOLA—CUBAN TROOPS IN COMBAT

Between July 12 and 15, 1975, the MPLA successfully captured Angola's capital, Luanda, but was immediately threatened from both the north and the south. In the north, FNLA troops attacked the MPLA but were stopped at Kinfangondo (12 mi N of Luanda). In the south, South

African troops crossed the border between Angola and Namibia on August 11 and seized the hydroelectric dams on the Cunene River which spanned the border. Within a few weeks, other South African troops captured the towns of Pereira d'Eça and Roçadas, thus blocking the route leading to the dams from the north. The South African forces advanced northward.[22]

Cuba reacted quickly to the dangers confronting the FNLA. Castro called for volunteers from the Cuban army to fight in Angola. Many who volunteered were black, possibly an attempt to demonstrate a racial bond with Angola.[23] In early September the Cuban merchantships *Viet Nam Heroico*, *Isla Coral*, and *La Plata*, packed with troops, vehicles, and 1,000 tons of gasoline, sailed 5,000 miles to the African nation. Even though Angola was a petroleum-producing nation, Castro wanted to reduce the possibility that his supply could be interrupted, so the *Viet Nam Heroico* carried 200 tons of gasoline in 55-gallon drums in the holds, which were left open for ventilation, and *La Plata* carried the drums strapped to the deck.

The United States held a secret, high-level talk with Cuba to express its consternation over Cuba's actions, but this had little effect. The Cuban troops landed in early October.[24]

The South African force driving northward from the Namibian border posed the most significant threat to the MPLA, so some of the recently arrived Cuban troops joined the MPLA troops moving against Nova Lisboa (today's Huambo, 300 mi SE of Luanda) and Lobito (220 mi S of Luanda). The remainder established training camps at Benguela, Saurimo, Cabinda, and Delatando.[25]

On October 6 Cuba and the MPLA clashed with the FNLA and South African troops at Norton de Matos and were badly beaten. While the Cubans had been crossing the Atlantic, the South Africans had apparently airlifted a few troops plus some armored cars into central Angola. These were supplied by C-130 aircraft flying into Nova Lisboa and Silva Porto (275 mi SE of Luanda).[26]

On October 23 the South Africans launched a major offensive. A mechanized column composed of armored cars, motorized infantry, and artillery manned by the South African army, Portuguese mercenaries, and FNLA fighters (loyal to Daniel Chipenda who had defected from the MPLA) attacked. On that day the column captured Sá da Bandeira (400 mi S of Luanda) and on the twenty-seventh the port of Moçâmedes (380 mi S of Luanda), without resistance. The column then fell back to Sá da Bandeira but then turned north against Benguela (250 mi S of Luanda) where the Cubans had one of their training camps.

The mechanized column detoured to Nova Lisboa on November 1. It then resumed toward Benguela. The Cubans blocked the column on November 4 with 122mm rocket fire, causing the South Africans to request heavy artillery which could outdistance the rockets. The next day, the Cubans abandoned Benguela and Lobito, and by November 11 (Independence Day) the South African column was advancing on Novo Redondo (120 mi S of Luanda).[27]

Castro reacted to the presence of the South African armored column by announcing "Operation Carlotta," a massive resupply of Angola, on November 5.[28] On the seventh Cuba began a thirteen-day airlift of a 650-man special forces battalion. The Cubans used old Bristol Britannia turboprop aircraft, making refueling stops in Barbados, Guinea-Bissau, and the Congo before landing in Luanda. The troops traveled as "tourists," carrying machine guns in briefcases. They packed 75mm cannons, 82mm mortars, and small arms into the aircrafts' cargo holds. Aircraft with normal take-off weights of 185,000 pounds were lifting off weighing 194,000 pounds. Pilots were flying over 200 hours per month. A round trip required 50 hours.[29]

Castro's resupply efforts by sea were no less dramatic. Perhaps five troop-laden ships had sailed from Cuba in late October, arriving in Angola during the middle of November. Cuba's only two passenger ships were fitted with cots, field kitchens, and additional latrines. Paper plates were used and plastic yogurt containers served as glasses. The ballast tanks were used for bathing and toilet water. Ships normally outfitted for 306 persons (passengers and crew) sailed with 1,000 on board in addition to armored cars, weapons, and munitions.[30]

BATTLE OF BRIDGE 14

Between December 9 and 12, Cuban and South African troops fought between Santa Comba (180 mi SE of Luanda) and Quibala (150 mi SE of Luanda); the Cubans were defeated. Among the Cuban casualties was the commander, Raúl Argüello, a veteran of the Cuban Revolution. He was killed when his vehicle hit a land mine. At the same time UNITA troops and another South African mechanized unit captured Luso (500 mi ESE of Luanda).[31]

Following these defeats, the number of Cuban troops airlifted to Angola more than doubled, from about 400 per week to perhaps a thousand. Among these troops were seasoned veterans of the Cuban Revolution and wars in Latin America, such as Victor Chueng Colas, Leopoldo Cintras Frías, Abelardo Colome Ibarra, and Raúl Menendez Tomassevich. By the end of January 1976, some 7,000 Cuban troops were in Angola. Cuba also prepared to send at least one artillery regiment and a motorized infantry battalion.[32]

And, Cuba no longer was having to go it alone in aiding the MPLA. On November 13, 1975, Soviet military advisors had arrived in Angola. In early 1976 the Soviets began providing IL-62 jet transports to the Cubans, significantly increasing their airlift potential. These aircraft introduced fresh troops and rotated veterans into the mid-1980s.[33]

MPLA'S NORTHERN OFFENSIVE

On January 4, 1976, the Cuban-supported MPLA captured Uije (150 mi N of Luanda) and the major airbase 25 miles to the east the following day from the FNLA. On the twelfth, the MPLA took the port of Ambriz (125 Mi N of Luanda). As a consequence, the troops from Zaire, who had supported the FNLA, pulled back across their border.[34]

In mid-January, the South Africans withdrew from Cela and Santa Comba deep in Angola to a position just north of the Angolan-Namibian border. This was probably influenced by a number of factors. First, the surge in Cuban troops required South Africa to make a decision to either increase its army in Angola or withdraw. Second, the United States stopped supplying Angolans opposed to the MPLA. And third, the Cubans temporarily stopped airlifting troops to Angola, which provided a graceful way out for its opponents.[35]

Cuba resumed airlifting troops to Angola in late February 1976 at a reduced rate.[36] In that month, the MPLA captured the last UNITA stronghold and drove its rivals into neighboring countries. The MPLA also had to battle a new faction, the Front for the Liberation of the Cabinda Enclave (FLEC), led by Francisco Xavier Lubtoa.[37]

By March 1977 the MPLA controlled enough of the country to permit Castro to pay a state visit. However, in May Nito Alves and José Van Dunem attempted an unsuccessful coup against Agostinho Neto. Cuban troops helped defeat the rebels. In July, an additional 4,000 Cuban troops were introduced into Angola. In spite of this, the UNITA was able to regroup and launch an offensive against the MPLA in December. The Cuban-supported MPLA was able to counterattack beginning in April 1978.[38]

In September 1979 Neto died while undergoing surgery in the Soviet Union. José Eduardo dos Santos succeeded him. Throughout the late 1970s, the MPLA aggressively eliminated potential dissenters.[39]

The fighting dragged on for years while Fidel directed operations from Havana. Brig. Gen. Juan Escalona, Chief of the Command Post, stated:

> For over two years every day, without fail, between 2:30 and 3:00 in the afternoon I was advised I had a visitor. I knew the Commander in Chief had arrived. He would stay in the Armed Forces Ministry until the early hours of dawn. The entire Angolan operation was directed by Fidel minute by minute.[40]

South African forces frequently crossed into Angola to destroy South-West African People's Organization (SWAPO) training bases. More critically, the MPLA could not root out the UNITA (which had emerged as its principal opposition) and became, therefore, increasingly dependent upon Cuban combat troops. By 1987 some 24,500 Cuban troops held defensive positions in Angola. The MPLA controlled the larger population centers while the UNITA held the countryside.[41]

BEGINNING OF THE END

By the late 1980s, the world balance of power was changing. The Soviet Union was disintegrating, and along with it, Cuba's capacity to continue its commitment to the MPLA. Throughout the 1980s, the MPLA grew weaker as the UNITA grew stronger, in large measure due to UNITA's support from South Africa and increasingly the United States.

In November 1987 the MPLA was in full retreat following a defeat at Mavinga (650 mi SE of Luanda). Cuba's most successful general, Arnaldo Ochoa Sanchez, and 15,000 Cuban reinforcements, including frontline pilots, were rushed to Angola. Ochoa remarked, "I have been sent to a lost war so that I will be blamed for the defeat."[42]

On January 13, 1988, South African-led forces attacked three MPLA brigades east of Cuito Cuanavale (580 mi SE of Luanda). The Cubans wanted these MPLA troops to retreat and then consolidate a new position; they were either unwilling or incapable of doing so. On February 15 the South Africans crashed through the MLPA's defenses and encircled the 59th MLPA Brigade. Seven Cuban tanks counterattacked; all were destroyed but the 59th Brigade was able to escape. Cuban General Cintra Frias now arrived on the scene to take command of field operations (Ochoa remained the senior Cuban in Angola) and the defenses finally held at Cuito Cuanavale.[43]

Both sides maneuvered on the battlefield to gain advantages at the negotiating table. Should the South Africans attack, Castro instructed Ochoa to "be ready to counter-attack with as many aircraft as possible to completely destroy the Ruacana water reservoirs and transformers [on the border with South African-controlled Namiba]."[44] Apparently, the MLPA knew nothing of these orders; it had a tacit understanding with the South Africans that the Ruacana dam complex was off-limits. Finally, in late 1988 Cuba agreed to withdraw by July 1, 1991, leaving the MPLA to its own fate.[45]

ANGOLAN OBSERVATIONS

During 1975 the Cuban army saved the MPLA from defeat by its internal rivals and external enemies. However, Cuba's military rescue committed that Caribbean nation to the long-term protection of the MPLA regime which required not only military but also economic aid. In the long run, this was unsustainable. The MPLA's internal rivals were numerically superior, although initially disorganized; but throughout the 1980s the MPLA's rivals grew stronger as the United States and South Africa became increasingly willing to supply them with aid.

Cuba's initial military success may be attributed to Castro's willingness to raise the ante beyond what either the United States or the Union of South Africa was willing to do in 1975. The Cuban commitment probably peaked near 36,000 troops, and possibly 150,000 troops rotated through Angola.[46]

Although Cuba has not released data concerning its casualties, they are estimated to be 3,000 killed (including Gen. Raul Arguello) and 3,000 wounded. These figures do not include the casualties related to disease. Although Cuban logistics were primitive, having to resort to a few aging commercial aircraft, small cargo ships, and large fishing vessels to support a major, long range military operation, nonetheless, these assets got the job done.[47]

Castro's massive military commitment to Angola revealed inequities within Cuban society. The commanding officer of Cuban air units in Angola during the mid-1970s, Gen. Rafael del Pino, revealed, after defecting to the United States in May 1987,

> The people, the officers resist going to Angola. This is not only because . . . we have converted ourselves into a mercenary army . . . but it is that our officers see that the problem is that neither the sons of the members of the Politburo [n]or the sons of the principal leaders of the government go to Angola, do not go into military service.[48]

Also, the Cuban economy was adversely affected. To fight on the scale required in Angola forced Cuba to call up its reservists. Many of these individuals were the most technically trained people on the island. As they were removed from their normal jobs, the economy suffered. For example, aircraft required two full crews to make the flight across the Atlantic. These additional crews came from small Cuban airlines, effectively shutting them down. And in spite of attempts to protect the sugar industry, as men were increasingly pulled from the fields, production dropped and, as a consequence, so did Cuban hard currency.[49]

The intervention by the South African army was a political failure for that nation. Although it won battles in 1975, the Union of South Africa, possessing no international support due to its racist policies, could not take political advantage of these victories. During 1975 it committed perhaps 2,000 combat troops to Angola and held a reserve force of some 4,000 men near the border. The subsequent policy of providing support for the UNITA, which at times included employing South African armor and aircraft, was much more successful.[50]

ETHIOPIAN BACKGROUND

In 1974 widespread national strikes crippled Ethiopia as demonstrations and riots spread against the authoritarian regime of Haile Selassie. The military refused to take action against the people. The *Dergue* (Armed Forces Coordinating Committee) emerged out of the confusion as a powerful political element. By late summer the *Dergue* arrested the Prime Minister and over one hundred other officials of the government. The *Dergue* finally seized power on September 12, deposed the Emperor, and established the Ethiopian Provisional Military Government. Fidel Castro was the first foreign head of state to visit Ethiopia following these events.

Over the next few months, the military government systematically destroyed the remaining civil leadership. Executions were common. However, at the same time, Ethiopia was to fight ethnic Somalis who lived in the Ogaden Desert in its northwest corner and wanted to be made part of Somalia. This fighting had profound implications for Ethiopia, since many ethnic groups who desired independence were within its borders.

Somalia had renewed its interest in annexing the Ogaden Province in 1969. Gen. Mohammad Siad Barre, who had come to power in that year through a coup, desired to incorporate those regions outside the nation which had Somali majorities. These included parts of Ethiopia, Djibouti, and Kenya. In 1974 Siad Barre provided the Soviet Union a naval base at Berbera in exchange for weapons and training, which allowed him to aggressively pursue his ambitions. Some of these weapons and training ultimately reached the "West Somali Liberation Front" (WSLF), which was fighting to separate the Ogaden Desert from Ethiopia and join it to Somalia.[51]

When the deposed Ethiopian Emperor died in August 1975, a number of grass-roots organizations demanded increased civil rights. The military government struck swiftly, openly murdering the opposition. These massacres intimidated those who survived. On February 3, 1977, Brig. Gen. Teferi Bante, head of the highly volatile *Dergue*, was killed in a coup led by Lt. Gen. Mengistu Haile Mariam—a gunfight literally errupted during a military council meeting. The Cuban news media hailed this as a great victory.[52]

Later in February, Gen. Arnaldo Ochoa, commander of the Cuban troops in Angola, headed a military delegation to Addis Ababa. This was followed by a two-day, unannounced visit by Castro, who tried in vain to resolve the border differences between Ethiopia and Somalia. In April Ethiopia asked the United States to withdraw its personnel from that country.[53]

However, by April the Somali separatists won some clear victories in the northeast, and fighting also erupted in southeastern Ethiopia. In May Mengistu traveled to Moscow seeking military hardware; the request was granted. This infuriated the Somalis, who after all had a friendship treaty with the Soviet Union. As a consequence, Somalia increased its aid to the WSLF and on June 17 Somali troops invaded Ogaden forcing the Cubans and Soviets to openly choose sides. Both Cuba and the Soviet Union believed that Ethiopia was more important to their long-term interests than Somalia.[54]

OPPOSING SIDES IN ETHIOPIA

In 1975 the Ethiopian army was composed of almost 41,000 troops. It possessed almost no armor or tracked vehicles, essential for desert fighting. Because of poor leadership, training, and equipment, it had little fighting ability.[55]

The WSLF had about 6,000 fighters. Many had been trained by the Cubans before Castro chose to side with Ethiopia and were supplied from Somalia.[56]

The Somali army was composed of 23,000 men. It possessed 250 tanks and 310 armored personnel carriers, mostly older Soviet equipment. Although its leadership, training, and equipment were poor, they were superior to those of the Ethiopian army.[57]

Prior to December 1977, no Cuban combat troops were in Ethiopia.

OPENING STRATEGIES IN ETHIOPIA

In July 1977 Somalia chose to escalate the fighting from guerrilla actions to open warfare in order to take advantage of its superior army vis-a-vis Ethiopia. Its strategy was to seize the Ogaden Desert and then threaten the heartland of Ethiopia. Initially, Ethiopian strategy was purely defensive.

THE FIRST SOMALI OFFENSIVE

Throughout the summer of 1977, the Ethiopian army lost ground on both the northwest and southwest fronts against the guerrillas while Mengistu carried out bloody purges against those suspected of opposing his rule in Ethiopia. Guerrillas sabotaged the Addis Ababa-to-Djibouti single-track railroad, which carried over half of Ethiopia's foreign trade, by destroying five bridges. Meanwhile, in July Somalia reacted to Cuban and Soviet assistance to Ethiopia by expelling its Soviet military advisors and accepting military aid from the United States and Great Britain.[58]

On July 17 a Somali force of 250 tanks, twelve mechanized brigades, and thirty war planes invaded the Ogaden Desert. By August the Somali army had seized 112 hamlets and towns and much of the desert. On the eighteenth Ethiopia declared a mass mobilization, and in September Cuban military help to Ethiopia began to increase. These were not enough to reverse the defeats. As a consequence of Cuba's actions, Somalia expelled the Cuban chargé d'affaires. Late in September the Somali army captured the city of Jijiga (375 mi N of Addis Ababa) and the Kara Marda Pass which was the gateway to central Ethiopia.[59]

By October Ethiopia had received large quantities of military hardware from the Soviet Union, but the Ethiopian army was totally unprepared to employ these. The Ethiopian Foreign Minister traveled to Cuba to seek Cuban training and combat troops as a last resort. However, by October 31 the Somali advance had been halted.[60]

THE SECOND SOMALI OFFENSIVE

On November 13 Somalia expelled all Soviets, took back its base concessions, and aborted its 1974 friendship treaty. It also broke diplomatic relations with Cuba. On the twenty-second Somalia launched a second offensive; the objective was the city of Harar (250 mi E of Addis Ababa). On December 22 Cuba began a secret, massive airlift by Soviet aircraft of its combat troops from Angola, the People's Republic of the Congo, and the Caribbean to Ethiopia. The Cuban combat force grew from 400 men in December 1977 to 16,000 men in April 1978.[61]

ETHIOPIA—CUBAN TROOPS IN COMBAT

In January 1978 Raúl Castro flew to Addis Ababa and then on to Moscow. On January 24, the Ethiopian and Cuban troops counterattacked from Harar. The Somalis sustained 3,000 casualties and began to retreat. In February Cuban troops launched a major offensive and recaptured much of the lost desert. On March 5 the Kara Marda Pass was recaptured and by the eighth the Somali army had been driven back into its own territory and was in a state of shambles. The fighting was over.[62]

In 1981 Ethiopia, supported by Cuban and Russian advisors (but not combat troops) invaded Somalia, attempting to drive Siad Barre from power. This failed in part because the United States provided Somalia $50 million in military aid. By 1984 the Ethiopian army was fighting six separatist guerrilla movements and the country was in chaos. Peace between Ethiopia and Somalia was agreed to on April 6, 1988, and the last Cuban left Ethiopia on September 9, 1989.[63]

ETHIOPIAN OBSERVATIONS

In 1977 Cuban combat troops were able to snatch victory from defeat because of the introduction of an overwhelming force (16,000 men) against Somalia in a little more than seven weeks. Although farther from Cuba, logistics were easier than the Angolan operation because many Cuban troops were pulled from Angola and the Republic of the Congo, and more importantly, the Soviet Union provided most of the air transportation. Cuban casualties are cited as being high, although no numbers are offered.[64]

As in Angola, Fidel Castro attempted to direct combat operations from Cuba. Division Gen. Leopoldo Cintra Frías stated:

> We maintained permanent contact with the Commander in Chief; daily he was sent cables with information. He replied to everything and gave pertinent instructions. . . . He would order you to place a cannon in a place, how to do it, with how many men, etc. He had it all at his fingertips.[65]

GENERAL OBSERVATIONS

Foremost, Cuba's fighting in Africa was at its own intiative and not that of the Soviet Union. General Cintra Frías, who served in both Angola and Ethiopia, stated, "The Soviets were never able to control us although I think that was their intention on more than one occasion."[66] José Raúl Alfonso, a former member of the Cuban intelligence community, stated, "the opinion [of those going to Angola in 1975] was that the Soviets did not know what we were going to do, so much so that Fidel told us that if things went wrong, we should not expect aid from them, not even from the Socialist camp."[67]

In some respects, the Cuban experience in Africa paralleled that of the United States in Vietnam. The Cuban army could win battles, but because Cuba did not understand the nature of the struggle, these victories did not lead to political success. In Angola particularly, Cuba saw this as a struggle against colonialism and capitalism where, in fact, it was primarily an internal feud between competing tribes. And, like Lyndon Johnson for Vietnam, Fidel Castro for Africa attempted to fight the war from his command post at home.

In the context of the cold war, Cuba's efforts in Africa were a waste of resources. Cuba's interventions were costly in men and treasure, contributing to a sharp downturn in its domestic economy. Additionally, Cuba's military actions in Africa cost Cuba any possible rapprochement with the United States. Far less significant, these military actions did win Castro the good will of some black Africans who perceived neocolonialism as their greatest threat.[68]

By late 1977 Cuba and the Soviet Union more clearly agreed upon foreign policy, as was demonstrated by their cooperation in Ethiopia, which had been somewhat lacking in Angola. One consequence of Cuba's troops fighting in Africa was that Soviet pilots and technicians replaced Cubans in the defenses of the Caribbean island so that the Cubans could serve in Africa. Also, from 1970 to 1979 Soviet troops in Cuba increased from 1,000 men to some 5,000 men, and in 1979 Cuba acknowledged that a Soviet combat brigade was stationed on the island.[69] Sarcastically, the *People's Daily* of Peking wrote:

> Question: What's the largest country in the world?
> Answer: Cuba. Its heart is in Havana; its government is in Moscow; its graveyards are in
>   Angola and Ethiopia; and its people are in Miami.[70]

One essential psychological, and therefore also political, factor in the Cuban involvement was the fact that many Cuban soldiers were either black or of mixed race.

One source states that over 300,000 Cuban military personnel and civilian experts served in Africa. It also states that of the 50,000 Cubans sent to Angola, half caught AIDS and that 10,000 Cubans died as a consequence of Cuban activity in Africa, although these numbers seem high. All Cubans had left Africa by May 1991.[71]

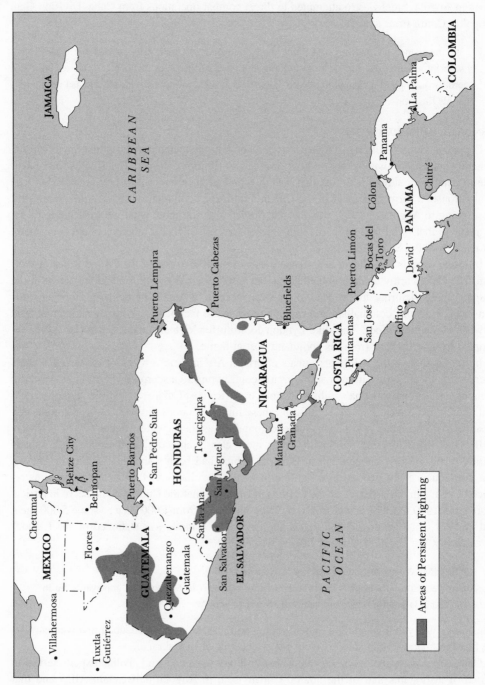

Map 8. Fidel's Legacy in Central America, 1985.

CHAPTER 36

THE ERA OF FIDEL'S LEGACY, 1974–91

We have no scorched-earth policy, we have a policy of scorched communists.
—José Efraín Ríos Montt, 1982, President of Guatemala

THE SPARK

The failure of the *Foco* and Urban strategies caused Fidel Castro to reexamine guerrilla operations and to devise a new strategy. Beginning in the mid- to late 1970s, Cuba once again renewed its efforts to help bring Marxist governments to power in the Caribbean basin through the use of guerrilla warfare.

BACKGROUND

Mao Tse-tung of China, Vo Nguyen Giap of Vietnam, and Che Guevara of Cuba were the leading Communist theoreticians on guerrilla warfare. All had conducted successful campaigns and had written extensively on the subject. Fidel Castro had never been included in this elite circle. After all, his tactics during the Cuban Revolution did not have the flair or daring of those of Che or of his own brother Raúl. Fidel, although a vociferous advocate of guerrilla warfare, had written little on the subject. And yet, Fidel was the symbol of revolution.

In the mid-1970s Fidel and the radical left reassessed their tactics due to the numerous failures of guerrilla endeavors throughout Latin America during the preceeding fifteen years. They were also inspired by the American failure in Vietnam and the Soviet-backed victories in Africa and Asia. Additionally, there had been a rapprochement between Cuba and the Soviet Union concerning the desire to support Latin American guerrilla movements.[1] In June 1974 Castro hosted a conference for Latin American Communist parties. The twenty-four parties that attended represented the Soviet philosophy of political versus military confrontation. Notwithstanding, the conference's declaration stated that it was the "right and duty of all revolutionary forces to answer counterrevolutionary violence with revolutionary violence."[2]

OPPOSING FORCES

The opposing sides remained unchanged from the earlier *foco* wars with increasing participation by the Cuban and U.S. militaries (see chapters 29 and 30). Nevertheless, the American defeat in Vietnam did place many self-imposed constraints upon U.S. support to its Latin American allies.

OPENING STRATEGIES

If the radical left were to be victorious in the future, the lessons of the Cuban Revolution needed to be correctly interpreted. Rural guerrilla warfare and urban guerrilla warfare had each contributed to the defeat of Batista, but neither alone would have caused his downfall. Factionalism within the guerrilla movements had to be eliminated. The support of the United States government for the regime under attack had to be neutralized. American and world opinion had to be influenced in favor of the guerrilla movement. The guerrillas needed to improve their supply lines to Cuba. And the radical left had to win the support of the franchised population and hold it long enough to secure power if a Marxist's state were to be created.[3]

The U.S. strategy was in flux. The United States had sustained a defeat in Vietnam that caused a tidal wave of public opposition to U.S. military involvement in foreign nations. Also, the U.S. citizens elected Jimmy Carter president in 1976. His foreign policy began to emphasize human rights. This came into conflict with the U.S. strategy of militarily aiding those opposed to Communism regardless of their record on human rights.

NICARAGUA, 1974–90

Prior to late 1974 the leftist guerrillas in Nicaragua were generally referred to as Sandinistas, but in fact they were far from united.[4] Many had died but nothing had changed. The Somoza family, which first came to power in 1934, remained in complete control.[5]

On the night of December 27, 1974, fortunes began to turn for the radical left. In the capital of Managua, the guerrillas seized the home of José María Castillo who was hosting numerous dignitaries including the U.S. ambassador, Turner B. Shelton. Fortunately, Shelton had departed before the guerrillas attacked. They killed the host, two national guardsmen (within Nicaragua the army was known as the national guard), and a chauffeur. After two days of negotiations, the guerrillas won the release of fourteen political prisoners, including Daniel Ortega,[6] and an estimated two million dollars in ransom. On December 30, accompanied by an archbishop, the Mexican and Spanish ambassadors to Nicaragua, and the Papal Nuncio, the guerrillas along with their booty were flown to Havana on board a Nicaraguan air force plane. Immediately, President Anastasio Somoza Debayle (the second son and namesake of the old assassinated dictator) declared a state of siege and increased repression.[7]

In spite of the spectacular success, the Sandinistas remained plagued by factionalism. These factions were all Marxist, but they disagreed on the tactics to be used to win power and who would govern after victory. This factionalism negatively influenced the amount of aid that Fidel Castro was willing to give. In May 1977 the three primary Sandinista factions agreed to a unified strategy: They would build public support around daily issues, including support from democratic, anti-Somoza groups; unify into a single vanguard; mobilize mass support for insurrection; and construct a Sandinista army for an uninterrupted offensive.[8]

Also at this time, a group of professional businessmen and clergy, later to be known as the "Twelve," denounced Somoza and called for a new government to include the Sandinistas. The Twelve and others opposed to Somoza formed the Broad Opposition Front (*Frente Amplio Opositor*—FAO).

In January 1978 the assassination of Pedro Joaquin Chamorro, editor of the newspaper *La Prensa*, galvanized public opinion against the Somoza regime. Spontaneous riots and strikes followed for two weeks. On February 21 a spontaneous insurrection erupted in the capital's Indian barrio of Monimbo. Elite troops restored order. Numerous uprisings occurred during the next six months, some of which were instigated by the Sandinistas.[9]

On August 22 Edén Pastora[10] (*nom de guerre Commandante Cero*) led twenty-five Sandinista guerrillas disguised as national guardsmen and seized the Nicaraguan Chamber of Deputies. They took 1,500 hostages including the President's son. Somoza paid a $10 million-dollar ransom, surrendered political prisoners, and provided the guerrillas safe passage to Panama. This success by the guerrillas triggered massive acts of defiance against the Somoza regime.[11]

The FAO called for a nationwide strike to begin on August 24 and by the end of the month it was widely successful. In early September the national guard broke the strike—some 50 people were killed, perhaps 200 injured, and hundreds more arrested. On September 9, the Sandinista faction, the "Insurrectional Tendency," attacked and captured the cities of Masaya, León, Chinandega, and Estelí. The Sandinistas were joined by poorly armed civilians. Somoza recaptured each city, one at a time, using his best troops, the 700-man "Somoza Combat Battalion," commanded by his son, Maj. Anastasio Somoza Portocarrero. Civilian losses were high. Jaime Wheelock of the Sandinista faction "Proletarian Tendency" criticized the attacks as being premature, thus undermining public support for the Sandinistas.[12] However, the Sandinistas did gain combat experience, urban mobilization skills, recruits, and captured equipment. Some 5,000 persons died.[13]

Cuba now played a more direct role. Throughout 1978 a high-ranking member of the America Department (*Departamento America*—AD)[14] of the Cuban Communist Party, Armando Ulises Estrada, made a number of secret trips to Nicaragua and Costa Rica attempting to better unite the Sandinista factions. The Sandinista factions, appreciating their shortage of munitions and the opportunity currently at hand, agreed to cooperate. As a consequence, Cuba significantly increased the supply of weapons, munitions, and training. First the weapons were flown to Panama. Then they were flown to the town of Liberia, Costa Rica. Costa Rica virtually ceded a 15-mile stretch along its border with Nicaragua to the Sandinistas to serve as their base.[15]

In January 1979 the Sandinistas announced a new offensive, targeting the national guard and the occupation of the major cities. On February 21 (the forty-fifth anniversary of Sandino's assassination), the Sandinistas attacked numerous national guard outposts. On April 9, some 250 guerrillas captured the town of Estelí (85 mi N of Managua) and held it through five days of aerial attacks. When recapturing the town, the national guard executed many including hospital workers who had treated wounded guerrillas.[16]

On May 4 Sandinista guerrillas attacked the national guard in the capital, Managua, and in other cities. Somoza immediately arrested numerous opponents, some of whom were freed after American protests. Initially, the guard retreated into the Infantry Training School, Managua airport, and air force headquarters, but soon counterattacked. After one month of fighting the guard drove the guerrillas out of Managua.[17]

Also beginning in May, the Somoza regime suffered one international setback after another.[18] On the twentieth Mexico broke diplomatic relations with the Somoza government citing its "horrific genocide" against its own people. Mexico's actions were soon followed by

Ecuador (June 17), Panama (June 18), Brazil (June 25), and Peru (June 26). Also on June 17 Bolivia, Colombia, and Venezuela recognized the Sandinistas as legitimate belligerents. On the twenty-third the OAS took the unprecedented step of endorsing the Sandinista-backed Junta of the Government of National Reconstruction instead of the Somoza regime.[19]

Some 5,000 Sandinista guerrillas supported by 15,000 civilians launched what proved to be their final offensive on May 28. A force attacked from Costa Rica along the southwest coast. Humberto Ortega directed guerrilla operations by radio. The Cubans, who earlier had set up an operations center in San José, Costa Rica, maintained contact with the Sandinistas and Havana during the preparations for the final offensive. The AD-run center was headed by Julian López Díaz, who later became the Cuban ambassador to Sandinista-run Nicaragua.[20]

By now, the guerrillas had received significant numbers of Belgian-made assault rifles as well as other supplies from Cuba. At the same time, guerrillas launched attacks in the northeast and on the outskirts of Managua. Initially, the national guard under Gen. José Somoza (the President's half-brother) drove the invaders back toward Costa Rica. However, on June 3 heavy fighting broke out in Managua and on the fifth the Sandinistas captured León (50 mi W of Managua) and other important towns in the northwest.[21]

The Sandinistas spearheaded popular uprisings in the cities. Urban guerrillas besieged garrisons and blocked transportation routes. The Sandinistas held the road between the airport and Managua, thus giving them access to foreign journalists and the world press. On June 11 Somoza ordered an aerial bombardment of the capital, which appeared more to be a punishment against the poor for supporting the Sandinistas than surgical strikes against guerrillas. Some accounts place the number of casualties as high as 10,000 persons.[22] On the twenty-eighth the Sandinistas withdrew from the capital to prevent additional civilian casualties. While this was happening, ABC television reporter William Stewart was executed by the national guard on June 20; this was a public relations disaster for Somoza.[23]

The fighting continued throughout July. Among those now fighting was an International Brigade that included members of the Palestine Liberation Organization (PLO).[24] The United States finally pressured Somoza into accepting the inevitable and resigning. On July 17, 1979, Somoza fled to Paraguay. The Communists had achieved their first victory since that of the Cuban Revolution in 1959, in spite of the fact that the Nicaraguan national guard fought hard almost to the bitter end. One estimate of the cost of the war was 60,000 dead (out of a population of 2.5 million persons), 250,000 displaced persons, and $5 billion in property damage.[25]

However, the fighting did not end with the Sandinista victory. In 1979 the Sandinistas had called for "a struggle for the true union of the Central American peoples within one country, beginning with support for national liberation movements in neighboring states."[26] The new Marxist-Leninist regime in Nicaragua now directly supported the radical left in El Salvador and in Guatemala. The regime also began building a large conventional military force, thereby threatening to change the balance of power within Central America.

To contain and possibly to eliminate the Sandinista government, the new Reagan administration, which took office in January 1981, began militarily strengthening Nicaragua's neighbors (Honduras, El Salvador, and Guatemala) and "clandestinely" aiding various Nicaraguans groups opposed to the new Sandinista government. Collectively they became known as the Democratic Nicaraguan Front (*Frente Democratica Nicaraguense*—FDN), generally referred to as the *Contras* by the international press and as the "freedom fighters" by the Reagan administration.[27]

American support for the *Contras* began covertly in late 1981, but this soon became an "open" secret. Initially the CIA spent $19 million to train 500 guerrillas to operate in Honduras, El Salvador, and Nicaragua. The original mission of the guerrillas was to interdict clandestine arm shipments from the Sandinistas to the Salvadoran leftist guerrillas.[28] Contra leader Edgar Chamorro later revealed that "the FDN was started with the cooperation of the Argentine advisers; the Hondurans who provided the territory, logistical support, military facilities, and some training; and the Americans, who gave the money and overall supervision."[29]

Between 1981 and 1984 the *Contra* force grew from 500 guerrillas to about 12,000. Initially, the *Contras* operated across the Nicaraguan-Honduran border. In 1981 two more guerrilla groups were established among the Miskito Indians on the east coast of Nicaragua. The following year another front was opened across the Nicaraguan–Costa Rican border when Eden Pastora declared against those governing in Managua. Thus, Nicaragua was under attack from the north, east, and south. The Sandinistas controlled the cities and open ground while the *Contras* transversed the mountains and coastal swamps from their safe havens. The number of attacks carried out by the *Contras* escalated from fifteen in 1981 to seventy-eight in 1982, and over 600 in 1983. The Sandinista government responded by significantly increasing the size of its army and militia.[30]

In 1983 representatives from Colombia, Mexico, Venezuela, and Panama proposed a peace plan. President Reagan declared his support for the effort; however, neither the United States nor Nicaragua took any steps to cooperate with the Contadora (named for the island where the meeting occurred) peace initiative.[31]

By 1984 American tactics had evolved to include using the *Contras* and CIA operatives to attack Nicaragua's infrastructure. In 1984 CIA operatives (possibly *Contras*) mined the Nicaraguan harbors of Sandino, Corinto, and El Bluff, attempting to weaken an already dismal economy. These mines damaged a number of ships. Nicaragua charged in the World Court that the United States had violated international law. The court found in favor of Nicaragua but the United States refused to recognize the court's decision.[32]

In October 1984 the United States suffered a public relations disaster. The U.S. media acquired a copy of a CIA manual entitled *Psychological Operations in Guerrilla Warfare*, published for the *Contras*. In a section entitled "Selective Use of Violence for Propagandistic Effects," the manual recommends, "It is possible to neutralize carefully selected and planned targets, such as court judges, *mesta* judges, police and State Security officials, . . . etc."[33]

As a consequence of the mining, the operations manual, and *Contra* attacks against the port of Corinto, the U.S. Congress suspended *Contra* funding in April 1985. However, within a few days Sandinista leader Daniel Ortega traveled to Moscow, giving credibility to the Reagan administration's claim of direct Soviet involvement within Central America. In June the U.S. House of Representatives overwhelmingly approved $27 million "humanitarian" aid for the *Contras*.[34]

By late 1984 the *Contras* became increasingly restricted. The Sandinista government convinced some of the Miskito Indians to stop fighting. Also, the Costa Rican government increasingly restricted the use of its territory by the *Contras*. The Nicaraguan army became more aggressive in pursuing the *Contras* across the Honduran border. Those *Contras* operating deep in Nicaragua were now dependent upon air supply. On August 1, 1985, *Contras* operating out of Honduras attacked the Nicaraguan town of La Trinidad (75 mi N of Managua). Only half of the attackers escaped uninjured.[35]

Figure 27. The Era of Fidel's Legacy (1974–91). Nicaraguan soldiers wearing U.S-style jungle fatigues are standing in front of Soviet-supplied BTR-60 armored personnel carriers and BM-21 multiple rocket launches in the mid-1990s. When the Soviets withdrew their military aid from Fidel
Castro, complex hardware such as these vehicles became very difficult if not impossible for the pro-
Cuban forces to maintain. *Courtesy Julio Montes.*

In late 1986 the "Iran-*Contra* Affair" exploded in the press. The perpetrators schemed to sell
arms to moderate elements within revolutionary Iran in order to gain influence for the release
of U.S. hostages held in the Middle East. The money earned from these weapon sales would be
used to fund the *Contras*. This illegal, poorly executed fiasco threatened the continuation of
congressional funding for the *Contras*.[36]

In January 1987 President Oscar Arias of Costa Rica proposed a new peace initiative for
Central America. The "Arias Accord" evolved into the Guatemala Peace Agreement of August
7, 1987. Basically, the five Central American nations of Guatemala, Honduras, El Salvador,
Costa Rica, and Panama called for all nations to end their military aid into the region.[37]

The fate of the *Contras* was momentarily rescued in the U.S. Congress due to two events in
December 1987. The first was a 4,000-man *Contra* attack deep within Nicaragua against the
towns of Siuna, Bonanza, and Rosita; this demonstrated a robustness many thought did not exist. And the second was the defection of Maj. Roger Miranda Bengochea, chief aide to the
Nicaraguan Defense Minister, Humberto Ortega. In December 1987 Miranda testified that the
Cuban and Soviet military advisors in Nicaragua had agreed to double the size of the Nicaraguan military to 59,000 men and then equip it with twelve MiG-21 fighters, an additional
squadron of Mi-24 attack helicopters, and medium-range surface-to-air missiles. Miranda also
testified that Nicaragua was supporting the radical left in Guatemala and El Salvador.[38]

Finally, in February 1988 the U.S. Congress cut off all aid to the *Contras*, and just when it appeared that the *Contras* would wither and die, the Soviet Union imploded. As a consequence, the Sandinista regime in Nicaragua stopped receiving aid from the Communist nations. On April 1, 1988, the Sandinista government and a faction of the *Contras* concluded a cease-fire at Sapoa, Nicaragua. This pleased neither the Reagan administration nor the more militant *Contras* but it led to an armed truce.[39]

In order to continue in power, Sandinista leader Daniel Ortega gambled that he could win an internationally supervised presidential election. He lost the gamble. Surprisingly, in February 1990 Violeta Chamorro defeated Ortega and the Sandinista government fell; the war with the *Contras* ended. Some 30,000 Nicaraguans died in the conflict between 1980 and 1990. The economic consequences of exporting revolution, of ten years of an American embargo, and of numerous *Contra* attacks were devastating. Nicaragua was left on its own to reintegrate into society some 12,000 *Contra* guerrillas and tens of thousands of former Sandinista soldiers, most of whom remained well armed.[40]

EL SALVADOR, 1980–91

The violence in El Salvador took on a new intensity in 1980 following the Sandinista victory in Nicaragua. Prior to 1980 the Salvadoran war had been a struggle between five leftist organizations and the government. In May 1980 these factions met in Havana at the invitation of Fidel Castro. In exchange for Cuban support, the guerrillas agreed to coordinate their activities in El Salvador and abroad and to adopt the name the United Revolutionary Directorate (*Directorio Revolucionario Unido*—DRU); soon they became known as the Farabundo Martí National Liberation Front (*Frente Farabundo Martí para la Liberacion Nacional*—FMLN).[41]

The Cuban aid was immediate. In 1980 Shafik Handal, General Secretary of the Communist Party of El Salvador, arranged to have arms smuggled from Bulgaria, Czechoslovakia, East Germany, Hungary, Vietnam, and Ethiopia into El Salvador. They were shipped to Cuba and then airlifted to Nicaragua.[42] From there, the arms were transported to El Salvador by a variety of air, land, and water routes. Trucks fitted with secret compartments carried arms through Honduras. Small craft brought arms from Nicaragua's Pacific ports across the Gulf of Fonseca. Other craft transported munitions from Nicaragua's northwest coast to the numerous inlets that dot the coast of El Salvador. Light aircraft were also used to fly weapons to the guerrillas. Also, Salvadoran guerrillas trained in Nicaragua and in Cuba, possibly in units as large as battalions (250 to 300 men).[43]

Aid from the Communist world did create a crisis between the two most powerful Salvadoran organizations as they vied for power. In 1983 Salvador Cayetano Carpio,[44] leader of the 3,000-member Popular Liberation Forces (*Fuerzas de Liberación Popular*—FPL), mysteriously died and Joaquin Villalobos Huezo,[45] leader of the 4,000-man People's Revolutionary Army (*Ejército Revolucionario del Pueblo*—ERP), emerged as the most prominent guerrilla leader. Villalobos, a pragmatist, appealed to a wide audience among the radical left. Among his new supporters were former lieutenants of Carpio, including Carpio's deputy, the noted female guerrilla Mélida Anaya Montes.[46]

By 1980 El Salvador was in crisis. On January 22, some 200 Salvadorans died in an antigovernment protest. On March 24 Salvadoran archbishop Oscar Romero, an outspoken critic of the government, was assassinated. In December President Carter suspended military aid to the Salvadoran government due to its human rights abuses.[47]

In January 1981 the FMLN proclaimed the "final offensive" and attempted to expand its stronghold beyond the north-central areas so that it could proclaim a provisional government and gain international recognition. On the first, the FMLN destroyed one of the longest bridges in El Salvador, "*El Puente de Oro*" (the Golden Bridge) in the department of Usulutan. To capture and defend territory required the guerrillas to field brigade-size units (3,000 men). The FMLN also opened two newspapers and three radio stations that broadcasted from Managua, Nicaragua, and Mexico City. Salpress (the Salvadoran Press), a guerrilla news service established in 1980, distributed features worldwide. In August 1981 France and Mexico recognized the FMLN as a legitimate entity. And in 1983, the FMLN hired a U.S. public relations firm to market its position.[48]

During 1981 the weakness of the Salvadoran government and its armed forces were so pronounced that a guerrilla victory seemed possible; the guerrillas were attempting to defeat the Salvadoran army in direct combat. In July the new Reagan administration resumed military aid to El Salvador. It escalated from $12 million under Carter to $85 million under Reagan. The effectiveness of the U.S. aid was limited. Finding instructors and a place to train proved to be nagging problems. The U.S. Congress froze the number of U.S. trainers at fifty-five individuals as a consequence of the fear of repeating the Vietnam experience. Venezuelan trainers were enlisted to quietly fill the gap. However, a U.S. State Department employee revealed their participation to the press and consequently the Venezuelan government withdrew its soldiers under domestic pressure.[49]

Between January and May 1982, the United States trained approximately 500 cadets at Fort Benning, Georgia, and the "General Ramón Belloso" light infantry battalion of 900 men at Fort Bragg, North Carolina. Also, the U.S. cajoled Honduras into building a training center in northern Honduras where both Salvadoran and Honduran troops were trained.[50]

On January 2, 1982, the FMLN attacked air force headquarters at Ilopango (7 Mi E of San Salvador) and destroyed or damaged twelve aircraft and seven helicopters. This was almost half of the Salvadoran air force's strength. The United States immediately replaced the losses. A year later the FMLN attacked the 1st Brigade's headquarters outside of San Salvador. By now the guerrillas controlled one-third of the country.[51]

In 1983 the Salvadoran government initiated the Nation Campaign Plan. It focused on political (including military), economic, and social development in the departments of San Vicente and Usulutan in eastern El Salvador where the guerrillas were most active. On December 31, 1983, the FMLN destroyed the second longest bridge in El Salvador, the Cuscatlan Bridge, also located in Usulutan Department. During this time, the extreme right formed death squads to kill suspected guerrillas and their sympathizers. Between 1982 and 1985 the guerrillas wilted under the constant pressure from the military.[52] The guerrillas attempted a few large-scale operations, such as the attack on the government's communication outpost on the slopes of San Salvador volcano, but in general, these failed. The guerrillas could not win control of an area where they could establish a provisional government.

The FMLN adopted a new strategy, that of attacking the national economy and demoralizing the army.[53] The guerrillas broke into small units, generally ten to fifteen members. They concentrated on kidnappings, executions, and economic sabotage, focusing on destroying electric production and fresh water supply systems. The guerrillas planted mines and set booby traps, typically made from readily available commercial material. These accounted for some 80 percent of the army's casualties. Approximately sixty soldiers were seriously injured each month and undoubtedly large numbers of civilians as well; this resulted in some 5,000 amputees in the army alone. North Americans became prime targets. Ricardo Calvaria, an ERP spokesman, stated, "in the long run killing Yankees is a form of undermining Reagan's policies."[54]

During 1985 the El Salvador military received $454 million in aid from the United States which allowed for significantly upgrading its capabilities. American advisors urged the Salvadoran army to use small, self-contained commando-like groups to keep the guerrillas on the run. The government also began a propaganda campaign aimed at convincing the guerrilla rank and file to lay down its arms on the promise of full pardon.

In September 1985 the guerrillas kidnapped President José Napoleon Duarte's daughter, Ines. In order to secure the army's agreement to the exchange of prisoners that won his daughter's release, Duarte conceded greater autonomy to the military in the war against the guerrillas. In January 1986 the FMLN attacked and virtually destroyed the town of Juayua in Sonsonate Province.

By the end of 1986 the army had to resort to press gangs in order to forcefully fill its ranks. Each barracks had its own press gang and the vast majority of those gathered were poor and uneducated. The well-to-do easily escaped military service. On October 2, 1986, the government passed a law attempting to better enforce the compulsory military service for men and women over eighteen as required by the constitution. In practice, little changed. The well-to-do found ways to evade service.

Beginning in 1986 the government adopted a new strategy. American reconnaissance aircraft flying from Palmerola, Honduras, flew surveillance missions over guerrilla-held territory. When a concentration of people was located, the site was attacked by the Salvadoran air force. The objectives were to wear down the guerrillas and to drive the civilians out of the area. Twelve "free-fire" zones were established in the Chalatenango region. Anyone found there was regarded as the enemy.

Following the devastating earthquake on October 10, 1986, the guerrillas declared a unilateral truce. This was more the result of the need to catch their breath than for humanitarian reasons.

By 1988 the guerrillas appreciated that they were running out of time as the Soviet Union moved toward *perestroika*. The guerrillas knew that Cuba alone could not sustain their activity. They decided to carry the war to the cities so that the middle and upper classes would be threatened and forced to choose sides. If the guerrillas failed to achieve an outright victory, perhaps such an initiative would strengthen their hand at any future negotiating table for a compromise peace. In part this hope was based on the changing attitude within the United States. Now that the international Communist threat was rapidly disintegrating, more members of the U.S. Congress were pressing for a compromise settlement within El Salvador.

In November 1989 the FMLN announced a "final offensive" for a second time. This was patterned on the Nicaraguan example: First you create the impression that the government is under a state of siege and then you topple it with a massive assault. On November 11 the FMLN launched an all-out attack. On November 21 the FMLN captured and held hostage the OAS' General Secretary, João Baena Soares, in the Sheraton Hotel in San Salvador. The United States flew the elite commando unit "Delta Force" to El Salvador but by the time it arrived the General Secretary had been rescued by Salvadorian special forces.[55]

The population did not rise up in support of the FMLN nor did the army disintegrate. The guerrillas suffered large casualties during the offensive and had to abandon the attack. The guerrillas did demonstrate a vitality that surprised some in the Salvadoran army and many in the United States. At this critical time, the credibility of the Salvadoran military was significantly damaged when on November 16 six prominent Jesuit priests working at the Universidad Centroamericana, along with their housekeeper and her fifteen-year-old daughter, were dragged from their beds and murdered by a U.S.-trained special forces unit. This act placed U.S. support in jeopardy. These events reinforced the belief of many members of the U.S. Congress that a political compromise was the best solution.

The guerrillas lost the battle for the cities but were offered a political compromise, primarily because the U.S. Congress desired out of the conflict. In fact, the guerrillas' sponsor—Cuba—had become impotent and they were faced with the dismal reality of going it alone. Following two years of negotiations, the guerrillas were reintegrated into society in 1992. The nation had sustained severe economic damage and was overflowing with weapons. As part of the compromise, the government dismantled a large part of the army. During the decade-long struggle, the Salvadorian army had grown from 20,000 men to some 65,000. More than 40,000 soldiers and guerrillas were repatriated to civilian life. Also, one hundred officers were dismissed from the Salvadorian army for human rights violations. Although the Communist ideology was discredited, high unemployment and an overabundance of weapons led to significant lawlessness and, in the remote regions of the nation, anarchy.

HONDURAS, 1982–91

Although suffering from a plethora of political, social, and economic problems, initially Honduras was not the focus of Castro-supported insurgency. This fact plus its strategic location—sharing borders with Guatemala, Nicaragua, and El Salvador—made it the keystone in American strategy for maintaining control in Central America following the downfall of the Somoza government in Nicaragua.[56]

The Honduran military was unique among those of Central America. Prior to World War II, it was highly decentralized with commanders and units possessing strong regional loyalties. The creation of a national army began very late by regional standards. The first national military training school for officers was not established until the 1940s. Professionalization was expedited by a May 25, 1954, U.S.-Honduran treaty whereby the United States provided military aid in exchange for unlimited access to Honduran products.[57]

Under the 1957 constitution, the Honduran army became virtually independent of civilian control. The senior officers chose the chief of the armed forces and the armed forces had the right to disobey civilian authority if they believed it unconstitutional. This made the military the most important political force within Honduras throughout the era of the cold war.

By 1980 the military had governed Honduras for seventeen years; under pressure from the United States, elections were held for a national assembly to be followed in eighteen months by presidential elections.[58]

Although Honduras had not been directly involved in the recent regional fighting, a few of its army's officers had been active on the periphery. Apparently, independent-minded Honduran commanders illicitly sold arms to the Sandinistas prior to their victory over Somoza in Nicaragua. Also, ultraleft guerrillas were shipping arms through Honduras possibly with the collusion of some Honduran officers. Additionally, Salvadoran guerrillas from the Popular

Liberation Forces (*Fuerzas Liberacion Popular*—FLP) and the Revolutionary Army of the Poor (*Ejercito Revolucionaio del Pobre*—ERP) were using a demilitarized zone along the Honduran-Salvadoran border as safe havens. This zone had been established following the 1969 border war (see chapter 32).[59]

The new Reagan administration significantly increased military aid to the Honduran government. In particular, it wanted to eliminate the guerrilla havens within the demilitarized zone. In October 1980 the United States orchestrated a treaty between Honduras and El Salvador which provided for joint patrols and gave the Salvadoran army the right to enter the havens when pursuing guerrillas. In fact, the joint patrols began before the treaty had been negotiated. These led to a massacre on May 14, 1980, when some 600 Salvadorans were killed while trying to cross the Sumpul River which separated the two nations. A second massacre occurred in March 1981 at the Lempa River.[60]

In November 1981 Liberal Suazo Córdova, backed by an ultra-Conservative military faction headed by Col. Gustavo Alvarez,[61] won the presidency. The United States endeavored to forge an informal military coalition to include Honduras, Guatemala, and El Salvador. By mid-1982 this had not come together possibly because the Guatemalans still smarted from their treatment by the Carter administration. So increasingly the U.S. strategy became to build up Honduras and to support the *Contras* operating out of Honduras and Costa Rica.[62]

Fighting intensified in Honduras. In July 1982 Honduran guerrillas blew up a generating plant in the capital, Tegucigalpa. In August Honduran and Nicaraguan troops clashed along the border and the Honduran army was placed on full alert. In November *Newsweek* revealed that the Honduran border town of Negroponte was controlled by the *Contras* who were using it as a haven and staging point in their operations against Nicaragua.[63]

The United States and Honduras began a series of military exercises which escalated to previously unseen proportions within the hemisphere.[64] In May 1982 Honduran General Alvarez signed a secret agreement with the United States to build the Regional Training Center (*Centro Regional Entrenamiento Militar*—CREM) at Puerto Castilla (150 mi NNE of Tegucigalpa) and to upgrade three Honduran airfields—Palmerola, Golosón (near La Ceiba), and La Mesa (near San Pedro Sula). The first U.S. trainers and Salvadoran troops to be trained arrived in June. The Palmerola Air Base, some 50 miles from the Nicaraguan border, became the focal point of U.S. aid.[65]

In September 1983 the Honduran army destroyed a guerrilla column in Olancho. Among the dead was the North American Roman Catholic priest, James Guadalupe Carney.[66]

In March 1984 a group of young officers forced Alvarez and four senior generals to resign; they permitted Suazo to remain as President. Air force Gen. Walter López now took command of the armed forces. These young officers believed that Alvarez was politically too ambitious and had conceded too much to the United States for too little. They wanted to renegotiate (1) the use of the CREM training center where twice as many Salvadorans as Hondurans were trained; (2) the presence of the *Contras* in their country; (3) the terms of the 1954 military pact with the United States; (4) the status of the Salvadoran troops in Honduras; and (5) a settlement of their border dispute with El Salvador.[67]

In May, 60,000 demonstrators in Tegucigalpa and 40,000 in San Pedro Sula protested U.S. involvement in Honduras. On September 28 Honduras blocked the admission of Salvadoran troops to CREM. Finally, the Honduran government required that the training camp be closed in June 1985.[68]

Hondurans became increasingly concerned as the U.S. Congress twice rejected Reagan's request in 1984 for $28 million to fund the *Contras*, since some 15,000 were inside Honduras. One Honduran officer observed, "If they are guerrillas, why aren't they in the mountains? They are a bunch of dilettantes, who spend their lives in their casino. They will never overthrow the Sandinistas."[69] In August 1984 Honduras ordered various *Contra* facilities closed. In January 1985 it expelled the *Contra* leader Steadman for holding a press conference in Tegucigalpa. But in the long run, the new Honduran military leadership was unable to get significant concessions from the United States.

Honduran and Nicaraguan troops clashed along the border. In September 1985 one Honduran soldier was killed and two Nicaraguan helicopters badly damaged. In December 1986 the Sandinistas attacked *Contra* camps in southeastern Honduras. Honduras had ignored earlier, smaller incursions. This time Honduras responded with a cross-border artillery barrage followed by a raid by Super Mystere fighter-bombers against the town of Wiwili. In March 1988 a large-scale Sandinista incursion into Honduras influenced the United States to dispatch troops to Honduras.[70]

Elsewhere, the fate of the *Contra*-Sandinista conflict was being decided by the two protagonists. In the summer of 1989, Honduras, with the tacit support of the new George Bush administration, expelled the remaining *Contras*.[71]

GUATEMALA, 1974–91

By 1974 Guatemala was relatively peaceful due to the earlier defeats of the radical left. The Guatemalan radical left regrouped in order to renew the "unfinished revolution" of Arbenz and the *foco* wars; these roots gave the guerrillas a strong sense of identity. Although presidential elections were held in 1974, 1978, and 1982, the poor voter turnouts belied a fear of reprisals against potential voters from the extreme left and the reactionary right as well as a lack of confidence in the political system in spite of the (unenforced) mandatory requirement to vote.

On February 4, 1976, an earthquake killed 23,000 people and destroyed half of the nation's inadequate infrastructure. During the next three years, the prime mission of the army became the reconstruction of that infrastructure. The guerrillas took advantage of the army's distraction to infiltrate new areas of operations.[72]

Survivors of the Rebel Armed Forces (*Fuerzas Armadas Rebeldes*—FAR) and the Guatemalan Workers Party (*Partido Guatemalteco del Trabajo*—PGT) traveled to Cuba, Vietnam, and other nations that had experienced recent revolutions to examine their tactics. Upon their return, these radical leftists helped form the Guerrilla Army of the Poor (*Ejercito Guerrillero de Los Pobres*—EGP) in the remote Ixan region, some 250 miles north of Guatemala City. The members of the EGP rejected the strategy of the 1960s and 1970s, labeling it as "improvised action," and developed a new, comprehensive plan. First, they rejected belief in the brevity of the struggle as promised in the *foco* strategy and prepared for prolonged warfare. Second, they wanted to establish a base and political infrastructure in a remote but populated region. Third, they sought the support of the Indian population which the radical left had previously ignored.

While the radical left was reorganizing, both it and the reactionary right renewed their reigns of terror. In October 1978 the right-wing ESA published the names of thirty-eight individuals "sentenced to death." Within two days Oliverio Castaneda, president of the University's student association, was murdered; his name had been on the list. In January 1980 the Jesuits in Guatemala declared that the death squads had murdered 3,252 persons in the first ten months of 1979.[73]

In rapid succession, the radical left assassinated the former Minister of Defense, Gen. Rafael Arriaga Bosque (September 29, 1977); assassinated the Conservative politician Jorge David García (December 27); and kidnapped former Foreign Minister Roberto Herrera Ibarguen (December 31). The kidnappers released Herrera Ibarguen on January 30, 1978, after a ransom was paid.[74]

In 1977 the Carter administration conditioned the continuation of economic and military assistance to the Guatemalan government on improvements in its human rights practices. The government believed this to be an infringement of its sovereignty, refused to comply, and as a consequence the United States "publicly" terminated military aid. Apparently not all U.S. military advisors were withdrawn and some spare parts for military hardware reached Guatemala. Also, the United States continued economic aid. As its readiness deteriorated, the Guatemalan military began losing control of the countryside. The capabilities of the guerrillas, aided through Cuba, improved.[75]

To offset the loss of American military aid, the Guatemalan army purchased weapons far and wide. The Israeli-made GALIL rifle replaced the American M-1; Israeli- and Swiss-produced aircraft substituted for American models; heavy machine guns were purchased from Belgium; and artillery pieces were acquired from Argentina, Spain, and Yugoslavia. Also, as American training ceased, schools had to be established and doctrine developed. However, these were stopgap measures and in the long run could not fill the void created by the partial American withdrawal.[76]

As order broke down, vigilantism increased. Indians were frequently victims of the violence, particularly from the reactionary right. At least some of the time, their political actions were orchestrated by the radical left. In May 1978 some 700 Kekchis demonstrated in Panzós (135 mi NE of Guatemala City). Soldiers killed over 140 and wounded another 300 of the demonstrators. Following this tragedy, the reactionary right tortured and killed hundreds of Indians attempting to eliminate through terror the possibility of the Indians joining the radical left as had been the case in the successful Nicaraguan revolution.[77]

In January 1980 Indians from El Quiché (75 mi NW of Guatemala City) marched on the capital for a second time, protesting disappearances. On January 30, thirty Indians occupied the Spanish Embassy and on the following day they took the Spanish ambassador, Máximo Cajal y López, hostage. Against the wishes of the Spanish Ambassador, the Guatemalan police stormed the embassy. The Indians fought back with fire bombs. The Ambassador escaped with his clothes on fire. Thirty-nine people, including all but one of the Indians, died. The surviving Indian was kidnapped from a hospital and murdered. The violence against the Indians escalated. Amnesty International placed the death tool at 5,000 Guatemalans, mostly Indians, between 1978 and 1981.[78]

The military government believed many within the Roman Catholic clergy to be openly supporting the radical left, so the reactionary right struck at church members. Between January 1980 and July 1981, at least ten priests were killed by paramilitary groups. By July 1980, within El Quiché Department in northern Guatemala, three priests had been murdered, one kidnapped, and the bishop unsuccessfully ambushed. As a consequence, the Church suspended pastoral activities in the area and withdrew fifty priests and nuns.[79]

The Guatemalan radical left began to focus more upon military targets than civilian ones. Many of its operations were centered against the Verapaz oil region bordering Mexico.[80] However, the radical left was unable to take full advantage of the government's loss of U.S. aid because it remained disunited. In the fall of 1980 factions, meeting at Castro's "request" in Managua, Nicaragua, agreed to unify. In exchange, Castro agreed to increase support. However, the cooperation among guerrillas improved only marginally. In spite of this, by 1982 the guerrillas controlled 80 percent of the country. They had some 12,000 men and women under arms and perhaps 100,000 active sympathizers.[81]

In November 1981 the Guatemalan government began creating and arming the Civilian Self-Defense Patrols (*Patrullas de Autodefensa Civil*—PAC), a paramilitary civilian defense organization. Apparently, the PAC grew rapidly: By mid-1982 some 25,000 peasants were incorporated; by early 1983 there were 350,000 members; and by early 1985 there were 900,000 members. These individuals were drawn from a population of some 9 million people. Many were induced to join the PAC through a program entitled "guns and beans" (*fusiles y frijoles*); the peasants were given food and medical help in exchange for joining PAC. Patrol duty was obligatory in rural areas for those between sixteen and fifty years of age on punishment by death. In 1987 the requirement was extended to those between fifteen and fifty-five years of age. A member served a twenty-four-hour shift every eighth day. Mostly the PAC members were armed with old carbines and shotguns. In some cases the civilian defense patrols became the tools of the reactionary right, committing massacres; they have been accused of genocide.[82]

In February 1982 the four leading guerrilla organizations formed a coalition known as the Guatemalan National Revolutionary Union (*Union Revolucionaria Nacional Guatemalteca*—URNG). This was a condition of Fidel Castro in exchange for continued support.[83] The Organization of the Armed People (*Organizacion del Pueblo en Armas*—OAP), led by Rodrigo Asturias,[84] was the strongest element. Asturias began to abandon ambushes as a tactic, believing that they did not cause enough casualties. Instead, this guerrilla focused on attacking army posts. The guerrillas frequently achieved total surprise; it was not unusual for the guerrillas to attack at night or during a tropical rainstorm. Their objectives varied from capturing arms to kidnapping the commanding officers. The guerrillas' intelligence was very good.

In 1982 the guerrillas attempted to "liberate" those regions in which they already operated with little opposition—El Quiche, Huehuetenango, Sacatepequez, Alta Verapaz, Baja Verapaz, and Chimaltenango—an area of some 10,000 square miles. The objective was to gain political recognition of this "liberated territory" by the United Nations so that the guerrillas could achieve belligerent status. This would allow them to have access to international forums as well as full recognition and support by the non-Western bloc. The geographical key to the plan was Chimaltenango, only 45 miles from the national capital, Guatemala City. Chimaltenango had been a guerrilla hotbed since the mid-1970s. The guerrillas tried to isolate Chimaltenango by blocking the roads by felling trees, digging trenches, and planting Claymore mines.[85]

On March 23, 1982, Gen. José Efraín Ríos Montt,[86] a born-again Christian, seized the government and prevented newly elected Gen. Angel Aníbal Guevara from taking office. Ríos Montt was supported by the younger officers who were appalled by the harshness of the conflict. He closed Congress and abrogated the constitution. He declared, "we will shoot anyone who breaks the law."[87] The Reagan administration quickly recognized the new government.[88]

The Guatemalan army formulated the "Victory 82" strategy. This strategy united government activities under a military district commander which, in addition to executing military strategy, empowered him to significantly improve social services. In fact, the government had lost control over these. Prior to the creation of the interagency coordinators (*coordinadores inter-institucionales*) who worked for the military district commander, government bureaucrats—teachers, doctors, roadworkers, and the like—were frequently absent from their jobs up to half the time and the government pretended that the problem did not exist.

Victory 82 (and its annual successors) focused on regaining control of the countryside. Initially, the military established bases in the mountains from which troops launched searches for the enemy rather than reacting to its attack; increased the activity of special forces such as airborne troops and intelligence collecting; and created a Department of Psychological Operations. Next, the military established "model villages."

The model villages (*Aldeas Modelo*) plan (officially, Aid Program for Areas in Conflict, *Programa para Ayuda a Areas en Conflicto*—PAAC) was based upon an Israeli concept used in the occupied West Bank and Gaza. Cuba claimed that Israelis were involved in setting up the project.[89]

The purpose was to draw the villagers out of guerrilla-controlled territory. Frequently, the guerrillas forced the villagers to provide for their needs and when necessary to serve as human shields. The living conditions in the model villages were a significant improvement over those in the guerrilla-controlled territory; however, the peasants were given no choice. Their former homes were destroyed and crops burned.

On May 12, 1982, guerrillas including ten Indians and leftists from the Popular front and the Committee for Peasant Unity (*Frente Popular*—FP-31) seized the Brazilian embassy and took about ten hostages, including the ambassador. The government allowed them to hold a press conference in which they denounced the security forces and gave them safe passage to Mexico in exchange for the release of the hostages.[90]

The Ríos Montt government had irritated many, including the right-wing National Liberation Movement (*Movimiento de Liberacion Nacional*—MLN), the Catholic Church, the Guatemalan wealthy, and even the United States. The MLN, which possessed a 5,000-man private army, resented the prominence Ríos Montt gave to junior officers. The Catholic Church opposed the human rights abuses and the favoritism now afforded to born-again Christians. The wealthy were opposed to a new 10-percent value added tax. And, the United States did not like the fact that Ríos Montt was not willing to support it against Nicaragua's leftist government. On August 8, 1983, the Minister of Defense, Gen. Oscar Humberto Mejía Victores, overthrew Ríos Montt.[91]

In mid-1983 the guerrillas launched new attacks in the remote regions and these escalated through 1985. In November 1983 the United States temporarily suspended all aid to Guatemala when the bodies of U.S. Agency for International Development (AID) workers Felipe Ralac Xiloj and Julieta Sánchez Castillo were discovered near the Guatemalan border with Mexico. Meanwhile, on July 1, 1984, the military promoted elections for a national constitutional assembly. Discord reigned as the assembly argued over yet another constitution (the fourth in forty years) and its own salary (which proved to be most generous). In 1985 the provisional government of Gen. Mejía Victores regained U.S. military aid. In 1985 the U.S. Congress authorized $45.5 million in aid to Guatemala. On January 14, 1986, the military handed the presidency over to the recently elected civilian Vinicio Cerezo Arévalo.[92]

Following the return to civilian rule, the right-wing death squads escalated their activities. As a consequence, on February 5 President Cerezo ordered a raid on the government's Technical Investigations Department (*Departamento de Investigaciones Tecnicas*—DIT) which was known to be linked with the death squads. Some 600 DIT agents were arrested and the agency abolished.[93]

The reinstatement of U.S. military aid to the Guatemalan army, coupled with the decline of Communist aid through Cuba for the guerrillas, led to the near collapse of the radical left by 1991. However, the worldwide collapse of Communism influenced the United States into pressuring the Guatemalan government to compromise with the radical left.

The military dominated Guatemalan politics throughout the cold war.[94] Although military officers were in theory accountable to the civil judiciary, in practice, they frequently were not. This long, bloody conflict eroded discipline and corrupted some officers. During the three decades of conflict, some 100,000 Guatemalans died and almost as many disappeared and probably perished. Also, more than 500,000 refugees fled Guatemala.[95]

COLOMBIA, 1974–91

The M-19, the fourth major Communist guerrilla group in Colombia, began operations in January 1974 when the FARC, ELN and EPL were in retreat. The M-19 derived its name from the contested presidential election of April 19, 1970, when former President Gustavo Rojas Pinilla was defeated. Its ideology was Marxist with a veneer of selected ideas of Simón Bolívar. The M-19 envisioned expanding into the "Bolivarian" nations—Venezuela, Ecuador, Peru, and Bolivia. Its activities centered in the cities. In January 1974, M-19 stole the sword and spurs of Simón Bolívar from a museum in Bogotá. It soon focused its operations on kidnappings. On February 15, 1976, it kidnapped José Raquel Mercado, the president of the Colombian Confederation of Workers. Its demands not met, M-19 executed Mercado on April 19. Between 1974 and 1978, M-19 kidnapped 417 persons, raising $6 million in ransom money from many of these.[96]

In 1978, M-19 scored a major, yet fleeting success. It stole 4,000 weapons from an army arsenal in northern Bogotá. Within a month, the army recovered most of the arms and arrested many of those responsible. M-19 turned its emphasis from urban to rural operations.[97]

In March 1979 M-19, the FARC, and the ELN (now led by Nicolás Rodríguez Bautista) began closer cooperation. By the end of the year, the FARC extended its operations into the departments of El Valle, Meta, Cundinamarca, and the territory of Arauca (northeastern Colombia). The recently elected Julio Turbay Ayala administration (1978–82) imposed an antiterrorist law that gave government forces significant latitude in fighting guerrillas. Numerous violations of human rights occurred. However, by the end of 1979 the military had confined the ELN to the central Magdalena region.[98]

On February 27, 1980, the M-19 guerrillas, led by Rosenberg Pabon Pabon, seized the Dominican Republic Embassy in Bogotá. They captured the American, Mexican, Uruguay, and Venezuelan ambassadors, fifteen other diplomats, and the Papal Nuncio. They were held hostage for sixty-one days. As part of the negotiated settlement, the guerrillas were flown to Cuba and given asylum.[99]

In the summer of 1980, Cuba arranged a meeting among the three most powerful guerrilla forces—the FARC, the ELN, and M-19. These Leftists adequately resolved their ideological differences to rejuvenate a coordinated guerrilla war against the Colombian government.[100]

In February 1981 Cuban-trained guerrillas clandestinely landed in Colombia from the fishing vessel *Freddie*. Pabon was among the passengers and was subsequently captured by the Colombia government. As a result, Colombia suspended diplomatic relations with Cuba on March 23. On November 14 the Colombia navy intercepted and sank the motorboat *El Karina* attempting to land more guerrillas and weapons on Colombia's Pacific coast.[101]

Striking out at the United States, M-19 on January 19, 1981, kidnapped and executed U.S. citizen Chester A. Bitterman, who was a linguist at the Summer Institute of Linguistics in Bogotá. The Leftists accused him of being a CIA spy.[102]

At this time, Fidel Castro attempted to exploit the drug trade to support the Radical Left in its effort to seize power. Between October 1981 and March 1982, the Colombian Jaime Guillot Lara purchased weapons and carried money from Cuba to M-19 guerrillas. In exchange, Guillot's marijuana-laden ships were given sanctuary in Cuban waters. President Turbay asked the OAS to create an Inter-American naval force to intercept weapons being shipped to Colombia from Cuba and Nicaragua.[103]

In 1981, M-19 suffered a significant defeat. The Colombian military intercepted and destroyed a large band of well-armed guerrillas attempting to infiltrate from Ecuador by using the San Miguel River. Many of the guerrillas had been trained by the Sandinistas in Nicaragua.

In spite of the setbacks for the guerrillas, the Colombian government was under increasing national and international pressure to reach an accommodation with the Radical Left. On March 23, 1981, President Julio Turbay signed an amnesty law for the guerrillas and some 1,500 fighters accepted. On June 20, 1982, shortly before relinquishing office, Turbay lifted the state of siege, which had been in effect continuously for thirty-four years. Although the guerrillas had not been eliminated, they were on the defensive. The FARC still operated in more than a dozen isolated pockets and had about 1,000 fighters; the EPL and the ELN were reduced to a few hundred fighters.[104]

Turbay's successor, Belisario Betancur (1982–86), a Conservative, was elected president. His unexpected victory was in large measure attributed to this proposed amnesty, "Peace for Colombia" (*La Paz por Colombia*). During his August 7, 1982, inaugural address, Betancur offered amnesty to the guerrillas without conditions; they did not have to surrender their weapons. Later the amnesty offer was extended to guerrillas in prison. The three major guerrilla factions—the FARC, the ELN, and M-19—agreed to the truce. The agreement held for about one year; however, many on both sides opposed the amnesty and it finally broke down.[105]

In July 1983 the ELN began a new offensive. It dynamited three American-owned buildings in the city of Bucaramanga (280 mi N of Bogotá). On October 7 the ELN led violent demonstrations at the national university in which eleven persons were injured. On November 22, 1983, the ELN kidnapped the brother of President Betancur and released him unharmed on December 7.

In March and August 1984 the government signed still other truces with the guerrilla factions (excluding the ELN) promising political reforms in exchange for a cease-fire. These truces were attempts by the government to emulate a successful cease-fire that had taken place between the Venezuelan government and their guerrillas. Unlike the circumstance in Venezuela, the Colombian government was negotiating from a position of weakness. In Venezuela, the guerrillas had been decisively defeated prior to being offered an amnesty. This was not the case in Colombia. As a result of its weakness, the government permitted the guerrillas to keep their organization, arms, and uniforms.[106]

In spite of these disappointments, the government was committed to the peace plan and began a one-year trial period. It initiated political and social changes, all of which were criticized by the guerrillas as being halfhearted. Fighting renewed. In April 1985 three pitched battles took place. Government troops laid siege to a major M-19 stronghold near Corinto in Cauca Province (225 mi SW of Bogotá). After three weeks of fighting, during which both sides sustained numerous casualties, the guerrillas slipped through government lines. The only government success was the defection of Luís Alberto Rodríguez, a deputy commander in the FARC.[107]

In November 1985, M-19 seized control of the palace of justice in Bogotá. The Colombian military insisted on an assault, and the President gave the order. Over one hundred people died including eleven supreme court justices. This attack caused M-19 to lose popular support.[108]

In April 1986 Virgilio Barco, a Liberal, was elected president (1986–90), again partly because of a promise to end the struggle with the guerrillas. Now the ELN emerged as the most aggressive Leftists, having as many as 50,000 sympathizers. Within four months violence ranging from kidnappings to massacres were commonplace. During November alone, 70 guerrillas and an equal number of soldiers were killed during battles and some 200 policemen were seriously wounded. Scores of *campesinos* were massacred. Oil installations valued at $50 million were sabotaged. On the other side, low-level military officers used torture and assassinated members of the Radical Left.[109]

During 1986 the FARC began yet another armed truce with the government as a consequence of the Uribe Accords. Most of the FARC's combatants were demobilized and the FARC created the mass-based political party, the Patriotic Union (*Unión Patriotica*—UP). The accord was largely enforced by the strong hand of the FARC's leader, Manuel Marulanda. The Patriotic Union enjoyed almost immediate political success in local and regional elections. It ran Jaime Pardo Leal in the 1986 presidential elections. However, right-wing death squads assassinated Pardo shortly after he urged the government to act against them. As a consequence, the FARC remobilized many of its fighters and the major guerrilla groups formed a coalition known as the "Simón Bolívar Guerrilla Coordination."[110]

Right-wing death squads attempted to sabotage the local elections in March 1988. This was the first popular election of mayors in Colombia; previously, mayors had been appointed by the central government. Six hundred members of the Patriotic Union, including seventeen mayoral candidates, were murdered. In March, twenty-three trade unionists, who were also members of the Patriot Union, were dragged from their beds during the early morning hours and executed in the coastal region of Uraba. By late 1988 the Colombian government was cited for human-rights abuses by Amnesty International. The FARC resumed its offensive against the government, kidnapping numerous officials.[111]

On May 29, 1988, M-19 kidnapped two-time Conservative presidential candidate Alvaro Gómez. He was released on July 20—Independence Day.[112]

In late 1988 the government sent army troops under Gen. Luís Cabrales to northeastern Colombia, a banana-growing region. Here, Leftist guerrillas, Rightist death squads, drug lords, and the private armies of estate owners operated with near impunity from the government. Following the kidnapping of twenty-two soldiers, Cabrales demonstrated his firepower against several villages suspected of being sympathetic to the guerrillas. The guerrillas immediately released the soldiers. Cabrales, supported by the landowners, instituted a citizens identification program;

liberal politicians objected, arguing that the death squads had access to the information. Cabrales was soon relieved.[113]

Increasingly, right-wing death squads killed Colombians on the Left. On November 11, 1988, death squad members attacked suspected Leftists in the city of Segovia (170 mi NNW of Bogotá) with machine guns and grenades. During an hour-long rampage, they killed 47 civilians and wounded 200. In the hamlet of Pinalitio they killed 14 peasants who were watching a cock fight.[114]

In 1989 President Barco reached terms with some members of M-19 and the FARC; but the ELN and EPL would not agree. The agreement caused some of the guerrillas to lay down their arms. Former guerrillas created the Democratic Alliance political party and ran for political office. As a concession to the Leftists, Barco stripped the military of the right to arm civilians, but he was unsuccessful in disarming the right-wing militias.

Shortly, the two most prominent Leftist presidential candidates were assassinated. On March 22, 1990, Bernardo Jaramillo, the Patriotic Union candidate, was assassinated in the "secured" Bogotá airport. Carlos Pizarro, leader of the Democratic Alliance (and former M-19 guerrilla), was assassinated by a gunman while flying as a passenger on April 26.[115] As a consequence, perhaps 10,000 guerrillas renewed the armed struggle (6,000 fighters from the FARC; 2,500 fighters from the ELN; and 500 fighters from the EPL).[116]

Between February and July 1991, a special assembly wrote a new constitution to replace the 1896 document. On the day that the special representatives were selected (December 9, 1990), the Colombian army seized the FARC's public headquarters in Casa Verde, Department of Meta (90 mi SE of Bogotá), causing more of the Radical Left to take up arms again.[117]

Once again, the government attempted to negotiate a truce with the FARC in early 1991. As the negotiations dragged out, the guerrillas began attacking Colombia's oil installations in hope of influencing the talks to their advantage. The ELN, which had rejected the talks, carried the violence to an extreme.[118]

Colombia's Radical Left did not give up with the ending of the cold war. It continued the fight, choosing to use drug money to finance its operations (see chapter 38). The number killed in Colombia between 1964 and 1991 is unknown. A 1985 publication estimated 20,000 Colombians had died up to that point in time. In mid-1988 FARC leader Manuel Marulanda illogically boasted, "[the guerrillas] may have to cleanse Colombian society by killing all the men of violence."[119]

GRENADA, 1983

The New Jewel (Joint Endeavour for the Welfare, Education and Liberation of the People) Movement, a pro-Cuban Marxist group, seized control of the island of Grenada, a former British colony, in March 1979. By 1983 the United States had became increasingly concerned over the construction of a major airstrip that was nearing completion at Point Salines. The airstrip was capable of handling the largest of Soviet aircraft. In October of that year, leftist radicals overthrew one of their own, Prime Minister Maurice Bishop, and chaos spread over the island. The American public became alarmed for the safety of some 1,000 American medical students who were on the island. The tiny nations that composed the Organization of Eastern Caribbean States requested that the United States intervene. These circumstances provided the Reagan administration with an opportunity to eliminate a pro-Castro government while rescuing the students.[120]

At dawn on October 25, 1983, five hundred U.S. Army Rangers parachuted from Air Force C-130 transports onto the Point Salines airstrip at the southwest tip of the island. The Cuban defenders had been alerted to the possibility of an attack when earlier in the morning one of their sentries discovered American commandos. The Cubans immediately opened fire.[121]

While the fight raged at Point Salines, some 250 Marines landed by helicopters at the Pearls airfield on the eastern side of the island. The Marines met little resistance and easily captured the airfield. Cargo aircraft landed M-60 tanks, armored personnel carriers, artillery, and additional troops.[122]

During the Grenada invasion, a number of American commando operations failed due to poor planning and the enemy's alertness. A twenty-two-man naval SEAL (Sea-Air-Land) team sent to rescue the British figurehead Governor-General, Sir Paul Scoon, and his family, was trapped by superior gunfire and had to be rescued by an AC-130 aircraft gunship. An Army Special Forces "Delta" team sent to rescue political prisoners held in the Richmond Hill Prison also took casualties. The prison was protected by nearby Fort Frederick. Gunfire from the Grenadian People's Revolutionary Armed Forces stationed at the fort drove back the helicopters in which the U.S. soldiers were ambushed. Nonetheless, within a few days the operation was over. The 6,000 American combat troops overwhelmed the 784 Cubans (636 construction workers with military training, 43 military advisors, and 18 diplomats) as well as the few hundred Grenadian soldiers who chose to fight. Casualties were: the United States, 19 killed and 152 wounded; Cuba, 25 killed and 59 wounded; and Grenada, 67 killed and 358 wounded.[123]

In spite of the military glitches, the invasion was a huge political success for the United States. The Reagan administration had seized an opportunity created by an internal dispute among the radical left on Grenada to take control of the island.

OBSERVATIONS

Fidel Castro's efforts to champion revolution in Latin America collapsed with the implosion of the Soviet Union. In 1995 Castro stated:

> The Soviet union has been accused of promoting subversion in Latin America, and what I am able to tell you is that the USSR was opposed to that activity. . . . the only place where we [Cubans] did not intent to promote revolution [was Mexico]. . . . in the rest, without exception, we intended it.

In the same article, former Cuban intelligence officer José Raúl Alfonso added, "The Soviets always opposed Cuban aid to guerrilla movements because they feared Cuba would steal the limelight in the political relations with Communist parties in Latin America."[124]

The nations of the Caribbean Basin were the last major battlegrounds of the cold war. Although many of these struggles were sparked and fueled by the superpowers through their allies, these small nations were the ones that suffered the incalculable social, economic, and political damage resulting from the contest-by-proxy.

Communism did not create the injustices of the Caribbean basin, it simply tried to exploit them. And neither did the defeat of Communism remove these centuries-old problems. They remained, and in many respects were exacerbated by the wars.

The United States' strategic tenet that outside Communist support was essential for the sustenance of the guerrilla wars of the Caribbean Basin proved correct. The ending of the cold war caused the collapse of support from the Soviet Union, but it also created the desire of the

United States to end the fighting as rapidly as possible. As a consequence, the United States sought to compromise with the disenfranchised radical left. Although organized fighting ended for the most part, many of the nations in the region were left in shambles, their economies destroyed, and banditry common.

Castro's new strategy, begun in the 1970s, initially proved successful in Nicaragua. Victory was achieved through a coalition that included Communists and non-Communists temporarily united against the Somoza dictatorship. Once the United Front had defeated the dictatorship, the Communists were in the best position to gain control of the new government because of their superior organization, long-range planning, help from Cuba, and control of the weapons. The Nicaraguan revolution became the model for the extreme left during the 1980s as the Cuban Revolution had been during the 1960s. The Nicaraguan revolution possessed a sophistication not found in the *foco* and urban strategies. In Nicaragua, the Sandinistas reconfirmed numerous lessons of the Cuban Revolution that had been ignored during the 1960s and early 1970s.

First, in order for a guerrilla force to win control of a government, it had to broaden the base of its support beyond a narrow ideology and had to include a significant amount of the population. This was accomplished in Nicaragua, as in Cuba, largely due to the stupidity and brutality of those who ruled. Once in power, the guerrillas retained this broad support long enough to secure their hold, and a Marxist state was born.

Second, a successful Latin American guerrilla movement had to neutralize international support for its enemy, particularly that coming from the United States. This was accomplished by the Sandinistas through the use of propaganda, which internationalized the conflict. During the late 1970s, this was aided by the *laissez faire* policies of the Carter administration.

Third, in order to win, a Latin American guerrilla movement had to have substantial outside help. This the Sandinistas obtained from Cuba.

In El Salvador, the radical left's experience appears to confirm that the most critical tactical decision for a guerrilla movement was when to openly oppose government troops. The Salvadoran guerrillas acted prematurely in 1981 and sustained a major defeat. They were never fully able to regain the initiative.

Not all guerrilla movements of the 1970s and 1980s were Castro inspired, but they did offer fertile ground for Castro to gain influence. Strong evidence suggests that he took advantage of many of these opportunities.[125]

On April 4, 1989, Fidel Castro and Mikhail Gorbachev signed a friendship treaty that condemned force as a foreign policy tool. Also about this time, Gorbachev told President Bush that the Soviet Union had decided to stop sending weapons to Nicaragua. And on August 5, 1989, the Cuban Communist Party prohibited the circulation of the Soviet publications *Moscow News* and *Sputnik* because they "justify bourgeois democracy" and had a "fascination for the American way of life."[126]

Cuba paid a high price in treasure for its support of leftist guerrillas; by 1991 the Cuban economy was in a shambles. With the collapse of the Soviet Union, Fidel Castro became the sole champion of the radical left in Latin America, but he was no longer capable of exploiting his status.

CHAPTER 37

PERU: THE SHINING PATH, 1980–92

Destroy imperialist domination, principally that of Yankee imperialism in our case, and ward off the other superpower, Russia, and the other imperialist powers.

—A Shining Path pamphlet

THE SPARK

During the night of May 17, 1980, guerrillas from the "Shining Path" burned ballot boxes in the remote Andean town of Chuschi (198 mi SE of Lima) located in the department of Ayacucho; the boxes were to be used in the presidential election scheduled for the next day. This was the Shining Path's first act of violence against the Peruvian government. The decision by Abímael Guzmán[1] (*nombre de guerra*, *Camarada* Gonzalo) to split from the Maoist Communist Party of Peru—Red Flag (*Partido Comunista de Peru—Bandera Roja*) and to create the Communist Party of Peru—by way of the Shining Path of Mariátegui[2] (*Partido Comunista de Peru en el Sendero Luminoso de José Mariátegui*) in 1970 led inevitably to what Guzmán called "popular war."[3]

BACKGROUND

The principal guerrilla movement that terrorized Peru during the 1980s and early 1990s was the inspiration of one man, Abímael Guzmán. Guzmán taught at the University of San Cristóbal de Huamanga in the department of Ayacucho for seventeen years (1962 to 1979). This was the poorest region of Peru; it had the lowest income per capita and the least share of the gross national product among the twenty-four departments[4] into which Peru was divided. In addition to the economic problems, the Indian culture of the Andean highlands had never been integrated into the post-conquest Peruvian culture.[5]

OPPOSING FORCES

The Shining Path defined its enemy as anyone who participated within Peruvian society. Therefore, almost no one was immune from attack. The Shining Path attacked the Chinese, the Indian, the Israeli, the Soviet, and the United States embassies to emphasize the nationalist origins of the movement. The Shining Path commonly referred to the franchised left as "parliamentary cretins," regardless of how extreme their political rhetoric might be.[6]

During his decade-and-a-half of teaching at the University of Huamanga, Guzmán gathered a loyal cadre of lieutenants, most of whom came to the university as students. He was also able to build a rapport among the poor through his teaching and those of his former students. The University of Huamanga was the ideal location to carry on such activity since the school had been reopened in 1959 in order to help improve the standard of living among the poor of the Andean highlands.[7] Many of the graduates returned to their small, rural communities in the departments of Huancavelica, Apurímac, and Ayacucho as teachers. They were among the few in those communities who had an education and thus were greatly respected.[8]

The Shining Path recruited its rank and file from a variety of sources including university and secondary students, women, professionals, and Andean Indians. Shining Path recruiters took advantage of the Marxist-oriented Student Revolutionary Front (*Frente Estudiantil Revolucionario—FER*), which had been founded in the early 1970s, by visiting campuses throughout Peru ostensibly as members of the FER but in reality spreading the doctrine and recruiting followers for the Shining Path.[9]

Another group susceptible to Shining Path recruitment was the thousands of secondary school students who were unable to pass the demanding entrance examination of the Peruvian university system. Each year approximately 250,000 students were turned away from the public and private universities and were thrown into the almost nonexistent job market. Another targeted group was women, particularly those in the lower class. Frequently, women were the trigger persons in major assassinations.[10]

Andean Indians were also targeted for recruitment. The Shining Path manipulated primitive superstitions with some success. The most exploited myth was the prophesied return of "Inkari," an Inca king, who the Shining Path implied was Abímael Guzmán.[11]

The Shining Path evolved into five levels of membership. At the bottom were the "sympathizers." They took part in demonstrations, provided resources, transported supplies, and carried messages. Next were the "activists." They supported the "popular schools," distributed propaganda, and spread civil unrest. Above them were the "militants." They were guerrillas who committed acts of violence. Next were the "commanders." They were responsible for the military and political decisions within their regions. At the top was the "cupula," a handful of people who directed the national strategy.[12]

In 1980 the Shining Path established its first military school, "Initiation of the Armed Struggle 80" (*Inicio de la Lucha Armada 80*). Exactly how many full- and part-time guerrillas the Shining Path fielded is unclear; the number appears to be between 2,000 and 8,000 men.[13]

The Shining Path armed itself by stealing weapons and dynamite. Large quantities of the latter were stored at numerous mining sites throughout Peru.[14]

The Shining Path was politically and strategically centralized but tactically decentralized. This permitted Guzmán and the inner council to retain national direction of the movement without running the risks in tactical operations such as those that had destroyed the leadership of the urban guerrillas in Argentina, Brazil, and Uruguay (see chapter 31). The Shining Path held national congresses in 1979, 1982, 1985, and 1988, during which ideology and strategy were discussed. On the tactical level, regional commanders were allowed considerable autonomy.[15]

The Shining Path's opponent was the Peruvian political system. It was emerging from more than three decades of bitter conflict between the senior military and populist *Aprista* Party (see chapter 15). Many within the old landed aristocracy had been disenfranchised through reforms initiated by Gen. Juan Velasco (military president between 1968 and 1975); however, the working and peasant classes had not been the primary beneficiaries of these changes since the government retained control over many of these assets through nationalization.[16]

The Peruvian military was large but not well suited to fight a "popular war." The Peruvian army numbered 75,000 men, two-thirds of whom were conscripts. Conscription was for two years; service could be far from home; training was poor; and pay amounted to $12 a month. This made the soldiers vulnerable to being corrupted by the Shining Path and drug traffickers. The privileged could easily avoid military service. All army units were under-strength, some by 40 percent; as a consequence, they could not effectively train. Only a few "elite" army units were up to strength.[17]

Most arms and equipment were obsolescent or obsolete. The navy possessed the largest submarine force in Latin America (8 boats), a moderate-size surface force (3 cruisers and 7 destroyers); and a 3,000-man marine corps brigade. The air force operated 112 combat aircraft, including 32 Canberra bombers, 24 A-37B attack aircraft, 24 Mirage fighters, 11 Soviet-built attack helicopters, 50 transport and utility helicopters, and 67 general-purpose aircraft. In general, aircraft readiness was poor. Additionally, there were three national police forces totaling 60,000 personnel.[18]

OPENING STRATEGIES

The Shining Path's strategy was to destroy the existing political, economic, and social structure of Peru and to recreate a society based upon Guzmán's unique interpretation of Mao. Guzmán believed that the only way to recreate Peru was through "popular war." Guzmán repeatedly said that the struggle might last for fifty to one hundred years.[19]

The Shining Path believed the first step down the long road to a recreated Peru was to build an alternate educational system to that of the government's. Guzmán developed instructions for the indoctrination of people. The teaching techniques were tailored to the audience, whether it be illiterate peasants or university students. The goal of these schools and other vehicles of propaganda was to make the Shining Path and the masses increasingly indistinguishable. Once "popular schools" won sufficient converts in a region, local officials were to be intimidated or assassinated and public property and that belonging to the bourgeois was to be destroyed.

These acts would also destabilize the government, thus causing a power vacuum and allowing the Shining Path to create a support base. Once a support base was established, guerrilla activity would follow. Operating from support bases the Shining Path would eliminate the need for base camps (or as Ché called them, *focos*) which had proven to be vulnerable during the *foco* wars (see chapters 29 and 30).

Tactically, the Shining Path planned to attack simultaneously on multiple fronts and always sought to achieve surprise. Once the government concentrated large forces in the region, the guerrillas would melt into the population. It was hoped that these tactics would cause government forces to try to defend everywhere while at the same time attempt to mount an offensive.[20]

The Shining Path considered terrorism, sabotage, assassination, and subversion important tools for undermining the stability of the state. It chose targets that were expensive to repair and replace or those that would impact the lives of as many Peruvians as possible—favorite targets were the high-tension towers used to transmit electricity. Minor government officials in the regions dominated by the Shining Path were to be executed, frequently in front of those who had elected them, if they refused to comply with the demands of the Shining Path. Also, high-ranking officials were targeted for assassination. Through these acts, the Shining Path hoped to demonstrate the inability of the police services to provide protection, drain resources from so-cial programs, intimidate its opposition, and heighten the feelings of injustice.

To exploit drug trafficking as a source of revenue, Shining Path teams (typically thirty members) operated in drug-producing regions. They identified government supporters and enforcers for the traffickers. These individuals were eliminated by either driving them out or killing them. Popular Committees (*comités populares*) composed of Shining Path sympathizers were then placed in charge of these "liberated" towns. The Shining Path would then provide protection against the government and the traffickers alike to the drug-growing farmers and, for a percentage, would serve as the middlemen in the sale of the crop.[21]

The Shining Path offered traffickers stable production, protection from the government, and a weakening of central authority. The Shining Path increased production by demanding a strong work ethic. It closed bars, executed homosexuals, and banished prostitutes. The Shining Path also protected numerous clandestine airfields used to fly the cocaine paste to processing centers in Colombia and elsewhere.[22]

The Peruvian government was in a phase of transition between military and civilian rule and as a consequence had no national strategy to fight an internal guerrilla war. President Fernando Belaúnde, who had been ousted by the military twelve years earlier, wanted to reduce the military's ability to intervene in civil affairs. He cut the military's budget, restricted its intelli-gence-gathering capabilities, and created a National Defense System. This system required in-teraction between civilian and military leaders; he hoped this would undermine independent political action by the military. Unfortunately, the civilians who had recently returned to power remained aloft from their military compatriots.

These changes reduced the military's capacity to fight the guerrillas. President Belaúnde had no concept of how to deal with the Shining Path and the military now focused on external threats from its neighbors, Ecuador and Chile. Also, the fifty-year struggle between the senior military and the *Aprista* Party had created estrangements among the various branches of the armed services as well as strained their relationships with the various national police organiza-tions (see chapter 15).[23]

THE 1980 SHINING PATH OFFENSIVE

In 1980 the Shining Path began its operations in the isolated south-central highlands (north-ern Ayacucho, northwestern Apurimác, and eastern Huancavelica Departments). There, the pre-dominantly Indian communities possessed a centuries-old tradition of resisting the rule by the Spanish-influenced, White coastal elite. Additionally, the indigenous population was upset with the government for having dammed the Mantaro River. By 1982 the Shining Path dominated much of this region, governing through its "Popular Committees."

On the local level, the military reacted by employing "dirty war" tactics; hundreds of sus-pects disappeared.[24] The legal system of Peru was as ill-prepared to address a terrorist threat as the military. Only a few laws dating from the 1970s addressing civil disturbance had applica-tion to terrorist activities. Control of the government had only recently reverted to the civil-ians,[25] thereby severely tempering the passing of any legislation that might limit civil rights. The first law concerning terrorism was not passed until March 10, 1981.[26] Many suspected of being members of the Shining Path were arrested, but most were later released because of lack of evidence, frustrating the police and armed forces. Between April 1980 and May 1981, al-most 500 acts of violence were attributed to the Shining Path.[27]

THE 1981 GOVERNMENT COUNTEROFFENSIVE

In June 1981 the Belaúnde administration began the first counteroffensive against the Shining Path. The operation was conducted by the newly formed Peruvian Investigative Police (*Policia de Investigaciones del Perú*—PIP) supported by two special forces units, the *Sinchis* and the *Llapan Aticcs*.[28] These operations failed due to insufficient planning, logistics, and communications. Many of the units were not even equipped with radios.[29]

In March 1982 a sizable Shining Path guerrilla band seized the city of Ayacucho (207 mi SE of Lima) and freed 247 prisoners from jail before disappearing into the countryside. By mid-1982 the Shining Path practically controlled the department of Ayacucho, forcing businesses to pay them for protection.[30]

On July 1, 1982, Congress passed Law 23414 requiring all captured terrorists to be brought to Lima for trial. This was an attempt to assure adequate protection for the court as well as a magistrate qualified to handle a terrorist case. Although this decision lessened the threat of violence against the judicial system, which had been experienced in the regional courts, it overburdened the courts of Lima. The long "paper trail" caused by the centralization added delays, and ultimately Law 24499 of April 22, 1986, rescinded the earlier law.

On December 21, 1982, President Belaúnde declared a state of emergency and ordered the military to establish martial law in the departments of Ayacucho and Apurímac and many constitutional rights were suspended.[31] On December 23, three air force planes carrying some 450 soldiers and marines landed in Ayacucho. Government troops occupied numerous towns in a show of force and carried out numerous ceremonies in an attempt to reestablish authority. The security forces could not distinguish between the Shining Path and the local inhabitants. Numerous human rights abuses occurred. This undermined the credibility and the morale of the army. The Popular Committees, which had been governing Shining Path-controlled areas, went underground. Guzmán ordered his forces to melt away rather than defend the areas they controlled. As a result, the Indians, who had welcomed the Shining Path, felt betrayed.[32]

In an attempt to undermine the appeal of the Shining Path, President Belaúnde proposed an economic assistance plan. However, floods in the north, a drought in the south, and an external debt crisis doomed his plan.

THE OPENING STRUGGLE FOR THE UPPER HUALLAGA VALLEY

During the early 1980s, the Shining Path extended its operations into the Upper Huallaga Valley (about the size of Massachusetts), already known for its coca production.[33] Shining Path members quietly assimilated into the local population and carefully began their education program. Apparently, these efforts were orchestrated by Osmán Morote Barrionuevo,[34] believed to be the second in command of the Shining Path. The presence of the Shining Path in the valley surfaced in December 1983 when it attacked the Civil Guard (*Guardia Civil*) station in Nuevo Progreso, killing three guard members.[35]

As the growers (poor subsistence farmers for the most part) became increasingly victimized by the drug traffickers on the one hand and the government's coca-eradication programs on the other, the Shining Path emerged as their champion. The Shining Path provided protection and helped negotiate better prices for the coca leaves, for a fee. By 1985 the Shining Path had established a strong presence. The guerrillas were able to equate the government's antinarcotics initiatives with drug use in the United States. The Shining Path justified its role by arguing that consumption, not production, was the problem. A foreign expert observed, "You'll have imperialists cutting down coca trees in front of a crying peasant woman. Mao could not have thought of anything better."[36]

"OPERATION BRANCO"

In May of 1984 the government launched its first antinarcotics operations in the Upper Huallaga Valley with substantial funding from the U.S. Drug Enforcement Agency (DEA). Initially conceived as a fifteen-day operation, it revealed the extent of the interconnection between drugs and terrorism not previously appreciated. As a result, the operation was extended to thirty days. During the operation, twenty-five clandestine airfields and several hidden laboratories were destroyed although only a modest amount of drugs was seized. Concerned that the United States would be upset if its funds were spent on antiterrorist activities, the Ministry of the Interior restricted the operation exclusively to antinarcotic work. At the same time the army was sent into the valley. This effort was disastrous since a number of high-ranking officers involved in the operation accepted bribes from the Shining Path. Following "Operation Branco," violence increased in the Upper Huallaga Valley.[37]

CREATING CIVIL DEFENSE HAMLETS

In 1983 the government began relocating the inhabitants of entire hamlets to more defensible sites and established Civil Defense Committees (*Comités de Defensa Civil*) and organized peasant patrols (*rondas campesinas*). These communities were called "masses" or "mounds" (*montoneras*) by the general population and "flocks of sheep" (*mesnadas*) by the Shining Path.[38] For the relocated villagers the experience was traumatic. Many were forced to move from ancestral lands, their tenure on which dated back to before memory, and they were forced to live with people whom they had long viewed with suspicion. Such attitudes were not uncommon between neighboring, yet geographically isolated hamlets. Also, living conditions in the "Civil Defense Hamlets" were frequently worse than in their poverty-stricken villages. Their fragile subsistence economies and delicate ecological balance were disrupted. Many farmers were given no land to work and the few, substandard public services deteriorated.[39]

The hostility toward the forced relocation fostered the belief among some of the peasants that supporting the Shining Path was analogous to fighting for one's land. The few Civil Defense Committees that were created were ill-prepared to defend themselves and received little support from the government. The Shining Path targeted these communities. Among the more bloody attacks, the Shining Path occupied the town of Rumi Rumi in December 1987 and brutally murdered town leaders and male youths. The peasantry was caught between two forces with both willing and able to inflict punishment but neither capable of providing protection.[40]

THE 1984 SHINING PATH OFFENSIVE

The Shining Path moved to recapture the initiative. While the government sent more troops into the south-central highlands, the Shining Path opened new fronts. It moved into the north-central highland departments of Junín, Huánuco, and Pasco. Junín held strategic importance, for it was the primary source of Lima's food, water, and electricity. The Shining Path also began operations in the extreme north to win control of drug routes. It spread in the south to Puno, attempting to open a corridor to Bolivia through which supplies might be introduced. And in the capital of Lima, the Shining Path would work to undermine confidence in the government.[41]

In 1984 Gen. Adrian Huamán Centero, a *"cholo"* (mixed European and Indian ancestry) and fluent in the Quechua dialect, was appointed military chief of the emergency zone of Ayacucho. He endeavored to win the peasants through economic and social assistance. This was expensive and coincided with the economic crisis of 1984. Because of his frankness with the media, he was removed by the end of the year.[42]

Also in 1984, the Shining Path toppled eight high-tension electricity towers in the Mantaro Valley, plunging one-third of the country into darkness. It also dynamited the trans-Andes oil pipeline (*Oleodueto Norperunano*); both acts of sabotage cost the nation millions in repairs and lost revenues. On December 4 Lima was blacked out and a giant bonfire in the shape of a hammer and sickle was lit on a hillside overlooking Lima.

In January 1985 Lima airport was blacked out as the Pope's aircraft was approaching to land and again a bonfire in the shape of a hammer and sickle appeared in the hills. In the interior the Shining Path murdered peasants for aiding the military and in turn government forces shot anyone suspected of supporting the Shining Path.

THE 1985 PRESIDENTIAL ELECTION

As the mid-1985 elections approached, the guerrillas intensified their activities. Through intimidation the Shining Path prevented a significant percentage of the population from voting, which was mandatory under Peruvian law. Voter turnout was especially low in the southern highlands departments of Ayacucho, Apurímac, and Huacavelica. Winning candidate Alan García declared that he would not tolerate human rights abuses by government forces. He formed a commission whose task it was to recommend a plan to deal with the Shining Path. It recommended emergency economic assistance to impoverished areas, a selective amnesty, and a dialogue with the guerrillas. García attempted to win the loyalty of the senior officers by appointing them to important and lucrative political positions. This strategy created a rift between these senior officers and their subordinates who believed that the generals had sold out the military institution.[43]

The discovery of a mass grave provided the new administration with the public support needed to ask the independent-minded army to explain its tactics. President García ordered the military to report to Congress within seventy-two hours concerning the grave. Gen. Sinesio Jarama, Chief of the Joint Chiefs of Staff, and Gen. Wilfredo Mori, Chief of the Second Military Region and the fifth ranking officer in the army, reported to a special Senate subcommittee on September 16, 1985. The graves were the result of government forces' operations near the village of Accomarca (210 mi SE of Lima) in Ayacucho Department between August 13 and 15. As a consequence of the killings, Generals Jarama and Mori were retired and Lt. Telmo Hurtado, who admitted responsibility, was tried by a military court. As a result of this event, military operations in the emergency zone stagnated. The Shining Path exploited this government malaise and punished those who had cooperated with government forces.[44]

THE SHINING PATH ATTACKS LIMA

By mid-1986 the Shining Path increasingly attacked the capital through bombings and assassinations and attempted to cut off its food supply. This latter objective was not well thought through. Lima imported much of its food by sea through Callao and the Shining Path had no means to interdict this source. Second, the peasants, who supplied Lima, were not subsistence farmers. They sold their excess to buy other agricultural necessities. Therefore, the Shining Path's strategy to cut Lima's food supply was also adversely affecting the peasants.[45]

In May, Rear Adm. Carlos Ponce Canessa was assassinated in his car while stopped at a traffic light. The Admiral had commanded the marine corps (*Infantes de Marina*) which had units operating against the Shining Path in Huanta. As a consequence of these actions, President García declared Lima an emergency zone, thereby giving the military martial rule throughout the capital as it already had over a dozen provinces in the central Andes.[46]

PRISONS REVOLT

On June 18 and 19, 1986, Shining Path prisoners in El Frontin and Lurigancho prisons rebelled and seized control of the facilities. According to army intelligence, those in the prisons had planned and continued to plan the terrorist attacks on Lima. These riots were brutally suppressed by the military; many prisoners were killed after they surrendered. Between 300 and 1,000 Shining Path members were killed, including Antonio Díaz Martínez, a chief strategist for the movement. Shocked by the massacres, García had one hundred guards jailed; the Minister of Justice resigned. García's actions increased the distrust that the field commanders had for the President. Many officers now wanted written instructions detailing what to attack and how to execute their orders; some chose inaction. The massacres did cause the Shining Path to scale back its operations in the capital.[47]

In late 1986 the Shining Path again focused its efforts in the Andean highlands. In September, the Shining Path attacked the small, impoverished village of Cochas (135 mi E of Lima) in Ayacucho Department. The villagers attempted to defend themselves with whatever was at hand. As a consequence, eight villagers were killed and the village was burned down. Since the government could not protect the numerous, small mountain villages, many were deserted as the people sought refuge in either the cities or the jungle.[48]

On January 15, 1987, the Shining Path simultaneously attacked the electricity-transmission infrastructure in six provinces, two textile factories, banks, and television stations. A week later the Shining Path blacked out much of the nation through a coordinated attack on the power grid. On the thirtieth it assassinated Dr. Cesar López Silva, the National Secretary of the APRA Party.[49]

By early 1987 the war settled into a stalemate. The Shining Path had regained some influence in the southern highlands following the Accomarca massacre but had not been able to sufficiently disrupt political, economic, and social activity in Lima. In part, this was due to the Shining Path's inability to win over the miners of Pasco and Junín. Following the Shining Path's assassination of the popular mayor of San Juan de Salinas in 1987, the populace told government agents where to find Shining Path cell members in Puno (525 mi SE of Lima). This was a major setback for the guerrillas in southern Peru.[50]

In June 1987 the government created the Special Tribunal which was dedicated exclusively to trying insurgents under Law 24700. In spite of substantial financial incentives, it was difficult to find those willing to serve. After two months of work (January 1 through March 8, 1988) the tribunal was dissolved by the Supreme Court due to a lack of progress. The Supreme Court directed that the fourteen criminal tribunals of Lima share the terrorist caseload.[51]

THE CONTINUING STRUGGLE FOR THE UPPER HUALLAGA VALLEY

By 1987 the Shining Path brought vast regions of the Tocache Province under its control, making them "liberated zones." These included Belaúnde's "marginal Highway" and the two important towns of Tocache and Uchize (246 mi NE of Lima). On May 31, 1987, the Shining

Path assaulted the Civil Guard post near the town of Uchize. The assault lasted for four hours before the defenders ran out of ammunition. Ten of those who surrendered were killed, three by public execution. The public was outraged by the failure of the army to rescue the besieged defenders. On July 3, 1988, the terrorists ambushed a military convoy between Tingo Maria and Monzón, killing thirteen soldiers. Outmaneuvered, the government was frequently forced to abandon control of areas for brief periods.[52]

By January 1989 the Shining Path's influence in the interior had spread northeast toward the Brazilian frontier and the Peruvian river port of Pucallpa (303 mi NE of Lima). Within a year the Shining Path spread into the Ene Valley to the outskirts of the provincial capital of Satipo. The Shining Path succeeded in winning the hearts and minds of the people even though the farmers of the valley may have had a very superficial understanding of the movement's ideology. The income earned from its drug activities was estimated to be as much as $30 million per year and it allowed the Shining Path to finance its operations.[53]

THE SHINING PATH CHANGES ITS STRATEGY

Beginning in late 1987 the Shining Path modified its strategy. The control of isolated areas in the highlands and terrorist attacks within Lima and other cities was not sufficiently weakening the government. Also, the Shining Path was losing influence to the less radical, left-wing *Túpac Amaru* Revolutionary Movement (*Movimiento Revolucionario Túpac Amaru*—MRTA) and the *Túpac Amaru* had successfully infiltrated the Shining Path's command structure in Lima. At their national congress in 1988, the Shining Path abandoned its sectarian approach and attempted to appeal to a broader constituency—trade unionists; the rural dispossessed, who had fled to the cities; and professionals such as lawyers, engineers, teachers, minor bureaucrats, and medical personnel. It successfully infiltrated the National Federation of Peruvian Hotel Workers (*Federación de Trabajadores en Hoteles del Peru*) and the Peruvian Public Education Workers Union (*Sindicato Unico de Trabajadores de la Educación Pública*).

The Shining Path renewed its urban offensive. This change in strategy was helped by a judicial ruling that declared that prosecuting individuals *solely* for being members of support groups of the Shining Path would violate their constitutional rights. Focusing upon Lima, numerous public activities were held by support organizations at the University of San Marcos. The Shining Path also organized its first public marches. In March sympathizers demonstrated in the *Plaza del Congreso*; the presence of troops and tanks did not intimidate them.[54]

Attacks continued in the highlands. On November 21, 1988, twenty-two soldiers and a number of civilians were killed in Ayacucho Department when some 220 pounds of dynamite exploded under two pickup trucks in which they were riding. The soldiers had abandoned the use of military vehicles because these were being targeted. In February 1989 fifty guerrillas destroyed the private agricultural cooperative at Cahuide in the department of Junín. They murdered men, killed animals, destroyed the machinery, and disappeared back into the mountains. In April the Shining Path killed 26 unarmed members of a self-defense committee at Carhuapampa in the southern department of Ancash just north of Lima. Gen. Sinecio Jarama observed, "It no longer causes any outcry or dismay to hear that a policeman, mayor or official has been killed. Only when there are massacres of 20 or more people do we take notice."[55]

By August 1988, thirty-six provinces in seven departments were under a state of siege.

THE 1989 MUNICIPAL ELECTIONS

The Shining Path assassinated some 120 mayoral candidates and local officials, while an additional 500 candidates withdrew from their contests. Almost 60 percent of the voters either did not cast their ballots or intentionally spoiled them, some out of fear and others out of sympathy. In June 1989 the Shining Path dynamited a bus in downtown Lima, killing five persons and seriously wounding fourteen, including members of the presidential guard. On June 17 the Shining Path destroyed sixteen electrical towers in the highlands of Pinacocha, plunging Lima and other coastal cities into darkness. The following month Shining Path guerrillas destroyed the army base at Madre Mía in the Department of Huánuco; the battle lasted four hours. On November 9 the Shining Path assassinated the former defense minister, Gen. Enrique López-Albujar. In April 1990 the guerrillas attacked the army base at Santa Lucía in the Upper Huallaga Valley where U.S. support personnel were located.[56]

A Peruvian Senate Human Rights Commission report stated that 1989 was the bloodiest year of the decade for political violence in Peru. It stated that 3,198 persons were killed and estimated that the violence, which had begun in 1980, had cost Peru $3.2 billion. Some in the military continued to use "dirty war" tactics. The army massacred some thirty peasants from the village of Cayara (228 mi SE of Lima) in the department of Ayacucho. The government's special prosecutor who was investigating the case, Carlos Escobar, had to seek political asylum in the United States.[57]

CIVIL DEFENSE HAMLETS INITIATE AN OFFENSIVE

By the end of 1989 a syndicate of 85 Civil Defense Committees led by Pompeyo Rivera Torres (*nombre de guerra Huayhuaco*) had established control over much of La Mar Province. As a reward, President García presented 200 hunting rifles to the committees. On March 1, 1990, some 200 peasants ambushed 20 guerrillas near Cochas (135 mi E of Lima) in the department of Junín. Nine guerrillas were hacked to pieces.[58]

THE 1990 PRESIDENTIAL ELECTION

Absenteeism by voters within those southern Andean departments where the Shining Path was particularly strong ran as high as 35 percent. The April election was won by political newcomer Alberto Fujimori. Through internal economic reforms and an improving world economy, he was able to reduce Peru's inflation from 7,650 percent in 1990 to 139 percent in 1991.[59]

Fujimori replaced the leadership within the military and police with individuals who were loyal to him. Ex-Israeli officers began training elite army and navy units. In 1990 the army replaced its aging Soviet-built Mi-8 Soviet transport helicopters with Mi-17s; this increased transport capacity from twenty-four to thirty troops per helicopter. These improvements permitted well-trained troops to be airlifted into the Mantaro Valley (189 miles of Lima), to hunt down guerrillas who were blowing up electric towers. Also, these elite units began incursions into the shantytowns around Lima searching for the enemy.[60]

The Shining Path struck back, targeting religious organizations. In May 1991 five missionaries and social workers were tried for "crimes against peasants" in the village of Huasahuasi (108 mi NE of Lima) in the department of Junín and shot in the head. Within a week the Shining Path assassinated a provincial director of Catholic charity. Next, a Canadian evangelist was murdered in Lima.[61]

During 1991 the Shining Path turned the shantytowns in the San Juan de Lurigancho Valley on the outskirts of Lima into a battlefield. The government forces ruled the slums by day and the Shining Path by night. Neither side took prisoners.[62]

At 11 P.M. on April 5, 1992, President Fujimori declared a state of emergency and suspended the constitution, the Congress, and the judiciary process. His action, supported by the military, was a "self-coup d'etat" (*autogolpe*). This extreme step was popular within Peru and unpopular among the international community. The United States and others cut off economic and military aid to Peru.[63] Fujimori created the National Anti-Terrorist Directorate (*Dirección Nacional de Lucha contra Terrorismo*—DINCOTE). He declared martial law against terrorists; he moved trials from civil to military courts; he approved the introduction of the life sentence.[64]

New life was injected into the Civil Defense Hamlets. The army initiated joint patrols with the peasants and began to use the peasants as scouts, translators, and intelligence gatherers. Membership within the village militias (*rondas campesinas*) was expanded from 14,000 members to some 50,000 by 1993. Also, these militias were given better training and better weapons than their predecessors. By 1993 the *rondas* were retaking control of the Andean highlands from the Shining Path.[65]

By November a new congress drafted another constitution which was narrowly approved by the people. Although the Shining Path did try to disrupt the political process, its actions were neither intense nor well organized.[66]

Guzmán appreciated that the tide was turning against him in the highlands. In July 1992 the Shining Path detonated a car bomb made of 1,300 pounds of dynamite in the upscale Lima suburb of Miraflores. The blast killed 13 persons, wounded 22, and left 500 homeless. It followed this by machine-gun attacks against police stations and additional bomb blasts.[67]

THE CAPTURE OF GUZMÁN

On September 12, 1992, Abímael Guzmán, Elvia Iparraguirre (second in command), and six other leaders of the Shining Path were captured at the dance academy of ballerina Maritza Garrida Lecca in Surco, a middle-class suburb of Lima. Guzmán had been forced to move to Lima because he had developed a skin ailment from hiding out in the high altitude of the Andes Mountains. Guzmán was sentenced to life in prison and fined 25 billion dollars.[68]

OBSERVATIONS

The capture of Abímael Guzmán, the messianic leader of the Shining Path, decapitated the Shining Path. The movement continued for years following his capture and committed acts of violence, acting very much like a chicken with its head cut off. Beginning in 2002 the Shining Path began to once again threaten Peruvian stability.

The Shining Path possessed numerous other weaknesses that contributed to its demise. Its sectarian philosophy limited its capacity to grow; not even members of the slightly less extreme, political left trusted the Shining Path. The Shining Path's marriage of convenience with drug traffickers undermined its claim to the moral high ground.[69]

The government also made its share of mistakes. The civilians, who returned to power in 1980 as the Shining Path was initiating violence, never created a strategy to deal with the threat. Therefore, for more than ten years the government's countersubversive strategy was left to the military commanders in the Emergency Zones. Not surprisingly, they chose to fight violence with violence. These commanders and many of their subordinates were changed every

December. Therefore, each year increasingly experienced guerrillas were fighting against a new group of novices. Even after the election of President García, who opposed "dirty war" tactics, the civilian leadership offered no alternative strategy to the military.[70]

The Shining Path was the only serious Communist revolutionary movement within Latin America that did not owe its allegiance to Moscow or Havana. Apparently, between 1980 and 1992 the struggle between the Shining Path and the Peruvian government caused some 25,000 deaths and cost $22 billion in damage to the nation's infrastructure.[71]

Map 9. Colombia's Drug War, 1982–2001.

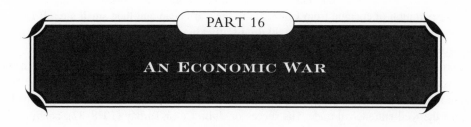

PART 16

AN ECONOMIC WAR

CHAPTER 38

COLOMBIA'S DRUG WAR, 1982–2001

Last year [1987] I said we were on the verge of the abyss. Today, I think we are in the abyss.
—former Colombian President Misael Pastrana Borrero

THE SPARK

Proclaiming a single event as the defining moment when the Colombian drug war began would be an oversimplification. May 1982, when the Radical Left FARC decided to use drug money to finance its efforts to overthrow the Colombian government, is an important transition date. This joining together of the Radical Left and the drug czars created a new reality that multiplied the destructive capabilities of both.[1]

BACKGROUND

Colombia had evolved very differently than most Latin American nations. During the nineteenth century the overarching cause for conflict had been "separation versus union"—would Colombia evolve into a modern nation-state, or would it remain a confederation of provinces, or would it further split apart? Unlike in Argentina and Brazil, nineteenth-century wars did not resolve this question in Colombia (see companion volume). Superimposed upon this unresolved conflict between separation or union was the twentieth-century interclass conflict between the haves and the have-nots. Thus, from 1947 until the end of the cold war (see chapters 20, 29, 30, 37), it was difficult to discern the loyalties and motivations of individual Colombians.[2]

Although the use of drugs had deep roots among indigenous peoples within Colombia, the export of these illegal substances did not explode until the mid-1960s when marijuana production mushroomed. Smugglers, who had previously transported emeralds and other high-value items in order to avoid customs duties, transitioned to the lucrative marijuana trade. Within a decade cocaine became the drug of choice and smugglers quickly responded. Cocaine smuggling was revolutionized in the 1970s by Carlos Lehder Rivas when he transformed the

373

transportation system from one that relied on human "mules" into one using large aircraft in the transportation of cocaine from Colombia to the Caribbean and then small aircraft from the Caribbean to the United States. By 1980 drug trafficking amounted to some $3 billion a year, the equivalent of all legal exports combined.[3]

Through the mid-1970s the Colombian government pretty much ignored the illegal narcotics business. Large quantities of dollars were exchanged openly at the *Banco de la República* with no questions asked. Finally, President Alfonso López Michelsen (1974–78) began the fight against the well-entrenched trade. His successor, Julio César Turbay (1978–82), continued the struggle. Turbay ordered the military to blockade the Guajira Peninsula (Colombia's northernmost projection). It did so for two years, seizing 6,000 tons of marijuana and some 300 boats and planes. The United States' concern over the rapidly growing import of drugs prompted a new level of cooperation. In 1979 the United States and Colombia signed an extradition treaty whereby those in Colombia accused of crimes in the United States could be extradited. In return, Colombia received increasing military aid throughout the period from the United States.[4]

Cooperation between Colombia and the United States against the drug traffickers did not last. The U.S. Congress significantly restricted the use of military equipment provided to Colombia for fear that it would be used against the Leftist guerrillas and not just the drug dealers. As a result, in March 1980 Colombia lifted the blockade of the Guajira Peninsula to reassign its limited assets to fight the Leftist guerrillas elsewhere and because of the exposure to corruption of those fighting the drug dealers.[5]

In May 1982 at the seventh party conference held in Cumaral (100 mi SE of Bogotá), the Radical Left FARC decided to finance their expanded military operations against the Colombian government through the exploitation of the drug trade. The FARC was not a monolith and some of its elements already had a long association with the drug czars. Now, the FARC taxed production, sold protection, and recruited those that narcotrafficking pushed to the margins of society.[6]

At about the same time, drug traffickers began to increase their influence throughout Colombia. They protected peasant farmers from beatings, kidnappings, rapes, and murders from any quarter. They easily acquired farmland that hundreds of landowners had abandoned to escape forced payments for protection to the Leftist guerrillas or the Rightist death squads (see chapter 36). As a consequence, by the mid-1980s drug smuggling, guerrilla warfare, and banditry became intertwined, making it almost impossible to separate them.[7]

OPPOSING SIDES

By the mid- to late 1990s, six heavily armed entities operated in Colombia: the Colombian government's forces; numerous Leftist guerrilla groups; the drug dealers; paramilitary self-defense forces; right-wing death squads; and elements of the U.S. armed forces.[8]

The Colombian government possessed numerous combat organizations. In 1986, the Colombian army was composed of 53,000 men, of whom 24,000 were conscripts. The army was organized into brigades and several included horse cavalry. The army relied heavily on mortars rather than artillery given the rugged terrain. The air force possessed 71 helicopters, of which 45 were gunships; in addition, it possessed fixed-wing fighters and logistics aircraft. The National Police Force was composed of 50,000 men; in the late 1980s Gen. Miguel Gómez, its commander, created the Elite Force which was trained by and patterned on the British SAS (Special Air Services). Additionally, the individual provinces maintained 38,000 *carabineros* (state police).[9]

The largest guerrilla force was the FARC which could field some 15,000 combatants, nominally led by the seventy-plus-year-old Manuel Marulanda. They were scattered throughout Colombia in "fronts" typically composed of 500 individuals. These were well-armed units with some fronts having more automatic weapons than the government's infantry battalions. Local FARC commanders had significant autonomy.[10] The second largest guerrilla force—the ELN—possessed 3,000 to 5,000 fighters. The death from hepatitis of its cofounder, Father Manuel Pérez, in February 1998 may have caused its current leader, Nicolás Bautista, to alter the ELN's ideology. It was in part based on radical Liberation Theology.[11]

The first of some 130 paramilitary self-defense forces was formed from peasants in 1987. These forces initially existed primarily in cattle-rasing regions and were funded by the cattle barons. They were trained by British and Israeli soldiers of fortune and received some of their arms from Colombian military officers who were sympathetic to their cause and others from the Black Market. Within a few years some paramilitary self-defense forces found it more profitable to rely on the drug czars for financing.[12]

The right-wing death squads also appeared in the late 1980s. Among others, they attracted some retired military and policemen.[13]

Figure 28. Colombia's Drug War (1982–2001). Conscripts (draftees) are being trained. These young soldiers potentially could face numerous enemies—leftist guerrillas, right-wing militias, and drug dealers. *Courtesy of Dr. Tom Marks.*

By the year 2000 the United States had approximately 200 military and advisors in Colombia.[14]

OPENING STRATEGIES

The drug czars and the Leftist guerrillas shared some short-term interests: the need to control territory; the desire for money; and the continued instability of the Colombian government. The drug czars needed land to produce coca while the Leftist guerrillas desired it for a *foco*, or safe haven. Both needed money. This was the measure of success for the drug czars and the Leftist guerrillas desired it to finance their revolution. For the drug czars, the weaker the government the less it could interfere with its illegal activities. For the Leftist guerrillas, the weaker the government the sooner they could achieve victory. But this was where the interests of the drug czars and the Leftist guerrillas parted. For the drug czars, the ideal government was a weak democracy, but for the Leftist guerrillas, the ideal government was themselves. To achieve these strategies, both the drug czars and the Leftist guerrillas used intimidation through terrorism.

The paramilitary self-defense forces were aligned with the drug traffickers against the Leftist guerrillas. Initially, the objective of both was to keep the guerrillas out of cattle country where they were killing and kidnapping wealthy owners. However, by the mid-1990s the operations of the self-defense forces extended far beyond cattle country. Since some in the government shared the goals of the paramilitary self-defense forces, they frequently ignored their brutal attacks against the Left. The operational strategy of the paramilitary self-defense forces was to eliminate the leadership of the Radical Left.[15]

For the right-wing death squads, their goal was to perpetuate the weak democracy so that they could control remote areas and exploit the chaos to their political and economic advantage. Their principal operational strategy was intimidation through assassination and kidnapping. Labor leaders and journalists were their frequent targets.

Initially, those who governed Colombia chose to ignore the drug trade. This changed in late 1986 when the government adopted an offensive strategy. This relied heavily on intelligence, some gathered through very sophisticated electronics made available by the United States.[16]

For the United States, the goal was to end the exportation and control of drugs from Colombia. Its operational strategy was to improve the antidrug operational capabilities of Colombian forces by providing equipment, intelligence, and financial support. U.S. military presence was to be kept to a minimum.

Nowhere in Latin America are military operations more influenced by topography than in Colombia. Knowing the distance between locations is insufficient to even begin to guess the needed traveling time. The topography of Colombia abruptly changes from jungle valleys to huge mountains and then plummets back into a jungle. The topography can even limit helicopter operations because some areas are persistently shrouded by low-lying clouds.[17]

COLOMBIA NATIONALIZES THE DRUG WAR

President Belisario Betancur Cuartas (1982–86) took a nationalistic approach to the drug problem. He refused to honor the extradition treaty with the United States, preferring to use Colombian courts. He appointed Rodrigo Lara Bonilla head of the Justice Ministry who aggressively sought the destruction of the trade in cooperation with U.S. agencies. However, an assassin killed Lara in Bogotá on April 30, 1984. As a consequence, the Betancur government carried out a massive crackdown against the drug czars and signed an extradition order for drug czar Carlos Lehder (not yet in custody). In July the first aerial spraying of marijuana began.[18]

As a consequence of the government's crackdown, key Colombian drug czars fled to Panama where they paid President Manuel Noriega some $5 million for protection. This ultimately led to the U.S. military intervention "Operation Just Causes" in December 1989 and the removal of Noriega from power. While in Panama, drug czars Jorge Luis Ochoa and Pablo Escobar offered the Colombian government a deal whereby they would withdraw from the drug trade, help fight against it in the future, and repatriate billions of dollars in exchange for their "reincorporation" into Colombian society.[19]

Refusing to accept the drug dealers' proposal, President Betancur intensified the war on the drug czars. As a consequence, the drug czars diversified their methods of operations and increased their attacks on the Colombian judiciary. Between 1981 and 1986 they assassinated some fifty judges; attorneys general also became favorite targets. In January 1987 Justice Minister Enrique Parejo Gonzalez survived an assassination attempt in Budapest, Hungary. The United States found it necessary to evacuate dependents from its embassy because of the threats from the drug traffickers.[20]

By the late 1980s the illegal drug industry grew into Colombia's principal foreign exchange earner, even exceeding coffee. The earnings of the Medellín cartel were between two and four billion dollars a year, which exceeded many Fortune 500 companies.[21]

The assassination of Guillermo Cano Isaza (publisher of Colombia's second-largest newspaper *El Espectador*) forced Colombia's new president, Virgilio Barco (1986–90), to intensify the use of the armed forces against the drug czars. The army carried out over 1,500 raids, seizing 500 suspects and a large cache of weapons. The armed forces also began to monitor the import and export of chemicals used by the narcotics industry. They tightened the enforcement of transportation regulations covering ground, air, and water.

On February 4, 1987, an elite police unit captured Carlos Lehder and he was whisked away to a U.S. jail that same day.[22] Also, on November 21 the government captured drug czar Jorge Luis Ochoa; however, he was released on a legal technicality by Justice Minister Enrique Low Murtra.[23]

ESCOBAR DECLARES WAR

At the end of 1987, Pablo Escobar Guevara, the then-reigning drug king, declared war against the Colombian government. Escobar had won the loyalty of many in the lower classes by funding public projects, particularly housing. In Medellín, the "drug capital," a large housing complex even bore his name.[24]

Escobar ordered a series of high-level assassinations and kidnappings. In January 1988 Attorney General Carlos Mauro Hoyos Jiménez, who was investigating the release of Ochoa, was murdered; on January 11, Andrés Pastrana, the Social Conservative candidate for mayor of Bogotá, was kidnapped; and on August 18, 1989, Luis Carlos Galán, Liberal candidate for the presidency, was assassinated. During the search for Hoyos' killers, government forces rescued Pastrana.[25]

The Barco government's principal reaction was the restriction of civil liberties. The military and police arrested some 10,000 individuals and seized 134 aircraft belonging to suspected drug dealers. On August 22, 1988, five individuals were arrested for the murder of Galán.[26]

Escobar and other drug czars responded. The next day, August 23, they blew up the offices of the two major political parties in Bogotá. In Medellín, the drug czars blew up nine banks.

Initially, Escobar and his cohorts were victorious, in part because of the ability to pay large bounties for the assassination of civilian and military leaders. Bonuses were given for killing officers and members of the Elite Force. The influence of the drug czars was demonstrated in 1988 when Judge Marta González issued warrants for the arrest of three drug czars, three army officers, and other government officials. Since she could get no one to serve these warrants, the judge fled the country.[27]

Escobar continued his rampage. In July and August 1989, drug *sicarios* (paid assassins) murdered the governor of the department of Antioquia, a district superior court judge, and the chief of police of Medellín. Escobar orchestrated the dynamiting of a jeep in Medellín killing eight policemen. Next gunmen dynamited a government truck, wounding ten members of the elite antidrug force, killing eight civilians, and wounding 120 more. On November 27 a bomb exploded on an *Avianca* (Colombian national airline) jet, killing 107 persons. On December 6 a suicide driver detonated 1,000 pounds of dynamite outside the Administration Security Department in Bogotá and destroyed the building.[28]

Slowly, government forces began gaining the upper hand against Escobar. On December 15, 1989, the Elite Force and the Narcotics Brigade killed drug kingpin Gonzalo Rodríguez Gacha and six others in a running gun battle. This led to the destruction of cocaine-processing factories, clandestine airstrips, and weapons caches. Once again, drug czars offered a truce, and it was rejected. In March and April 1990, the drug czars financed the assassinations of two Leftist presidential candidates, both of whom supported extradition (see chapter 36).[29]

As the intelligence system improved, so did government successes. Numerous government raids thwarted bombings aimed at disrupting the May 27, 1990, national elections. Among those arrested was the brother of Pablo Escobar's chief bodyguard.[30]

In September 1990 Escobar carried out a series of kidnappings of high-profile individuals, perhaps preparing to ransom himself should the need arise. Among those seized were Francisco Santos (editor of the newspaper *El Tiempo*) and his son; the journalist Diane Turbay (daughter of former President Julio Cesar Turbay); and Maruja Pachon (a television commentator and wife of a senator). This strategy paid dividends. Pachon was released in exchange for the abolishment of extradition to the United States for drug traffickers. Finally in July 1991 Escobar surrendered and was imprisoned under conditions he had negotiated.[31]

In July 1992 Escobar escaped from his "gilded cage" and for over a year remained one step ahead of the 1,500-man "Search Block" unit assigned to his recapture. Although Escobar placed a $30,000 bounty on the heads of the Search Block officers, it was his own men who were killed. Some twenty-six of Escobar's closest associates, including his brother-in-law, were killed. The end came in December 1993 when Pablo Escobar and his bodyguard were gunned down in a western suburb of Bogotá. Escobar had extracted a heavy price from Colombian society. He had caused the deaths of an attorney general, a justice minister, three presidential candidates, some two hundred judges, a thousand police officers, and hundreds of other Colombians. The death of Escobar was widely celebrated by his enemies and competitors alike, and resulted in the dismantling of the Medellín drug cartel. But it did not alter the intensity of the Drug War.[32]

THE RESURGENCE OF THE RADICAL LEFT

On January 29, 1992, the ELN boldly attacked urban targets. They blew up three pipelines on the outskirts of Barrancabermeja (270 mi N of Bogotá), causing oil to gush into the streams

Figure 29. Colombia's Drug War (1982–2001). Hooded Colombian soldiers guard Medellín, a center of drug activity. Due to the numerous assassinations of government forces, these soldiers hide their identity. *Courtesy of Dr. Tom Marks.*

that supplied the drinking water for the slums of the city. Although a local public relations disaster for the ELN, nationally it won the ELN recruits among the impoverished. Throughout the 1990s Colombia's petroleum infrastructure became the ELN's principal target as it represented the wealthy elite. Throughout 1995 it dynamited on average three pipelines a month, and this intensity increased. In July 1997 the guerrillas shot down a helicopter flying engineers to repair one of the numerous breaks the guerrillas had caused; twenty-four persons died. By 1997 oil companies were paying a "war tax" of $1.25 a barrel to the Colombian government and perhaps additional money to other combatants for protection.[33]

THE DRUG WAR CONTINUES

In July 1995 the government captured drug czar José Santacruz Londono (*El Gordo*—"The Fat One") in a Bogotá restaurant. Shortly afterward, other key lieutenants were also captured. Santacruz' cartel, operating out of Cali (200 mi SW of Bogotá), distributed perhaps 80 percent of the world's cocaine, the value of which was estimated to be $7 billion a year in the United States alone. He was sentenced to fifteen years in prison. As the major cartels fell one by one, perhaps forty mid-sized ones took their place.[34]

THE PARAMILITARY UNITE

By 1995 Carlos Castaño had united the various paramilitary militias in the north under the Self-Defense Peasants of Cordoba and Urabá (*Autodefensas Campesinas de Cordoba y Urabá*) and began extending their operations southward. Thus the paramilitary militias evolved from being a regional operative to a national one. This significantly changed the dynamics of the fight. Now many of the major fights were between the paramilitaries and the Leftist guerrillas without the army being directly involved.[35]

A GOVERNMENT SCANDAL

In August 1995 President Ernesto Samper (1994–98) was accused of taking a $6 million campaign contribution from the Cali drug cartel. These charges had been made in 1994, but this time significant evidence supported the allegation. Appreciating that the government was in a weak position, the Radical Left rejected the government's peace proposal and began a new offensive. On August 20 President Samper was forced to impose a ninety-day state of emergency to save his government.[36]

The revelation that Samper's campaign had used drug money had international repercussions for Colombia. In March 1996 the United States "decertified" Colombia. Additionally, the U.S. Ambassador to Colombia, Myles Frechette, began making frequent public comments concerning corruption and human rights abuses. On March 5 Assistant Secretary for International Narcotics Robert Gelbard stated, "There is no doubt at this point that the administration of President Ernesto Samper receives significant financial aid from the Colombian drug lords."[37] As a consequence, Colombia lost significant direct U.S. military aid during 1996 and again in 1997, plus the U.S. government vetoed numerous loans to Colombia from multilateral development banks.[38]

A COORDINATED STRATEGY

In early 1996 the FARC initiated a new strategy that coordinated attacks by its terrorists, guerrillas, and militias. In mid-April some 150 FARC fighters attacked a six-vehicle army convoy near the border with Ecuador. That same day the ELN kidnapped Representative Josez Maya, a congressional peace envoy. On August 30 the FARC overwhelmed an army unit at Las Delicias, Putumayo (360 mi S of Bogotá). Mostly composed of conscripts, some sixty soldiers were killed or wounded and the remaining sixty taken hostage. This attack was one of twenty-two simultaneous assaults carried out by the FARC on this day. These overwhelmed the army's ability to respond.[39]

In September 1996 the FARC seized the hamlet of Mocoa (295 mi SSW of Bogotá). Since the FARC controlled the local unpaved airstrip, the military was forced to send an armored rescue column down a road through guerrilla-controlled territory. Additionally, the guerrillas captured small army outposts in the southern region of Putumayo, Guavaire, and Caqueta killing a few hundred soldiers.[40]

In July 1997 the paramilitary self-defense forces struck back. One hundred members seized the town of Mapiripán (124 mi S of Bogotá) and tortured to death thirty suspected guerrilla sympathizers. Their decapitated heads were mounted on lampposts as a reminder.[41]

Nationwide elections occurred on October 26, 1997, for governors and other local officials. In many cases no candidates ran for office. Voter turnout was very low, particularly in the remote areas.[42]

The FARC's offensive continued. In late February 1998 it ambushed 154 soldiers of the 52nd Counter-guerrilla Battalion at El Billar (in Caqueta Department south of Bogotá) and decimated the troops. Next, the FARC introduced its own homemade armored vehicles. The first use was against Puerto Lleras (80 mi SE of Bogotá) on March 24, 1998. A second "armor" attack using two armored agricultural tractors and 300 fighters occurred a week later against Vista Hermosa, Meta (85 mi SE of Bogotá).[43]

While the Radical Left attacked the government, the right-wing death squads ravaged parts of the country. Some fifty persons died at their hands near Puerto Asis in southern Colombia. Three police officers were arrested on February 20, 1998, accused of killing the mayor-elect of Bolívar. And human rights activist Jesús María Valle Jaramillo was gunned down in his law office in Medellín. In early May, a few days before presidential elections, right-wing paramilitaries seized control of some poor barrios in Barrancabermeja and rounded up suspected leftist supporters. They executed eight in a public square and abducted forty-two hostages, three of whom were later found dead. The atrocities continued.[44]

PRESIDENTIAL ELECTIONS

The nation focused on the May 31, 1998, presidential election; Andrés Pastrana (1998–2002) won a subsequent runoff between the top vote-getters on June 21. The Radical Left immediately demonstrated its strength to the new President. On July 7 the FARC attacked 23 locations simultaneously. Several hundred fighters attacked and overran Puerto Rico, Meta, southeast of Bogotá, employing homemade mortars and two improvised armored vehicles, one an armored bulldozer. Three policemen were killed; five wounded (and then executed); and 28 taken hostage. In August some 1,200 Leftist guerrillas attacked an army company (mostly conscripts) at the counter-narcotics police base at Miraflores, Guaviare (140 mi SE of Bogotá). The government lost 30 soldiers killed, 50 wounded, and 100 taken hostage.[45]

These Leftist successes, principally aimed at securing hostages, caused President Pastrana to meet face-to-face with FARC leaders. In February 1999 Pastrana conceded to them a temporary demilitarized zone (*Zona de Despeje*) running from the eastern slope of the Andes Mountains through the eastern lowlands as the Leftists' price for opening negotiations. Although *la zona* (the size of Iowa) represented about one-third the territory of Colombia, it was inhabited by only one-fortieth of the population. Also during this time, Leftist guerrillas were able to increase their fire power through the acquisition of East German-manufactured modern machine guns acquired through illegal channels.[46]

Not to be outdone for headlines, the ELN hijacked an Avianca airliner and forced it to land in northwestern Colombia in April 1999. The hijackers escaped by canoe into the jungle with 46 hostages. The following month, the ELN executed one of its most spectacular kidnappings. It took 150 worshipers hostage from a church in a wealthy barrio of Cali. In both cases most of the captives were released or ransomed over time.[47]

On May 21 the Pastrana government extended the concession of *la zona* to the FARC. As a consequence the Defense Minister, Rodrigo Lloreda, and some ten generals resigned in protest.[48]

The FARC launched massive attacks from *la zona* in all directions during July and November 1999 and again in July 2000. Bridges and power stations were blown up and twenty villages attacked. The FARC employed a few locally made, armored tractors. The army responded by putting 120,000 reservists on alert and government troops finally pushed these excursions back into *la zona* but only after sustaining heavy casualties.[49]

Police and military units were not the only targets of the Radical Left. On August 15, 1999, the ELN kidnapped Catholic Bishop José de Jesús Quintero. It released him on September 20 demanding that the Vatican transfer him and another bishop whom the ELN accused of being sympathetic to the right-wing paramilitaries.[50]

Not only was the government fighting the Leftists and Rightists, but the drug czars as well. On October 13 the government arrested thirty-one members of a drug cartel allegedly headed by Alejandro Madrigal. In November two major drug traffickers were extradited to the United States: Fernando José Flores and Jaime Orlando.[51]

In April 2000 Pastrana also pulled government troops out of a 1,120-square-mile area (half the size of Delaware) in the north, thereby creating a safe haven for the ELN. In protest, numerous top government officials resigned.[52]

PLAN COLOMBIA

In mid-2000 the Pastrana administration initiated Plan Colombia, which had been developed with the assistance of the United States. This $7.5 billion plan called for the social, economic, and political (particularly judicial) reforms and the strengthening of the military. Colombia did not fully fund the plan and the safe havens conceded to the guerrillas precluded extending military operations into some of the most important coca-growing areas. The United States provided $1.3 billion for Plan Colombia over two years. Of this, $700 million went to counterdrug activities, the centerpiece of which was the creation of the Colombian army's Counter Narcotics Brigade.[53]

THE FARC STRIKES BACK

In early September 2000, some 600 FARC fighters attacked a communications relay center for television and phone services in western Colombia but were unable to take control during two days of fighting. On October 20 the FARC launched a major offensive from the northwest far from *la zona*, attempting to drive government troops and police out of Dabeiba (75 mi NW of Medellín). This town was the gateway to Medellín from the northwest. The government airlifted elements of the 4th Brigade as a relief force, and it dropped directly into an ambush. The brigade sustained one hundred dead and lost one Black Hawk helicopter. The army persevered and drove the guerrillas back into hiding.[54]

Four days earlier, on October 16, the government dismissed 89 officers and 299 soldiers who were accused of misconduct.[55] Regardless, the attacks by the Radical Left continued. In late October the FARC overran the hamlet of Mitú in far eastern Colombia. In response, Colombian paratroopers with the cooperation of the Brazilian government used an airstrip at Querai, Brazil (45 mi E of Mitú) to launch a strike against the FARC. The operation cost the lives of 150 soldiers, seven civilians, and only five FARC guerrillas. To make matters worse, the FARC escaped with some forty police hostages. In February 2001 President Pastrana met again with FARC leaders in *la zona*. They agreed once more to extend the temporary status of *la zona* for another eight months.[56]

Throughout these years of chaos, Colombian public opinion increasingly turned against the guerrillas and drug traffickers. On August 7, 2002, Alvaro Uribe became the new president of Colombia. He renounced the guerrilla safe havens and initiated an offensive against the guerrillas and narcotraffickers.

OBSERVATIONS

The Colombian Drug War has disintegrated into a free-for-all. It is hard to conceive of a winner in this war. For Colombia, the Drug War continues to impede the country's evolution into a modern nation-state. This is evident by the fact that during the past three decades Colombia has been economically prosperous in a macro sense and yet income distribution remains one of the most skewed in Latin America. Some 55 percent of the population lives in poverty. And, Colombia continues to have one of the highest homicide rates in the world. Within Colombia of the early twenty-first century, regionalism still dominates centralism—politically, economically, and socially.[57]

For Colombia's fighting forces, the multiplicity of enemies, the difficulty of the terrain, the on-again, off-again support from the United States, and intelligence leaks have made it impossible to achieve a decisive victory.[58]

The Leftist guerrillas, particularly the FARC, may be militarily stronger today than at any time in the past. For one thing, they have achieved financial self-sufficiency. They collect annually some $170 million from drug-related activities and another $160 million from extortion. The ELN has also demonstrated resiliency.[59]

But for the Leftist guerrillas, illegal drug money has also corrupted their people and hurt their image. They are becoming increasingly difficult to distinguish from the drug traffickers. Also, the FARC's complex command structure of five blockading fronts (*bloques de frente*), two joint commands (*comandos conjuntos*), two mobile blockades (*bloques moviles*), sixty-six fronts (*cuadrillas*), fourteen columns (*columnas*), four urban fronts (*urbana frentes*), two units (*unidades*), and one school (*escuela*) reflects an organizational weakness. The FARC lacks central control and is more of a confederation than a union.[60]

For the United States, if its strategy of eliminating drug control and exportation from Colombia proves successful, it will mean a significant reduction in drug trafficking over the midterm—perhaps five years. After all, 80 percent of all cocaine comes from Colombia. However, the drug trade has proven to be incredibly adaptive, and it is unreasonable to expect that such a success would have a lasting effect.

Those running the drug industry may be the only winners. True, the few "czars" are gone, but they have been replaced by many "barons." Apparently, Latin American cocaine production has increased by 60 to 100 percent over the last twenty years. Colombia alone not only produces 80 percent of the world's cocaine but also 70 percent of the heroin consumed on the east coast of the United States.[61]

The drug war still rages after some twenty years; therefore, even a guesstimate as to total casualties would be premature. During the decade of the 1990s, some 35,000 people died as a consequence of fighting in Colombia. Additionally, in the year 2000 another 4,000 Colombians died: some 2,000 noncombatants; 1,000 Leftist guerrillas and drug mercenaries; 500 policemen; 300 soldiers; and 100 paramilitary self-defense force members. By the year 2000 there were one million internal refugees in Colombia, and this was increasing by more than 100,000 persons a year.[62]

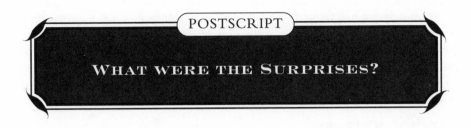

POSTSCRIPT

WHAT WERE THE SURPRISES?

War is composed of nothing but surprises.

—Napoleon Bonaparte

What were those discoveries which most surprised me concerning twentieth-century Latin American military operations?

STRATEGIC SURPRISES

First, Latin America, and the Caribbean basin in particular, was profoundly altered by World War II. As this world conflict was drawing to a close, a rejuvenated Latin American Left, which encompassed extremes from democrats to radicals, emerged and sought to overthrow the reactionary Right which had dominated the region since independence. Within a few years, the United States' world strategy of containment smothered this initiative. Leftists were forced to choose between either accepting a U.S.-condoned status-quo, which in some cases was very antidemocratic, or seeking a violent solution.

Second, the United States' policy toward Latin American during the cold war was an aberration of its past practices where commercial and not political ideology was a prime motivator. Prior to the cold war, the United States intervened based on its domestic politics and economics. Should the United States return to this pre-cold war paradigm, questions such as "How deeply will the United States intervene in Colombia to fight the drug wars?" will have more to do with what happens in the United States and less to do with what happens in Colombia. This does not mean that events in Colombia will be irrelevant but they will be secondary.

Third, opening strategies during Latin America's twentieth-century wars were rarely successful and soon abandoned—most often because their creators grossly underestimated the task. In 1932 Bolivian military leaders planned to conquer the Chaco with 605 trucks, but only twenty-five were purchased. In fact, once war began, the Bolivian army had to acquire a few thousand trucks between 1932 and 1935 and still lost the war. In 1955, Fidel Castro's initial strategy was to seize a radio station in Santiago (as well as other strategic sites), broadcast a *pronunciamiento* against Fulgencio Batista, and then march on Havana. Military disasters caused this strategy to be abandoned and guerrilla warfare was adopted.

Within South America the era of the professional officer corps began to supplement the *caudillo* at the end of the nineteenth century. This professionalization did not begin to arrive in the Caribbean until decades later. There, the United States initiated the process with the hope that a professional officer corps would lead to more stable and democratic governments. The United States only got half its wish. An unintended consequence of a U.S.-promoted professional officer corps in the Caribbean was the likes of Rafael Trujillo who took control of the American creation and brutally exploited his country.

And, the *caudillo* was never totally displaced by a professional officer corps. This explains why it was possible to have *caudillo*-inspired coup d'etats and institutional-inspired coup d'etats occurring at the same time.

OPERATIONAL SURPRISES

The United States introduced clandestine military operations as its primary strategy beginning with the Guatemalan Revolution of 1954. Initially, the adoption of this strategy was caused by the Eisenhower administration's desire to reduce conventional military forces in order to save money. By the end of the cold war in the early 1990s, both the United States and its allies plus the Communists were exploiting this strategy to the maximum. This leaves a nasty legacy for the future—the United States which championed democratic values choosing undemocratic means in an attempt to get there.

TACTICAL SURPRISES

As during the nineteenth century, the exploitation of new weapons was dependent upon their maturity, the ability to service them, *and the local evolution of doctrine on how to employ them*. During the 1941 Peru-Ecuador border war, the Peruvians dispersed their twelve tanks and used them to support infantry, thus sacrificing the value of concentration. True, this proved to be irrelevant due to the weakness of the Ecuadorians. In the Malvinas War of 1982, the Argentines successfully created a doctrine for employing the five air-launched Exocet missiles in their inventory but at least three of these missiles either failed to explode or did not acquire targets—this is a high percentage of failures given the investment in the missiles.

As we move into the twenty-first century, we transition out of the "cold war" and into a new age of "accelerated globalization." Obviously, many of the old causes for conflict in Latin America will continue to spark fighting into the future. The most challenging question is whether the individuals frustrated by the economic, social, and political inequities now further exacerbated by the accelerated globalization, will find an ideology that will unite them and provide direction so that they may attempt to violently influence the future.

NOTES

PREFACE

1. "South America: Armies in Command," *Time* Magazine, 23–24 (December 27, 1968), 23.

2. In 1951 Congressman Donald L. Jackson, mocking the Guatemalan military, stated, "If someone would confiscate those two tanks they have, they would be much more peaceful." U.S. House of Representatives, Committee on Foreign Affairs, *Selective Executive Session Hearings of the Committee, 1951–56* (Washington, D.C.: Government Printing Office, 1980), 16: 393.

3. Guillermo Plazas Olarte, "Conflicto con el Perú, 1932–1934," in *Historia de las fuerzas militares de Colombia, ejército*, ed. Alvaro Valencia Tovar, 3 vols. (Bogota: Planta, 1993), 3: 41; Jesús Torres Almeyda, "Primeros decenios del siglo XX," in *Historia de las fuerzas militares de Colombia, armada*, ed. Alvaro Valencia Tovar (Bogota: Planta, 1993), 329; Guillermo S. Faura Gaig, *Los ríos de la amazonia peruana* (Lima: El Centro de Estudios Historicos Militares del Peru, 1962), 329.

4. *World Almanac and Book of Facts 1993* (New York: World Almanac Press, 1992), 697; John J. Finan, "Colombia (1948 until 1959)," in D. M. Condit et al., *Challenge and Response in Internal Conflict*, vol. 3 of *The Experience in Africa and Latin America*, 3 vols. (Washington, D.C.: The American University, 1968), 3: 411; Barbara A. Tenenbaum, ed., *Encyclopedia of Latin American History and Culture*, 5 vols. (New York: Charles Scribner's Sons, 1996), 5: 425–26.

5. Ramón Cesar Bejarano, *Síntesis de la guerra del Chaco* (Asuncíon: Editorial Toledo, 1982), 69; Bureau of the Census, *Historical Statistics of the United States Colonial Times to 1957* (Washington, D.C.: Government Printing Office, 1961), 735.

6. *Webster's New International Dictionary of the English Language*, 2d ed. (Springfield: G. & C. Merriam Company, 1961), 2134.

INTRODUCTION

1. Cristián García-Godoy, *The San Martín Papers* (Washington, D.C.: The San Martín Society, 1988), 5.

2. Jay Mallin Sr., "The Military and Transition in Cuba," by International Research 2000 Inc, 1995), 10. Ernesto Betancourt, Director of *Radio Martí*, states that between 400,000 and 500,000 Cubans served in Africa. Ernesto F. Betancourt, "Cuba in Africa," a paper delivered at the Latin American Studies Association's XV International Congress Conference (September 21–23, 1989, San Juan, Puerto Rico), 12.

3. U.S. House of Representatives, 80th Congress, 1st Session, Document 3836, 471–72. In the early challenges—Bolivia (1952), Guatemala (1954), Cuba (1959), and the Dominican Republic (1965)—perhaps the United States correctly evaluated the extent of Communist involvement twice, when it did not intervene in Bolivia and did in the Dominican Republic.

4. *Correio da Manhã* (Rio de Janeiro), June 21, 1958, 1; Moniz Bandeira, *Brasil-Estados Unidos: A rivalidade emergente (1950–1988),* (Rio de Janeiro: Ed. Civilização Braseira, 1989), 262–63.

5. President John F. Kennedy stated in a September 13, 1962, news conference that "if Cuba should ever attempt to export its aggressive purposes by force or the threat of force against any nation in this hemisphere or become an offensive military base of significant capacity for the Soviet Union, then this country will do whatever must be done to protect its own security and that of its allies." *Public Papers of the Presidents: John F. Kennedy*, 3 vols. (Washington, D.C.: Government Printing Office, 1962–64), 2: 674.

6. Arthur P. Whitaker, *The United States and South America: The Northern Republics* (Westport, Conn.: Greenwood Press, 1974), 168.

7. James Daniel Richardson, *A Compilation of the Messages and the Papers of the Presidents*, 22 vols. (New York: Bureau of National Literature, 1897–1917), 14: 6921–24.

8. Robert L. Scheina, *Latin America: A Naval History, 1810–1987* (Annapolis: U.S. Naval Institute Press, 1987), 304–20.

CHAPTER ONE

1. Richardson, *A Compilation*, 10: 4537–38.

2. José Vicente Concha (1867–1929) had presidential aspirations and did not want to be associated with a treaty that might lose control of the isthmus.

3. Eduardo Lemaitre, *Panamá y su separación de Colombia*, 4th ed. (Bogotá: Amazonas Editores Ltda, 1993), 356.

4. The text of the Hay-Herrán Treaty is in Senate Document 456, 63rd Congress, 2nd Session, 57–72.

5. Lemaitre, *Panamá,* 379.

6. ibid.

7. "Colombia's Treatment of the Treaty," *Literary Digest* 27: 9; 246–47 (August 29, 1903), 246; see also "Proposed Panama Secession," *Literary Digest* 27: 12; 343–45 (September 19, 1903), which begins, "The suggestion that the United States indorse and assist secession in a sister republic to get a canal route (considered in these columns August 29), continues to be warmly discussed in the American press."

8. Dwight Carroll Miner, *The Fight for the Panama Route* (New York: Columbia University Press, 1940), 350.

9. U.S. Marines and sailors had been called upon twice during the early twentieth century to guard the Panama railroad from the continuing Colombian civil wars. The first was between November 22 and December 4, 1901, and the second was between September 17 and November 18, 1902.

10. L. G. Carr Laughton, *The Naval Pocket-Book* (London: W. Thacker, Spink, 1903), 219–20.

11. *Foreign Relations of the United States*, multiple vols. (Washington, D.C.: U.S. Department of State, 1861–), year 1903: 247.

12. ibid., 270.

13. In Roosevelt's 1903 annual message, he quoted remarks by Secretary of State William Seward and Attorney General James Speed in 1865 which argued that the United States' guarantee of Colombian sovereignty and property in the 1846 treaty applied only to external aggression. Richardson, *A Compilation*, 15: 6808.

14. *Foreign Relations 1903*, 248, 250, 254–55; Enrique Román Bazurto, *Proas en tres mares* (Bogotá: Imprenta de las Fuerzas Militares, n.d.), 52.

15. *Foreign Relations 1903*, 268–70.

16. John Nikol and Francis X. Holbrook, "Naval Operations in the Panama Revolution 1903," *The American Neptune* 37: 4; 253–61 (October 1977), 259.

17. Richardson, *A Compilation*, 15: 6814.

18. A Marine Corps battalion ranged in size from 325 to 425 officers and men. In September 1902 the Marines established a floating battalion and this was generally maintained in the Caribbean when not ashore during a crisis.

A regiment was two battalions. A brigade varied from 1,400 to 2,800 officers and men. In 1904 the Panama Expeditionary Brigade was 1,400 officers and men; in 1906 the 1st Provisional Brigade to Cuba was 2,893; and in 1912 the Provisional Brigade to Cuba was about 1,600. Brigades were provisional and pulled together when needed. Research provided by Patrick Roth.

CHAPTER TWO

1. Antônio Pimentel Winz, "Plácido de Castro e a integração do Acre," *Navigator Subsídios para a Historia Marítima do Brasil* 10: 46–66 (December 1974): 52.

2. José Maria Bello, *A History of Modern Brazil, 1889–1964* (Stanford: Stanford University Press, 1966), 186–87; Winz, "Plácido de Castro," 46.

3. Hernâni Donato, *Dicionário das batalhas brasileiras* (São Paulo: IBRASA, 1987), 164.

4. Winz, "Plácido de Castro," 52–53; Donato, *Dicionário,* 165; Gordon Ireland, *Boundaries, Possessions, and Conflicts in South America* (Cambridge: Harvard University Press, 1938), 45.

5. Following the surrender of Luís Gálvez in March 1900, a large number of persons from northern Brazil organized an expedition to take Acre from the Bolivians. Their less adventurous but more practical countrymen labeled their undertaking the "Expedition of Poets" (*Expedição dos Poetas*). The participants called it the "Expedition of Floriano Peixoto."

6. Winz, "Plácido de Castro," 54.

7. Ireland, *Boundary Disputes*, 45–46; Bello, *A History of Modern Brazil*, 187; Donato, *Dicionário*, 165; Winz, "Plácido de Castro," 54.

8. Ireland, *Boundary Disputes*, 46.

9. Winz, "Plácido de Castro," 55.

10. ibid.

11. ibid., 55–56.

12. Brazil acquired the Acre and a small amount of territory to the south for two million pounds sterling. Also, Brazil agreed to build the Madeira to Marmoré railroad and paid the "Bolivian Trading Company 110,000 pounds as compensation." Donato, *Dicionário*, 165; Ireland, *Boundary Disputes*, 47; Bello, *A History of Modern Brazil*, 188.

13. Harold Osborne, *Bolivia: A Land Divided* (London: Royal Institute of International Affairs, 1954), 59.

CHAPTER THREE

1. Francisco Madero (1873–1913) was the younger son of a wealthy family of cotton planters from Chihuahua. He had been educated by Jesuits in Saltillo, in France, and in California and had traveled to Europe. He was elected mayor of his town but the Porfirio Díaz government did not recognize the election. Madero was an honest liberal idealist with no

administrative or military experience. He was further handicapped by greedy relatives belonging to the landed aristocracy. Madero's small stature (five feet), and his squeaky voice did not contribute to his ability to deal with men who were accustomed to taking the law into their own hands.

2. José de la Cruz Porfirio Díaz (1830–1915) was an experienced soldier. He fought as a Liberal against Santa Anna and served in the War of the *Reforma*. Díaz emerged from the war against Maximilian as Mexico's most accomplished general. On several occasions, he was an unsuccessful presidential candidate who ultimately seized the government by force in 1876. Until 1910 Díaz maintained a stable political system that supposedly adhered to the Constitution of 1857.

3. The Plan of San Luis Potosi called for suffrage, no reelection, reestablishing of public liberties, the right of workers to organize, and an end to concessions to foreigners. José Vasconcelos, *Breve Historia de México* (Mexico: Editorial Polis, 1944), 566.

4. J. Patrick McHenry, *A Short History of Mexico* (New York: Dolphin Books, 1970), 151; Jesus Romero Flores, *La revolución mexicana* (Mexico: Talleres Gráficos de la Nación, 1960), 30–31; Daniel Gutierrez Santos, *Historia militar de Mexico, 1876–1914* (Mexico: Ediciones Ateneo, S.A., 1955), 53–58.

5. Reau Campbell, *Campbell's New Revised Complete Guide and Descriptive Book of Mexico* (Chicago: Rogers & Smith, 1907), 51; Kurt F. Reinhardt, "Positivism in Mexico," *The Americas* 2: 1; 93–98 (July 1945).

6. Francisco Bulnes, *El Verdadero Díaz y la Revolución* (México: Editora Nacional, 1967), 372–75; Francisco Bulnes, *The Whole Truth about Mexico* (New York: M. Bulnes Book Company, 1916), 146–47.

7. Vasconcelos, *Breve Historia*, 564–65; Pauline R. Kibbe, *A Guide to Mexican History* (Mexico: Editorial Minutiae Mexicana, 1966), 58; Bulnes, *The Whole Truth*, 21–22.

8. Vasconcelos, *Breve Historia*, 563–67; Bulnes, *El Verdadero Díaz*, 380–92; Guillermo Mendoza Vallejo and Luís Garfías Magaña, "El Ejército Mexicano de 1860 a 1913," *El Ejército Mexicano* (Mexico: Secretaria de la Defensa Nacional, 1979), 324.

9. Luís Garfías M., *The Mexican Revolution* (Mexico City: Panorama Editorial, S.A., 1987), 11. Michel C. Meyer and William L. Sherman, *The Course of Mexican History* (New York: Oxford University Press, 1979), 466, place the Mexican population at 15,160,000 in 1910.

10. Thomas A. Janvier, "The Mexican Army," *Harper's New Monthly Magazine* 79: 474; 813–27 (November 1889), 827.

11. Mendoza and Garfías, "El Ejército Mexicano de 1860 a 1913," 326–29; Garfías M., *The Mexican Revolution*, 11; Meyer and Sherman, *The Course*, 454.

12. Bulnes, *The Whole Truth*, 146.

13. Moisés González Navarro, "Social Aspects of the Mexican Revolution," *Journal of World History* 8: 2; 281–89 (1964), 383.

14. Francisco "Pancho" Villa (1878–1923) the pseudonym for Doroteo Arango, was a classic *caudillo*. He was generous to those who followed him and brutal to those who opposed him. Villa was from peasant stock and had been driven to banditry at an early age. Villa possessed little education. He had an intuition for military tactics and led by example. Villa was an excellent horseman. Frequently, he championed the rights of the oppressed, running large landowners out of the country. In October 1910 Villa led fifteen men into rebellion against Porfirio Díaz. His following at the Battle of Celaya in August 1915 was perhaps 50,000

men scattered throughout northern Mexico. See Rubén Osorio, *La familia secreta de Pancho Villa una historia oral*, trans. by John Klingemann (Alpine: Sul Ross State University, 2000), for details concerning Villa's early life.

15. Emiliano Zapata (1880–1919), an Indian, inherited a small plot of land and supplemented this income by working as a muleteer and a stable master. As a young man he protested the seizure of the *ejidos* in his birthplace, Anenecuilco. Because of his actions he was forcefully conscripted into the 9th Cavalry Regiment. Due to the intercession of influential aristocrats, he remained in the army for only six months. Zapata wanted to break up the great estates and redistribute the lands, in particular the sugar estates in his home state of Morelos. He wanted to reestablish the *ejidos* or community-held lands of the Indian villages. In November 1911 Zapata issued his Plan of Ayala in which he stated opposition to the manner in which Madero was delaying his addressing of the agrarian problems. Zapata had no political ambitions. He was extremely provincial in vision. Agents of Pablo González assassinated Zapata.

16. Luís Garfías Magana, "E' Ejército Mexicano de 1913 a 1938," *Ejército Mexicano* (Mexico: Secretaria de la Defensa Nacional, 1979), 368.

17. Pascual Orozco (1882–1915) was a muleteer and a shopkeeper prior to the revolution. Like Emiliano Zapata, Orozco was a quiet, retiring person. On the battlefield he was confident, brave, and prudent.

18. Mendoza and Garfías, "El Ejército Mexicano de 1860 a 1913," 326; *Anales gráficos de la historia militar de México 1810–1991* (Mexico: Editorial Gustavo Casasola, S.A., 1991), 174; Gutierrez, *Historia militar*, 50–51.

19. *Anales gráficos* 176; Costa Soto, *Historia militar de México* (Mexico: Impreso en los Talleros Gráficos de la Nación, 1947), 93: Mendoza and Garfías, "El Ejército Mexicano de 1860 a 1913," 329–31; Garfías, *The Mexican Revolution*, 28; McHenry, *A Short History*, 151.

20. Meyer and Sherman, *The Course*, 502.

21. Mendoza and Garfías, "El Ejército Mexicano de 1860 a 1913," 331–34; Garfías, *The Mexican Revolution*, 31–32.

22. Garfías, *The Mexican Revolution*, 32.

23. Costa Soto, *Historia military*, 95; Garfías, *The Mexican Revolution*, 33; Romero, *La revolución*, 36; Meyer and Sherman, *The Course*, 502.

24. Meyer and Sherman, *The Course*, 503; Mendoza and Garfías, "El Ejército Mexicano de 1860 a 1913," 275–76; Gutierrez, *Historia military*, 74–83; Garfías, *The Mexican Revolution*, 34–36; Costa Soto, *Historia military*, 98–99.

25. Jésus Romero Flores, *Anales Historicos de la revolución mexicana*, 4 vols. (Mexico: El Nacional, 1939), 1: 189–205; Manuel Rodríguez Lapuente, *Breve Historia Gráfica de la revolución mexicana*, 2d ed. (Mexico: Ediciones G. Gili, 1987), 28; McHenry, *A Short History*, 152–53.

26. Vasconcelos, *Breve Historia*, 567; Mendoza and Garfías, "El Ejército Mexicano de 1860 a 1913," 336–37.

27. Garfías, *The Mexican Revolution*, 46–47; Vasconcelos, *Breve Historia*, 568–69.

28. McHenry, *A Short History*, 155; Mendoza and Garfías, "El Ejército Mexicano de 1860 a 1913," 338–39; *Anales gráficos*, 210; Gutierrez, *Historia militar*, 97–100.

29. Mendoza and Garfías, "El Ejército Mexicano de 1860 a 1913," 339–40; Garfías, *The Mexican Revolution*, 57–59; *Anales gráficos*, 211–13.

30. Mendoza and Garfías, "El Ejército Mexicano de 1860 a 1913," 340; Garfías, *The Mexican Revolution*, 60; *Anales gráficos*, 116–19; Gutierrez, *Historia militar*, 100–4.

31. Gutierrez, *Historia militar*, 105–8; Mendoza and Garfías, "El Ejército Mexicano de 1860 a 1913," 341–42; Garfías, *The Mexican Revolution*, 62–63.

32. Victoriano Huerta (1854–1916) was born in the state of Jalisco and was a pure Huichol Indian. As a very young man he served as the aide to Gen. Donato Guerra, who used his influence to have Huerta admitted to the National Military Academy. He took part in the coup that brought Porfirio Díaz to power in 1876. During the *Porfiriato*, Huerta fought in the campaigns against the Yaqui and Mayan Indians. Huerta was a good student but not particularly trusted by those who knew him. He led federal forces against Emiliano Zapata during the interim presidency of Leon de la Barra and earned a reputation for cruelty. Following Huerta's defeat of General Orozco in 1912, Huerta would not account for one million pesos of the War Department's funds and was retired. Madero recalled Huerta to command federal troops defending the National Palace against rebels led by Félix Díaz. Huerta was a good tactician although his strategy for dealing with the Félix Díaz revolt was indecisive. Huerta has been accused of being perpetually intoxicated.

33. Mendoza and Garfías, "El Ejército Mexicano de 1860 a 1913," 342–48; Costa Soto, *Historia military*, 103–4; Garfías, *The Mexican Revolution*, 65–67.

34. Mendoza and Garfías, "El Ejército Mexicano de 1860 a 1913," 348–49; Garfías, *The Mexican Revolution*, 70–71; Costa Soto, *Historia militar*, 104–5.

35. Costa Soto, *Historia militar*, 105–6; *Anales gráficos*, 247–49; Romero, *La revolución*, 45.

36. Gutierrez, *Historia militar*, 128–32; Mendoza and Garfías, "El Ejército Mexicano de 1860 a 1913," 351–52; Garfías, *The Mexican Revolution*, 73–75.

37. Mendoza and Garfías, "El Ejército Mexicano de 1860 a 1913," 354; Garfías, *The Mexican Revolution*, 76–78; Romero, *La revolución*, 46.

38. Garfías, *The Mexican Revolution*, 78.

39. Henry Lane Wilson had been appointed ambassador by President William Taft and was primarily concerned with representing American business interests.

40. Mendoza and Garfías, "El Ejército Mexicano de 1860 a 1913," 354–57; Vasconcelos, *Breve Historia*, 574–82; Garfías, *The Mexican Revolution*, 84–87; Kibbe, *A Guide*, 62.

41. Vasconcelos, *Breve Historia*, 569.

42. Venustiano Carranza (1859–1920) was a senator from the state of Coahuila under Porfirio Díaz and a member of the landed aristocracy. He joined Madero's cause and was appointed governor of Coahuila in 1911. Carranza was a shrewd politician but possessed little military talent.

43. Romero, *La revolución*, 48–49; Garfías, "El Ejército Mexicano de 1913 a 1938," 364.

44. Michael C. Meyer, "The Militarization of Mexico, 1913–1914," *The Americas* 27: 3; 293–306 (January 1971): 294; Vasconcelos, *Breve Historia*, 586–87; Garfías, *The Mexican Revolution*, 91.

45. Alvero Obregón (1880–1928), prior to the revolution, had been a farm hand and factory worker and was not well traveled. Obregón had little formal education. However, he possessed an amazing amount of natural military talent. He brought with him to the Constitutionalist army the loyalty of many Yaqui Indians.

46. Garfías, *The Mexican Revolution*, 92–95.

47. Garfías, "El Ejército Mexicano de 1913 a 1938," 373–75; Garfías, *The Mexican Revolution*, 99; Costa Soto, *Historia militar*, 108.

48. Costa Soto, *Historia militar*, 109–10.

49. Garfías, *The Mexican Revolution*, 100, 115; *Anales gráficos*, 278–86.

50. Garfías, "El Ejército Mexicano de 1913 a 1938," 375–77; Garfías, *The Mexican Revolution*, 104–5.

51. Garfías, *The Mexican Revolution*, 113.

52. Garfías, "El Ejército Mexicano de 1913 a 1938," 379.

53. Garfías, "El Ejército Mexicano de 1913 a 1938," 384–86; Garfías, *The Mexican Revolution*, 120; Costa Soto, *Historia militar*, 111–12; *Anales gráficos*, 299.

54. Garfías, "El Ejército Mexicano de 1913 a 1938," 386–88; *Anales gráficos*, 307; Garfías, *The Mexican Revolution*, 120–21.

55. Meyer, "Militarization," 298–300; Meyer and Sherman, *The Course*, 525–26; Gutierrez, *Historia military*, 148–51.

56. Meyer, "Militarization," 302.

57. Vasconcelos, *Breve Historia*, 588–89.

58. On April 9, 1914, Huerta's forces arrested nine American sailors for unknowingly entering a prohibited zone in Tampico. Once the Mexican authorities learned they were Americans, they were immediately released, apologized to, and escorted to the waterfront. The incident took about half an hour. The commander of a U.S. battleship division, Rear Adm. Henry Mayo, demanded a formal apology and a salute to the flag. The local commander apologized but Huerta refused a formal apology and a salute. McHenry, *A Short History*, 164.

59. McHenry, *A Short History*, 164–65; Costa Soto, *Historia military*, 115; *Anales gráficos*, 324–27; Romero, *La revolución*, 55–56.

60. McHenry, *A Short History*, 165.

61. Costa Soto, *Historia militar*, 117–18; Garfías, "El Ejército Mexicano de 1913 a 1938," 342; Garfías, *The Mexican Revolution*, 117–18; *Anales gráficos*, 331–38.

62. Garfías, *The Mexican Revolution*, 123–24; *Anales gráficos*, 319–20.

63. Garfías, *The Mexican Revolution*, 122, 126; Costa Soto, *Historia militar*, 116–17, 269, 297.

64. Garfías, "El Ejército Mexicano de 1913 a 1938," 397–99; Garfías, *The Mexican Revolution*, 126; *Anales gráficos*, 339, 345.

65. McHenry, *A Short History*, 166.

66. Garfías, "El Ejército Mexicano de 1913 a 1938," 403–5.

67. Garfías, *The Mexican Revolution*, 139–40; Costa Soto, *Historia militar*, 124; Romero, *La revolución*, 64.

68. Costa Soto, *Historia military*, 125; Garfías, *The Mexican Revolution*, 142.

69. McHenry, *A Short History*, 169; Garfías, "El Ejército Mexicano de 1913 a 1938," 408; Meyer and Sherman, *The Course*, 539.

70. Garfías, *The Mexican Revolution*, 145–47; Garfías, "El Ejército Mexicano de 1913 a 1938," 409.

71. Garfías, *The Mexican Revolution*, 148.

72. Garfías, "El Ejército Mexicano de 1913 a 1938," 411–12; Garfias, *The Mexican Revolution*, 150–51.

73. Garfías, "El Ejército Mexicano de 1913 a 1938," 413–15; Garfías, *The Mexican Revolution*, 152–54; *Anales gráficos*, 318–21.

74. Obregón was in such pain that he put a pistol to his head and pulled the trigger only to find that the gun was empty. McHenry, *A Short History*, 169.

75. Garfías, "El Ejército Mexicano de 1913 a 1938," 416–17; Garfías, *The Mexican Revolution*, 155–56; Costa Soto, *Historia militar*, 129–31.

76. Meyer and Sherman, *The Course*, 539.

77. Kibbe, *A Guide*, 65–66; *Anales gráficos*, 416–18; Romero, *La revolución*, 68–69.

78. Vasconcelos, *Breve Historia*, 615–16.

79. F. A. Kirkpatrick, *Latin America: A Brief History* (New York: Macmillan, 1939), 349.

80. Harold Davis, *History of Latin America* (New York: The Ronald Press Co., 968), 618.

CHAPTER FOUR

1. Meyer and Sherman, *The Course*, 587; David Marley, *Wars of the Americas* (Santa Barbara: ABC-CLIO, 1998), 643.

2. John W. F. Dulles, *Yesterday in Mexico* (Austin: University of Texas Press, 1972), 296–97; Charles C. Cumberland, *Mexican Revolution: The Constitutional Years* (Austin: University of Texas Press, 1974), 417.

3. Dulles, *Yesterday*, 298–99.

4. ibid., 300; Francis McCullagh, *Red Mexico* (New York: Louis Carrier, 1928), 63–64.

5. Dulles, *Yesterday*, 299–300.

6. Antonio Ríus Faciuo, *Mejico cristero* (Mexico: Editorial Patria, S.A., 1960), 14–15.

7. Emilio Portes Gil, *The Conflict between the Civil Power and the Clergy* (Mexico: Press of the Ministry of Foreign Affairs, 1935), 103.

8. William F. Montavon, *The Facts Concerning the Mexican Problem* (Washington, D.C.: National Catholic Welfare Conference, 1926), 5–19; Ríus, *Mejico cristero*, 18–20; Marley, *Wars*, 642.

9. Ríus, *Mejico cristero*, 48–53; Dulles, *Yesterday*, 302–3.

10. Ríus, *Mejico cristero*, 47–48.

11. ibid., 69–77.

12. Garfias, "El ejército mexicano," 457; *Anales gráficos*, 510; Marley, *Wars*, 643.

13. Ríus, *Mejico cristero*, 257–59; Elizabeth Salas, *Soldaderas in the Mexican Military* (Austin: University of Texas Press, 1990), 49; Dulles, *Yesterday*, 309–10.

14. Salas, *Soldaderas*, 49–50; Garfias, "El ejército mexicano," 438–57; *Anales gráficos*, 506–7.

15. Dulles, *Yesterday*, 305–8.

16. *Anales gráficos*, 509–10.

17. Ríus, *Mejico cristero*, 245–46; *Anales gráficos*, 511; Alfonso Taracena, *La verdadera revolución mexicana*, 12 vols. plus (México: Editiorial Jus, 1960–63), 12: 187–88; Dulles, *Yesterday*, 310; Marley, *Wars*, 643.

18. Archbishop Mora y del Río died on April 22 and Bishop Ignacio Valdespino on May 12 while in exile in San Antonio, Texas.

19. Meyer and Sherman, *The Course*, 588.

20. Anales gráficos, 512; Ríus, *Mejico cristero*, 299; Dulles, *Yesterday*, 310–11; Cota Soto, *Historia militar*, 155.

21. Dulles, *Yesterday*, 311.

22. Dulles, *Yesterday*, 311–15; Ríus, *Mejico cristero*, 315–30; Marley, *Wars*, 643.

23. Ríus, *Mejico cristero*, 340–44; *Anales gráficos*, 518–19.

24. Ríus, *Mejico cristero*, 369–78; Dulles, *Yesterday*, 358–59.

25. Dulles, *Yesterday*, 463; *Anales gráficos*, 520; Marley, *Wars*, 643.

26. Marley, *Wars*, 643.

27. Dulles, *Yesterday*, 425.

28. Cota Soto, *Historia military*, 160; Marley, *Wars*, 644.

29. Meyer and Sherman, *The Course*, 591.

30. ibid.; Marley, *Wars*, 644.

31. H. McKennie Goodpasture, *Cross and Sword* (New York: Orbis Books, 1989), 203; Alberto María Carreño, *Paginas de historia mexicana* (Mexico: Ediciones Victoria, 1936), 3: 361–62 [apparently volumes 1 & 2 were not published].

32. J. de Jesús Nieto López, *Diccionario histórico del México contemporáneo (1900–1982)*, (Mexico City: Alhambra Mexicana, 1991), 157.

According to Dulles the War Ministry estimated the number of deaths to be between 800 and 1,000 persons. These figures may refer only to the losses of the Mexican army and police. Contemporary accounts set the total number of deaths much higher. Dulles, *Yesterday*, 463.

33. Dulles, *Yesterday*, 512.

CHAPTER FIVE

1. Eight Latin American nations declared war against the Central Powers: Brazil, Costa Rica, Cuba, Guatemala, Haiti, Honduras, Nicaragua, and Panama. Five broke diplomatic relations: Bolivia, the Dominican Republic, Ecuador, Peru, and Uruguay. Seven remained neutral: Argentina, Chile, Colombia, Mexico, Paraguay, El Salvador, and Venezuela.

2. Brasil, Ministério das Relações Exteriores, *Relatório 1917–18*, 2: special appendix, 169.

3. "Latin American Trade," *The Navy* (Washington), 8: 451–55 (November 1914), 451–55.

4. "Then, also, there are hundreds of thousands of Germans in South Brazil, and rumor has it that they are drilling and have found arms." "River Plate News," *Fairplay* 68: 915 (May 31, 1917), 915.

5. *The Statesman's Year-Book: Statistical and Historical Annual of the States of the World* (New York: St. Martin's Press, 1918), 723.

6. Brasil, Ministério das Relações Exteriores, *Relatório 1916–17*, 1: 1.

7. Naval War College, *International Law Documents 1917*, 64. See also Brasil, Ministério das Relações Exteriores, *Relatório 1917–18*, 1: 23.

8. "Attitude of South America," U.S. Naval Institute *Proceedings*, 43: 1094 (May 1917): 1094.

9. Brazil had ratified the convention on January 5, 1914.

10. A total of forty-four ships is listed in Arthur Oscar Saldanha da Gama, *A marinha do Brasil na primeira guerra mundial* (Rio de Janeiro: CAPEMI Editora e Gráfica Ltda., 1982), 24–25. The *Belmonte* (ex-*Valesia*) is not listed because the Brazilian navy employed this ship. Brasil, Ministério das Relações Exteriores, *Relatório 1917–18*, 1: 136–41, 2: special appendix, 165–81.

11. David Healy, "Admiral William B. Caperton and United States Naval Diplomacy in the South America, 1917–1919," *Latin American Studies* 8: 297–323 (November 1976): 297–323.

12. da Gama, *A marinha do Brasil na primeira guerra*, 12–14.

13. ibid., 41–42.

14. ibid., 43–46.

15. ibid., 38–39.

16. "German Plots Revealed," U.S. Naval Institute *Proceedings* 43: 3082 (December 1917), 3082.

17. Percy Alvin Martin, *Latin America and the War* (Baltimore: The Johns Hopkins Press, 1925), 72–73; "South America," U.S. Naval Institute *Proceedings* 43: 3082 (December 1917), 3082.

18. The German gunboat *Eber* had been stationed in southwest Africa before the outbreak of war. On August 31, 1914, the gunboat handed over her two 105mm guns, her six revolving cannons, and most of the crew to the auxiliary cruiser *Cap Trafalgar* (former liner), near the Brazilian island of Trinidade. With a skeleton crew and no weapons, the *Eber* reached Bahia, Brazil, where she was interned.

19. Brasil, Ministério das Relações Exteriores, *Relatório 1917–18*, 116–17.

20. Walton L. Robinson, "Brazilian Navy in the World War," U.S. Naval Institute *Proceedings* 62: 1712–20 (December 1936): 1717.

21. da Gama, *A marinha do Brasil na primeira guerra* 130–35; Renato de Almeida [Guillobel], *Memórias* (n.p.: Serviço Gráfico da Fundação [Getúlio Vargas], 1973), 113.

22. Paulo de Q. Duarte, *Dias de guerra no Atlântico sul* (Rio de Janeiro: Biblioteca do Exército, 1968), 10–13.

23. da Gama, *A marinha do Brasil na primeira guerra* 146–54. A number of accounts credit the destroyer *Rio Grande do Norte* with sinking a U-boat. See P. C. Burns, "Brazilian Navy," *Armed Forces Journal International* 113: 27 (December 1975), 27. Writings concerning U-boat losses do not support this claim. See Robert M. Grant, "Known Sunk: German Submarine War Losses, 1914–1918," U.S. Naval Institute *Proceedings* 64: 66–77 (January 1938), 66–77; *História do Brasil*, 2d ed. (São Paulo: Divisão de Publicações do Grupo Folha, 1997), 193.

24. da Gama, *A marinha do Brasil na primeira guerra*, 93–96.

25. Martin, *Latin America and the War*, 2; *História Naval Brasileira*, 5: 2 (Rio de Janeiro: Serviço de Documentação Geral da Marinha, 1985), 111.

26. British Vessels Captured and Destroyed by the Enemy, tables D and E. The seven do not include *Taquari*, which lost eight men in an attack but the ship did not sink.

27. Initially, forty-five ships were requisitioned from the Germans. Two, the *Acari* (ex-*Ebenburg*), and the *Maceió* (ex-*Santa Anna*), were torpedoed and lost.

28. Brazil sold the first to Poland and the second to Great Britain; both were scrapped. Brasil, Ministério das Relações Exteriores, Relatório 1920, ix–xxxv. See Scheina, Latin America, 133–38.

CHAPTER SIX

1. Dana G. Munro, *Intervention and Dollar Diplomacy in the Caribbean 1900–1921* (Princeton: Princeton University Press, 1964), 353; Marley, *Wars*, 612.

2. Frances Maclean, "They Didn't Speak Our Language; We Didn't Speak Theirs," *Smithsonian* 44–55 (January 1993), 44–46; R. Ernest Dupuy and William H. Baumer, *The Little Wars of the United States* (New York: Hawthorn Books, 1968), 145.

3. Samuel Flagg Bemis, *The Latin American Policy of the United States* (New York: Harcourt, Brace and Company, 1943), 144–45.

4. Richardson, *A Compilation*, 15: 6923.

5. Carl Kelsey, "The American Intervention in Haiti and the Dominican Republic," *Annuals of the American Academy of Political and Social Science for the Year 1921*, 134.

6. Harry Allanson Ellsworth, *One Hundred Eighty Landings of the United States Marine Corps 1800–1934* (Washington, D.C.: History and Museum Division, Headquarters, U.S. Marine Corps, 1974), 88–89.

7. Kelsey, "The American Intervention," 134–35.

8. Maclean, "They Didn't Speak Our Language," 46–47.

9. Kelsey, "The American Intervention," 135–36; Dupuy and Baumer, *The Little Wars*, 146.

10. *Annual Reports of the Navy Department 1915* (Washington, D.C.: Government Printing Office, 1916), 763; Dupuy and Baumer, *The Little Wars*, 146; Kelsey, "The American Intervention," 136.

11. *Annual Reports of the Navy Department 1915*, 763.

12. *Cacos* in Haitian Creole has been translated to mean "mean red ant" and "bird of prey." Maclean, "They Didn't Speak Our Language," 46.

13. Walter H. Posner, "American Marines in Haiti, 1915–1922," *The Americas* 30: 3; 231–66 (January 1964), 241.

14. Graham A. Cosmas, "*Cacos* and *Caudillos*: Marines and Counterinsurgency in Hispaniola, 1915–24," in *New Interpretations of Naval History*, ed. by William R. Roberts and Jack Sweetman (Annapolis: Naval Institute Press, 1991), 299.

15. Lars Schoultz, *Beneath the United States* (Cambridge: Harvard University Press, 1998), 232–33; Julius Pratt, *America's Colonial Experiment* (New York: Prentice-Hall, 1951), 148–49; Kelsey, "The American Intervention," 136.

16. Marley, *Wars*, 612–13; Dupuy and Baumer, *The Little Wars*, 148.

17. The three squad leaders—Capt. William P. Upshur, First Lt. Edward A. Ostermann, and Gunnery Sgt. Dan Daly—were awarded Congressional Medals of Honor. Dupuy and Baumer, *The Little Wars*, 149.

18. The first three men through the drain—Maj. Smedley Butler, Sgt. Ross L. Iams, and Pvt. Samuel Gross—received Congressional Medals of Honor.

19. Dupuy and Baumer, *The Little Wars*, 149–50; Patrick Bellegarde-Smith, *Haiti: The Breached Citadel* (Boulder: Westview Press, 1990), 80.

20. *Annual Reports of the Navy Department 1915*, 763; Kelsey, "The American Intervention," 138–39; Posner, "American Marines in Haiti," 250.

21. Cosmas, "*Cacos* and *Caudillos*," 294; Dupuy and Baumer, *The Little Wars*, 151–52.

22. Dupuy and Baumer, *The Little Wars*, 152–53.

23. Ellsworth, *One Hundred Eighty Landings*, 90.

24. Bellegarde-Smith, *Haiti*, 83; J. A. H. Hopkins and Melinda Alexander, *Machine-Gun Diplomacy* (New York: Lewis Copeland Company, 1928), 93–94.

25. Pratt, *America's Colonial Experiment*, 149.

26. Bellegarde-Smith, *Haiti*, 80, 85.

27. Schoultz, *Beneath the United States*, 233.

28. Posner, "American Marines in Haiti," 251.

CHAPTER SEVEN

1. Sumner Welles, *Naboth's Vineyard: The Dominican Republic 1844–1924*, 2 vols. (New York: Payson & Clarke, 1928), 2: 768; Stephen M. Fuller and Graham A. Cosmas, *Marines in the Dominican Republic 1916–1924* (Washington, D.C.: U.S. Government Printing Office, 1974), 7–9.

2. Carl Kelsey, "American Intervention in Haiti and the Dominican Republic," *Annuals of the American Academy of Political and Social Science* 6: 113–202 (March 1922), 175.

3. The Dominican Republic and the United States signed an agreement whereby the United States assumed the responsibility for paying all the Dominican Republic's debts, foreign and domestic, and was given charge of all custom houses.

4. Welles, *Naboth's Vineyard*, 2: 699–708.

5. *Foreign Relations of the United States 1916*, 224; Welles, *Naboth's Vineyard*, 2: 769–72; Ellsworth, *One Hundred and Eighty Landings*, 69; Luis F. Mejia, *De Lilis a Trujillo* (Caracas: Editorial Elite, 1944), 125–28.

6. Bruce J. Calder, "*Caudillos* and *Gavilleros* versus the United States Marines: Guerrilla Insurgency during the Dominican Intervention, 1916–1924," *Hispanic American Historical Review* 58: 4; 649–75 (1978), 652–53; Welles, *Naboth's Vineyard*, 2: 908.

7. Fuller and Cosmas, *Marines*, 11; Ellsworth, *One Hundred and Eighty Landings*, 70; John M. Collins, *America's Small Wars* (Washington, D.C.: Brassey's, 1991), 219.

8. Fuller and Cosmas, *Marines*, 14–22; Welles, *Naboth's Vineyard*, 2: 776–77; Mejia, *De Lilis a Trujillo*, 129; Marley, *Wars*, 614.

9. Williams received a Congressional Medal of Honor. Fuller and Cosmas, *Marines*, 26; Mejia, *De Lilis a Trujillo*, 130; Marley, *Wars*, 614.

10. Welles, *Naboth's Vineyard*, 2: 749–50.

11. Welles, *Naboth's Vineyard*, 2: 794.

12. J. Marino Inchaustegui, *Historia dominicana*, 2 vols. (Ciudad Trujillo: Impresora Dominicana, 1955), 2: 130; Welles, *Naboth's Vineyard*, 2: 797.

13. Mejia, *De Lilis a Trujillo*, 146–47.

14. Calder, "*Caudillos*," 652; Dupuy and Baumer, *The Little Wars*, 156.

15. Welles, *Naboth's Vineyard*, 2: 824–36; Mejia, *De Lilis a Trujillo*, 175.

16. "Favors Body with 'Teeth'; Harding Says Covenant Has Failed 'Beyond Restoration,'" *New York Times* 1, 12 (August 29, 1920), 1, 12.

17. Inchaustegui, *Historia dominicana*, 2: 135–37.

18. Warren Zimmermann, "Jingoes," *Wilson Quarterly* 22: 2 (Spring 1998), 62.

19. Dupuy and Baumer, *The Little Wars*, 157.

20. Inchaustegui, *Historia dominicana*, 2: 133.

21. Schoultz, *Beneath the United States*, 231.

22. Ellsworth, *One Hundred and Eighty Landings*, 71.

23. Daniel Gustavo Benavídes, "Yrigoyen y la intervención de Estados Unidos en Santo Domingo," *Todo Es Historia* 42: 229; 74–84 (May–June 1986), 76.

CHAPTER EIGHT

1. Augusto César Sandino (1893–1933) was the illegitimate son of a wealthy landowner and an Indian servant. He lived with his mother and used her family name until his teen years. When his father remarried, Augusto was brought into his household and treated as the first-born. He changed his middle name from Calderón to César after learning that his first name, Augusto, was identical to the first emperor of ancient Rome, Augustus Caesar. In 1920 Sandino wounded a man during an argument and spent the next years as a nomad. He worked as a miner, a plantation hand, and a mechanic. In 1923 he worked for American oil companies in Tampico, Mexico, a country that but a few years earlier had endured a profound social revolution. He returned to Nicaragua in June 1926 with $5,000 in savings and a .44 caliber Smith & Wesson revolver. Sandino worked for a short while as an assistant paymaster at the

American-owned San Albino gold mine. He then raised a small following and joined the Liberals in their attempt to overthrow the Conservative Díaz. Sandino was a skilled orator and was not shy in promoting himself. He minted gold coins that bore his image and he renamed the town of El Jícaro to Ciudad Sandino. Although Sandino was supported by the Communist-dominated All American Anti-Imperialist League and other pro-Communist organizations, he never proclaimed to be a Marxist.

2. *Sandino: The Testimony of a Nicaraguan Patriot 1921–34*, compiled and edited by Sergio Ramírez (Princeton: Princeton University Press, 1990), 70.

3. Congressional Record, 69th Cong, 2d Sess, "Affairs in Nicaragua" (House Doc No. 633), (January 10, 1927), 1324–26.

4. J. Fred Rippy, *The Caribbean Danger Zone* (New York: G. P. Putnam's Sons, 1940), 166–69.

5. Alfred Barnaby Thomas, *Latin America: A History* (New York: The Macmillan Company, 1956), 597; Rippy, *The Caribbean*, 170–72.

6. Rippy, *The Caribbean*, 172–77.

7. Rippy, *The Caribbean*, 178; Dupuy and Baumer, *The Little Wars*, 158–59.

8. Bemis, *The Latin American Policy*, 186–89; "Nicaragua," *O.N.I. Monthly Information Bulletin* 11: 1; 1–13 (July 1928), 2.

9. C. B. Carter, "The Kentucky Feud in Nicaragua," *The World's Work* 312–30 (1927), 312–13; Walter LaFeber, *Inevitable Revolutions* (New York: W. W. Norton, 1983), 64–65.

10. Lejeune Cummins, *Quijote on a Burro* (Mexico City: La Impresora Azteca, 1958), 5; Carter, "The Kentucky Feud," 320; Marley, *Wars*, 640.

11. Cummins, *Quijote*, 6; Carter, "The Kentucky Feud," 320; "Nicaragua," *O.N.I.*, 2–4; Marley, *Wars*, 640.

12. "Nicaragua," *O.N.I.*, 3–4.

13. Cummins, *Quijote*, 14; Carter, "The Kentucky Feud," 321; LaFeber, *Inevitable Revolutions*, 65; Marley, *Wars*, 640.

14. Marley, *Wars*, 640; "Nicaragua," *O.N.I.*, 4.

15. U.S. Department of State, *A Brief History of the Relations between the United States and Nicaragua, 1909–1928* (Washington, D.C.: Government Printing Office, 1928), 45–46; Bernard C. Nalty, *The United States Marines in Nicaragua* (Washington, D.C.: Historical Branch, G–3 Division, Headquarters, U.S. Marine Corps, revised 1962), 14.

16. "Nicaragua," *O.N.I.*, 5; Marley, *Wars*, 641; Henry L. Stimson, *American Policy in Nicaragua* (New York: Scribner's, 1927), 26–27; Henry L. Stimson and McGeorge Bundy, *On Active Duty in Peace and War* (New York: Harper & Brothers, 1948), 110–16.

17. Cummins, *Quijote*, 23–26; "Nicaragua," *O.N.I.*, 5; Marley, *Wars*, 641.

18. *Latin-American Yearbook for 1920 for Investors and Merchants* (New York: Criterion Publishing Syndicate, Inc., 1920), 521; "Nicaragua," *O.N.I.*, 1; Carter, "The Kentucky Feud," 314.

19. Julian C. Smith et al., *A Review of the Organization and Operations of the Guardia Nacional de Nicaragua* (Washington, D.C.: Headquarters, U.S. Marine Corps, n.d.), 12–16; *Annual Reports of the Navy Department 1929* (Washington, D.C.: Government Printing Office, 1930), 6; Cummins, *Quijote*, 23.

20. Carter, "The Kentucky Feud," 317–18; Evans F. Carlson, "*The Guardia Nacional de Nicaragua*," *The Marine Corps Gazette* 21: 3; 7–20 (August 1937), 7; Smith, *A Review*, 12–16; LaFeber, *Inevitable Revolutions*, 65–66.

21. Bernard C. Nalty, "Nicaragua (1927–1933)," in *Challenge and Response in Internal Conflict*, ed. by D. M. Condit et al., 3 vols. (Washington, D.C.: The American University Press, 1968), 3: 163; "Combat Operations in Nicaragua," *The Marine Corps Gazette* 14: 1; 16–30 (January 1929), 21; 14: 2; 81–94 (June 1929), 91; 14: 3; 170–79 (September 1929), 170.

22. Cummins, *Quijote*, 58.

23. "The United States Marines in Nicaragua" (Marine Corps Historical Reference Series No. 21), 23–26, 57–58; Nalty, "Nicaragua (1927–1933)," 160; LaFeber, *Inevitable Revolutions*, 66; Cummins, *Quijote*, 57–58.

24. Cummins, *Quijote*, 37, 51, 57, 60; *Sandino*, 68–90.

25. Sandino wrote, "the lesson of the battle of El Ocotal [July 16, 1927] convinced me that it was a foolish thing for us to die in pitched battles against the United States, and that it was preferable to maintain our protest for as long as possible." *Sandino*, 162.

26. *Sandino*, 89; Cummins, *Quijote*, 25–29, 49–55; Nalty, "Nicaragua (1927–1933)," 161.

27. "Nicaragua," *O.N.I.*, 1; Charles R. Sanderson, "The Supply Service in Western Nicaragua," *The Marine Corps Gazette* 17: 1, 41–44 (May 1932), 41–44; Nalty, "Nicaragua (1927–1933)," 159, 164.

28. Glendell L. Fitzgerald, "Combat Reports of Operations in Nicaragua," *The Marine Corps Gazette* 13: 4; 241–47 (December 1928), 242–47; Cummins, *Quijote*, 52.

29. U.S. Department of State, *A Brief History*, 50–54.

30. *Sandino*, 78; Nalty, "Nicaragua (1927–1933)," 159; Nalty, *The United States Marines*, 16; Cummins, *Quijote*, 51.

31. Nalty, *The United States Marines*, 17; *Sandino*, 88; Marley, *Wars*, 642; Dupuy and Baumer, *The Little Wars*, 162.

32. Nalty, *The United States Marines*, 17–18.

33. *Sandino*, 89, 102; Nalty, *The United States Marines*, 18; Marley, *Wars*, 642.

34. This may have been the second plane shot down by anti-aircraft fire in Latin America. The first was probably during the Paraguayan civil war of 1922–23.

35. *Sandino*, 114; Cummins, *Quijote*, 59–60.

36. Nalty, *The United States Marines*, 21.

37. Dupuy and Baumer, *The Little Wars*, 162–63; *Congressional Record*, 70th Congress, 1st Session (December 8, 1927), 261–62; Nalty, *The United States Marines*, 21.

38. Nalty, *The United States Marines*, 21; Cummins, *Quijote*, 60–63; Dupuy and Baumer, *The Little Wars*, 163; *Sandino*, 151–53.

39. Cummins, *Quijote*, 63.

40. Cummins, *Quijote*, 63–64; Nalty, *The United States Marines*, 22; Dupuy and Baumer, *The Little Wars*, 163.

Aviation expert C. G. Grey wrote, "The value of aircraft in warfare over difficult country has been thoroughly demonstrated by the U.S. Marines. In fact, it is believed that the attack at Chipote by four 'corsair' aircraft was the first aeroplane attack, unsupported by ground troops, ever made against a fortified position. These four aircraft, by the use of fixed and free guns, bombs and hand grenades, routed 1,500 well-armed bandits from a fortified position on the side of a mountain. Not a single man or machine was lost, and it was estimated that it would have required an extra regiment of troops and heavy casualties to have taken the position with ground troops." *Jane's All the World's Aircraft* (London: various publishers, 1912), 1928: 30b.

For a description of the siege and aerial assault from Sandino's point of view see *Sandino*, 162–67.

41. Cummins, *Quijote*, 67–68; *Sandino*, 185–86.

42. Nalty, *The United States Marines*, 22–23; Cummins, *Quijote*, 71–72.

43. Cummins, *Quijote*, 68; *Sandino*, 198–99.

44. Merritt A. Edson, "The Coco Patrol," *The Marine Corps Gazette* 20: 4; 40–41, 60–72 (November 1936); Cummins, *Quijote*, 73–75; Nalty, *The United States Marines*, 24–25.

45. Nalty, *The United States Marines*, 27; Cummins, *Quijote*, 33–34; Dupuy and Baumer, *The Little Wars*, 164.

46. Cummins, *Quijote*, 76.

47. Nalty, *The United States Marines*, 28.

48. Herman Hanneken, "A Discussion of the *Voluntario* Troops in Nicaragua," *Marine Corps Gazette* 26: 4; 120, 247–66 (November 1942), 120; Nalty, *The United States Marines*, 29.

49. Dupuy and Baumer, *The Little Wars*, 166.

50. Cummins, *Quijote*, 37.

51. ibid., 36; *Sandino*, 266–67.

52. Nalty, *The United States Marines*, 29.

53. Nalty, "Nicaragua (1927–1933)," 160; Nalty, *The United States Marines*, 30; *Sandino*, 333–34.

54. Cummins, *Quijote*, 86.

55. Nalty, *The United States Marines*, 31; Cummins, *Quijote*, 40–43, 86.

56. *Annual Reports of the Navy Department 1931* (Washington, D.C.: Government Printing Office, 1932), 373–74; Nalty, *The United States Marines*, 31; Cummins, *Quijote*, 88–90.

57. Cummins, *Quijote*, 90.

58. ibid., 91–92; *Foreign Relations* 1931, 3: 828–29.

59. *Foreign Relations* 1932, 5: 933; LaFeber, *Inevitable Revolutions*, 67; Nalty, *The United States Marines*, 22.

60. The Statues at Large of the United States of America 47: 1, 439; Cummins, *Quijote*, 94, 113–25, 129–36, 143–56.

61. Nalty, *The United States Marines*, 32–33.

62. Cummins, *Quijote*, 93.

63. ibid., 95.

64. ibid., 96.

65. Anastasio "Tacho" Somoza García (1896–1956) was born in Carazo, department of San Marcos, and was a member of the working class. He studied advertising in Philadelphia where he met the daughter of a wealthy Nicaraguan whom he married. He mastered English and used it to his advantage. Somoza possessed no military training. He was shrewd, brutal, and professed to be pro-United States in order to win its backing. He had four loves—power, wealth, women, and baseball.

66. Wilfred P. Deac, "Fire from the Hills," *Military History* 38–45 (August 1990), 45; LaFeber, *Inevitable Revolutions*, 68.

67. Cummins, *Quijote*, 97.

68. Nalty, *The United States Marines*, 33.

69. LaFeber, *Inevitable Revolutions*, 68; Cummins, *Quijote*, 45.

70. Cummins, *Quijote*, 49–57, 98–103.

71. Nalty, "Nicaragua (1927–1933)," 167; Marley, *Wars*, 642. Somoza claimed that Sandino's execution had the approval of the U.S. Minister, Arthur Bliss Lane. Lane denied this. LaFeber, *Inevitable Revolutions*, 68.

72. Donald Marquand Dozer, *Are We Good Neighbors?* (Gainesville: University of Florida Press, 1959), 11. Bruce Calder argues that at least some of the Dominican guerrillas were ideologically motivated as well. "Were the [Dominican] insurgents politically conscious? If so, at what level? Many bits of evidence indicate that all the guerrillas had at least inchoate political motives." Calder, "*Caudillos*," 659.

73. Nalty, *The United States Marines*, 34.

74. Smith, *A Review*, 100–1; Cummins *Quijote*, 82, 86–87.

75. *Sandino*, 276.

76. Nalty, "Nicaragua (1927–1933)," 165; Marvin Goldwert, *The Constabulary in the Dominican Republic and Nicaragua* (Gainsville: University of Florida, 1962), 49; Smith, *A Review*, 24, 42; Harold N. Denny, *Dollars for Bullets* (New York: The Dial Press, 1929), 338.

CHAPTER NINE

1. "Operational Histories of South American Battleships," *Warship International* 94: 438–39 (1972), 438.

2. David Caddick, "The Brazilian Navy," *Navy* 26: 144–46 (May 1921), 146; "The Iconoclast Abroad," *Shipping Illustrated* 33: 290 (December 31, 1910), 290.

3. Donato, *Dicionário*, 169.

4. "The handling of the Brazilian warships sans officers was a novel sight to us. I confess that I never saw evolutions performed in smarter style than those undergone by the mutinous warships. . . . I doubt whether a flag officer of rank would have done any better." "The Iconoclast Abroad," 290.

5. Donato, *Dicionário*, 169; Caddick, "The Brazilian Navy," 146; "Iconoclast Abroad," 290. The Brazilian navy forestalled another mutiny in 1919. Scheina, *Latin America*, 107.

6. Present were the battleship *Almirante Latorre*; armored cruiser *O'Higgins*; destroyers *Aldea*, *Hyatt*, *Lunch*, *Orella*, *Riquelme*, *Serrano*, and *Videla*; and the submarines *Simpson*, *O'Brien*, and a number of H-class boats. Rodrigo Fuenzalida Bade, *La armada de Chile*, 2d ed., 4 vols. (Valparaíso: Talleres Empresa Periodistica, 1978), 4: 1175.

7. Scheina, *Latin America*, 107–8.

8. These were: (1) full pay for the enlisted men; (2) that the millionaires of Chile loan 300 million pesos to the government; (3) that all government-owned, uncultivated land be divided among the workmen; (4) that the government continue public works; (5) that employment be provided for the unemployed; (6) that the sailors be given free clothing allowance; (7) that the rations be improved; (8) that the rations include more sugar; (9) that navy-yard watchmen be replaced by sailors; (10) that contract pilots no longer be employed; (11) that service trade [officer] schools be closed for two years; and, (12) that retirement for enlisted men be optional at fifteen years but compulsory at twenty years of service. Scheina, *Latin America*, 108.

9. William F. Sater, "The Abortive Kronstadt: The Chilean Naval Mutiny of 1931," *Hispanic American Historical Review* 60: 2; 239–68 (May 1980), 239–48; Fuenzalida, *La Armada*, 4: 1176–77.

10. Scheina, *Latin America*, 108–9.

11. Those sailing were the protected cruiser *Blanco Encalada*; submarine tender *Araucano*; submarines *Capitán Thompson, Almirante Simpson, H-1, H-2, H-4,* and five coast guard craft. Fuenzalida, *La armada*, 4: 1179.

12. Edgardo Von Schroeders, *El delegado del gobierno y el motín de la escuadra* (Santiago: Sociedad Imprenta y Litografía Universo, 1933), 17–26, 58–60, 98–99.

13. Sater, "The Abortive Kronstadt," 247.

14. "Chilean Naval Mutiny," *Monthly Information Bulletin* 14; 11–20 (July–October 1931), 14, 17; Fuenzalida, *La armada*, 4: 1180.

15. Rodolfo Martínez V., *Historia de la fuerza aérea de Chile*, 2 vols. (n.p., n.d.), 1: 159–65.

16. Scheina, *Latin America*, 112, 359.

17. The *Almirante Latorre* carried four 4-inch AA guns mounted during her 1929–31 refit in England. Six of the destroyers had one 3-inch AA gun each. The only other AA guns were machine guns scattered among the fleet.

18. Ramón Vergara Montero, *Por rutas extraviadas* (Santiago: Imprenta Universitaria, 1933), 38–61; Fuenzalida states that one aircraft was damaged and had to make an emergency landing between Coquimbo and Ovalle. Fuenzalida, *La armada*, 4: 1180.

19. Sater, "The Abortive Kronstadt," 253.

20. ibid., 258–59; *Mercurio* (Santiago), October 12, 1931, 18.

21. "Brazil," *The Navy* 16: 179 (July 1911), 179.

CHAPTER TEN

1. Robert V. Daniels, *A Documentary History of Communism*, rev. ed., 2 vols. (Hanover, N.H.: University Press of New England, 1984), 2: 83–87.

2. Latin American Communist parties established prior to World War II were Argentina (1918), Mexico (1919), Guatemala (1921), Uruguay (1921), Brazil (1922), Chile (1922), Colombia (1922), Cuba (1925), Honduras (1927), Paraguay (1928), El Salvador (1930), Venezuela (1931), and Peru (1933). See Charles Hobday, compiler, *Communist and Marxist Parties of the World* (Burnt Mill, Essex, United Kingdom: Longman, 1986).

3. Salvador de Madariaga, *Latin America between the Eagle and the Bear* (New York: Frederick A. Praeger, 1973), 138.

4. Madariaga, *Latin America*, 138–39.

5. Daniel James, *Mexico and the Americas* (New York: Frederick A. Praeger, 1963), 333.

6. Robert Alexander, *Communism in Latin America* (New Brunswick: Rutgers University Press, 1957), 322–23; Rollie E. Poppino, *International Communism in Latin America* (New York: The Free Press of Glencoe, 1964), 64.

7. James, *Mexico*, 333; Wilfrid Parsons, *Mexican Martydom* (New York: Macmillan Company, 1936), 207; Alexander, *Communism in Latin America*, 325.

8. Alexander, *Communism in Latin America*, 329.

9. Dulles, *Yesterday in Mexico*, 480; James, *Mexico*, 333.

10. James, *Mexico*, 334.

11. Meyer and Sherman, *The Course*, 592; Alexander, *Communism in Latin America*, 329.

12. Robert J. Alexander, *Communism in Latin America*, 319.

13. Alexander, *Communism in Latin America*, 177–85.

14. Scheina, *Latin America*, 107–8.

15. *Las grandes lunchas revolucionarias del proletariado chileno*, quoted from Juraj Domic K., *Poltica militar del partiado comunista de Chile* (Santiago: TT.GG. Instituto Geográfico Militar, 1988), 27.

16. Domic, *Poltica militar*, 28; Alexander, *Communism in Latin America*, 186.

17. Poppino, *International Communism*, 70; Domic, *Poltica militar*, 28.

18. Domic, *Poltica militar*, 28.

19. Harvey Levenstein, "Canada and the Suppression of the Salvadorian Revolution of 1932," *The Canadian Historical Review* 62 (4), 451–69 (1981), 452–53.

20. Kenneth J. Grieb, "The United States and the Rise of General Maximiliano Hernández Martínez," *Journal of Latin American Studies* 3: 2; 151–72 (November 1971), 152.

21. Alexander, *Communism in Latin America*, 368; Poppino, *International Communism*, 142.

22. Maxilimiano Hernández Martínez (1882–1966) was born in San Salvador. He was educated at the Colegio Nacional de San Salvador and the Colegio Militar of Guatemala. He became a lieutenant in 1903; a captain and major in 1906; a lieutenant colonel in 1909; a colonel in 1914; and a brigadier general in 1919. He participated in the fighting against Guatemala in 1906. He served as the Chief of Staff and as the Secretary of War.

23. Agustín Farabundo Martí (1893–1932) was an intellectual associated with the national university. He reputedly adopted his surname to honor the Cuban patriot José Martí. In 1920 Martí took part in some of the first strikes to occur in El Salvador. He was exiled that year for having provoked a duel with a former professor. Martí joined the Red Battalions in Mexico and became a sergeant. He traveled to New York City to the headquarters of the Anti-Imperialist League. From New York, Martí traveled to Nicaragua where he worked with Augusto Sandino as his personal secretary for almost a year before they disagreed over ideology. Martí was appointed the Salvadorian representative of the *Socorro Rojo Internacional* (Red Aid Society in El Salvador), which grew significantly in influence. He returned to El Salvador in 1930. Martí was arrested just prior to the Communist-led uprising in 1932 and shot on February 1, 1932, after a brief court-martial.

24. Alexander, Communism in Latin America, 368.

25. Sonsonate, Izalco, San Salvador, Colón, Tacuba, and Ahuachapán.

26. Thomas P. Anderson, *Matanza* (Willimantic: Curbstone Press, 1992), 92–121; Edelberto Torres Rivas, "Crisis and Conflict, 1930 to the present," in Central America since Independence, ed. by Leslie Bethell (Cambridge: Cambridge University Press, 1991), 105, places the number at less than fifty deaths.

27. Anderson, *Matanza*, 120–23; Poppino, International Communism, 141–42; Levenstein, "Canada," 451; Torres, "Crisis." Twenty-five thousand violent deaths is a suspiciously high number given El Salvador's population of about 1.8 million people.

28. Alexander, *Communism in Latin America*, 93–102, 107–9.

29. ibid., 109–11; Poppino, *International Communism*, 144–45.

30. João Pandia Calogeras, *A History of Brazil*, trans. by Percy Alvin Martin (Chapel Hill: Univ. of North Carolina Press, 1939), 346–47. On April 21, 1945, President Vargas released Prestes and 147 other accused conspirators under a general amnesty.

CHAPTER ELEVEN

1. Initially a *fortin* was a military post established primarily to protect against Indians and bandits. Typically, it was made up of a few huts, a barrack, a corral, and, most critically,

a watering hole; sometimes the site was surrounded by a trench. José Carlos Marcet, *Datos para una reseña cronológica sobre antecedentes, dersarrollo y resultado de la guerra del Chaco* (Asuncion: n.p., 1974), 109–12.

2. Daniel Salamanca, *Mensajes y memorias postumas* (Cochabamba, Bolivia: Editorial Canelas, S.A., 1976), 14–15; David Alvestegui, *Salamanca: su gravitación sobre el destino de Bolivia*, 4 vols. (Buenos Aires: Imprenta Lopez, 1962–70), 3: 379, 390; Rogelio Ayala Moreira, *Por qué no ganamos la guerra del Chaco* (La Paz: Talleres Gráficos Bolinianos, 1959), 112–20; Félix Tabera, *Picuiba: apuntes para la historia de la guerra del Chaco* (La Paz: Ed. Don Bosco, 1960), 96; Roberto Querejazu Calvo, *Masamaklay* (La Paz: Empresa Industrial Gráfica E. Burillo, 1965), 40.

3. Juan Esteban Vacca, *Notas del la pasada guerra del Chaco* (Buenos Aires: Círculo Militar, 1938), 290–91; Antonio González, *La guerra del Chaco* (São Paulo: Tipografia Cupolo, 1941), 24–25. Three distinct areas made up the Chaco. The Austral or southern Chaco lay south of the Bermejo River and is today the Argentine province named Chaco. The Central Chaco lay between the Bermejo and Pilcomayo Rivers. This disputed territory was ceded by Paraguay to Argentina as a result of the lost War of the Triple Alliance. The Chaco Boreal, or northern Chaco, is bordered by the Pilcomayo River on the south and the Paraguay River on the east; the foothills of the Andes form its northern and western frontiers.

4. Jurg Meister, *Francisco Solano López Nationalheld oder Kriegsverbrecher?* (Osnabrück: Biblio Verlag, 1987), 391. Only nineteen of the 410 French settlers remained; the rest returned to France. The Mennonites produced above all vegetables and milk and, therefore, were important to the Paraguayan army. They were exempt from military service.

5. David H. Zook Jr., *The Conduct of the Chaco War* (New Haven: Bookman Assoc., 1960), 63.

A persistent misconception is that the discovery of oil in the Chaco had fostered the war. In fact, oil had been discovered much earlier. In 1924 a French engineer announced the discovery of vast oil deposits in the Chaco. Both Bolivia and Paraguay granted concession for the exploration and exploitation to major multinational corporations. Within a short period of time, Standard Oil of New Jersey was operating under a Bolivian concession. However, this activity had no apparent influence upon the decision to go to war.

6. Querejazu, *Masamaklay*, 92–102, 166; Vicente Rivarola, *Memorias diplomáticas*, 3 vols. (Buenos Aires: Ed. Ayacucho, 1952), 3: 292–94.

7. R. W. Thompson, an inexperienced reporter for the London *Morning Post* sent to the Chaco in 1935, was taken in by the Paraguayans. He wrote that prior to the war, "The Paraguayans built fort for fort, but their 'forts' were little more than mud enclosures in which the garrison of a 'corporal and three men' would be lucky to share a cast-off 1910 Argentine rifle between them." R. W. Thompson, *An Echo of Trumpets* (London: George Allen & Unwin, 1964), 31.

8. José Carlos Marcet, *Antecedentes, desarrollo y resultado de la guerra del Chaco* (Asunción: n.p., 1974), 19; César Sánchez Bonifato, *La ultima guerra en Sudamerica* (Buenos Aires: Editorial Korrigan, 1974), 34–51. The Bolivians claim that a French pilot sabotaged their planes and bombs. A civilian JU-34 flew the 10-kilogram bombs from El Alto via Cochabamba—Santa Cruz to Puerto Suarez where one Bréguet and one Fokker should have dropped them on the Paraguayans. However, the Bréguet crash-landed near San Fermin while the Fokker was damaged while landing at Potosí. The only operational aircraft present, a Caudron trainer piloted by a Swiss, [first name unknown] Haberlin, flew some spare parts

from La Paz to Potosí so that finally the Fokker could attack on December 15, 1928. After all that, the bombs did not explode. Jurg Meister, "Der Chaco-Konflikt 1928–1938," 3 vols. (Woodford, Australia: unpublished manuscript, n.d.), 1: 25–38; Georg von Rauch, "The Green Hell Air War," *Air Enthusiast* 207–13 (No. 2, n.d.), 209.

9. Bolivia had to agree to a 50-percent reduction in the number of men in the army as one of the conditions for obtaining the U.S. Dillon-Read loan of $24 million. The army was to be reduced from 9,450 in 1930 to 3,600 men. The strength in 1930 was actually 7,000 and it was reduced to 5,539 men.

10. Vacca, *Notas*, 309; Adrian English, *Armed Forces in Latin America* (London: Jane's, 1984), 77; Angel R. Ríos, *La defensa del Chaco* (Buenos Aires: Ed. Ayacucho, 1950), 105; Carlos José Fernández, *La guerra del Chaco*, 6 vols. (Buenos Aires: Pellegrini Impresores, 1955–76), 1: 25 and 6: 34.

11. Jurg Meister, "Der Chaco-Konflikt," (unpublished manuscript, 4 binders), 1: 39–51; González, *La guerra*, 36–44; Marcial Samaniego, "Situación del las fuerzas armadas de la nación en el decenio de a pre–guerra del Chaco," in *Historia Militar del Paraguay*, 3 vols. (Asunción: Academia de Historia Militar del Paraguay, 1984–88), 1: 28–30.

12. Meister, "Der Chaco-Konflikt," 1: 52–71; Víctor Ayala Queirolo, "Los ejércitos de la guerra del Chaco," in *Historia militar del Paraguay*, 3 vols. (Asunción: Academia de Historia Militar del Paraguay, 1984–88), 1: 70–73; Samaniego, "Situación," 70–73: González, *La guerra*, 17–19, 44–45; Vacca, *Notas*, 295–97, 327–28.

13. Dan Hagedorn and Antonio L. Sapienza, *Aircraft of the Chaco War 1932–35* (Atglen, Pa.: Schiffer Military/Aviation History, 1997), 18–128; Samaniego, "Situación," 41–42; Rauch, "The Green Hell," 209.

14. Samaniego, "Situación," 31–32, 40.

15. Meister, "Der Chaco-Konflikt," 1: 72–97; González, *La guerra*, 19; Bejarano, *Síntesis*, 69.

16. For a contemporary analysis of the Bolivian army which held it in high regard, see the formerly classified assessment in U.S. Office of Naval Intelligence *Monthly Information Bulletin* 1–10 (October 1925), 1–10.

17. Vacca, *Notas*, 307–8.

18. Hans Kundt (1869–1939) came to Bolivia in August 1911 as the head of a 13-man German military mission with the rank of colonel and served as Chief of Staff from 1911–1914. He and the mission returned to Germany with the outbreak of World War I, rising between 1914 and 1918 to the rank of brigadier general within the German army. Kundt returned in 1920 to Bolivia as a private citizen. He adopted Bolivian citizenship to circumvent restrictions in the Versailles Treaty that prohibited German military missions and served as the Chief of Staff of the Bolivian army from 1921–26 and 1929–30. Prior to the Chaco War, some in the international community held Kundt in high regard. "Bolivia," U.S. Office of Naval Intelligence *Monthly Information Bulletin* 1–10 (October 1925), 7. However, the French were skeptical of his abilities and passed along their opinions to Estigarribia while he was at their *Ecole de Guerre*. In 1926 German Gen. Ernst Kabisch had some negative things to say about Kundt in the German press. Also, some Bolivian officers were jealous of Kundt's higher pay and faster promotion rate. In 1930 Kundt was exiled from Bolivia by the 1930 junta because of his support for the Siles government. Following the early Bolivian defeats in the Chaco, Kundt was recalled and arrived in La Paz on December 6, 1932, to great adulation.

19. Kurt von Borde, *Deutsche unter fremden Fahnen* (Berlin: Schlieffen Verlag, 1938), 298.

20. Angel Rodríguez, *Autopsia de una guerra* (Santiago de Chile: Ed. Ercilla, 1940), 12.

21. President Salamanca told General Carlos Quintanilla in August 1932, "Execute the order . . . if it has merit it will be yours, if it presents problems, they will be mine." Roberto Querejazu Calvo, *Masamaklay*, 55.

22. Meister, "Der Chaco-Konflikt," 1: 98–113; Vacca, *Notas*, 85–285, 295–97; Ayala, "Los ejércitos," 68–69, 72–73.

23. Hagedorn and Sapienza, *Aircraft of the Chaco War*, 18–128; von Rauch, "The Green Hell," 209.

24. There were three other, shorter railway lines penetrating the Chaco, but they had little strategic value. Vacca, *Notas*, 291.

25. Manuel Maria Oliver, *La guerra en el Chaco boreal* (Buenos Aires: Roldán Editor, 1935), 12, 65; Fernández, *La guerra*, 1: 93–94; Aquiles Vergara Vicuña, *Historia de la guerra del Chaco*, 7 vols. (Santiago de Chile: Ed. Nascimento, 1935), 1: 166.

26. Juan Bautista Ayala, *Planes de operaciones del la guerra del Chaco* (Asunción: Escuela Técnica Salesiana, 1969), 49–64; Juan Bautista Ayala, *La guerra del Chaco hasta Campo Via* (Buenos Aires: Tall. Gráf. Aconcagua, 1959), 54–59, 71–72; Meister, "Der Chaco-Konflikt," 1: 125–40.

27. Ayala, *Planes*, 31–43; Zook, *The Conduct*, 88–90; Tabera, *Picuiba*, 120–21; Meister, "Der Chaco-Konflikt," 1: 125–40.

28. Tabera, *Picuiba*, 137–40; Ernesto Scarone, *Ataque y retoma del fortin Carlos A. López* (Asunción, n.p., 1973), 64–92; Fernández, *La guerra*, I, 69, 83–86; Oscar Moscoso, *Recuerdo de la guerra del Chaco* (Sucre: Tip. Salesiana, 1939), 61–71.

29. José Félix Estigarribia (1888–1940) served in rebel ranks during the 1908 revolution. Estigarribia joined the Paraguayan army in 1910 and attended the Colegio Nacional in Asunción. Between March and May 1913, he served in a military mission to Chile. In July 1922 Estigarribia participated in the defense of Asunción against revolutionary forces. As a result, he was promoted to major on November 13, 1922. Between 1924 and 1927 Estigarribia studied in France, first in Nance and then as a member of the first class of the Escuela Superior de Guerra in Paris. On March 1, 1928, Estigarribia was named Chief of the General Staff and later that year was named professor of tactics at the Escuela Militar. In 1931 he was appointed inspector general of the Army. When the Chaco War began, Estigarribia was a lieutenant colonel. He was promoted to colonel on October 1, 1932, following the Paraguayan victory at Boquerón. He rapidly advanced through the senior ranks, becoming General of the Army on September 16, 1935. He was named Commander in Chief of the Armed Forces four days later. Estigarribia never left the Chaco during the war. President Ayala visited him thirty times, almost always by aircraft. Ultimately, Estigarribia would be elected president in 1939. He was killed in an aircraft crash on February 18, 1940.

30. English, *Armed Forces*, 77; Harris G. Warren, *Paraguay An Informal History* (Norman: University of Oklahoma Press, 1949), 296.

31. Rojas was then made the Commander of the 4th Army Corps which existed only on paper in Asunción and was soon dismissed.

32. José Estigarribia, *The Epic of the Chaco War* (Austin: University of Texas Press, 1950), 37–39; Zook, *The Conduct*, 93–94; Meister, "Der Chaco-Konflikt," 1: 158–71.

33. Fernández, *La guerra*, 1: 170; Heriberto Florentin, *Lo que he visto en Boquerón* (Buenos Aires: Ed. Asunción, 1957), 161; Nicolás Delgado, *Historia de la guerra del Chaco*, 2 vols. (Asunción: Imp. Militar, 1943), 1: 14; Estigarribia, *The Epic*, 43.

34. Jurg Meister, "Documentation Air Operations during the Chaco-War 1932 to 1935," (Canowindra, Australia: unpublished manuscript, 1997), 6.

35. Meister, "Der Chaco-Konflikt," 1: 158–71.

36. Zook, *The Conduct*, 101; Fernández, *La guerra*, I, 219–25, 245, 267–72, 293, 314–17; Florentin, *Boquerón*, 201, 235–36; Alberto Taborga, *Boquerón* (La Paz: Lib. y. Ed. "Juventud," 1970), 64–66, 81–86; David Toro Ruiloa, *Mi Actuación en la guerra del Chaco* (La Paz: Ed. Renacimiento, 1941), 16.

37. Rivarola, *Memorias diplomáticas*, 2: 203.

38. Vergara Vicuña, *Historia*, 1: 126, 438, 484–93, II 223–23, 248–52; Fernandez, *La guerra*, 2: 60–63.

39. Enrique Peñaranda de Castillo (1892–1969) was born in Sorata, La Paz Province. He entered the Military Academy in 1907 and graduated as a second lieutenant of infantry in 1910. He was assigned to the "Tarija" Regiment guarding the Chaco until 1915. He again returned to the Chaco garrison in 1919. Later, as a lieutenant colonel, Peñaranda commanded the "Colorado" Regiment then stationed in Potosí. He returned for a third tour in the Chaco in 1929 when he commanded the "Loa" Regiment garrisoned at Villa Montes. Just prior to the fighting, Peñaranda established the following *fortins*: Cabezón, Platanillos, Loa, Bolívar, and Camacho. He received his baptism of fire at Corrales and Toledo on July 27 and 28, 1932.

40. Vergara Vicuña, *Historia*, 1: 513–16; Ayala Moreira, *Por qué no ganamos*, 186.

41. Fernández, *La guerra*, 1: 306–06, 2: 69–75, 279–80; Delgado, *Historia de la guerra*, 1: 39–41; Vergara Vicuña, *Historia*, 1: 519, 2: 291–95.

42. Belaieff and the other White Russians joined the Paraguayan army in late 1930. Guided by Indians, Belaieff led the expedition that discovered Lake Pitiantuta in March 1931. For accounts of the service and fate of some of these men, see González, *La guerra*, 232–33; Bonifato, *La ultima guerra*, 70–71.

43. Marcet, *Antecedentes*, 32–33.

44. Toro, *Mi actuacion*, 39–41; Moscoso, *Recuerdo*, 236–238; Julio Guerrero, *Peñaranda ante la historia* (La Paz: Imp. Interdencia Gral. de Guerra, 1937), 31–35. Enrique Vidaurre, *Acciones militares en Toledo y Fernández* (La Paz: Lit. e Imp. Unidas, 1940), 57–91; Julio Díaz Arguedas, *Los elegidos en la gloria* (La Paz: Imp. Intendencia Gral. de Guerra, 1937), 290–91; Paraguay, *Los partes del conductor* (Asunción: Aydantia General Sección Historia e Imprenta, 1950), 62–63.

45. Marcet, *Antecedentes*, 33–34; Fernández, *La guerra*, 2: 252–61, 302–03; Estigarribia, *The Epic*, 69–70; Moscoso, *Recuerdo*, 181–86.

46. Zook, *The Conduct*, 143; Marcet, *Antecedentes*, 35–36.

47. Republic Argentina, Ministerio de Relaciones Exteriores y Culto, *La neutralidad Argentina en el conflicto Boliviano-Paraguayo* (Buenos Aires: Talleres S.A. Cosa Jacobo Peuser Ltda., 1933), 6–66.

48. Moscoso, *Recuerdo*, 207, 217–19, 223–25; Estigarribia, *The Epic*, 75; Rafael Franco, *Dos batallas de la guerra del Chaco* (Buenos Aires: Editorial Yegros, 1959), 20–22; Paraguay, *Partes del conductor*, 71, 77.

49. Meister, "Der Chaco-Konflikt," 1: 198–223; Estigarribia, *The Epic*, 77–78; Moscos, *Recuedro*, 235, 241; Paraguary, *Partes del conductor*, 92–95; Vergara Vicuña, *Historia*, 4: 374–79, 426–27.

50. Meister, "Der Chaco-Konflikt," 1: 224–62; Marcet, *Antecedentes*, 39–40.

51. David Toro Ruilova (1898–1977) was born in Sucre. He entered the Military Academy and graduated as a second lieutenant of artillery in 1915. He ascended the ranks rapidly. Toro became a lieutenant in 1919, a captain in 1920, and a major in 1925. He served as the aide to General Kundt, was a professor of war and artillery at the Military Academy, and served as the military attache to Argentina. During the war, a cavalry corps that Toro commanded was destroyed at the Battle of Picuiba (November 1934) but Toro was absolved of blame. At the end of the war, Toro led a cavalry brigade into La Paz ostensibly to provide General Peñaranda an escort but in reality to overthrow the government of President Tejada which occurred on May 17, 1936.

52. Moscoso, *Recuerdo*, 262–66; Toro, *Mi actuación*, 49; Vergara Vicuña, *Historia*, 4: 633; Rivarola, *Memorias diplomáticas*, 3: 28.

53. Zook, *The Conduct*, 163; Estigarribia, *The Epic*, 107; Paraguay, *Partes del conductor*, 141; Vergara Vicuña, *Historia*, 5: 126–27; Rios, *La defensa*, 176–78.

54. Marcet, *Antecedentes*, 44–45. The first Christmas armistice of 1933 (twenty-four hours), was arranged by the Pope. The second one, from December 19, 1933, to January 8, 1934, was instigated by the League of Nations.

55. Meister, "Der Chaco-Konflikt," 263–72; Marcet, *Antecedentes*, 46–50.

56. Estigarribia, *The Epic*, 151–53; Marcet, *Antecedentes*, 50; Vergara Vicuña, *Historia*, 5: 510, 534–43.

57. Estigarribia, *The Epic*, 166–68; Marcet, *Antecedentes*, 51–52; Paraguay, *Partes del conductor*, 189–92.

58. Estigarribia, *The Epic*, 172; Toro, *Mi actuación*, 77; Díaz Arguedas, *La guerra*, 110.

59. Marcet, *Antecedentes*, 53.

60. Estigarribia, *The Epic*, 72–78; Toro, *Mi actuación*, 80; Marcet, *Antecedentes*, 53; Díaz Arguedas, *La guerra*, 220–23.

61. Julio Díaz Arguedas, *Como fue derrocado el hombre símbolo* (La Paz: Empresa Editora "Universo," 1957), 99–111; Marcet, *Antecedentes*, 54.

62. Toro, *Mi actuación*, 93–94; Díaz Arguedas, *La guerra*, 238–41; Estigarribia, *The Epic*, 178.

63. von Rauch, "The Green Hell," 212.

64. Estigarribia, *The Epic*, 179–83; Vergara Vicuña, *Historia*, 6: 179–85, 193–98; Paraguay, *Partes del conductor*, 207–10.

65. Díaz Arguedas, *Como fue derrocado*, 178.

66. Díaz Arguedas, *Como fue derrocado*, 186–204, 207–33, 288–89; Marcet, *Antecedentes*, 56.

67. Meister, "Der Chaco-Konflikt," 2: 1–15.

68. Toro, *Mi actuación*, 154–82, 189–220; Estigarribia, *The Epic*, 186; Vergara Vicuña, *Historia*, 6: 391–94, 438–43; Paraguay, *Partes del conductor*, 217–18.

69. Meister, "Der Chaco-Konflikt" 2: 277–86.

70. Rivarola, *Memorias diplomáticas*, 3: 166–74, 192.

71. Meister, "Der Chaco-Konflikt," 1: 123–30; Marcet, *Antecedentes*, 56–57.

72. von Rauch, "The Green Hell," 213; Vergara Vicuña, *Historia,* 6: 592–695, 615–16.

73. Díaz Arguedas, *La guerra*, 297–306; Estigarribia, *The Epic*, 190–94; Paraguay, *Partes del conductor*, 223–25, 229–30; Toro, *Mi actuación*, 305–7.

74. Estigarribia, *The Epic*, 194–204; Vergara Vicuña, *Historia*, 7: 35–76, 135–43, 164–66, 182–93, 203–15, 250–55, 260–65, 308–15, 365–71; Díaz Arguedas, *La guerra*, 326–31.

75. Paraguay still had twenty to thirty thousand men in uniform but not all at the front. Some were working on unarmed road-building gangs, others in obscure desk jobs in the rear, and at least ten thousand were working at the naval arsenal. Meister, "Der Chaco-Konflikt," 2: 181–91.

76. Estigarribia, *The Epic*, 195–99; Rios, *La defensa del Chaco*, 308–9, 316–19; Rivarola, *Memorias diplomáticas*, 3: 247, 266. But in 1934 Bolivia had to import Chilean miners to work in the tin mines because so many of the Bolivian miners had been mobilized.

77. Bejarano, *Síntesis*, 69; Paraguay, *Los Partes*, 267–68; Loveman, *For la Patria*, 107–8.

78. "Actually, neither country was right until the Chaco War decided the issue." Warren, *Paraguay*, 288.

79. Meister, "Der Chaco-Konflikt," 3: 223–48; Bejarano, *Síntesis*, 69; Hugo Pol, *La Campaña del Chaco* (La Paz: n.p., 1945), 47, 90; Brian Loveman, *For la Patria* (Wilmington: Scholarly Resources, 1999), 112–13.

80. Zook, *The Conduct*, 199, 236.

81. Vergara Vicuña, *Historia*, 4: 325–29.

82. English, *Armed Forces*, 78, 343; Meister, "Der Chaco-Konflikt," 3: 223–48.

83. Rios, *La defensa del Chaco*, 99–101; Ayala, *La Guerra*, 78–79.

84. A British report proclaimed, "I rallied to the 'under-dog' with all my heart to proclaim the Paraguayan cause in the columns of the *Morning Post*." Thompson, *An Echo*, 33.

85. T. Wewege-Smith, *Gran Chaco Adventure* (London: Hutchinson, 1937), 250.

86. Meister, "Der Chaco-Konflikt," 3: 269–76; González, *La Guerra*, 200.

87. Meister, "Der Chaco-Konflikt," 3: 276a–76e.

CHAPTER TWELVE

1. Faura, *Los ríos*, 437; Bryce Wood, *The United States and Latin American Wars 1932–1942* (New York: Columbia University Press, 1966), 175; Plazas, "Conflicto," 16, 20–21; Frederick Pike, *The Modern History of Peru* (London: Weidenfeld & Nicolson, 1967), 266; Ronald Bruce St. John, *The Foreign Policy of Peru* (Boulder: Lynne Rienner, 1992), 174.

2. Oscar Benavides (1876–1945), born into a wealthy and influential family, entered a military secondary school at the age of fourteen. In 1906 he graduated first in his class from *Escuela Superior de Guerra*, which had been established in 1904. Benavides studied in France and served on military commissions to Germany and Austria. His success against Colombia in 1911 made him a national hero. In 1913 he was appointed army Chief of Staff. In February 1914 Benavides led a *golpe* against civilian President Guillermo Billinghurst who was attempting to reduce the power of the Peruvian military. Benavides then relinquished power to José Pardo, a civilian. In 1916 Benavides led a military mission to France. He was Minister Plenipotentiary to Italy between 1917 and 1920. The following year the Leguía government exiled him. Benavides served as Minister Plenipotentiary to Spain in 1931 and to Great Britain in 1932 and 1933.

3. Fernando Romero, *Las fuerzas de la marina en el nor-oriente y la guerra fluvial* (Lima: Armada de Peru, 1935), 44–46; Fernando Romero, *Notas para una historia de la marina fuvial de guerra* (Lima: La Punta, 1959), 115–16; Ireland, *Boundaries*, 185–95.

4. Wood, *The United States*, 170–71.

5. The treaty was ratified in Bogotá on March 19, 1928. Félix Denegri Luna, *Peru and Ecuador: Notes for the History of a Frontier* (Lima: Universidad Católica del Perú, 1996), 234–37; Faura, *Los Ríos*, 436; Wood, *The United States*, 169, 174–75; Georg von Rauch, "The Leticia Conflict," *Air Enthusiast* 26: 1–8 (December 1984–March 1985): 2; Jesus Maria Henao and Gerardo Arrubla, *History of Colombia* (Chapel Hill: University of North Carolina Press, 1958), 548–49.

General Oscar Benavides, expressing the perception held by many Peruvians, wrote on November 10, 1932, "The Colombian minister to Peru should be proud of his work! Cleverly exploiting in his public speeches the exaggerated egotism, the immeasurable vanity of [Peruvian President] Augusto Leguía . . . he was able to present to his country the welcome surprise of extending its territorial domain over areas it never had claimed even in its most exaggerated demands." Wood, *The United States*, 187.

6. Plazas, "Conflicto," 16.

7. Romero, *Las fuerzas*, 49–51; Romero, *Notas*, 150; Faura, *Los ríos*, 437; Torres Almeyda, "Primeros decenios," 4: 315.

8. Both of Peru's cruisers suffered from boiler problems. New boilers were purchased from Great Britain and delivered to Balboa, Panama. Initially, the United States would not permit the installation to take place there. Wood, *The United States*, 420–41; *Conway's All the World's Fighting Ships 1922–46* (London: Conway Maritime Press, 1980), 415, 423–24; Torres, "Primeros decenios," 315; English, *Armed Forces*, 169.

9. English, *Armed Forces*, 391–92.

10. Herbert Boy (1897–1973) was born in Duisburg, Germany. He volunteered for service in World War I and joined the 25th Infantry Regiment. He fought at the Battle of Champagne and was wounded twice. Boy then transferred to the aviation branch and became a pilot in the 14th Squadron. Following the war Boy traveled to Colombia where in January 1924 he began flying for SCADTA (*Sociedad Colombo-Alemana de Transporte Aéreo*), which had been founded in Barranquilla in 1919. He soon became the company's chief pilot. At the outbreak of fighting in 1932, the Colombian government made him an honorary major in the army and he served as a liaison between the national command and the field commanders. Boy supervised the acquisition of aircraft, the recruiting and training of pilots, and the construction of airfields. Boy flew in the raid against Tarapacá. He commanded Colombian aircraft involved in the dogfight above Güeppí. Boy returned to commercial aviation in July 1934 and was awarded the Cruz of Boyacá. In 1948 he became a Colombian citizen.

11. José Manuel Villalobos Barradas, "Fuerza aérea colombiana," *Historia de las fuerzas militares de Colombia*, directed by Alvaro Valencia Tovar, 6 vols. (Bogotá: Planeta Colombiana Editorial S.A., 1993), 5: 51; von Rauch, "The Leticia Conflict," 2–3; Plazas, "Conflicto," 29–30.

12. Alfredo Vázquez Cobo (1869–1941) was born in Cali and educated in France as an engineer. He fought for the *Gobiernistas* during the Thousand Days War with the rank of colonel and later general. Vázquez Cobo was one of the signatories of the peace treaty on board the U.S. battleship *Wisconsin* in November 1902. He served as Minister of War during the Marroquín administration and Minister of Foreign Relations during the Reyes administration. He signed the Vázquez Cobo-Martínez Treaty with Brazil. Vázquez Cobo was an unsuccessful presidential candidate in 1930.

13. Plazas, "Conflicto," 16–18, 31–32; von Rauch, "The Leticia Conflict," 2, 5; Faura, *Los ríos*, 439; Wood, *The United States*, 180; English, *Armed Forces*, 169.

14. There is much controversy concerning the number of Colombian and Peruvian soldiers in the *selva* at the time the conflict started. Many books incorrectly place the number of Peruvian soldiers in September 1932 at about 500 men. See Romero, *Las fuerzas*, 48–49; Romero, *Notas*, 149; Faura, *Los ríos*, 437.

Plazas asserts that thirty Colombian soldiers were at Leticia when the conflict began. This was possibly the number planned but not sent prior to September 1, 1932. Plazas, "Conflicto," 16.

15. At the time the orders were placed with Curtiss-Wright, the company was in serious financial trouble. Its stock had plummeted from $30 a share to 75 cents a share. The Colombian orders may have saved the company from collapse. The Colombian and Bolivian (see chapter 11) purchases of Junkers aircraft allowed that firm to overcome a critical period in its existence. Villalobos, "Fuerza aérea," 53, 79–80; Von Rauch, "The Leticia Conflict," 4; English, *Armed Forces*, 182, 392.

16. Torres, "Primeros decenios," 320–22; Plazas, "Conflicto," 30; Wood, *The United States*, 180.

17. Wood, *The United States*, 180.

18. ibid., 180; Villalobos, "Fuerza Aérea," 51.

19. Faura, *Los ríos*, 439.

20. Torres, "Primeros decenios," 322–25.

21. Efraín Rojas Acevedo (1887–unk) was one of the founders of the Superior War School (*Escuela Superior de Guerra*) in 1909. In 1928 he served as military attaché to Chile. Rojas led a mission to the United States in 1934.

22. Torres, "Primeros decenios," 323; Plazas, "Conflicto," 36.

23. von Rauch, "The Leticia Conflict," 5–6; Villalobos, "Fuerza aérea," 63–64; Torres, "Primeros decenios," 325–26; Romero, *Las fuerzas*, 65–67; Wood, *The United States*, 210–11.

24. Plazas, "Conflicto," 38–41; Villalobos, "Fuerza aérea," 70–72; Romero, *Las fuerzas*, 80–83; von Rauch, "The Leticia Conflict," 6–7.

25. Torres, "Primeros decenios," 331; Plazas, "Conflicto," 38.

26. Romero, *Las fuerzas*, 89–92; Torres, "Primeros decenios," 330.

27. Wood, *The United States*, 229; English, *Armed Forces*, 382.

28. Scheina, *Latin America*, 122; Wood, *The United States*, 169–70.

29. St. Johns, *The Foreign Policy*, 175–76; Pike, *The Modern History*, 268–69; Plazas, "Conflicto," 41–42.

30. Plazas, "Conflicto," 47; Torres, "Primeros decenios," 331; Romero, *Las fuerzas*, 97; von Rauch, "The Leticia Conflict," 7.

31. Daniel M. Masterson, *Militarism and Politics in Latin America, Peru from Sánchez Cerro to Sendero Luminoso* (Westport: Greenwood Press, 1991), 53; Ireland, *Boundaries*, 202–5; Wood, *The United States*, 249–51.

32. von Rauch, "The Leticia Conflict," 8.

33. Plazas, "Conflicto," 47–48; von Rauch, "The Leticia Conflict," 8.

34. von Rauch, "The Leticia Conflict," 8.

35. von Rauch, "The Leticia Conflict," 8; Masterson, *Militarism*, 51.

36. English, *Armed Forces*, 169.

CHAPTER THIRTEEN

1. Masterson, *Militarism*, 71; Julio Tobar Donoso, *La invasión peruana y protocolo de Rio antecedentes y explicación histórica* (Quito: Banco Central del Ecuador, 1982), 72.

2. Latino Américo [pseudonym], *La cuestión de limites entre el Perú y el Ecuador* (Bueons Aires: Libreria e Imprenta de Mayo, 1910), 9; Julio Tobar Donoso and Alfredo Luna Tobar, *Derecho territorial ecuatoriano* (Quito: Ed. del Sol, 1979), 20; "La historia de dos vecinos" (Quito), *Hoy* 4 (October 25, 1998), 4.

3. Denegri, *Peru*, 2; Franciso A. Cornicelli, "Las raíces centenarias del conflicto limítrofe Perú–Ecuador," *Armas y Geoestrategia* (Buenos Aires), 1: 2; 63–78 (Winter 1981), 63–64.

4. Francisco de Requena spent almost thirty years in the Amazon Basin. He served as the Governor of Maynas and Quijos. Requena returned to Spain in the late 1780s and worked in the Council of the Indies (*Consejo de Indias*).

5. F. Morales Padrón, "La frontera peruano-ecuatoriana," *Estudios Americanos* (Sevilla), 2: 7; 455–66 (September 1950), 457; Américo, *La cuestión*, 87; Tobar and Luna, *Derecho terrirorial*, 32.

6. Denegri, *Peru*, 53–55.

7. ibid., 48.

8. Morales, "La Frontera," 457; Américo, *La cuestión*, 36–39; Denegri, *Peru*, 47, 58–59.

9. Tobar and Luna, *Derecho territorial*, 90; Denegri, *Peru*, 94–95.

10. Denegri, *Peru*, 97–101; Cornicelli, "Las raíces," 65–67.

11. Américo, *La cuestión*, 42; Denegri, *Peru*, 164–66.

12. Denegri, *Peru*, 202–7; Cornicelli, "Las Raíces," 68.

13. Romero, *Marina fluvial*, 103–6; Faura, *Los ríos*, 368–69; Denegri, *Peru*, 213–15.

14. Tobar and Luna, *Derecho terrirorial*, 175; Cornicelli, "Las Raíces," 70.

15. Bryce Wood, *Aggression and History: The Case of Ecuador and Peru* (Ann Arbor: University Microfilms International, 1978), 78–79.

16. Alberto Carbone, "La segunda guerra del amazonas," *Defensa* 33: 60–64 (January 1981), 61; Denegri, *Peru*, 257.

17. Masterson, *Militarism*, 57, 66, 69.

18. Charles K. Kliment and Vladimír Francev, *Czechoslovak Armored Fighting Vehicles 1918–1948* (Atglen, Pa.: Schiffer Military/Aviation History, 1997), 116–17; Carbone, "La segunda Guerra," 61; Wood, *Aggression*, 65–66.

19. Wood, *Aggression*, 66–68.

20. Tobar Donoso, *La invasión peruana*, 137–38.

21. Carbone, "La segunda guerra," 62; Wood, *Aggression*, 76–77.

22. Wood, *Aggression*, 76; Carbone, "La segunda guerra," 62.

23. Eloy G. Ureta (1892–1965) was born in northern Peru at Chiclayo. He graduated from the Chorrillos Military Academy in 1913 and attended the Advanced War School in 1922. Ureta received additional education in Europe. In July 1932 as a lieutenant colonel, he was chief of staff to Col. Manuel Ruiz Bravo who recaptured Trujillo from the *Apristas*. In 1936 Colonel Ureta commanded the Third Army Division stationed at Arequipa. He also was the Director of the Escuela Superior de Guerra, where plans were developed for the possibility of war with Ecuador. In early 1941, now a general, Ureta was given command of all military forces in northern Peru. He became a national hero as a consequence of the 1941 war with Ecuador and was given the title of marshal in 1946.

24. Eloy G. Ureta, *Apuntes sobre una campaña (1941)* (Madrid: Editorial Antorcha, 1953), 67–69.

25. Wood, *Aggression*, 112; Masterson, *Militarism*, 70–71.

26. Ureta, *Apuntes*, 42: Carbone, "La segunda Guerra," 62; Vernon E. Megee, "An Aerial Blitzkrieg in Miniature," *The Marine Corps Gazette* 26: 1; 7–8, 63 (March 1942), 7.

27. Carbone, "La segunda guerra," 62–63; Wood, *Aggression*, 66–68; Ureta, *Apuntes*, 75–78.

28. Carbone, "La segunda guerra," 63.

29. Ureta, *Apuntes*, 69–70, 364; Carbone, "La segunda guerra," 63.

30. Humberto Araujo Arana, *Antecedentes y choques fronterizos, ocupación y desocupación peruana de territorio ecuatoriano en 1941–1942*, 3 vols. (Lima: n.p., 1963–69), 3: 211–19; Miguel Monteza Taur, *El conflicto militar del Peru con el Ecuador 1941* (Lima: Editorial Arica, 1976), 58.

31. Carbone, "La segunda guerra," 63; Megee, "An Aerial Blitzkrieg," 7; Ureta, *Apuntes*, 364–65; Araujo, *Antecedentes y choques fronterizos*, 3: 254.

32. Megee, "An Aerial Blitzkrieg," 8, 63; Ureta, *Apuntes*, 143–46.

33. Araujo Arana, *Antecedentes*, 3: 314.

34. Megee, "An Aerial Blitzkrieg," 8, 63; David H. Zook Jr., *Zarumilla-Marañon: The Ecuador-Peru Dispute* (New York: Bookman Associates, 1964), 183; Carbone, "La segunda guerra," 63.

35. Carbone, "La segunda guerra," 63.

36. Wood, *Aggression*, 120; Carbone, "La segunda guerra," 63; Masterson, *Militarism*, 71–72.

37. Carbone, "La segunda guerra," 61; Masterson, *Militarism*, 72; Denegri, *Peru*, 268.

38. Adrian English, "Flash in the Pan? The Peruvian-Ecuadorian Clash," *Jane's Intelligence Review* 7: 3; 141–43 (March 1985), 141.

39. Megee, "An Aerial Blitzkrieg," 8.

40. Denegri, *Peru*, 256.

41. Ureta, *Apuntes*, 456–65.

42. Masterson, *Militarism*, 74.

43. David Spencer, "The Peruvian-Ecuadorian conflict of 1981," *El Dorado* 8: 2; 88–91, 103 (1998), 88; Beth A. Simmons, *Territorial Disputes and Their Resolution: The Case of Ecuador and Peru* (Washington, D.C.: United States Institute of Peace, 1999), 11.

44. Cornicelli, "Las raíces," 71–74; Simmons, *Territorial Disputes*, 10–11; Glenn R. Weidner, "Operation Safe Border: The Ecuador-Peru Crisis," *Joint Forces Quarterly* 11: 52–58 (Spring 1996), 53.

45. Spencer, "The Peruvian-Ecuadorian conflict," 88–91, 103.

46. Spencer, "The Peruvian-Ecuadorian conflict," 88–91, 103; David Oliver, "Condor Conflict," *Airforce Monthly* 25–29 (December 1995), 25.

47. "Peru-Ecuador Dispute Dies Down," *Jane's Intelligence Review* 2: 4; 6 (April 1995), 6.

48. English, "Flash in the Pan?" 142.

49. Simmons, *Territorial Disputes*, 11.

50. English, "Flash in the Pan?" 142–43.

51. ibid., 143.

52. ibid.

53. Weidner, "Operation Safe Border," 53; David Spencer, "Tiwinza: The Cenepa River Valley War," *El Dorado* 8: 3; 136–39, 141–45, 147–48 (1998), 136–37.

54. Spencer, "Tiwinza," 136–39, 141–45, 147–48.

55. Oliver, "Condor Conflict," 25–26; Spencer, "Tiwinza," 136–39, 141–45, 147–48.

56. "Peru-Ecuador Dispute," 6; Oliver, "Condor Conflict," 26–29; Spencer, "Tiwinza," 136–39, 141–45, 147–48.

57. Weidner, "Operation Safe Border," 53.

58. Spencer, "Tiwinza," 136–37.

59. "Peru-Ecuador Dispute," 6; Spencer, "Tiwinza," 136–39, 141–45, 147–48; Simmons, *Territorial Disputes*, 12.

60. Simmons, *Territorial Disputes*, 12–13.

CHAPTER FOURTEEN

1. Jordan Young, "Military Aspects of the 1930 Brazilian Revolution," *Hispanic American Historical Review* 44: 2; 180–96 (May 1964), 180.

2. Luís Carlos Prestes (1898–1990) was born in Pôrto Alegre, Rio Grande do Sul. His father was an army lieutenant who had risen through the ranks, and his mother was a school teacher. Prestes attended the high school Colégio Militar in Rio de Janeiro and the two-year Escola Militar de Realengo, graduating in 1920 as a lieutenant in the Army Corps of Engineers. Between 1920 and 1922 he was assigned to a railway construction battalion that was working in Deodoro, a suburb of Rio de Janeiro. Prestes was involved in the July 1922 conspiracy but since he was confined to his bed by typhus at the time of the rebellion, the full degree of his participation may not have been appreciated. He was transferred to the backlands of Rio Grande do Sul, away from federal and state capitals.

3. Ernest A. Duff, "Luís Carlos Prestes and the Revolution of 1924," *Luso-Brazilian Review*, 6: 1; 3–16 (June 1967), 9, 11.

4. The Militar Club (*Clube Militar*) was founded on June 26, 1887. Its members remained active in politics, frequently covertly, until the consolidation of political power by Gentulio Vargas in 1930. Between 1897 and 1901 President Prudente de Morais closed the club for plotting against his government.

5. John W. F. Dulles, *Vargas of Brazil: A Political Biography* (Austin: University of Texas Press, 1967), 20–21; Calogeras, *A History*, 329.

6. Dulles, *Vargas*, 21–23; John W. F. Dulles, *Anarchists and Communists in Brazil, 1900–1935* (Austin: University of Texas Press, 1973), 180; Louis [*sic*] Carlos Prestes, "How I became a Communist," *World Marxist Review*, 16: 1: 114–22 (January 1973), 115–16.

7. Duff, "Luís Carlos Prestes," 6.

8. Duff, "Luís Carlos Prestes," 8; Dulles, *Anarchists*, 239–40.

9. The most important of these short-lived rebellions took place at Aracajú, Bahia, on July 13; at Manaos, Amazonas, on July 23; and at Belem, Pará, on July 26. Manaos even declared itself a republic. Duff, "Luís Carlos Prestes," 8.

10. Duff, "Luís Carlos Prestes," 8–9.

11. Robert J. Alexander, "Brazilian 'Tenentismo'" *Hispanic American Historical Review* 36: 2; 229–42 (May 1956), 230; Dulles, *Vargas*, 29–34; Duff, "Luís Carlos Prestes," 10.

12. Hercolino Cascardo (1900–67) remained in exile until 1930 when he returned to Brazil under a general amnesty. In 1935 Cascardo became one of the founders of the National Liberation Alliance (*Aliança Nacional Liberatadora*—ANL). Before his death he was promoted to the rank of fleet admiral in the naval reserve.

13. Dulles, *Anarchists*, 245; Scheina, *Latin America*, 77–79.

14. Italo Landucci, *Cenas e episódios da coluna Prestes* (São Paulo: Editora Brasiliense, 1947), 25; Duff, "Luís Carlos Prestes," 10.

15. Until the 1970s, in northern Brazil politically powerful individuals were known as "colonels" in spite of the fact that they may have seen no military service. The use of the title was based on the practices of the *Guardia Nacional* (disestablished in 1918), in which officers were frequently appointed from the rich and powerful. In southern Brazil the term *caudilho* was used.

16. Duff, "Luís Carlos Prestes," 10–12.

17. Dulles, *Vargas*, 34–41; Dulles, *Anarchists*, 246; Alexander, "Brazilian 'Tenentismo,'" 230–31.

18. John D. Wirth, "Tenentismo in the Brazilian Revolution of 1930," *Hispanic American Historical Review* 44: 2; 161–79 (May 1964), 165–67.

19. Bello, *A History of Modern Brazil*, 261–70; Dulles, *Vargas*, 44–57; Thomas Skidmore, *Politics in Brazil, 1930–1964* (New York: Oxford University Press, 1967), 4.

20. Young, "Military Aspects," 180–81; Dulles, *Vargas*, 62; Wirth, "Tenentismo," 168.

21. Young, "Military Aspects," 190–91.

22. ibid., 192–94; *Foreign Relations 1930*, 1: 439–43.

23. Dulles, *Vargas*, 67–76; Young, "Military Aspects," 190–96; John J. Johnson, *The Military in Society in Latin America* (Stanford: Stanford University Press, 1964), 204–5; Wirth, "Tenentismo," 168; Young, "Military Aspects," 195–96.

24. Dulles, *Vargas*, 79; Young, "Military Aspects," 181; Wirth, "Tenentismo," 168–69, 178–79; Alexander, "Brazilian 'Tenentismo,'" 233–42. Johnson does not believe that Vargas was completely in charge. Johnson, *The Military in Society*, 206.

25. *Foreign Relations 1932*, 5: 397–99; Jackson Flores Jr., "The Brazilian Air War," *Air Enthusiast* 35: 64–73 (January–April 1988), 65.

26. *Foreign Relations 1932*, 5: 404–5.

27. *Foreign Relations 1932*, 5: 390–91; Dulles, *Vargas*, 98–116; Skidmore, *Politics in Brazil*, 17–18.

28. Flores, "The Brazilian Air War," 65.

29. *Foreign Relations 1932*, 5: 401–2, 424–26; Flores, "The Brazilian Air War," 64–65.

30. *Foreign Relations 1932*, 5: 425–26.

31. In addition to Prestes, numerous *tenentes* rose to national prominence. Among the most important were the following: Eduardo Gomes became the first commander of the Brazilian air force and was an unsuccessful presidential candidate in 1945 and 1955; Estillac Leal became Minister of War in 1951–52; Juarez Távora rose to prominence in northeast Brazil and was an unsuccessful presidential candidate in 1955. See Duff, "Luís Carlos Prestes," 12–13; Alexander, *Communism in Latin America*, 102.

32. Prestes, "How I became a Communist," 116.

33. ibid.

CHAPTER FIFTEEN

1. Luís Sánchez Cerro (1889–1933) was born in Piura in northern Peru and was of mixed Indian and European heritage (a *cholo*). His family possessed modest wealth. Sánchez Cerro enlisted in the army as a private in 1910. Within a few months he was sent to the *Escuela Militar de Chorrillos* and graduated as a second lieutenant in 1914. In that year he was

wounded in the *golpe* that overthrew President Guillermo Billinghurst. Sánchez Cerro took part in unsuccessful coups against President Leguía in 1919 and 1922. Reinstated in the army, he was sent to Italy, Spain, and France on military missions. In 1929 Sánchez Cerro was promoted to lieutenant colonel and given command of a battalion stationed at Arequipa. He died in Lima from an assassin's bullet on April 30, 1933.

2. Pike, *The Modern History of Peru*, 252–53, 266–67; Masterson, *Militarism*, 33–34, 44, 51; *Vision del Peru en el siglo XX*, 2 vols. (Lima: Ediciones Libreria Studivm, S.A., 1962–63), 1: 307, 321.

3. Victor Raúl Haya de la Torre (1895–1979) was born in Trujillo into a distinguished and cultured family of modest wealth. His family claimed to be of "pure" European ancestry although Victor's physiognomy could lead one to question that claim. As a teen he was active in youth movements, particularly those concerned with the fate of the Peruvian Indians. He studied law in Trujillo and Lima between 1915 and 1917 and was active in student politics. In 1919 Haya de la Torre helped craft an alliance between students and textile workers who organized a strike for the eight-hour work day. On May 23, 1923, he led a massive demonstration against President Leguía's plan to dedicate Peru to the "Sacred Heart of Jesus," for which Haya de la Torre was imprisoned. He began a hunger strike. The government, fearing the death of this popular young leader while in prison, deported him to Panama on October 9. Haya de la Torre traveled widely, including Central America, Mexico, the United States, Western Europe, and the Soviet Union. He had access to many great intellectuals including the Mexican José Vasconcelos and the Russian Leon Trotsky. In 1930, when Leguía was overthrown, Haya de la Torre was in Europe, having recently been deported from Central America due to the influence of the United States. He returned to Peru in August 1931. He was an outstanding orator and is quoted at the beginning of this chapter (see Pike, *The Modern History of Peru*, 240–41).

4. Masterson, *Militarism*, 40–41, 44–47; Rex A. Hudson, ed., *Peru: A Country Study*, 4th ed. (Washington, D.C.: Headquarters, Department of the Army, 1993), 41; Jorge Ortíz Sotelo, "Las rebeliones navales del Callao 1932 y 1948" (A paper presented to the 13th Naval History Symposium, Annapolis, Md., 1997), 1–2.

Robert Alexander implies that Sánchez Cerro "stole" the election. Robert Alexander, ed., *Aprismo* (n.p.: Kent State University, 1973), 10–11.

5. Luigi R. Einaudi, *Peruvian Military Relations with the United States* (Santa Monica: Rand Corporation, June 1970), 14; Ortíz, "Las rebeliones navales," 1–2.

6. Thomas M. Davis Jr., "The *Indigenismo* of the Peruvian *Aprista* Party: A Reinterpretation," *Hispanic American Historical Review* 51: 4; 626–45 (November 1971), 632–33; Germán Arciniegas, *The State of Latin America* (New York: Alfred A. Knopf, 1952), 85–87; Pike, *The Modern History of Peru*, 239.

7. Masterson, *Militarism*, 30–31, 63, 104–5.

8. ibid., 24–34, 91.

9. Article 213, 1933 Peruvian Constitution.

10. Pike, *The Modern History of Peru*, 262.

11. Masterson, *Militarism*, 47–48.

12. Masterson, *Militarism*, 48; Pike, *The Modern History of Peru*, 263–64.

13. Pike, *The Modern History of Peru*, 264–65; Alexander, *Aprismo*, 11; Masterson, *Militarism*, 48.

14. In early 1932 the Peruvian cruisers *Almirante Grau* and *Coronel Bolognesi* were in the U.S. naval base at Balboa, Panama Canal Zone. There their crews came into contact with dissident *Apristas* who had recently been expelled from Peru.

Pedro Ugarteche, *Sánchez Cerro papeles y recuerdos de un presidente de Perú*, 3 vols. (Lima: Editorial Universitaria, 1969), 3: 86–88; "Mutiny in the Peruvian Navy," *Monthly Information Bulletin* 19–21 (July–October 1932), 19; Ortíz, "rebeliones navales," 3–4.

15. Ortíz, "rebeliones navales," 4; "Mutiny in the Peruvian Navy," 19; Ugarteche, *Sánchez Cerro*, 3: 86.

16. Ortíz, "rebeliones navales," 4; Ugarteche, *Sánchez Cerro*, 3: 86.

17. Ortíz, "rebeliones navales," 4.

18. Ugarteche, *Sánchez Cerro*, 3: 92–93.

19. Ugarteche, *Sánchez Cerro*, 3: 92–93; Ortíz, "rebeliones navales," 4–5.

20. Ortíz, "rebeliones navales," 5; Ugarteche, *Sanchez Cerro*, 3: 87.

According to "Mutiny in the Peruvian Navy," a submarine fired a torpedo across the bow of the *Almirante Grau* and a white flag was immediately hoisted. Then the cruiser *Coronel Bolognesi* fired several 3-inch shells at the submarine without effect. Reportedly, at this point the submarine returned fire. It is unlikely that the government would have endeavored to induce the surrender by firing an expensive and not always predictable torpedo as a warning shot.

21. Jorge Basadre observed, "The official version classified the insurrection as communist; but it had *Aprista* origin." Jorge Basadre, *Historia de la república del Perú* 7th ed., 10 vols. (Lima: Edicionial Universitaria, 1983), 10: 231. See also Ortíz, "rebeliones navales," 5; Masterson, *Militarism*, 48–49.

22. Basadre, *Historia de la república*, 10: 233–34.

23. Arciniegas, *The State*, 84.

24. Basadre, *Historia de la república*, 10: 234–36.

25. ibid., 10: 236–37.

26. Pike states that before fleeing Trujillo, the *Aprista* leadership ordered the execution of the military captives. Basadre states that there is no proof of this. Pike, *The Modern History of Peru*, 265–66; Basadre, *Historia de la república*, 10: 237.

27. Basadre, *Historia de la república*, 10: 241–45; Masterson, *Militarism*, 51–52.

28. Masterson, *Militarism*, 52. The *Apristas* claimed that General Benavides was responsible for the assassination. Alexander, *Aprismo*, 11.

29. Daniel M. Masterson, "Soldiers, Sailors, and *Apristas*: Conspiracy and Power Politics in Peru, 1932–1948," in *The Underside of Latin American History*, ed. by John F. Bratzel and Daniel M. Masterson (East Lansing: Michigan State University, 1977), 26–27; Alexander, *Aprismo*, 11–12; Pike, *The Modern History of Peru*, 269–71.

30. Masterson, *Militarism*, 54–55; Pike, *The Modern History of Peru*, 272–73.

31. Masterson, *Militarism*, 55–56.

32. ibid., 58–59.

33. ibid., 67–68, 80–81; R. J. Owens, *Peru* (London: Oxford University Press, 1966), 55.

34. Masterson, "Soldiers," 27; Masterson, *Militarism*, 79–80.

35. Pike, *The Modern History of Peru*, 283–86; Alexander, *Aprismo*, 12–13; Owens, *Peru*, 56.

36. Victor Villanueva, *La Sublevación aprista del 48: La tragedia de un pueblo y un partido* (Lima: Milla Batres, 1973), 191–92; Masterson, *Militarism*, 89, 94–95, 106.

37. Ortíz, "rebeliones navales," 5; Masterson, "Soldiers," 27–28.

38. Pike, *The Modern History of Peru*, 285–86; Masterson, *Militarism*, 98–101.

39. Masterson, *Militarism*, 103.

40. ibid., 112–14.

41. Masterson, "Soldiers," 30–31; Masterson, *Militarism*, 115–16.

42. José del Carmen Marín Arista (1899–1980) was born in San Miguel de Guyabamba and was principally of Indian descent. He entered the *Escuela Militar de Chorrillos* in 1917 and graduated first in his class. On two occasions he trained in France between 1921 and 1939. In 1939 Marín graduated with honors from the Superior War College in Paris. During the 1940s he directed the preparatory *Colegio Militar Leoncio Prado* and the *Escuela Militar de Chorrillos*. In July 1950 Marín became the first director of the Center for High Military Studies. He was one of the few senior officers who was not anti-*Aprista*.

43. Villanueva, *La sublevación*, 114–17; Pike, *The Modern History of Peru*, 287–88.

44. Villanueva, *La sublevación*, 118–26; Ortíz, "rebeliones navales," 6; Masterson, *Militarism*, 118.

45. Ortíz, "rebeliones navales," 6; Masterson, *Militarism*, 118–19.

46. Ortíz, "rebeliones navales," 6–7.

47. Masterson, "Soldiers," 34–35; Masterson, *Militarism*, 119.

48. Ortíz, "rebeliones navales," 7–8.

49. ibid., 8; Jorge Ortíz Sotelo, *Escuela naval de Peru (Historia Ilustrada* (Callao: Escuela Naval del Peru, 1981), 128; Alexander, *Aprismo*, 13; Masterson, *Militarism*, 119–20.

50. Manuel A. Odría (1897–1974) was born in Tarma, central Peru, into a moderately wealthy family. He entered the *Escuela Militar de Chorrillos* in 1915 and graduated first in his class. He also attended the Escuela Superior de Guerra Naval and was promoted to lieutenant colonel in 1936. Odría commanded the 1st Light Division during the 1941 war with Ecuador and was among those acclaimed as national heroes. As a brigadier general he served as an instructor at *Escuela Superior de Guerra Naval*. In January 1947 Odría served in President Bustamante's cabinet and was the leading anti-*Aprista*.

51. Masterson, *Militarism*, 122–23; Arciniegas, *The State*, 79.

52. Glynn Mapes, "Changing a Nation: Ruling Junta in Peru Takes a Different Tack, Seeks Social Revision," *Wall Street Journal* 174: 1, 19 (August 22, 1969), 19.

53. Daniel M. Masterson, "Caudillismo and Institutional Change: Manuel Odría and the Peruvian Armed Forces, 1948–1956," *The Americas* 40: 4; 479–89 (April 1984), 484; Luigi R. Einaudi, *The Peruvian Military: A Summary Political Analysis* (Santa Monica: The Rand Corporation, 1969), 7–8; José Pareja Paz Soldán, *Derecho constitucional peruano* (Lima: Ediciones Libería Studium, 1966), 402; *Vision del Peru*, 1: 331.

54. Alexander, *Aprismo*, 13–14; Arciniegas, *The State*, 79–80.

55. Pike, *The Modern History of Peru*, 291; Masterson, *Militarism*, 135. In April 1954 Haya de la Torre was permitted to leave Peru under safe conduct.

56. Pike, *The Modern History of Peru*, 289–91.

57. Masterson, *Militarism*, 144–45.

58. Alexander, *Aprismo*, 14–15; Masterson, *Militarism*, 146.

59. Einaudi, *Peruvian Military Relation*, 14; Alexander, *Aprismo*, 15–16; Pike, *The Modern History of Peru*, 296.

60. Pike, *The Modern History of Peru*, 298–99; Alexander, *Aprismo*, 16–17; Masterson, *Militarism*, 169–74.

61. Masterson, *Militarism*, 174–77; Lyle N. McAlister, "Peru," in *The Military in Latin America Socio-Political Evolution: Four Case Studies*, ed. by Lyle N. McAlister, Anthony P. Maingot, and Robert A. Potash (Washington, D.C.: Center for Research in Social Science Systems, 1970), 59–67.

62. Pike, *The Modern History of Peru*, 301–2; McAlister, "Peru," 60.

63. Pike, *The Modern History of Peru*, 305–6.

64. Alexander, *Aprismo*, 48–49.

65. Juan Velasco Alvardo (1910–77) was born in the northern department of Piura. One of eleven children, he came from modest economic origins. A *cholo* (a person of mixed Indian and European blood), he worked as a "shoeshine boy" during his youth. Velasco entered the army as a private in 1929 and apparently was the top performer in a competitive examination that permitted him to attend the military academy beginning in 1930. He graduated first in his class. His assignments included instructor at the *Escuela Oficiales* and the *Escuela Superior de Guerra*. He served as director of the *Escuela Militar de Chorrillos* and the *Escuela de Infantería*. In 1959 he was promoted to brigadier general and served as the Peruvian military attaché to France between 1962 and 1963. In that year he was promoted to division general and became the Peruvian delegate to the Inter-American Defense Board in Washington, D.C.

66. Malcolm W. Browne, "Peru Speculates on Countercoup," *New York Times* (November 3, 1968), 27. Three Air Force lieutenant generals were passed over—Roland Gervasi, José Heiges, and Jorge Soldi. Along with General López, they were known as "The Italian Club." All had been trained in Italy during the 1930s and were young pilots during the 1941 war with Ecuador.

67. Richard N. Goodwin, "Letter from Peru," *New Yorker* 45: 41–109 (May 17, 1969), 68–70; Val Clear, "Report from Lima," *Fortune* 79: 55–56, 58 (March 1969), 56; Mapes, "Changing a Nation," 19; Gustavo Valcarcel, "Peruvian Paradoxes," Moscow *New Times* (January 13, 1969), 20–22; Clear, "Report from Lima," 56.

68. Malcolm W. Browne, "Peru's Junta Allows a Former Enemy to Return," *New York Times* (February 23, 1969), 14.

69. Clear, "Report from Lima," 58; Malcolm W. Browne, "Peru's Leaders Talk of Plans: 'We Shall Not Stop,'" *New York Times* (June 28, 1969), 6; Benjamin Welles, "U.S. Cautious on Peru Reform," *New York Times* (June 26, 1969), 4; "Grace Company Funds Seized by Peru in New Land Reform," *New York Times* (June 27, 1969), 6.

70. Masterson, *Militarism*, 23; Hudson, *Peru*, 50–51, 230–31.

71. Richard Patch, "The Peruvian Elections of 1963: A New President and a Challenge," *American University's Field Staff Reports Service West Coast South America Series* 10: 1–14 (July 1963), 1, 6; Lisa North, *Civil-Military Relations in Argentina, Chile, and Peru* (Berkeley: Institute of International Studies, University of California, 1966), 48–53; Masterson, *Militarism* 91–93.

72. Browne, "Peru's Junta," 14.

73. Article 275 of the 1979 Peruvian Constitution and Article 213 of the 1933 Peruvian Constitution. See also Hudson, *Peru*, 278.

CHAPTER SIXTEEN

1. Isaac F. Rojas (1906–93) entered the Naval Academy in 1923 and graduated in 1929, ranked second in a class of thirty-four. He served on board many ships and was stationed in

England for a few years. Rojas commanded the coast guard ship *Pueyrredón*, and was Superintendent of the Naval Academy between 1953 and 1955. Following the overthrow of Perón,
Rojas served as Vice President of Argentina between 1955 and 1958. He was promoted to
full admiral in 1958 and retired. In 1963 he headed the failed coup attempt and was jailed on
the island of Martín García. He and President Carlos Menem, a *Peronista*, publicly reconciled in 1990.

2. Eduardo Lonardi (1896–1956), the son of an Italian immigrant, graduated second in
his class from the Military Academy, specializing in artillery, in 1916. Later he studied at the
National War College (*Escuela Superior de Guerra*), and then was assigned to the General
Staff. In 1938 Lonardi served as the military attaché to Chile. He presided over the Argentine
delegation to the Inter-American Defense Board (*La Junta de Defensa Interamericana*) in
Washington between 1942 and 1948. In 1951 Lonardi commanded the First Army which was
headquartered in Rosario. He rivaled Gen. Benjamín Menéndez for the leadership of the conspiracy to overthrow Juan Perón. At the last minute he backed away from the plot. Many
officers under his command were openly sympathetic to the failed coup against Perón attempted
in September. Lonardi was among the numerous high-ranking officers purged from the army
following the failed plot. Lonardi was imprisoned for almost one year for conspiring against
Perón, being released in December 1953.

3. Juan Perón (1895–1974) was born in Lobos, Buenos Aires, grew up in Santa Cruz,
and was educated in Buenos Aires. He entered the Military Academy in 1911 and graduated
in 1913 as Second Lieutenant of Infantry. In 1924 Perón became a captain. In 1926 Perón
attended the Superior War School and graduated near the top of the class. He was assigned to
the army General Staff in 1929. In 1931 he supported Gen. José Agustín P. Justo in his bid
for power. Justo ultimately came to power, and Perón was assigned to the Superior War School
as an instructor in military history. Beginning in 1936 Perón served as the military attaché to
Chile; in 1938 he was accused of espionage and withdrawn. Perón was sent to Italy and
Germany in 1938–39 to study mountain operations. There he became sympathetic to fascism.
Returning to Argentina in 1940, he was made Director of the Mountain Instruction Center
the following year and promoted to colonel. Perón helped form the United Officers Group
(*Grupo Oficiales Unidos*—GOU), and became its most prominent spokesman. This clique,
mostly composed of midlevel officers, was anti-Marxist, anti-American, and anti-Jewish. He
was prominent in the successful June 4, 1943, coup. Perón was rewarded as he rapidly rose
through the positions of assistant to the Secretary of War, Secretary of Work and Social Security, Secretary of War, and Vice President. He was elected President of Argentina in 1946.
Exiled in 1955, he eventually settled in Spain. Perón returned to the presidency in 1973 and
died in 1975.

4. For the *Justicialista*, or *Peronista*, Party, the seventeenth of October was considered
its founding date. While Perón governed, this was Argentina's most important national holiday.

5. María Eva ["Evita"] Duarte de Perón (1919–52) was born out of wedlock and moved
from Junín to Buenos Aires at the age of sixteen. She worked as a part-time radio "soap-
opera" actress. Meeting Juan Perón in October 1943 at a party at *Radio Belgrano*, she became his mistress. Evita and Juan married in late October 1945. She headed the feminine
branch of the Peronist Party, directed the Eva Perón Social Aid Foundation, and dominated
the ministries of health and labor. Her bid to become vice president during the 1951 election
was blocked by the army. Evita transformed herself from a dark-haired, would-be actress into
a blond, charismatic leader of the *descamisados*. She died of cancer in Buenos Aires on July
26, 1952.

6. Juan Carlos Christensen, *Historia Argentina sin mitos* (Buenos Aires: Grupo Editor Latinoamericano, 1990), 619–20; Alain Rouquié, *Poder militar y sociedad politica en la Argentina, 1943–1973*, 2 vols. (Buenos Aires: Emece Editores, 1982), 2: 65–68; George Pendle, *Argentina* (New York: Oxford University Press, 1963), 97–98.

7. Marvin Goldwert, *Democracy, Militarism, and Nationalism in Argentina, 1930–1966* (Austin: University of Texas Press, 1972), 102–3.

The I.Ae.27 *Pulqui I* was the first jet built in Latin America; its first flight was in 1947. This was followed by the I.Ae.33 *Pulqui II*, two of which were built. The *Pulqui II* was a single-seat, swept-wing, jet-propelled fighter. The aircraft was propelled by two Rolls Royce Nene engines. German engineer Kurt Tank, then living in Cordoba, Argentina, designed these aircraft. They were similar to the U.S. Sabre F-86 and the Russian MiG-15, all of which evolved out of the same school of aeronautical design.

8. Edwin Lieuwen, *Arms and Politics in Latin America* (New York: Frederick A. Praeger, Inc., 1960), 69–70.

9. Goldwert, *Democracy*, 103–4, 113–14.

10. *The Statesman's Year-Book 1955*, 792–93; Arthur P. Whitaker, *Argentine Upheaval* (New York: Praeger, 1956), 65–66; Russell H. Fitzibbon, "Argentina after Eva Peron," *Yale Review* 43: 32–45 (Autumn 1952), 35–36.

11. Isidoro J. Ruíz Moreno, *La marina revolucionaria (1874–1963)* (Buenos Aires: Planeta, 1998), 183–87; Robert A. Potash, *The Army & Politics in Argentina, 1945–1962* (Stanford: Stanford University Press, 1980), 180; Raymond Estep, *The Argentine Armed Forces and Government* (Maxwell Air Force Base, Ala.: Air University, 1970), 13.

12. Gerhard Masur, *Nationalism in Latin America* (New York: The Macmillan Company, 1966), 186–87; Potash, *The Army*, 171–76.

13. Goldwert, *Democracy*, 101.

14. Rouquié, *Poder militar*, 2: 90; Ruíz, *La marina*, 187–89; Anibal O. Olivieri, *Dos veces rebelde* (Buenos Aires: Ediciones Sigla, 1958), 33–37; Estep, *The Argentine Armed Forces*, 14.

15. Rouquié, *Poder militar*, 2: 91–93; Potash, *The Army*, 134–37; Olivieri, *Dos veces rebelde*, 43–48.

16. Samuel Toranzo Calderón (1897–1992), began his military career in the army and transferred to the marine corps during the 1930s. Calderón had been an early supporter of Perón and his social programs.

17. Ruíz, *La marina*, 193–94; Olivieri, *Dos veces rebelde*, 120–28; Rouquié, *Poder militar*, 2: 108–11; Potash, *The Army*, 181–87.

18. Luis Alberto Romero, *Los golpes militares, 1812–1955* (Buenos Aires: Carlos Perez Editor, S.A., 1969), 152.

19. Potash, *The Army*, 188–89; Ruíz, *La marina*, 195–96.

20. Ruíz, *La marina*, 196–97.

21. Ruíz, *La marina*, 197; Olivieri, *Dos veces rebelde*, 105–40; Miguel Angel Cavallo, *Puerto Belgrano, hora cero: la marina se subleva* (Buenos Aires: Fundamental Editiores, 1956), 36–46; Guillermo D. Plater, *Una gran lección* (Buenos Aires: Almafuerte, 1956), 27–35.

22. Buenos Aires *Democracia* (August 18, 1955), 2–3; Ruíz, *La marina*, 198.

23. "Reanudanse en la fecha todas las actividades," Buenos Aires *La Nacion* (June 20, 1955), 1–2.

24. Rouquié, *Poder militar*, 2: 110; Potash, *The Army*, 188; Cavallo, *Puerto Belgrano*, 21, 41; Goldwert, *Democracy*, 129–30.

25. Potash, *The Army*, 189; *Ejército argentino cronología militar Argentina 1806–1980* (Buenos Aires: Comando en Jefe de Ejército, 1982), 358.

26. "Argentine Navy's Role in the Overthrow of the Peron Regime," *ONI Review* 10: 624–29 (December 1955), 624–29; Ruíz, *La marina*, 197; Olivieri, *Dos veces rebelde*, 105–40; Cavallo, *Puerto Belgrano*, 36–46; Plater, *Una gran lección*, 27–35.

27. "En su fallo," 2–3; Rouquié, *Poder militar*, 2: 108–9; Potash, *The Army*, 191.

28. "Reanudanse en la fecha," 1–2; Potash, *The Army*, 195.

29. Cavallo, *Puerto Belgrano*, 55.

30. Goldwert, *Democracy*, 132–33.

31. Pedro Aramburu (1903–70) became a brigadier general in December 1952 and a major general in December 1954. He was an unsuccessful presidential candidate in 1963. Aramburu was kidnapped and assassinated by *Montoneros*. He was reputed for his honesty.

32. Potash, *The Army*, 195–96; Ruíz, *La marina*, 203–4.

33. Potash, *The Army*, 199.

34. ibid., 199.

35. "Lonardi y la revolución del 55," *Todo es Historia* 186: 43–52 (March 1981), 44–46; Rouquié, *Poder militar*, 2: 116–22.

36. "Lonardi y la revolución del 55," 44–45; Potash, *The Army*, 181, 197.

37. Rouquié, *Poder militar*, 2: 117.

38. Romero, *Los golpes militares*, 157; Ruíz, *La marina*, 206–7.

39. "Argentine Navy's Role," 624–29.

40. "Lonardi y la revolución del 55," 46–47; Potash, *The Army*, 201.

41. Ruíz, *La marina*, 208–10.

42. The original commanding officer had been relieved when he refused to open fire on the storage tanks.

43. Rouquié, *Poder militar*, 2: 119; Ruíz, *La marina*, 210–11.

44. Ruíz, *La marina*, 212.

45. Text of message provided courtesy of Admiral Isaac F. Rojas.

46. Text of conditions provided courtesy of Admiral Rojas.

47. Text provided courtesy of Admiral Rojas.

48. Text of message provided courtesy of Admiral Rojas.

49. *Ejército argentino cronología*, 359.

50. Rouquié, *Poder militar*, 2: 121; John Edwin Fagg, *Latin America: A General History* (New York: The MacMillan Company, 1963), 955.

51. Admiral Rojas also held the position of chief of naval operations as a rear admiral. Rear Adm. Teodoro Hartung became the navy minister. In May 1958 Congress elevated Rojas to full admiral over his own objections. The decision passed both houses by unanimous vote.

52. "Argentine Navy's Role," *ONI Review* 624–29.

53. Potash, *The Army*, 215.

54. Whitaker, *Argentine Upheaval*, 36–37; Goldwert, *Democracy*, 164; Masur, *Nationalism*, 190.

55. Christensen, *Historia Argentina*, 137; Goldwert, *Democracy*, 165–66.

56. Goldwert, *Democracy*, 166; Fagg, *Latin America*, 956.

57. Harold F. Peterson, *Argentina and the United States* (New York: University Publishers, Inc., 1964), 506–7.

58. Christensen, *Historia Argentina*, 640; Goldwert, *Democracy*, 168–69; Potash, *The Army*, 265–66.

59. Potash, *The Army*, 288–90; Ruíz, *La Marina*, 222–23.

60. Potash, *The Army*, 290–91.

61. Goldwert, *Democracy*, 178–79; Potash, *The Army*, 292–93, 305–7.

62. Carlos Severo Toranzo Montero (1902–77) throughout the 1930s and 1940s criticized the army for its role in politics. In 1932 he was jailed for espousing free elections. Toranzo Montero was retired as a lieutenant colonel in 1950. He was jailed again in 1951 for his anti-Perón activities but released in 1953 and resided in Uruguay. Two years later he joined the "liberating Revolution" in Córdoba. He was reincorporated into the army as a general. In 1958 Toranzo Montero was appointed as the Argentine representative to the Inter-American Defense Board in Washington, D.C.

63. Potash, *The Army*, 314–19; Goldwert, *Democracy*, 179–80.

64. Goldwert, *Democracy*, 180–81; Faustino Svencions, *Argentine Foreign Policy and World Events 1958 to 1982: A Survey* (Washington, D.C.: National Defense University, 1984), 7.

65. Potash, *The Army*, 323.

66. Potash, *The Army*, 330–31; Goldwert, *Democracy*, 183.

67. Estep, *The Argentine Armed Forces*, 29; Potash, *The Army*, 340–44; Svencions, *Argentine Foreign Policy*, 9.

68. Whitaker, *Argentina*, 165; Goldwert, *Democracy*, 185–87; Christensen, *Historia Argentina*, 641; Ruíz, *La marina*, 224–25; Fagg, *Latin America*, 958.

69. Goldwert, *Democracy*, 188–89; Potash, *The Army*, 1–10.

70. Goldwert, *Democracy*, 188–89.

71. Potash, *The Army*, 26–28; Goldwert, *Democracy*, 190.

72. Potash, *The Army*, 34–38; Goldwert, *Democracy*, 190–91.

73. Potash, *The Army*, 48–50.

74. ibid., 51–60; Edwin Lieuwen, *Generals vs. Presidents* (New York: Frederick A. Praeger, 1964), 19–20; Estep, *The Argentine Armed Forces*, 33.

75. Goldwert, *Democracy*, 191–92.

76. ibid., 67.

77. Potash, *The Army*, 93–95; Ruíz, *La marina*, 228–29.

78. Potash, *The Army*, 98–103; Ruíz, *La marina*, 228–61; Estep, *The Argentine Armed Forces*, 34; Goldwert, *Democracy*, 194.

79. Peter Ranis, "Background to the 1965 Argentine Elections," *The World Today* 21: 192–209 (May 1965), 201–2; James R. Scobie, *Argentina: A City and a Nation* (New York: Oxford University Press, 1964), 220–21.

80. Thomas M. Millington, "President Arturo Illia and the Argentine Military," *Journal of Inter-American Studies* 6: 405–24 (July 1964), 409; Goldwert, *Democracy*, 200–1.

81. Potash, *The Army*, 186–93; "Illia Defied by Army Chief; Troops Seize Key Positions," *New York Times* (June 28, 1966): 1, 15; Christensen, *Historia Argentina*, 642–44.

82. Ruíz, *La marina*, 215–16. However, Goldwert concludes, "Naval rebellion was doomed without a land base, and General Lonardi seemed prepared to provide this essential element." Goldwert, *Democracy*, 135.

According to Arguindeguy, "she was assigned the name *17 de Octubre* which had no significance at all to the Argentine Navy . . . and includes the later falsification of the Argentine commissioning date [which was actually April 12, 1951]. . . . This is an opportune place to correct the historical record." Pablo E. Arguindeguy, *Apuntes sobre los buques de la armada argentina* (Buenos Aires: Departamento de Estudios Historicos Navales, 1972), 5: 2633.

83. Loveman, *For la Patria*, 122–24.

CHAPTER SEVENTEEN

1. Jürgen Rohwer, *Axis Submarine Successes, 1939–45* (Annapolis: Naval Institute Press, 1983), 69–124; Arthur Oscar Saldanha da Gama, *A marinha do Brasil na segunda guerra mundial* (Rio de Janeiro: CAPAMI Editora e Gráfica Ltda, 1982), 276–77.

2. National Archives, Records of the Office of Naval Intelligence, Records of the Division of Pan-American Affairs and U.S. naval missions, summary of naval staff conversations and agreements with American representatives, August–October 1942, entry 49, Box 1.

3. U.S. Department of State, *Foreign Relations 1942*, xxiii.

4. The Rio meeting also led to the establishment of the Inter-American Defense Board to coordinate military and technical matters throughout the hemisphere. Gordon Connell-Smith, *Inter-American System* (London: Oxford University Press, 1966), 120–23.

5. Frank D. McCann, "Brazil, the United States and World War II: A Commentary," *Diplomatic History* 3: 1; 59–76 (Winter 1979), 59–61.

6. Between December 1942 and June 1943, some 1,985 aircraft were delivered to Great Britain and North Africa via Brazil. W. F. Craven and J. L. Cate, eds., *The Army Air Force in World War II* 7 vols. (Chicago: University of Chicago Press, 1948–58), 7:76.

7. According to Garzke and Dulin, the *Richelieu* was completed but not combat ready. William H. Garzke Jr., and Robert O. Dulin Jr., *Battleships: Allied Battleships in World War II* (Annapolis: Naval Institute Press, 1980), 85–86.

8. Scheina, *Latin America*, 133–38.

9. Early in the war, seventeen of thirty-two German merchantships caught in Brazilian waters attempted to run a British blockade and return to Germany. A number of them were intercepted inside the security zone by British warships and sunk or scuttled by their own crews. On December 11, 1940, a British warship caught the Brazilian merchantship *Siqueira Campos*, which had sailed from Lisbon, Portugal, for Rio de Janeiro carrying a cargo of German-manufactured arms destined for the Brazilian army. The ship was taken to Gibraltar and detained. This infuriated the Brazilians. It took the intercession of the United States before the ship was allowed to proceed. In another incident, the merchantship *Buarque*, en route to the United States from Brazil, both neutral, was boarded by a British inspection party and commandeered for allegedly carrying contraband. On December 1 a more serious event occurred. The British auxiliary cruiser *Calvin Castle* stopped the Brazilian merchantship *Itapé* off the São Tomé lighthouse and removed twenty-five Germans and two Italians. And on January 18, 1941, a British party from the auxiliary cruiser *Asturias* boarded the French merchantship *Mendoza* in Brazilian territorial waters. Samuel E. Morison, *History of United States Naval Operations in World War II* (Boston: Little, Brown, 1947–62), 1: 37; Jürgen Rohwer, "Operações navais da Alemanha no litoral do Brasil durante a segunda guerra mundial," *Navigator Subsidios para a Historia Maritima do Brasil* 18: 3–38 (January–December 1982), 5–6.

10. da Gama, *A marinha do Brasil na segunda guerra*, 10–11; Jürgen Rohwer and Gerhard Hümmelchen, *Chronology of War at Sea, 1939–1945*, 2 vols. (New York: Arco Publishing, 1973), 1: 68.

11. Morison, *History of U. S. Naval Operations*, 1: 378; Stetson Conn and Byron Fairchild, *The Western Hemisphere: The Framework of Hemisphere Defense* (Washington, D.C.: Office of the Chief of Military History, 1960), 306.

12. da Gama, *A marinha do Brasil na segunda guerra*, 19, 276; Rohwer, *Axis Submarine Successes*, 69–124.

13. Karl Dönitz, *Memoirs: Ten Years and Twenty Days* (London: Weidenfeld and Nicolson, 1958), 239.

14. Frank M. Garcia, "Brazil Attacks Axis Submarines," New York *Times* (May 29, 1942), 1. The Ministry of Aeronautics and Brazil's Air Forces had been formerly established on January 20, 1941.

15. Rohwer, "Operacoes navais," 14–15; Donitz, *Memoirs*, 239.

16. Conn and Fairchild, *The Western Hemisphere*, 267, 271.

17. Ricardo Bonalume Neto, *A nossa segunda guerra* (Rio de Janeiro: Expressão e Cultura, 1995), 88–89.

The establishment of the Brazilian air force as a separate service under a Ministry of Aeronautics (which was in charge of civil aviation as well), was motivated by political, rather than military considerations. Ironically, the newly established air force would fight under the command of the U.S. Navy in the South Atlantic, and under the U.S. Army Air Force in Italy.

18. "Brazil," U.S. Naval Institute *Proceedings* 65: 436; 901–2 (June 1939), 902.

19. "Brazil," U.S. Naval Institute *Proceedings* 65: 441; 1658 (November 1939), 1658.

20. The *Marcilio Dias* and *Greenhalgh* were commissioned on November 29, 1943, and the *Mariz e Barros* in 1944.

21. "Brazil," U.S. Naval Institute *Proceedings* 68: 475; 1337–38 (September 1942).

22. Conn and Fairchild, *The Western Hemisphere*, 272–78, 284–312.

23. ibid., 295–96, 317.

24. Morison, *History of U. S. Naval Operations*, 1: 378–79.

25. President Vargas' decision to put the Brazilian armed forces under U.S. command was so radical that, when Admiral Ingram reported it to the Secretary of the Navy, Frank J. Knox, during the latter's visit to Brazil in September 1942, Knox suspected it might be a ploy. See Neto, *Segunda guerra*, 34–36.

26. da Gama, *A marinha do Brasil na segunda guerra*, 141–285; Morison, *History of U. S. Naval Operations*, 1: 387–89.

27. Rohwer, "Operações navais," 16–17; Morison, *History of U. S. Naval Operations*, 1: 387; Rohwer, *Axis Submarine Successes*, 158, 183.

28. Neto, *Segunda guerra*, 95–96.

29. Rohwer, *Axis Submarine Successes*, 158, 183.

30. da Gama, *A marinha do Brasil na segunda guerra*, 98–100.

31. Conn and Fairchild, *The Western Hemisphere*, 328.

32. John W. F. Dulles, *Castello Branco: The Making of a Brazilian President* (College Station, Texas: A & M University Press, 1978), 66.

33. McCann, "Brazil," 72–73. Frank D. McCann, "The *Forca Expedicionária Brasileira* in the Italian Campaign, 1944–45," *Army History* 26: 1–11 (Spring 1993), 1.

34. Conn and Fairchild, *The Western Hemisphere*, 328.

35. Dulles, *Castello Branco*, 66.

36. The new division included the 1st, 6th, and 11th Infantry Regiments and the 9th Engineer Battalion.

37. The division had nine infantry battalions organized into three regiments. There were four 12-gun battalions of artillery; three of 105mm howitzers; and one of 155mm howitzers. In addition the division had an engineer and medical battalion and various support elements.

38. Dulles, *Castello Branco*, 66–68.

39. ibid., 74–79.

40. Dominick Graham and Shelford Bidwell, *Tug of War: The Battle for Italy 1943–45* (London: Hodder and Stoughton, 1986), 241–347.

41. Dulles, *Castello Branco*, 79–81.

42. ibid., 84.

43. Craven and Cate, *The Army Air Force*, 7: 450.

44. Dulles, *Castello Branco*, 88–90.

45. Brazilian participants were the 3rd Battalion, 6th Infantry Regiment, and the divisional reconnaissance troop (a cavalry unit with M8 armored cars), supporting the 2nd Battalion, 1st Field Howitzer Regiment.

46. Dulles, *Castello Branco*, 99.

47. ibid., 101–3.

48. ibid., 125–32.

49. ibid., 130–32. McCann, "The *Forca Expedicionária Brasileira*," 8.

50. Neto, *Segunda guerra*, 114–15.

51. Dulles, *Castello Branco*, 150–57; McCann, "The *Forca Expedicionária Brasileira*," 8.

52. The Brazilian light cruiser *Bahia* operated on station 13, located on the equator at 30' West longitude. On July 4 the *Bahia* was conducting antiaircraft exercises, firing her 20mm guns against a kite streamed abaft. Apparently, a gunner shot down the kite, and, in the course of firing, unintentionally hit a rack of depth charges stowed on the stern, which exploded. The *Bahia*'s guns had not been fitted with protective guide rails that would have prevented their barrels from firing at dangerous angles. In a matter of minutes the ship lost all power and 367 men took to the lifeboats. Less than half of the crew survived; four U.S. Navy radiomen were among the lost. The disaster was not discovered until July 8, when the Brazilian cruiser *Rio Grande do Sul* arrived on the scene to relieve the *Bahia*. One lifeboat reached the coast of Brazil.

53. Mexicans contributed to the purchase of war material for the Republicans in Europe and the Americas, probably with Spanish money, and helped to transport them to Spain. Items purchased in Europe were loaded in merchantships carrying papers for disembarkation in Veracruz. At least seven of these ships attempted to run the Nationalist blockade and enter Spanish ports held by the Republicans. Six of them succeeded. Mexico also supported the activities of the Republican ambassador from Spain. He chartered merchantships to collect war materials in Mexico and ship them to Spain. Mexico provided the largest number of Latin American volunteers to fight for Republican Spain. At least 464 Mexicans fought in the International Brigade and some 200 others served with additional units. Two Mexicans became Republican generals, Juan Bautista Gomez and Alfaro Sigieros (also known as David Alfaro Xiqueiros). At least twenty Mexicans fought on the side of the Nationalists.

54. Enrique Cárdenas de la Peña, *Gesta en el golfo: La segunda guerra mundial y México*, 2 vols. (México: Editorial Primicias, 1966), 167–72.

55. Conn and Fairchild, *The Western Hemisphere*, 336.

56. Enrique Cárdenas de la Peña, *Semblanza marítima del México independiente y revolucionario*, 2 vols. (México: Secretarìa de Marina, 1970), 1: 259.

57. Scheina, *Latin America*, 167–68.

58. Cárdenas, *Gesta en el golfo*, 56–91; Cárdenas, *Semblanza marítima* 1: 259–63, 2: doc. 73; Rohwer, *Axis Submarine Successes*, 76–112.

59. Cárdenas, *Gesta en el golfo*, 189; Cárdenas, *Semblanza marítima*, 1: 261–62.

60. Conn and Fairchild, *The Western Hemisphere*, 349.

61. Paul V. Walsh, "Fuerza Aérea Expedicionária Mexicana," *El Dorado* 6:2; 74–80 [late 1993]. The Mexican aircraft were assigned to the U.S. 58th Fighter Group.

62. da Gama, *A marinha do Brasil na segunda guerra*, 164–73; Duarte, *Dias*, 293–94.

63. Graham and Bidwell, *Tug of War*, 401.

64. da Gama, *A marinha do Brasil na segunda guerra*, 197, 276–77.

65. Claudio Moreira Bento, "Brazil's Involvement in World War II: The Fiftieth Anniversary," *Army History* 26: 29–30 (Spring 1993), 29.

66. Cárdenas, *Semblanza marítima*, 1: 263; Cárdenas, *Gesta en el golfo*, 129.

67. McCann, "Brazil," 73.

68. Stanley Hilton, "The United States, Brazil, and the Cold War, 1945–60: End of the Special Relationship," *The Journal of American History* 68: 3; 599–624 (December 1981), 611.

Frank McCann concluded, "Brazil's rejection of further overseas military operations in the Korean and Vietnam Wars is partly related to the national perception that the United States did not adequately appreciate its contribution in World War II." McCann, "The *Forca Expedicionária Brasileira*," 9.

CHAPTER EIGHTEEN

1. Jorge Ubico (1878–1946) failed to meet the military academy's academic standards but acquired the rank of lieutenant in 1897 through political manipulation. In 1901 he was second in command of the "Canales" Battalion during a skirmish with El Salvador. In 1906 he again participated in an action against El Salvador and was promoted to colonel. Between 1918 and 1920 Ubico headed sanitation campaigns against yellow fever. He was promoted to brigadier general in 1920 and became chief of the General Staff. A year later he became military commandant of Guatemala and Minister of War. In 1922 Ubico was promoted to general of division. He was an unsuccessful candidate for the presidency in 1922 and 1926.

2. Preston James, *Latin America* (New York: Odyssey Press, 1942), 684; Walter La Feber, *Inevitable Revolutions* (New York: W.W. Norton, 1983), 98–99.

3. *The Statesman's Year-Book 1944*, 1000, 1278; *The Statesman's Year-Book 1947*, 831; *The Statesman's Year-Book 1948*, 1116; Charles D. Ameringer, *The Caribbean Legion* (University Park: Pennsylvania State University Press, 1996), 1–4.

4. Marcia Olander, "Costa Rica in 1948: Cold War or Local War?" *The Americas* 52: 4; 465–93 (April 1996), 475; Daniel P. Hagedorn, *Central American and Caribbean Air Forces* (Tonbridge: An Air-Britain Publication, 1993), 38.

5. Ameringer, *The Caribbean Legion*, 8–9, 73–74.

6. Juan "Juancito" Rodríguez García (unk.), a prominent rancher from La Vega, led troops in the 1912 revolt and was given the title of "general." He served as a deputy to the national congress between 1934 and 1942. By the 1940s, he was the second richest man in the Dominican Republic to Rafael Trujillo. By then Somosa was stealing cattle from Rodríguez' ranch. Rodríguez voted in favor of renaming the city of Santo Domingo, Ciudad Trujillo. He fled the Dominican Republic on February 1, 1946, taking a significant fortune with him.

7. José ("Don Pepe") Figueres Ferrer (1906–90) was born in San Ramón, Costa Rica, to parents who had emigrated from Spain. He possessed little formal education beyond the high school level. Figueres was in the United States between 1924 and 1928 and spent much of his time in the Boston Public Library reading. Returning to Costa Rica, he became a successful farmer and manufacturer. Figueres was expelled from Costa Rica in July 1942 for publicly criticizing the government for not protecting the property of German and Italian citizens following a U-boat attack on a United Fruit Company ship. He returned to Costa Rica in 1944 and was a founder of the Social Democratic Party (*Partido Social Democrata* —PSD). He became the militant leader of the Costa Rican left. But as Figueres said, "You can't make chocolate [rebellion] without cacao [weapons]" (Ameringer, *The Caribbean Legion*, 64). So, in 1947 he signed the "Caribbean Pact" along with other regional dissidents which called for the overthrow of the Caribbean dictators and promised the weapons to do so. Figueres served as President of Costa Rica between 1953 and 1958 and again between 1970 and 1974.

8. Ameringer, *The Caribbean Legion*, 66–67; Charles D. Ameringer, *Don Pepe* (Albuquerque: University of New Mexico, 1978), 40.

9. Helen Schooley, *Conflict in Central America* (Harlow: Longman, 1987), 49–50; Raymond Estep, *The Latin American Nations Today* (Maxwell Air Force Base, Ala.: Air University, 1964), 133; "Coffee-Country Revolt," *Newsweek* 23 (April 17, 1944): 65.

10. "Coffee-Country Revolt," 65.

11. "El Salvador Coup Said to Oust Ruler," New York *Times* (April 4, 1944), 5; Patricia Parkman, *Insurrectionary Civil Strikes in Latin America 1931–61* (Cambridge: Albert Einstein Institution, 1990), 33.

12. "Salvadoreans Name Menendez President," New York *Times* (May 10, 1944), 2; "El Salvador Elated as Ex-ruler Leaves," New York *Times* (May 12, 1944), 3; "El Salvador Still Torn," New York *Times* (May 17, 1944), 3.

13. "Revolt Casts Out Salvador Regime," New York *Times* (October 22, 1944), 30; "Guatemala Blocks the Funds of Ubico," New York *Times* (October 26, 1944), 9; "Anti-Revolution Treaty," New York *Times* (October 31, 1944), 5; Estep, *The Latin American Nations*, 134.

14. Keesing's Contemporary Archives VII (1948–50), p. 8911A.

15. "El Salvador Revolt Deposes President," New York *Times* (December 15, 1948), 1; "Junta Takes Over in San Salvador," New York *Times* (December 16, 1948), 19; "El Salvador Opens 3-Day Poll Today," New York *Times* (March 26, 1950), 17; "El Salvador's Election," New York *Times* (April 24, 1950), 9.

16. Dana Munro, *The Latin American Republics* (New York: Appleton-Century-Crofts, 1950), 450–81; Dana Munro, *The Five Republics of Central America* (New York: Oxford University Press, 1918), 50–54; Medardo Mejía, *El movimiento obrero en la revolution de octubre* (Guatemala: Tipografía Nacional, 1949), 86–87.

17. Mejía, *El movimiento obrero*, 47–51; Parkman, *Insurrectionary Civil Strikes*, 34–35.

18. "Guatemalan Students Out," New York *Times* (June 24, 1944), 7; "Guatemala under Military Junta as Unrest Forces President Out," New York *Times* (July 2, 1944), 7; Parkman, *Insurrectionary Civil Strikes*, 34–35.

19. Mejía, *El movimiento obrero*, 72; Parkman, *Insurrectionary Civil Strikes*, 35.

20. "Guatemalan Disquiet Believed Mounting," New York *Times* (August 28, 1944), 12; "Candidate Arrives in Guatemala," New York *Times* (September 3, 1944), 7; "Latin Publisher Buried," New York *Times* (October 3, 1944), 8.

21. Jacobo Arbenz Guzmán (1913–71) was born in Quezaltenango. His father was a Swiss immigrant and his mother a Guatemalan. He graduated from the *Escuela Politécnica*, the military officers' academy, in 1935. In 1939 he married into a wealthy Salvadoran family, which allegedly had Communist connections. Arbenz reached the rank of captain in the Guatemalan army before resigning and leaving Guatemala due to dissatisfaction with the Ponce regime. His last assignment was as cadet corps commander at the *Escuela Politécnica*. He was appointed Minister of Defense in 1945. He conspired with President Arévalo to assassinate General Arana.

22. Francisco Javier Arana (1905–49) was the commanding officer of the elite *Guardia de Honor* tank corps stationed in the capital in 1944. Between 1945 and 1949 he was the chief of the Guatemalan armed forces and suppressed a number of Conservative plots against the Arévalo government. He and Arbenz developed a rivalry for the 1950 presidential elections, Arana courting Conservatives and Arbenz Liberals. Arana was accused of plotting a take over of the government and was shot on July 18, 1949, while resisting arrest by Arbenz' partisans.

23. Juan José Arévalo Bermejo (1904–90), born in Taxisco, Santa Rosa, graduated from the *Escuela Normal* in 1922. Initially working in the Ministry of Education, he voluntarily went into exile in Argentina, where he received a doctorate in philosophy in 1934. Arévalo taught at La Plata University. Arévalo was an excellent pamphleteer and very anti-United States. He returned to Guatemala in 1944 to campaign for the presidency which he won in December. Arévalo's two foreign policy goals were to create a Central American federation and to eliminate right-wing dictators. He conspired with his hand-picked successor, General Arbenz, to assassinate General Arana in 1949. Following his term as president that ended in 1950, Arévalo resided in Mexico. In 1962 he announced that he would run for president. On March 29, 1963, he attempted to secretly cross into Guatemala; this precipitated the military to overthrow President Ydígoras Fuentes, thereby denying Arévalo the possibility to run for office. Finally, Arévalo returned to Guatemala City during the 1980s. Six feet tall and two hundred pounds, he projected a powerful image.

24. "Guatemala Ousts Regime in Revolt," New York *Times* (October 21, 1944), 5.

25. Mejía, *El movimiento obrero*, 88.

26. Julio Alberto Yon, "Guatemala, A Sad and Bloody Case of Insurgency" (Research paper, Naval War College, Newport, R.I., 1990), 3.

27. Fitzhugh Turner, "Communism in the Caribbean," *New York Herald Tribune* (February 8, 1950), 1. This was the first of a five-part series of articles that were published between February 8 and 13, all by the same title.

28. Tulio Halperín Donghi, *The Contemporary History of Latin America* (Durham, N.C.: Duke University Press, 1993), 239; *Jane's Fighting Ships* (London: various publishers, since 1898), 1950–51: 176.

29. Juan Bosch Gaviño (1909–), born in La Vega, the Dominican Republic, published a collection of short stories in 1933. He was jailed in 1934 for suspicion of taking part in an assassination plot against Rafael Trujillo. Freed the next year, he edited the newspaper *Listín Diario*. Bosch fled the Dominican Republic in 1937. He resided in Cuba, Costa Rica, Bolivia, Chile, and Venezuela, making numerous political contacts. He was a cofounder of the Dominican Revolutionary Party (*Partido Revolucionario Dominicano*—PRD), during 1939 in Havana, Cuba. Between 1948 and 1952 he served as Cuban President Carlos Prío Socarrás' private secretary.

30. Ameringer, *The Caribbean Legion*, 32–35.

31. ibid., 35–36.

32. ibid., 36; Ameringer, *Don Pepe*, 39.

33. Ameringer, *The Caribbean Legion*, 36–42.

34. ibid., 42–46.

35. ibid., 53–55.

36. ibid., 55–56.

37. Miguel Angel Ramírez (unk.) was vice consul in New York in 1930 when Trujillo seized power and accepted exile rather than return to the Dominican Republic. He worked as a merchant and wholesaler before becoming involved in the anti-Trujillo movement.

38. Ameringer, *The Caribbean Legion*, 57–62.

39. Schooley, *Conflict*, 73–74; Estep, *The Latin American Nations*, 191; Halperín, *The Contemporary History*, 239; La Feber, *Inevitable Revolutions*, 103.

40. Ameringer, *Don Pepe*, 50; "Arguello Takes Nicaragua Office," New York *Times* (May 2, 1947), 5.

41. Eduardo Crawley, *Dictators Never Die* (New York: St. Martin's Press, 1979), 101–6.

42. Crawley, *Dictators*, 106–8; "Nicaraguan Panic Is Laid to Somoza," New York *Times* (September 25, 1947), 21.

43. Olander, "Costa Rica," 467; Schooley, *Conflict*, 100; Ameringer, *Don Pepe*, 43–47; "Costa Rican Vote Clouded by 'Fraud,'" New York *Times* (February 10, 1948), 17; "Ulate is Declared Costa Rican Victor," New York *Times* (February 29, 1948), 9; "Costa Rica Annuls Presidential Election; Ulate Disappears as Supporter is Killed," New York *Times* (March 2, 1948), 15.

44. Ameringer, *Don Pepe*, 50.

45. Ameringer, *The Caribbean Legion*, 68–71; Ameringer, *Don Pepe*, 48–51; Schooley, *Conflict*, 100.

46. Ameringer, *The Caribbean Legion*, 71–72; Ameringer, *Don Pepe*, 53.

47. Olander, "Costa Rica," 476; Ameringer, *Don Pepe*, 53; Hagedorn, *Central American and Caribbean Air Forces*, 126.

48. Robert G. Breene Jr., ed., *Latin American Political Yearbook 1997* (New Brunswick: Transaction Publishers, 1998), 86.

49. Hagedorn, *Central American and Caribbean Air Forces*, 124; Ameringer, *Don Pepe*, 56–57; Charles D. Ameringer, *The Democratic Left in Exile* (Coral Gables: University of Miami Press, 1974), 72–74.

50. Ameringer, *The Caribbean Legion*, 72–73; Ameringer, *Don Pepe*, 54–58.

51. Olander, "Costa Rica," 473; Ameringer, *The Caribbean Legion*, 74; Kyle Longley, "Peaceful Costa Rica, The First Battleground: The United States and the Costa Rican Revolution of 1948," *The Americas* 50: 2; 149–75 (October 1993), 171.

52. Olander, "Costa Rica," 479–80; Ameringer, *Don Pepe*, 62–63.

53. Olander, "Costa Rica," 475; Herbert K. Tillema, *International Armed Conflict Since 1945* (Boulder, Colo.: Westview Press, 1991), 22–23; Ameringer, *The Caribbean Legion*, 75; "Picado Surrenders in Costa Rica Seen," New York *Times* (April 17, 1948), 1; "Costa Rica Leader Sees Big Job Ahead," New York *Times* (April 27, 1948), 14.

54. Alberto Carbone, "Duelo en la frontera: Figueres vs Somoza," *Defensa* 80: 60–62 (December 1984), 61.

55. Ameringer, *The Caribbean Legion*, 87.

56. Crawley, *Dictators*, 109–10; Schooley, *Conflict*, 100; Ameringer, *The Caribbean Legion*, 88–93.

57. Ameringer, *The Caribbean Legion*, 95–99.

58. ibid., 99.

59. ibid., 99–104.

60. ibid., 104–9; John Dienst and Dan Hagedorn, *North American F-51 Mustangs in Latin American Air Force Service* (Arlington, Tex.: Aerofax, 1985), 3.

61. Crawley, *Dictators*, 112–13; Ameringer, *Don Pepe*, 121–22; Dienst and Hagedorn, *North American F-51 Mustangs*, 12–13; Carbone, "Duelo," 62.

62. Ameringer, *Don Pepe*, 122–23; Dienst and Hagedorn, *North American F-51 Mustangs*, 11–13.

63. Crawley, *Dictators*, 99, 113; Carbone, "Duelo," 62; Estep, *The Latin American Nations*, 80.

64. Cordell Hull, *The Memoirs of Cordell Hull*, 2 vols. (New York: Macmillan, 1948), 1: 334; William W. Bishop Jr., *International Law*, 3d ed. (Boston: Little, Brown, 1971), 339–42; Gerhard von Glahn, *Law among Nations* (New York: Macmillan, 1965), 467.

65. Bureau of Public Affairs, Historical Office, "Historical Study: U.S. Policy toward Latin America, 1933–1974" (Washington, D.C.: U.S. Department of State, 1975), 34–39; Ameringer, *The Caribbean Legion*, 137–40.

66. Spruille Braden (1894–1978) was educated at Yale University and between 1912 and 1919 he worked for American mining companies in Chile. Between 1935 and 1939 he served as chairman of the American delegation to the Chaco Peace Conference. Braden served as the U.S. ambassador to Colombia (1939–42), to Cuba (1942–45), and to Argentina (May–October 1945). He was recalled from Argentina after publicly criticizing presidential candidate Juan Perón. Beginning in late 1945, Braden served as the Assistant Secretary of State for Inter-American Affairs, before resigning in June 1947. He then served as a consultant to many companies with Latin American interests. In 1961 Braden favored the invasion of Cuba. By 1963 he was on the national council of the John Birch Society. He opposed the return of the canal to Panama.

67. Ameringer, *The Caribbean Legion*, 11–26, 137–40.

CHAPTER NINETEEN

1. Enrique Volta Gaona, *La revolución de 1947* (Asunción: Editora Litocolor, 1982), 39–44.

2. Dennis M. Hanratty and Sandra W. Meditz, *Paraguay: A Country Study* (Washington, D.C.: Government Printing Office, 1990), 39; Carlos Borche, *Campos de concentración en América* (Montevideo: Comité Nacional de Ayuda al Pueblo Paraguayo, 1945), 81.

3. In December 1928 a relatively unknown Maj. Rafael Franco (1897–1973) launched an unprovoked attack against the Bolivian *fortín* Vanguardia in protest of what he believed to be Paraguay's lack of preparation for war (see chapter 11). This action brought him to national attention. Although relieved of command, he was soon restored when the Chaco War erupted. He held numerous important commands during the war and was among Paraguay's most distinguished officers. On February 17, 1936, he led a successful coup against the liberal President Ayala and his primary supporter, Gen. José Estigarribia. Shortly after achieving power, Franco sold a significant quantity of worn-out weapons (including the notorious Spanish "*mataparaguayo*" [Paraguayan killers] Mauser rifles) to the Swiss arms merchant

Thorvald G. Ehrlich. Many Paraguayan nationalists feared that the Chaco War had not ended the conflict, and were outraged by the sale. This sale and Franco's announced reform program, which called for the redistribution of land and the protection of workers' rights, contributed to his overthrow on August 15, 1937, by military leaders loyal to the Liberal Party. Franco was sent into exile where he formed the *Febreristas* Party. He was the political leader and symbol of the disappointed Chaco War veterans who believed that their sacrifices had not been recognized nor had they been adequately rewarded.

4. Volta Gaona, *La revolución*, 20–21.

5. Hanratty and Meditz, *Paraguay*, 40.

6. Antonio E. Gonzalez, *La rebelión de Concepción* (Buenos Aires: n.p., 1947), 109–10; Thomas, *Latin America: A History*, 338.

7. Gonzalez, *La rebelión*, 110; *The Statesman's Year-Book 1947*, 1134.

8. Smith came from an American family that had immigrated to Paraguay, and had been the commanding officer of a Paraguayan Division during the Chaco War.

9. Volta Gaona, *La revolución*, 124–29.

10. ibid., 142–47.

11. Captain Bozzano had been in charge of the construction of the two gunboats in Italy prior to the Chaco War. During the war he commanded the naval arsenal in Asuncíon that employed some 2,000 workers.

12. Volta Gaona, *La revolución*, 148–49.

13. Alfredo Stroessner Mattiauda (1912–) was the son of a German immigrant father and a Paraguayan mother. He entered the Francisco López Military Academy in 1929 and graduated after three years of study on October 1, 1932, due to the outbreak of the Chaco War. During the war, he was twice decorated for bravery, once after the Battle of Boquerón (1932), and again after the Battle of El Carmen (1934). By the end of the Chaco War, Stroessner had reached the rank of 1st lieutenant. In October 1940, at the rank of major, he was sent to Brazil for artillery training. Between 1941 and 1943 he served as a regimental aide and on a board of examiners for artillery officers. In 1943 Stroessner attended the Paraguayan Superior War School. After graduating, he served as the commanding officer of Paraguay's principal artillery unit and in 1946 was assigned to the General Staff Headquarters. In 1954 Stroessner seized the presidency and held it until 1989.

14. Volta Gaona, *La revolución*, 175–79.

15. ibid., 198–202.

16. ibid., 207–239.

17. ibid., 122–23.

18. ibid., 245–46.

19. Hanratty and Meditz, *Paraguay*, 40–41.

20. Thomas, *Latin America: A History*, 338.

21. Volta Gaona, *La revolución*, 285.

CHAPTER TWENTY

1. Germán Arciniegas, *The State of Latin America* (New York: Alfred A. Knopf, 1952), 162; Alberto Andrade Amaya, "Violencia política y conflictos internos," in *Historia de las fuerzas militares de Colombia*, 6 vols. (Bogotá: Planeta, 1993), 3: 65; John Walton, *Reluctant Rebels* (New York: Columbia University Press, 1984), 74.

2. James M. Daniel, *Rural Violence in Colombia Since 1946* (Washington, D.C.: Special Research Operations Office, American University, 1965), 25; Walton, *Reluctant Rebels*, 82–85.

3. Gary Valenza, "Colombia's Quiet War," *Strategy & Tactics* 197: 45–56 (May/June 1999), 49; Walton, *Reluctant Rebels*, 85–87.

4. Daniel, *Rural Violence*, 35–37; Arciniegas, *The State*, 158–59.

5. Finan, "Colombia," 3: 411; Valenza, "Colombia's Quiet War," 48.

6. Arciniegas, *The State*, 161–62.

7. Daniel, *Rural Violence*, 63, 153, 157.

8. Andrade, "Violencia política," 3: 66–73.

9. Walton, *Reluctant Rebels*, 90–91; Andrade, "Violencia política," 3: 74.

10. Andrade, "Violencia política," 3: 66–71; John D. Martz, *Colombia: A Contemporary Political Survey* (Chapel Hill, N.C.: University of North Carolina Press, 1962), 61; Jeanne Kuebler, "Smoldering Colombia," *Editorial Research Reports* 11: 5, 562–82 (August 1965), 575.

11. Walton, *Reluctant Rebels*, 91; E. J. Hobsbawn, "The Revolutionary Situation in Colombia," *The World Today* 19: 6; 248–58 (June 1963), 250.

12. Martz, *Colombia*, 49.

13. ibid., 96.

14. Carleton Beals, *Latin America: World in Revolution* (New York: Abelard-Schuman, 1963), 182.

15. Martz, *Colombia*, 116.

16. Daniel, *Rural Violence*, 68–72; Valenza, "Colombia's Quiet War," 50; Hobsbawn, "The Revolutionary Situation," 250–51.

17. Gustavo Rojas Pinilla (1900–75) graduated from the Colombian military academy in 1920 as a lieutenant of artillery. He voluntarily left the service to study civil engineering in the United States. Rojas returned to Colombia and rejoined the army during the Leticia Conflict. During the 1940s he commanded the outpost at Tarapacá and later the Palacé Battalion. He then served as subdirector of the Superior War College and the Chief of the Department of Civil Aviation within the Colombian Armed Forces. Rojas commanded the 1st and 3rd Brigades and was promoted to general in October 1949. He served as the subchief of the Inter-American Defense Board in Washington and became the Commanding General of the Armed Forces in November 1952, a post created by President Gómez in April 1951. However, friction soon developed between the two men.

18. W. O. Galbraith, *Colombia* (London: Oxford University Press, 1966), 152; Andrade, "Violencia política," 3: 87.

19. Andrade, "Violencia política," 3: 94–95; Martz, *Colombia*, 177; Daniel, *Rural Violence*, 214; United States, Department of the Army, *Special Warfare Area Handbook for Colombia* (Washington, D.C.: Foreign Areas Study Division, The American University, 1961), 367.

20. Galbraith, *Colombia*, 153; Harry Bernstein, *Venezuela and Colombia* (Englewood Cliffs, N.J.: Prentice-Hall, 1965), 141.

21. Lieuwen, *Arms*, 89; Valenza, "Colombia's Quiet War," 50.

22. Andrade, "Violencia política," 3: 96; Germán Guzmán Campos, Orlando Fals Borda, and Eduardo Umaña Luna, *La violencia en Colombia*, vol. 1, *Monografías Sociologicas* No.

12 (Bogotá: Facultad de Sociologia, Universidad Nacional, 1962), 97; Walton, *Reluctant Rebels*, 91, 97.

23. Finan, "Colombia (1948 until 1958)," 412; J. León Helguera, "The Changing Role of the Military in Colombia," *Journal of Inter-American Studies* 3: 3, 351–57 (July 1961), 356; Daniel, *Rural Violence*, 96, 214.

24. Andrade, "Violencia política," 3: 107–10; Hobsbawn, "The Revolutionary Situation," 251; Walton, *Reluctant Rebels*, 97.

25. Prior to the plebiscite, the agreement was changed to require passage of all legislation in Congress and lesser legislative bodies by the vote of a two-thirds majority.

26. The plebiscite also called for civil service reform, the granting of political equality to women, and the allocation of not less than 10 percent of the national budget to public education.

27. Martz, *Colombia*, 277–78.

28. Valenza, "Colombia's Quiet War," 50.

29. ibid.

30. ibid., 51.

31. Finan, "Colombia," 411; Arciniegas, *The State*, 155.

CHAPTER TWENTY-ONE

1. Hubert Herring, *A History of Latin America* (New York: Alfred A. Knopf, 1955), 494; Arciniegas, *The State*, 187–88, 195.

2. The Inter-American Defense Board was created by the Rio de Janeiro meeting of American ministers in January 1942. The board's mission is to study and recommend measures necessary to defend the hemisphere. The board meets in Washington, D.C., and the first meeting took place on March 30, 1942.

3. Raymond Estep, "United States Military Aid to Latin America," (Maxwell Air Force Base, Ala.: Air University, 1966), 20–21; Roger L. Buck, "The Role of the Naval Mission in United States–Latin American Relations," (Newport, R.I.: M.A. thesis, Naval War College, 1967), 27.

4. F. Parkinson, *Latin America, The Cold War, & The World Powers* (Thousand Oaks, Calif.: Sage Publications, 1974), 21–35; John Lewis Gaddis, *Strategy of Containment* (Oxford: Oxford University Press, 1982), 89–126; Paul Kennedy, *Rise and Fall of Great Powers* (New York: Vintage Books, 1987), 382–83; LaFeber, *The American Age*, 528–31.

5. Russell W. Ramsey, "The Colombian Battalion in Korean and Suez," *Journal of Inter-American Studies* 9: 4; 541–60 (October 1967), 552.

6. *The Statesman's Year-Book 1950*, 874; U.S. House of Representatives, Committee on Foreign Affairs, *Military Assistance Programs*, Part 2 (Washington, D.C.: U.S. Government Printing Office, 1976), 390.

7. *The Statesman's Year-Book 1950*, 874; *Jane's Fighting Ships 1950–51*, 160.

8. Arciniegas, *The State*, 191–94.

9. "Colombian Frigates in the Korean War," *ONI Review* 18: 525–50 (December 1953), 548–50; *The History of the United Nations Forces*, 5 vols. (Seoul: The Ministry of National Defense, n.d.), 3: 175–76.

10. Alberto Ruiz Novoa, *Enseñanzas de la campaña de Corea: aplicables al ejército de Colombia* (Bogotá: Antares, 1956), 170.

11. Ruiz, *Enseñanzas*, 170–71; *History of the United Nations Forces*, 3: 175–76.

12. "Colombian Frigates," 548–50; Ruiz, *Enseñanzas*, 175–76.

13. *History of the United Nations Forces*, 3: 176–77; Román, *Proas*, 104–7.

14. "Colombian Frigates," 548–50; *History of the United Nations Forces*, 3: 178–79; Román, *Proas*, 106–8.

15. Alvaro Valencia Tovar, "Participación en fuerzas de las Naciones Unidas," in *Historia de las fuerzas militares de Colombia*, 3: 174; Ramsey, "The Colombian Battalion," 547; U.S. House, Foreign Affairs, *Military Assistance*, 390.

16. Ruiz, *Enseñanzas*, 150–51; Valencia, "Participación," 3: 176–86; Alberto Carbone, "Corea: la saga del batallón Colombia," *Defensa* 34: 58–61 (February 1981), 61; Ramsey, "The Colombian Battalion," 547.

17. Ruiz, *Enseñanzas*, 150–61; Valencia, "Participación," 3: 193.

18. Ruiz, *Enseñanzas*, 161–62; Valencia, "Participación," 3: 199; Carbone, "Corea," 61.

19. Ruiz, *Enseñanzas*, 162–64; Carbone, "Corea," 61; Ramsey, "The Colombian Battalion," 547–48.

20. U.S. House, Foreign Affairs, *Military Assistance*, 408.

21. John Child, *Unequal Alliance: The Inter-American Military System, 1939–1978* (Boulder, Colo.: Westview Press, 1980), 115–17; J. D. Hereford, R. S. Hansen, J. S. Rose, R. W. Richardson, and M. C. Jackson, "United States Military Assistance to Latin America" (Newport, R.I.: Naval War College, Groups Study, 1969), 30–31; J. Lloyd Mecham, *A Survey of United States-Latin American Relations* (Boston: Houghton Mifflin, 1965), 336.

22. Ramsey, "The Colombian Battalion," 554–55; Carbone, "Corea," 61.

23. Valencia, "Participación," 3: 201–3; Ramsey, "The Colombian Battalion," 548.

CHAPTER TWENTY-TWO

1. One hundred thirty-five schools were built, many for the rural Indians. The printing of classic writings was subsidized. And seventeen hospitals were constructed.

2. "Revolt Breaks Out in Guatemala after Shooting of Army's Leader," New York *Times* (July 19, 1949), 1; "Guatemala Calls on Reserves' Help," New York *Times* (July 20, 1949), 14; "Guatemala Rising Reported Quelled," New York *Times* (July 21, 1949), 17.

3. Yon, "Guatemala," 3.

4. Edward G. Miller, Assistant Secretary for Inter-American Affairs, testified before Congress in 1951, "I think it is probably futile to discuss whether or not Arévalo is a Communist. I think it would be hard to tell. Maybe he was not when he was installed as President. But, in any event, he became either a captive or the associate of this Communist-dominated labor movement, which from then on was practically the sole political force in the country." U.S. House of Representatives, Committee on Foreign Affairs, *Selective Executive Session Hearings of the Committee, 1951–56*, 16: 398.

5. In 1952 the U.S. State Department's assessment of Arbenz concluded: "He is an army officer. Of course, he is subject to control by the Communists, but he probably is not considered a Communist." U.S. House, F.A., *Selective Executive Session*, 16: 405.

6. Richard G. Massock, "The Pink Shows through Guatemala's Denial," *Washington Post* (November 15, 1953), 3B.

7. U.S. House, F.A., *Selective Executive Session*, 16: 463.

8. Guatemala also voted against a resolution favoring "the guarantee of human rights and freedoms of all persons." Guatemalan diplomats explained their action was because the United States had abstained from voting against "colonialism and foreign occupation."

9. Richard H. Immerman, *The CIA in Guatemala: The Foreign Policy of Intervention* (Austin: University of Texas Press, 1982), 118–22.

10. Stephen Schlesinger and Stephen Kinzer, *Bitter Fruit: The Untold Story of the American Coup in Guatemala* (New York: Doubleday, 1982), 102–3.

11. U.S. House, F.A., *Selective Executive Session*, 16: 467. CIA agent David Atlee Phillips described Ambassador Puerifoy, "The Ambassador was a flamboyant character, the only American envoy I ever knew to carry a pistol." David Atlee Phillips, *The Night Watch* (New York: Atheneum, 1977), 52.

12. "Guatemala Says Neighbors and U.S. Plot an Invasion," New York *Times* (January 30, 1954), A1; "Charges of Intervention in Guatemala Denied," United States, Department of State, *Bulletin* (Vol. 30), 251; Parkinson, *Latin America*, 40.

13. Parkinson, *Latin America*, 40–41.

14. ibid., 41.

15. Phillips, *The Night Watch*, 44.

16. ibid., 46.

17. ibid.

18. U.S. State Dept., *Foreign Relations 1954–55*, "The Ambassador in Guatemala (Puerifoy) to the Department of State" (June 27, 1954), 4: 1189–91.

19. Phillips, *The Night Watch*, 48.

20. Parkinson, *Latin America*, 43–46.

21. U.S. State Dept., *Foreign Relations 1954–55*, "Memorandum by the Director of the Central Intelligence Agency (Dulles) to the President (June 20, 1954)," 4: 1176.

22. Phillips, *The Night Watch*, 52.

23. ibid., 34–35; Loveman, *For la Patria*, 156–57.

24. Phillips, *The Night Watch*, 53.

CHAPTER TWENTY-THREE

1. Hudson and Hanratty, *Bolivia,* 30; Robert J. Alexander, *The Bolivian National Revolution* (New Brunswick, N.J.: Rutgers University Press, 1958), 23–25; Robert J. Alexander, *Bolivia: Past, Present, and Future of Its Politics* (New York: Praeger Publishers, 1982), 64–66.

2. Paul van Lindert and Otto Verkoren, *Bolivia in Focus* (London: Latin American Research Bureau, 1994), 16; Herbert S. Klein, *Bolivia* (Oxford: Oxford University Press, 1992), 197; Alexander, *The Bolivian National Revolution*, 7, 13–14, 42.

3. Lindert and Verkoren, *Bolivia*, 17–18; Luis Peñaloza C., *Historia del movimiento nacionalista revolucionario 1941–1952* (La Paz: Editorial Libreria "Juventud," 1963), 21; Richard W. Patch, "Peasantry and National Revolution: Bolivia," in *Nationalism in Latin America*, ed. by Samuel L. Baily (New York: Alfred A. Knopf, 1971), 163–64.

4. Peñaloza, *Historia*, 55–57; Arciniegas, *The State*, 126–30; William Brill, *Military Intervention in Bolivia: The Overthrew of Paz Estenssoro and the MNR* (Washington, D.C.: Institute for the Comparative Study of Political Systems, 1967), 7–8; "Bolivia: The Restrained Revolution," 126.

5. "Falange" is based on the Greek word "phalanx" which means "a group united for a common purpose." Typically the term has a military association.

6. Robert Barton, *A Short History of the Republic of Bolivia* (La Paz: Editorial Los Amigos del Libro, 1968), 247–48; Alexander, *The Bolivian National Revolution*, 27–30; Brill, *Military Intervention*, 6.

7. Herbert S. Klein, "David Toro and the Establishment of 'Military Socialism'" *Hispanic American Historical Review* 45: 1; 25–52 (February 1965), 35.

8. Cole Blasier, "The United States, Germany, and the Bolivian Revolutionaries (1941–1946)," *Hispanic American Historical Review* 52: 1; 26–54 (February 1972), 29–30; Humberto Vazquez Machicado, José de Mesa, and Teresa Gisbert, *Manual de la historia de Bolivia* (La Paz: Gisbert y Cia., S.A., 1963), 436–37; René Canelas López, *Teoría del motín y las sediciones en Bolivia* (La Paz: Editorial Los Amigos del Libro, 1983), 177–80; Alexander, *The Bolivian National Revolution*, 26; Valentin Abecia Baldivieso, *Breve historia de Bolivia* (Caracas: Academia Nacional de la Historia, 1985), 176.

9. Germán Busch (1904–39) was born in the department of Santa Cruz; his father was German and his mother Bolivian. He attended the Military Academy between 1922 and 1927, graduating as a second lieutenant of cavalry. In 1929 Gen. Hans Kundt brought him into the general staff (*Estado Mayor General*) as an aide. The bond between the two may be judged by the fact that they shared a secret written code. During the Chaco War Busch fought at many of the major battles including Boquerón (September 1932), Alihuata (October 1932), El Carmen (November 1934), and Picuiba (December 1934), and rose in rank from lieutenant to lieutenant colonel. Busch helped plan the defense of the Camiri oil fields. He was very popular among the soldiers. In May 1936 Busch played an important role in the overthrow of President José Luis Tejada and was appointed Chief of Staff (second in command), of the Bolivian army. He was also the Supreme Chief of the Legion of Ex-Combatants, the *Radépa*. His death has been attributed to suicide caused by alchohol, an unhappy love affair, and political pressure, as well as to murder.

10. Canelas, *Teoría del motín*, 185–86; Alexander, *The Bolivian National Revolution*, 26–28; Jonathan Kelley and Herbert S. Klein, *Revolution and the Rebirth of Inequality* (Berkeley: University of California Press, 1981), 91–92.

11. Peñaloza, *Historia*, 33–44; Alexander, *The Bolivian National Revolution*, 28–29; Vazquez et al., *Manual*, 438–40.

12. Jerry W. Knudson, "The Impact of the Catavi Mine Massacre of 1942 on Bolivian Politics and Public Opinion," *The Americas* 26: 3; 254–76 (January 1970), 254–55; Peñaloza, *Historia*, 52; Alexander, *Bolivia*, 70–71; Klein, *Bolivia*, 216–17.

13. Gualberto Villarroel López (1908–46) was born in the department of Cochabamba. Villarroel fought in the Chaco War and became a member of the secret *Radépa* lodge. Villarroel taught mathematics at the military academy where he gained popularity. As a major he was appointed subchief of the General Staff, a position normally held by a more senior officer. Villarroel became a protegé of German Minister Ernest Wendler whom Peñaranda expelled in 1941 for allegedly attempting to organize a coup d' etat against the Bolivian government.

14. Víctor Paz Estenssoro (1907–), born into a prominent family from the department of Tarija in the south, acquired a law degree from the University of La Paz in 1927. During the late 1920s and early 1930s, he held minor government jobs and worked as a professor of economics at the University of La Paz. Paz Estenssoro fought in the Chaco War as a warrant officer (*suboficial*), in an artillery battery. In 1941 he was a cofounder of the MNR. Elected to Congress, he won notoriety for his speeches following the Catavi mining massacre.

15. Peñaloza, *Historia*, 58–73; William S. Stokes, "The 'Revolucion Nacional' and the MNR in Bolivia," *Inter-American Economics Affairs* 12: 4; 28–53 (Spring 1969), 29; G. Earl Sanders, "The Quiet Experiment in American Diplomacy," *The Americas* 33: 1; 25–49 (July 1976), 29; Alexander, *The Bolivian National Revolution*, 34–35.

16. Arciniegas, *The State*, 123–24, 133–34. Today the lamppost bears a plaque honoring Villarroel and members of the presidential guard are posted at the spot.

17. Stokes, "The 'Revolucion Nacional,'" 31–32; Vazquez et al., *Manual*, 440–41; Canelas, *Teoría del motín*, 209–13; Alexander, *Bolivia*, 72–75; Alexander, *The Bolivian National Revolution*, 38.

18. Alexander, *The Bolivian National Revolution*, 39; Hudson and Hanratty, *Bolivia*, 34.

19. Hernán Siles Zuazo (1914–) was born in La Paz and his father had been President of Bolivia between 1926 and 1930. Siles Zuazo studied at the American Institute and the National University, both in La Paz. He was a cofounder of the MNR and was the vice presidential candidate of the party in 1952.

20. Juan Lechín Oquendo (1914–), son of a Lebanese salesman and an Indian mother, earned acclaim as a soccer player during his youth. He attended the *Instituto Americano* in La Paz. He became a miner and when less than twenty years of age was a founding member of the Bolivian Federation of Miners (*Federación Sindical de Trabajadores Mineros de Bolivia*—FSTMB). He fought in the Chaco War. In the mid-1940s he joined the MNR and in 1947 Lechín was elected a senator by the miners. Lechín was a Marxist. He was deported several times between 1947 and 1952.

21. Stokes, "The 'Revolucion Nacional,'" 32; Alexander, *The Bolivian National Revolution*, 39–40; Canelas, *Teoría del motín*, 219–23; Arciniegas, *The State*, 139.

22. Peñaloza, *Historia*, 257. See Klein, *Bolivia*, 224–25; Canelas, *Teoría del motín*, 223–24; Alexander, *Bolivia*, 78–79; Alexander, *The Bolivian National Revolution*, 40–41.

23. Mariano Baptista Gumucio, *Historia contemporánea de Bolivia 1930–1978*, 2d ed. (La Paz: Gisbert & Cia. S.A., 1978), 193; Alexander, *The Bolivian National Revolution*, 4, 145; *The Statesman's Year-Book 1953*, 816.

24. Arciniegas, *The State*, 122.

25. Peñaloza, *Historia*, 257.

26. ibid., 258–59; Brill, *Military Intervention*, 11.

27. Brill, *Military Intervention*, 12.

28. Peñaloza, *Historia*, 261–64; Canelas, *Teoría del motín*, 225–27; Brill, *Military Intervention*, 12.

29. Humberto Torres Ortíz (unk.) served as the commander of the 7th Division stationed in Roberé. Torres was appointed commander of the army in mid-1951.

30. Brill, *Military Intervention*, 11.

31. ibid., 12–13.

32. Peñaloza, *Historia*, 265–68.

33. ibid., 271–72; Brill, *Military Intervention*, 13–14; Hudson and Hanratty, *Bolivia*, 35.

34. Brill, *Military Intervention*, 14.

35. Following the revolution, Seleme emerged from the Chilean Embassy and claimed to be the head of the new government. The MNR brushed him aside and made him ambassador to Chile. Alexander, *Bolivia*, 81; Peñaloza, *Historia*, 271–78; Alexander, *The Bolivian National Revolution*, 44.

36. Peñaloza, *Historia*, 278–80; Brill, *Military Intervention*, 14; Alexander, *The Bolivian National Revolution*, 44.

37. Patch, "Peasantry," 124.

38. Alexander, *The Bolivian National Revolution*, 271. He adds, "On April 9, 1952, there began in Bolivia one of the major Latin American revolutions of the twentieth century. In some ways it reversed the course of Bolivian history since the coming of the Spanish conquistadores early in the sixteenth century." Alexander, *Bolivia*, 80.

39. Lindert and Verkoren, *Bolivia*, 19–20; Hudson and Hanratty, *Bolivia*, 35–36; Kelley and Klein, *Revolution*, 94–95.

40. Hudson and Hanratty, *Bolivia*, 35; Alexander, *Bolivia*, 93–94; Alexander, *The Bolivian National Revolution*, 142; Brill, *Military Intervention*, 15–17.

41. James V. Kohl, "National Revolution to Revolution of Restoration: Arms and Factional Politics in Bolivia," *Inter-American Economic Affairs* 39: 1; 3–30 (Summer 1985), 3.

42. Brill, *Military Intervention*, 17; Alexander, *The Bolivian National Revolution*, 47.

43. Hudson and Hanratty, *Bolivia*, 37.

44. Peñaloza, who has provided the most detailed account of the fighting, places the dead at 600 persons. Peñaloza, *Historia*, 288. See also Brill, *Military Intervention*, 14; Klein, *Bolivia*, 225.

CHAPTER TWENTY-FOUR

1. Fidel Castro (1927–) was born in the village of Biran in eastern Cuba and came from a fairly well-to-do plantation family. He was very active in student affairs at the University of Havana. Castro had the reputation of being a hothead and was unsuccessful in an attempt to become president of the student federation. In 1947 he joined an expedition that was training to overthrow Rafael Trujillo of the Dominican Republic. The plot failed, and Castro escaped arrest and returned to the university. The following year Castro headed a Cuban delegation to the anti-Colonial and anti-imperial student congress in Bogota, Colombia. Castro graduated from law school in 1950 and ran for Congress as a member of the Orthodox Party (*Partido del Pueblo Cubano—Ortodoxo*). On March 10, 1952, Fulgencio Batista executed a coup and annulled the election. Although he had a police record, prior to the July 26, 1953, attack on the Moncada Barracks, Castro was not well known throughout Cuba. Castro was sentenced to fifteen years in prison for the attack. He was released on May 15, 1955, under an amnesty to political prisoners. Following the successful revolution, Castro became Prime Minister in February 1959.

Castro is nearly six feet tall, possesses strong features, and has a commanding presence. His style is colorful and flamboyant; Castro evokes intense emotional response.

2. Raúl Castro (1931–) is in many respects the opposite of his brother Fidel. Raúl is slight in build, quiet in manner, and a man of few words. These characteristics mask the fact that he is very energetic. Raúl joined the Popular Socialist Party (*Partido Socialista Popular*), a Communist party in the early 1950s. Apparently, he kept this a secret from Fidel until the late 1950s. In 1952–53 he was a delegate to a Communist-front, international congress on the rights of youth held in Vienna, Austria. During this trip he visited Bucharest and Prague. In June 1953 he became a member of the Cuban Communist Youth and was arrested and briefly detained for carrying Communist propaganda. Raúl was sentenced to thirteen years in prison for his part in the July 26, 1953, attack on the Moncada Barracks. Following the successful revolution, he became Commander-in-Chief of the Cuban armed forces in February 1959, a position that he still holds.

3. Jules Dubois, *Fidel Castro: Rebel-Liberator or Dictator* (New York: The New Bobbs-Merrill Company, 1959), 36. Dubois was a correspondent for the *Chicago Tribune* who had close contact with the Cuban exiles in Miami during the 1950s. Also see R. Hart Phillips, *Cuba: Island of Paradox* (New York: McDowell, Obolensky, 1959), 266–67; Nathaniel Weyl, *Red Star over Cuba: The Russian Assault on the Western Hemisphere* (New York: The Devin-Adair Company, 1960), 104–5; Jay Mallin Sr., *History of the Cuban Armed Forces* (Reston, Va.: Ancient Mariner Press, 2000), 85–86.

4. Dubois, *Fidel Castro*, 38–39.

5. ibid., 26–83; Norman A. LaCarite, *Case Studies in Insurgency and Revolutionary Warfare: Cuba 1953–1959* (Washington, D.C.: American University, 1963), 87.

The date of the attack on the Moncada barracks is the origin of the term *26 de Julio* frequently adopted by Marxist guerrillas throughout Latin America as their name. The choice of the date upon which Fidel Castro carried out an unsuccessful, poorly planned attack, demonstrates the personal magnetism of the Cuban leader.

6. Howell Davies, ed., *The South American Handbook 1961* (London: Trade and Travel Publications, 1961), 817.

7. Ruben Fulgencio Batista (1901–73) was born in the town of Banes in eastern Cuba into a peasant family. Like his father, Fulencio began work as a sugar cane field laborer at 15 cents a day. After holding menial jobs, he joined the army in 1921. Batista was a soldier by day and a student by night. Leaving the army, he joined the Rural Guard (*Rural Guardia*), the branch of the army that functioned as a federal police. Batista returned to the regular army and was eventually promoted to sergeant due in large measure to the education he had earned and to hard work. Following the August 12, 1933, coup which removed Gerardo Machado from the presidency, chaotic conditions prevailed throughout Cuba. On September 4 Batista led a small number of sergeants, soldiers, and civilians in another coup. For more than six years, Batista remained the power behind the presidency. On July 14, 1940, he was elected president of Cuba. In 1944 Batista permitted free and honest elections and was voted out of office. He toured Latin America and settled in Daytona Beach, Florida. In 1948, running from Florida, Batista won a seat in the Cuban senate. He became a candidate for the presidency in 1952. Most believed that Roberto Agramonte of the Orthodox Party would win. On March 10, 1952, Batista led twenty-six men in a successful coup and seized the presidency. Following his overthrow on January 1, 1959, Batista sought haven first in the Dominican Republic and ultimately in Spain where he died.

8. Fidel Castro's defense speech was later published under the title of *History Will Absolve Me* (New York: Liberal Press, 1959).

9. Ernesto "Che" Guevara de la Serna (1928–68) was born and raised in Rosario, Argentina. His parents separated while he was young and Guevara spent most of his time with his mother, who had leftist leanings. Guevara was an asthmatic, but he did not permit this to interfere with a strenuous physical life. He studied medicine at the University of Buenos Aires. In 1952 he broke off his studies and began a transcontinental journey along with a friend. In Chile he temporarily worked as a guard for the American-owned Braden Copper Company. In Peru Che worked in a leprosarium located on the banks of the Amazon River. From there, he traveled to Colombia and Venezuela. In July and August 1952 Che spent a few weeks in the Miami, Florida, area; he remained beyond the length of his visa and was asked to leave. Guevara returned to Argentina and completed his medical degree in March 1953. In order to avoid conscription into the Argentine army, Guevara traveled to Bolivia, Peru, Ecuador, Panama, Costa Rica, and Guatemala between 1953 and 1955. While in Bolivia he worked in an agrarian reform office and later headed a leper colony near the city of Santa Cruz. In Guatemala he obtained a minor position in the agrarian reform program. When the Arbenz government fell, Guevara took refuge in the Argentine embassy. Within two months he was permitted to go to Mexico where he met the Castro brothers. Apparently, Guevara became a member of the Communist party in 1957. Che later said, "I was born in Argentina, I fought in Cuba, and I began to be a revolutionary in Guatemala." Andrew Sinclair, *Che Guevara* (New York: Viking Press, 1970), 1.

On February 7, 1959, the Cuban revolutionary government declared Guevara a Cuban citizen. Following the Cuban Revolution, Che ran Cuba's economy, first as president of the national bank (he signed the currency simply "Che") and then as Minister of Industries. He helped formulate foreign policy and helped organize and direct revolutionary warfare through-out Latin America. In late 1964 he addressed the United Nations. Then for three months, Che openly traveled throughout the world preaching revolution. Guevara's last public appearance in Cuba (or anywhere, for that matter) was in March 1965. After that he secretly went to the Congo and led a Cuban military group before going to Bolivia in 1968 where he was killed. Che's remains were exhumed from their grave in Bolivia and returned to Cuba on July 13, 1997; Fidel headed the entourage that received them. Che was buried in Santa Clara, the site of his most important victory during the Cuban Revolution.

Guevara earned the nickname "Che" from his Cuban colleagues because of his frequent use of the expression. "Che" is an Argentine colloquialism used to call a boy.

10. Wyatt MacGaffey et al., *Cuba* (New Haven: HRAF Press, 1962), 236.

11. Alberto Bayo (1892–unk.) graduated from the Spanish Academy of Infantry in 1915. During the 1920s he served in the Spanish Foreign Legion as the result of a sword duel which had not found favor with the Spanish King. Bayo saw extensive service in the air and on the ground fighting the Moors and Riffs in North Africa. He served as a colonel in the Republi-can Air Force during the Spanish Civil War. In 1936 Bayo commanded a failed Republican invasion of Majorca, one of the Balearic Islands. In 1938 he was authorized to establish a small guerrilla warfare school in Barcelona; however, it was soon overrun by the National-ists. Following the war, Bayo traveled to Cuba and then to Mexico. In 1948 he was asked by some Nicaraguans to train them in guerrilla warfare. He was rewarded for his teachings in part with the title of "general."

Following Castro's landing in Cuba, Bayo trained two more Cuban expeditions and con-ducted a fund-raising tour in the United States and Latin America to aid Castro's cause. After Castro's victory, Bayo taught guerrilla warfare in Cuba.

Bayo wrote a number of works on guerrilla warfare, including the manual *150 Questions for a Guerrilla* (Boulder, Colo.: Panther Publications, 1963).

12. MacGaffey, *Cuba*, 236; Ray Brennan, *Castro, Cuba, and Justice* (New York: Doubleday, 1959), 79–80.

13. Brennan, *Castro*, 98–99; Robert Taber, *M-26* (New York: Lyle Stuart, 1961), 56.

14. Lee Huberman and Paul Sweezy, *Cuba: Anatomy of a Revolution* (New York: Monthly Review Press, 1960), 63; Dickey Chapelle, "How Castro Won," in *Modern Guerrilla War-fare*, ed. by Franklin Mark Osanka (New York: Free Press of Glemcoe, 1962), 326–27. Dickey Chapelle was a reporter who wrote for *Life*, the *Saturday Evening Post, Reader's Digest*, and other periodicals. She accompanied Castro's rural guerrilla forces between Thanksgiving and Christmas of 1958.

15. Chapelle, "How Castro Won," 327–28.

16. ibid., 334–35; "Cuba; Caught in a War," *Time* (July 14, 1958), 29.

Che later wrote that it would have been better if the inexperienced guerrillas had been armed with single-shot weapons in order to conserve scarce ammunition. This would, how-ever, have negated the unsettling effect of the high volume of fire on government troops used late in the campaign to attack *cuartels*. Ernesto "Che" Guevara, *On Guerrilla Warfare* (New York: Frederick A. Praeger, 1961), 31.

17. Guevara, *On Guerrilla Warfare*.

18. Paul A. Jureidini et al., *Casebook on Insurgency and Revolutionary Warfare: 23 Summary Accounts* (Washington, D.C.: American University, 1962), 85.

19. Taber, *M-26*, 216.

20. *The Statesman's Year Book 1958*, ed. by S. H. Steinberg (London: Macmillan, 1958), 920; Taber, *M-26*, 60.

21. *Jane's Fighting Ships 1955–56*, 167–70; *The Statesman's Year Book 1958*, 920.

22. The *Granma* had been designed to carry eight passengers plus a small crew. Dubois, *Fidel Castro*, 138–40.

23. Dubois, *Fidel Castro*, 138.

24. The uprising in Santiago, led by Frank País, nearly succeeded. LaCarite, *Case Studies*, 49, 102; Dubois, *Fidel Castro*, 139; Mallin, *History*, 89–90.

25. Faustino Perez, "Yo vive en el Gramma," *Bohemia* 51: 2; 36–38, 178 (December 1959), 37; Mallin, *History*, 90–92.

26. Numbers vary slightly concerning those with Castro. Fermoselle, *The Evolution*, lists by name each he believes to be present during most of the important events. See also Dubois, *Fidel Castro*, 143–44; Taber, *M-26*, 66–70.

27. Che Guevara, *On Guerrilla Warfare*, 95–96.

28. Taber, *M-26*, 145–46; Phillips, *Cuba*.

29. Ernesto Guevara, "Combate de la Plata," *Verde Olivo* 2: 10; 46–49 (March 12, 1961), 47–49; Mallin, *History*, 94.

In hindsight, the U.S. Department of State wrote, "The character of the Batista regime in Cuba made a violent popular reaction almost inevitable." U.S. Dept. of State, *Cuba* (Washington, D.C.: Inter-American Series 66, Publication 7171, April 1966), 2–3.

30. Herbert L. Matthews, *The Cuban Story* (New York: George Braziller, 1961), 15–39; Jane Franklin, *Cuba and the United States* (Melbourne: Oceans Press, 1997), 16; Mallin, *History*, 95–97.

31. Guevara, "Combate," 47–49; Vincente Martínez, "Se acabo el saqueo policíaco a los comercios!" *Bohemia* 51: 3; 132 (January 18–25, 1959), 132; Ernesto Guevara, "El Refuerzo," *Verde Olivo* 2: 32; 4–6 (August 13, 1961), 4–6.

32. Phillips, *Cuba*, 331.

33. "Cuba Says Troops Slew Thirty Rebels," New York *Times* (November 16, 1957), 7; "Cuban Rebels Raid Rural Guard Post," New York *Times* (November 17, 1957), 35.

34. LaCarite, *Case Studies*, 103.

35. Régis Debray elaborates on the *foco* theory in *Revolution in the Revolution?* (New York: Monthly Review Press, 1967).

36. Chapelle, "How Castro Won," 328; Guevara, *On Guerrilla Warfare*, 95–97.

37. Mallin, "The Military," 2; Dubois, *Fidel Castro*, 150–54.

38. In the assault on the presidential palace, twenty-seven guerrillas and five soldiers died. The leader of the students who took over the radio station, José Antonio Echeverría, president of the Federation of University Students, was killed in a gun battle shortly after leaving the radio station. See Dubois, *Fidel Castro*, 152–53, 157–58; Franklin, *Cuba*, 16.

39. Franklin, *Cuba*, 16.

40. Dubois, *Fidel Castro*, 176–78; Fulgencio Batista, *Cuba Betrayed* (New York: Vantage Press, 1962), 67–68; Taber, *M-26*, 178.

41. Ramon Barquin, *Las lucha as guerrillas en Cuba: de la colonia a la Sierra Maestra* (Madrid: Plaejor, 1978), 477–83.

Ramon Barquin had attempted to organize a coup against the Batista government in April 1956 prior to Castro's landing. Barquin, who at the time was the army attaché in Washington, was arrested and imprisoned on Isla de Pinos. He was later exiled. See also Louis A. Perez, *Army Politics in Cuba 1898–1958* (Pittsburgh: University of Pittsburgh Press, 1976); "Cuba Sentences Three Rebels to Die," New York *Times* (September 27, 1957), 6; "Cuba Ousts Head of Mutiny Force," New York *Times* (September 10, 1957), 12.

42. Brennan, *Castro*, 171; Phillips, *Cuba*, 331–32; Chapelle, "How Castro Won," 328.

43. One underground member was chief clerk in the Office of Military and Air Attaché of the Cuban Embassy in the United States. In early 1957 he passed along information concerning Cuban arms purchases. This in turn was passed along to U.S. Congressman Adam Clayton Powell, who used the documentation to denounce U.S. arms shipments to Batista. Mario Llerena, *The Unsuspected Revolution* (Ithaca: Cornell University Press, 1978), 180–81; Dubois, *Fidel Castro* 212.

44. Brennan, *Castro*, 180; Special Operations Research Office, *Special Warfare Area Handbook for Cuba* (Washington, D.C.: American University, 1961), 396.

45. Phillips, *Cuba*, 291, 316–17; Brennan, *Castro*, 25–27, 64; Weyl, *Red Star*, 106.

46. Dubois, *Fidel Castro*, 281; Chapelle, "How Castro Won," 328; LaCarite, *Case Studies in Insurgency*, 84; Rene Ray Rivero, *Libertad y revolución* (n.p.: n.p., 1959), 49–53.

47. Merle Kling, "Cuba: A Case Study of a Successful Attempt to Seize Political Power by the Application of Unconventional Warfare," *The Annals of the American Academy of Political and Social Science* 341; 42–52 (May 1962), 48–49. A number of countries did take advantage of the opportunity to sell munitions to Cuba. The principal ones were the Dominican Republic, Nicaragua, and Great Britain. "Cuba," *Hispanic American Report* 11: 4; 202–5 (April 1958), 203; "Cuba," *Hispanic American Report* 11: 9; 494–98 (September 1958), 496–97; "Cuba," *Hispanic American Report* 11: 10; 550–53 (November 1958), 552; "Cuba," *Hispanic American Report* 11: 12; 668–71 (December 1958), 670–71.

48. Dubois, *Fidel Castro*, 244.

49. Rivero, *Libertad*, 50; MacGaffey, *Cuba*, 244; Taber, *M-26*, 221. Chapelle states, "I came to two conclusions about the curious B-26 performance: First, the claims of the pilots at their subsequent trials that they did everything short of court-martial to avoid killing noncombatants are entirely valid. . . . Second, the psychological impact of the B-26 operations on the people of rural Cuba will be a major barrier to friendly U.S.-Cuban relations for generations to come." Chapelle, "How Castro Won," 331, 333.

50. Chapelle, "How Castro Won," 329.

51. Dubois, *Fidel Castro*, 211.

52. MacGaffey et al., *Cuba*, 244; Dubois, *Fidel Castro*, 254. The official Communist Party newspaper stated that future attempts would also fail if the guerrilla movement continued to ignore Communist participation in policy formulation. Theodore Draper, *Castro's Revolution: Myths and Realities* (New York: Frederick A. Praeger, 1962), 13.

53. Rivero, *Libertad*, 58–59; Brennan, *Castro*, 227–31.

54. Rivero, *Libertad*, 54–56; Taber, *M-26*, 265–68; Dubois, *Fidel Castro*, 287–89.

55. Rivero, *Libertad*, 58–59.

56. ibid., 51, 60–61; Dubois, *Fidel Castro*, 284.

57. Taber, *M-26*, 270; Batista, *Cuba Betrayed*, 82–83.

58. MacGaffey et al., *Cuba*, 244; Dubois, *Fidel Castro*, 282; LaCarite, *Case Studies*, 81–82.

59. Batista, *Cuba Betrayed*, 81–83; Taber, *M-26*, 251–56.

60. Dubois, *Fidel Castro*, 274–75; Taber, *M-26*, 260, 274–75; Mallin, *History*, 101–2.

61. Costa Rican President José Figueres gave the arms to Castro. In March 1958 a shipment was delivered by a Costa Rican National Airlines aircraft. Its cargo was 125,000 rounds of ammunition, mortars and shells, approximately thirty machine guns and submachine guns, plus Mauser rifles. LaCarite, *Case Studies*, 117. In November of that year, President Wolfgang Larrazábal sent a planeload of arms directly to the Sierra Maestra. Llerena, *Unsuspected Revolution*, 311–12.

62. Camilo Cienfuegos (1931–59), born into a poor Havana family, earned an eighth grade education and received some informal education from a family acquaintance who was a Communist. In 1945 Cienfuegos joined an anti-Fascist group. In 1947 Cienfuegos was a member of the baseball team that won the national championship. He worked at a variety of jobs including sculpting before traveling to the United States where he lived for a short time. Cienfuegos joined Castro's group in Mexico and was a member of the expedition that sailed to Cuba on board the *Granma* in late 1956. He rose to the rank of *comandante*. Cienfuegos disappeared while flying solo from Camagüey to Havana in October 1959; no trace of the wreckage was found. Communists and anti-Communists accused each other of having assassinated Cienfuegos. Like Fidel, Camilo was an imposing figure. He was handsome and possessed red hair. He was athletic and quick of wit.

63. Dubois, *Fidel Castro*, 302–4.

64. ibid., 303–4.

65. Batista, *Cuba Betrayed*, 84–85, 94; Rivero, *Libertad*, 121; Dubois, *Fidel Castro*, 303–4.

66. Rivero, *Libertad*, 120. Batista alleged that the guerrillas bribed their way across the island. Mallin also supports these claims. Batista, *Cuba Betrayed*, 86–87; Mallin, *History*, 103–4.

67. Taber, *M-26*, 275–76; Dubois, *Fidel Castro*, 312.

68. Neill Macaulay, "Cuban Rebel Army: A Numerical Survey," *Hispanic American Historical Review* 58: 2; 284–95 (May 1978), 288–90.

69. Taber, *M-26*, 278.

70. Chapelle, "How Castro Won," 331; Taber, *M-26*, 278; R. Hart Phillips, "Castro's Power at Peak on Eve of Cuban Vote," New York *Times* (November 2, 1958), 4E.

71. U.S. 86th Cong., Senate, 1st and 2nd Sess., *Communist Threat to the United States through the Caribbean* (Washington, D.C.: Government Printing Office), 7: 687.

72. Dubois, *Fidel Castro*, 330–31.

73. ibid., 331; Rivero, *Libertad*, 137; Taber, *M-26*, 282–84.

74. Dubois, *Fidel Castro*, 311; Enrique Rodriguez Loeches, *Rumbo A Escambray* (Havana: Capitolio Nacional, 1960), 101–2; Eloy Gutiérrez Menoyo, "El II frente nacional del Escambray," *Combate* [San José, Costa Rica] 2: 7; 47–50 (July-August 1959), 47.

75. Alberto del Río Chaviano was more interested in lining his pockets and partying than doing battle with the guerrillas. Ironically, he had been the military chief of Oriente Province and had personally directed the roundup of those who, along with Castro, had attacked the Moncada Army barracks on July 26, 1953. Also, he commanded the 15,000 troops that had endeavored to hunt down Castro from May through August 1958.

76. Dubois, *Fidel Castro*, 336–37; Batista, *Cuba Betrayed*, 108–9; Mallin, *History*, 106.

77. Batista, *Cuba Betrayed*, 88–89, 100–1.

78. Dubois, *Fidel Castro*, 339; Batista, *Cuba Betrayed*, 113, 115–19.

79. Che wrote, "Guerrillas seldom can spare any forces to constitute a reserve. Yet, a reserve will be needed in desperate, unforeseen situations. One way to prepare for this need is to compose an elite platoon given special privileges. Call it 'The Joker' or 'Suicide Platoon.' Forge its reputation for heroism by committing it to the most difficult combat situations." Guevara, *On Guerrilla Warfare*, 48–49.

80. Dubois, *Fidel Castro*, 341.

81. ibid., 342–47; Batista, *Cuba Betrayed*, 127–39.

82. Phillips, *Cuba*, 404; "Dominican Republic," *Hispanic American Report* 12:1; 28–30 (January 1959), 28–29.

83. Llerena, *Unsuspected Revolution*, 72.

84. Macaulay, "The Cuban Rebel Army," 284–95; Mallin, *History*, 109.

85. In November 1959 an official of the Central Intelligence Agency testified before a Congressional subcommittee that available evidence did not warrant concluding that Fidel Castro was a Communist. U.S. 86th Cong. Senate, *Communist Threat*, 3: 162–64. During a number of interviews in 1958 and 1959, Castro stated that he was not a Communist. See "Inside Cuba's Revolution," *Look* 22: 24–30 (February 4, 1958); Dana Adams Schmidt, "Castro Stresses Land Reform Aim," New York *Times* (April 21, 1959), 1, 12. Castro did not publicly reveal his loyalty to Marxism-Leninism until his televised speech of December 2, 1961.

86. The American ambassador, Earl E. T. Smith, worked to keep Batista in power, but officials at the State Department and influential members of the U.S. Congress wanted to withdraw all military assistance and political support for the Batista regime. And, the Central Intelligence Agency was unclear as to the consequence of a Castro victory and withheld critical information from the ambassador. Earl E. T. Smith, *The Fourth Floor: An Account of the Castro Communist Revolution* (New York: Random House, 1962), 32–34.

87. For an analysis of coup d'etats in Latin America, see Merle Kling, "Toward a Theory of Power and Political Instability in Latin America," *The Western Political Quarterly* 9: 1; 21–35 (March 1956), 21–35; and William S. Stokes, "Violence as a Power Factor in Latin American Politics," *The Western Political Quarterly* 5: 3; 445–68 (September 1952).

88. While preparing in Mexico for his attack against Batista, Castro told Mario Llerena, "We are prepared to set up the Hotel Nacional in the mountains and resist for six months." Llerena, *Unsuspected Revolution*, 86, 119.

89. Jean-Paul Sartre, *Sartre on Cuba* (New York: Ballantine Books, 1961), and Huberman and Sweezy, *Cuba*.

90. Mallin, "The Military," 1. Hugh Thomas wrote of Fidel Castro, "A Marxist regime was established largely, it would seem, because of the will of a single man, and he was a most untypical Marxist at that." Llerena, *Unsuspected Revolution*, 11.

91. Carlos Franqui, *Diario de la revolución cubana* (Barcelona: R. Torres, 1976), 598, 732–33; LaCarite, *Case Studies*, 111; Taber, *M-26*, 210.

CHAPTER TWENTY-FIVE

1. The "Andean Hegemony" occurred between 1899 and 1945, during which time Venezuela was governed by dictators and democratic presidents, all military men and all natives of the state of Táchira in the Andean region. The era began in October 1899 when Gen. Cipriano Castro assumed power following the "Restoration Revolution." Pérez Jiménez, who governed from behind the scenes beginning in 1950 and publicly between 1952 and 1958, was also a native of Táchira. Libertad Olivo Garrido, *Estudio sobre el acceso y permanencia*

de los andinos en el poder militar 1945–1970 (Caracas: Circulo de las Fuerzas Armadas, 1993), 7–13.

2. Isaías Medina Angarita (1897–1953) was born in San Cristóbal, in the state of Táchira. In 1914 he graduated from the Venezuelan Military Academy. He served as Minister of War and Navy and in 1941 was elected by Congress to be the President of Venezuela. He was the first graduate of the military academy to hold that office. Medina modernized public education and the health system. He supported laws that promoted agriculture and oil exploration. On the other hand, Medina paid little attention to the military, giving it neither modern training nor equipment. Numerous senior officers lacked formal military education and professional skills. These circumstances provoked the rebellion of young, junior officers which led to Medina's downfall. Medina was exiled to the United States, but some years later, when seriously ill, he was permitted to return to Venezuela where he died.

3. Marcos Pérez Jiménez (1914–) was born in Michelena in the Andean Mountains. In 1933 he graduated as an artillery officer from the Military and Naval School, first in his class. Recognized for his academic excellence, he taught at various army schools. In Peru Pérez Jiménez attended the School for the Application of Artillery, where he graduated first in his class, and later he attended the Superior War College at Chorrillos. He served as the Chief of Staff of the army between 1945 and 1946 and Chief of Staff of the armed forces between 1946 and 1948. Pérez Jiménez participated in the overthrow of President Rómulo Gallegos in November 1948 and was a member of the junta that governed until December 1952. Then at the age of thirty-nine, he was declared the winner of the presidential election. Overthrown in January 1958, Pérez Jiménez fled first to the Dominican Republic and later to the United States. He was extradited from the United States in 1963, tried by the Venezuelan Supreme Court, and sent to prison. Freed in 1968, he briefly returned to Spain but was back in Venezuela within a year. Pérez Jiménez was elected as a senator from Caracas by a large majority. Notwithstanding, the Congress refused to permit him to take his seat on a technicality. Pérez Jiménez retired to Madrid, Spain.

4. Rómulo Betancourt Bello (1906–81), a son of Spanish immigrants from the Canarias Islands, was born in Guatire, Venezuela. He began his political life at the age of twenty and was at that time a militant Communist. In 1943 he founded the Democratic Action Party. In 1945 he served as the president of the junta that seized power from democratically elected Isaías Medina. Ousted by the military in 1948, Betancourt was forced into exile. He returned to Venezuela in January 1958 and in December he was elected President. At the end of his term in 1964, he retired to Berna, Switzerland. Betancourt returned to Venezuela at the beginning of the 1970s and died in New York City in 1981.

5. Carlos Delgado-Chalbaud Gómez (1909–50), born in Caracas, was the son of Vice Adm. Román Delgado-Chalbaud. He took part in the unsuccessful attempt organized by his father to overthrow the government of Gen. Juan Vicente Gómez. When this failed, Carlos Delgado-Chalbaud fled, ultimately to Europe. He graduated as an engineer from the Politechnical School of Saint Cyr, France. As a member of the *4th Règiment d'Ingènieurs* of the French army, he taught in French and North American military schools during World War I. In 1938 Delgado-Chalbaud was incorporated into the Venezuelan army with the rank of captain. He was one of the leaders who overthrew democratically elected Isaías Medina. While serving as the president of the governing junta, Delgado-Chalbaud was assassinated by a group led by an old *caudillo*, Rafael Simón Urbina. Delgado-Chalbaud was promoted to full colonel *post mortem*.

In spite of Venezuela's turbulent past, this was the first assassination of a serving chief executive.

6. Luis Felipe Llovera Páez (1913–77) was born in Ciudad Bolívar in eastern Venezuela. He graduated from the Military and Naval School in 1932 with honors as an infantry officer. Llovera attended the U.S. military school at Fort Benning, Georgia, and the *Escuela Superior de Guerra* in Chorrillos, Peru. He served as an instructor and commanded various infantry battalions. Llovera was a member of the ruling military junta during the late 1940s and early 1950s and was a confidant of Pérez Jiménez. Between 1952 and 1955 Llovera was the founding director of the Office of Special Presidential Studies which was responsible for the massive public works programs undertaken by Pérez Jiménez' government. Between 1955 and 1958 Llovera was the Minister of Communications. On January 23, 1958, he and his family fled Venezuela in the same aircraft as Pérez Jiménez. Llovera lived in Europe and South America until 1971, when he returned to Venezuela. He founded a political party that was based upon programs initiated by Pérez Jiménez. Llovera retired from politics shortly thereafter and died in Caracas.

7. On the morning of November 13, 1950, adventurers following the orders of Rafael Simón Urbina, a personal enemy of the junta president, overpowered guards and a chauffeur and abducted the president of the junta, Col. Delgado-Chalbaud, and his naval aid, Lt. Carlos Bacalao, from the presidential automobile in Caracas. They were taken to Urbina's house where Delgado-Chalbaud was assassinated and Bacalao wounded. Urbina was caught by the police and killed while trying to escape.

8. Fredy Rincón, *El nuevo ideal nacional y los planes económicos-militares de Pérez Jiménez, 1952–1959* (Caracas: Ediciones Centauro, 1982), 21–22; Ocarina Castilo D'Imperio, *Los años del bulldozer: iIdiolgía y política 1948–1958* (Caracas: Fondo Editorial Troykos/ Asociación de Profesores UCV/CENDES, 1990), 169; Juan José Marín Frechilla, *Planes, planos y projectos para Venezuela: 1908–1958* (Caracas: Universidad Central de Venezuela, 1994), 260–61.

9. Agustín Blanco Muñoz, *Habla el general Marcos Pérez Jiménez* (Caracas: CENDES/ Edit. José Martí, 1983), 121; Edecio La Riva Araujo, *Los fusiles de la paz* (Caracas: privately published, 1968), 51–54; *Comandantes del ejército venezolano: 1810–1985* (Caracas: Ejército, Dirección de Educación, 1985), 31–33; Iván Dario Giménez, *Los golpes de estado desde Castro hasta Caldera* (Caracas: Centralca, 1996), 97; Stockholm International Peace Research Institute (SIPRI), *Arms Trade Register: The Arms Trade with the Third World* (Stockholm: Almquist & Wiskel, 1974), 122–23; *Venezuela 1955* (Caracas: Ministerio de Relaciones Exteriores, 1955), 121.

10. Rincón, *El nuevo ideal nacional*, 126–27; Giménez, *Los golpes*, 97; SIPRI, *Arms Trade*, 121–23; Oscar Emilio Ghersi Gómez, "La moderización de la armada desde el 30 de marzo de 1949 al 10 de enero de 1958," *Revista de la Armada* 10: 42–47 (July 24, 1986), 42–47.

11. Giménez, *Los golpes*, 96–97; Luís H. Paredes, *Historia de la aviación militar venezolana* (Caracas: Ministerio de la Defensa, 1978), 359–441; *Fuentes para el estudio del 23 de enero 1958*, 2 vols. (Caracas: Congreso de la République, 1983–84), 1: 2, 35; 2: 2, 35.

12. Giménez, *Los golpes*, 98; SIPRI, *Arms Trade*, 122; *Venezuela 1955*, 125–27.

13. Castilo D'Imperio, *Los años*, 198; Juan Avendaño Lugo, *El militarismo en Venezuela: La dictadura de Pérez Jiménez* (Caracas: Ediciones Centauro, 1982), 285–86.

14. Avendaño Lugo, *El militarismo*, 288.

15. The Armed Forces Basic School (*Escuela Basica de las Fuerzas Armadas*) was established on August 8, 1954, as part of a reorganization of the military education system. The school's purpose was to unify the first two years of study for students of the four service academies. After completing two years of basic studies, the students would transfer to the service academy of their choice to complete two years of specialized training. In 1958 the Armed Forces Basic School moved to a new location and began operating independently from the Military Academy, where it had originally been located. For various reasons, including rivalry among the armed forces, the school closed within seven months. However, in 1988 the Armed Forces Basic School reopened in Maracay with a new studies program.

16. Hugo Enrique Trejo (1922–) was born in the city of Mérida in the Venezuelan Andes. He graduated from the Venezuelan Military School in January 1943 number one in his class. Trejo specialized in both infantry and artillery. He attended the senior war college in Spain. He participated in the October 18, 1945, coup against President Medina. One of the leaders in the movement against Pérez Jiménez in 1958, Trejo served as ambassador to Costa Rica until 1966. In the meantime, he was promoted to colonel in 1961. Trejo retired from the army in 1967.

17. Jesús María Castro León (1908–65), a grandson of Gen. Cipriano Castro, was born in the hamlet of Capacho in the Venezuelan Andes. He graduated from the Military Aviation School in 1937. He received additional flight training in the United States during the late 1940s. Castro served as Superintendent of the Military Aviation School and as Chief of Air General Staff, the second in command of the air force. Castro participated in the overthrow of Pérez Jiménez and was designated Minister of Defense. In July 1958 he was promoted to General of Brigade but within two weeks was accused of conspiring against the governing junta and was exiled. In April 1960 he clandestinely returned to Venezuela and headed an unsuccessful rebellion of army troops in the city of San Cristóbal in the Andes. Castro was tried by court-martial and found guilty. He died in prison in the Fortification of San Carlos in Caracas.

18. Agustín Blanco Muñoz, *El 23 de enero: habla la conspiración* (Caracas: Ediciones FACES–UCV/ATENEO, 1980), 197.

19. Maracay, capital of the state of Aragua, is considered the "military capital" of Venezuela. Numerous military installations including barracks, air bases, weapons factories, maintenance centers, arsenals, training centers, and hospitals are located there. These facilities were initiated by Gen. Vicente Gómez at the beginning of the twentieth century because he did not care to live in Caracas.

20. Army and marine regiments, battalions, and groups bear both a name and a number. For example, the army "*Bravos de Apure* Armored Battalion" is (since 1990 when the army changed the numbering system) the "414th *Bravos de Apure* Armored Battalion." However, the units are most commonly referred to by their name only.

21. Giménez, *Los golpes*, 101; *El 23 de enero y las fuerzas armadas venezolanas* (Caracas: Ministerio de la Defensa, 1990: 97–98; Luís Enrique Sucre and Tomás Enrique Carrillo Batalla, *1° de enero de 1958: el fracaso de un triunfo* (Caracas: Alarcón Fernández Editor, 1993), 121–29.

22. José Rodríguez Itrube, *Crónica de la década militar* (Caracas: Ediciones Nueva Politica, 1984), 512.

23. Very few military personnel were at their stations or ships. Most two-year conscripts came into the armed services at the same time; their tour of duty had just ended and the new

draftees had not yet arrived. Also, half of the officers and senior enlisted personnel were on holiday leave. Sucre and Carrillo, 1° de enero de 1958, 129–31.

24. Blanco Muñóz, El 23 de enero, 151–52. One Venom jet was damaged by antiaircraft fire and forced to land at the Maíquetia International Airport.

25. On July 14, 1949, the Naval Technical School, Warrant Officer School, and Sailors School were combined into the Naval Education Center (Centro de Entrenamiento Naval). In the early 1960s it received its current name, the Naval Education Center "Captain Felipe Santiago Esteves" (CANES).

26. Ricardo Sosa Ríos, Mar de leva (Caracas: Edreca Editores, 1979), 21–29.

27. The naval tug Felipe Larrazabal (ex-U.S. Discovery, ARS-3), transported a company from Marine Battalion No. 2 from Puerto Cabello to Turiamo Auxiliary Naval Base. A company from Marine Battalion No. 1 was carried from La Guaira to Turiamo in the transport Dos de Diciembre.

28. Blanco Muñóz, El 23 de enero, 97–99; Edito J. Ramírez, El 18 de octubre y la problemática venezolana actual 1945 y 1979 (Caracas: Avila Arte Editores, S.A., 1981), 248; Hugo Trejo, Revolución no ha terminado (Valencia, Venezuela: Vadell Hermanos Editores, 1977), 81–116.

29. The National Guard Troop School, founded in August 1937, educated the nucleus of professional troops belonging to the National Guard. This school should not be confused with the National Guard Academy, located near Caracas, which educated officers.

30. Sosa Ríos, Mar, 21–29.

31. Marcos Aurelio Moros Angulo would serve as the commander general of the army between 1958 and 1960.

32. Sucre and Carrillo, 1° de enero de 1958, 165–69; Sosa Ríos, Mar, 21–29; El 23 de enero y las fuerzas armadas venezolanas, 112.

33. Haroldo Rodríguez Figueroa graduated from the Venezuelan Naval Academy in 1955. He served as Commander of the Navy between June 1983 and June 1984 with the rank of vice admiral.

34. El 23 de enero y las fuerzas armadas venezolanas, 118; Blanco Muñoz, Habla el general, 261–66; Blanco Muñoz, El 23 de octubre, 88–92.

35. El 23 de enero y las fuerzas armadas venezolanas, 118; Blanco Muñoz, Habla el general, 261–66; Rodríguez Itrube, Crónica, 531.

36. Miguel J. Rodríguez Olivares, who graduated from the Venezuelan Naval Academy, became Commander of the Fleet in 1958. In October 1958 he became of member of the governing junta, representing the navy, after Rear Adm. Wolfgang Larrazábal's resignation as president; Dr. Edgar Sanabria was designated the new president. Rodríguez Olivares died of cancer in 1960, a few days before being designated Chief of Naval Staff, a position he never held. Promoted to rear admiral postmortem, he was buried with ex-president's honors.

37. "23 de enero: 25 años," El diario de caracas, Special Edition (January 23, 1983), 7–12.

38. Wolfgang Larrazábal Ugueto (1911–) was born at Carúpano in the state of Sucre. He graduated from the Military and Naval School in 1932. During his career he was the Director of the Naval School and commanded the gunboat General Urdaneta and the corvette Carabobo. Between 1947 and 1948 Capt. Wolfgang Larrazábal commanded the Venezuelan navy. In 1948 he was designated the naval attaché to the United States and the following year attended the U.S. Naval War College in Newport, Rhode Island. Upon returning to Venezu-

ela, he held administrative positions within the armed forces. In July 1957 he and his brother Carlos were promoted to rear admiral, the first Venezuelans to hold that rank in the twentieth century. In January 1958 Wolfgang Larrazábal was appointed the Commandant General of the Navy. Following the overthrow of Pérez Jiménez, he served as the president of the governing junta. Wolfgang Larrazábal retired in November 1958 in order to be a candidate for president in the December election. In 1959 he returned to active duty and was made ambassador to Chile. In 1960, along with his brother, he was promoted to vice admiral; both retired in 1962. In 1963 Wolfgang Larrazábal founded a political party and unsuccessfully ran for president. He subsequently performed diplomatic missions for the government.

39. Blanco Muñoz, *El 23 de enero*, 35.

40. ibid., 376–77; Sosa Ríos, *Mar*, 21–22.

41. "23 de enero: 25 años," 7–12; Blanco Muñoz, *El 23 de enero*, 14, 65, 330; Giménez, *Los golpes*, 108–9.

42. Pedro Quevedo would serve as Commander General of the Army between 1960 and 1964.

43. "23 de enero: 25 años," 7–12; Blanco Muñoz, *El 23 de enero*, 14, 65, 330; *El 23 de enero y las fuerzas armadas venezolanas*, 188.

44. "23 de enero: 25 años," 7–12; Blanco Muñoz, *El 23 de enero*, 14, 65, 330.

45. Giménez, *Los golpes*, 109.

46. ibid., 118–19; José Rivas Rivas, compiler, *Un año en el gobierno de Wolfgang Larrazabal* (Caracas: Pensamiento Vivo, C.A. within *Historia gráfica de Venezuela*, volume 3, 1980), (April 1958), 29.

47. Rivas, *Un año en el gobierno* (May 1958), 7–13; Richard M. Nixon, *Seis crisis* (Barcelona: Ediciones G.P., 1967), 209–65.

48. Carlos Larrazábal Ugueto (1909–86), like his brother Wolfgang, graduated from the Military and Naval School in 1932. His advanced education included studying at the U.S. Naval War College in Newport, Rhode Island. He was promoted to rear admiral in 1957 and vice admiral in 1960. In January 1958 he was appointed Minister of Industry and Commerce by Pérez Jiménez. With the overthrow of Pérez Jiménez, Carlos Larrazábal became the Commander of the Navy, a position he held until retiring in 1962.

49. Giménez, *Los golpes*, 113–17; Rivas, *Un año en el gobierno* (July–August 1958), 5–11.

50. Giménez, *Los golpes*, 118–19; Rivas, *Un año en el gobierno* (September 1958), 3–16.

51. "Venezuela: Democracy under Fire," *On Record* 1; 9; 1–64 (New York), 9; Robert J. Alexander, *Venezuelan Democratic Revolution* (New Brunswick, N.J.: Rutgers University Press, 1964), 51–52, 106, 114.

52. "Caracas Upsets a Military Coup," New York *Times* (July 24, 1958), 1, 8.

53. On January 24, 1958, *El Universal* placed the number of deaths at 161 persons and wounded at 472. *El Nacional* gave 300 persons killed and 1,000 hurt. These were the two most important daily newspapers.

CHAPTER TWENTY-SIX

1. "Nicaragua," *Hispanic American Report* 12: 2; 83–85 (February 1959), 83–84.

2. "Dominican Republic," *Hispanic American Report* 12: 6; 323–24 (June 1959), 324; Fabián Escalante, *The Secret War* (Melbourne: Ocean Press, 1995), 17–18.

3. The literature is very contradictory as to what motivated Morgan and Gutiérrez Menoyo. Castro, who later executed Morgan and exiled Gutiérrez Menoyo (in March 1961), portrays the two as traitors to the Cuban Revolution who exposed the Trujillo-backed plot out of fear of having their participation discovered. See Escalante, *The Secret War*, 18–22.

Other authors imply that Morgan and Gutiérrez Menoyo were still loyal to the Cuban Revolution (but not Castro and Communism) and were acting as patriots when they informed Castro of the plot. See the School of Inter-American Affairs, University of New Mexico, "Post-World War II Political Developments in Latin America," pp. 1–78 in U.S. Senate, 86th Cong., 2nd Sess., Doc. 125, *United States-Latin American Relations* (Washington, D.C.: U.S. Government Printing Office, 1960), 76.

4. Escalante, *The Secret War*, 22–23.

5. ibid., 23–27.

6. ibid., 27.

7. ibid., 27–29; Franklin, *Cuba*, 22; Mallin, *History*, 110.

8. "Dominican Republic," *Hispanic American Report* 12: 8; 436–37 (August 1959), 436.

9. "Dominican Republic," *Hispanic American Report* 12: 2; 91–93 (February 1959), 92.

10. The School of Inter-American Affairs, University of New Mexico, "Post-World War II Political Developments in Latin America," 76; Mallin, *History*, 191.

11. Jules Dubois, *Operation America* (New York: Walker and Company, 1963), 73; U.S. Dept. of State, *Inter-American Efforts to Relieve International Tensions in the Western Hemisphere, 1959–1960* (Washington, D.C.: U.S. Government Printing Office, 1962), 17, 133–34; Robert L. Scheina, "The Cuban Navy," in *The Soviet and Other Communist Navies*, ed. by James L. George (Annapolis: Naval Institute Press, 1986), 25.

12. "Haiti," *Hispanic American Report* 12: 2; 90–91 (February 1959), 90–91.

13. "Invaders Reported Mopped up in Haiti," New York *Times* (August 21, 1959), 6; "Invaders Cuban, Haiti Maintains," New York *Times* (August 25, 1959), 13; "Haiti," *Hispanic American Report* 12: 8; 434–36 (August 1959), 434–35; "Haiti," *Hispanic American Report* 12: 9; 489–90 (September 1959), 489.

14. "Haiti," *Hispanic American Report* 12: 2; 90–91 (February 1959), 90–91.

15. Dubois, *Operation America*, 106; U.S. Dept. of State, *Inter-American Efforts*, 7; Fermoselle, *The Evolution*, 348–49; "Panama," *Hispanic American Report* 12: 4; 204–5 (April 1959), 204–5; "Panama," *Hispanic American Report* 12: 5; 262–64 (May 1959), 262; "Panama," *Hispanic American Report* 12: 6; 318–19 (June 1959), 319; Mallin, *History*, 190.

16. U.S. Dept. of State, *Inter-American Efforts*, 13; "Nicaragua," *Hispanic American Report* 12: 6; 316–17 (June 1959), 316.

17. "Nicaragua," *Hispanic American Report* 12: 7; 372–73 (July 1959), 372–73.

18. Dubois, *Operation America*, 242; U.S., U.S. Dept. of State, *Inter-American Efforts*, 10, 13–15.

19. "Nicaragua," *Hispanic American Report* 12: 10; 538–39 (October 1959), 538; "Nicaragua," *Hispanic American Report* 12: 11; 595 (November 1959), 595.

20. "Nicaragua," *Hispanic American Report* 12: 12; 658–60 (December 1959), 658.

21. "Nicaragua," *Hispanic American Report* 12: 1; 17–18 (January 1959), 17–18.

22. "Nicaragua," *Hispanic American Report* 12: 12; 589–60 (December 1959), 659–60.

CHAPTER TWENTY-SEVEN

1. *Operation Zapata: The "Ultrasensitive" Report and Testimony of the Board of Inquiry on the Bay of Pigs* (Frederick, Md.: Aletheia Books, University Publications of America, 1981), 3; Escalante, *The Secret War*, 45.

2. U.S. Senate, 87th Cong., 1st Sess. Rept. 994, Part 1, *Final Report of the Committee on Commerce* (Washington, D.C.: Government Printing Office, 1961), 511; U. S. Department of State, "Events in United States–Cuban Relations" (Prepared for the Committee on Foreign Relations, U.S. Senate), (Washington, D.C.: Government Printing Office, 1962), 4; Emily Hatchwell and Simon Calder, *Cuba* (London: Latin American Bureau [Research and Action], 1995), 19; Hernando Clavo and Katlijn Declercq, *The Cuban Exile Movement*, trans. by Mary Todd (Melbourne: Ocean Press, 2000), 2.

3. Clavo and Declercq, *The Cuban Exile Movement*, 3; Franklin, *Cuba*, 23–25; Konstantin Tarasov and Vyacheslav Zubenko, *The CIA in Latin America* (Moscow: Progess Publishers, 1984), 207.

4. "Communists take over 90 miles from U.S.," *U.S. News and World Report* 48: 62–66, 68 (June 20, 1960), 62–66; U.S. Dept of State, "Events in United States–Cuban Relations," 15–19; Franklin, *Cuba*, 28.

5. Escalante, *The Secret War*, 67.

6. Huber Matos Benítez (unk), teacher and small landowner, joined the anti-Batista guerrillas in early 1958 when he flew into Cuba on an aircraft that was delivering weapons and ammunition from Costa Rica. Following his arrest, Matos was tried and sentenced to twenty years in prison for treason. Freed in 1979, he traveled first to Costa Rica and then to Venezuela where he founded the Movement Independent and Democratic Cuba (*Cuba Independente y Democrática*—CID). In 1981 Matos established the radio station "La Voz del CID," a short-wave broadcasting station in Central America.

7. Manuel Francisco Artime Buesa (1932–) was educated as a psychiatrist. He joined the anti-Batista guerrillas in the Sierra Maestra late in 1958. Because of his previous anti-Batista activities, he was given the rank of lieutenant. In early 1959 he wrote and published *Comunismo para que?* Following the arrest of Huber Matos, Artime resigned from the Revolutionary movement and sought refuge in a Latin American embassy. From there, he fled to the United States. Artime announced the founding of the Movement for the Recovery of the Revolution (*Movimiento para la Recuperación de la Revolución*—MRR), on June 5, 1960, while in Costa Rica. He became the political officer of Brigade 2506 and was captured on the beach at the Bay of Pigs. Artime was among those exchanged for medical supplies.

8. Escalante, *The Secret War*, 30–38; Mallin, *History*, 116–18.

9. Mallin, *History*, 125–26.

10. Avrahm G. Mezerick, ed., *Cuba and the United States*, 2 vols. (New York: International Review Service, 1962–63), 2: 39.

11. Fermoselle, *The Evolution*, 269–71; *Operation Zapata*, 74–75; Franklin, *Cuba*, 25–26.

12. Mallin, *History*, 115; Fermoselle, *The Evolution*, 269–71.

13. David R. Mets, *Land-Based Air Power in Third World Crises* (Maxwell Air Force Base, Ala.: Air University Press, 1986), 71; *Operation Zapata*, 72, 74–75, 128, 134, 141.

14. *Operation Zapata*, 141.

15. Fermoselle, *The Evolution*, 272–73; Orlando Castro Hidalgo, *Spy for Fidel* (Miami: E. A. Seemann Publishing, 1971), 27; Clavo and Declercq, *The Cuban Exile Movement*, 3.

16. *Operation Zapata*, xi, 3–4.

17. ibid., 6–7; Felix I. Rodríguez and John Weisman, *Shadow Warrior* (New York: Simon and Schuster, 1989), 60, 64.

18. Mallin, *History*, 125–29.

19. Dan Hagedorn and Leif Hellstrom, *Foreign Invaders* (Leicester, England: Midland Publishing Limited, 1994), 126; *Operation Zapata*, 38, 69–70.

20. Each soldier trained for the assault on Cuba was assigned a number starting at 2000. Soldier 2506, Carlos Rodríguez Santana, fell to his death during a training accident. To honor him, his number was assigned to the brigade. Rodríguez and Weisman, *Shadow Warrior*, 54.

21. Phillips, *The Night Watch*, 89–90, 97; Escalante, *The Secret War*, 47; Franklin, *Cuba*, 26–34.

22. Federal Communication agents confiscated the two-way radios issued by the CIA to Cubans training in Florida because "non-U.S. citizens cannot broadcast in U.S. Territory." Fermoselle, *The Evolution*, 275. David Atlee Phillips wrote that the CIA never anticipated a general uprising of the Cuban people against Castro. Phillips, *The Night Watch*, 97.

23. "Despite the shortcomings pointed out in the assessment, the Joint Chiefs of Staff consider that timely execution of this plan has a fair chance of ultimate success and, even if it does not achieve immediately the full results desired, could contribute to the eventual overthrow of the Castro regime." From JCSM-57-61, "Military Evaluation of the CIA Paramilitary Plan—Cuba," in *Operation Zapata*, 10, 42, 85.

24. Félix Rodríguez (1941–), alias Máximo Gómez among others, received military training in Central America during 1960–61 at the sponsorship of the CIA. He was one of the fifteen members of the 35-man infiltration team that evaded capture following the Bay of Pigs. He hid in the Venezuelan Embassy in Cuba for five months. Rodríguez joined the U.S. Army in 1963 and fought in Vietnam; he was wounded and retired from the service. In 1968 the CIA sent him to Bolivia to help track down Che Guevara. In 1985 Rodríguez advised the Salvadoran government in the fight against the Communist guerrillas. He was asked by U.S. Marine Lt. Col. Oliver North to assist in his project to arm the *Contras* and became linked to the Iran-*Contra* scandal.

25. *Bahia de Cochinos* is literally translated as "Bay of Pigs." However, in the region *Cochinos* are also a type of fish. Mallin, *History*, 130.

26. *Operation Zapata*, 13, 80.

27. Fermoselle, *The Evolution*, 278; *Operation Zapata*, 80–81, 95.

28. Mallin, *History*, 145–46; *Operation Zapata*, xii.

29. *Operation Zapata*, 18, 96–97; Escalante, *The Secret War*, 86; Mallin, *History*, 131–32.

30. *Operation Zapata*, 18; Hagedorn and Hellstrom, *Foreign Invaders*, 127; Mallin, *History*, 133–35.

31. Phillips, *The Night Watch*, 102, 106–07; Hagedorn and Hellstrom, *Foreign Invaders*, 127; Franklin, *Cuba*, 39–40.

32. *Operation Zapata*, 20–21; Mallin, *History*, 135.

33. *Operation Zapata*, 21, 24, 38, 119; Hagedorn and Hellstrom, *Foreign Invaders*, 127.

34. *Operation Zapata*, 41.

35. Mallin, *History*, 135.

36. *Operation Zapata*, 22.

37. ibid., 22, 24.

38. ibid., 22, 36, 132; Mallin, *History*, 137–38.

39. *Operation Zapata*, 23–24, 132.

40. ibid., 23, 34, 36; Hagedorn and Hellstrom, *Foreign Invaders*, 129; Mallin, *History*, 138–39.

41. Fermoselle, *The Evolution*, 276–77.

42. Mallin, *History*, 135–36.

43. ibid., 137.

44. *Operation Zapata*, 24; Hagedorn and Hellstrom, *Foreign Invaders*, 129; Mallin, *History*, 142–44.

45. *Operation Zapata*, 24, 132, 135.

46. ibid., 24, 132.

47. ibid., 25, 37.

48. Phillips, *The Night Watch*, 109; Castro Hidalgo, *Spy for Fidel*, 10–12; Mallin, *History*, 139–40.

49. *Operation Zapata*, 25; Mallin, *History*, 144–45.

50. *Operation Zapata*, 26.

51. ibid., 26–27, 90, 121–23; Mallin, *History*, 146; Phillips, *The Night Watch*, 109.

52. *Operation Zapata*, 27–29.

53. ibid., 28–29, 32, 121; Mallin, *History*, 150.

54. *Operation Zapata*, 133; Mallin, *History*, 152.

55. Those captured were tried in Havana between March 29 and April 7, 1962. Convicted, they lost their Cuban citizenship and were fined $62 million. In lieu of the fine, the prisoners were sentenced to 30 years at hard labor. On April 14 Cuba released the 60 wounded prisoners, who were flown to Miami. On December 23–24, 1962, some 1,053 brigade members were exchanged with the United States for $53 million worth of medicine and baby food. Nine members were retained in prison, allegedly for crimes committed during the Batista era. The last brigade member was released on October 17, 1986. Franklin, *Cuba*, 51; Fermoselle, *The Evolution*, 280.

56. Rafael del Pino Díaz (1938–) was born in western Cuba into a middle-class family. In 1953 he took part in a demonstration against Batista and was arrested. His parents sent him to school in Knoxville, Tennessee, to remove him from Cuba. Returning to Cuba, del Pino joined the 26th of July Movement in 1956. He was arrested in January 1957. When released, he traveled to Panama and Venezuela. In Venezuela he joined the conspirators against Marcos Pérez Jiménez. In January 1958 del Pino was injured and captured. Following Pérez Jiménez' overthrow one month later, del Pino joined the 26th of July Movement in Caracas. In June 1958 he returned to Cuba and eventually joined the guerrillas in the mountains. Following the Cuban Revolution he joined Castro's new air force. In April 1962 he shot down two aircraft over the Bay of Pigs. In 1957 del Pino commanded Cuban air units in Angola. By 1982 he had achieved the rank of brigade general. Del Pino studied at the Soviet Yuri Gagarin Aviation School. Between April and May 1987, he traveled to the Soviet Union to coordinate a joint exercise with the Soviet air force. On May 28 of that year, del Pino defected, flying to Florida in a twin-engine Cessna 402 aircraft with some family members.

57. Hagedorn and Hellstrom, *Foreign Invaders*, 130–31; *Operation Zapata*, 29, 34; Clavo and Declercq, *The Cuban Exile Movement*, 6.

58. U.S. Dept of State, "Events in United States–Cuban Relations," 21; *Operation Zapata*, x; Franklin, *Cuba*, 46.

59. *Agresiones de Estados Unidos a Cuba, 1787–1976* (La Habana: Editorial de Ciencias Sociales, 1979), 81–169; Rodríguez and Weisman, *Shadow Warrior*, 105–8.

60. Eloy Gutiérrez Menoyo (1934–) was born in Spain. His family immigrated to Cuba in 1946, having supported the losing side in the Spanish Civil War (1936–39). Family members were soon engaged in anti-Batista activity. In 1957 Eloy was in charge of the logistics for his elder brother's unsuccessful attack on Batista's presidential palace. Eloy fled to the Escambray Mountains where in November 1957 he formed a guerrilla group to fight Batista, reaching the rank of major which was the highest possible in the Revolutionary army. He fled Cuba in January 1961, following his involvement in the plot and counterplot between Fidel Castro and Rafael Trujillo (see chapter 26). Following Eloy's capture in 1965, he spent twenty-two years in prison, during which time he received numerous beatings that left him partially deaf and blind. The Spanish government negotiated his release and he was freed on Christmas Day 1986. He has become an advocate for dialogue with Castro and organized the group Cuban Change *(Cambio Cubano)*. With the permission of Castro's government, Gutiérrez Menoyo returned to Cuba in June 1995 and met with Fidel.

61. "Alpha" for the beginning and "66" for the initial number of members. Clavo and Declercq, *The Cuban Exile Movement*, 27.

62. *Agresiones*, 94, 99, 107; Escalante, *The Secret War*, 180, 185, 189.

63. Franklin, *Cuba*, 52, 55, 64.

64. Jay Mallin Sr., "Covering Cuba" [unpublished manuscript, 1998]; "Miami," 3; *Agresiones*, 129; Clavo and Declercq, *The Cuban Exile Movement*, 174.

65. *Agresiones*, 92; Rodríguez and Weisman, *Shadow Warrior*, 111–12.

66. Miguel Acoca and Robert K. Brown, "A Plot to Destroy JFK and Invade Cuba," *Soldier of Fortune* 12–14, 17–21, 60–61 (Spring 1976), 12–14.

67. Escalante, *The Secret War*, 52.

68. *Alleged Assassination Plots Involving Foreign Leaders* (New York: W. W. Norton, 1976), 140–76; Clavo and Declercq, *The Cuban Exile Movement*, 7; Franklin, *Cuba*, 43–46.

69. Rodríguez and Weisman, *Shadow Warrior*, 118–19.

70. Howard Jones, *Quest for Security: A History of U.S. Foreign Relations*, 2 vols. (New York: McGraw-Hill, 1996), 2: 567–75.

71. *Alleged Assassination Plots*, 173; Bradley Earl Ayers, *The War that Never Was* (Indianapolis: Bobbs-Merrill, 1976), 15, 57–66; Franklin, *Cuba*, 63.

72. Rodríguez and Weisman, *Shadow Warrior*, 120–23; *Alleged Assassination Plots*, 177; Clavo and Declercq, *The Cuban Exile Movement*, 29.

73. Rodríguez and Weisman, *Shadow Warrior*, 124–25; *Agresiones*, 128.

74. Clavo and Declercq, *The Cuban Exile Movement*, 10–13; Alfonso Chardy, "Alpha 66 reports gun battle off Cuba's coast," *The Miami Herald* (January 4, 1991), 1B–2B; David Hancock, "Alpha 66 on alert after reports from Cuba," *The Miami Herald* (June 8, 1993), 48; Tarasov and Zubenko, *The CIA*, 227–37.

75. On January 2, 1961, Cuban Foreign Minister Raúl Roa García formally charged in the United Nations that the United States was training Cuban émigrés in Guatemala for an invasion of Cuba. The Security Council refused to investigate the matter. Franklin, *Cuba*, 34. Also, Miami newspapers were filled with rumors of the pending invasion.

76. *Operation Zapata*, 98; Franklin, *Cuba*, 41.

77. Phillips, *The Night Watch*, 110.

78. Sergo Mikoyan, son and private secretary to Soviet First Deputy Premier Anastas Mikoyan, recalled: "The main idea [of sending the missiles] was the defense of Fidel's regime. Khrushchev has some reasons to think the United States would repeat the Bay of Pigs, but not make mistakes anymore."

Georgi Shaknazarov, a confidant of several high-ranking officials instrumental in the Cuban missile crisis, observed: "That is why it seems to me Khrushchev decided to put missiles in Cuba. At some point . . . we had no doubt the United States would repeat the attack on Cuba after the Bay of Pigs." James G. Blight and David A. Welch, *On the Brink: Americans and Soviets Reexamine the Cuban Missile Crisis* (New York: Hill and Wang, 1989), 238, 258.

79. U.S. Dept. of State, "Events in United States-Cuban Relations," 22; David Wise and Thomas B. Ross, *The Invisible Government* (New York: Random House, 1964), 287.

80. Hatchwell and Calder, *Cuba*, 20.

81. Rodríguez and Weisman, *Shadow Warrior*, 110.

82. Daniel P. Hagedorn, *Central American and Caribbean Air Forces*, 28–33; Scheina, "The Cuban Navy," 328.

CHAPTER TWENTY-EIGHT

1. "Venezuelan 'Plot': Bomb Attack on Radio Stations," London *Times* (January 4, 1960), 10; Rómulo Betancourt, *Tres años de Gobierno democático (1959–1962),* 3 vols. (Caracas: Imprenta nacional, 1962), 2: 231.

2. Gerard Cartay Ramírez, *Politica y Partidos modernos en Venezuela* (Caracas: Ediciones Centauro, 1983), 138–41; Jesús Sanoja Hernández, "Mirando al MIR," *El Nacional* A–6 (April 9, 1999), A–6.

3. "Castro Leon Jailed," New York *Times* (April 24, 1960), 35.

4. Juan de Onis, "Case on Trujillo Impresses Panel," New York *Times* (July 21, 1960), 1–2; "Dominican Dictatorship," London *Times* (August 22, 1960), 9; Pedro Corso, "La subversión castrista en Venezuela" [Valencia] *El Carabobeño* (August 13, 1985), 4.

5. Carlos Soto Tamayo, *Rómulo: democracia con garra* (Caracas: S/E, 1986), 384–85.

6. "Left Wing Extremists Behind Venezuela Riots," London *Times* (November 30, 1960), 11; "Venezuela Informs O.A.S. Dominicans Plot an Attack," New York *Times* (December 1, 1960), 1, 3.

7. Soto Tamayo, *Rómulo*, 266–69.

8. Antonio Briceño Linares (1913–) was born in Carvajal, state of Trujillo, in the Andes. He graduated as an ensign from the Military and Naval School in February 1937. In 1939 Briceño received his wings as a pilot from the Military Aviation School. Between 1940 and 1943 he served in both naval and army aviation. In 1943 Briceño formally passed to the ranks of army aviation, which became the Venezuelan air force in 1949. He undertook numerous study programs in the United States—at the U.S. Naval Air Station, Pensacola, in 1940; at the Naval Air Station, Corpus Christi, in 1945; at the U.S. Air Force Tactical Aviation School, Tyndall Field in the late 1940s; at the U.S. Air Force Command and Staff School, Maxwell Air Force Base, in 1951; at American University, Washington, D.C., studying aviation and administration in the early 1950s. Between 1953 and 1955 Briceño was the Director of the Venezuelan Air Force Academy. Next he served as air attaché to Washington and in 1958 was named the Chairman of the Board of the Venezuelan national airlines. Briceño served as Commandant General of the air force between 1958 and 1961 and then as Minister of Defense between 1961 and 1964. In 1964 he was promoted to General of Division and

designated the Venezuelan Chief of Delegation to the Inter-American Defense Board, Washington. He retired in 1967 and later served as ambassador to Italy and West Germany.

9. Carlos Capriles Ayala and Rafael Del Naranco, *Todos los golpes a la democracia venezolana* (Caracas: Consorcio de Ediciones Capriles, 1992), 93–97; Iván D. Jiménez Sánchez, *Los golpes de estado desde Castro hasta Caldera* (Caracas: Cetralca, 1996), 119–20; Soto Tamayo, *Rómulo*, 272–76.

10. "Venezuela Cuts Ties with Havana," New York *Times* (November 12, 1961), 34.

11. The theory has been put forward that Vice Adm. Carlos Larrazábal was the true leader of this subversion against President Betancourt. The principal proponent of this theory is Rear Adm. Ricardo Sosa Ríos, Larrazábal's brother-in-law, who replaced him as commander of the navy in February 1962. Admiral Larrazábal, until his death in 1986, denied this charge. Nevertheless, in 1997, the thirty-fifth anniversary of the failed plot, retired naval Capt. Pedro Medina Silva, who was second in command of the insurrection at Puerto Cabello, stated in an interview that Vice Adm. Carlos Larrazábal was the true leader of the conspiracy. Other senior officers he identified as being involved were Brigade Generals Pedro José Quevedo (Commandant General of the Army), Miguel de la Rosa (Commandant General of the Air Force), and Carlos Luís Araque (Commandant General of the National Guard). Sosa Ríos, *Mar*, 68–69, 82–83, 86–87; Agustín Blanco Muñoz, *La conspiración cívico militar; guairazo, barcelonazo y porteñazo* (Caracas: Ediciones UCV-FACES, 1981), 18–21, 56–58, 88–90, 201–2; "A 35 años del porteñazo: perdono, pero no olvido," *Quinto Día* (Caracas, May 6–13, 1997), 16.

12. Sosa Ríos, *Mar*, 85–87; Blanco Muñoz, *Conspiración*, 285–87.

13. This action is considered the first attack by Castroites against the Venezuelan government. Soto Tamayo, *Rómulo*, 283.

14. ibid., 402–3.

15. Blanco Muñoz, *Conspiración*, 92–118.

16. José Constantino Seijas Villalobos (1923–76), graduated from the U.S. Naval Academy in 1945, was promoted to rear admiral in July 1967, and in 1969 became Commander of the Navy. In July 1971 he became a vice admiral, in 1972 Chief of Joint Staff of the armed forces, and in 1974 Inspector General of the armed forces and Vice Minister of Defense.

17. Sosa Ríos, *Mar*, 65–68; Betancourt, *Tres años*, 3: 78–79; Jiménez Sánchez, *Los golpes*, 121–23.

18. Sosa Ríos, *Mar*, 65.

19. Blanco Muñoz, *Conspiración*, 120–50; Sosa Ríos, *Mar*, 67.

20. "Venezuela Bans Reds' Activities," New York *Times* (May 11, 1962), 1, 14.

21. Jesús Carbonell Izquierdo (1922–) graduated from the Venezuelan Naval Academy in January 1943. In 1967 he became Commander of the Navy with the rank of rear admiral; in 1969, armed forces Chief of the Joint Staff; in 1970, Inspector General of the armed forces (Vice Minister of Defense), as vice admiral; in 1971, Minister of Defense. He was the third naval officer to hold this last position. The first was Vice Adm. Lino de Clemente y Palacios, who on April 19, 1810, was designated Secretary of War and Navy for the "Junta Patriota," and the second was Rear Adm. José Ramon Yépez between 1875 and 1879.

22. Blanco Muñoz, *Conspiración*, 113–65; Sosa Ríos, *Mar*, 65, 71; Victor Hugo Morales Monasterios, *Del porteñazo al Perú* (Caracas: Editorial Domingo Fuentes, 1971), 54–55.

23. Sosa Ríos, *Mar*, 71–72; Morales Monasterios, *Del porteñazo*, 55.

24. Sosa Ríos, *Mar*, 71–72; Morales Monasterios, *Del porteñazo*, 55–56.

25. Captain Ponte Rodríguez, removed as chief of the second section in the naval chief of staff a few weeks prior to the rebellion, was awaiting assignment. Commander Medina Silva was second in command of the Puerto Cabello Naval Base. Lieutenant Morales Monasterios had been the commanding officer of the marines' "Simón Bolívar" Battalion since January 9, 1962, and under direct orders from the Commander of the Navy. A few days before the rebellion, the Lieutenant had been designated assistant naval attaché in London, a position he never filled.

26. Vice Adm. Justo Pastor Fernández Márquez, who graduated from the Venezuelan Naval Academy in July 1956, became Commander of the Navy in June 1984. Morales Monasterios, *Del porteñazo*, 56–57; Sosa Ríos, *Mar*, 73.

27. Morales Monasterios, *Del porteñazo*, 56–58.

28. ibid., 76.

29. Alípio Márquez, *Vida de cuartel* (Caracas: Ediciones Garrado, 1977), 297–98.

30. Morales, *Del porteñazo*, 57–60, 63–65; Sosa Ríos, *Mar*, 75–76; Blanco Muñoz, *Conspiración*, 37–38.

31. Morales Monasterios, *Del porteñazo*, 66–68; 77; Sosa Ríos, *Mar*, 74–77.

32. Blanco Muñoz, *Conspiración*, 38; Morales Monasterios, *Del porteñazo*, 68–69, 71–83; Sosa Ríos, *Mar*, 75–78.

33. Captain Ponte Rodríguez died in prison of a heart attack on July 24, 1964. Commander Medina Silva escaped from prison after a short incarceration and lived in exile until 1970, at which time he was permitted to return. Commander Morales Monasterios was held in prison until 1968, when he was deported to West Germany. He lived there for five years, then was permitted to return to Venezuela. None of the condemned naval officers served a full sentence. The punishment for the majority was dismissal from the service.

CHAPTER TWENTY-NINE

1. Kenneth O. Gilmore, "Cuba's Brazen Blueprint for Subversion," *Readers Digest* 87: 520; 67–75 (August 15, 1965), 71–74; "Castro's Cuba: A U.S. Problem Becomes a Threat to the World," *U.S. News and World Report* 51–54 (February 10, 1964), 52.

2. Franklin Mark Osanka, *Modern Guerrilla Warfare* (New York: The Free Press of Glencoe, 1962), 344.

3. John D. Waghelstein, "Ruminations of a Pachyderm or What I Learned in the Counterinsurgency Business," *Small Wars and Insurgencies* 5: 3; 360–78 (Winter 1994), 362.

4. Che Guevara's book, *La guerra de guerrillas*, was published in Havana in 1960 by the Departamento de Instruccion of the Armed Forces Ministry. His article, "Guerra de guerrillas: un Método," was first published in *Cuba Socialista* in September 1962. It was reprinted by *Bohemia* the following year. The book is a basic how-to volume (a small paperback so it would fit into the pockets of guerrillas).

5. Guevara's belief that guerrilla warfare could lead to a general revolution and that it is not always necessary to wait for the existence of all the conditions for revolution but that they may be induced differed from the theories of the other two Communist theoreticians on guerilla warfare, Mao and Giap. Guevara first addressed the application of these theories to the remainder of Latin America in a speech to the *Nuestro Tiempo* Association in Havana on January 27, 1959. Andrés Suárez, *Cuba: Castroism and Communism, 1959–1966* (Cambridge: M.I.T. Press, 1967), 39–43; John D. Waghelstein, "A Latin-American Insurgency Status Report," *Military Review* 47: 2; 42–47 (February 1987), 43.

6. Luigi Valsalice, *La guerrilla castrista en Venezuela y sus protagonistas 1962–1969* (Caracas: Ediciones Centauro, 1979), 8–9; Julián Rodríguez B., "Venezuela y Cuba en 1960" [Caracas] *Ultimas Noticias/Suplemento Cultural* (May 2, 1999), 10.

7. Waghelstein, "Ruminations," 361.

8. Carlos Soto Tamayo, *Rómulo: democracia con garra* (Caracas: n.p., 1988), 315–16.

9. Rómulo Betancourt, *Tres años de gobierno democrático* (1959–1962), 3 vols. (Caracas: Imprenta Nacional, 1962), 2: 332.

10. Eleazar Díaz Rangel, "Los cubanos revelan secretos de sus desembarcos en Venezuela," [Madrid] *Tribuna Venezolana* 12–21 (June 1997), 21.

11. Soto Tamayo, *Rómulo*, 317–18; F. Parkinson, *Latin America, the Cold War, and the World Powers 1945–1973* (Newbury Park, Calif.: Sage, 1974), 185.

12. Soto Tamayo, *Rómulo*, 319; Marley, *Wars*, 664.

13. "When the Chips Are Down on Cuba," *U.S. News and World Report* (February 5, 1962), 27; "Crushing Rout of Communists in Venezuela," London *Observer* (January 28, 1962), 3; Betancourt, *Tres años*, 2: 306.

14. "Daily Report—Latin America," *Foreign Broadcasting Information Service*: 172 (September 2, 1964), 1; 212 (October 29, 1964), 1; 246 (December 18, 1964), 1. Valsalice, *La guerrilla castrista*, 145–47.

15. "When the Chips Are Down," 27; Bertram B. Johansson, "Castro Drafts 'Calendar,'" *Christian Science Monitor* (April 20, 1962), 5.

16. "Venezuela," *Deadline Data of World Affairs*, 46–47; Bertram B. Johansson, "Soviet Action Stings Castro," *Christian Science Monitor* (October 29, 1962), 1; "Venezuela Calls Up her Military Forces," New York *Times* (October 28, 1962), 1.

17. "Venezuela," *Deadline Data*, 48; Valsalice, *La guerrilla castrista*, 46.

18. "Venezuela," *Deadline Data*, 53.

19. ibid., 54.

20. "Venezuela Balks Assassins' Plot," New York *Times* (June 13, 1963), 1, 8; "Venezuelan Roundup Modified," *Christian Science Monitor* (June 15, 1963), 10.

21. Soto Tamayo, *Rómulo*, 321; "Drive Against the Left in Venezuela," London *Times* (October 2, 1963), 10; Waghelstein, "Ruminations," 361.

22. "Venezuela Rosier than Red in the Hemisphere," *Time* 82; 41–42 (November 1, 1963), 42.

23. Soto Tamayo, *Rómulo*, 321; "Venezuela," *Deadline Data*, 60–62; "Venezuela Terrorists Are Defied," *Washington Post* (December 1, 1963), 1, 22.

24. Charles W. Wiley and Richard J. Booklet, "New 'Vietnams' in Latin America," *The American Legion* 80: 3; 18–21, 46–47 (March 1966), 20; Paul Finch, "Venezuelan Terrorists Seize Plane," *Washington Post* (November 29, 1963), 1; Romulo Betancourt, "The Venezuelan Miracle," *The Reporter* 31: 3; 37–41 (August 13, 1964), 39.

25. "Where U.S. Won and Castro Lost in Latin America," *U.S. News and World Report* (December 16, 1963), 92–94; Richard Jeder, "Venezuela Votes in Heavy Turnout Despite Terror," New York *Times* (December 2, 1963), 1, 3.

26. Parkinson, *Latin America*, 186.

27. "Return of the FALN," *Time* (July 24, 1964), 36.

28. Soto Tamayo, *Rómulo*, 329; Agustín Blanco Muñoz, *La lucha armada hablan 6 comandantes* (Caracas: UCV/FACES, 1981), 284–85, 384.

29. "Daily Report—Latin America," *Foreign Broadcasting Information Service*: 71 (April 14, 1965), 1; 146 (July 30, 1965), 1; 146 (August 13, 1965), 1; 184 (September 23, 1965), 1; "Where Castro Brews Trouble for the U.S.," *U.S. News and World Report* 59: 16; 38–40 (October 18, 1965), 38.

30. "One War that the Communists Are Losing," *U.S. News and World Report* 46: 20; 86–88 (November 14, 1966), 87; Waghelstein, "Ruminations," 361.

31. "Daily Report—Latin America," 46: 1 (March 7, 1966), 1; Lewis H. Diuguid, "Venezuela Elects President to Succeed Leoni," *Washington Post* (December 1, 1968), A27.

32. During the 1930s the PCC drew most of its support from the squatter villages that began to grow around Bogotá. During the 1940s and 1950s, the PCC had some influence within the "republics."

33. Manuel Marulanda Vélez (1930–), was born Pedro Antonio Marín, a peasant, and did not obtain a formal education. He adopted the name Manuel Marulanda Vélez in tribute to an assassinated union leader who had opposed sending Colombian troops to fight in Korea. In 1948 he organized a Liberal guerrilla band which fought the Conservative government of Mariana Ospina. His tactics have traditionally been very conservative. Andrés Cala, "The Enigmatic Guerrilla: FARC's Manuel Marulanda," *Current History* 56–59 (February 2000), 57–58.

34. Valenza, "Colombia's Quiet War," 51.

35. ibid., 51.

36. Mario Antonio Yon Sosa (1932–70) was of half-Chinese origin. He received training at Fort Gulick in the Canal Zone.

37. Luis Augusto Turcius Lima (1941–66) was from the lower class. His early education was in a private Catholic school and a public vocation college (high school). After graduating from the Guatemalan Military Academy, he was trained for six months at Fort Benning, Georgia.

38. Miguel Ydígoras claimed that the first Communist plot against his government began on February 15, 1959, when Raúl and Rolando Lorenzana unsuccessfully attempted to organize an Indian rebellion. Miguel Ydígoras, *My War with Communism*, trans. by Mario Rosenthal (Englewood Cliffs, N.J.: Prentice-Hall, 1963), 20.

39. Alan Howard, "With the Guerrillas in Guatemala," New York *Times Magazine* (June 26, 1966), 8–25. The Retalhulen Air Base placed the CIA-supported Cuban air force approximately 775 miles from Havana and 1,050 miles from Miami. Ydígoras claimed that the plot was Communist inspired. Ydígoras, *My War*, 169.

40. Felix Belair Jr., "Carrier on Guard: Destroyers Also Take Posts in Response to Two Nations' Pleas," New York *Times* (November 18, 1960), 1, 3; L. Fletcher Prouty, *The Secret Team: The CIA and Its Allies in Control of the World* (Englewood Cliffs, N.J.: Prentice-Hall, 1973), 46; "Guatemala," *Hispanic American Report* 15: 1; 19–21 (March 1962), 19.

41. "Guatemala," *Hispanic American Report* 15: 2; 116–18 (April 1962), 116; Richard Gott, *Guerrilla Movements in Latin America* (London: Thomas Nelson, 1970), 38–40.

42. Schlesinger and Kinzer, *Bitter Fruit*, 241–42.

43. Debray, *Revolution*, 44.

44. Herbert Wendt, *The Red, White, and Black Continent* (New York: Doubleday, 1966), 162–66; "Guatemala," *Hispanic American Report* 16: 3; 237–40 (May 1963), 237–38. Juan Arevelo's comments concerning the United States, in his book *The Shark and the Sardines* (New York: Lyle Stuart, 1961), surely did not endear him to the Ambassador.

45. Hector Alejandro Gramajo Morales, *De la guerra . . . A la guerra* (Gautemala: Fondo de Cultura Editorial, 1995), 99–102.

46. Adolfo Gilly, "The Guerrilla Movement in Guatemala" *Monthly Review* 1: 9–40 (May 1965), and 2: 7–41 (June 1965), 1: 20.

47. Gramajo, *De la guerra*, 462–64.

48. Robert H. Holden, "The Real Diplomacy of Violence: United States Military Power in Central America, 1950–1990," *The International History Review* 15; 2; 283–322 (May 1993), 312.

49. The Trotskyite Hugo Blanco emerged as the leader of some 2,000 *campesinos* (poor farmers) in the Convención Valley in 1958. Blanco worked to overturn the centuries-old land distribution system. In November 1962 Blanco led a small band to a police station. They sought arms in order to confront an armed party led by a local landlord. In the struggle that followed, a policeman was killed. Blanco and his following were hunted down and he was captured on May 29, 1963. Blanco was sentenced to twenty years incarceration but was pardoned on December 22, 1970. Mario A. Malpica, *Biografía de la revolución* (Lima: Ediciones Ensayos Sociales, 1967), 468–69; Victor Villanueva, *Hugo Blanco y la rebelión campesina* (Lima: Editorial Juan Mejia, 1967).

50. Javier Heraud (1942–63), was educated at Markham, the English public school in Lima, and the Catholic University. His family was prominent in society.

51. Gott, *Guerrilla Movements*, 248–51.

52. Luis de la Puente Uceda (1926–65) was the son of a Peruvian landowner and a distant relative of Haya de la Torre, founder of the *Aprista* party. Following the coup d'etat by Manuel Odria in 1948, the APRA was declared illegal and de la Puente and other *Apristas* were exiled. De la Puente secretly returned to Peru in 1954 to lead an insurrection against Odria's regime. He was captured and imprisoned. Prior to the elections of 1956 de la Puente and other political prisoners were released. In 1959 he attended the first National Agrarian Reform Forum in Havana, Cuba. Once de la Puente returned to Peru, he led the radicals during their break with the *Aprista* party and formed the APRA *Rebelde*.

53. The most important law was the decree 1444 on March 28, 1963.

54. Béjar was pardoned following the overthrow of President Fernando Belaúnde Terry in 1968.

55. Gott, *Guerilla Movements*, 231–85.

56. Center for Strategic Studies, *Dominican Action—1965: Intervention or Cooperation* (Washington, D.C.: Georgetown University Press, 1966), 27.

57. Lawrence M. Greenberg, "The U.S. Dominican Intervention: Success Story," *Parameters* 17: 4, 18–29 (December 1987), 21.

58. *The Dominican Intervention 1965* (Carlisle Barracks, Pa.: U.S. Army War College, 1984), 9.

59. Eldredge R. Long Jr., "The Dominican Crisis 1965: An Experiment in International Peace Keeping," Thesis, U.S. Naval War College, Newport, R.I., 1967, 39.

60. Yale H. Ferguson, "The Dominican Intervention of 1965: Recent Interpretations," *International Organization* 27: 515–48 (Autumn 1973), 530; Greenberg, "The U.S. Dominican Intervention," 23–24.

61. Alberto Carbone, "1965: La FIP en Santo Domingo," *Defensa* 43: 78–81 (November 1981), 78–81.

62. Greenberg, "The U.S. Dominican Intervention," 25–26.

63. ibid., 26, 29. In February 1973 Colonel Caamaño was killed while clandestinely leading a band of pro-Castro guerrillas back to the Dominican Republic. Gonzalo de Bethencourt, "La Guerrilla de las mulas," *Defensa* 68: 70–77 (December 1983), 73.

64. Jules Régis Debray (1940–) was a student of the French Communist Louis Althusser. He lectured at the University of Havana and found favor with Fidel Castro and Che Guevara. Debray argued that military leadership needed to be given primacy over political leadership when necessary. This reversed the priorities of the revolutionary teachings of Leninists. Debray was permitted access to guerrillas who supported Castro. He was captured in Bolivia in late July 1967 while leaving one of Che Guevara's camps. He was sentenced to thirty years in jail for his complicity in Guevara's activities, but served only three years. Debray became a fierce critic of the Cuban Revolution, and one of Che's daughters, among others, accused Debray of betraying her father to the Bolivians without being tortured.

65. The French as well as the first English edition were published in 1967. See Debray, *Revolution*. Also see Rolondo E. Bonachea, ed., *Che: Selected Works of Ernesto Guevara* (Cambridge: M.I.T. Press, 1969), 32.

CHAPTER THIRTY

1. Apparently, the Khrushchev-Kennedy agreement ending the Cuban Missile Crisis provided that the United States would stop supporting and work to prevent Cuban émigrés from attacking the island and withdraw its surface-to-surface missiles from Turkey. The Soviet Union would withdraw its surface-to-surface missiles from Cuba and not introduce offensive weapons to the island. Parkinson, *Latin America*, 185, 215.

2. Havana Domestic Service (July 26, 1967), cited in the *Foreign Broadcast Information Service* 6: h15.

3. Peter Shearman, *The Soviet Union and Cuba* (New York: Routledge & Kegan Paul, 1987), 15–17; Suárez, *Cuba*, 243; Waghelstein, "A Latin-American Insurgency," 43; Parkinson, *Latin America*, 218–20.

4. Although it was widely known that the Cuban government supported leftist guerrilla movements, that government did not officially acknowledge the extent of its activities until 1997 when the book *Secretos de generales* (Habana: Editorial SI-MAR, S.A., 1996), by Luis Baez.

5. The United States established the Latin American Training Center–Ground Division in the Panama Canal Zone in 1946. This was renamed the U.S. Army School of the Americas in July 1963 and Spanish was made the official language. The school suspended operations in October 1984 to comply with the terms of the 1977 Panama Canal Treaty. It reopened in early 1985 at Fort Benning, Georgia. During much of its existence the school was under attack by political liberals, who dubbed it "the school of dictators." The School of the Americas trained over 61,000 Latin American military, paramilitary, police, and civilians. Gary L. Arnold, "IMET in Latin America," *Military Review* 47: 2; 30–41 (February 1987), 33.

6. Waghelstein, "Ruminations," 361–62.

7. Arnold, "IMET," 33.

8. Díaz Rangel, "Los cubanos," 12–13; Ramón Maceiras, "Ochoa y la guerrilla venezolana" [Caracas] *Zeta* 768 (August 10, 1989), 23.

9. Díaz Rangel, "Los cubanos," 12–13; Maceiras, "Ochoa," 13; "El Che quiso incorporarse en el 60 a la lucha armada en Venezuela," [Caracas] *El Mundo* (June 14, 1997), 2; "Fidel Castro casi muere en invasión a Venezuela," [Caracas] *El Globo* (June 25, 1997), 8.

10. Arnaldo Ochoa Sánchez (1940–89), born of peasant origins, joined the Cuban Revolutionary army in 1958 in the Sierra Maestra. He fought under the command of Camilo Cienfuegos. Following the Revolution, Ochoa fought against the anti-Castro guerrillas in the Escambray Mountains. He also fought at the Bay of Pigs in April 1962. In 1966 he was sent to Venezuela to train and to command local guerrillas. Returning to Cuba two years later as a lieutenant colonel, he was assigned to the Special Operations Group under the direct command of Fidel and Rául Castro. Its task was to plan and to direct the operation for revenge against those Bolivians directly responsible for the execution of Che Guevera. Speculation is that Ochoa carried out the operation using Argentine and French terrorists to assassinate Bolivians, including the President, Gen. René Barrientos Ortuño, and a former president, Gen. Juan José Torres. Also during the 1960s, he served in the Congo, and in the early 1970s Ochoa commanded a Cuban force in Sierra Leone. He studied at the Soviet Frunze Academy and became fluent in Russian. During early 1976 Ochoa commanded 12,000 Cuban troops in Angola. In February 1977 he commanded a Cuban mission to Ethiopia. Ochoa was promoted to General of Division. He returned to Ethiopia where he remained for several years. Beginning in 1983 he served in Nicaragua supporting the Sandinista government for two years. In January 1984 Ochoa was awarded Cuba's highest military declaration, "Hero of the Republic of Cuba and the Máximo Gómez Order, First Degree." In the late 1980s Ochoa returned to Angola. His military decisions were highly criticized by Fidel Castro and Ochoa was recalled to Havana. On June 14, 1989, he was arrested, accused of narcotics trafficking, confessed, tried, condemned to death, and shot on July 13. Speculation is that Fidel felt threatened by Ochoa's popularity and eliminated the potential rival; Ochoa confessed to safeguard his family.

"El vengador del "Che" murió a manos de Fidel," [Caracas] *Zeta* 768 (August 10, 1988), 20–22; Nina Negrón, "Diccionario de la revolución," [Caracas] *Primicia* (January 19, 1999), 44; Mallin, *History*, 338–67; Rui Ferreira, "Castro Dice que Cuban Sí Apoyo la Subversión," [Miami] *El Nuevo Mundo* (July 4, 1998), A01.

11. Leopoldo Cintra Frías (1941–) fought in the Cuban Revolution where he earned the rank of lieutenant. In 1960 he studied artillery in Czechoslovakia. During 1975 Cintra fought in Angola against South African forces. He commanded a tank unit in Ethiopia during 1978. He reached the rank of brigade general and is a member of the Cuban Communist Party.

12. Among the army units that pursued the guerrillas were "Hunter" (*Cazadores*) battalions created in 1963. These were light infantry units organized, trained, and equipped for counterinsurgency warfare. They could be distinguished by their green berets. The majority of the officers, warrants, and senior enlisted (*suboficiales*) were trained by U.S. Rangers and Special Forces. These "Hunter" battalions were so successful that between 1963 and 1967 thirteen battalions were created. At the end of the armed struggle against the rural guerrillas, these battalions were amalgamated into the 73rd "Hunter Brigade." In the 1980s the Salvadoran army created "Hunter" battalions based on the advice of Venezuelan military advisors sent to Central America. In 1999 Venezuela created the 23rd "Hunter Brigade." It is being used to combat narco-trafficking along the frontier with Colombia.

13. Díaz Rangel, "Los cubanos," 15.

14. ibid., 16; Maceiras, "Ochoa," 13.

15. "War on Subversion," *Time* 88 (December 23, 1966), 29; "Caracas Terrorists Attack U.S. Buildings," *The Washington Post* (November 26, 1966), A14; "Venezuela—Rooting Out the Rebels," *Newsweek* 68 (December 26, 1966), 37.

16. "War on Subversion," 29; Drew Pearson, "Terrorism in Venezuela," *The Washington Post* (January 15, 1967), E7.

17. Ulises Rosales del Toro (1942–) fought in the Cuban Revolution. He attended a number of Soviet military schools, including the Voroshilov Military Academy. In 1963 Rosales served in Algeria and in 1975 he fought in Angola. In December 1981 he became Chief of the General Staff. By 1997 Rosales reached the rank of General of Division. Rosales is the first substitute for the Minister of the Revolutionary Armed Forces, Raúl Castro.

18. Raúl Menéndez Tomassevich (1929–) fought in the Cuban Revolution and at the Bay of Pigs. Between 1961 and 1962 he was the Chief of the *Lucha Contra Bandidos (LCB)* in the Escambray Mountains. In July 1966 "Tomas" (his nickname) headed a mission to Guinea Bissau. He attended the Soviet Voroshilov Military Academy. During the 1970s, Menéndez served as Chief of the Cuban Military Mission to Angola. He earned the rank of General of Division and became the vice minister of the Revolutionary Armed Forces.

19. Díaz Rangel, "Los cubanos," 12; "Libro revela los secretos de la lucha anticomunista. Militares de Cuba confiesan episodios de guerrilla venezolana," [Caracas] *El Nacional* (March 29, 1997), A2; Soto Tamayo, *Rómulo,* 330–31; Díaz Rangel, "Los cubanos," 16; Agustín Blanco Muñoz, *La izquierda revolucionaria insurge* (Caracas: Ediciones FACES/UCV, 1981), 331; Blanco Muñoz, *La lucha armada,* 171, 274; Carlos Soto Tamayo, *Inteligencia militar y subversión armada* (Caracas: Ministerio de la Defensa, 1982), 168–90.

During a February 1989 visit to Venezuela, Fidel Castro asked President Carlos Andrés Pérez to locate and return to Cuba the remains of the three Cubans who lost their lives during the Machurucuto landing. Pérez ordered a search and the remains of two were located and returned. Marcos Tarre, "Los muertos de Machurucuto," [Caracas] *Letra G* (February 13, 1994), 11.

20. Baez, *Secretos,* 108.

21. "Hace 20 años tres buques cubanos repletos de guerrilleros intentaron atracar en Venezuela," [Caracas] *Ultimas Noticias* (September 7, 1988), 4; Solís Martínez, "La persecución en Caliente," [Caracas] *El Universal* (April 10, 1995), 1–5; "Venezuela Seizes Ship; Cuba Objects," *Washington Post* (November 21, 1968), E1.

22. "For the Record," *Washington Post* (December 20, 1968), A18.

23. Valenza, "Colombia's Quiet War," 52; U.S. Senate, 90th Cong., 2d Sess., *Survey of the Alliance for Progress, Insurgency in Latin America* (Washington, D.C.: Government Printing Office, 1968), 17.

24. "The Month in Review—Colombia," *Current History* 186 (September 1970), 186.

25. Estep, *Guerrilla Warfare,* 37.

26. Peter Calvert, *Guatemalan Insurgency and American Security* (London: Institute for Conflict Studies, No. 167, 1984), 8–9.

27. César Montes (1942–) had long been a social revolutionary. At the age of thirteen, he was expelled from Catholic school for opinions concerning the 1954 overthrow of the Arbenz government. At eighteen years of age, he led a student demonstration and three years later he joined the guerrillas in the hills.

28. Calvert, *Guatemalan Insurgency,* 9.

29. Henry Giniger, "Guatemala Is a Battleground," New York *Times Magazine* (June 16, 1968), 22; Carlos Caballero Jurado and Nigel Thomas, *Central American Wars 1959–89* (London: Osprey Publishing, 1990), 10.

30. George Black, *Garrison Guatemala* (London: Zed Press, 1984), 101–4.

31. Giniger, "Guatemala Is a Battleground," 25.

32. Calvert, *Guatemalan Insurgency*, 9.

33. Schooley, *Conflict*, 25; Calvert, *Guatemalan Insurgency*, 9.

34. The new Federal Police was a civilian agency responsible for law enforcement related to the central government such as passport controls, among others. There were also two state police agencies, the Civil Police and the Military Police. The state Civil Police was primarily responsible for criminal activity, such as bank robberies and narcotics sales. The state Military Police were uniformed, military-trained, and responsible for public order. The name "Military Police" was adopted in 1964; some states, such as Rio Grande do Sul, retained the old name, Military Brigade.

35. Donato, *Dicionário*, 195, 341.

36. By the late 1960s, Brazil had numerous Communist parties. The Brazilian Communist Party (*Partido Comunista Brasileiro*—PCB) was established in 1922 and was affiliated with the Soviet Union (see chapter 10). It gained legal status in 1946. In February 1962 a splinter group founded the Communist Party of Brazil (*Partido Comunista do Brasil*—PC do B); it was aligned with China. In April 1968 a splinter group was expelled from the PCB for revolutionary deviations and founded the Brazilian Revolutionary Communist Party (*Partido Comunista Brasileiro Revolucionário*—PCBR). In addition, there were parties with strong Communist tendencies: the National Liberation Alliance (*Aliança Nacional Libertadora*—ANL), Revolutionary Armed Vanguard-Palmares (*Vanguarda Armada Revolucionária-Palmares*—VAR-Palmares), the Popular Revolutionary Vanguard (*Vanguarda Popular Revolutionária*—VPR), and others.

37. Donato, *Dicionário*, 524.

38. The Popular Revolutionary Vanguard was composed of dissidents from the National Revolutionary Movement (*Movimento Nacional Revolucionário*), which had been founded in 1964.

39. Donato, *Dicionário*, 285.

40. Jay Mallin, "'Che' Guevara: Some Documentary Puzzles at the End of a Long Journey," *Journal of Inter-American Studies and World Affairs* 10:1; 74–84 (1968), 79; Parkinson, *Latin America*, 217.

41. Haydee Tamara Bunke, *nom de guerre* "Tania" (1937–67), was born in Argentina to German parents who had fled Nazi Germany. Her father was a Communist and her mother a Jew. The family returned to East Germany following World War II and Bunke became a translator. She met Che Guevara in 1960 while traveling in a trade mission to Cuba, and they became romantically involved. She immigrated to Cuba and was eventually assigned as an undercover agent to Bolivia. Bunke was killed during the destruction of Guevara's guerrilla band. Her remains were returned to Cuba and interred with her compatriots, including Che, at Santa Clara in 1997.

42. Mallin, "'Che,'" 80; George Andrew Roth, "I Was Arrested with Regis Debray," *Evergreen Review* (February 1968), 45–47, 81–97; Marc Hutten, "How Guerrillas Were Beaten by the Jungle: 30 Years Sought for Debray," London *Times* (October 28, 1967), 8.

43. Richard Gott, "Che, Debray, and the CIA," *The Nation* (November 20, 1967), 524; Jay Mallin, ed., *Che Guevara on Revolution* (New York: Delta Books, 1970), 208.

44. Gott, *Guerrilla Movements*, 404, 448; Jean Larteguy, *The Guerrillas* (New York: World Publishing, 1970), 241.

45. Waghelstein, "Ruminations," 362; Michèle Ray, "The Execution of Che by the CIA," *Ramparts* 23–37 (March 1968), 37.

46. Robin Blackburn and Perry Anderson, "The Ordeal of Regis Debray," London *Observer* (August 27, 1967), 7; John D. Waghelstein, "'Che's' Bolivian Adventure," *Military Review* 59: 8; 39–48 (August 1979), 42.

47. Waghelstein, "'Che's' Bolivian Adventure," 42.

48. Gott, *Guerrilla Movements*, 471.

49. Mallin, "'Che,'" 81.

50. The five survivors were Gido "Inti" Peredo, a second Bolivian, and three Cubans; all five escaped to Chile. Following Che's death, the Army of National Liberation (*Ejército de Liberación Nacional*), formed from pre-Guevara elements, became the primary practitioner of guerrilla warfare in Bolivia. Although it frequently captured national headlines, it never posed a serious threat to the Bolivian government. "Guevara Force Said to Elude Trap," New York *Times* (November 30, 1967), 25.

51. Mallin, "'Che,'" 84; Marley, *Wars*, 666; Gott, *Guerrilla Movements*, 475.

52. *Congressional Record*, 90th Cong., 1st Sess. (May 16, 1967), 113: 12818–822.

53. [La Paz] *Presencia* (October 11, 1967), quoted in Mallin, "'Che,'" 82.

54. Waghelstein, "Ruminations," 362.

55. Gott, *Guerrilla Movements*, 83.

56. "Terror From the Extremes," *Time* 80 (October 19, 1962), 32.

57. Eugenio Hernandez, "Cuban-Soviet Relations: Divergence and Convergence" (Washington, D.C.: Georgetown University, Latin American Studies Program, Occasional Paper No. 3, 1980), 9; Georgie Anne Geyer, *Guerrilla Prince* (Boston: Little, Brown, 1991), 326–27.

58. Ferreira, "Castro," A01.

CHAPTER THIRTY-ONE

1. Richard L. Clutterbuck, *Protest and the Urban Guerrilla* (New York: Abelard-Schuman, 1974), 284–85; Peter Janke, "Terrorism in Argentina," *Journal of the Royal United Services Institute for Defence Studies* 119, 3 (September 1974), 44.

2. James Kohl and John Litt, *Urban Guerrilla Warfare in Latin America* (Cambridge, Mass.: MIT Press, 1974), 143–44, 191; João Quartim, *Dictatorship and Armed Struggle in Brazil* (New York: Monthly Review Press, 1972), 131; Alain Labrousse, *The Tupamaros: Urban Guerrillas in Uruguay* (n.p.: Harmondsworth, Penguin, 1973), 115–16.

3. Robert Moss, "Urban Guerrillas in Latin America," The Institute for the Study of Conflict, London, *Conflict Studies* 8 (October 1970), 6.

4. An Argentine Montonero admitted, "[W]e put things into practice before making up theories about them." Kohl and Litt, *Urban Guerrilla Warfare*, 380–81.

5. Carlos Marighela (1911–69) was born in El Salvador, Bahia States, Brazil. He was the son of a Negro mother and an Italian immigrant father. Because of his size and the color of his skin, he was called "the ebony giant" in Brazilian newspapers. He joined the Communist party in 1922 (at the age of eleven), and was frequently arrested, tortured, and shot due to his activities. In 1967 he completed a break with the Communist party because he disagreed with the peaceful strategy it had publicly adopted. Marighela's theories on guerrilla warfare were outlined in his "Minimanual of the Urban Guerrilla," first published in *Tricontinental Bimonthly*, Havana (January–February 1970), 16–56. The work has been reissued numerous times in a variety of languages.

6. Abraham Guillen (1913–unk) was born in Spain. He immigrated to Argentina and during the 1960s became one of the most prolific writers encouraging urban revolution. His principal work was *Estrategia de la guerra urbana manuales del pueblo* (Montevideo: Manuales del Pueblo, 1966).

7. "Guerrilla Politics in Argentina," The Institute for the Study of Conflict, London, *Conflict Studies* 63 (October 1975), 10.

8. Raúl Sendic (1925–89) was of Serb-Sicilian descent. Twice during the late 1950s he was defeated in elections while running as a Socialist. Sendic gave up law studies in order to organize poverty-stricken sugar workers, leading them in strikes during the early 1960s. In July 1963 he led the first *Tupamaro* attack against a gun club 80 miles outside Montevideo. He was captured in December 1964 but released. Sendic was captured again in 1970. In September 1971 he was freed by Tupamaro during a daring, massive jail break. The following September Sendic was shot in the face and again captured. He was tortured while imprisoned. In 1985 Sendic and other *Tupamaros* were freed under an amnesty. He reentered politics. Sendic died of Charcot's disease in France.

9. *Generals and Tupamaros: the Struggle for Power in Uruguay, 1969–1973* (London: Latin American Review of Books, 1974), preface.

10. Tupac Amaru II, the last Inca, led an unsuccessful revolt against the Spanish at the end of the colonial era.

11. Estep, *Guerrilla Warfare*, 57.

12. Moss, "Urban Guerrillas," 13.

13. Jay Mallin, "The Military vs Urban Guerrillas," *Marine Corps Gazette* 57: 1; 18–25 (January 1973), 20; Moss, "Urban Guerrillas," 14.

14. Mallin, "The Military vs Urban Guerrillas," 20.

15. ibid., 19.

16. Moss, "Urban Guerrillas," 14.

17. Mallin, "The Military vs Urban Guerrillas," 19–20.

18. ibid., 24–25.

19. ibid., 21.

20. ibid., 24.

21. Raymond Estep, *Guerrilla Warfare in Latin America, 1963–1975* (Maxwell Air Force Base, Ala.: Air University Institute for Professional Development, 1975), 62.

22. Kohl and Litt, *Urban Guerrilla Warfare*, 302.

23. Mallin, "The Military vs Urban Guerrillas," 24–25.

24. Johnson, "Guerrilla Politics," 4, 13–14; Mallin, "The Military vs Urban Guerrillas," 24–25.

25. Carlos Marighela, *For the Liberation of Brazil* (Middlesex: Penguin Books, 1971), 57–58.

26. Estep, *Guerrilla Warfare*, 50–51.

27. Charles B. Elbrick, the U.S. Ambassador, was kidnapped in Rio de Janeiro on September 4, 1969. He was released after fifteen government prisoners were flown to Mexico. Nobuo Okuchi, the Japanese Consul General in São Paulo, was kidnapped in March 1970. He was released after five prisoners were freed. Ehrenfried von Holleben, the West German Ambassador, was kidnapped in June. He was freed after forty prisoners were flown to Algeria. Giovanni Enrico Bucher, the Swiss Ambassador, was kidnapped on December 7. He was freed after seventy prisoners were flown to Chile.

28. Luís Mir, *A revolução impossíve* (São Paulo: Editora Best Seller, 1994), 696–97, 717.

29. Richard Gillespie, "A Critique of the Urban Guerrilla: Argentina, Uruguay, and Brazil," *Conflict Quarterly* 1: 2; 39–53 (Fall 1980), 43.

30. "Peronism meant before all else loyalty to the person of Perón. Peronists, it seemed, could be either Fascists or Marxists, but not both at once. That feat only Perón himself could perform." Johnson, "Guerrilla Politics," 2.

31. Janke, "Terrorism," 44.

32. Among the most publicized attacks by the ERP were the following: On May 23, 1971, it kidnapped Stanley Silvester, a manager of Swift Packing House in the province of Santa Fe; on March 21, 1972, it murdered Oberdam Sallustro, President of Fiat Argentina, and on April 10 it murdered Gen. Juan Carlos Sanchez, commander of the army's Second Corps, and the politician Roberto Mario Uzal.

33. "Como Murio Aramburu," *La Causa Peronista* 1: 9; 25–30 (September 3, 1974), 25–30.

34. Kenneth F. Johnson, "Peronism: The Final Gamble," The Institute for the Study of Conflict, London, *Conflict Study* 42 (January 1974), 7.

35. Johnson, "Peronism," 10.

36. Janke, "Terrorism," 47.

37. "Copó un grupo terrorista un comando ejército," *La Prensa* (September 7, 1973), 1, 6.

38. "Efectuóse el sepelio de Rucci, quien fue asesinado el martes, *La Nacion* (September 27, 1973), 1.

39. Law 20.642 passed on June 25, 1974, and was enacted on the twenty-ninth.

40. "El frente rural," *El Combatiente* 7: 3–4 (June 12, 1974), 3–4; Johnson, "Guerrilla Politics," 3.

41. "Desarrollo del acto visto desde la casa de gobierno," *La Prensa* (May 2, 1974), 7; "Hubo incidentes ella desconcentración," *La Prensa* (May 2, 1974), 9.

42. The AAA was allegedly linked to the right-wing Perónist deputy Alberto Brito Lima and López Rega, a confidant of Isabel Martínez de Perón, the Social Welfare Minister. Rega was accused in Congress of using ministry funds to finance the AAA. Johnson, "Guerrilla Politics," 8–9.

43. Johnson, "Guerrilla Politics," 16.

44. "Atacaron terroristas un arsenal militar," *La Prensa* (December 24, 1975), 1–2.

45. "Fue asesinado el doctor Mor Roig," *La Nacion* (July 16, 1974), 1, 10.

46. "Dos empresarios fueron secuestrados en olivos," *La Nacion* (September 20, 1974), 1, 12.

47. The National Executive Power, February 5, 1975, Decree "S," 261.

48. "Contra un avión de la fuerza aérea se atentó en el aeropuerto de Tucumán" *La Pensa* (August 29, 1975), 1, 6; "Sangriento intento extremista en Formosa *La Nacion* (October 6, 1975), 1, 10.

49. Decree 2770 created an Internal Security Council to coordinate the campaign against the guerrillas; Decree 2771 allowed the Defense Council to operationally control civil law enforcement agencies in the struggle against the guerrillas; and Decree 2772 allowed the armed forces, under the command of the President, to be used for security and military operations against the guerrillas.

50. Among the more publicized assassinations were: October 3, 1974, Juan Mario Russo, former Secretary General of the Timber Trade Union; December 14, Antonio dos Santos Larangeira, an industrialist; February 14, 1975, Hipolito Acuña, a Radical Civil Union deputy from Santa Fe Province; February 26, John Patrick Egan, U.S. Consul; June 4, Rául Gameloni, Manager of the ACINDAR plant; June 10, Juan Enrique Pelayes, a trade-union leader; October 28, Alberto Salas, personnel director for Fiat; December 17, Alberto Manuel Campos, Mayor of San Martin; February 26, 1976, Héctor Minetti, manager of the Liqueur Company.

51. Gillespie, "A Critique of the Urban Guerrilla," 47.

52. In January 1989 a movement named "Everything for the Nation" (*Todo para el Pueblo*) attacked an army garrison at La Tablada, outside Buenos Aires. Many had been *Montoneros*. The attack was a failure; the entire force was killed or captured.

53. Mallin, "The Military vs Urban Guerrillas," 25.

CHAPTER THIRTY-TWO

1. Longino Becerra, *Evolución histórica de Honduras* (Tegucigalpa: Baktun Editorial, 1994), 182; Ralph Lee Woodward Jr., *Central America: A Nation Divided*, 2d ed. (New York: Oxford University Press, 1985), 275; Alberto Carbone, "El Salvador-Honduras: la guerra de las 100 horas," *Defensa* 25; 72–79 (May 1980), 72–74.

2. *Historia de El Salvador*, 2 vols. (Mexico: Ministerio de Educación El Salvador, 1990–94), 2: 224–25; David E. Spencer, "The 1969 Hundred Hours War: It Wasn't about Soccer," (Unpublished manuscript, 1991), 2.

3. Victor Bulmer-Thomas, "Honduras since 1930," in *Central America since Independence*, ed. by Leslie Bethell (Cambridge: Cambridge University Press, 1991), 214; Dan Hagedorn, "From *Caudillos* to Coin," *Air Enthusiast* 31: 55–70 (July–November 1986), 68; Schooley, *Conflict*, 39.

4. Jay Mallin, "Salvador-Honduras War, 1969," *Air University Review* 21: 3; 87–92 (March–April 1970), 87–89; English, *Armed Forces*, 285; Schooley, *Conflict*, 38–39.

5. "The El Salvador-Honduras War," *Strategic Survey 1969* (London: Institute for Strategic Studies, 1970), 57; Hagedorn, *Central American and Caribbean Air Forces*, 73; Carbone, "El Salvador-Honduras," 74.

6. Mallin, "Salvador-Honduras War," 87; "The El Salvador-Honduras War," 55; Carbone, "El Salvador-Honduras," 72.

7. Normally conscription should have provided El Salvador with over 20,000 recruits each year. Therefore, conscription must have been very selective.

8. Spencer, "The 1969 Hundred Hours War," 3.

9. ibid.

10. The trainers could be used for strafing and other combat missions. English, *Armed Forces*, 285, 408; Hagedorn, *Central American and Caribbean Air Forces*, 88–89; Carbone, "El Salvador-Honduras," 78.

11. English, *Armed Forces*, 408; Carbone, "El Salvador-Honduras," 78; Thomas P. Anderson, *The War of the Dispossessed* (Lincoln: University of Nebraska Press, 1981), 116.

12. Carbone, "El Salvador-Honduras," 76; Anderson, *The War*, 112; Becerra, *Evolución Histórica*, 191; Spencer, "The 1969 Hundred Hours War," 4–5.

13. Hagedorn, *Central American and Caribbean Air Forces*, 73–74; Mallin, "Salvador-Honduras War," 89.

14. Spencer, "The 1969 Hundred Hours War," 6.

15. ibid., 8.

16. J. Wilfredo Sánchez V., *Ticante* (Tegucigalpa: Corporacion Editora Nacional, 1983), 63.

17. Spencer, "The 1969 Hundred Hours War," 10; *Historia de El Salvador*, 2: 227.

18. Spencer, "The 1969 Hundred Hours War," 11–12.

19. ibid., 14.

20. *Historia de El Salvador*, 2: 228; Spencer, "The 1969 Hundred Hours War," 15.

21. Carbone, "El Salvador-Honduras," 77.

22. Hagedorn, *Central American and Caribbean Air Forces*, 74; Carbone, "El Salvador-Honduras," 74; Victor Manuel Mendez y Reyes, *La guerra que yo viví* (San Salvador: n.p., 1972), 152–54.

23. Hagedorn, *Central American and Caribbean Air Forces*, 74–75; Spencer, "The 1969 Hundred Hours War," 12–13.

24. Mallin, "Salvador-Honduras War," 91.

25. ibid., 91–92; Woodward, *Central America*, 275.

26. Becerra, *Evolución histórica*, 191; English, *Armed Forces*, 286; Mallin, "Salvador-Honduras War," 92.

27. Mallin, "Salvador-Honduras War," 91; Bulmer-Thomas, "Honduras," 215.

28. *Historia de El Salvador*, 2: 228–29; "The El Salvador-Honduras War," 60–61; Schooley, *Conflict*, 39.

29. English, *Armed Forces*, 286.

CHAPTER THIRTY-THREE

1. Admiral Anaya before the Rattenbach Commission in *Gente* (December 8, 1983), 29; Martin Middlebrook, *The Battle for the 'Malvinas'* (London: Viking, 1989), 7; Siro de Martin, "Notas y comentarios," *Boletín del Centro Naval* 748: 77–98 (January–March 1987), 82.

2. Scheina, *Latin America*, 379–81.

3. Admiral Lombardo was ordered to keep the plan a secret, so only Rear Adm. Carlos Garcia Boll, chief of naval aviation; Rear Adm. Gualter Allara, commander of the fleet; and Rear Adm. Carlos Büsser, head of the Argentine marines, and a few of their most trusted subordinates participated in its preparations. They revised a plan that had been prepared by Admiral Anaya in 1977. Middlebrook, *The Battle*, 2.

4. O. R. Cardoso, R. Kirschbaum, and E. van der Kooy, *Falklands—The Secret Plot* (Surrey: Preston Editions, 1987), 1–6, 27; Carlos A. Büsser, "La recuperacion de Malvinas," *Boletin del Centro Naval* 748: 13–32 (January–March 1987), 13–15.

5. Martin Middlebrook, *The Battle*, 7–10; Martin, "Notas y Comentarios," 82; General Leopoldo Galtieri before the Rattenbach Commission, *Gente* (December 8, 1983), 15; Büsser, "La recuperacion," 20.

6. Amphibious Task Force 40 was composed of the British-designed Type 42 destroyers *Santisima Trinidad* (flagship) and the *Hercules*, the corvettes *Drummond* and *Granville*, the submarine *Santa Fé*, the landing ship tank *Cabo San Antonio*, the icebreaker *Almirante Irizar*, and the cargo transport *Isla de las Estados*.
Covering Task Force 20 was made up of the light carrier *25 de Mayo*; the destroyers *Bouchard*, *Piedrabuena*, *and* Py; the fleet tanker *Punta Médanos*; and the fleet tug *Alférez Sobral*.

7. September 16, 1982, interview with Rear Adm. Carlos Büsser; September 16, 1982, interview with Lt. Cmdr. Hugo Santillán.

8. September 15, 1982, interview with Capt. Carlos Coli and Cmdr. Jorge Acosta concerning fleet operations.

9. Scheina, *Latin America: A Naval History*, 255–63.

10. Jeffery Ethell and Alfred Price, *Air War South Atlantic* (New York: Macmillan, 1983), 229; "Las operaciones de ataque," *Aeroespacio* 429: 50–61 (September–October 1982).

11. *The Military Balance 1981–1982* (London: Institute for Strategic Studies, 1981), 92.

12. "Americas' Falklands War," *The Weekend Australian* 17 (March 10–11, 1984), 17.

13. Brenda Ralph Lewis, "Unexpected War in the Falklands," *Strategy and Tactics* 103: 122–29 (September–October 1985), 122–23; Secretary of State for Defence, *The Falklands Campaign: The Lessons* (London: Her Majesty's Stationery Office, 1982), 6, 37–38.

14. *The Military Balance 1981–1982*, 27–28; Secretary of State for Defence, *The Falklands Campaign*, 6, 42–43.

15. *The Military Balance 1981–1982*, 29; Secretary of State for Defence, *The Falklands Campaign*, 44; Ethell and Price, *Air War*, 229.

16. Perhaps mesmerized by the political as opposed to the military solutions that resulted from the fate of other British colonies throughout the world, Argentine leaders apparently believed that the British would negotiate the fate of the islands rather than fight. Also, the composition of Argentine body politics made it next to impossible to negotiate within a time frame set against the backdrop of a British task force steaming south.

17. *Informe Rattenbach: el drama de Malvinas* (Buenos Aires: Ediciones Espartaco, 1988), 195–97; Ejercito Argentino, *Informe oficial de ejército argentino conflicto Malvinas*, 2 vols. (Buenos Aires: Ejército Argentino, 1983), 2: annex 9.

18. September 30, 1983, interview with Argentine Navy's Malvinas Analysis Group; Secretary of State for Defence, *The Falklands Campaign*, 7.

19. The precise location of the attack is not agreed upon; however, it was at or near 55°24' south latitude and 60°32' west longitude.

20. Some 321 of the *General Belgrano*'s crew died. The Argentine navy has calculated that 272 died during or shortly after the impact of the torpedo and 49 died at sea or after rescue from injuries and exposure. There were 819 survivors.

21. September 30, 1983, interview with Rear Adm. Gualter Alara, Commander of Task Force 79; September 13, 1982, interview with Capt. José Tejo, commanding officer of the *Santísima Trinidad*.

22. Rolando L. Alano, "Santa Bárbara, qué debut!" *Aeroespacio* 433: 44–45 (May–June 1983).

23. Ethell and Price, *Air War*, 53, 248–51; September 16, 1982, interview with Rear Adm. Carlos Büsser.

24. Rubén O. Moro, *South Atlantic Conflict: The War for the Malvinas* (New York: Praeger, 1989), 89–91, 143, 184–87; "La FAA y la fuerza de tareas británica," *Aeroespacio* 429: 32–48 (September–October 1982), 41; Ethell and Price, *Air War*, 234–35.

25. September 23, 1983, interview with Capt. Fernando Azcueta, Commander of the *San Luis*; September 27, 1983, interview with Capt. Eulogio Moya, Commander of the Argentine Submarine Command.

26. September 30, 1983, interview with Argentine navy's Malvinas Analysis Group; September 29, 1983, interview with pilots from T-34 Squadron.

27. September 13, 1982, interview with senior Argentine naval aviators.

28. Secretary of State for Defence, *The Falklands Campaign*, 9.

29. September 13, 1982, interview with Argentine senior naval aviators; September 13, 1982, interview with Lt. Cmdr. Rodolfo Castro Fox, Commander of Naval Attack Squadron Three.

30. Secretary of State for Defence, *The Falklands Campaign*, 9; Ethell and Price, *Air War*, 238–41.

31. September 15, 1983, interview with Cmdr. Jorge Colombo, Commander of the Super Etendard Squadron; Secretary of State for Defence, *The Falklands Campaign*, 9.

32. September 13, 1982, interview with senior Argentine naval aviators.

33. Secretary of State for Defence, *The Falklands Campaign*, 10; Ejercito Argentino, *Informe oficial*, 1: 74.

34. Luis Alberto Terencio, "El día mas negro de la flota," *Aeroespacio* 431: 18–26 (January–February 1983); Secretary of State for Defence, *The Falklands Campaign*, 10–11.

35. September 9, 1982, interview with Cmdr. Julio Pérez, in charge of the special detachment responsible for the installation of the Exocet in the Malvinas.

36. Secretary of State for Defence, *The Falklands Campaign*, 12.

37. Jurg Meister, *Der Krieg um die Falkland-Inseln 1982* (Osnabrück: Biblio-Verlag, 1984), 177–83; "La FAA en la guerra de las Malvinas," *Aerospacio* 429: 12–20 (September–October 1982), 12–20; Luís Dorna, "Helicópteros en las Malvinas," *Aeroespacio* 437: 14–24 (January–February 1984); Pio Matassi, *Malvinas, La batalla aérea* (Buenos Aires: Aeroespacio, n.d.), 74–75.

38. Robert L. Scheina, "Argentine Jointness and the Malvinas," *Joint Forces Quarterly* 5: 95–101 (Summer 1994), 100–1; Alberto Miguez, "Argentina's Defense Impasse," *International Defense Review* 21: 1581–84 (December 1988), 1582.

CHAPTER THIRTY–FOUR

1. Ismael Huerta hints that the decision to intervene occurred in June 1973. Ismael Huerta, *Volvería a ser marino*, 2 vols. (Santiago: Editorial Andrés Bello, 1988), 2: 62. Sergio Huidobro states that the decision was made on July 4. Sergio Huidobro Justiniano, *Decision naval* (Valparaíso: Imprenta de la Armada, 1989), 139.

2. José Toribio Merino Castro, *Bitacora de un almirante memorias*, 3d ed. (Santiago: Editorial Andres Bello, 1998), 178–88; Carlos U. López, *Allende and the Military: An Historical Perspective* (Washington, D.C.: Council for Inter-American Security Educational Institute, n.d.), 1.

3. United States, 94th Cong., 1st sess., Senate, Select Committee to Study Governmental Operations with Respect to Intelligence Activities, *Covert Action in Chile 1963–1973* (Washington, D.C.: Government Printing Office, 1975), 57; Robert L. Borosage and John Marks, "Destabilizing Chile," in *The CIA File*, ed. by Robert L. Borosage and John Marks (New York: Grossman Publishers, 1976), 79; William Blum, *The CIA: A Forgotten History* (London: Zed Books, 1986), 232–35.

4. U.S. 94th Cong., Senate, *Covert Action in Chile*, 58–59; John M. Collins, *America's Small Wars: Lessons for the Future* (New York: Brassey's, Inc., 1991), 165; Blum, *The CIA*, 237.

5. López, *Allende*, 3.

6. Paul Sigmund, *Soviet Policy in Cuba and Chile* (Carlisle, Pa.: Strategic Studies Institute, U.S. Army War College,1980), 12–13; Bynum Weathers Jr., *The Role of the Military in Chilean Politics, 1810–1980* (Maxwell Air Force Base, Ala.: Documentary Research Division, Air University Library, 1980), 160.

7. Collins, *America's Small Wars*, 165.

8. Blum, *The CIA*, 238; Collins, *America's Small Wars*, 165.

9. Borosage and Marks, "Destabilizing Chile," 84; U.S. 94th Cong., Senate, *Covert Action in Chile*, 37–38; Adam Schesch and Patricia Garrett, "The Case of Chile," in *Uncloaking the CIA,* ed. by Howard Frazier (New York: Free Press, 1978), 48.

10. *Strategic Survey 1973* (London: International Institute for Strategic Studies, 1974), 79; Sigmund, *Soviet Policy*, 14.

11. Augusto Pinochet Ugarte (1915–), born in Valparaíso, entered the Military Academy in 1932 and graduated in 1936. He specialized in military geography and has written a number of works related to the subject. His early assignments included being an instructor at the Military Academy, the War College, and the Ecuadorian War College. In 1970, with the rank of division general, Pinochet was appointed as the Commander of the Military District of the Province of Santiago, one of the most influential commands in the army.

12. Paul E. Sigmund, *The Overthrow of Allende* (Pittsburgh: University of Pittsburgh Press, 1977), 162–63; López, *Allende*, 5.

13. Sigmund, *Soviet Policy*, 14.

14. Borosage and Marks, "Destabilizing Chile," 86; Blum, *The CIA*, 238–39; *Strategic Survey 1973*, 80.

15. U.S. 94th Cong., Senate, *Covert Action in Chile*, 26, 31, 36; Borosage and Marks, "Destabilizing Chile," 86; Sigmund, *The Overthrow of Allende*, 115–118, 121.

16. López, *Allende*, 7.

17. Thomas G. Sanders, "The Military Government in Chile, Part I: The Coup," *Fieldstaff Reports, West Coast South America Series*, 22 vols., 1: 5; Albert L. Michaels, "Background to a Coup: Civil-Military Relations in Twentieth-Century Chile and the Overthrow of Salvador Allende," in *Civilian Control of the Military*, ed. by Claude E. Welch Jr. (Albany: State University of New York Press, 1976), 300.

18. Frederick M. Nunn, *The Military in Chilean History* (Albuquerque: University of New Mexico Press, 1976), 280–82; Sigmund, *The Overthrow of Allende*, 196–202; Blum, *The CIA*, 241.

19. Weathers, *The Role of the Military*, 166; Sigmund, *The Overthrow of Allende*, 202–4.

20. Sigmund, *The Overthrow of Allende*, 209–111; Borosage and Marks, "Destabilizing Chile," 86–87.

21. Weathers, *The Role of the Military*, 169.

22. Sigmund, *The Overthrow of Allende*, 213–14; Nunn, *The Military in Chilean History*, 284; James R. Whalen, *Out of the Ashes* (Washington, D.C.: Regnery Gateway, 1989), 404.

23. José Toribio Merino (1915–96), born in La Serena, entered the Naval Academy in 1931 and graduated in 1936. During World War II he served on board the old U.S. cruiser *Raleigh*. Between 1956 and 1957 Merino served at the Chilean naval mission in Great Britain. During his career, he commanded numerous ships and by 1970 he was the senior officer with a command afloat.

24. Huidobro, *Decision naval*, 208–11; López, *Allende*, 11–12.

25. López, *Allende*, 12–13; Weathers, *The Role of the Military*, 172.

26. López, *Allende*, 13.

27. Weathers, *The Role of the Military*, 174–75.

28. López, *Allende*, 13.

29. U.S. 94th Cong., Senate, *Covert Action in Chile*, 61; López, *Allende*, 13–14.

30. Huidobro, *Decision naval*, 211–21; López, *Allende*, 14.

31. López, *Allende*, 14–15.

32. ibid., 1; *The Military Balance 1972–73* (London: International Institute for Strategic Studies, 1972), 58.

33. Sigmund, *Soviet Policy*, 14.

34. ibid., 13.

35. *Libro blanco del cambio de gobierno en Chile* (Santiago: Editiorial Lord Cochrane, 1973), 103–8.

36. López, *Allende*, 5; López, *Chile: A Brief Naval History*, 90.

Shortly after the September 11, 1973, coup, the military government published the *White Book of the Change of Government in Chile* (Santiago: Empresa Editora Nacional, [1973]). This 258-page work provides analysis and documentation of the military preparations and planned assassinations by the Popular Unity. Thomas Sanders questions the authenticity of Plan Z, the plan to assassinate the leadership of the Chilean military. He concludes, "in October [1973] the Junta made public a 'Plan Z,' according to which the UP, stimulated by Cubans, had planned to murder the top military chiefs on September 19 and take power. The 'White Book' of Plan Z, however, is not convincing, though the materials do show that the UP also had a contingency plan directed against a military coup and had been arming frantically to prepare for it." Sanders, "The Military Government in Chile," 9.

37. Huidobro, *Decision naval*, 240–41; James Whalen, *Allende: Death of a Marxist Dream* (Westport: Arlington House, 1981), 24; López, *Allende*, 15; Sanders, "The Military Government in Chile," 8.

38. Sanders, "The Military Government in Chile," 9; López, *Allende*, 15; Augusto Pinochet, *The Critical Day* (Santiago: Editorial Renacimiento, 1982), 127.

39. Begun in 1960, "Unitas" was a multinational naval exercise initiated by the United States which emphasized antisubmarine warfare.

40. López, *Allende*, 15.

41. ibid.; Pinochet, *The Critical Day*, 127.

42. López, *Allende*, 15.

43. Whalen, *Allende*, 167–71; Pinochet, *The Critical Day*, 128–36; Weathers, *The Role of the Military*, 179; Sanders, "The Military Government in Chile," 8.

44. Sigmund, *Soviet Policy*, 18.

45. Whalen, *Ashes*, 580.

46. Pinochet, *The Critical Day*, 139.

CHAPTER THIRTY-FIVE

1. Daniel Tretiak, "Cuba and the Soviet Union: The Growing Accommodation, 1964–1965," *Orbis* 10: 2; 439–58 (1967), 443–44; William J. Durch, "The Cuban Military in Africa and the Middle East: From Algeria to Angola," *Studies in Comparative Communism* 11: 1, 2, 34–74 (Spring/Summer 1978), 36–37.

2. Martin D. Gensler, "Cuba's 'Second Vietnam': Bolivia," *The Yale Review* 60: 3, 342–65 (March 1971), 344–46; Gerhard Drekonja-Kornat, "Understanding Cuba's Presence in Africa," *Journal of Inter-American Studies and World Affairs* 25: 1, 121–29 (February 1983), 123–24.

3. R. D. Heinl Jr., "A Red Foreign Legion," *Detriot News* (February 8, 1976), 1; Nicolas Lang, "Les cubains en Afrique noire," *Est & Ouest* (Paris), 386: 21–24 (June 16–30, 1967), 23. The camp was closed when Kwame Nkrumah was ousted by the military on 1966.

4. Peter Grose, "Algeria Charges Morocco Forces Invade in Sahara," New York *Times* (October 15, 1963), 1; Peter Grose, "Moroccans Trap Attacking Force of 200 at Oasis," New York *Times* (October 28, 1963), 10; Peter Grose, "Armaments Race by East and West in Africa Feud," New York *Times* (October 30, 1963), 1 and 3; "Algerian Disputes Arms-Aid Reports," New York *Times* (October 31, 1963), 4; Peter Grose, "Morocco Breaks Ties with Cuba over Algeria Aid," New York *Times* (November 1, 1963), 2; Tad Szulc, "Cuba Began Role in Zanzibar in '61,' " New York *Times* (January 23, 1964), 3; Peter Braestrup, "Algerian 'Purge' Sought by Army," New York *Times* (January 27, 1964), 3; "Russian Built Tanks Landed in Algeria," London *Times* (October 28, 1963), 10; "Cuban Volunteers in Algeria," New York *Times* (October 30, 1963), 7.

5. "Cuban President Greeted in Algiers on State Visit," New York *Times* (October 13, 1964), 15; Parkinson, *Latin America*, 190.

6. Gabriel García Márquez, "Cuba in Angola: Operation Carlotta," in *Fidel Castro Speeches*, ed. by Michael Taber (New York: Pathfinder Press, 1984), 339; Durch, "The Cuban Military," 54–58.

7. Herminio Portell-Vila, "Castro's Adventure in Africa," *International Security Review* 26–59 (Spring 1979), 29; Jay Mallin, "Che Guevara: Some Documentary Puzzles at the End of a Long Journey," *Journal of Inter-American Studies* 10: 1; 74–84 (January 1968), 77–78.

8. Rene Gauze, *The Politics of Congo Brazzaville*, ed. by Virginia Thompson and Richard Adloff, No. 129 (Stanford, Calif.: Hoover Institution Press, 1973), 161.

9. Baez, *Secretos*, 62.

10. Lloyd Garrison, "Rising Reported in Brazzaville," New York *Times* (June 29, 1966), 1; Richard Eder, "Cuban Force Rises in Congo Republic," New York *Times* (October 23, 1966), 20.

11. "Angola—An Easy Route and an Olive Branch," *Time* (February 23, 1976), 18; "Cuban Troops: Cats'-Paws for Soviet Intrigues," *U.S. News and World Report* 79: 23, 27 (December 8, 1975), 27.

12. García, "Cuba," 343. Rodriguez was released following the April 1974 revolution in Portugal and became a member of the Communist Party Central Committee in Cuba.

13. "Cuban Troops: Cats'-Paws," 27; Geoffrey Godsell, "Angola Impasse: Its Meaning for U.S.," *The Christian Science Monitor* 68: 34, 1 (January 14, 1976), 1; "Cuba," *Facts on File Yearbook 1973*, 752–53 (New York: Facts on File, 1973), 752; "The Cubans in Search of Yemen," *Foreign Report* 6–7 (June 26, 1974), 6; Brian Crozier, "The Soviet Presence in Somalia," *Conflict Studies*, 54 (February 1975), 9.

14. Jay Mallin, *Cuba and Angola* (Miami: Research Institute for Cuban Studies, University of Miami, 1987), 3–4; Mallin, *History*, 290–94.

15. García, "Cuba," 340; Hearings before the Subcommittee of African Affairs of the Committee on Foreign Relations, U.S. Senate, 94th Cong., 2nd Sess. *U.S. Involvement in Civil War in Angola* (Washington, D.C.: Government Printing Office, 1978), 17, 175–185; Kenneth Adelman, "Report from Angola," *Foreign Affairs* 53: 3; 558–74 (April 1975), 568.

16. John Marcum, *The Angolan Revolution Exile Politics and Guerrilla Warfare (1962–1976)*, (Cambridge, Mass.: The MIP Press, 1978), 40; Arthur Klinghoffer, *The Angolan War: A Study in Soviet Policy in the Third World* (Boulder: Westview Press, 1980), 11.

17. Portell-Vila, "Castro's Adventure," 40.

18. Don Oberdorfer, "Cuban Intervention in Angola Intrigues World Capitals," *Washington Post* (February 18, 1976), A6; James Nelson Goodsell, "More than One-Tenth of Cuban Army in Angola," *The Christian Science Monitor* 68: 40, 1, 9 (January 22, 1976), 9; W. Martin James III, *A Political History of the Civil War in Angola 1974–1990* (New Brunswick, N.J.: Transaction Publishers, 1992), 62–64.

19. García, "Cuba," 340.

20. *The Military Balance 1975–1976* (London: International Institute for Strategic Studies, 1975), 44.

21. Durch, "The Cuban Military," 64; "White Troops among Forces Advancing on Angolan Capital," London *Times* (November 17, 1975), 1.

22. *Keesing's Contemporary Archives* (1975), 2479; *Strategic Survey* 1975; Wilfred Burchett, *Southern Africa Stands Up* (New York: Urizen Books, 1978), xxi–xxii.

23. Klinghoffer, *The Angola War*, 111; Fermoselle, *The Evolution*, 401; Oberdorfer, "Cuban Intervention in Angola," A6; David Deutschmann, ed., *Changing the History of Africa* (Melbourne: Ocean Press, 1989), 43; Burchett, *Southern Africa Stands Up*, 90.

24. David Binder, "U.S. and Cubans Discussed Links in Talks in 1975," New York *Times* (March 29, 1977), 8.

25. García, "Cuba," 341–42; Michael T. Kaufman, "Angolans in Luanda Area Try to Regroup," New York *Times* (November 6, 1975), 37; Mallin, *History*, 293–94.

26. Durch, "The Cuban Military," 66; Nicholas Ashford, "Arms Race among Rival Factions turns Angola Conflict into an International Issue," London *Times* (September 25, 1975), 6.

27. Durch, "The Cuban Military," 68–69; "Decolonization-Angola," *Strategic Survey 1975* (London: International Institute for Strategic Studies, 1976), 34; Burchett, *Southern Africa*, xxii.

28. The fifth of November, 1975, was the 132nd anniversary of a slave rebellion in Cuba that was led by a black woman named Carlota.

29. García, "Cuba," 346–48; Goodsell, "More than One-tenth of Cuban Army," 9; U.S. Senate, "Angola," 17; Mallin, *Cuba and Angola*, 6–7; Deutschmann, *Changing the History*, 51; Mallin, *History*, 295.

30. García, "Cuba," 349; Deutschmann, *Changing the History*, 52.

31. *Strategic Survey 1975*, 36; Mallin, *History*, 296.

32. Goodsell, "More than One-tenth of Cuban Army," 1; David Shipler, "Soviet Officials Playing Down Involvement in Angolan War," New York *Times* (December 18, 1975), 15; Durch, "The Cuban Military," 68; Mallin, *Cuba and Angola*, 7.

33. Jim Dingeman, "Angola, Portugal in Africa," *Strategy and Tactics* 56: 22–29 (May–June 1976), 28; "Soviets Raise the Ante," *Washington Star* (November 15, 1975), 4; Hugh MacDonald, *Aeroflot: Soviet Air Transport Since 1923* (London: Putnam, 1975), 219.

34. Burchett, *Southern Africa*, xxiv.

35. The U.S. Congress passed the Tunney Amendment (the Senate on December 19, 1975, and the House on January 27, 1976), which shut off all U.S. aid to the National Front and the Popular Movement. Charles Corddry, "South Africa Orders Angola Pullout," *Baltimore Sun* (January 23, 1976), 4.

On March 27 the South African army pulled out of Angola, having received assurances from the MPLA for the security of the Cunene Dam complex. Durch, "The Cuban Military," 69.

36. John Maclean, "Cuba Resumes Airlift to Bolster Angola Force," *Chicago Tribune* (February 27, 1976), 2.

37. Leon Dash, "A Long March in Angola," *Washington Post* (August 7–13, 1977, seven-part series)—No. 1 "Ambushing an Unwary Enemy" (August 7), A1, A22; No. 2 "War Without Frontiers, Battle Lines" (August 8), A1, A20; No. 3 "What Leads Guerrillas to Fight On?" (August 9), A1, A8; No. 4 "Captives Walk a Rock Road" (August 10), A1, A8; No. 5 "Politics Taught By Fable—Guerrillas Paint NETO as Pro-White" (August 11), A1, A24; No. 6 "Colonialism Gone, Racism Remains" (August 12), A1, A20; No. 7 "UNITA: Self-Criticism Deep in a Hidden Forest" (August 13), A1, A10; Ray Moseley, "Angola's Marxist Leaders Battle Rebels and Crippled Economy," New York *Times* (November 28, 1976), 1; "Cuba Reported to Send More Troops to Angola," New York *Times* (September 12, 1977), 11.

38. Fermoselle, *The Evolution*, 404.

39. ibid., 404–5.

40. Baez, *Secretos*, 441.

41. Laffin, *War Annual* 1, 1986: 17; Mallin, *History*, 303.

42. Willem Steenkamp, *South Africa's Border War 1966–1989* (Gibraltar: Ashanti Publishing Limited, 1989), 255.

43. ibid., 356.

44. ibid.

45. Laffin, *War Annual* 5, 1991: 13; Steenkamp, *South Africa's Border War*, 356.

46. Fermoselle, *The Evolution*, 403.

47. ibid., 402–4; the French handbook *Quid 1992* states that the Cubans lost 8,000 men between 1975 and 1978, which seems too high. *Quid 1992* (Paris: Éditions Robert Laffont, 1991), 864; García, "Cuba," 347–50.

48. Mallin, *Cuba and Angola*, 14.

49. Jorge I. Dominguez, "The Cuban Operations in Angola: Costs and Benefits for the Armed Forces," *Cuban Studies* 10–19 (January 1978), 12.

50. Fermoselle, *The Evolution*, 402–3.

51. ibid., 406.

52. Mallin, *History*, 202; Nelson P. Valdés, "Cuban Foreign Policy in the Horn of Africa," *Cuban Studies* 10:1, 49–89 (January 1980), 52.

53. Valdés, "Cuban Foreign Policy," 52–53; David B. Ottaway, "Soviet Wooing of Ethiopia May Push Somalia Towards U.S.," *Washington Post* (February 28, 1977), A20; "Castro Ends Secretive Ethiopian Visit, No Hint on Aid Issue," *Washington Post* (March 19, 1977), A21; "Castro: Playing Kissinger in the Horn?" *Washington Post* (March 18, 1977), A19.

54. Valdés, "Cuban Foreign Policy," 54–55; Mallin, *History*, 203–4.

55. *The Military Balance of Power 1975–76*, 41–42.

56. Valdés, "Cuban Foreign Policy," 54.

57. *The Military Balance of Power 1975–76*, 43.

58. Valdés, "Cuban Foreign Policy," 54.

59. ibid.; Mallin, *History*, 204.

60. Valdés, "Cuban Foreign Policy," 55–56.

61. ibid., 57–58; Mallin, *History*, 204–5.

62. Valdés, "Cuban Foreign Policy," 60–61; Mallin, *History*, 205–6.

63. Laffin, *War Annual* 1, 1986: 65; Mallin, *History*, 207.

64. Valdés, "Cuban Foreign Policy," 60–61; Fermoselle, *The Evolution*, 407.

65. Baez, *Secretos*, 488.

66. ibid., 490.

67. Ferreira, "Castro," A01.

68. Drekonja-Kornat, "Understanding Cuba's Presence," 125–38.

69. Fermoselle, *The Evolution*, 407.

70. Bridgland, *The War for Africa*, 335.

71. *Quid 1997* (Paris: Éditions Robert Laffont, 1996), 1165.

CHAPTER THIRTY-SIX

1. Soviet-backed, initially successful takeovers occurred in Afghanistan, Angola, Ethiopia, Kampuchea, Laos, Mozambique, and South Yemen. In August 1968 Castro publicly supported the Soviet decision to invade Czechoslovakia. Beginning in the early 1970s, the Soviet Union increased the quantity and quality of its defense aid to Cuba. Shearman, *The Soviet Union*, 22–25.

2. William E. Ratliff, *Castroism and Communism in Latin America* (Washington, D.C.: Enterprise Institute for Public Policy Research, 1976), 217–18.

3. Waghelstein, "A Latin-American Insurgency," 45–46.

4. Richard H. Shultz Jr., "The Soviet Union and Central America," in *Guerrilla Warfare and Counterinsurgency* (Lexington, Ky.: Lexington Books, 1989), 378.

5. Modern guerrilla warfare in Nicaragua began in 1961 with the unsuccessful attempt led by Carlos Fonseca Amador to invade Nicaragua with the help of Fidel Castro. Fonseca had studied at the University of Managua. In 1957 he visited the Soviet Union and during the early 1960s was in Cuba. While in Havana, Fonseca helped create the National Liberation Front (*Frente de Liberacion Nacional*—FLN), which subsequently changed its name to the National Sandinista Liberation Front—FSLN to honor Augusto Sandino, the guerrilla leader who battled U.S. Marines between 1927 and 1933 (see chapter 8).

In 1963 Fonseca returned to Nicaragua to head covert guerrilla activities in Managua. Following an urban terrorist campaign in 1966, he moved his theater of operations to the mountainous northern department of Matagala. Sandinista activity triggered a massive counterinsurgency operation by the Nicaraguan national guard. In August 1967 the national guard crushed a principal Sandinista force in southwestern Nicaragua. It overoptimistically declared the campaign a success. For almost a decade the Sandinistas occasionally captured the national headlines.

6. Daniel Ortega Saaverda (1945–) was born in the small village of La Libertad. His father worked as an accountant for a mining firm and fought for Augusto Sandino. Both of his parents were arrested during the 1940s by the Somoza regime. Ortega's family moved to Managua. He briefly studied for the priesthood in El Salvador and law at the University of Central America, Managua. Ortega joined the Sandinistas in 1963 and undertook missions as an urban guerrilla. He was arrested for bombing vehicles at the U.S. embassy. In 1964 he was arrested in Guatemala and turned over to the Somoza government. While being held he was severely tortured. In November 1967 he was charged with bank robbery and sentenced to eight years in jail. He was freed in December 1974 in a prisoner exchange. He joined the Sandinista National Directorate in 1975 but made few public pronouncements. Daniel and his brother

Humberto were elected president and vice president, respectively, in November 1984 for a six-year term. He lost the presidency to Violeta Barrios de Chamorro in 1990.

7. Since only the privileged exercised many of these rights, their restriction had little impact. A state of siege was imposed and a special military court was created to try those accused of subversion.

8. Gen. Reynaldo Perez Vega, Chief Military Aide to President Somoza, was kidnapped and executed on March 8, 1978.

9. John A. Booth, *The End of the Beginning: the Nicaraguan Revolution* (Boulder, Colo.: Westview Press, 1982), 162–65; Marley, *Wars*, 667.

10. Edén Pastora Gómez (1937–) was a longtime member of the Sandinista National Liberation Front. Following the Sandinista victory in 1979, he was given a government position from which he resigned in 1981. He appeared in Costa Rica in 1982, criticized the Sandinista government, and formed the Revolutionary Sandinista Front. He allied his group with the Revolutionary Democratic Alliance but withdrew his group when the alliance united with the *Contras* which included many former supporters of the Somoza regime. On May 30, 1984, Pastora escaped an assassination plot when a bomb hidden in a journalist's camera exploded. Also in 1984, the Costa Rican government expelled Pastora, who then took up residence in Venezuela.

11. Schooley, *Conflict*, 78; Caballero and Thomas, *Central American Wars*, 20.

12. U.S. Dept. of State, Bureau of Public Affairs, "Cuban Support for Terrorism and Insurgency in the Western Hemisphere," statement of Thomas O. Enders, Assistant Secretary for Inter-American Affairs, before the Subcommittee on Security and Terrorism of the Senate Committee on the Judiciary, March 12, 1982, 1.

13. Schooley, *Conflict*, 78–79; Caballero and Thomas, *Central American Wars*, 20.

14. The America Department (AD), was a small but elite intelligence service set up by Fidel Castro in 1974 to conduct subversive operations throughout the hemisphere. It was headed by Manuel Piñeiro Losada, who had served under Raúl Castro during the revolution. The AD was instrumental in bringing together the various leftist groups in each of the Central American countries. Mallin, *History*, 189.

15. Costa Rica's democratic government had long opposed Somoza's authoritarian regime. Apparently it chose to ignore the use of its territory by Cuba, Panama, and Venezuela to funnel aid to the Sandinistas. David Nolan, *The Ideology of the Sandinistas and the Nicaraguan Revolution* (Miami: University of Miami Press, 1984), 97–98; Uri Ra'anan et al., *Hydra of Carnage* (Lexington, Ky.: Lexington Books, 1986), 323–24.

16. Schooley, *Conflict*, 80–81.

17. Caballero and Thomas, *Central American Wars*, 20; Marley, *Wars*, 667.

18. On November 17, 1978, the Inter-American Commission on Human Rights accused the Somoza government of victimizing all sectors of the population. The AFL-CIO began limited boycotts of Nicaraguan products to protest the repression of labor unions.

19. Schooley, *Conflict*, 81.

20. The operations center was under the command of Julian López Díaz, a member of Cuba's American Department and subsequently the Cuban Ambassador to Nicaragua. Ra'anan, *Hydra*, 323–24; U.S. Dept. of State, "Cuba's Renewed Support for Violence in Latin America," Special Report 90, December 14, 1981.

21. Schooley, *Conflict*, 81.

22. This seems high considering that given the destruction caused by the 1972 earthquake not many population concentations existed in Managua.

23. Schooley, *Conflict*, 82.

24. Ra'anan, *Hydra*, 319.

25. Schooley, *Conflict*, 82; Laffin, *War Annual* 2, 157, places the deaths at 45,000 persons.

26. Laffin, *War Annual* 1, 114.

27. Caballero and Thomas, *Central American Wars*, 20–21.

28. Walter LaFeber, *Inevitable Revolutions: The United States in Central America* (Ontario: Penguin Books, 1984), 296; Tom Barry and Deb Preusch, *The Central American Fact Book* (New York: Grove Press, 1986), 91; Don Oberdorfer and Patrick E. Tyler, "Reagan Backs Action Plan for Central America: Political, Paramilitary Steps Included," *Washington Post* (February 14, 1982), A1, A4.

29. Richard Lapper and James Painter, *Honduras State for Sale* (London: Latin American Bureau, 1985), 86; Caballero and Thomas, *Central American Wars*, 20–21.

30. Schooley, *Conflict*, 254; Laffin, *War Annual* 2, 157–58; Marley, *Wars*, 668.

31. Laffin, *War Annual* 1, 113.

32. Thomas Leonard, *Central America and United States Policies, 1820s–1980s* (Claremont, Calif.: Regina Books, 1985), 58; Jorge I. Dominguez and Marc Lindenburg, *Central America: Current Crisis and Future Prospects* (New York: Foreign Policy Association, 1984, Headline Series, No., 271), 59.

33. Tayacán, *Psychological Operations in Guerrilla Warfare* (New York: Vintage Books, 1985), 57.

34. Jill Smolowe, "Oh, Brother—Not Again," *Time* (December 28, 1987), 33.

35. Caballero and Thomas, *Central American Wars*, 22–23.

36. Ed Magnuson, "Here Comes the Prosecutor," *Time* (November 30, 1987), 17.

37. Laffin, *War Annual* 5, 37.

38. Laffin, *War Annual* 3, 69; Jill Smolowe, "Tales of a Sandinista Defector," *Time* (December 21, 1987), 47.

39. Caballero and Thomas, *Central American Wars*, 22–23.

40. Laffin, *War Annual* 2, 55–58.

41. The five groups were the Popular Liberation Forces (*Fuerzas Populares de Liberacion*—FPL), the Armed Forces of Liberation (*Fuerzas Armadas de Liberacion*—FAL), the Armed Forces of National Liberation (*Fuerzas Armadas Revolucionarias Nacionales*—FARN), the Revolutionary Party of Central American Workers (*Partido Revolucionario de Trajadores Centroamericanos*—PRTC), and the People's Revolutionary Army (*Ejército Revolucionario del Pueblo*—ERP).

42. Ra'anan, *Hydra*, 329, 335–39, 342–44; Juan de Onis, "Soviet-Bloc Nations Said to Pledge Arms to Salvador Rebels," *New York Times* (February 6, 1981), A1, A7.

The Palestine Liberation Organization claimed to have supplied pilots to Nicaragua and to the Salvadoran guerrillas as well as instructors. "PLO Guerrillas serve in Nicaragua, El Salvador and Angola, Arafat said," *Wall Street Journal* (January 14, 1982), 1; Ra'anan, *Hydra*, 315–16.

43. Testimony of Fred C. Ikle, U.S. Under Secretary of Defense for Policy, before the Subcommittee on Western Hemisphere Affairs at the Senate Foreign Relations Committee (December 15, 1981), 4–5; Hedrick Smith, "A Former Salvadoran Rebel Chief Tells of Arms

for Nicaragua," New York *Times* (July 12, 1984), A10; Larry Rohter, "Sandinista is Pushing Peace Plan," New York *Times* (March 21, 1985), A3; Sam Dillon, "Base for Ferrying Arms to El Salvador Found in Nicaragua," *Washington Post* (September 21, 1983), A29, A34; Robert J. McCartney, "Rebels Use Harsher Methods," *Washington Post* (June 18, 1984), A1, A19.

44. Salvador Cayetano Carpio (1920–83) joined the outlawed El Salvadoran Communist Party in 1947 and eventually became the Secretary General. He believed that the struggle would ultimately lead to direct confrontation with the United States. Carpio committed suicide in Managua after the murder of Comrade Anna María over the issue of whether to negotiate with the government.

45. Joaquin Villalobos Huezo (1951–) is shrouded in mystery. He was born possibly in Santa Ana or Sonsonate, El Salvador. He probably came from the middle class, attended the University of El Salvador, and studied economics. He became involved in the politics of the university. He joined the ERP in 1973 and within a year rose to the executive directorate. Villalobos is credited with helping to create the FMLN. Following the compromise settlement of the war, he entered mainstream politics and as a consequence he was expelled from the FMLN by those who had refused to accept the compromise.

46. Mélida Anaya Montes (1931–83), was stabbed to death in Managua, Nicaragua, shortly after the death of Carpio.

47. Marley, *Wars*, 667; Caballero and Thomas, *Central American Wars*, 13–14.

48. Caballero and Thomas, *Central American Wars*, 14.

49. Waghelstein, "Ruminations," 364.

50. ibid.

51. Caballero and Thomas, *Central American Wars*, 14; Marley, *Wars*, 668.

52. The government's efforts sustained a setback on October 23, 1984, when Lt. Col. Domingo Monterrosa was killed in a helicopter crash. Through personal example, he had become the cutting edge of the government's attack on the guerrilla forces. Radio Venceremos, one of the guerrilla stations, claimed that their forces had shot down the Huey helicopter with machine-gun fire.

53. Shultz, "The Soviet Union," 380.

54. "El Salvador: Inside Guerrilla Territory," *Time* (January 20, 1986), 30.

55. *Facts on File 1989*, 870; Keeing's *Record of World Events 1989*, 37038.

56. Lapper and Painter, *Honduras*, 75; Caballero and Thomas, *Central American Wars*, 17.

57. Arnold, "IMET," 33.

58. Lapper and Painter, *Honduras*, 43–45, 77–78.

59. ibid., 75–76, 81.

60. ibid.

61. Gustavo Alvarez Martínez (1937–89), attended the Argentine *Escuela Militar* between 1958 and 1962 and later the Peruvian *Colegio Superior de Guerra*. He was also trained at the School of the Americas. His assignments included Commander of the 4th Infantry Battalion at La Ceiba, Commander of Military Zone II at San Pedro Sula, and Chief of the Public Security Forces in 1980. In this last position, Alvarez commanded the secret police. President Suazo Córdova appointed him Commander in Chief of the armed forces in November 1981 and he was promoted to general in April 1982. Ideologically, Alvarez was ultraconservative. In 1984 a junta of young officers ousted him from power. Alvarez was assassinated in Tegucigalpa; the Popular Liberation Front claimed responsibility.

62. Lapper and Painter, *Honduras*, 84.

63. ibid., *Honduras*, 5–6.

64. The largest exercises were:

February 1983	"Big Pine I"	1,600 U.S. and 4,000 Hondurans
August 1983	"Big Pine II"	5,500 U.S. and 3,000 Hondurans
February 1985	"Big Pine III"	3,000 U.S. and 5,000 Hondurans
April 1985	"Universal Trek 85"	7,000 U.S. and 2,300 Hondurans

See Lapper and Painter, *Honduras*, 124–27, for a complete listing.

65. Lapper and Painter, *Honduras*, 5–6, 90; Dominguez and Lindenburg, *Central America*, 63.

66. Lapper and Painter, *Honduras*, 6.

67. ibid., 103–6.

68. ibid., 6.

69. ibid., 109.

70. Laffin, *War Annual* 2, 158; Laffin, *War Annual* 3, 69; Lapper and Painter, *Honduras*, 7; Caballero and Thomas, *Central American Wars*, 18.

71. Caballero and Thomas, *Central American Wars*, 22–23.

72. Gramajo, *De la guerra*, 116–17.

73. Schooley, *Conflict*, 174.

74. ibid., 178.

75. Calvert, *Guatemalan Insurgency*, 9; Caballero and Thomas, *Central American Wars*, 10.

76. Gramajo, *De la guerra*, 117–19; Calvert, *Guatemalan Insurgency*, 9.

77. Calvert, *Guatemalan Insurgency*, 11.

78. Schooley, *Conflict*, 178–79. The Spanish government broke diplomatic relations with Guatemala over the incident on February 1. Calvert, *Guatemalan Insurgency*, 11.

79. Schooley, *Conflict*, 148–49.

80. ibid., 179.

81. U.S. Dept. of State, "Cuban Support for Terrorism," 2.

82. Schooley, *Conflict*, 175, 180.

83. Rex A. Hudson, *Castro's America Department* (Washington, D.C.: Cuban-American Foundation, 1988), 38.

84. Rodrigo Asturias' father, Miguel Angel Asturias, won the Noble Prize for literature in 1967.

85. Schooley, *Conflict*, 179.

86. José Efraín Ríos Montt (1926–), joined the Protestant fundamentalist Church of the Complete Word in 1978.

87. Schooley, *Conflict*, 27.

88. Marley, *Wars*, 668; Caballero and Thomas, *Central American Wars*, 11.

89. Schooley, *Conflict*, 180.

90. ibid., 179; *Facts on File 1982*, 426.

91. Schooley, *Conflict*, 28–29, 149; Calvert, *Guatemalan Insurgency*, 15.

92. Schooley, *Conflict*, 30.

93. ibid., 175.

94. Black, *Garrison Guatemala*, 31.

95. Gramajo, *De la guerra*, 157–58; Schooley, *Conflict*, 207.

96. Jonathan Hartlyn, "Colombia: Old Problems, New Opportunties," *Current History* 62–65, 82–84 (February 1983), 65; Valenza, "Colombia's Quiet War," 53; Laffin, *War Annual* 1, 35.

97. Hartlyn, "Colombia," 65, 83.

98. John D. Martz, "Colombia's Search for Peace," *Current History* 125–28, 145–47 (March 1989), 125.

99. U.S. Dept. of State, "Cuban Support for Terrorism," 2; Valenza, "Colombia's Quiet War," 53.

100. U.S. Dept. of State, "Cuban Support for Terrorism," 2; "The Month in Review Colombia," *Current History*, 188 (April 1980), 188; "The Month in Review Colombia," *Current History*, 233 (May 1980), 233.

101. U.S. Dept. of State, "Cuban Support for Terrorism," 2; Germán Castro Caicedo, *El Karina* (Bogotá: Plaza & Janes Editores, 1987).

102. "The Month in Review Colombia," *Current History*, 236 (May 1981), 236.

103. U.S. Dept. of State, "Cuban Support for Terrorism," 2; "The Month in Review Colombia," *Current History*, 236 (May 1982), 236.

104. Harvey F. Kline, "New Directions in Colombia?" *Current History*, 65–68, 83 (February 1985), 66.

105. Hartlyn, "Colombia," 84; Kline, "New Directions," 67; Martz, "Colombia's Search," 126.

106. Laffin, *War Annual* 1, 35; "The Month in Review Colombia," *Current History*, 348 (October 1984), 348.

107. Laffin, *War Annual* 1, 36; Laffin, *War Annual* 2, 61.

108. Martz, "Colombia's Search," 125–26; Laffin, *War Annual* 2, 62; Valenza, "Colombia's Quiet War," 53.

109. Valenza, "Colombia's Quiet War," 53; Martz, "Colombia's Search," 125; Bruce Michael Bagley, "Colombian Politics: Crisis or Continuity?" *Current History*, 21–24, 40–41 (January 1987), 24.

110. By the year 2001 some 4,000 UP affiliates had been murdered. Only four assassins have been convicted. Martz, "Colombia's Search," 126; Laffin, *War Annual* 2, 61–62; Valenza, "Colombia's Quiet War," 52.

111. Laffin, *War Annual* 3, 83; Martz, "Colombia's Search," 125.

112. Martz, "Colombia's Search," 127.

113. Laffin, *War Annual* 4, 75; Laffin, *War Annual* 5, 61.

114. Martz, "Colombia's Search," 127; Laffin, *War Annual* 4, 75–76.

115. Hanratty and Meditz, *Colombia*, xxxii; Laffin, *War Annual* 5, 64.

116. Laffin, *War Annual* 5, 64.

117. Arlene B. Tickner, "Colombia: Chronicle of a Crisis Foretold," *Current History*, 61–65 (February 1998), 62.

118. Laffin, *War Annual* 6, 61.

119. Laffin, *War Annual* 3, 84; Laffin, *War Annual* 1, 37.

120. Collins, *America's Small Wars*, 195–96, 260.

121. Marty Kufus, "U.S. Special-Operations KIA's on Grenada," *Strategy & Tactics* 126: 40–44 (April–May 1989), 40–41.

122. ibid., 41.

123. ibid., 42–44; Daniel P. Bolger, "Operation URGENT FURY and Its Critics," *Military Review* 66: 7; 58–69 (July 1986), 287.

124. Ferreira, "Castro," A1; "Revolution, then, came to be Castro's supreme vocation. Castro sees revolution not as a last resort but as a channel for self-expression—an escape valve for his accumulated resentments and hates. He actually needs revolution as the addict needs his drugs." Llerena, *Unsuspected Revolution*, 203.

125. Caesar D. Sereseres, "Lessons from Central America's Revolutionary Wars, 1972–1984," in *The Lessons of Recent Wars in the Third World*, 2 vols. (Lexington: Lexington Books, 1985), 1: 180.

126. Bill Keller, "Gobachev Signs Treaty with Cuba," New York *Times* (April 5, 1989), A8; Mikhail Gorbachev, *Memoirs* (New York: Doubleday, 1995), 501; "The Month in Review," *Current History* 88: 540; 363–68 (October 1989), 364.

CHAPTER THIRTY–SEVEN

1. Abímael Guzmán Reinoso (1934–) received his primary and secondary education at the private Catholic school La Salle, in Arequipa located in southern Peru in the Andean highlands. Guzmán received a doctorate degree in philosophy from the University San Agustín de Arequipa where he also taught for a short while. In 1962 he began teaching philosophy and social science in the education department at the University of San Cristóbal de Huamanga in Ayacucho. In 1971 Guzmán became director of personnel at the University of Huamanga and was thus able to mold the faculty and staff. In 1979 the military government detained Guzmán but he was released during the transition to civilian rule. Guzmán soon disappeared from sight. Many questioned whether Guzmán, known to have been in poor health, was still alive. In 1988 the extreme left newspaper *El Diario* published the "interview of the century" with Guzmán which was widely accepted as being authentic. Guzmán's followers have referred to him as the "fourth sword of Marxism"—Marx, Lenin, and Mao being his only true predecessors.

2. José Carlos Mariátegui (1894–1930) was born into poverty and was sickly throughout his life. Through his superior talents as a writer and ideologist, he gained national prominence. Between 1919 and 1923 Mariátegui traveled throughout western Europe where he became an adherent to Marxism. After returning to Peru, both of his legs were amputated as a result of his childhood illnesses. Supporting himself as a freelance writer, his home became a meeting place for the intellectual left. He founded the Socialist Party of Peru (*Partido Socialista del Perú*), in 1928 and edited his principle ideological writings into the book *Siete ensayos de interpretacion de la realidad peruana* which has been printed numerous times beginning in 1928. The following year Mariátegui organized the Peruvian General Federation of Workers (*Central General de Trabajadores del Peru*). He believed that socialism was the solution to Peru's political, economic, and social problems.

3. Masterson, *Militarism*, 275; Brian Train, "Apocalypse Next: The Struggle for Peru," *Strategy and Tactics* 179: 43–55 (March/April 1996), 51; "Our Red Flag Is Flying in Peru," (New York: Committee to Support the Revolution in Peru, ca. 1990), 8.

4. Peru is divided into three regions (Amazonas, Grau, and Nor Oriental del Marañón), all along the northern frontier; one Constitutional Province (Callao); and twenty-four departments. These departments are subdivided into provinces.

5. Gabriela Tarazona-Sevillano, *Sendero Luminoso and the Threat of Narcoterrorism* (Washington, D.C.: Praeger Published with The Center of Strategy and International Studies,

1990), 4; Jill Smolowe, "His Turn to Lose," *Time* 140: 13; 47–48 (September 28, 1992), 47–48.

6. Luis Arce Borja, "Linea militar, sendero y el ejército guerrillero popular," *El Diario* (insert, January 6, 1988), viii; Train, "Apocalypse Next," 43–44, 47; Robert B. Davis, *"Sendero Luminoso* and Peru's Struggle for Survival," *Military Review* 70: 1; 79–88 (January 1990), 82; "Our Red Flag," 5–6.

7. The University of San Cristóbal de Huamanga, was created in 1677 and began to function in 1704. The University was closed in 1876. It was ordered reopened in 1957 and resumed classes in 1959. In 1986 some 6,000 students were attending the university.

8. Train, "Apocalypse Next," 47.

9. David Scott Palmer, "The Origins and Evolution of Sendero Luminoso," *Comparative Politics* 18: 2; 127–46 (January 1986), 127–46; Train, "Apocalypse Next," 47.

10. Masterson, *Militarism*, 278; Tarazona-Sevillano, *Sendero Luminoso*, 35, 76–78; Train, "Apocalypse Next," 47.

11. In 1572 Túpac Amaru I, the last Inca emperor, led a revolt against the Spaniards. It failed and he was beheaded. Legend says that the head is growing a new body under the ground and when the process is complete "Inkari" will rise up and restore the old Inca kingdom. Ronald Wright, *A Journey in the Two Worlds of Peru: Cut Stones and Cross Roads* (New York: Viking, 1984), 130–31.

12. Tarazona-Sevillano, *Sendero Luminoso*, 67–70; Carlos Iván Degregori, *Sendero Luminoso*, 2 parts (Lima: Instituto de Estudios Peruanos, 1988), 2: 41–44.

13. Train, "Apocalypse Next," 49, 52.

14. ibid., 51.

15. Luis Arce Borja, "Linea militar," vi; Raúl Gonzáles, "Las conferencias senderistas," *Quehacer* (August 30, 1984), 19–20; "La cuarta guerra," *Caretas* (September 2, 1985), 24A; Train, "Apocalypse Next," 48.

16. Train, "Apocalypse Next," 46.

17. Masterson, *Militarism*, 285–87; Daniel W. Fitz-Simons, "Sendero Luminoso: Case Study in Insurgency," *Parameters* 23: 2; 64–73 (Summer 1993), 69; *The Military Balance 1980–81*, 84.

18. *The Military Balance 1980–81*, 84.

19. "Our Red Flag," 6; Tarazona-Sevillano, *Sendero Luminoso*, 29–30.

20. Luis Arce Borja, "Linea militar," viii.

21. Train, "Apocalypse Next," 50.

22. Tarazona-Sevillano, *Sendero Luminoso*, 118; John Laffin, *War Annual*, beginning with volume 3, expanded title becomes *The World in Conflict . . . War Annual* (London: Brassey's Defence Publishers, 1986–), 4: 153.

23. Enrique Obando Arbulú, "Subversion and Antisubversion in Peru, 1980–92: A View from Lima," *Low Intensity Conflict & Law Enforcement* 2: 2; 318–30 (Autumn 1993), 320–21.

24. Obando, "Subversion," 321.

25. Peru's current constitution was promulgated on July 12, 1979, and entered into effect on July 28, 1980.

26. Legislative Decree 46. Liberals successfully campaigned to have it succeeded by Law 24651 on March 19, 1987. Under this second law individuals could not be investigated without due cause. Law 24651 in turn was replaced by Law 24953 on December 7, 1988.

27. Tarazona-Sevillano, *Sendero Luminoso*, 127.

28. The *"Sinchis"* was created within the Civil Guard and the *"Llapan Aticcs"* ("legendary Inca warrior qualities") within the Peruvian army during 1965 to combat the rural guerrilla threat.

29. Tarazona-Sevillano, *Sendero Luminoso*, 89.

30. Gustavo Gorriti, "Morir en Huamanaga," *Caretas* 688 (March 8, 1982), 12–15; "Our Red Flag," 9; Davis, "Sendero Luminoso," 84; Train, "Apocalypse Next," 51.

31. Those suspended the right to assemble, travel internally without restrictions, and the sanctity of the residence. Security forces could search and arrest without warrants. Civil authority rested with a senior military officer appointed by the President. Civil judicial authority is also restricted.

32. Davis, "Sendero Luminoso," 84; Americas Watch Committee, *Abdicating Democratic Authority: Human Rights in Peru* (New York: Americas Watch, October 1984), and Amnesty International, *Peru: Torture and Extrajudicial Execution* (New York: Amnesty International, August 1983).

33. Tarazona-Sevillano, *Sendero Luminoso*, 110, 114, 127; Train, "Apocalypse Next," 50.

34. Osmán Morote Barrionuevo (1945–) was the son of the former president of the University of San Cristóbal. In 1975 he became a faculty member following a trip to China. Morote was a cofounder of the Shining Path and a member of the National Central Committee. He was captured by the government in June 1988; the following month he was released for "lack of evidence." Captured a second time, Morote remains in prison.

35. Gustavo Gorriti, "Sendero en la Selva," *Caretas* 10–15, 72 (May 7, 1984), 11–14.

36. Alan Riding, "Rebels Disputing Coca Eradication in Peru," New York *Times* (January 26, 1989), A10; Masterson, *Militarism*, 281.

37. "La misión de Mariano," *Caretas* 14–17, 72 (May 28, 1984), 17; Jóse Gonzales, "Se despunta Sendero?" *Debate* 47: 33–39 (November–December 1987), 36.

38. Degregori, *Sendero Luminoso*, 2: 47–50.

39. ibid., 2: 41.

40. Hugo Ned Alarcón, "Rumi Rumi, La massacre," *Caretas* 48–49 (December 21, 1987), 48–49; "Our Red Flag," 2.

41. Davis, "Sendero Luminoso," 85; "Our Red Flag," 3, 9.

42. Obando, "Subversion," 321–22; Tarazona-Sevillano, *Sendero Luminoso*, 92.

43. Obando, "Subversion," 322–23; Train, "Apocalypse Next," 51–52.

44. Laffin, *War Annual* 2, 177–79.

45. Obando, "Subversion," 324–25.

46. Masterson, *Militarism*, 280.

47. Laffin, *War Annual* 2, 180; Obando, "Subversion," 323; Masterson, *Militarism*, 280–81; "Our Red Flag," 10.

48. Abilio Arroyo and Gustavo Gorriti, "Masacre en Cochas Pueblos inermes," *Caretas* 923: 45–46, 72 (September 29, 1986), 45–46, 72.

49. Laffin, *War Annual* 2, 180.

50. Davis, "Sendero Luminoso," 85.

51. Tarazona-Sevillano, *Sendero Luminoso*, 87–88.

52. Laffin, *War Annual* 4, 153; Tarazona-Sevillano, *Sendero Luminoso*, 159.

53. Tarazona-Sevillano, *Sendero Luminoso*, 126; Laffin, *War Annual* 6, 171; Davis, "Sendero Luminoso," 82.

54. Davis, "Shining Path," 85–86; Tarazona-Sevillano, *Sendero Luminoso*, 53, 66–67.

55. Laffin, *War Annual* 4, 153.

56. Train, "Apocalypse Next," 52; "Derriban 16 torres de energia en el centro," (Lima) *Nacional* (June 17, 1989), 14; "Our Red Flag," 4, 16–17.

57. Laffin, *War Annual* 6, 170.

58. "El famoso Huayhuaco," *Caretas* 37 (December 11, 1989), 37; Laffin, *War Annual* 6, 170.

59. Train, "Apocalypse Next," 52–53; "Our Red Flag," 13–15.

60. Fitz-Simons, "Sendero Luminoso," 71–72; John Everett-Heath, *Helicopters in Combat* (London: Arms and Armour, 1992), 121.

61. Laffin, *War Annual* 6, 169–71.

62. ibid., 171–72.

63. On April 24, 1992, a Peruvian fighter fired on and damaged an unarmed U.S. Air Force C-130 aircraft that was flying an antidrug surveillance mission. One crew member was killed and two wounded. The incident occurred in daylight in clear weather.

64. Breene, *Latin American Political Yearbook 1997*, 171.

65. Don Podesta, "Joint Patrols Challenge Peru's Rebels," *The Washington Post* (September 8, 1992), A14; Train, "Apocalypse Next," 53; Obando, "Subversion," 325.

66. Train, "Apocalypse Next," 53.

67. Russell Watson and Brook Larmer, "It's Your Turn to Lose," *Newsweek* (September 28, 1992), 28–29; Obando, "Subversion," 328–29; Nicolás de Bari Hermoza Ríos, *Fuerzas armadas del Peru lecciones de este siglo* (Lima: FIMART S.A., 1996), 175.

68. Corinne Schmidt, "Capture in Peru Police Report Capture of 'Shining Path' Leader," *The Washington Post* (September 13, 1992), A8.

69. Fitz-Simons, "Sendero Luminoso," 68.

70. Obando, "Subversion," 321.

71. Fitz-Simons, "Sendero Luminoso," 64; "Our Red Flag," 20. The newspaper *Expreso* placed the figure at more than 14,000 dead for the period between 1980 and mid-1989. Government figures are about one-half that number. See "Mas de 14 mil muertos por violencia terroista," *Expreso* (July 13, 1989), 4. Between 1980 and 1989 the Shining Path had knocked down 1,205 electric towers. The Peruvian National Electric Company estimated the cost of repairs at $600 million. "En últimos 10 años fueron derribadas 1,205 torres," *Expreso* (January 14, 1990), 13.

CHAPTER THIRTY-EIGHT

1. Tom Marks, "Colombian Crossroads," *Soldier of Fortune* 56–61, 72 (September 2001), 58.

2. Tickner, "Colombia," 61; Kline, "New Directions." 67.

3. Bruce M. Bagley, "Colombia and the War on Drugs," in *Regional Security Issues* (Washington, D.C.: National Defense University, 1991), 343–47.

4. Bagley, "Colombia," 351; Kline, "New Directions," 67.

5. Bagley, "Colombia," 352.

6. Marks, "Colombian Crossroads," 58.

7. ibid., 57.

8. Valenza, "Colombia's Quiet War," 51.

9. Laffin, *War Annual* 2, 63–64; Laffin, *War Annual* 5, 63; Adrian English, "The Colombian Armed Forces—An Update," *Jane's Intelligence Review* 7: 5 (September 1995), 424–26.

10. Valenza, "Colombia's Quiet War," 52; Cala, "The Enigmatic Guerrilla," 56; Joseph R. Nuñez, *Fighting the Hobbesian Trinity in Colombia: A New Strategy for Peace* (Carlisle: Strategic Studies Institute, 2001), 8; Marks, "Colombian Crossroads," 58.

11. Valenza, "Colombia's Quiet War," 52.

12. Nuñez, *Fighting*, 7; Laffin, *War Annual* 6, 59, 63.

13. Bagley, "Colombia," 345.

14. Michael Shifter, "The United States and Colombia: Partners in Ambiguity," *Current History* 51–55 (February 2000), 51.

15. Nuñez, *Fighting*, 6–7; Tom Marks, "Colombian Crossroads Part II," *Soldier of Fortune* 44–49, 70 (October 2001), 49.

16. Laffin, *War Annual* 5, 63.

17. ibid., 2: 62–63.

18. Bagley, "Colombia," 352–53; Kline, "New Directions," 68.

19. Bagley, "Colombia," 353–54; Kline, "New Directions," 68.

20. Bagley, "Colombia," 354–55; "The Month in Review Foreign Policy," *Current History* 143–44 (March 1985), 143.

21. Bagley, "Colombia," 343.

22. On May 19, 1988, Carlos Lehder was convicted in a Jacksonville, Florida, court and sentenced to life plus 135 years and fine $350,000.

23. Laffin, *War Annual* 2, 63; Bagley, "Colombia," 356; Martz, "Colombia's Search," 128.

24. Laffin, *War Annual* 3, 83.

25. Martz, "Colombia's Search," 127; Laffin, *War Annual* 3, 83.

26. Martz, Colombia's Search," 128; "The Month in Review Colombia," *Current History* 364 (October 1989), 364.

27. Laffin, *War Annual* 4, 76.

28. Hanratty and Meditz, *Colombia*, xxxi; Laffin, *War Annual* 5, 63.

29. Dennis M. Hanratty and Sandra W. Meditz, eds., *Colombia: A Country Study*, 4th ed., (Washington, D.C.: U.S. Government Printing Office, 1990), xxxi; Laffin, *War Annual* 5, 63–64.

30. Laffin, *War Annual* 5, 65.

31. ibid., 66; Laffin, *War Annual* 6, 60.

32. Laffin, *War Annual* 6, 65–66; "A Drug Trade Primer for the Late 1990s," *Current History* 150–53 (April 1998), 151.

33. Laffin, *War Annual* 6, 65; Laffin, *War Annual* 7, 45; Laffin, *War Annual* 8, 96–97.

34. Laffin, *War Annual* 7, 46.

35. Nuñez, *Fighting*, 9; Tickner, "Colombia," 63.

36. Breene, *Latin American Political Yearbook 1997*, 19–20; Laffin, *War Annual* 7, 46.

37. Laffin, *War Annual* 8, 93.

38. ibid.; Marks, "Colombian Crossroads," 59; Tickner, "Colombia," 64–65.

39. Marks, "Colombian Crossroads," 59–60.

40. Laffin, *War Annual* 8, 94–95.

41. Tickner, "Colombia," 64.

42. ibid., 65.

43. Laffin, *War Annual* 8, 94–95; David Spencer, "Improv[ised] Armour Alive in Colombia," *Tank TV* 1–3 (December 1999), 2.

44. "The Month in Review Colombia," *Current History* 190 (April 1998), 190; 290–91 (September 1998), 290.

45. Spencer, "Improv[ised] Armour," 3.

46. Marks, "Colombian Crossroads," 59–60; Marks, "Colombian Crossroads Part II," 44; Breene, *Latin American Political Yearbook 1997*, 118–22.

47. "The Month in Review Colombia," *Current History* 300 (September 1999), 300; Shifter, "The United States," 53.

48. "The Month in Review Colombia," *Current History* 300 (September 1999), 300.

49. Marks, "Colombian Crossroads," 60; "The Month in Review Colombia," *Current History* 300 (September 1999), 300.

50. "The Month in Review Colombia," *Current History* 397 (November 1999), 397.

51. "The Month in Review Colombia," *Current History* 442 (December 1999), 442; 43 (October 1999), 43.

52. "The Month in Review Colombia," *Current History* 294–95 (September 2000), 294–95.

53. Marks, "Colombian Crossroads Part II," 49; "The Month in Review Colombia," *Current History* 88 (February 2000), 88; John A. Cope, "Colombia's War: Toward a New Strategy," *Strategic Forum* 194: 1–8 (October 2002), 4–5.

54. "The Month in Review Colombia," *Current History* 396–97 (September 2000), 396; Marks, "Colombian Crossroads," 61.

55. "The Month in Review Colombia," *Current History* 440–41 (October 2000), 441.

56. William W. Mendel, "Colombia y las amenazas a la seguridad regional," *Military Review*, Hispano-American 3–18 (July–August 2001), 13.

57. Hanratty and Meditz, *Colombia*, xxviii; Bagley, "Colombia," 343–44; Tickner, "Colombia," 62; Martz, "Colombia's Search," 125.

58. David C. Jordan, *Drug Politics: Dirty Money and Democracies* (Norman: University of Oklahoma Press, 1999), 168; Laffin, *War Annual* 2, 64.

59. Cala, "The Enigmatic Guerrilla," 59.

60. Marks, "Colombian Crossroads Part II," 46.

61. "A Drug Trade Primer," 151–52; Shifter, "The United States," 52.

62. Nuñez, *Fighting*, 7; Laffin, *War Annual* 5, 66; Valenza, "Colombia's Quiet War," 55, 59.

Latin America's Wars, 1900–2001 drew upon numerous sources. Their short citations, which were used throughout this volume except for the initial citation, are listed below and the page number where the full citation may be found is provided.

Sources related to Latin America's wars become increasingly scarce as the twentieth century progresses. Works describing every detail of the Mexican Revolution, the Chaco War, and other early conflicts are abundant. However, moving on into the cold war era beginning in the 1960s, sources become much more difficult to find, particularly from the side of the radical left. The cold war conflicts did not end until the 1990s. For the most part, the Cuban archives remains closed and only a few individuals, with Fidel Castro's permission, have written about the fighting. A handful of "retired" leftist guerrillas have begun to grant interviews to newspaper reporters and their stories have added to our knowledge, particularly concerning events in Venezuela. A few works serve as a starting point for researching the fighting in the cold war era. Worthy of special attention are John Laffin's eight editions of *The World in Conflict* (title varies slightly); the U.S. Army's area handbook series, the volumes of which are cited in this work under the names of the editors; and Helen Schooley's *Conflict in Central America*. Full citations of these works may be found by consulting the author index.

Valencia Tovar, Alvaro, *Historia de las fuerzas militares*, 387n3

Valencia Tovar, Alvaro, "Participación," 436n15

Valenza, Gary, "Colombia's Quiet War," 434n3

Valsalice, Luigi, *La guerrilla castrista*, 460n6

van der Kooy, E., *Falklands*, 471n4

van Lindert, Paul, *Bolivia*, 437n2

Vasconcelos, Josí, *Breve historia*, 390n3

Vazquez Machicado, Humberto, *Manual*, 438n8

"Venezuela," *Deadline Data*, 460n16

"Venezuela 1955," 448n9

"Venezuela Balks Assassins' Plot," 460n20

"Venezuela Bans Reds' Activities," 458n20

"Venezuela Calls Up her Military Forces," 460n16

"Venezuela Cuts Ties with Havana," 458n10

"Venezuela: Democracy under Fire," 451n51

"Venezuela Informs O.A.S.," 457n6

"Venezuela—Rooting Out the Rebels," 464n15

"Venezuela Rosier," 460n22

"Venezuela Seizes Ship," 465n21

"Venezuela Terrorists Are Defied," 460n23

"Venezuelan 'Plot,'" 457n1

"Venezuelan Roundup Modified," 460n20

Vergara Montero, Ramón, *Por rutas*, 403n18

Vergara Vicuña, Aquiles, *Historia*, 407n25

Verkoren, Otto, *Bolivia*, 437n2

Vidaurre, Enrique, *Acciones militares*, 408n44

Villalobos Barradas, José Manuel, "Fuerza aérea," 411n11

Villanueva, Victor, *Hugo Blanco*, 462n49

Villanueva, Victor, *La Sublevación*, 418n36

Vision del Peru, 419n53

Volta Gaona, Enrique, *La revolución*, 432n1

von Borde, Kurt, *Deutsche unter fremden Fahnen*, 407n19

von Glahn, Gerhard, *Law among Nations*, 432n64

von Rauch, Georg, "The Green Hell," 406n8

von Rauch, Georg, "The Leticia Conflict," 411n5

von Schroeders, Edgardo, *El delegado*, 403n12

Waghelstein, John D., "'Che's' Bolivian Adventure," 467n46

Waghelstein, John D., "A Latin-American Insurgency," 459n5

Waghelstein, John D., "Ruminations," 459n3

Walsh, Paul V., "Fuerza Aérea," 428n61

Walton, John., *Reluctant Rebels*, 433n1

"War on Subversion," *Time*, 464n15

Warren, Harris G., *Paraguay*, 407n30

Watson, Russell, "It's Your Turn to Lose," 488n67

Weathers, Bynum, Jr., *The Role of the Military*, 473n6

Webster's New International Dictionary, 387n6

Weidner, Glenn R., "Operation Safe Border," 414n44

Weisman, John, *Shadow Warrior*, 454n17

Welch, David A., *On the Brink*, 457n78

Welles, Benjamin, "U.S. Cautious," 420n69

Welles, Sumner, *Naboth's Vineyard*, 397n1

Wendt, Herbert, *The Red, White, and Black Continent*, 461n44

Wewege-Smith, T., *Gran Chaco*, 410n85

Weyl, Nathaniel, *Red Star*, 440n3

Whalen, James, *Allende*, 475n37

Whalan, James R., *Out of the Ashes*, 474n22

"When the Chips Are Down," 460n13

"Where Castro Brews Trouble," 460n29

"Where U.S. Won and Castro Lost," 460n25

Whitaker, Arthur P., *Argentine Upheaval*, 422n10

Whitaker, Arthur P., *The United States and South America*, 388n6

"White Troops among Forces," 477n21

White Book of the Change of Government in Chile, 475n36

Wiley, Charles W., "New 'Vietnams,'" 460n24

Winz, Antônio Pimentel, "Plácido de Castro," 389n1

Wirth, John D., "Tenentismo," 416n18

Wise, David, *The Invisible Government*, 457n79

Wood, Bryce, *Aggression*, 413n15

Wood, Bryce, *The United States*, 410n1

Woodward, Ralph Lee, Jr., *Central America*, 470n1

World Almanac, 387n4

Wright, Ronald, *A Journey*, 486n11

Ydígoras, Miguel, *My War*, 461n38

Yon, Julio Alberto, "Guatemala," 430n26

Young, Jordan, "Military Aspects," 415n1

Zimmermann, Warren, "Jingoes," 398n18

Zook, David H., Jr., *The Conduct*, 405n5

Zook, David H., Jr., *Zarumilla-Marañon*, 414n34

Zubenko, Vyacheslav, *The CIA*, 453n3

INDEX

*Numbers in italics refer to figures or maps.
*Numbers in **bold** indicate biographical sketches.

505

ABOUT THE AUTHOR

Robert L. Scheina, Ph.D., is a professor of history at the National Defense University and a leading authority on Latin American military history. He has published hundreds of articles and four other books on Latin America, including *Latin America: A Naval History, 1810–1987*, the seminal work on the subject. He is also the author of *Santa Anna: A Curse upon Mexico*, a volume in the Brassey's "Military Profiles" series, and *Latin America's Wars, Vol. 1: The Age of the* Caudillo*, 1791–1899*. He lives in Crofton, Maryland.

3M